Preface

The Need to Teach C

It's a fact of life, the C language tends to dominate many programming applications these days. Just take a look at the job advertisements for programmers and it is clear that a large proportion of work requires at least a knowledge of C. C may be regarded as the de-facto systems implementation language with C++ emerging, as a dominant language that will be used by programmers well into the twenty-first century.

Although many academic courses in universities and colleges prescribe for good reason, languages such as Pascal, Modula-2 or Ada as the first language, increasingly there is pressure from both the computing industry and student population to teach C.

As this book illustrates, the approach taken in teaching C as the first language to students, need not differ from the traditional way of teaching, say Pascal. Much emphasis is placed on top-down design, structured programming and clearly written code.

Audience

I have assumed that you have no prior knowledge of computer programming. The book has been written for use on the ACM-recommended curriculum for CS I and is aimed at a broad audience of students in science, engineering and business where a knowledge of programming is thought to be essential. For Computer Science majors, the book also provides an introduction to many of the topics found in data structures that are covered .n the CS2 course.

The book may also be used as the text for a variety of introductory programming courses on C and C++.

Overview

Chapters 1 thru 7 provide you with a gradual introduction to the fundamentals of programming where much emphasis is placed upon good practice involving program design and the implementation of structured programs. Chapters 8 thru 14 introduce data structures. Chapter 15 covers aspects of the C language not covered by the preceding chapters. Chapters 16 thru 18 extend your knowledge of ANSI C by introducing extensions to the language through C++.

In addition to an exposition of C and C++, the text contains a comprehensive appraisal of many topics found in data structures - arrays, records, recursion, linked lists, queues, stacks and binary trees; in data processing - sorting, searching, merging, report writing and data validation; and in programming-structured programming, modularity, data abstraction and object-oriented programming.

The emphasis throughout the book is on the use of carefully chosen examples that highlight the features of the language being studied. Explanation about the language is put into context with the example programs.

iii

The development of the language statements and the programs are taken in manageable steps, to enable you to build a firm foundation of knowledge. The type of programming examples used are simple enough to give you confidence at each stage of learning to program.

Synopsis

Chapter I introduces you to the hardware and software that you are likely to use when writing, testing, and implementing programs. These days it is quite common for a student who enters an introductory programming course to have some knowledge of hardware and the use of computers, through say, word processing or spreadsheet applications. For this reason the chapter moves quickly through the equipment used in a computer system to the software likely to be encountered in a programming environment. Levels of programming languages, and the use of an editor, compiler and linker are explained in this chapter. Finally having set the scene about the programming environment you are introduced to the meaning of programming, problem solving and designing algorithms. By the end of the chapter the main components of a program - sequence, selection and repetition have been introduced.

Since the majority of programs that we write are to do with processing data, chapter 2 provides you with an explanation of the types of data that you are likely to use, and how this data is described in a program. This chapter provides the first introduction to the syntax of the language through a generic format that is easy to recognize and assimilate. When you have gained more experience in the use of the language you can always make reference to the formal definition of the syntax given in appendix E.

Chapter 3 provides you with more "nuts and bolts" of the language to enable you to write arithmetic expressions in C. The chapter also introduces the standard C library and explains how routines from the library are used to provide for input of data to the computer and the output of results. At this point you have enough information to attempt writing simple programs consisting of sequences of instructions.

The design of computer programs is a recurrent theme throughout the book. For this reason the whole of chapter 4 is devoted to the top-down design of programs and focuses on problem analysis, algorithm design, data dictionaries, desk checks, screen layouts for input and output, coding the program and the results of a program being run on the computer.

Chapter 5 explains in detail how functions are used to build programs. This chapter tackles the all too thorny issues of parameter-passing mechanisms in C. Traditionally students find this area difficult, however, by introducing the material in a systematic way and in the context of the need to pass parameters, it is possible to increase your confidence of this material and let you to use functions and parameters as a most natural way of constructing programs in future chapters. This chapter also gives you the first introduction to the use of pointers, which are of such importance in the C language.

Having laid a firm foundation of knowledge for top-down design and the use of functions in constructing computer programs it is now possible to introduce you to further constructs within the language. Chapter 6 concentrates on the flow of control in a computer program and introduces the selection statements if , if else, and switch. However, as a means of making tile presentation of C look more akin to other high-level languages I have deliberately included the use of enumerated data types in this chapter to enable the creation of a Boolean type. Data validation is also introduced in this chapter.

Chapter 7 is about looping structures. The chapter covers the three looping structures while, do. . while and for, and the applicability of each kind of loop. This chapter may be considered as the first milestone in the book. By now you have covered the fundamentals of programming and it is necessary to turn your attention to data structures.

Chapter 8 is devoted to the one-dimensional array. Within this chapter the use of loops, in particular for loops, is given greater attention. Although the data type *string* was introduced as early as chapter 2, it is only now that more emphasis can be put on the implementation of strings.

Although pointers were first introduced in chapter 5, their importance in C is such that they warrant a separate chapter. Chapter 9 explains how pointers are used to access the contents of an array, and how the memory space to store data in arrays can be created at run-time using dynamic memory allocation. The chapter also explains arrays of pointers and pointers to functions.

The only means of data input and output up to and including chapter 9 is via keyboard input and screen output. Clearly when dealing with larger volumes of data it is more practical to use data files for the storage of information. Having discussed the idea of a pointer it is now possible to introduce you to data streams and text files. Chapter 10 covers the creation of text files held on disk, accessing, the components of the file and the creation of reports that may be printed. The contents of this chapter opens up the scope of the programming problems that can be examined.

Chapter 11 continues the theme of arrays by examining structures (records) that can be stored in one-dimensional arrays. The chapter also covers the use of two and three-dimensional arrays. This chapter can be considered as a second milestone within the book, since the case studies show the culmination of the fundamentals of programming together with the use of arrays, structures and text files.

Chapter 12 is about programming techniques that are used later in the book and may be rewarded as a precursor to the material covered on the CS2 course. The first of these is recursion, which offers an alternative to looping when attempting to solve a certain type of problem. The use of recursion is set into context by exploring sorting and searching algorithms that require either non-recursive or recursive methods for their implementation. This chapter also introduces two standard recursive functions, qsort and bsearch used to sort and search the contents of arrays.

Chapter 13 extends your knowledge of file formats and file processing by introducing binary files. The advantages of binary files over text files and the methods of accessing the files and maintaining the files are discussed. The chapter also covers the use of direct access files. As far back as chapter 9 the dynamic allocation of memory to array structures was introduced. Chapter 14 takes a look at other structures such as linked lists, queues, stacks and binary trees that also use dynamic memory allocation. The material provides useful prerequisite information to later chapters on data abstraction and object-oriented programming. Once again this material serves as an introduction to the CS2 course.

It is inevitable that in designing the layout of material for a book, some of the features of the C language do not always fit within the earlier chapter headings. For this reason chapter 15 is included as a "catch all" chapter that includes a number of miscellaneous, yet important topics in the C language.

Since C++ is based upon ANSI C, no modem text on the C language would be complete without some mention of how C++ can be regarded as an extension of C. Tile extensions of C should be viewed in three areas - procedural changes, data abstraction and object-oriented programming. At this point in the text you should have acquired sufficient knowledge and skills in the use of C to be confident about programming. Using this new foundation of knowledge it is a straightforward matter to teach you the differences between C and C++, and foster a desire to go forward and learn more about object-oriented programming techniques.

Chapter 16 provides you with an introduction to C++ as a procedural language. It highlights many of the differences between C and C++, and emphasizes the incompatibilities that exist between ANSI C and C++.

Chapter 17 introduces the topic of data abstraction and how the technique is implemented in C++. Several of the examples in this chapter require you to have read and understood chapter 14. Within this chapter the topics of classes, constructors and operator overloading are explained, that are the cornerstone of object-oriented programming.

Finally chapter 18 introduces the topic of object-oriented programming and flow the techniques are implemented in C++. The chapter covers the advantages of object-oriented programming over traditional procedural programming. The chapter expands upon the work of chapter 17 and introduces the topics of inheritance, polymorphism and object-oriented design.

Language and Computer Requirements

Studying from this book can be more effective and enjoyable if a computer is used for running both the example programs and your own answers to the programming problems.

All the programs written for the examples and die answers up to and including chapter 15 have been compiled using DEC C, JPI TopSpeed C, Microsoft Visual C++ and Borland Turbo C++ to ensure their portability between UNIX, MSDOS and Windows environments on a Digital Personal DEC Station and an

IBM compatible computer. In fact any C compiler that is compliant with ANSI/ISO 9899-1990 C can be used for the implementation of the programs found in the first fifteen chapters.

The programs for both the examples and answers found in the chapters 16, 17 and 18 have been compiled using IPI TopSpeed C++ and Microsoft Visual C++.

Pedagogical Features

Objectives

Each chapter begins with a set of learning objectives that you should be capable of achieving.

Margin Notes for Quick Reference

A set of margin notes for C and C++ Syntax, C++ features, Style Matters and Cautions are available in the margins to enable you to make a quick reference to important aspects of the text.

Case Studies

Many chapters contain fully designed case studies with comprehensive documentation, program listings and output.

Example Programs

All chapters contain example programs, in addition to the case studies, and are used to demonstrate the key features of each chapter. All computer programs are followed by a listing of the output from the program.

End of Chapter Summary

Every chapter contains a summary of the key points raised. This provides you with a check list of the topics that you should understand before progressing to the next chapter.

Review Questions

All chapters contain review questions to enable you to test and re-enforce your knowledge.

Programming Exercises

All chapters contain pencil-and-paper exercises designed to test your understanding of aspects of the programming topics introduced in the chapter. These should be tackled before the programming problems.

Programming Problems

All chapters contain a set of problems that require the use of a computer to solve. You are expected to write fully working solutions to each problem.

Supplements

Program Disk

You may download the example programs, including case study programs, listed in every chapter in this book. The program disk is available through the Jones and Bartlett World Wide Web site on the Internet at: **http://www.jbpub.com/disks/**

Instructor's Guide

Available to each professor is an instructor's guide for the book that contains, hints and tips on teaching the material, together with all the answers to the review questions and the answers to the programming exercises and problems that do not appear in Appendix D.

Acknowledgments

I am also most grateful to the reviewers whose comments I found to be most constructive and helpful and have gone towards shaping this book into its present form.

Michael van Biema, Columbia University; Ernest L. Carey, Utah Valley State College; Kevin Croteau, Francis Marion University; Kathy Cupp, Oklahoma City Community College; Lennart Edblom, Umea University; Jack R. Hagemeister, Washington State University; Linda S. Halsted, St. Michael's College; D. D. Hearn, University of Illinois at Urbana Champaign; Rob Langsner, University of Nevada, Reno; Stephen P. Leach, Florida State University; Charles McDowell, University of California Santa Cruz; Scott W. McLeod, Riverside Community College; Walter L. Ruzzo, University of Washington; David L. Syler, Tri State University; La Toria H. Tookes, Paul D. Camp Community College; and Matthew O. Ward, Worcester Polytechnical Institute.

BJH - Oxford, England 1997

Brief Contents

Table of Contents

Appendix A - Summary of ANSI C Standard Library Functions   627

Appendix B - Miscellany   651

Appendix C - Selected Answers   655

Index   705

Through C to C++

Chapter 1
Programming Environment

The modern world of high technology could not have been realized without the development of computers. They have become commonplace in business, industry, research, and the home. Their power enables them to solve both complex and repetitive problems accurately; problems that in the past would have either not been possible or taken humans a considerable time to complete.

Human imagination and creativity is the key to applying computers to more diverse applications in the future. This book encourages you to apply your own creativity and problem-solving skills to harness the unique strengths of computers and computer programs.

Chapter 1 begins with a brief introduction to the hardware and software that make up a typical computing environment in which programmers work. This is followed by an approach to problem solving that is designed to get you thinking along the right lines before writing your first computer program. By the end of the chapter, you should have an understanding of the following topics:

☐ The hardware units that make up a computer system.

☐ The different levels of computer languages.

☐ The need to translate languages into a form that the computer can recognize.

☐ The stages in the implementation of a computer program.

☐ The purpose of a computer program and its relationship to data and results.

☐ The stages involved in writing a computer program.

☐ The elements of simple problem solving.

1.1 A Digital Computer

A digital computer is an electronic machine capable of storing instructions and executing them at a very high speed. For example, an instruction can be executed in 1/100,000,000 of 1 second. The term **digital** implies that all information is represented by numbers within the computer. The numbers are stored as binary numbers, base 2, since it is convenient to physically represent the binary digits, bits 1 and 0, as two respective voltage levels. If we could inspect these numbers within the computer, we might see a digital trace, similar to that illustrated in Figure 1.1, showing the respective voltage levels of the bits that represent a number. The peaks in the trace represent bit value 1, and the troughs represent bit value 0. The trace shows a wave pattern of 10010110, which represents a binary number.

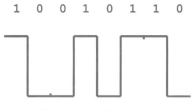

Figure 1.1 A digital trace

A digital computer stores information in the **main memory**. The main memory is composed of many millions of storage cells. The unique numeric address of each cell identifies the location of the cell within the memory. Figure 1.2 illustrates several separately addressed storage cells which contain information in a binary format in the main memory of a computer.

The main memory is used to store data and program instructions temporarily. **Data** is the name given to facts and figures, for example, the names of employees and the number of hours worked by each employee. A computer **program** consists of a series of instructions for the computer to execute and provides a method for processing data, for example, information for weekly payroll calculations. A computer can execute only program instructions that are stored in the main memory.

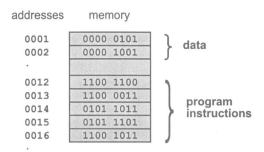

Figure 1.2 Data and instructions in memory

The **central processing unit** (CPU) is the heart of any computer; it executes program instructions and controls the flow of information.

2

The CPU consists of two subunits. The **arithmetic and logic unit** (ALU) performs the processes of arithmetic, logical operations, and comparisons on data, whereas the **control unit** fetches the instructions from main memory, interprets and executes them, and coordinates the flow of information throughout the computer system.

Figure 1.3 illustrates a computer model that contains the CPU, main memory, and three other units - input, secondary storage, and output - known as **peripheral units**.

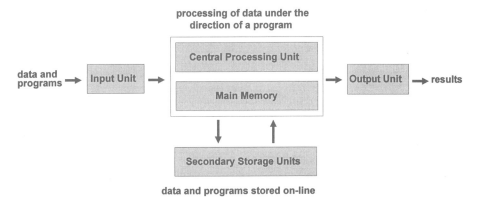

Figure 1.3 A computer model

An **input unit** allows data and computer programs to be input into the computer model.

Since the main memory is used only to store programs and data temporarily, it is necessary to have **secondary storage units** to provide a permanent storage facility. Programs and data are transferred to and from the secondary storage units to the main memory only when they are required.

An **output unit** transfers results from the main memory and secondary storage units to the outside world.

1.2 Input and Output Units

The most popular input unit used in a computer system is a **keyboard**. A keyboard is an input device modeled after a typewriter keyboard but with additional keys. The layout of a popular keyboard is depicted in Figure 1.4. Both data and programs can be keyed into the computer by using such a keyboard.

A television screen or **monitor** is an output device that can display information as it is being typed into a computer. The display provides a means of visually checking that the correct information is being entered. A monitor has a dual function; in addition to displaying information entered at the keyboard, the monitor can display information that has been processed by the computer. Figure 1.5 illustrates a typical monitor that is used in a computer system.

Because a monitor cannot produce a hard copy of the output, most computer systems include a **printer** as another output unit. Printers vary in their speed of output; **dot matrix printers** print characters composed from dots at a rate of up to 150 characters per second, and **laser printers** print complete pages in seconds using a technology similar to that of a photocopier. Figure 1.6 illustrates both types of printers.

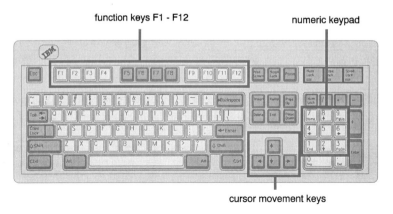

Figure 1.4 The layout of a popular keyboard

It is worth mentioning that there are other types of input and output units; however, these units are for specialized use and do not normally form part of a program development environment. For example, bar code readers are input units that detect stock codes on supermarket merchandise. Magnetic ink character readers detect bank account numbers and branch codes on bank checks. Optical character and mark readers detect information written on documents. Similarly, output units include graph and map plotters, synthezized speech units, and digital-to-analog output converters for controlling machinery.

Figure 1.5 A monitor

1.3 Secondary Storage Units

These units can be broadly subdivided into the following categories:

☐ **Hard disk** units that use a magnetic medium to store information and have a storage capacity of up to many thousands of millions of characters. A **character** may be regarded as a letter of the alphabet in either upper case or lower case, a decimal digit, a punctuation symbol, or a special character - but more of this later!

4

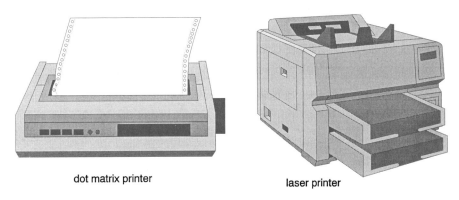

dot matrix printer   laser printer

Figure 1.6 A selection of printers

- □ **Floppy disk** units that have, depending upon their size and density, a storage capacity of up to several million characters, on one exchangeable magnetic disk. The term exchangeable implies that several disks may be swapped on the same disk drive unit.

- □ **Optical** and **magneto/optical** exchangeable disks with a storage capacity of up to hundreds of millions of characters on one exchangeable disk.

- □ **Magnetic tape** units with a storage capacity of up to 100,000,000 characters on one tape.

Information is also encoded onto magnetic and optical media using binary codes, since it is possible to represent the bits 1 and 0 by directions of magnetization, and on optical media, such as compact disks, by the presence or absence of pits etched into the disk surface by a laser beam.

The magnetic and optical disk units transfer information to and from the CPU at speeds of several millions of characters per second. When dealing with disk-based media, access to the information is direct and fast. By comparison, access speeds to information held on magnetic tape can be slow, since the contents of the tape must be read sequentially before information can be retrieved.

Since information can be read from or written to both tape and disk, these media can also be regarded as sources for the input and output of information.

The most common form of secondary storage medium that you are likely to use is the floppy disk. In comparison with hard disks, access to information on floppy disks is slow. Figure 1.7 illustrates two popular sizes of floppy disks. Note that storage capacities are shown in Kilobytes (Kbytes) and Megabytes (Mbytes). A **byte** is eight binary digits (bits), which is a sufficient storage space for storing a single character. Although the term **Kilobyte** implies 1,000 bytes, it is strictly 1,024 bytes (2^{10}); similarly a **Megabyte** is 1,048,576 bytes (2^{20}), not 1,000,000 bytes as its name implies.

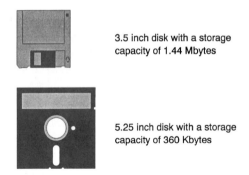

3.5 inch disk with a storage capacity of 1.44 Mbytes

5.25 inch disk with a storage capacity of 360 Kbytes

Figure 1.7 Popular floppy disks

1.4 Computer Configurations

You are likely to come across three different ways in which computer equipment is configured. The stand-alone **personal computer** (shown in Figure 1.8) consists of an outer casing, or box, that contains the central processing unit, main memory, secondary storage devices such as a hard disk, and floppy disk drives, a power supply, and various interface cards to permit linking the CPU to other devices. The personal computer has as standard a keyboard and monitor. In addition to these peripherals, a device known as a **mouse** is used to point at items displayed on the monitor, and as such may be regarded as an input device because it signals an input to a response. The stand-alone computer will probably be connected to a printer.

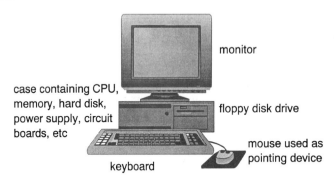

monitor

case containing CPU, memory, hard disk, power supply, circuit boards, etc

floppy disk drive

mouse used as pointing device

keyboard

Figure 1.8 A stand-alone personal computer

A second configuration that is extremely popular is a **network** of computers. Computers can be joined together on a network in several ways, but the subject of network configuration is of little importance in this chapter. The main points to consider are that a network usually contains a larger more powerful computer known as a **file server** to which all the other computers are connected. The file server has two major purposes: to store and distribute essential software and information that is of common use to all the users on the network and to permit the sharing of other peripheral devices, such as printers and plotters.

Each terminal on the network can be a personal computer or **workstation** (a powerful computer with components similar to a PC) with its own local processing power and capability to store information. Figure 1.9 illustrates a small network in which three personal computers are connected to the file server in order to obtain access to shared computer software and a single printer.

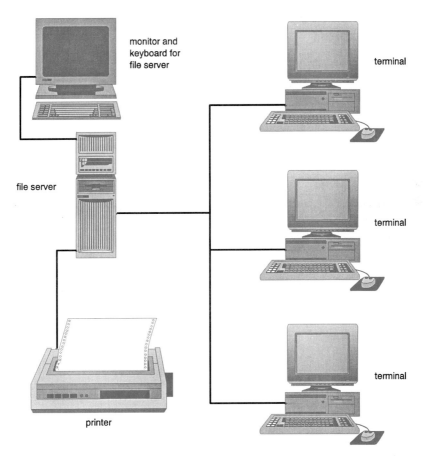

Figure 1.9 A network of personal computers

A third form of computer configuration is a **time-sharing** system in which dumb terminals are connected to a central computer (see Figure 1.10). Time-sharing implies that the central computer shares or rations its processing power among a group of users, servicing each one in turn, at such a high speed that to the users it appears they have their own computer. A **dumb terminal** is essentially a combined input and output device in the form of a keyboard and a monitor. A dumb terminal has no processing power and relies solely upon the central computer for access to software packages and to process information.

7

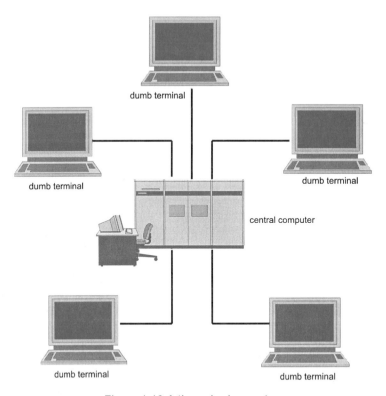

Figure 1.10 A time-sharing system

1.5 Computer Languages

A computer language is a set of instructions used for writing computer programs. There are essentially three levels of language, high, low, and machine code. C is a high-level language and was designed and implemented in 1972 by Dennis Ritchie of Bell Laboratories. However, the first American National Standards Institute (ANSI) Standard for the language was not completed until 1990. A standard is essentially a definition of the format or grammar of the language statements, the meaning or semantics of the statements, and sometimes recommendations on how the language should be implemented on a computer.

Figure 1.11 illustrates several statements in a C program that adds two numbers together and returns the result. As this example illustrates, **high-level languages** contain statements that are written with English words, arithmetic operations, and symbols. Such languages are not designed specifically for any one brand of computer or any specific architecture.

The **architecture** of a computer is its type of CPU, memory size, and internal features. A program written in C to run on one computer architecture that also runs without modification on a different architecture and produces exactly the same results is said to be **portable** between the two computers.

```
int sum(void)
{
        int X = 5;
        int Y = 9;
        int Z;

        Z = X + Y;
        return Z;
}
```

Figure 1.11 Part of a high-level program

The version of C used in this book conforms to the American National Standards Institute/ International Standards Organization (ANSI/ISO) 9899-1990 Standard. High-level languages remain portable between computers only if the language statements used conform to those defined in the standard for the language. However, software manufacturers tend to add enhancements to languages, creating in effect a dialect of the language. Computers also vary in their CPU and memory architectures. The more differences in dialects of a language and architectures of computers that exist, the less portable the language is likely to be.

Low-level languages contain statements that use mnemonic codes (codes suggesting their meaning) to represent operations that are specific to the architecture of the computer. Each low-level language has instructions that correspond closely to the built-in operations of a specific computer. Since different CPU architectures use different low-level languages, a program written for one CPU architecture will not run on a different CPU architecture. Despite the many low-level languages in existence, they all adhere to the same broad principles of language structure. Figure 1.12 illustrates the same instruction segment as Figure 1.11, but using a low-level language.

```
add     ax, bx
pop     bx
pop     bp
retf
```

Figure 1.12 An example of assembly-level code

This program segment adds two numbers and stores the result in memory. This type of programming is obviously not as clear as the previous segment of code written in C. However, the function of both pieces of code are identical.

Programs are often written in low-level languages when the execution speed of the program is critical to the application and the use of a high-level language might produce a program that does not run fast enough. Examples of such applications are computer animations and graphics programs.

Machine-code statements are even harder to interpret mentally. They are normally written using one of the number bases 2, 8, or 16. The program segment in Figure 1.13 performs the same addition function as the high-level and low-level program segments in Figures 1.11 and 1.12. However, it is coded in base 2 binary and requires the aid of a reference manual in order to decipher its meaning.

Figure 1.13 Example of machine-level code

In the days before the use of high-level or low-level languages machine code was the only means of programming a computer. The use of machine-code today is limited to the inspection and interpretation of the contents of computer memory.

1.6 Program Implementation

Four phases are associated with the implementation of a program on a computer system. These phases are illustrated in Figure 1.14.

Phase 1 - The creation of a C program in text mode using the editor.

In order to type a C program at the keyboard and save the program on a disk, it is necessary to run a program called an **editor**. In addition to enabling program entry, an editor allows a program to be retrieved from disk and amended as necessary. A C program is stored in text mode so that the programmer can read the program as it was written. The C program does not require translation to a machine recognizable form at this stage. In phase 1 the format of the program is known as **source code**.

Phase 2 - The translation of a program using a compiler.

A computer stores and uses information in a binary format; therefore, the computer cannot understand programs written in either high-level or low-level languages. Source code written in either a high-level or low-level language must be translated into a binary machine code that the computer can recognize. Translation is possible by using a supplied program, a translator, to translate high-level or low-level language statements into machine code.

Translation to machine code from a high-level language is performed by a **compiler** and from a low-level language by an **assembler**. The compiler or assembler is resident in the main memory of the computer and uses the high-level or low-level program code as input data. The output from the translator is a program in machine-readable code known as **object code**. In addition to translation, a compiler or assembler reports on any grammatical errors made by the programmer in the language statements of the program.

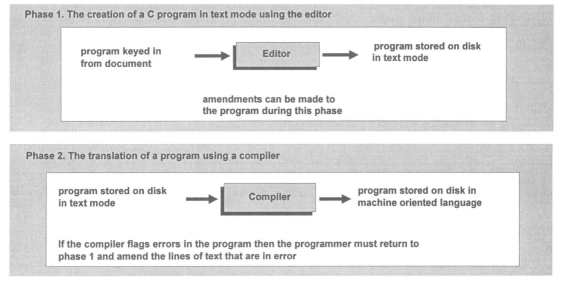

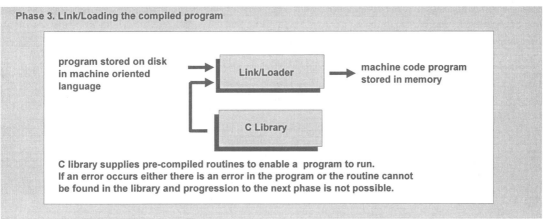

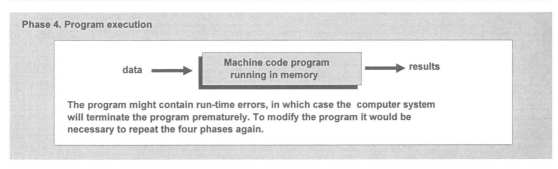

Figure 1.14 Four phases of program implementation

Different compilers are normally associated with different computer architectures. The same program compiled on different computer architectures will produce different machine codes. Therefore, the portability of a program refers only to the program in source code and not machine code.

C is noted for its translation into efficient machine-level code, portability of source code, power and flexibility of language statements, and the use of a standard library. The **standard library** contains a large repertoire of precompiled routines that are useful for writing programs.

Phase 3 - Link/loading the compiled program.

Before a compiled C program can be run or executed by the computer, it must be converted into an executable form. One function of the **link/loader** is to take the object program and combine it with any necessary software (already in machine-readable form) to enable the computer to run the program. For example, input and output routines that are supplied from the C library will need linking into the program to allow data to be input at a keyboard and results to be displayed on a monitor. The complete machine-code program is then loaded into memory ready for execution.

Phase 4 - Program execution.

After the command to run or execute the program is invoked, the program may request data input; this data is then processed and the results are output. As an example, Figure 1.15 illustrates that a program has been used to input data into the computer, process the data, and then output the results from the computer program in the form of a report. You should not be concerned at this stage with the meaning of the statements in the program.

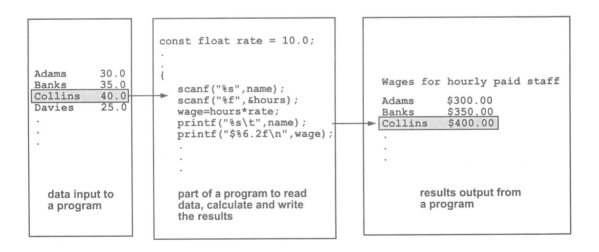

Figure 1.15 Data, program and results

12

It is possible for a program to fail during the execution stage, in which case it must be stopped from any further execution. If modifications to the program are required, it is necessary to perform the amendments from phase 1 and repeat the four phases.

A layer of software known as an **operating system** exists below the user's program, and controls the computer system. An operating system has many roles; one important aspect is to supervise the execution of user-written programs. Such supervision includes the premature termination of a program that attempts to execute an illegal operation, such as dividing a number by zero or reading from a data file that has not been opened. UNIX and MSDOS are two popular operating systems.

1.7 What is Programming?

The development of a computer program can be broken down broadly into the five activities that are illustrated in Figure 1.16 and described in the following sections.

Problem Analysis

The first activity involves studying the problem, in order to understand the nature of the problem and determine how to solve it.

Designing and Testing an Algorithm

An **algorithm** is a solution to a problem and normally consists of a series of steps. The algorithm may be represented by either a flowchart or a narrative of the solution known as **pseudocode**. The use of flowcharts to represent algorithms will be covered in the next section. Later in the book you will be shown how to use pseudocode.

Having designed a solution, the next step is to trace through the algorithm with test data to verify that the solution contains no logical errors. **Logical errors** are mistakes in the design of a program, such as a branch to a wrong statement, or the use of a wrong mathematical formula.

Coding the Algorithm

The third activity is to use a suitable computer language to code the algorithm into a corresponding computer program. The operations defined in the flowchart or pseudocode should translate directly into instructions in a high-level language.

Testing the Code

During the fourth activity the program must be compiled, and at this stage the compiler will list any errors in the way the grammar of the language has been used. These errors are known as **syntax errors** and are associated with the wrong construction of language statements.

However, this is not the whole story. At the stages of design and after coding the program, it is necessary to test the solution to the problem and verify that the program does indeed function correctly. Programs can be tested, either by the programmer tracing through the design and program code or by **peer-group** inspection. In the latter technique, members of the programming team review the accuracy of a design or program and determine whether it meets the original specification. Further testing, using suitable test data, is always carried out with the program being run on a computer.

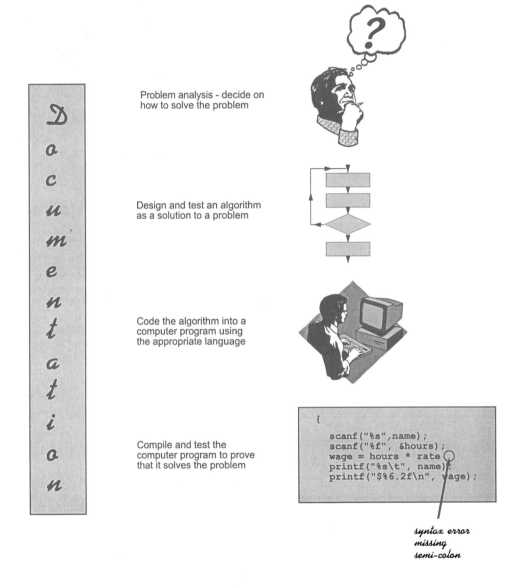

Problem analysis - decide on how to solve the problem

Design and test an algorithm as a solution to a problem

Code the algorithm into a computer program using the appropriate language

Compile and test the computer program to prove that it solves the problem

```
{

    scanf("%s",name);
    scanf("%f", &hours);
    wage = hours * rate
    printf("%s\t", name);
    printf("$%6.2f\n", wage);
```

syntax error missing semi-colon

Documentation

Figure 1.16 Development of a computer program

Documentation

Despite documentation being discussed as the fifth activity in programming, it is used and produced during the other four activities, and for this reason documentation can be regarded as an activity that occurs throughout the entire programming cycle.

A computer program is not usually static. Over a period of time it may be changed and indeed evolve as the computer project to which it contributes evolves. Documentation involves documenting the purpose of the program, the method of solution, the stages of testing that it has undergone, and other necessary facts. The documentation of a program will usually conform to the in-house standards of an organization. In this book, documentation will consist of writing comments into a program to show what each part is meant to do. Documentation also includes the design, information used to design and test the program, and predicted results.

Programming, therefore, contains the activities of problem analysis, designing an algorithm, coding a program from the algorithm, testing the code, and documenting the program.

1.8 Designing Algorithms

In this section you will be introduced to flowcharts as a means of expressing an algorithm. A **flowchart** is a pictorial method of representing a solution to a problem. A flowchart contains a description of how to solve a problem written in a style independent of any programming language. A flowchart is composed from the series of symbols illustrated in Figure 1.17.

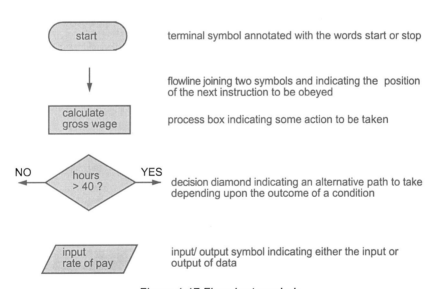

Figure 1.17 Flowchart symbols

15

Algorithm Example 1.1: A Sequence of Instructions

A person is paid a weekly wage based upon the number of hours worked per week and the hourly rate of pay. Design and represent an algorithm in the form of a flowchart to input the rate of pay and the number of hours worked, calculate the gross wage, and output the result.

The solution is given in Figure 1.18. Notice that the sequence of events begins at start and is taken in the order *input rate of pay*, *input hours worked*, *calculate gross wage,* and *output gross wage*. When this algorithm is coded into a computer language, input of the data is assumed to be through a keyboard and the output of the result to a monitor.

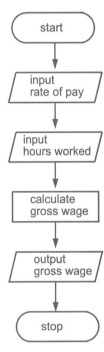

Figure 1.18 A sequence of instructions

At this first stage of creating an algorithm, it is possible to test the design. This form of testing is known as a **desk check** and requires the use of representative test data. Suppose the *rate of pay* is $10 and the number of *hours worked* is 35. The calculation based upon this data will be of the form *gross wage = hourly rate x hours worked*, which computes to be $350. This value would then be displayed (output) on the monitor.

The names of the items of data from the flowchart can be represented as headings in a table. The desk check involves tracing through the flowchart and annotating the table with the values of the data. In this exercise the data will comprise a one-line entry in the following table:

rate of pay	hours worked	gross wage
10	35	350

Algorithm Example 1.2: Selection Between Instructions

If an hourly employee is paid overtime at the rate of 1.5 x hourly rate for working more than 40 hours, then the method of calculating the gross wage will depend upon the number of hours worked.

If the number of hours worked is greater than 40 hours, then the

gross wage with overtime = 1.5 x hourly rate x (hours worked - 40) + 40 x hourly rate

else

gross wage = hourly rate x hours worked

The solution to this example is given in Figure 1.19. Notice that the flowchart contains a new symbol in the shape of a decision diamond. This symbol represents a condition. The result of the condition will be either *yes* or *no*; and the two arrowed lines emerging from the symbol indicate these two possible paths. Using the condition, it is possible to select which instruction to execute next.

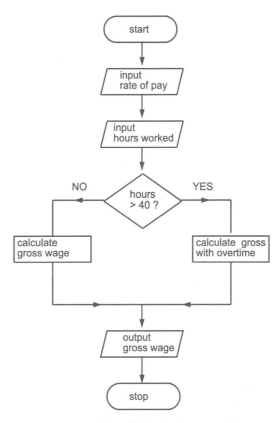

Figure 1.19 Flowchart showing selection

To apply a desk check to this design, you will need to choose two sets of data, that is one set to test each branch in the flowchart. If the first set of data is a rate of pay of $10 and the number of hours worked is 35, then the answer to the question *hours > 40 ?* will be *no*, and the gross wage will be calculated using the second formula; the output is a gross wage of $350. However, if the second set of test data is a rate of pay of $10 and the number of hours worked is 50, then the answer to the question *hours > 40 ?* will be *yes,* and the gross wage will be calculated using the first formula; the output is a gross wage of $550.

The names of the items of data that appear as headings in the following table are supplemented by the condition hours > 40.

rate of pay	hours worked	hours > 40?	gross wage
10	35	no	350
10	50	yes	550

Algorithm Example 1.3: Repetition

If a small company employs five workers, and if each employee is paid at the same hourly rate, it is possible to design an algorithm to calculate the gross weekly wage for each employee. We will assume that the same rate of pay is made for regular and overtime hours. The algorithm given in Example 1.1 can be modified so that the steps to input the number of hours worked, calculate the gross wage, and output the gross wage are repeated for each employee. If a counter is increased by one every time the gross wage is calculated and output for an employee, then when the counter reaches the value five, the steps will not need to be repeated again and the algorithm can stop. The flowchart for this algorithm is given in Figure 1.20. Notice that a **loop** has been created by asking the question *counter = 5 ?* If the answer is *no,* then a flow line is drawn that loops back into the flowchart to input the hours worked for the next employee and calculate and output the wage for that employee. Because the five employees are all paid at the same hourly rate, it will not be necessary to include the input rate of pay step within the loop; so the step has been placed before the entry into the loop. In using a counter to record the number of employees wages that have been processed, it is necessary to initialize this value to zero prior to entry into the loop.

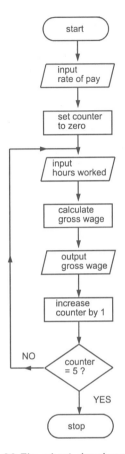

Figure 1.20 Flowchart showing repetition

The test data for this problem is assumed to be an hourly rate of $10 per hour and the values 35, 40, 45, 50, and 38 respectively, for the number of hours worked by each employee.

rate of pay	hours worked	gross wage	counter	counter = 5?
10			0	
	35	350	1	no
	40	400	2	no
	45	450	3	no
	50	500	4	no
	38	380	5	yes

19

These three algorithms have introduced you to three important structures in computer programming:

sequence: A series of instructions that the computer executes one after another in the order specified.

selection: Depending upon the result of a condition, the computer will select a different sequence of instructions to execute.

repetition: Depending upon the result of a condition, the computer may repeat a sequence of instructions a number of times.

These structures will be explained in detail in the context of the C language throughout this book.

The fourth example illustrates the use of three structures in one algorithm.

Algorithm Example 1.4: Sequence, Selection, and Repetition

The final example is an algorithm that calculates the gross weekly wages for five employees; overtime is paid at 1.5 x hourly rate for employees working more than 40 hours per week. You may assume that all employees are paid at the same hourly rate. The flowchart in Figure 1.20 can be modified so that the step calculate gross wage is replaced by the selection shown in Figure 1.21.

If the test data is chosen to be the same as that given in Example 1.3, then the following desk check can be made on the algorithm.

rate of pay	hours worked	hours > 40?	gross wage	counter	counter = 5?
10				0	
	35	no	350	1	no
	40	no	400	2	no
	45	yes	475	3	no
	50	yes	550	4	no
	38	no	380	5	yes

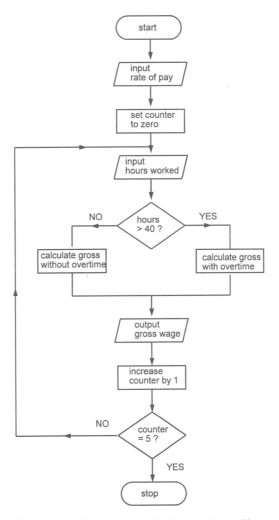

Figure 1.21 Sequence, selection and repetition

Summary

☐ A digital computer consists of the central processing unit and main memory as well as peripherals in the form of input, output, and secondary storage units.

☐ Data is input to the computer and processed under the direction of a program to produce results at an output unit.

☐ Common input units are a keyboard and a mouse, and common output units are a monitor and printer.

21

□ Secondary storage media include fixed hard disks, removable floppy disks, removable magneto/ optical disks, and removable tapes. These items may also be considered as input/ output devices, since all permit both reading and writing.

□ Computers can be either stand-alone devices or part of a computer network that contains many workstations.

□ The advantages of networks are that software and hardware peripherals can be shared between the network users and processing power is distributed over the network by virtue of each terminal having its own processing power.

□ In a time-sharing system, a central computer may service many dumb terminals.

□ There are three levels of computer language: high (for example, C), low (assembly-level language), and machine code (binary representation).

□ Programs written in a high-level language, such as C, must be compiled, linked, and loaded into memory before they can be executed by a computer.

□ The supervision of the running of a program on a computer is one of the tasks of the operating system.

□ Programming consists of analysing the problem, designing an algorithm, coding the algorithm into a computer program, testing the computer program, and supplying sufficient documentation so that the program can easily be understood and modified by others.

□ Algorithm design can be represented in the form of a flowchart.

□ Three constructs form the basis of writing computer programs, sequence, selection and repetition.

Review Questions

1. What are bits?

2. How are bits represented inside a digital computer?

3. How are bits represented on magnetic disks and optical disks?

4. What is stored in the main memory of a computer?

5. What is a program?

6. What is data?

7. What is the purpose of the arithmetic and logic unit?

8. What is the purpose of the control unit?

9. What are the five major hardware units of a digital computer system, and how are these represented in a typical personal computer?

10. Discuss the relative capacities of the various storage media.

11. What is a byte?

12. List three input units and three output units.

13. What are the most common input and output units in a C development environment ?

14. What are the major advantages of computer networks?

15. Why is it necessary to translate a C program into a machine-oriented language ?

16. What does a compiler do?

17. List the four phases that occur before a C program can be executed by a computer.

18. Define program portability.

19. Why are low-level languages not considered to be portable ?

20. List the activities involved in program design.

21. What is a flowchart?

22. What is a desk check?

23. Name three structures used in programming.

24. What is documentation?

25. What is peer-group evaluation?

Programming Exercises

26. Draw a flowchart to represent making a cup of instant coffee. Use the following operations in the correct logical order in your answer.

stir contents of cup
switch electric power on kettle
start
get cup and saucer
put one teaspoon of instant coffee into cup
wait for water in kettle to boil
put one teaspoon of sugar into cup
stop
pour boiling water into cup
fill electric kettle with water
switch off electric kettle

27. Devise an algorithm for crossing a road on foot, by inserting the operations and conditions into the correct logical sequence on the flowchart illustrated in Figure 1.22. The algorithm should take into account that a marked crossing may be nearby.

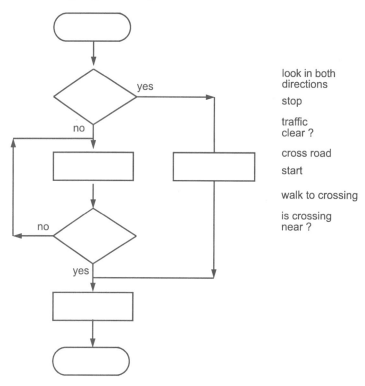

look in both
directions

stop

traffic
clear ?

cross road

start

walk to crossing

is crossing
near ?

Figure 1.22

28. Construct an algorithm using a flowchart to count and output the natural numbers from 10 to 15, inclusive. You should initialize your number counter to 10, output this value, increase the number counter by 1, and then test to see if the counter is less than or equal to 15. If the value is not greater than 15, repeat the output and incremental steps until the condition becomes false. Desk check the algorithm.

29. Modify the algorithm represented by the flowchart in Example 1.4 to handle any number of employees (not just five employees as stated in the problem). The data 10, 35, 40, 45, 50, 38, 60, -1 represents the rate of pay (first number) followed by a series of numbers representing the number of hours worked by each employee. The data string is terminated with the value -1. In redrawing the flowchart do not use a counter, but detect when the data terminator -1 is input in order to exit from the loop. Desk check the algorithm. Hint - place the decision to exit from the loop at the beginning of the loop.

30. Figure 1.14 illustrates the four phases of program implementation. Use this figure to complete the flowchart illustrated in Figure 1.23 so that the operations and conditions appear in logical sequence.

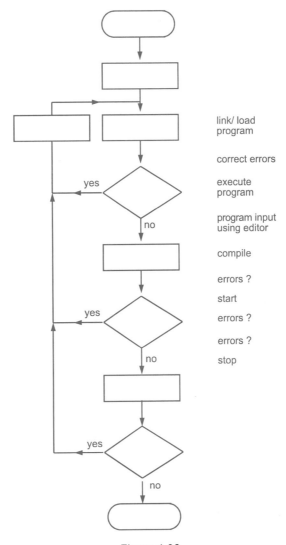

link/ load
program

correct errors

execute
program

program input
using editor

compile

errors ?

start

errors ?

errors ?

stop

Figure 1.23

31. Assume that the words in a sentence occupy no more than one line, are separated by a single space, and that the sentence is terminated by a period. Devise an algorithm in the form of a flowchart to read single characters from a sentence and count how many words are in the sentence.

32. The lengths of four sides of a regular quadrilateral and one internal angle are input to a computer. Design an algorithm, represented as a flowchart, to categorize the shape of the quadrilateral as a square, rhombus, rectangle, or parallelogram.

The rules for determining the shape of the regular quadrilateral are given in the following table:

25

name of shape	right angle between two sides?	all sides equal?
square	yes	yes
rectangle	yes	no
rhombus	no	yes
parallelogram	no	no

Programming Problems

The following questions require you to use your computer. You are not expected to understand the meaning of the instructions in the following programs; however, you can probably guess what they do.

33 (a) Input and save the following C program on your computer.

```
#include <stdio.h>
void main(void)
{
   printf("This is my first C program!");
}
```

(b) Compile the program. If it contains errors, then compare it with the program in 33 (a) and you will probably find your errors. Correct the errors and recompile the program.
(c) Link/load the program.
(d) Run the program.

Note: Depending upon the environment you are using steps (c) and (d) may be combined into one step.

34 (a) Input and save the following C program on your computer (it contains deliberate errors).

```
#include <stdio.h>
void main(void)
{
   printf("Computing can be fun ")
   print("provided you get it right!");
}
```

(b) Compile the program and study the error messages. Can you deduce what and where the errors are?
(c) Return to the editor and correct the line `printf("Computing can be fun ")`. Recompile the program. At this stage it should be error free. If it still contains errors, then compare your program with the program in 33 (a).
(d) If the program compiles without errors, then link/load the program. This will produce an error. Can you guess at this stage what it is?
(e) Return to the editor and correct the line `print("provided you get it right!");`.
(f) Recompile the program, and if it is error free then link/ load the program. If this operation is successful, then run the program.

26

Chapter 2
Data

If data are facts and figures, how can we represent these in the C language?

This chapter contains information about data found in everyday life. It explores the different characteristics of data such as type, size, and format and introduces you to four data types: *integer*, *real*, *character,* and *string*. The methods of declaring these types of data and documenting their meaning in a C program is also examined. By the end of the chapter, you should have an understanding of the following topics:

☐   How to recognize data and classify it by type.

☐   The identification of variables and constants.

☐   How to represent variables and constants in a program.

☐   Conversion between different number bases.

2.1 What is Data?

We first encountered the term data in Chapter 1 where it was defined as the name given to facts and figures. The word data has found its way into everyday language. The Concise Oxford Dictionary definition of data is "1 known facts or things used as a basis for inference or reckoning. 2 quantities or characters operated on by a computer etc". Put another way, data can be numbers, groups of characters, or both that represent facts. Examples of data are all around us. Consider the diagram of a road sign, Figure 2.1, that you might come across when traveling through Massachusetts. A group of characters represents a name, for example, Boston, and a positive whole number represents a distance, for example, 40 miles.

Marlborough	15
Boston	40
Gloucester	60

Figure 2.1 A road sign

Figure 2.2 illustrates a thermometer that measures the temperature outdoors. The scale on the thermometer is graduated in both degrees Fahrenheit and degrees Celsius. The illustration makes clear that the temperature outside is cold - either $+14^\circ$ Fahrenheit or -10° Celsius. Either a positive or a negative whole number represents the temperature.

Figure 2.3 illustrates a menu. Groups of characters represent the names of the items of food or drink, and a number containing a decimal fraction, represents the price of each item.

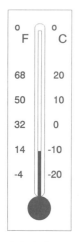

Figure 2.2 A thermometer

Ben's Breakfast Bar

MENU

Eggs - scrambled or fried	$ 2.75
Blueberry Pancakes	$ 4.00
Bagel with cream cheese	$ 1.50
English Muffin	$ 0.95
Yogurt	$ 1.00
Corned Beef Hash	$ 1.75
Toast	$ 0.75
Home Fries	$ 1.00
Tea or Coffee	$ 0.75
Hot Chocolate	$ 0.95

all prices exclude local taxes

Figure 2.3 A menu

Figure 2.4 illustrates a sales receipt. The name of the cashier is represented by a group of characters; the date is represented by whole numbers indicating month, day, and year; and the time of day by whole numbers and a single character. The names of the purchases are represented by groups of characters, and the quantities purchased by whole numbers. The unit cost, purchase price, subtotal, sales tax, total, cash amount, and change are all represented by numbers containing decimal fractions.

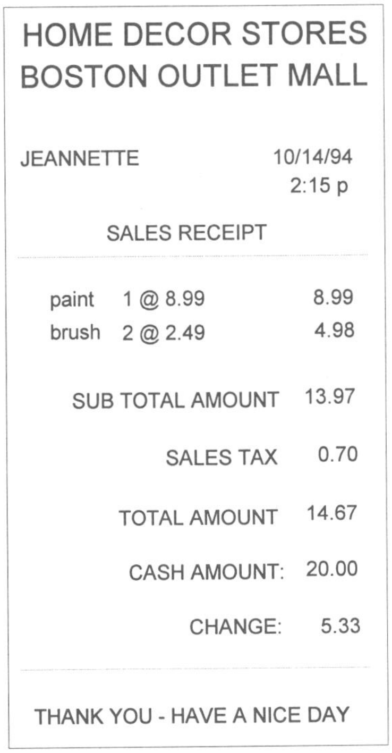

```
HOME DECOR STORES
BOSTON OUTLET MALL


JEANNETTE                    10/14/94
                               2:15 p

         SALES RECEIPT


paint    1 @ 8.99              8.99
brush    2 @ 2.49              4.98


    SUB TOTAL AMOUNT          13.97

            SALES TAX          0.70

        TOTAL AMOUNT          14.67

       CASH AMOUNT:           20.00

            CHANGE:            5.33


THANK YOU - HAVE A NICE DAY
```

Figure 2.4 A sales receipt

These few examples show that data can take the form of whole numbers, such as distances, temperatures, hours, minutes, month, day, and year; numbers with a decimal fraction, such as amounts of money; single characters such as *a* or *p* as codes for a.m. or p.m. respectively; and finally groups of characters, such as names of towns, items of food and drink on a menu, names of people, and names of purchases.

2.2 Types of Data

Using the data from the previous section it is possible to identify four data types: **integer** (positive or negative whole numbers), **real** (numbers with a decimal fraction), **character** (a single character), and **string** (a group of characters). For example, in Figure 2.1 the name of the city Boston is composed of a group of characters and is known as a string data type. The distance to Boston of 40 miles, is a whole number and is known as an integer data type.

The thermometer shown in Figure 2.2 contains two temperature scales. Both temperature scales use positive and negative numbers. If you assume that the accuracy of the scale is to a whole number of degrees, then the positive or negative whole numbers are of data type integer.

The menu shown in Figure 2.3 contains a mixture of data. The names of items of food and drink are of data type string; the prices contain a decimal fraction and are numbers of data type real.

The sales receipt shown in Figure 2.4 contains the name of the sales assistant and the names of the purchases and is of data type string. The date expressed as month, day, and year are data type integers; and the time in hours and minutes are represented by integers followed by either *a* or *p* of data type character. The quantity of goods purchased is a whole number and is of data type integer. The unit cost and purchase price of the goods, subtotal, sales tax, total, cash amount, and change are all numbers of data type real.

2.3 Data Types

Integer and real numbers are stored within specific formats in the memory of a computer. However, we need not be concerned with the organization of this data in memory in order to utilize the data types in the C language. In this section you will learn that the ranges of values that can be stored in a computer's memory depend upon the data types being used.

Integer Numbers

Integers are stored within a fixed number of bytes. The range of integer values that can be stored in the memory of a computer is machine dependent. A common size for integer storage is two bytes, which gives the range of integers that can be stored as -32768 to +32767. In C the type integer can be described as

```
int
```

However, if larger integers are to be stored, then they can be declared as:

```
long    int
```

which increases integer storage to four bytes and gives the range of integers that can be stored as -2147483648 to + 2147483647.

Both integer and long integer can be qualified as being

```
unsigned        int
unsigned long   int
```

in which case the range of numbers that can be stored are 0 to +65535 and 0 to +4294967295 respectively.

Real Numbers

Real numbers are stored within a fixed number of bytes using a floating-point representation of the number. The number of bytes can vary between four, eight, and ten; however, four is common. Real numbers have two parts, a **mantissa** (the fractional part) and an **exponent** (the power to which the base of the number must be raised in order to give the correct value of the number when multiplied by the mantissa). For example 437.875 can be rewritten as 0.437875×10^3, where 0.437875 is the mantissa and 3 is the exponent.

A four-byte organization of a real number will give a maximum value of 3.4×10^{38} and a minimum value of 1.17×10^{-38} with an accuracy of 6 decimal digits. The majority of decimal fractions do not convert exactly into binary fractions; therefore, the representation of a real number is not always accurate. In C the type real can be described as

```
float
```

The more storage space that is allocated to the mantissa, the greater the precision of the real number being represented. Allocating more storage space to the exponent increases the range of real numbers that can be stored. If the storage allocated to real numbers is increased to 8 bytes, then a precision of 15 decimal digits with a maximum value of 1.79×10^{308} and the smallest value of 2.22×10^{-308} is possible. Real numbers are represented to a greater range and accuracy in C if they are declared as

```
double
```

When the result of a computation is too large to be represented, the number has **overflowed** storage. Conversely, when a result is too small to be represented, the number has **underflowed** storage and the computer will probably return the result as zero.

Characters

A character is stored in a single byte of memory using a 7-bit binary code. The list of American Standard Code for Information Interchange (ASCII) character codes is given in Table 2.1. Notice that characters are not confined to letters of the alphabet but can be digits and other symbols.

In C the type declaration for a character is described as

```
char
```

and is used to denote a single character taken from the ASCII character set. A character is stored using its ASCII code, which is an integer in the range 0 to 127.

Strings

The type declaration string is not implicitly defined as part of the C language. A **string** is stored as a set of characters within consecutive memory locations. Each character is stored as the binary representation of its ASCII code and occupies one byte of memory. The end of the string is denoted by the null character, which is automatically appended to the string. A **null** character has an ASCII code of zero.

2.4 Variables

Data may be thought of as occupying areas of the computer's memory in the same way as people occupy houses in a street. To distinguish different families in different houses, we could use either the surname of the family or the number of the house. To distinguish data in different areas of memory, we could give the data a name or use the numeric memory address where the data is stored.

Table 2.1 ASCII codes for characters

Code	Character	Code	Character	Code	Character
000	NUL	043	+	086	V
001	SOH	044	,	087	W
002	STX	045	-	088	X
003	ETX	046	.	089	Y
004	EOT	047	/	090	Z
005	ENQ	048	0	091	[
006	ACK	049	1	092	\
007	BEL	050	2	093	]
008	BS	051	3	094	^
009	HT	052	4	095	_
010	LF	053	5	096	`
011	VT	054	6	097	a
012	FF	055	7	098	b
013	CR	056	8	099	c
014	SO	057	9	100	d
015	SI	058	:	101	e
016	DLE	059	;	102	f
017	DC1	060	<	103	g
018	DC2	061	=	104	h
019	DC3	062	>	105	i
020	DC4	063	?	106	j
021	NAK	064	@	107	k
022	STN	065	A	108	l
023	ETB	066	B	109	m
024	AN	067	C	110	n
025	EM	068	D	111	o
026	SUB	069	E	112	p
027	ESC	070	F	113	q
028	FS	071	G	114	r
029	GS	072	H	115	s
030	RS	073	I	116	t
031	US	074	J	117	u
032	space	075	K	118	v
033	!	076	L	119	w
034	"	077	M	120	x
035	#	078	N	121	y
036	$	079	O	122	z
037	%	080	P	123	{
038	&	081	Q	124		
039	'	082	R	125	}
040	(	083	S	126	~
041	)	084	T	127	del
042	*	085	U		

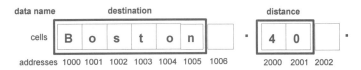

Figure 2.5 Data referred to by name

In C it is much easier to refer to data by name and let the computer do the work of finding out where in memory the data is stored. Figure 2.5 illustrates how data can be stored across the storage cells and accessed by the names given to the groups of cells and not the addresses of the cells. Although the contents of these cells have been illustrated as characters, within the memory they are stored as binary numbers.

When a program that uses these data names is executed, the instructions may change the contents of some, if not all, of the groups of cells. Because of this change or variation in the data, the data names are known as **variables**. A programmer is required to compose many different types of names in a program, of which variables are just one type. The collective name given to all these names is **identifiers**. C uses the following rules for the composition of identifiers.

An identifier may contain combinations of letters of the alphabet (both-upper case A-Z and lower-case a-z), an underscore character _ and decimal digits, provided the identifier begins with either a letter or an underscore character. C distinguishes between the use of upper-case and lower-case letters in an identifier. Identifiers can normally be of any length; however, the particular implementation of C being used may recognize only a certain number of characters. An identifier must not be the same as C keywords listed in Figure 2.6.

auto	double	int	struct
break	else	long	switch
case	enum	register	typedef
char	extern	return	union
const	float	short	unsigned
continue	for	signed	void
default	goto	sizeof	volatile
do	if	static	while

Figure 2.6 Keywords

The C compiler looks for certain **keywords**, words with special meanings when it compiles a program. Keywords are treated as reserved words - reserved for use by the compiler. We will use keywords in program statements, but not as identifiers.

Style Matters:

composing useful identifiers

A programmer should always compose identifiers so they convey meaning. The identifiers `name`, `street`, `town`, and `zipcode` imply the meaning of the data that they represent, unlike the nondescriptive identifiers `N`, `S`, `T` and `Z`. When an identifier is constructed from more than one word, each word should either begin with an upper-case letter or be separated from the next by an underscore; an identifier should be easy to read, and its meaning should be clear. Examples of legal identifiers are `SubTotal`, `sales_tax`, `unit_cost`, and `rate_of_pay`.

2.5 Variable Declaration

A C program contains data declarations and instructions. The data declarations must appear before the instructions, since they describe the type of data used by the instructions.

If the values of the data in the storage cells can be changed by the instructions in a computer program, then the values of the data vary and the data identifiers are known as variables. The syntax for making a variable declaration follows.

C Syntax:

variable
declaration

data type   identifier list ;

For example, the data declarations for the road sign shown in Figure 2.1 might be

```
char    destination[12];
int     distance;
```

Caution:

possible
program-
ming
error

Because the name of a destination was defined as a *string* , it is necessary to declare it as type char with twelve consecutive memory locations set aside for storing the largest string. The string "Marlborough" has eleven characters, but it is necessary to include one more character for storing the end-of-string null terminator. The null terminator is automatically appended to the string; therefore, it is necessary to ensure that enough memory has been designated, and hence the declaration char destination[12]. Failure to declare this extra character may result in other data being corrupted by the character string.

Data declarations for the thermometer and the menu shown in Figure 2.2 and 2.3 respectively might be:

```
int     Fahrenheit_temp;
int     Celsius_temp;
```

and

```
char    menu_item[26];
float   price;
```

The largest string in menu_item was "Eggs - scrambled or fried"; this string contains twenty-five characters including spaces, hence the declaration char menu_item[26]. Notice that the declaration of the name of the breakfast bar, the title and the last line of the menu, and the currency sign have not been included, since these are not variable quantities. Only the items of food and drink and the prices will vary according to the data being used.

34

The data declarations for the sales receipt shown in Figure 2.4 follow. Once again information that does not change, for example, the name and address of the store and messages, have not been declared as variables.

```
char    name[10];
int     month;
int     day;
int     year;
int     hours;
int     minutes;
char    am_pm;
char    description[6];
int     quantity;
float   unit_cost;
float   price;
float   sub_total;
float   sales_tax;
float   total;
float   cash;
float   change;
```

Note the declaration of a single character, am_pm, does not require the storage length to be stated after the variable name, as is the case with strings.

To reduce the number of lines used in declaring variables, it is permissible to group the declarations according to their data types. For example, the previous list of declarations can be rewritten on fewer lines; however, this style is harder to read.

```
char    am_pm, name[10], description[6];
int     month, day, year, hours, minutes, quantity;
float   unit_cost, price, sub_total, sales_tax, total, cash, change;
```

When defining the lengths of strings, it is necessary to allocate only enough memory to store the largest string plus the terminating null character. You might adopt the habit of allocating the same arbitrary amount of memory to every string. In the sales-receipt example both the name of the cashier and the name of a product might have been allocated an arbitrary ten characters.

Variables can be initialized at the point of declaration. If JEANNETTE is the only cashier in the store, it is permissible to declare

```
char    name[10] = "JEANNETTE";
```

or

```
char    name[] = "JEANNETTE";
```

Style matters:

string initialization

In this latter case it was not necessary to specify the amount of memory to allocate to the string, since the number of characters found in the string "JEANNETTE" can be calculated at the time of compilation. Both declarations are equivalent; however, the style of the second declaration is preferable because it is less prone to error than the first.

35

2.6 Constant Declaration

Many programs have data values that remain constant during the running of the program. In the previous example, if the name of the cashier never changed during the running of the program, then that name could be declared as a **constant**. Other examples of items of data that remain constant could be the rate of sales tax at 5%, mathematical PI at 3.14159, and the Earth's gravitational constant (g) at the surface 9.80665 ms^{-2}.

The syntax for a constant declaration follows

C Syntax:

constant declaration

$$const \quad data\, type \quad identifier \quad = \quad value\,;$$

Such constants can be declared in a C program as

```
const   char    name[]      = "JEANNETTE";
const   float   tax_rate    = 0.05;
const   float   PI          = 3.14159;
const   float   g           = 9.80065;
```

Integer constants can be defined as being long, if the letter L or l appears after the number, for example 12345678L.

Integer constants can be defined as being unsigned if the letter U or u appears after the number, for example 43456U.

A floating constant can be represented in either decimal notation or in scientific notation using the letter E or e to denote the exponent, for example, 1234.56 and 0.7865E+02.

Floating constants are, by default, stored in double precision. If single precision is required then either the letters F or f should appear after the number, for example, 6.784f.

Character constants are enclosed between single apostrophes, for example 'A', and can be declared as follows:

```
const   char    letter = 'A';
```

String constants are enclosed between double quotes, for example, "abracadabra", and the compiler marks the end of the string with a null character. A constant string can be declared as follows:

```
const   char    magic[] = "abracadabra";
```

2.7 Number Bases

In the C language numbers can be represented in octal (base 8), decimal (base 10) and hexadecimal (base 16). Despite all information being stored in the computer in binary (base 2) there is no equivalent representation for binary numbers in the C language. One reason for this is that binary numbers tend to be long and cumbersome, for example, the number 0111111111111111 is 32767 in decimal. The hexadecimal system is used as a shorthand method of representing binary numbers. Table 2.2 shows that a hexadecimal digit is a convenient representation of four bits; for example, 0111111111111111 is 7FFF in hexadecimal (don't worry about how this conversion is done at the moment). Therefore, in applications where it is necessary to refer to individual bits within the computer, the hexadecimal number system may be used.

Table 2.2 Number bases 2, 8, 10 and 16

binary	octal	decimal	hexadecimal
0000	0	0	0
0001	1	1	1
0010	2	2	2
0011	3	3	3
0100	4	4	4
0101	5	5	5
0110	6	6	6
0111	7	7	7
1000	10	8	8
1001	11	9	9
1010	12	10	A
1011	13	11	B
1100	14	12	C
1101	15	13	D
1110	16	14	E
1111	17	15	F

To a lesser extent an octal number system may also be used as a shorthand notation for binary numbers, since an octal digit can represent three bits.

Decimal integer constants contain the digits 0 to 9 and must not begin with 0 (zero), for example, 237, 18567, and -789.

Octal integer constants contain the digits 0 to 7 and must begin with 0 (zero), for example 017, 05643, and 0234.

Hexadecimal integer constants contain the digits 0 to 9 and the letters a to f, or A to F and must begin with 0x, for example 0x12FF, 0x56ABC, and 0x89A345.

In describing the data types for octal and hexadecimal numbers, it is permissible to use the same declarations as for decimal integers. Therefore, the types `int` and `long int`, qualified with `unsigned`, are appropriate in the following examples:

```
unsigned int A = 0347;
```

is used to initialize the variable A with the octal number 347.

```
unsigned long int B = 0x56A7C
```

is used to initialize the variable B with the hexadecimal number 56A7C.

2.8 Number Conversion

In this section we will consider several algorithms for converting from one number system to another.

Decimal to Binary, Octal, and Hexadecimal

To convert an integer decimal number to number base 2, 8, or 16, use the following algorithm:

1. *The decimal number is treated as a numerator and the number base as the denominator.*
2. *Divide the numerator by the denominator to obtain the integral quotient and the remainder.*
3. *The remainder becomes the (next) least significant digit in the conversion.*
4. *When the integral quotient is zero, the conversion is complete.*
5. *The integral quotient is taken to be the new numerator.*
6. *Repeat from step 2.*

Figure 2.7 uses the algorithm to convert a decimal number (75) to a binary number.

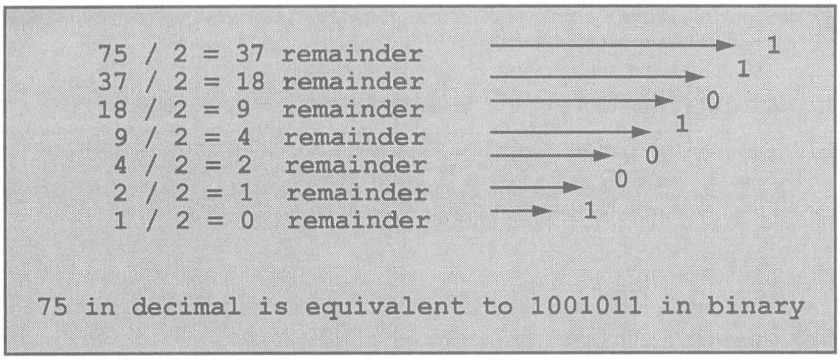

```
75 / 2 = 37  remainder                          1
37 / 2 = 18  remainder                        1
18 / 2 = 9   remainder                      0
 9 / 2 = 4   remainder                    1
 4 / 2 = 2   remainder                  0
 2 / 2 = 1   remainder                0
 1 / 2 = 0   remainder              1


75 in decimal is equivalent to 1001011 in binary
```

Figure 2.7 Conversion decimal to binary

Figure 2.8 illustrates the conversion of a decimal (3947) to hexadecimal.

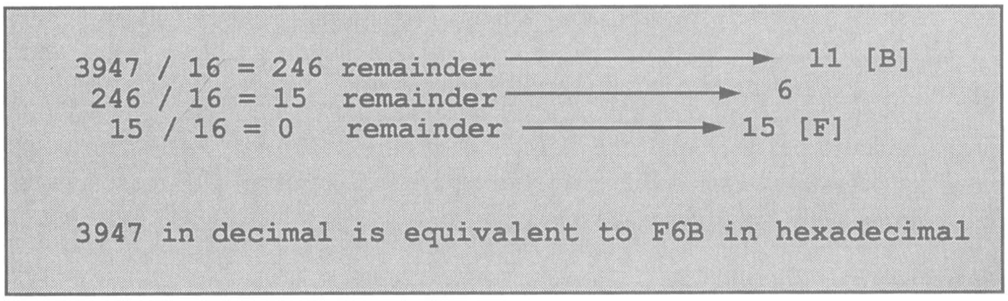

```
3947 / 16 = 246  remainder              11  [B]
 246 / 16 = 15   remainder               6
  15 / 16 = 0    remainder              15  [F]


3947 in decimal is equivalent to F6B in hexadecimal
```

Figure 2.8 Conversion decimal to hexadecimal

A similar approach is taken to convert a decimal number to octal. What is the equivalent octal number to 435 in decimal? (The answer is 663, but can you do the conversion?)

Binary, Octal, and Hexadecimal to Decimal

Use the following algorithm to convert an integer binary, octal, or hexadecimal number to a decimal number.

Each digit in the number (base n) represents the base n raised to a power, with the least significant digit representing n^0, the next most significant digit n^1, the next most significant digit n^2, and so on. Each of these values represents the appropriate weight of the respective digits in the number. The sum of the product of each of the weights with their respective digits is calculated and is equivalent to the decimal number.

From this general algorithm, it follows that each binary digit represents the base 2 raised to a power with the least significant digit representing 2^0, the next most significant digit 2^1, the next most significant digit 2^2, and so on. For example, the binary number 01110011 is $1x2^6+1x2^5+1x2^4+1x2^1+1x2^0 = 64+32+16+2+1 = 115$.

Each octal digit represents the base 8 raised to a power with the least significant digit representing 8^0, the next most significant digit 8^1, the next most significant digit 8^2, and so on. For example, the octal number 05643 is $5x8^3+6x8^2+4x8^1+3x8^0$, which is equivalent to 2979 in decimal.

Finally, each hexadecimal digit represents the base 16 raised to a power with the least significant digit representing 16^0, the next most significant digit 16^1, the next most significant 16^2, and so on. For example, the hexadecimal number 0x12FF is $1x16^3+2x16^2+15x16^1+15x16^0$, which is equivalent to 4863 in decimal.

Conversion between Binary, Octal, and Hexadecimal

A binary number can be converted to octal by partitioning the bit string into groups of three bits starting at the least significant end of the number and evaluating each group as an octal digit. For example,

0111001100011110 = 0 | 111 | 001 | 100 | 011 | 110 = 071436.

A binary number can be converted to hexadecimal by partitioning the bit string into groups of four bits, starting at the least significant end of the number and evaluating each group as a hexadecimal digit. For example,

0111001100011110 = 0111 | 0011 | 0001 | 1110 = 731E.

These two examples show that to convert either an octal or hexadecimal number to binary requires representing each digit as its respective three-bit or four-bit binary number. For example,

06504 = 110101000100 and

0x32FC = 0011001011111100.

Finally, the simplest method to convert from octal to hexadecimal and vice versa is to convert either number to its equivalent binary number and then convert accordingly. For example,

071436 = 0111001100011110 = 0111 | 0011 | 0001 | 1110 = 731E

Summary

- [ ] Data is composed of characters and numbers that represent facts and figures.

- [ ] The integer data type is `int`; however, `long int` may be used to represent a wider range of integers. Both `int` and `long int` may be qualified as being `unsigned`.

- [ ] The real data type is `float`; however, `double` can be used to improve the accuracy of storage of real numbers.

- [ ] The character data type is `char`.

- [ ] The data type string is not implicitly defined in the language and must be explicitly defined in a program as a variable or constant of type `char`, qualified by the amount of storage space to set aside for all the characters in the string plus one byte for the terminating null character.

- [ ] The size of data that can be stored in a computer's memory is limited by its type and must fit between a predefined range.

- [ ] Data must conform to set formats.

- [ ] Data stored in the memory of a computer can be referenced through a data name invented by the programmer and should be self-documenting.

- [ ] Data names must conform to the rules for identifiers.

- [ ] All the variables used in a C program must be declared before they can be used by instructions contained in the program.

- [ ] Variable data declaration specifies the type of data followed by the name of the data.

- [ ] Variables may be initialized at the point of declaration.

- [ ] Data values that do not change during the running of a program may be declared as constants.

- [ ] Integers can be expressed as octal, decimal, or hexadecimal numbers. However, there is no representation for binary numbers in C.

Review Questions

1. Describe the meaning of the data types integer, real, character, and string.

2. How are the four types listed in question (1) represented as data types in C?

3. How would you declare an integer variable that had a value of one million?

4. What is the effect of qualifying an integer as being `unsigned`?

5. Distinguish between the mantissa and exponent of a real number.

6. True or false - real numbers may be described as having the type `float` or `double`.

7. True or false - a character is stored as an integer value.

8. True or false - an identifier may begin with an underscore.

9. True or false - the following declaration is sufficient to store the string "apple":

```
char fruit[5];
```

10. Why is a string terminated with a null character?

11. What range of signed integers can be stored within 2 bytes?

12. What is the smallest real number that can be stored as type `float`?

13. What is underflow and overflow?

14. What is a variable?

15. Is `return` a keyword?

16. What is a constant?

17. Is the following declaration correct?

```
const float;
```

18. True or false - an identifier described as being a constant may have its initial value changed by statements in a program.

19. Is the syntax of the following declaration correct?

```
constant float tax = 0.05;
```

20. True or false - 71 is a legal octal constant.

21. True or false - 0x3FF is a legal hexadecimal constant.

22. True or false - 03276 is a legal decimal constant.

23. True or false - an unsigned integer constant is written with the letter U after the number.

24. True or false - floating constants are stored by default in double precision.

25. True or false - single precision real constants contain the letter f after the number.

Programming Exercises

26. From the illustrations in Figures 2.9 and 2.10 of items found in everyday life, discuss what you consider to be data and classify the data by type as variables declared in a C program.

COMMUTER RAIL FARES

Zone	One-Way	Half-Fare	Monthly Pass	Family Fare
1	2.00	1.00	64.00	8.00
2	2.25	1.10	72.00	9.00
3	2.50	1.25	82.00	10.00
4	3.00	1.50	94.00	12.00
5	3.25	1.60	104.00	13.00
6	3.50	1.75	112.00	14.00
7	3.75	1.85	120.00	15.00
8	4.00	2.00	128.00	16.00

Figure 2.9 Commuter rail fares

World forecasts

City	Today
Acapulco	90/79 s
Athens	79/59 pc
Bangkok	90/78 pc
Beijing	62/38 pc
Berlin	63/51 r
Bermuda	81/74 pc
Budapest	72/52 pc
Buenos Aries	83/62 pc
Cairo	89/ 68 pc
Dublin	53/ 39 c
Frankfurt	63/56 sh
Hong Kong	84/74 s

Note

The numbers refer to high and low temperatures in degrees Fahrenheit, and the abbreviations describe the following weather conditions.

s - sunny
pc - partial cloud
r - rain
c - cloud

Figure 2.10 Temperatures around the world

27. Identify the illegal variable names in the following list of identifiers. Explain why you think the names are illegal.

(a) PriceOfBricks (b) net-pay (c) X1   (d) cost of paper
(e) INTEGER   (f) ?X?Y   (g) 1856AD (h) float

28. Describe the types of the following items of data:

(a) "Lexington" (b) ';'   (c) +156   (d) 2147483647
(e) 247.9   (f) 0.732E+01F (g) 0173 (h) 0xAB0
(i) 2179U   (j) 23.96f

29. Use Table 2.1 to determine the integer values of the ASCII codes of the following characters:

(a) A   (b) M   (c) *   (d) a
(e) m   (f) NUL   (g) 9

30. Write the following numbers using the E notation for real numbers; only one nonzero digit should precede the decimal point.

(a) -874.458   (b) +0.00123456   (c) 123456789.0

31. Explain why the following numbers cannot be stored as numbers of type `float` within the ranges defined in this chapter. Suggest how you would change the data type to accommodate the numbers in the memory of the computer.

(a) 30.16E+38   (b) 1234567890.1234567 (c) -0.000456E-39

32. If a computer stored real numbers to an accuracy of 6 decimal digits and a signed 2 digit exponent in the range -38 to +38, comment upon the representation of the following data:

(a) 3.7948×10^{16}.   (b) -2.6394782   (c) 739.4621348
(d) $-17694.327 \times 10^{35}$ (e) $0.000000471 \times 10^{-34}$

33. Write suitable type declarations for the following constants:

(a) 0213   (b) 45678   (c) 0xFABC46   (d) "The Big Apple!"

34. Convert the following numbers into decimal values.

(a) 0234   (b) 0x56ABC   (c) 01011011

35. Convert the decimal number 87456 into binary, octal and hexadecimal numbers.

36. Draw a flowchart to convert a decimal number to hexadecimal.

37. Draw a flowchart to convert an eight-bit binary number to decimal.

Programming Problems

The following questions require you to use your computer. At this stage you are not expected to understand the meaning of the instructions in the following programs, however, you should by now understand the declarations. Input, save, compile, and run each program.

38. Identify the variable declaration in this program. After the program has been run explain the significance of the number printed on the line after the character. Hint - refer to Table 2.1.

```
#include <stdio.h>
void main(void)
{
   char single_character;
```

```
    printf("input a single character ");
    scanf("%c", &single_character);
    printf("%d\n", single_character);
}
```

39. Edit the program from question (38), so that the following lines of code appear after the last statement in the program and before the closing brace }.

```
    printf("%o\n", single_character);
    printf("%X\n", single_character);
```

Compile and run the edited program; then explain the significance of the three numbers that appear on new lines after the character? Hint - convert the decimal number to octal and hexadecimal.

40. Identify the variable declaration in the following program. After compiling and running the program, explain the significance of the two numbers that are printed below the hexadecimal number.

```
#include <stdio.h>

void main(void)
{
    unsigned int hex_number;

    printf("input a four digit hexadecimal number ");
    scanf("%x", &hex_number);

    printf("%o\n", hex_number);
    printf("%d\n", hex_number);
}
```

41. Edit the preceding program to change the name of the variable to dec_number throughout the program. Edit the prompt to read input an unsigned four digit integer, and change "%x" to "%d" in the scanf statement. From the coding in the two programs shown in questions (38) and (40), deduce what new language statements are required to print the equivalent of the input decimal integer as an octal number and as a hexadecimal number.

Run the program and check that the decimal integer has been converted correctly to octal and hexadecimal values.

Chapter 3
Arithmetic, Input and Output

We are all familiar with the arithmetic of numbers, but how can we represent this knowledge and mathematical notation in the C language?

Up to now we have talked about the input and output of data in terms of keyboard input and screen output; but how can we get the computer to read data from a keyboard and display information on a screen?

This chapter addresses these issues; in particular, the following points are covered.

- □ Assignment.
- □ The construction of arithmetic expressions for the purpose of calculation.
- □ The order of evaluation of arithmetic expressions.
- □ C library functions.
- □ The main function.
- □ *Printf* routine to provide formatted output to a screen.
- □ *Scanf* routine to read data entered at a keyboard.

3.1 Assignment

Arithmetic operations are among the most fundamental instructions that can be included in a program. To understand arithmetic operations, it is helpful to conceptualize how a computer uses memory. In Section 2.4 we saw that data can be referenced by name in the memory of a computer. Figure 3.1 illustrates numbers being referenced by the names A, B, and C in three separate locations in memory.

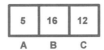

Figure 3.1 Numbers stored by name

The **arithmetic operators** + (addition), - (subtraction), * (multiplication), / (division), and % (remainder) can be used to make calculations on the stored numeric data. For example, A = B + C adds the contents of B to the contents of C and stores the result in A, destroying or overwriting the previous contents of A. Therefore, after the computer executes the statement A = B + C, the contents of A is changed. The result of this computation is shown in Figure 3.2. Similar before and after situations can be applied to other computations as illustrated in Figure 3.3.

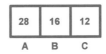

Figure 3.2 Result of the computation A=B+C

The syntax of an **assignment statement** is

C Syntax:

assignment

    identifier = expression

where the character = is known as an **assignment operator**. For example, from Figure 3.3

```
A = B + C + D
X = Y - Z
tax = price * tax_rate
time = distance / speed
C = A % B
```

are all examples of assignment statements.

The destination of an assignment will always be on the left-hand side of an assignment. A = 9 implies that A is assigned the value 9. The statement 9 = A has no meaning, since 9 is not a legal variable name. However, A = B implies that A is assigned the value of B, whereas B = A implies that B is assigned the value of A.

In the last example in Figure 3.3, the expression `counter = counter + 1` may seem a little unusual, since the variable counter appears on both sides of the expression. The statement should be read as follows: on the right-hand side of the expression, the current value of counter (3) is increased by 1, giving a result

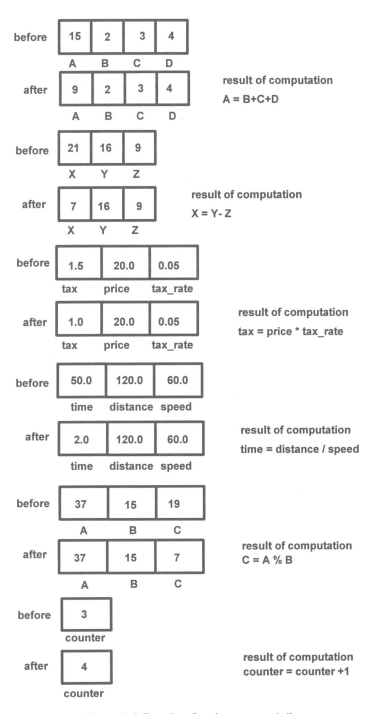

Figure 3.3 Results of various computations

of (4). This result is then assigned to the variable on the left-hand side of the expression, which also happens to be the variable counter. The old value of counter (3) is overwritten or destroyed by the new value (4). The effect of this statement has been to increase the value of the variable counter by 1.

The arithmetic operators in C can be divided into three categories.

unary operators

+ **unary plus**
- **unary minus**

have one operand and are used to represent positive or negative numbers, for example, -A, and +B.

binary multiplicative operators

* **multiplication**
/ **division**
% **remainder**

binary additive operators

+ **addition**
- **subtraction**

all have two operands, for example, A * B, A / B, A % B, A + B, and A - B.

The storage of integer and real numbers are organized differently and use different amounts of memory. Therefore, when operands are of different types, one or more of the operands must be converted to the type that can safely accommodate both values before any arithmetic can be performed. Type conversion can be implicit, in which case it is performed automatically when evaluating arithmetic expressions.

For example, an operation involving an integer type and a long integer type would promote the integer type to the long integer type for the purpose of performing arithmetic. However, the original type declaration for the integer variable does not change.

Type conversion is performed automatically when the type of the expression on the right-hand side of an assignment does not match the type of the variable on the left-hand side. In this case the value on the right-hand side of the assignment is converted to the type of the variable on the left-hand side.

```
int A;
float B;

B = A;
```

For example, the expression B = A implies that the value of A will be treated as a type float in order to perform the assignment. However, once again the original type declaration for integer A does not change.

Type conversion may also be explicit through the use of a **cast** operation. The syntax of this operation is

> (*type*) *expression*

where *type* in parenthesis indicates the type to which the expression should be converted. For example,

```
float   alpha;
int     beta;

alpha = (float) beta;
```

The cast expression, `(float) beta`, is used to convert `beta` in the expression to a number of type `float`. This does not imply that `beta` has changed its type from `int` to `float`; only the value has been converted to type `float` in the expression.

Integers, reals, and characters use different amounts of memory for storing data of a named type. For example, an integer (`int`) might require 2 bytes; a real number (`float`) 6 bytes, and a single character (`char`) 1 byte.

The operator **sizeof** has the syntax

> *sizeof (type)*

and will return an integral value corresponding to the number of bytes a particular data type requires to store data. For example,

```
sizeof(int)
```

might return 2 bytes for a personal computer or 4 bytes for a workstation.

```
sizeof(float)
```

might return 6 bytes.

3.2 Operator Precedence

If an expression was written as `A+B*C-D/E`, how would it be evaluated? There is a need to introduce a set of rules for the evaluation of such expressions. All operators have an associated hierarchy that determines the **order of precedence** for evaluating an expression.

Unary operators have a higher order of precedence than multiplicative operators, and multiplicative operators have a higher order of precedence than additive operators (see Table 3.1).

Expressions are evaluated by taking the operators with a higher priority before those of a lower priority. Generally, where operators are of the same priority, the expression is evaluated from left to right.

Expressions in parenthesis will be evaluated before non parenthesized expressions. Parenthesis, although not an operator, can be considered as having an order of precedence after unary operators.

The expression `A+B*C-D/E` can be evaluated by inspecting the operators and grouping operations according to the above rules. This process is illustrated in Figure 3.4; the numbers indicate the order of evaluation. The equivalent algebraic expression is given at each stage of the evaluation.

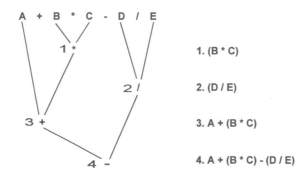

*Figure 3.4 Evaluation of A+B*C-D/E*

The expression `(X*X+Y*Y)/(A+B)` can be evaluated in the same way, as illustrated in Figure 3.5.

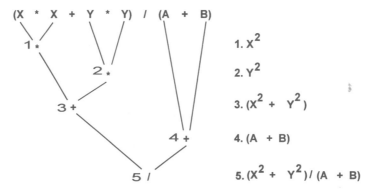

*Figure 3.5 Evaluation of (X*X+Y*Y)/(A+B)*

You should adopt the habit of using parenthesis in order to make the meaning of an expression as clear as possible. For example, the algebraic expression $\frac{UV}{WX}$ can be written in C as `U*V/W/X`; however, `(U*V)/(W*X)` is easier to understand. Similarly, $X^2+Y^2+\frac{4}{Z^2}x(X+Y)$

would be written in C as `(X*X)+(Y*Y)+4*(X+Y)/(Z*Z)`.

With the exception of the % remainder operator, which must have integer operands, all other operators can have integer or real operands or a mixture of both.

In a division, if both the operands are integer, then the fractional remainder in the result will be truncated.

Table 3.1 illustrates the priority level of the operators discussed in the previous section.

Table 3.1 Priority levels of operators

priority level	type	operator	symbol	example
2	unary	negate	–	`-A`
		plus	+	`+B`
		size	`sizeof`	`sizeof(int)`
3	cast	a data type	`(type)`	`(float)`
4	multiplicative	multiply	*	`A * B`
		divide	/	`A / B`
		remainder	%	`A % B`
5	additive	add	+	`A + B`
		subtract	–	`A - B`
15	assignment	equals	=	`A = B`

3.3 The Standard Library

In common with such high-level computer languages as Ada and Modula-2, C contains no statements in the definition of the language for the input and output of data. These languages are supplied with libraries that contain routines for input, and output as well as other routines. Whenever data is to be input or results output, the most appropriate routines from the libraries should be used.

A compiler **directive** is an instruction to the compiler, rather than an instruction to be compiled and translated into machine code. The #include directive makes it possible to include any previously written character file in the source file. A **header file** defines certain values, symbols, and routines; is written in C; and is supplied with the compiler. Header files are always given the suffix .h by convention. Input and output routines are all defined in the header file <stdio.h>; therefore, it is necessary to write the directive #include <stdio.h> at the beginning of a program if any of these routines are to be used in the program.

The ANSI C **standard library** is rich in routines that assist the programmer in developing software. The standard library is divided into fifteen parts, and each part is described by a header. The most common header files that you will encounter in this book are

<float.h>	characteristics of floating types
<limits.h>	sizes of integral types
<math.h>	mathematics
<stdio.h>	input/ output
<stdlib.h>	general utilities
<string.h>	string handling

A comprehensive account of the fifteen header files appears in Appendix A.

When routines from the standard library are used in a program, the programmer must include the appropriate header names at the beginning of the program.

3.4 Library Functions

When you use a C compiler, you will normally have access to an appropriate copy of the C library reference manual. This manual contains a description of all the library functions in the fifteen header files. A **library function** is a routine stored in the standard C library that you may include in your program without having to write it yourself.

The function **strcpy** (string copy) from the header file `<string.h>` is an example of a library function; `strcpy` is to strings, what = is to numbers.

The function `strcpy` copies a source string into a destination string. For example, given the declaration

```
char source[] = "abracadabra";
char destination[80];
```

the result of the statement

```
strcpy(destination, source);
```

is to overwrite the contents of `destination` with the character string contained in `source`. The function also copies the terminating null character from source to destination. The result of this assignment is illustrated in Figure 3.6.

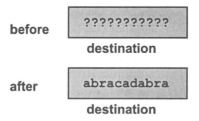

Figure 3.6 String assignment using the function strcpy

This example illustrates that a function is defined for a particular purpose, in this case copying a string. The function may be used in a program by including the appropriate header file at the beginning of the program, in this case the compiler directive `#include <string.h>` would appear at the beginning of the the source file. The function is used, in this case, by supplying it with the argument strings `source` and `destination`.

3.5 The Main Function

A C program is organized into functions - **main** represents the function where program execution must begin and, as the name suggests, is the main or controlling function. This function is written by the programmer and may include prewritten functions, such as `strcpy` from the C library.

A minimum format for a C program that includes the `main` function is defined as

C syntax:

format of program that includes the main function

compiler directives
void main(void)
{
  declaration of constants and/ or variables, followed by a
  sequence of instructions
}

For example, a program to copy one string to another and display the result of the copied string might be written as follows:

```
#include <string.h>
#include <stdio.h>

void main(void)
{
   char source[]="abracadabra";
   char destination[80];

   strcpy(destination, source);
   printf("%s", destination);
}
```

Two compiler directives are specified at the beginning of the program.

```
#include <string.h>
#include <stdio.h>
```

The inclusion of the first directive is necessary because the header `<string.h>` contains a reference to the function `strcpy`. However, it has been necessary to include the header `<stdio.h>` in order to use another library function `printf` in the program. The format of `printf` will be explained in the next section. For now, all you need to know is that `printf` is used to display the contents of the destination string.

The first line of the function `main` is described as:

```
void main(void)
```

At this point in the book you are not expected to understand the significance of the reserved word `void`. A full explanation of the use of `void` appears in Chapter 5.

The declarations of constants and variables and the language statements that make up the sequence of instructions contained within a function are delimited by the opening brace { and closing brace }. The declarations and executable statements within the function are separated by semicolons. However, there are no semicolons after the function heading `void main(void)`, or after the delimiting braces.

3.6 Output

The function `printf` is found in the standard library header file `<stdio.h>`. The purpose of `printf` is to display formatted data on a standard output device, which is normally the screen of a monitor.

The format of `printf` is:

C Syntax:

printf function

printf("control string", arg1, arg2, ... argn);

where the control string inside the quotes is the actual output and the arguments, if present, help to define the format of the output. A control string may contain up to three different character sequences and any combination of these sequences.

Ordinary Characters in Control Strings

A control string may contain alphabetic or numeric characters that are meant to be displayed verbatim. For example,

```
printf("computing is fun!");
```

will display the output as

```
computing is fun!_
```

In processing the control string, the characters are displayed on the screen of a monitor or any other default output device, and (assuming the output device is a monitor) the cursor _ remains on the same line as the string.

Escape Sequence Characters in Control Strings

How do we print single characters? The obvious answer would be to print them in the same way as a character string containing only one character. However, what if the character cannot be written in this way because it is an invisible non printing character, such as a tabulation or new line? C provides a special notation, the **escape sequence**, to deal specifically with printing invisible characters. The escape sequence characters appear in Appendix B. Here we cover only two of them.

    \n new line
    \t horizontal tab

For example,

```
printf("C programming is easy\n");
```

will display the output as

```
C programming is easy
```

_

In processing the control string, the characters are displayed, and the cursor _ moves to the next line below the letter C. The escape sequence characters \n generate the new line.

The following code utilizes the new line and tab characters.

```
printf("dollars\tcents\n\n");
```

will display the output as

```
dollars    cents
```


_

In processing the control string the string, dollars is displayed, the cursor then moves to the next preset tabulation (this will vary in size for different computer systems), and the string cents is displayed. The cursor _ then moves down two lines (\n\n) to below the letter d.

Format Specification Characters in Control Strings

Format specifications define the format of arguments following the control string. If it is required to output numbers, then the control string in a printf statement must specify the type of the number to output. A simplified version of the control string has the following structure;

"%type"

where type is one of the following values and denotes the number being output.

- **c**   integer ASCII code as a single character
- **d**   signed decimal integer
- **E**   floating-point number in exponential format
- **f**   floating-point number

The type d may be preceded by the letter l to indicate that it is a long integer. Table 3.2 illustrates the minimum control strings required to output numbers.

Table 3.2 Using printf with format specifications

type	explanation	example	output
c	a single character	printf("%c",65);	A
d	signed decimal integer	printf("%d",-1234);	-1234
E	signed decimal integer with E notation	printf("%E",123.45);	1.2345000E+02
f	standard signed decimal notation with six digits after the decimal point	printf("%f",54.321);	54.321000

If the requirement is to output numbers according to a set format, then it is possible to modify the control string so that it takes the form

"%width . precision type"

Width is a number that represents the minimum size of the field for displaying a number. The number is right justified unless a negative width is used, in which case the number is displayed left justified. If the value to be printed is larger than the width specified, then the width is automatically expanded to accommodate the number. Regardless of the value of the width, the displayed number will never be truncated. Thus no field width may be specified, and a number will still be displayed.

The precision after the decimal point is optional and indicates the number of decimal places to display a number of type `float` or `double`.

Assuming `alpha` has been assigned the value of 31678, the code

```
printf("%8d", alpha);
```

will display the output as

```
^^^31678_
```

In processing the control string, the value of `alpha` is displayed in a field width of 8 digits (`%8d`) and is right justified in the field. The left-hand side of the field will be filled with three spaces (indicated in this context by the character ^). The cursor _ remains on the same line as the number.

For the following statement, `beta` has been assigned the value of 1.2345.

```
printf("%-10.4f", beta);
```

The output is displayed as

```
1.2345^^^^_
```

In processing the control string, the value of `beta` is displayed left justified in a field width of 10 characters and 4 decimal places (`%-10.4f`). The decimal point is included in the calculation of the field width. The cursor _ remains on the same line as the output following the four trailing spaces after the number.

For the next example, `delta` has been assigned the value 123456789.0:

```
printf("%12.4E", delta);
```

The output is displayed as

```
^^1.2346E+08_
```

In processing the control string, the value of `delta` is displayed in E notation to four decimal places. Notice that the figure in the fourth place is rounded from 5 to 6, since the fifth decimal place was greater than 5. The number is right justified in a field width of 12 characters with two spaces to the left of the field. The cursor _ remains on the same line as the number.

Control Strings with a Mixture of Text and Types

In the following code, alpha has been assigned the value 31678

```
printf("alpha = %5d\n", alpha);
```

The output is displayed as

```
alpha = 31678
_
```

In processing the control string, the string literal is displayed followed by the value of alpha in a field width of 5 digits (%5d). The cursor _ moves to the beginning of a new line below the letter a of alpha.

In the following code, cash has been assigned the value 20.0.

```
printf("CASH AMOUNT\t\t%5.2f\n", cash);
```

will display the output as

```
CASH AMOUNT                    20.00
_
```

In processing the control string, the string literal is displayed, the cursor moves through two tabulation positions \t\t, and the value for cash is then displayed as a floating-point number having a field width of 5 characters with 2 decimal places (%5.2f). The cursor _ then moves to the beginning of the next line below the letter C.

Output of Single Character and String Variables

Single character and string variables can also be output using the printf function. The type specifier in the control string is given the following values:

c   single character
s   string

For example, assuming hours, minutes, and am_pm are 2, 15, and p, respectively,

```
printf("\t\t\t%2d:%2d %c\n", hours, minutes, am_pm);
```

will display the output as

```
                2:15 p
_
```

In processing the control string, the cursor moves through three tabulation positions \t\t\t, and the value of hours is displayed in a field width of 2 digits (%2d). A colon : is then displayed, since it forms part of the control string. The value of minutes is displayed in a field width of 2 digits (%2d). A space is then displayed, since this also forms part of the control string. A value for am_pm is displayed as a single character (%c). The cursor _ then moves to the beginning of the next line (\n).

A more complex example follows.

```
printf("%s\t%d @ %4.2f\t%5.2f\n", article, quantity, unit_cost, price);
```

Assuming `article`, `quantity`, `unit_cost`, and `price` are brush, 2, 2.49, and 4.98, respectively, `printf` will display output as

```
brush           2 @ 2.49            4.98
```
—

In processing the control string, the value of `article` is displayed as a string `%s`, and the cursor moves to the next tabulation position `\t`. The value of `quantity` is displayed `%d`. Note when the field width is omitted the number is displayed in a width suitable for the size of the number. The three characters space@space are displayed as part of the control string, followed by the value of `unit_cost` using a field width of 4 characters with 2 decimal places (`%4.2f`). The cursor _ moves through to the next tabulation position `\t`, and the value of `price` is displayed on a field width of 5 characters with 2 decimal places (`%5.2f`). The cursor then moves down one line `\n` to below the letter b.

3.7 Input

Now that we have considered outputting data in some detail, we turn out attention to how data is input into computer memory for manipulation by a C program. The function `scanf` is found in the standard library header file `<stdio.h>`. The purpose of `scanf` is to read characters from a standard input device, normally a keyboard, and store the converted data at the addresses given by the arguments. The address indicates a particular memory cell. Therefore, before examining `scanf` in more detail, we need to briefly consider the concept of a memory address.

The variables that have been introduced so far in the text have been associated with `int`, `float`, `double` or `char` types. It is understood that a declaration of the form

```
int largest = 32767;
```

implies that the identifier `largest` contains, or stores, the value 32767.

Pictorially, `largest` might be seen as a box containing the value 32767, as shown in Figure 3.7. This box represents an area of computer memory used for storing the integer `largest`. The address of this area of memory is denoted by `&largest`, where `&` is the **address operator**.

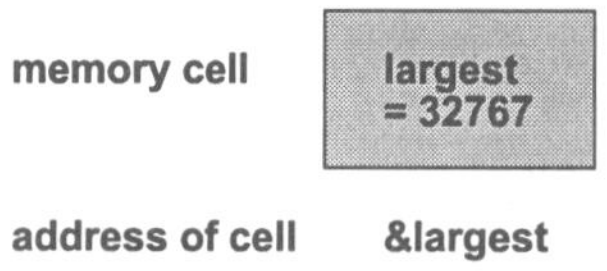

memory cell   largest = 32767

address of cell   &largest

Figure 3.7 Identifying variables by address

The reason we need to understand the address operator in order to use scanf is that when using scanf to input a number or a single character, the address of the variable is used and not simply the variable name.

The format of scanf is

C Syntax:

scanf("control string", arg1, arg2, ... argn);

scanf
function

where the control string defines how the input is to be converted.

A simplified version of the control string has the following structure

"% type"

where type is one of the following values and denotes the number being input.

c   single character
d   signed decimal integer
f   signed floating-point value
lf l is used to prefix types f as double and d as long

scanf will read past any initial **white-space characters** (space, horizontal or vertical tab, form-feed, or new-line character) when reading numbers and will continue to read the characters being input, up to the next white-space character after the number.

Table 3.3 illustrates how numbers can be read from an input device using the scanf function.

Table 3.3 Use of scanf to input data

type	data type	explanation	example statement	input	assignment
c	char	a single character	scanf("%c",&alpha);	A	alpha='A' [65]
d	int	decimal integer	scanf("%d",&beta);	1234	beta=1234
f	float	decimal value in either standard or E notation	scanf("%f",&delta);	-765.32	delta=-765.32
lf	double	decimal value in either standard or E notation	scanf("%lf",&epsilon);	1.123456E+56	epsilon=1.123456E+56

The control string is not confined to the input of one item of data as the following examples illustrate:

scanf("%d%d%d", &month, &day, &year); will read three decimal integers and store the values at the addresses of month, day, and, year respectively.

scanf("%d%d%c", &hours, &minutes, &am_pm); will read two decimal integers and a single character and store the values at the addresses of hours, minutes, and am_pm, respectively.

`scanf("%d%f%lf", &first, &second, &third);` will read a decimal integer, a floating point real, and a double precision real and store the values at the addresses of `first`, `second`, and `third`, respectively. The input data does not need to appear on one line. The data for this example could be input as

```
12345   0.9876
-6.3456789E-19
```

The `scanf` function regards white-space characters as field delimiters. Because a space separates the integer from the real number, the field for the integer number will contain 12345 and the field for the real number will contain 0.9876. A new line character separates the two real numbers; therefore, the field for the second real will contain -6.3456789E-19.

Caution:

possible
error
situation

When using scanf to input a number, the address of the variable is used and not simply the variable name.

3.8 Comments

Comments are used to document a program. The compiler ignores any text that appears between the symbols /* and */. Comments help people who write, test, and maintain programs. Well written comments do the following:

- ☐ State the author of the program and the date it was last amended.

- ☐ Identify the name of the source file.

- ☐ Identify the purpose of a function.

- ☐ Describe each major algorithmic step.

- ☐ Clarify any potentially confusing statements.

- ☐ Clarify the usage of some variables and constants.

Comments can be listed on the same line as language statements, or they can be listed on one or more lines. Comments cannot be nested one within another. Since the compiler ignores comments and replaces each comment by a single space character, such comments do not appear as output when the program is running.

Caution:

Potential
program-
ming
error

*If you forget to terminate a comment with a closing */, the compiler will ignore the lines in the program up to the next occurrence of a closing delimiter.*

3.9 Program Examples

Now that you have the skills to input, process, and output data, you can begin to examine their use in simple programs.

Program Example 3.1: Using Arithmetic Operators

Program Example 3.1 demonstrates the use of the operators +, -, *, /, and % on two integer operands. The program requires no input since the variables `first` and `second` have been initialized with the integer values 23 and 5, respectively. Notice that it is permissible to write expressions within `printf` statements.

```
/*
chap_3\ex_1.c
program to demonstrate the use of arithmetic operators on integer values
*/

#include <stdio.h>

void main(void)
{
    int first  = 23;
    int second = 5;

    printf("sum        %d\n", first + second);
    printf("difference %d\n", first - second);
    printf("product    %d\n", first * second);
    printf("quotient   %d\n", first / second);
    printf("remainder  %d\n", first % second);
}
```

Results

```
sum        28
difference 18
product    115
quotient   4
remainder  3
```

Program Example 3.2: Calculation of the Surface Area and Volume of a Sphere

Program Example 3.2 allows the user to input the radius of a sphere and calculate and display the surface area and volume of the sphere.

The formula for the surface area is *4 x pi x r^2* and the volume is *(r/3) x surface area.*

```
/*
chap_3\ex_2.c
program to input the radius of a sphere and display
the surface area and volume of the sphere
*/

#include <stdio.h>

void main(void)
{
   const  float pi = 3.14159;

   float radius;
   float surface_area;
   float volume;

   printf("input radius of sphere ");
   scanf("%f", &radius);

   surface_area = 4*pi*radius*radius;
   volume = surface_area * radius / 3;

   printf("surface area of sphere %-10.2f\n", surface_area);
   printf("volume of sphere %-10.2f\n", volume);
}
```

Results

```
input radius of sphere 10.0
surface area of sphere 1256.64
volume of sphere 4188.79
```

Style Matters:

the use of prompts

Notice in Program Example 3.2 that when input is required from the keyboard, a prompt is displayed on the screen using printf, prior to the scanf. Without this prompt the user of the program would not know what to enter or when to enter data from the keyboard. The majority of programs in this book require the user to input data from a keyboard. The programs are **interactive**; the computer is reacting to the data being input at run time by the user. Get into the good habit of always providing prompts on the screen to create a user-friendly environment in which to work.

Program Example 3.3: Uses of Printf

Program Example 3.3 illustrates some of the ways in which `printf` can be used to display numbers and strings. In this example several variables are declared and initialized and their respective values output using different control strings in the `printf` statements. Remember that the escape sequence `\t` provides a tabulation, `\n` a new line, and any format specification that contains a negative width implies that the number will be left justified.

```c
/*
chap_3\ex_3.c
program to demonstrate some of the different ways in which printf can
be used to display numbers and strings
*/

#include <stdio.h>

void main(void)
{
        int       A = 32;
        long int  B = 123456789L;
        float     C = 67.123;
        double    D = 0.987654321E+20;
        char      letter = 'Z';
        char      string[] = "Popocatapetl";

        printf("value of A\t %-10d\n", A);
        printf("         B\t %-15ld\n", B);
        printf("         C\t %10.4f\n", C);
        printf("         D\t %20.8E\n\n", D);
        printf("         letter\t %c\n", letter);
        printf("         string\t %s\n", string);
}
```

Results

```
value of A 32
         B 123456789
         C    67.1230
         D       9.87654321E+19

         letter  Z
         string  Popocatapetl
```

Program Example 3.4: Uses of Scanf

Program Example 3.4 uses scanf to input values from a keyboard. Then the program uses printf to display the values that had been input at the keyboard.

Caution:

possible
error
situation

When using scanf to input a number or a single character, the address of the variable, not simply the variable name, is used.

```
/*
chap_3\ex_4.c
program to demonstrate the various uses of scanf
*/

#include <stdio.h>

void main(void)
{
        int      alpha;
        float    beta;
        double   gamma;

        printf("input integer value for alpha ");
        scanf("%d", &alpha);
        printf("input float value (10 characters) for beta ");
        scanf("%f", &beta);
        printf("input double value (15 characters) for gamma ");
        scanf("%lf", &gamma);

        printf("\n\n");
        printf("alpha    = %-5d\n", alpha);
        printf("beta     = %10.4f\n", beta);
        printf("gamma    = %15.4e\n", gamma);
}
```

Results

```
input integer value for alpha 31678
input float value (10 characters) for beta 1.23456789
input double value (15 characters) for gamma 9.876543210E-15

alpha       = 31678
beta        =     1.2346
gamma       =        9.8765e-15
```

Program Example 3.5: Range of Data Types with Printf

In Program Example 3.5 the `printf` routine is used to display the ranges for the data types introduced in the previous chapter. Since all ranges are given in the header files `<limits.h>` and `<float.h>`, it is possible to include these files at the beginning of the program and display the constants defined in them. From the header file `<limits.h>`, the constants SCHAR_MIN, SCHAR_MAX, INT_MIN, INT_MAX, LONG_MIN, and LONG_MAX represent the minimum and maximum values for characters, integers, and long integers, respectively. From the header file `<float.h>`, FLT_MIN, FLT_MAX, DBL_MIN, and DBL_MAX represent the smallest and largest single-precision and double-precision floating-point numbers, respectively.

```c
/*
chap_3\ex_5.c
program to illustrate the ranges for the data types:
char, int, long int, float, double
*/

#include <stdio.h>
#include <limits.h>
#include <float.h>

void main(void)
{
        /* range of characters */

        printf("char min: %d\n",SCHAR_MIN);
        printf("char max: %d\n\n",SCHAR_MAX);

        /* range of integers */

        printf("int min: %d\n",INT_MIN);
        printf("int max: %d\n",INT_MAX);

        /* range of long integers */

        printf("long int min: %ld\n",LONG_MIN);
        printf("long int max: %ld\n\n",LONG_MAX);

        /* range of float */

        printf("float smallest: %15.9E\n",FLT_MIN);
        printf("float max: %15.9E\n\n",FLT_MAX);

        /* range of double */

        printf("double smallest: %25.16E\n",DBL_MIN);
        printf("double max: %25.16E\n\n",DBL_MAX);
}
```

Results

```
char min: -128
char max: 127

int min: -32768
int max: 32767
long int min: -2147483648
long int max: 2147483647

float smallest: 1.175494351E-38
float max: 3.402823466E+38

double smallest: 2.2250738585072014E-308
double max:    1.7976931348623151E+308
```

Summary

☐ Numeric data that reside in memory locations can be manipulated arithmetically by use of the following operators: +(addition); - (subtraction); * (multiplication); / (division); % (remainder).

☐ With the exception of the % remainder operator, which must have integer operands, all other operators can have integer or real operands or a mixture of both.

☐ Arithmetic expressions in C are evaluated in order of highest to lowest operator precedence (see Table 3.1). Expressions in parenthesis have higher precedence than non parenthesized expressions. Where operators have equal precedence, the expressions are generally evaluated from left to right.

☐ The result of a computation is assigned to a variable using the = assignment operator.

☐ When operands are of different types, one or more of the operands must be converted to the type that can safely accommodate the values before the operation can be performed. The conversion can occur in one of two ways: (1) implicitly, by which C automatically converts the value on the right-hand side of the assignment to the type of the variable on the left-hand side, or (2) by use of the cast operation, which the programmer must write into the program code.

☐ All input and output depends on the use of the appropriate library functions, including printf and scanf. Such functions are found in the library file denoted by the header <stdio.h>.

☐ The appropriate header must be included at the beginning of a program if functions or constants from the header file are to be used in the program.

☐ The function `strcpy` is used to copy strings and can be found in the header `<string.h>`.

☐ The header `<limits.h>` contains the machine-dependent maximum and minimum values for each integer type.

☐ The header `<float.h>` contains the machine-dependent range and precision for real numbers.

☐ The function `printf` is used to display formatted numbers, together with strings and characters. The contents of the control string is used to format the information to be printed.

☐ The memory address of a variable can be obtained by using the address operator `&`.

☐ The function `scanf` is used to input data from the default input device, such as a keyboard. Particular care must be exercised when using `scanf`, since the data being input <u>must conform exactly</u> to the requirements of the control string.

☐ The `#include` directive is used to include any previously written files into a program, such as library header files.

☐ A C program is organized into functions, with `void main(void)` being the controlling function from which program execution must begin.

☐ All the statements within a function are bracketed by the use of braces.

☐ Statements within a function are separated from each other by a semicolon.

☐ Comments are documentation items embedded in a program for the benefit of human readers; comments are ignored by the compiler. In C, comments are delimited by the symbols /* and */, respectively, and may be contained on a single line or spread over multiple lines.

Review Questions

1. Which operator calculates the remainder after the division of two integer numbers?

2. What is the result of the integer division 3/2?

3. If the variable counter has an initial value of 8, what is the value of counter = counter + 1?

4. Describe the term *operator precedence*.

5. What is the result of evaluating the expression 2 * 6 + 20 / 4?

6. True or false - the multiplication operator has a higher priority than the subtraction operator.

7. What does the expression `(int)alpha` do, if `alpha` is a declared as a real number?

8. What is the purpose of the `sizeof` operator?

9. What is the result of the expression `sizeof(double)`?

10. What is the purpose of a standard library in C?

11. Distinguish between a compiler directive and a language statement.

12. What is a header file?

13. What is the purpose of the `<stdio.h>` header file?

14. True or false - `&number` is the address of the variable `number`.

15. If different data types are involved in an arithmetic expression, which data type is the result?

16. How can you change the data type of an expression?

17. What is a control string?

18. What is an escape sequence?

19. How does an escape sequence represent a new line character?

20. What is the difference when the expressions `(double) (x/y)` and `(double)x/(double)y` are evaluated? Assume that both `x` and `y` are integers.

Programming Exercises

21. What are the values of the following variables after the execution of the respective assignments?

(a)
```
B = A;
C = A;
D = A;
```
A	B	C	D
36	98	45	29

(b)
```
D = A + B + C + D;
```
A	B	C	D
10	14	29	36

(c)
```
A = B - 2;
```
A	B
17	50

(d)
```
Y = X - Y;
```
X	Y
19	32

(e)
```
Z = X * Y;
```
X	Y	Z
18	3	27

(f)
```
B = B / A;
```
A	B
12.5	25.0

(g)   X = A / B;   A   B   X
                            16   3   25

(h)   Y = C % D;   C   D   Y
                            19   5   2

(i)   D = D + 1   D
                            34

22. Write the following expressions in C.

(a) $\dfrac{A+B}{C}$ (b) $\dfrac{W-X}{(Y+Z)}$ (c) $\dfrac{D-B}{2A}$ (d) $\dfrac{1}{2}(A^2+B^2)$

(e) $(A - B)(C - D)$ (f) $B^2 - 4AC$ (g) AX^2+BX+C

23. Find the errors in the following C expressions.

(a) A x B   (b) X*-Y   (c) (64+B)/-6   (d) (A-B)(A+B)

(e) -2 / A + -6   (f) $\dfrac{1}{2}*(X-Y)$

24. Rewrite the following C expressions as algebraic expressions.

(a) X + 2 / Y + 4   (b) A * B / (C + 2)   (c) U / V * W / X
(d) B * B - 4 * A * C   (e) A / B + C / D + E / F

25. How would you expect the following `printf` statements to display the information?

(a) `printf("Hello World");`
(b) `printf("\tname: ");`
(c) `printf("\tname: %s\n", name);` where name is declared as
    `char name[] ="Mickey Mouse";`
(d) `printf("a=%d\tb=%d\tc=%d\n", a, b, c);` where a = 3, b=4, and c=5.
(e) `printf("area covered %f10.2\n", area);` where area = 635.8658.

26. Discover the errors in the following statements.

(a) `scanf("%d", &alpha)` where alpha is a real number.
(b) `scanf("%f", beta)` where beta is a real number.
(c) `scanf("%2d%2d", &month, & day, &year);`
(d) `scanf("alpha = %-5d\n", alpha);` where alpha is defined as an unsigned integer.

Programming Problems

27. Investigate the contents of the <limits.h> and <float.h> header files for the version of ANSI C on the computer system you are using. Compare the values with those listed in Appendix A. If they are significantly different, then make a note of the specific differences. Rerun Program Example 3.5 and compare the results with those listed.

28. Write a program to output a message of your choice on the screen.

29. Write a program using the sizeof operator to determine the number of bytes the following data types use.

```
char
int
long int
float
double
```

30. Write programs to perform the following:

(a) Input the lengths of the two half axes of an ellipse; calculate and output the area of the ellipse. The formula for the area of an ellipse is *pi x a x b* where *a* and *b* are the respective lengths of the two half axes.

(b) Input the radius and height of a cylinder; calculate and output the volume of the cylinder. The formula for the volume of a cylinder is *pi x r²x h*, where *r* is the radius of the base of the cylinder and *h* is the perpendicular height of the cylinder.

Note - assume the value of *pi* to be an approximation of 3.14159.

31. Write a program to input the elapsed time in seconds since midnight. Calculate and output the number of hours, minutes, and seconds since midnight.

32. From your answer to question 26 Chapter 1, write a program that displays each operation for making a cup of coffee, taken in logical order from the flowchart.

33. We all keep loose change in our pockets. Write a program to calculate the total value of your loose change. You will need to input the number of half dollars, quarters, dimes, nickels, and pennies and then display the total value of the coinage in dollars and cents.

34. The interest payable on a loan is calculated according to the following equation:

$$interest = principal x \frac{rate}{100} x \frac{time}{365}$$

Write a program to input the principal amount borrowed, the rate as a percentage, and the time of the loan in days. Calculate and output the value of the interest.

Chapter 4
Program Design

Now that you have had a taste of writing simple computer programs, you are probably eager to get back to the computer and write more. Before you press another key, it is important for you to remember that programming involves more than typing statements into a computer. The first step in programming is to design and plan your programs away from the computer.

This chapter focuses your attention upon a prescriptive method for program development. By the end of the chapter you should have an understanding of the following topics:

☐ Designing programs from the top down.

☐ Using pseudocode in the construction of an algorithm.

☐ Testing algorithms.

☐ Planning the input and output.

☐ Coding algorithms into simple programs for the input and processing of data and the output of results.

4.1 Top-down Design

In attempting to solve a problem, it is far easier to divide the problem into parts and solve each part, rather than to try to solve the whole problem at one time. This approach is known as **top-down** design (and it is also known as **stepwise refinement**).

For example, consider the problem of how to calculate the time it takes to fill a rectangular swimming pool of uniform depth. The data available for this exercise is the size of the pool (length, width, and depth), the rate of water flow into the pool (20 gallons per minute), and the fact that a cubic foot of water has a capacity of 7.8 gallons.

The problem can be refined into the following four parts:

1. input the size of the pool
2. calculate the volume of the pool
3. calculate the time to fill the pool
4. output the results

Taken as a whole, the four parts represent the solution to the problem and form the basis of the algorithm for the main function. This top-down approach can be represented as the **structure chart** illustrated in Figure 4.1.

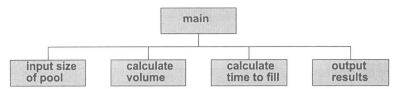

Figure 4.1 A structure chart

As the problems get harder, you will find it very beneficial to be able to divide the solution to a problem into parts, since it is far easier to work on just one part of the problem, rather than the whole problem.

In Chapter 1 you were introduced to a flowchart as a method of representing an algorithm. A structure chart is not the same as a flowchart. A structure chart shows how a hierarchical relationship can be identified between components of a program, whereas a flowchart shows the order in which instructions should be obeyed.

The four parts that represent the solution to this problem can also be represented in a flowchart as operations for input, processing, and output, as illustrated in Figure 4.2. This figure also shows how the four parts can be refined further into statements that can be easily coded into the C language.

Notice that each part in the first level of the solution has been given a number in the range 1 to 4. In top-down design it may be possible to refine each of these parts into smaller parts. For example,

1. input the size of the pool

has been refined to:

1.1 input length
1.2 input width
1.3 input depth

which in themselves have been represented as subdivisions of operation 1, hence the numbering convention 1.1, 1.2, 1.3.

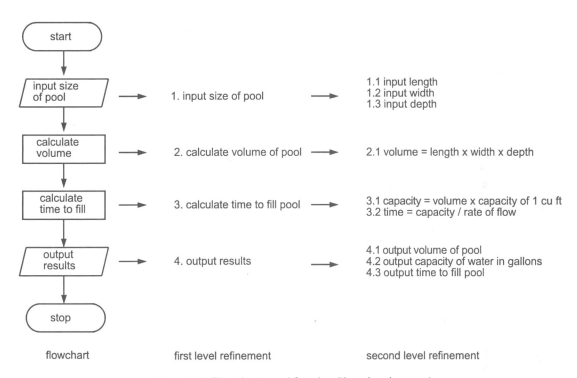

Figure 4.2 Flowchart used for algorithm development

The expression of the algorithm in words is known as **pseudocode**. As the problems become more advanced, you will notice that pseudocode is a mixture of statements written in English and C. However, do not make the mistake of thinking that pseudocode is just a description of the program statements in C. Used correctly, pseudocode helps to describe the operations in the algorithm prior to these statements being coded into C. To reinforce this point notice that the pseudocode in Figure 4.2 makes no reference to scanf and printf statements in the steps to input the size of the pool or output the results.

Top-down design will be used as the preferred method for designing algorithms throughout the rest of the book. This method will normally be expressed in pseudocode; however, as the problems get progressively harder we will also use structure charts. Do not feel that we have abandoned the flowchart as a means of expressing an algorithm; we will use the flowchart technique in describing some features of the language where it is important to understand the order of the C statements.

4.2 Program Design

Having been through the fundamentals of the meaning of data, data types, input and output, assignment, arithmetic, and the format of a program, it is now possible to use these elements to design and write programs that solve simple problems.

Before attempting to design and code a computer program, however, we need to state a few guidelines. These guidelines will be used in the following case studies, and should help you to develop a systematic approach to problem-solving and good programming habits. The seven necessary stages for developing a computer program are explained next.

1. Problem Analysis Document in English how you plan to tackle the problem from the information provided. Problem analysis should include sifting through the information and determining what data is to be input, how it is processed, and the information that is to be output. In the case of simple problems, little analysis will be required. Show any calculations that will be used on the data.

2. Algorithm Document in English, not C code, the sequence of operations that are necessary to solve the problem. This is in fact the algorithm or method of solving the problem, using a top-down design approach where applicable, and is represented in a pseudocode.

3. Data Dictionary Determine the items of data required. Classify this data into constants and variables and specify the data type for each constant and variable. At this stage, it is possible to write declarations in C to describe the constants and variables.

4. Desk Check Invent suitable test data such that the type and nature of the data is representative of the problem. Numerical data should be chosen for ease of calculation. Use the variables and constants defined in the data dictionary to construct headings for a table - similar to the tables created in section 1.8. Use the test data to trace through the algorithm line by line, obeying the instructions and modifying the values of the variables in the table as required. This desk check makes it possible to predict the results before the program is coded and run.

5. Screen Layout Design the final screen layout showing the screen text, specimen data that will be used, and expected results. This can be designed on ruled paper so that the column positions of each character in each line of output is known. The screen layout indicates prompts to the user for data and how the information related to any calculations is displayed. Designing the screen layout on paper helps the programmer write correct `scanf` and `printf` statements by pointing out the sorts of spacing, tabbing, line return, and other escape-sequence characters that will be needed in those statements.

6. Coding From the information documented in the algorithm, data dictionary, and screen layout, code the program using the C language. The process of compilation and linking will not be shown in the examples in this text, although it is assumed that these two stages have been completed before the program can be run.

7. Results If the compilation and linking stages are successful, run the program using the same test data and inspect whether the results are the same as predicted by the desk check.

Case Study: Travel Time

In this program a user inputs a distance to travel, in miles, and the speed of travel, in miles per hour. The program calculates the time it will take, in hours, to reach the destination.

Problem Analysis - Having input the distance and the speed, the formula *time = distance / speed* is used to calculate the time to travel the distance.

Algorithm - Programs that make calculations on input data and output the results, use a set order of instructions.

1. input data
2. use the data to calculate the information required
3. output the information

These three stages can be refined to produce a logical order of operations necessary for solving the problem. Notice that the first stage has been refined into two parts.

1.1 input distance to travel
1.2 input speed of travel

2. calculate time using the expression time = distance / speed
3. display the time of travel

Data Dictionary - Three items of data can be identified in this problem: distance, speed, and time. If distance and speed are whole numbers, then because of the calculation of time (distance/speed), the data type for the time must be a real number. The declaration for the data in this problem is:

```
int     distance;
int     speed;
float   time;
```

Desk Check - The distance can be chosen as 15 miles and the speed as 45 m.p.h.

variable	value
distance	15
speed	45
time	15/45 = 0.33

Ensure that the format of the `printf` function caters for at least two decimal places, since anything less will display an inaccurate result!

```
                          Screen Layout

123456789012345678901234567890123456789012345678901234567890
input distance to town 15
input speed of travel 45
time taken to reach town is 0.33 hours
```

```c
/*
chap_4\ex_1.c
program to calculate and output the time in hours, to travel a
distance input in miles, at an average speed input in mph
*/

#include <stdio.h>

void main(void)
{
        int     distance;
        int     speed;
        float   time

        printf("input distance to town ");
        scanf("%d", distance);

        printf("input speed of travel );
        scanf("%d", &speed);

        time = distance / speed;

        printf("time taken to reach town is %4.2f hours\n", time);
}
```

The lines shown in second color for this program contain errors that beginners tend to make. Can you identify the specific error in each case? Answers are provided in the next section.

4.3 Implementing a C Program

Regardless of the programming environment, the following stages are necessary to implement the C program developed in the previous section.

Invoke the editor, and type the program; save it to disk using the filename *ex_1.c*. The program is then compiled, which generates a report of errors and warnings. These errors are then corrected through the text editor. Typical error and warning diagnostics are as follows:

Syntax error, expected: ; [(=, in relation to the line `printf ("input distance to town ");`

This can be very misleading, since the error occurred on the previous line. You may notice that the data declaration `float time` has not been separated from the `printf` statement by a semicolon. Remember that the semicolon is used to separate statements in a program.

Error: Invalid string constant in relation to the line `printf ("input speed of travel );`

All string literals or constants are delimited by matching inverted commas or double quotes. The right-hand inverted commas are missing in this string.

Warning: Possible use of distance before assigned a value. This warning stems from the fact that the function `scanf` requires the address of a variable and not the name of the variable. The address operator is missing before the variable `distance` in the line `scanf ("%d", distance);`

After the errors are corrected the program is re-compiled, link/loaded, and run. The results of the program execution follow.

Results

```
input distance to town 15
input speed of travel 45
time taken to reach town is 0.00 hours
```

In comparing this result with the expected result of 0.33, clearly something has gone wrong! Look again at the calculation. Both distance and speed are integer values. The integer result of dividing 15 / 45 is 0.00 and not 0.33. Thus, the result 0 is converted to the type `float` on the left-hand side of the expression, which still results in 0.0.

Caution:

integer division

In this example it is necessary to perform a type conversion on distance and speed; therefore, the expression is modified to `time = (float) distance / (float) speed;`. After this modification, the program produces the expected results. If both the distance and the speed had been declared as float and not as integer in the program, the result would be correct without having to cast the types of both variables. The purpose of the example, however, is to warn you of the dangers of integer division.

4.4 String Input

C Syntax:

gets

In order to be able to program many of the examples given in this chapter, it is necessary to introduce a function that will allow the input of string data at the keyboard. The function is **gets** (get string) from the library header `<stdio.h>`. The syntax of the `gets` function is

gets (identifier)

All the characters entered at the keyboard will be stored until a new line character is input. For example, `gets (name)` where name has been declared as `char name[20]` will allow a string of less than 20 characters to be input. The system appends a null character at the end of the string.

4.5 The Input Buffer

When we input data at the keyboard where does it go? The answer is into a special location in the main memory that can store a fixed number of characters and is known as an **input buffer**. Consider what happens when the following code is executed by the computer.

```
scanf("%d", &first_price);
gets(first_name);
scanf("%d", &second_price);
.
.
```

The contents of the buffer is illustrated in Figure 4.3 after the characters 40 *new-line* have been input for the value of `first_price`. The `scanf` function consumes characters up to, but not including, the new-line character. The new-line character remains in the input buffer. The `gets` function consumes the new-line character. However, since this character is used by the function as a string delimiter, there is no opportunity to input data corresponding to the variable `first_name`, the computer executes the second `scanf` function and waits for the user to input a value corresponding to the variable `second_price`.

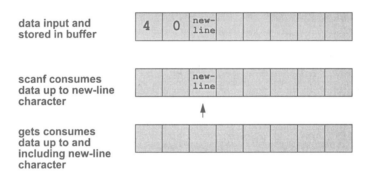

Figure 4.3 Input buffer

The solution to this problem is to clear the input buffer of the new-line character after the `scanf` function has consumed the necessary data. Although it is possible to use `scanf` to consume a single character, the library function **getchar** from the header `<stdio.h>` reads a single character. The syntax of the function is:

C Syntax:

getchar

getchar()

The function returns the ASCII code for the character that was consumed from the input buffer. In this case, however, this character is not required; therefore, the result of `getchar()` is not assigned to a variable.

The required modification to the code is

```
scanf("%d", &first_price);
getchar();
gets(first_name);
```

78

The function `getchar` can be used on its own, as illustrated by the code, or in an assignment statement. For example,

```
char reply;

reply = getchar();
```

.

assigns a single character input at the keyboard to the variable `reply`. The ASCII code of the character represents this value.

The following case studies illustrate how to develop programs that contain a sequence of instructions.

Case Study: Travel Time to a Known Destination

This case study is only a refinement of the previous case study. The user is first prompted to enter the name of the town so that it can be used in future textual output. Both the distance and speed are input, and the time taken to reach the town is calculated in the same manner as the previous case study.

Problem Analysis - The only new item here is the input of the name of the town. This name is used in the screen prompts and suggests to the user that the program has been customized to their requirements. The formula for calculating the time remains as *time = distance / speed*.

Algorithm

1. *input name of town*
2. *input distance*
3. *input speed*
4. *calculate time using the expression distance / speed*
5. *display time*

Data Dictionary - The only additional item of data is the name of a town, which is of type string. The other variables remain the same.

```
char    town[12];
int     distance;
int     speed;
float   time;
```

Desk Check - The value for town can be input as Marlborough; the distance and speed remain 15 miles and 45 m.p.h, respectively.

variable	value
town	Marlborough
distance	15
speed	45
time	0.33

```
Screen Layout
─────────────────────────────────────────────────────────
12345678901234567890123456789012345678901234567890
input name of town Marlborough
input distance to Marlborough 15
input speed of travel 45
time taken to reach Marlborough is 0.33 hours
```

```c
/*
chap_4\ex_2.c
program to calculate and output the time in hours, to travel a
distance input in miles, at an average speed input in mph
*/

#include <stdio.h>

void main(void)
{
        char    town[12];
        int     distance;
        int     speed;
        float   time;

        printf("input name of town ");
        gets(town);

        printf("input distance to %s ", town);
        scanf("%d", &distance);

        printf("input speed of travel ");
        scanf("%d", &speed);

        time = (float)distance / (float)speed;

        printf("time taken to reach %s is %4.2f hours\n", town, time);
}
```

Results

```
input name of town Marlborough
input distance to Marlborough 15
input speed of travel 45
time taken to reach Marlborough is 0.33 hours
```

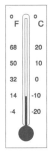

Case Study: Temperature Conversion

The thermometer illustrated in Chapter 2, Figure 2.2 shows two temperature scales, one in Fahrenheit and the other in Celsius. Write a program to input a temperature in degrees Fahrenheit and convert it to degrees Celsius.

Problem Analysis - The input data is a temperature in degrees Fahrenheit. The expression for conversion is *Celsius = (Fahrenheit - 32) * 5 / 9*. If both temperatures are recorded to an accuracy of 1 degree, then both items of data are integers.

Algorithm

1. input temperature in degrees Fahrenheit
2. convert temperature to degrees Celsius
3. display temperature in degrees Celsius

Data Dictionary - There are only two items of data in this example: a temperature in degrees Fahrenheit and its equivalent temperature in degrees Celsius. The declaration of the data in this example is

```
int Fahrenheit, Celsius;
```

Desk Check - Select 14 as the value for Fahrenheit.

variable   value
Fahrenheit 14
Celsius $(14-32)*5/9 = -18*5/9 = -10$

```
                        Screen Layout
┌──────────────────────────────────────────────────────────────┐
│12345678901234567890123456789012345678901234567890123456789 0  │
│input temperature in degrees F 14                               │
│equivalent temperature is -10 degrees C                         │
└──────────────────────────────────────────────────────────────┘
```

```
/*
chap_4\ex_3.c
program to input a temperature in degrees Fahrenheit and output the
temperature in degrees Celsius
*/

#include <stdio.h>

void main(void)
{
        int     Fahrenheit;
        int     Celsius;

        printf("input temperature in degrees F ");
        scanf("%d", &Fahrenheit);
        Celsius = (Fahrenheit - 32) * 5 / 9;
        printf("equivalent temperature is %3d degrees C\n", Celsius);
}
```

Results

```
input temperature in degrees F 14
equivalent temperature is -10 degrees C
```

Case Study: Cost of Newspapers

Write a program to input the name and cost in cents of three newspapers, calculate the total cost and average cost in cents, and display the results of the two computations.

Problem Analysis - By including the names of the papers in the prompts to input the price of the papers, the program is customized to the user's data. The total cost of the papers is obviously the sum of the three prices, and the average is calculated by dividing the total cost by 3. Since the price of the papers is assumed to be in cents and by default of integer type, the calculation for the average should produce an integer result.

Algorithm

first level of top-down design

1. *input data for newspapers*
2. *calculate costs*
3. *output results*

82

second level of top-down design

    1.1 input name of the first paper
    1.2 input the price of the first paper
    1.3 input name of the second paper
    1.4 input the price of the second paper
    1.5 input the name of the third paper
    1.6 input the price of the third paper

    2.1 calculate the total cost of all three papers
    2.2 calculate the average cost of the three papers

    3.1 display the total cost
    3.2 display the average cost

Data Dictionary - The names of the three newspapers, the individual costs of the three newspapers, the total cost, and average price are all items of data. The names of the newspapers are string variables, and the prices, total cost, and average price are integer variables.

```
char    name_paper_1[10], name_paper_2[10], name_paper_3[10];
int     price_paper_1, price_paper_2, price_paper_3;
int     total_cost, average;
```

Desk Check - The names of the papers are the Globe, Mercury, and Courier, and their respective costs are 40 cents, 50 cents and 60 cents.

variable	*value*
name_paper_1	Globe
price_paper_1	40
name_paper_2	Mercury
price_paper_2	50
name_paper_3	Courier
price_paper_3	60
total_cost	40+50+60 = 150
average	150 / 3 = 50

```
+------------------------------------------------------------------+
|                          Screen Layout                           |
+------------------------------------------------------------------+
|12345678901234567890123456789012345678901234567890123456789012345|
|name of first newspaper Globe                                     |
|price of Globe 40                                                 |
|name of second newspaper Mercury                                  |
|price of Mercury 50                                               |
|name of third newspaper Courier                                   |
|price of Courier 60                                               |
|total cost of three newspapers is 150c                            |
|average cost of newspapers is 50c                                 |
+------------------------------------------------------------------+
```

In the following program notice the use of the `getchar()` statement to flush the keyboard buffer of the unwanted new-line character.

```c
/*
chap_4\ex_4.c
program to input the names and prices of three newspapers, calculate
and output the total cost and average price of the papers
*/

#include <stdio.h>

void main(void)
{
        char    name_paper_1[10], name_paper_2[10], name_paper_3[10];
        int     price_paper_1, price_paper_2, price_paper_3;
        int     total_cost, average;

        printf("name of first newspaper ");
        gets(name_paper_1);
        printf("price of %s ", name_paper_1);
        scanf("%d", &price_paper_1);
        getchar();

        printf("name of second newspaper ");
        gets(name_paper_2);
        printf("price of %s ", name_paper_2);
        scanf("%d", &price_paper_2);
        getchar();

        printf("name of third newspaper ");
        gets(name_paper_3);
        printf("price of %s ", name_paper_3);
        scanf("%d", &price_paper_3);

        total_cost = price_paper_1 + price_paper_2 + price_paper_3;
        average = total_cost / 3;

        printf("total cost of three newspapers is %3dc\n", total_cost);
        printf("average price of newspapers is %2dc\n", average);
}
```

Results

```
name of first newspaper Globe
price of Globe
name of second newspaper Mercury
price of Mercury
name of third newspaper Courier
```

```
price of Courier 60
total cost of three newspapers is 150c
average price of newspapers is 50c
```

Case Study: Determining Paint Quantity

A rectangular living room has a total window area of 40 square feet and a total door area of 14 square feet. Write a program to input the length, width, and height of the room and calculate the area of available wall space. If a 1/2 gallon can of paint will cover 200 square feet of wall, calculate and display the number of cans required to paint the walls of the room. Note: the window and door areas and floor and ceiling are not to be painted.

Problem Analysis - In calculating the number of cans to purchase, it will be necessary to adjust the result of dividing the wall area by paint coverage to give a whole number of cans; otherwise, the calculation will result in a partial can of paint. A constant of 0.999 should be added to the theoretical number of cans before the result is truncated.

wall area = (2 * height * length) + (2 * height * width) - window area - door area
            = 2 * height * (length + width) - (window area + door area)
cans   = (wall area / paint cover) + 0.999

Since the variable cans is of type integer and it lies on the left-hand side of the assignment, the expression (wall area / paint cover) + 0.999 will be truncated to the nearest integer value. However, adding 0.999 to the result of the floating-point division, rounds any fractional left over amount to the next whole can.

Algorithm

first level of top-down design

> *1. input dimensions of room*
> *2. calculate number of cans*
> *3. output result*

second level of top-down design

> *1.1 input length*
> *1.2 input width*
> *1.3 input height*
>
> *2.1 calculate wall area*
> *2.2 calculate number of cans*
>
> *3.1 display number of cans*

Data Dictionary - The constants in this problem are the window and door areas and area of coverage of a can of paint. The dimensions of the room are to be input at the keyboard, and they (length, width, and height) should be treated as variables of type float. Before the number of cans of paint can be calculated, it is useful, but not necessary, to calculate the area of the walls to be painted. This variable will again be of type float. If it assumed that only half-gallon cans of paint can be used, then the number of cans will be of type integer.

Three constants can be identified in this problem:

```
const  float  paint_cover = 200.0;
const  float  window_area = 40.0;
const  float  door_area   = 14.0;
```

The variables are

```
float  length, width, height, wall_area;
int    NumberOfcans;
```

Desk Check - Length 30 feet, width 15 feet and height 8 feet.

variable	values
length	30
width	15
height	8
wall_area	2*8*(30+15) - (40 + 14) = 16*450 - 54 = 666
cans	(666 / 200) + 0.999 = 3.33 + 0.999 = 4 |.329

Because the variable cans is an integer, the decimal fraction 4.329 is truncated leaving a value of 4.

```
                        Screen Layout
  12345678901234567890123456789012345678901234567890
  input room dimensions
  length? 30.0
  width? 15.0
  height? 8.0
  number of cans to purchase = 4
```

```
/*
chap_4\ex_5.c
program to calculate the amount of paint needed to paint the walls
of a room
*/

#include <stdio.h>

void main(void)
{
        const   float   paint_cover  = 200.0;
        const   float   window_area  = 40.0;
        const   float   door_area    = 14.0;

        float   length, width, height;
        float   wall_area;
        int     cans;

        printf("input room dimensions\n");
        printf("length? ");
        scanf("%f", &length);
        printf("width? ");
        scanf("%f", &width);
        printf("height? ");
        scanf("%f", &height);

        wall_area = 2*height*(length + width)-(window_area + door_area);
        cans = (wall_area / paint_cover) + 0.999;

        printf("number of cans to purchase = %d\n", cans);
}
```

Results

```
input room dimensions
length? 30.0
width? 15.0
height? 8.0
number of cans to purchase  =  4
```

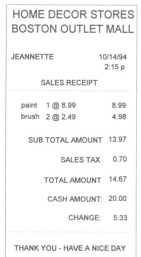

Case Study: Calculations for a Sales Receipt

The final example in this chapter is a program to display a sales receipt similar to that shown in Chapter 2, Figure 2.4. This example requires input of the date and time of the transaction, the names of the articles purchased, the quantity and unit price of the articles, and the amount of cash tendered for the purchase. The program then displays the names, quantities and unit prices of the articles and calculates and displays the costs, subtotal, sales tax, total, cash tendered and change.

Program Analysis - The data input to produce the sales receipt will be the date and time, the name, quantity, unit price of each item purchased, and the amount of cash tendered. Notice that this example is very restricted in that you can input only two items. The name of the check-out assistant is a constant.

The calculations on this data will produce the costs the items, a subtotal of all items, sales tax based on 5% of the subtotal, and the total amount (subtotal + sales tax). The change is the difference between the cash tendered and the total amount. You may assume that the cash tendered is always greater than or equal to the total amount.

Algorithm

first level of top-down design

    1. input data
    2. calculate necessary quantities to produce check-out slip
    3. display details of check-out slip

second level of top-down design

    1.1 input date and time of transaction
    1.2 input details of first article purchased
    1.3 input details of second article purchased
    1.4 input amount of cash tendered

    2.1 calculate cost of purchasing articles
    2.2 calculate sub-total
    2.3 calculate tax
    2.4 calculate total
    2.5 calculate change

3.1 display headings
3.2 display date and time of transaction
3.3 display sub-heading
3.4 display details of articles purchased
3.5 display sub-total
3.6 display tax
3.7 display total
3.8 display cash tendered
3.9 display change given
3.10 display final message

Data Dictionary - This data dictionary is similar to the one described in sections 2.5 and 2.6. However, since two articles are displayed on the sales receipt, it will be necessary to declare two variables each for the name of the article, the quantity purchased, the unit cost, and the price. The name of the cashier and the rate of sales tax are declared as constants.

```
const   float   tax_rate = 0.05;
const   char    name[] = "JEANNETTE";

        int     month, day, year;
        int     hours, minutes;
        char    am_pm;
        char    article_1[10], article_2[10];
        int     quantity_1, quantity_2;
        float   unit_cost_1, unit_cost_2;
        float   price_1, price_2;
        float   sub_total, tax, total, cash, change;
```

Desk Check - The test data can be taken directly from the illustration of the sales receipt in Figure 2.4.

variable	value
month	10
day	14
year	94
hours	2
minutes	15
am_pm	p
article_1	paint
quantity_1	1
unit_cost_1	8.99
article_2	brush
quantity_2	2
unit_cost_2	2.49

price_1	1 * 8.99 = 8.99
price_2	2 * 2.49 = 4.98
sub_total	8.99 + 4.98 = 13.97
tax	0.05 * 13.97 = 0.70
total	13.97 + 0.70 = 14.67
change	20.00 - 14.67 = 5.33

```
                    Screen Layout

12345678901234567890123456789012345678901234567890
input date as MM DD YY 10 14 94
input time as HH MM am or pm 2 15p
input name of first article paint
input quantity purchased 1
input unit price 8.99

input name of second article brush
input quantity purchased 2
input unit price 4.98

input amount of money tendered 20.00


  H O M E   D E C O R   S T O R E S
B O S T O N   O U T L E T   M A L L

JEANNETTE                10/14/94
                          2:15 P

        SALES RECEIPT
_____

paint   1 @ 8.99           8.99
brush   2 @ 2.49           4.98

SUB TOTAL AMOUNT          13.97
SALES TAX                  0.70
TOTAL AMOUNT             14.67
CASH AMOUNT              20.00
CHANGE                    5.33
_____


    THANK YOU - HAVE A NICE DAY
```

```
/*
chap_4\ex_6.c
program to produce a sales receipt
*/

#include <stdio.h>

void main(void)
{
        const   float   tax_rate = 0.05;
        const   char    name[] = "JEANNETTE";

                int     month, day, year;
                int     hours, minutes;
                char    am_pm;
                char    article_1[10], article_2[10]; /* names of articles */
                int     quantity_1, quantity_2;       /* quantities purchased */
                float   unit_cost_1, unit_cost_2;     /* individual costs */
                float   price_1, price_2;             /* quantity x unit_cost */
                float   sub_total, tax, total, cash, change;

        /* input data */

        printf("input date as MM DD YY ");
        scanf("%d%d%d", &month, &day, &year);

        printf("input time as HH MM am or pm ");
        scanf("%d%d%c", &hours, &minutes, &am_pm);
        getchar();

        printf("input name of first article ");
        gets(article_1);
        printf("input quantity purchased ");
        scanf("%d",&quantity_1);
        printf("input unit price ");
        scanf("%f",&unit_cost_1);
        getchar();

        printf("\ninput name of second article ");
        gets(article_2);
        printf("input quantity purchased ");
        scanf("%d",&quantity_2);
        printf("input unit price ");
        scanf("%f",&unit_cost_2);

        printf("\ninput amount of money tendered ");
        scanf("%f", &cash);
        printf("\n\n");
```

```
        /* calculate amounts for sales receipt */

        price_1 = quantity_1 * unit_cost_1;
        price_2 = quantity_2 * unit_cost_2;
        sub_total = price_1 + price_2;
        tax = tax_rate * sub_total;
        total = tax + sub_total;
        change = cash - total;

        /* display sales receipt */

        printf(" H O M E   D E C O R   S T O R E S\n");
        printf("B O S T O N   O U T L E T   M A L L\n\n");
        printf("%s\t\t%2d/%2d/%2d\n",name, month, day, year);
        printf("\t\t\t%2d:%2d %c\n\n", hours, minutes, am_pm);
        printf("\tSALES RECEIPT\n");
        printf("_____\n\n");
        printf("%s\t%d @ %4.2f\t%5.2f\n", article_1, quantity_1,
                                unit_cost_1, price_1);
        printf("%s\t%d @ %4.2f\t%5.2f\n\n", article_2, quantity_2,
                                unit_cost_2, price_2);
        printf("SUB TOTAL AMOUNT\t%5.2f\n", sub_total);
        printf("SALES TAX\t\t%5.2f\n", tax);
        printf("TOTAL AMOUNT\t\t%5.2f\n", total);
        printf("CASH AMOUNT\t\t%5.2f\n", cash);
        printf("CHANGE\t\t\t%5.2f\n\n", change);
        printf("_____\n\n");
        printf("  THANK YOU - HAVE A NICE DAY\n\n");
}
```

Results

```
input date as MM DD YY 10 14 94
input time as HH MM am or pm 2 15p
input name of first article paint
input quantity purchased 1
input unit price 8.99

input name of second article brush
input quantity purchased 2
input unit price 2.49

input amount of money tendered 20.00


  H O M E   D E C O R   S T O R E S
B O S T O N   O U T L E T   M A L L

JEANNETTE               10/14/94
                         2:15 p

       SALES RECEIPT
_____

paint  1 @ 8.99         8.99
brush  2 @ 2.49         4.98

SUB TOTAL AMOUNT       13.97
SALES TAX               0.70
TOTAL AMOUNT           14.67
CASH AMOUNT            20.00
CHANGE                  5.33


_____

   THANK YOU - HAVE A NICE DAY
```

Summary

□ To solve a problem, break it down into parts and attempt to solve the smaller problems, rather than tackle the problem as a whole. This approach to problem solving is known as top-down design or stepwise refinement.

□ A structure chart is a convenient way to organize a complex problem into a hierarchy of solution steps.

- ☐ A flowchart represents the logical order in which operations take place in order to solve a problem. It indicates the order of flow from one operation to the next.

- ☐ A top-down design can be represented in an English-like notation known as pseudocode. It is usually easier to show the decomposition of a problem using pseudocode than it is using a flowchart.

- ☐ Program design can be organized into seven steps:

  1. Problem analysis
  2. Algorithm
  3. Data dictionary
  4. Desk check
  5. Screen layout
  6. Coding
  7. Results, including compiling, link/loading, and running the program.

- ☐ Designing what the input of data and output of results will look like in an interactive computing environment will greatly facilitate the coding of the program.

- ☐ The program is coded from the algorithm, data dictionary, and screen layout.

- ☐ As a means of checking program accuracy, a program should be run for the first time with the same test data used during the desk-check.

Review Questions

1. What is an alternative term for top-down design?

2. True or false - a structure chart is the same as a flowchart.

3. What does a structure chart represent?

4. What is pseudocode?

5. True or false - pseudocode is written in C.

6. What is a data dictionary?

7. True or false - a desk check is used after the program has been written.

8. What is the purpose of a screen layout?

9. True or false - a program is coded from the data dictionary and the algorithm expressed in pseudocode.

10. At what stages in program design would test data be used?

Programming Exercises

In the answers to the following two questions you are expected to

(a) Draw a structure chart, illustrating the top-down approach to the design.
(b) Create an algorithm in pseudo-code.
(c) Invent suitable test data and desk check the algorithm.
(d) Produce a data dictionary for the variables and constants that are to be used in the program.
(e) Design a screen layout that illustrates the interactive nature of the algorithm.

11. A quotation for framing a photograph is based upon the following information:

The outside edge of the wooden frame is 6 inches longer and 6 inches wider than the photograph. The cost of the wood to make the frame is $2.50 per foot.

Two backing cards are required to be mounted with the photograph. Each card is 5.5 inches longer and 5.5 inches wider than the photograph. The cost of the backing card is $1.50 per square foot.

The photograph is to be protected under glass. The size of the glass is the same as a backing card. The cost of glass is $5.50 per square foot.

Computerize the process of supplying a fully itemized quotation for framing a photograph.

12. You plan to take a walking holiday in the Canadian Rockies. The trip is expected to last five days (unless the bears get you!). From the map of the area, you measure the distances you want to walk each day. The Canadian map you have is metric, with 1 centimeter equivalent to 0.78 kilometers. You estimate that because of the mountainous terrain your average speed of walking will be 1.5 miles per hour (you think in miles per hour, not kilometers per hour!).

Your task is to estimate how many miles you will walk each day and how long it will take you. Calculate the total distance you will have traveled by the end of the holiday and the total time you will spend walking between daily destinations. Note: 1 kilometer is equivalent to 0.625 miles.

Computerize the process of estimating the distances and times.

Programming Problems

13. From the full design in question 11, write a program to input the length and width of a photograph, and calculate and output a full quotation.

14. From the full design in question 12, write a program to input the map distances traveled on each leg of the journey and calculate the actual distances in miles and the time to walk between destinations.

15. From the top-down design expressed in pseudocode in section 4.1 derive a working program to calculate the time it takes to fill a rectangular swimming pool of uniform depth.

16. Write a program to input your name, height in inches, and weight in pounds; convert the height to centimeters and weight to kilograms and display the following results. Note: 1 inch = 2.54 centimeters and 1 pound = 0.4546 kilogram.

> PERSONAL DETAILS
> NAME: Henry Smithers
> HEIGHT (cm): 180
> WEIGHT (Kg): 75

17. Write a program to input the length and width of a rectangular garden, calculate the area of the lawn, and the cost of turfing the lawn if a 1.0 meter border is left around the perimeter of the garden. Assume the cost of turf is $2.00 per square meter. Display the result of these calculations.

18. Write a program to input an amount of money as a whole number, for example, $157, and display an analysis of the minimum number of $20, $10, $5, and $1 notes that make up this amount.

19. Write a program to input the length, width, and depths at the deepest and shallowest ends of a rectangular swimming pool that has a constant gradient between two opposite ends of the pool. Calculate the volume of water required to fill the pool and display this volume.

20. Return to the illustration of *Ben's Breakfast Bar* menu in Chapter 2, Figure 2.3.

Ben gives a discount of 25% on the cost of any three items of food purchased. Write a program to input the names and prices of three items chosen from the menu and output a fully itemized bill, including local tax at 5%.

21. A garage repair bill normally itemizes a description of the parts, the cost of the parts, the cost of labor, the sales tax, and the total amount due. Design a screen layout for such a repair bill. Write a program to input the necessary charges and display the bill.

22. Extend the algorithm developed in Chapter 1, section 1.8, Algorithm Example 1.1, to calculate the net pay for an employee after the following deductions:

Federal income tax at 15% gross pay;
Social security tax at 6.2% of gross pay
Payroll savings at 3% of gross pay
Retirement pension at 8.5% of gross pay;
Health insurance at $5.75 per employee.

Design a suitable layout for the employee's pay check. Write a program to input the hourly rate of pay, the number of hours worked in a week, calculate the deductions, and display the pay check.

Chapter 5
Functions

Functions fall into two categories. The first category is prewritten functions that are supplied with the standard C library and used in a program, for example, `printf`, `scanf`, `gets`, `getchar` and `strcpy`. The second category is programmer-defined functions that are written as part of a program. For example, the `main` function falls into this second category. Within this chapter the emphasis will be on the construction and use of programmer-defined functions.

By the end of this chapter you should have an understanding of the following topics:

- [ ] Constructing a function.
- [ ] Calling a function.
- [ ] Returning a value from a function.
- [ ] Passing data as arguments in a function call.
- [ ] The scope of identifiers.
- [ ] Designing a modular program.

5.1 Building Blocks

By now you have enough information to write small programs. However, at this stage it is important to explain how specific programmed activities can be formed into building blocks known as functions.

A **function** is a group of self-contained declarations and executable statements that perform an activity. It is very important to stress the words self-contained, since a function can be written and tested in isolation from the final program. A function can be thought of as a building block. Various functions, are written for various activities within a program. A complete program is built from many different functions, each having been tested before being used as part of the whole program.

5.2 Programmer-defined Functions

A C program normally consists of at least one function, the `main` function. In Program Example 5.1 a second function has been introduced to display a message. The program illustrates how to define a function within a program, how to call the function so that it can be executed, and how the computer returns to the main function after the function has been executed.

Program Example 5.1: Calling and Returning from a Function

```
/*
chap_5\ex_1.c
program to demonstrate how to construct a function call
*/

#include <stdio.h>

void display(void)
/* function to display a message */
{
   printf("function display has been called\n");
}

void main(void)
{
   printf("program execution starts at the main function\n");
   display();
   printf("returned to the main function\n");
}
```

Results

```
program execution starts at the main function
function display has been called
returned to the main function
```

The main function is executed before any other function. In this example the message program execution starts at the main function is displayed. The next line in the main function is display() and is the function call. A **function call** is simply the name of a function that signals the computer to branch to the actual function and perform the tasks it defines. The parentheses contain any arguments to be passed to the function from the caller. Such arguments form the **actual-parameter list** (in this case, there are no arguments). After reading the function call display() in the main function, the computer branches to the following function:

```
void display(void)
/* function to display a message */
{
   printf("function display has been called\n");
}
```

This syntax is the **function definition**. This particular function displays on the screen the message function display has been called.

After completing the function, the computer branches back to the next executable statement after the function call and the message returned to the main function is displayed. The main function has been completed and the program terminates.

Now that we have taken a first look at functions within the context of a program example, we must pause to understand the generic syntax of this important component.

A general form of function definition is:

C Syntax:

functions

```
return-type  function-name ( formal-parameter list )
{
    declarations
    statements
}
```

A **return-type** identifies the type of the value that the function will return to the caller. Possible return-types are: int, float, char, etc. If no data is being returned to the caller, the keyword void is used for the return-type.

The **formal-parameter list** indicates the data types for any arguments the function expects to receive from the caller. Each individual argument passed to the function must have its own corresponding parameter. If no arguments are being passed to the function, the keyword void is used in the formal parameter list.

Declarations refer to constant and variable declarations for use within the function.

Statements refer to the executable steps to be conducted within the function.

Caution:

potential error

Failure to include parentheses in a function call causes the compiler to ignore the call.

99

5.3 The Return Statement

Program Example 5.2 illustrates how the function sum returns the sum of two numbers to the main function. The return-type identifies the type of the value that the function will return to the caller.

C Syntax:

The syntax of the **return** statement is:

return
statement

return expression

where the expression may be omitted depending upon the use of the statement. Program Example 5.2 specifies the statement being used as

```
return first+second;
```

In Program Example 5.2 the return type for sum has been declared as int. The function sum invites the user to type in two numbers first and second. It is this value of first+second that is returned to the function sum by the return statement. The return statement has a dual purpose; it assigns a value to the function and also marks the position in the function where the computer must return to the calling program, in this case the main function.

Program Example 5.2: Returning a Value from a Function

```
/*
chap_5\ex_2.c
program to demonstrate calling a function that returns a value
*/

#include <stdio.h>

int sum(void)
/* function to return the sum of two values */
{
   int first, second; /* numbers to be input */

   printf("input first number ");
   scanf("%d", &first);
   printf("input second number ");
   scanf("%d", &second);
   return first + second;
}

void main(void)
{
   printf("sum of numbers is %d\n", sum() );
}
```

Results

```
input first number
input second number
sum of numbers is 80
```

Notice from Program Example 5.2 that it is quite acceptable to call a function from within a `printf` statement. For example, in `printf("sum of numbers is %d\n", sum());` the function `sum` is called before the `printf` statement can be executed. The function `sum` returns an integer value that is displayed using the control string `"%d"`.

If a function type is `void`, it is acceptable to use a `return` statement without an expression to force the computer to return to the caller. However, if the function type is `void` and the `return` statement is omitted, the computer will automatically return at the end of the function, as demonstrated in Program Example 5.1.

A function may contain several return statements (the relevance of this statement will not become apparent until the next chapter).

5.4 Value Parameters

There are two methods for passing arguments in C. The first method evaluates the argument and creates a local copy of the value, assigning it to the corresponding parameter in the function. In Program Example 5.3, the function `pieces` is used to return the number of pieces of wood that may be cut to a set size from a length of wood. The function call is made using the statement `pieces(L,S)` that contains two arguments `(L,S)`, both declared of type `float` in the function `main`. The formal-parameter list is coded as `(float length, float size)`. Notice that both the actual-parameter list and the formal-parameter list must contain the same number of arguments, in the same order and of the same data type.

Figure 5.1 illustrates that memory is allocated to storing the variables `L` and `S` in function `main`, and to storing the variables `length` and `size` in function `pieces`. Any changes to the parameters `length` and `size` would be localized to the function `pieces` and would not change the values of `L` and `S` in function `main`.

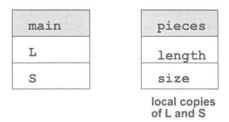

Figure 5.1 Passing parameters by value

101

Program Example 5.3: Parameters Passed by Value

```
/*
chap_5\ex_3.c
program to demonstrate the use of value arguments
*/

#include <stdio.h>

int pieces(float length, float size)
/*
function to calculate the number of pieces of wood that can be cut to a
set size from a length of wood */
{
        return (int) (length / size);
}

void main(void)
{
        float L; /* length of wood */
        float S; /* size of wood */

        printf("what is the length of the wood? ");
        scanf("%f", &L);

        printf("what size pieces do you want to cut? ");
        scanf("%f", &S);

        printf("number of pieces %d\n", pieces(L, S));
}
```

Results

```
what is the length of the wood? 10.0
what size pieces do you want to cut? 1.5
number of pieces 6
```

5.5 Reference Parameters

The second method of passing parameters involves passing character strings. This method will be extended to other types of data in this and future chapters.

When the argument is a character string, then a local copy of the string is not created and not stored in the data area of the function being called. Instead, the argument passes a memory address of where the argument is located to the corresponding function parameter. The memory address is a reference to the argument.

Program Example 5.4 contains a function get_data that invites a user to input a string. The function is called, and the address of the argument data_string is passed to the corresponding parameter string in the function get_data. Any reference to string in the function is a reference to the data contained at the address that was passed as an argument. Therefore, whatever value is input for string in the function get_data will be stored at the address of the argument, which is the memory location associated with the identifier data_string declared in the main function.

Since the parameter in the formal-parameter list is a character string, it must have square brackets after the identifier. The compiler has enough information about the size of the string from the declaration in the main function.

Program Example 5.4: Strings Passed by Reference

```
/*
chap_5\ex_4.c
program to demonstrate a string being passed as a reference parameter
*/

#include <stdio.h>

void get_data(char string[])
/* function to return a string */
{
   printf("input string ");
   gets(string);
}

void main(void)
{
   char data_string[80];

   get_data(data_string);
   printf("string input was %s", data_string);
}
```

Results

```
input string Hi Folks!
string input was Hi Folks!
```

Figure 5.2 illustrates how a character string is passed from the function get_data to the function main as a reference parameter. The original contents of data_string (is represented as ????? since the variable has not been initialized) will be overwritten by the new value "Hi Folks!".

the address of the argument data_string is
passed to the parameter string and not its contents

the value "Hi Folks!" input for string is stored at
the address passed as an argument

passing a parameter by reference changes
the contents of the argument's address

Figure 5.2 Passing a string parameter

Program Example 5.5 is an adaptation of Case Study: Cost of Newspapers in Chapter 4. In this modification, a function captures and returns the price of a newspaper. The first line of the function `paper_details` is given as

```
int paper_details(const char which_paper[])
```

An example of a statement used in the program to call this function is

```
price_paper_1 = paper_details(name_paper_1);
```

where `name_paper_1` is declared as: **const char name_paper_1[] = "Globe";**

Upon calling the function `paper_details`, the address of the memory location containing the string constant "Globe" is passed to the parameter `which_paper[]` in the formal parameter list. Figure 5.3 illustrates how the contents of the argument `name_paper_1` is accessed by reference, by the parameter `which_paper`, in the function `paper_details`.

Since the contents of the variable `name_paper_1` is a constant there is no requirement to declare and intialize this variable, but simply to use the string constant as the argument in the function call. Program Example 5.5 could be modified to pass a string literal argument "Globe" as follows.

```
price_paper_1 = paper_details("Globe");
```

Caution:

**potential
program-
ming error**

In both of these cases, if a character string is used as an argument and is not to be changed, then the reserved word `const` must be appended to the declaration of the string in the formal-parameter list. When `const` is present, the compiler will check that no assignment is made to the character string in the body of the function. The compiler should flag such an assignment as either an error or a warning.

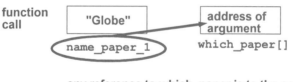

the address of the argument is passed to the
parameter which_paper and not its contents

any reference to which_paper is to the contents
of the address passed as argument

Figure 5.3 Passing a string constant

An advantage to be gained in using the function `paper_details` in this example stems from the reuse of the function. Notice that the function has been called three times from within the function `main` in order to return the prices of the three newspapers.

Program Example 5.5: String Constants passed by Reference

```
/*
chap_5\ex_5.c
program to input the prices of three newspapers, calculate
and output the total cost and average price of the papers
*/

#include <stdio.h>

int paper_details(const char which_paper[])
/*
function to return the price of a newspaper
*/
{
        int price;

        printf("price of %s ", which_paper);
        scanf("%d", &price);
        getchar();
        return price;
}

void main(void)
{
        const char name_paper_1[] = "Globe";
        const char name_paper_2[] = "Mercury";
        const char name_paper_3[] = "Courier";
```

```
int     price_paper_1, price_paper_2, price_paper_3;
int     total_cost, average;

price_paper_1 = paper_details(name_paper_1);
price_paper_2 = paper_details(name_paper_2);
price_paper_3 = paper_details(name_paper_3);

total_cost = price_paper_1 + price_paper_2 + price_paper_3;
average = total_cost / 3;

printf("total cost of three newspapers is %3dc\n", total_cost);
printf("average price of newspapers is %2dc\n", average);
}
```

Results

```
price of Globe 40
price of Mercury 50
price of Courier 60
total cost of three newspapers is 150c
average price of newspapers is 50c
```

5.6 Pointers

A **pointer** is an identifier that does not store data of type int, float, double, char, etc; but instead stores an address of where to find the data in memory. This address literally points to where the data is stored. The declaration

```
int *IntPointer;
```

implies that the variable IntPointer is a pointer to an integer. The asterisk * in front of IntPointer instructs the compiler that IntPointer is a variable pointer and not a variable of type integer.

The statement IntPointer = &largest; assigns the address of largest to IntPointer, causing IntPointer to point at the variable largest, as depicted in Figure 5.4. Remember **&** is an address operator and was described in Chapter 3.

The **indirection operator** * (asterisk) allows the programmer to identify the value of the datum that is being pointed at. For example in Figure 5.4, *IntPointer is the value INT_MAX.

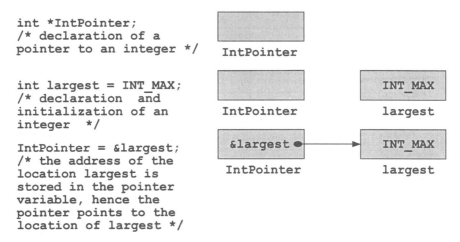

```
int *IntPointer;
/* declaration of a
pointer to an integer */
```

```
int largest = INT_MAX;
/* declaration  and
initialization of an
integer   */
```

```
IntPointer = &largest;
/* the address of the
location largest is
stored in the pointer
variable, hence the
pointer points to the
location of largest */
```

Figure 5.4 A pointer variable

Do not become confused between the use of the asterisk to declare a pointer as a variable and the use of the asterisk to gain access to the value of what is being pointed at. The asterisk is used in two different contexts; the first is for declaration and the second is for access to a datum.

Reference parameters, other than character strings, are possible in C. The formal parameters in a function are declared as pointers. The actual parameters (arguments) used in the function call are treated as addresses of the variables, not as the variables themselves.

For example, a function used to separate the whole part of a real number from its decimal fraction may be coded as

```
void split(float local_number, int *whole_number, float *fractional_part)
{
   *whole_number = local_number;
   *fractional_part = local_number - (int) local_number;
}
```

and called by `split(number, &whole, &fraction);` where `number`, `whole` and `fraction` are declared in the `main` function as `float number; int whole; float fraction;`

Figure 5.5 and Program Example 5.6 illustrate that `number` is passed to the function `split` as a local copy and that any changes to `local_number` in the function `split` do not alter `number` in the `main` function. The addresses `&whole` and `&fraction` are passed to the pointers `*whole_number` and `*fractional_part`. Any reference to `*whole_number` and `*fractional_part` in the function `split` must change the contents of `whole` and `fraction` in the `main` function.

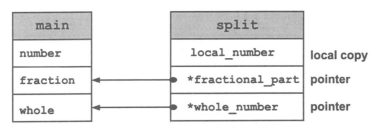

Figure 5.5 Pointer variables in a function

Program Example 5.6: Reference Parameters using Pointers and Addresses

```
/*
chap_5\ex_6.c
program to demonstrate the use of pointers in a formal parameter list
*/

#include <stdio.h>

void split(float local_number, int *whole_number, float *fractional_part)
{
        *whole_number = local_number;
        *fractional_part = local_number - (int) local_number;
}

void main(void)
{
        float number = 3.14159;
        float fraction;
        int    whole;

        split(number, &whole, &fraction);
        printf("whole %d\tfraction %f\n", whole, fraction);
}
```

Results

```
whole 3 fraction 0.141590
```

C Syntax:

function
prototype

A function **prototype** is a declaration of a function and consists of the first line of the function definition terminated by a semicolon. The syntax of a function prototype is given as

return-type function-name (formal-parameter list) ;

For example

```
void split(float local_number, int *whole_number, float *fractional_part);
```

is the function prototype of the function split defined in Program Example 5.6.

The final program in this section is an adaptation of Case Study: Determining Paint Quantity in Chapter 4. The modified program illustrates how functions may be used to break a program into separate parts. In this example two functions have been created - get_dimensions, and number_of_cans in addition to the function main. The function prototypes are

```
void get_dimensions(float *length, float *width, float *height);
int  number_of_cans(float length, float width, float height);
```

The function get_dimensions invites a user to input the length, width,and height of a room and passes these values back as reference parameters. However, within this function scanf has been used to input these values from the keyboard. You are in the habit, or should be, of using the address operator with the scanf function when inputting numbers. For example, scanf("%f", &length).

Now pause for a moment and think what you are doing. From the prototype it is clear that the variable length is a pointer. In other words length is already an address. Therefore, the variable length need not be qualified with the & address operator in the scanf function.

Data is passed to the function number_of_cans by value; in other words, a local copy of length, width and height are kept by this function. The function calculates and returns the number of cans of paint required.

Figure 5.6 illustrates how the parameters are organized for this program.

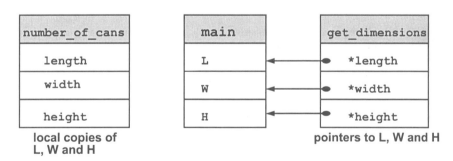

Figure 5.6 Value and reference parameters

Program Example 5.7: Value Parameters and Reference Parameters

```
/* chap_5\ex_7.c
program to calculate the amount of paint needed to paint the walls
of a room */

#include <stdio.h>
```

```
void get_dimensions(float *length, float *width, float *height)
/* function to pass the values for length, width and height as
reference parameters */

{
        printf("input room dimensions\n");
        printf("length? ");
        scanf("%f", length);
        printf("width? ");
        scanf("%f", width);
        printf("height? ");
        scanf("%f", height);
}

int number_of_cans(float length, float width, float height)
/* function to calculate the number of cans of paint */
{
        const    float    paint_cover    = 200.0;
        const    float    window_area    = 40.0;
        const    float    door_area      = 14.0;

        float wall_area;

        wall_area = 2*height*(length+width)-(window_area+door_area);
        return (wall_area / paint_cover) + 0.999;
}

void main(void)
{
        float    L; /* length of room */
        float    W; /* width of room */
        float    H; /* height of room */

        get_dimensions(&L, &W, &H);
        printf("number of cans to purchase = %d\n", number_of_cans(L,W,H));
}
```

Results

```
input room dimensions
length? 30.0
width? 15.0
height? 8.0
number of cans to purchase = 4
```

5.7 Scope

The **scope** of an identifier refers to the region of a program in which the identifier can be referenced.

A **block** begins with an open brace { and ends with a close brace } and contains declarations and executable statements. Identifiers that are declared within a block are said to have **block scope**, implying they are visible from their point of declaration to the end of the closing block. The term **visible** implies that the identifiers can be referred to or used within the block. For example, in the previous example the function `number_of_cans` contained the following four declarations:

```
int number_of_cans(float length, float width, float height)
{
        const   float   paint_cover     = 200.0;
        const   float   window_area     = 40.0;
        const   float   door_area       = 14.0;

        float wall_area;
           .
           .
}
```

The constants `paint_cover`, `window_area`, and `door_area`, and the variable `wall_area` all have block scope within the function `number_of_cans`. These identifiers are **local** to the function `number_of_cans` and are visible within the scope of the block, yet they cannot be referred to or used outside of the block.

Identifiers that represent function names do not lie within the scope of a block. However, such identifiers need to be referred to in other parts of a program; otherwise, it would not be possible to call a function. Function names are said to have **file scope**, implying that the identifiers can be referred to from their point of declaration to the end of the source file. In the Program Example 5.7, the names `get_dimensions` and `number_of_cans` have file scope and are used within the block of the `main` function. This fact is emphasised by the following skeletal code.

```
void get_dimensions(float *length, float *width, float *height)
{
     .
     .
}

int number_of_cans(float length, float width, float height)
{
     .
     .
}
```

```
void main(void)
{
        get_dimensions(&L, &W, &H);
        printf("number of cans to purchase = %d\n", number_of_cans(L,W,H));
}
```

Consider the following situation in which function `alpha` is called from within the block of function `main`, and the function `beta` is called from within the function `alpha`.

```
void alpha(void)
{
    beta();
    .
    .
}

void beta(void)
{
    .
    .
}

void main(void)
{
    alpha();
    .
    .
}
```

Function `alpha` has file scope from its point of declaration to the end of the source file and therefore can be used in the function `main`. Function `beta` has file scope from its point of declaration, after the block of `alpha`, to the end of the source file. Function `beta` cannot be called from the block of function `alpha`, since `beta` is not within its file scope. Function `alpha` contains a forward reference to function `beta`. A **forward reference** is a reference to an identifier before it has been declared.

The forward reference is resolved by declaring the prototypes of each function, except for `main`, before the definitions of the functions. All function names are then given file scope before they are called. The coding can be modified as follows.

```
void alpha(void);
void beta(void);

void alpha(void)
{
    beta();
    .
    .
}
```

```
void beta(void)
{
        .
        .
}

void main(void)
{
        alpha();
        .
        .
}
```

All constants, data types, and variables may be declared as having file scope, implying that all such identifiers are visible throughout the source file. Such a practice may force you to depart from the ethos that a function should be a group of self-contained declarations and executable statements. For this reason we will use identifiers that have file scope with caution throughout the book.

When a declaration inside a block names an identifier that is already visible, because it has file scope, the new declaration temporarily hides the old one and the identifier takes on a new meaning. At the end of the block, the identifier regains its old meaning. For example,

```
    int x;                  /* variable x has file scope */

    void delta(void)
    {
       int x;               /* variable x has block scope within function
                                delta, and the file scope version of x is hidden */
    }

    void main(void)
    {
       scanf("%d", &x);  /* since x has file scope it is visible in function
                .                main */
    }
```

Case Study: Modularity

In section 4.1 we stated that in attempting to solve a problem, it is far easier to divide the problem into parts and solve each part, rather than trying to solve the problem at one attempt. This approach is known as top-down design and can be represented in the form of a structure chart. An example of a structure chart for calculating the time taken to fill a rectangular swimming pool of uniform depth with water is illustrated again in Figure 5.7.

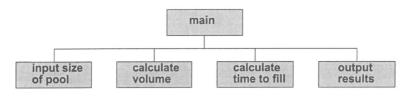

Figure 5.7 Structure chart for swimming pool

The implementation of this design would be much better, if the program code reflected the components of the structure chart. In the following program-design process each component in the structure chart is developed as a separate function.

Problem Analysis - Given the length, width, and depth (in feet) of the swimming pool, the volume is calculated from the following expression: *volume = length * width * depth*.

Since a cubic foot of water is equivalent to 7.8 gallons, the capacity of the water in the swimming pool is calculated from the following expression: *capacity = volume * 7.8*.

If the rate of flow of water into the pool is 20 gallons per minute, then the time (in hours) that it takes to fill the pool is calculated from the following expression: *time = capacity / 20 / 60*.

Algorithm for Function main

1. input the size of the pool
2. calculate the volume of the pool
3. calculate the time to fill the pool
4. output the results

Data Dictionary for the Function main This contains declarations for the length, width, and depth of the swimming pool, as well as declarations for the volume of the pool, capacity of the water, and the time taken to fill the pool.

```
float length, width, depth;
float volume, capacity, time;
```

Algorithm for Function pool_size

1.1 input length
1.2 input width
1.3 input depth

Data Dictionary for the Function pool_size The formal parameter list for this function contains three pointer parameters to reference the length, width, and depth of the pool. There are no local declarations. The function prototype is

```
void   pool_size(float *length, float *width, float *depth);
```

Algorithm for the Function pool_volume

2.1 volume = length * width * depth

Data Dictionary for the Function pool_volume The formal parameter list for this function contains three value parameters: length, width, and depth of the pool. There are no local declarations and the function returns the volume of the pool. The function prototype is

```
float   pool_volume(float length, float width, float depth);
```

Algorithm for Function time_to_fill

3.1 capacity = volume * capacity of 1 cubic foot
3.2 time = (capacity / rate of flow) / 60

Data Dictionary for the Function time_to_fill - The formal parameter list for this function contains two parameters: a value parameter for the volume and a reference parameter for the capacity. The function returns the time (in hours) to fill the pool. There are two local constant declarations representing the rate of flow of water and the capacity of 1 cubic foot of water. The function prototype is

```
float   time_to_fill(float volume, float *capacity);
```

and the local constants are

```
const float rate_of_flow = 20.0;
const float cubic_ft_capacity = 7.8;
```

Algorithm for the Function results

4.1 output volume of pool
4.2 output capacity of water in gallons
4.3 output time to fill pool

Data Dictionary for the Function results - The formal parameter list for this function contains three value parameters: the volume of the pool, capacity of the water, and time to fill the pool. There are no local declarations. The function prototype is

```
void    results(float volume, float capacity, float time);
```

Figure 5.8 is a further development of the structure chart given in Figure 5.7. The new structure chart illustrates how the choice of functions for the program can be reflected in the design. The arrowed lines in the chart indicate the parameters that are being passed to and from the main function and the values that are being returned by the functions pool_volume and time_to_fill.

115

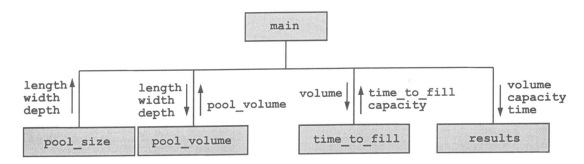

Figure 5.8 Revised structure chart

Test Data - length = 50 feet; width = 20 feet; depth = 5 feet

function	length	width	depth	volume	capacity	time
main	?	?	?	?	?	?
pool_size	50	20	5			
main	50	20	5			
pool_volume	50	20	5	5000		
main				5000		
time_to_fill				5000	39000	32.50
results				5000	39000	32.50

```
                       Screen Layout

12345678901234567890123456789012345678901234567890123456789 0

input size of pool in feet
length?  50.0
width?   20.0
depth?    5.0
volume of pool [cubic feet]    5000.0
capacity of water [gallons]   39000.0
time taken to fill [hours]       32.50
```

Figure 5.9 illustrates the organization of memory for dealing with the parameters in each of the functions. Notice that although the same names have been used in each function, value parameters are stored as local copies of the parameters in the function. You should understand by now that reference parameters are pointers to the arguments specified in the function call.

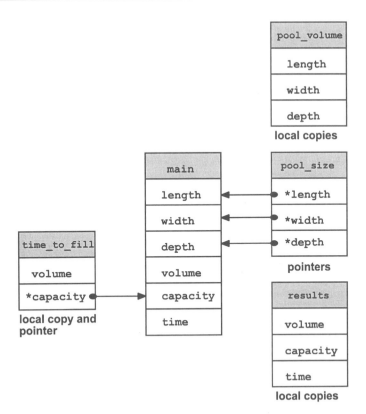

Figure 5.9 Value and reference parameters

```
/*
chap_5\ex_8.c
program to input the length, width and depth of a rectangular
swimming pool, and display the volume of the pool, capacity of
the water and time it takes to fill the pool
*/

#include <stdio.h>

void pool_size(float *length, float *width, float *depth)
/* function to pass the length, width and depth of the pool
as reference parameters */
{
   printf("input size of pool in feet\n");
   printf("length? ");
   scanf("%f",length);
   printf("width?   ");
```

```
    scanf("%f",width);
    printf("depth?   ");
    scanf("%f",depth);
}

float pool_volume(float length, float width, float depth)
/* function to return the volume of the pool in cubic feet */
{
    return length*width*depth;
}

float time_to_fill(float volume, float *capacity)
/* function to return the time in hours that it takes
to fill the pool and pass capacity as a reference parameter */
{
    /* rate of flow 20 gallons per minute */
    const float rate_of_flow    = 20.0;
    /* 1 cubic foot of water has a capacity of 7.8 gallons */
    const float cubic_ft_capacity = 7.8;

    *capacity = volume * cubic_ft_capacity;
    return  (*capacity / rate_of_flow) / 60.0;
}

void results(float volume, float capacity, float time)
/* function to display the volume and capacity of the water
and the time to fill the pool */
{
    printf("volume of pool [cubic feet] %8.1f\n", volume);
    printf("capacity of water [gallons] %8.1f\n", capacity);
    printf("time taken to fill [hours]  %8.2f\n", time);
}

void main(void)
{
    float length, width, depth;
    float volume, capacity, time;

    pool_size(&length, &width, &depth);
    volume = pool_volume(length, width, depth);
    time = time_to_fill(volume, &capacity);
    results(volume, capacity, time);
}
```

Results

```
input size of pool in feet
length?
width?
depth?
volume of pool [cubic feet]    5000.0
capacity of water [gallons]   39000.0
time taken to fill [hours]      32.50
```

5.8 Advantages of Using Functions

Incorporating functions into the initial design process and ultimately into the coding of the program has many advantages.

Modular Programming

Functions allow us to write a program in independent pieces that represent subsets of the overall programming problem. We can break complex programming problems into manageable functions. Members of a programming team can work independently on different functions, thus shortening the completion time for the overall program.

Efficiency of Code

Functions can be called more than once in a program, so we only have to write code once for tasks that will be performed multiple times.

Reuse

Functions can be used in programs other than the one for which they were originally written, for example, a function to display the time and date at the beginning of every program.

Testing

Functions may be tested independently of the rest of a program, so we don't have to wait until the whole program is completed to begin testing its accuracy and making corrections.

Summary

- ☐ A function should be written as a self-contained unit that represents a single programmed activity.

- ☐ When calling a function, the list of constants or variables after the function name is known as the actual-parameter list.

- ☐ The number of actual parameters must be the same as the number of corresponding formal-parameters.

- ☐ The order of the actual-parameters and the formal-parameters must be the same.

□ The data types of the corresponding actual-parameters and formal-parameters should be the same.

□ The names of the actual-parameters and formal-parameters can be the same or different.

□ Having executed a function, the computer returns to the next executable statement after the function call.

□ The computer will return to the calling function by either executing a `return` statement or reaching the physical end of the function.

□ The `return` statement may assign a value to the function and exit from the function.

□ A function may contain parameters and local constants, types, and variables.

□ Constants, types, and variables may have block scope or file scope.

Review Questions

1. What is a library function? Give examples of the library functions that have been covered this far in the text.

2. What is the syntax of a programmer-defined function?

3. Does every function return a value?

4. What is a formal-parameter list?

5. True or false - every function has a formal-parameter list.

6. What is an actual-parameter list?

7. True or false - a function may have many `return` statements.

8. True or false - a function may have no `return` statements.

9. Where does the computer return to upon exiting a function?

10. What is the scope of an identifier?

11. What is a block?

12. Distinguish between block scope and file scope.

13. Give an example of a parameter passed by value.

14. How is a value parameter represented, in the memory allocated to a function?

15. True or false - a string parameter is passed by value.

16. What is the meaning of the declaration `float *number`?

17. How do you interpret the statement `number = &minimum`, where `number` is taken to have the same meaning as expressed in question 16, and `minimum` is a floating-point variable?

18. What is a reference parameter?

19. How do you pass an integer as a reference parameter to a function?

20. When do you use `const` to qualify a parameter?

21. Define the term *modular programming*.

22. List three benefits to be gained by using functions to build a program.

Programming Exercises

23. Desk check the following code. What is output from function `main`?

```
int sum()
{
    int A = 12;
    int B = 13;

    return A+B;
}

void main(void)
{
    printf("sum %d\n", sum());
}
```

24. Desk check the following code. What is output from function `display`?

```
void display(const char message[])
{
    printf("%s\n", message);
}

void main(void)
{
    display("Hello World!");
}
```

25. Desk check the following code. What is output from function `display`?

```
void display(int A, int B)
{
    int C;

    C=A+B;
    printf("sum %d\n", C);
}

void main(void)
{
    display(25,13);
}
```

26. Desk check the following code. What is output from functions `value_only` and `main`?

```
void value_only(int A, int B)
{
    A = A - 1;
    B = B + 1;
    printf("A=%d B=%d\n", A, B);
}

void main(void);
{
    int A = 41;
    int B = 29;

    value_only(A, B);
    printf("A=%d B=%d\n", A, B);
}
```

27. Desk check the following code. What is output from function `main`?

```
void reference_only(int *A, int *B)
{
    *A = *A - 1;
    *B = *B + 1;
}


void main(void)
{
    int X = 41;
    int Y = 29;
```

```
    reference_only(&X, &Y);
    printf("X=%d Y=%d\n", X, Y);
}
```

28. State the errors in the following function calls and function prototypes

	function call	function declaration
(a)	`alpha;`	`void alpha(char d,char e,char f);`
(b)	`beta(A,B,C);`	`void beta(void);`
(c)	`delta(18,'*');`	`int delta(char  X, int Y);`
(d)	`gamma(X,Y);`	`void gamma(int i,int j,int k);`

29. What is the error in the following function?

```
void alpha(int number)
{
    return 2 * number;
}
```

30. In the following code, what is the value of `global` inside the function `over_ride`?

```
int global = 29;     /* integer variable with file scope */

void over_ride(void)
{
    int global = 56;   /* integer variable with block scope */
    .
    .
    .
}
```

Programming Problems

31. Write and test a function with the following prototype:

```
float input_datum(char prompt[]);
/* display the prompt string, input a floating point number referred to by
the prompt string, return this value */
```

32. Write and test functions with the following prototypes:

```
float circumference(float radius);
/* given the radius of a circle return the circumference */
float area(float radius);
/* given the radius of a circle return the area */
```

For questions 33, 34 and 35 you are expected to re-work your solutions to questions 11, 12, and 18 respectively, from Chapter 4.

33. Redesign your answer to question 11 to incorporate a modular design. Your design should incorporate three functions whose prototypes are given as

```
float cost_of_frame(float length, float width, float *length_wood);
/* given the length and width of the photograph, return the cost of the
wood to make the frame, and the length of wood */
float cost_of_card(float length, float width, float *area_card);
/* given the length and width of the photograph, return the total cost of
the backing cards, and the area of the card */
float cost_of_glass(float length, float width, float *area_glass);
/* given the length and width of the photograph, return the cost of the
glass for the frame, and the area of the glass */
```

Rewrite the program using the new functions to supply a fully itemized quotation for framing a photograph.

34. Redesign your answer to question 12 to incorporate a modular design. Your design should incorporate two functions whose prototypes are given as

```
float miles_per_day(float map_distance);
/* given the map distance for any one day of the journey, return the num-
ber of miles traveled for that day */
float time_per_day(float distance_in_miles);
/* given the distance traveled in miles per day, return the time taken to
complete the journey for one day */
```

Rewrite the program using the new functions to estimate the distance traveled and time spent walking per day and for the entire holiday.

35. Rewrite your answer to question 18 to calculate the number of $20, $10, $5, and $1 notes in a given amount of money and incorporate the following function prototype:

```
int number_of_notes(int *amount_of_money, int denomination);
/* given an amount of money return the number of notes that can be issued
for a given denomination; the amount of money remaining is the amount of
money left over, if any, after the transaction */
```

36. Write and test a function with the following prototype:

```
void time(  int  elapsed_seconds,
            int *hours,
            int *minutes,
            int *seconds);

/* given the number of elapsed seconds since midnight on one day only, cal-
culate and return as reference parameters the time in hours, minutes, and
seconds */
```

Chapter 6
Selection

Up to now all the programs have been constructed from a sequence of statements. Each time a program was run, the computer would execute the same statements. How do you write a program that requires different statements to be executed depending upon a set of conditions?

This chapter introduces the techniques of coding conditions and branching on the result of a condition to alternative statements in a program. By the end of the chapter you should have an understanding of the following topics:

- ☐ The syntax and use of the statements *if* and *if .. else*.

- ☐ The construction and evaluation of a conditional expression.

- ☐ The use of nested, or embedded selection statements.

- ☐ The declaration of variables of enumerated type.

- ☐ The use of logical operators in the construction of conditional expressions.

- ☐ The syntax and use of the *switch* statement.

6.1 If

Consider the following program that tells the user which garment to wear, depending on the weather.

Program Example 6.1: If Statement

```c
/*
chap_6\ex_1.c
program to demonstrate the if statement
*/

#include <stdio.h>
#include <string.h>

void main(void)
{
        const   char    yes = 'Y';

        char    reply;
        char    garment[9];

        strcpy(garment, "overcoat");

        printf("is it raining outside? answer Y[es] or N[o] ");
        scanf("%c", &reply);

        if (reply == yes) strcpy(garment, "raincoat");

        printf("before you go out today take your %s\n", garment);
}
```

Results from program being run twice

```
is it raining outside? answer Y[es] or N[o]
before you go out today take your overcoat

is it raining outside? answer Y[es] or N[o]
before you go out today take your raincoat
```

In tracing through the program, the following operations take place. The string variable `garment` is initialized to the value `"overcoat"`. The user is then requested to input whether it is raining or not. If the answer to the question is Y (yes), then the value of `garment` is changed to `"raincoat"`. However, if the answer to the question is N (no), then the value of `garment` remains unaltered. Finally the computer tells the user which garment to take before venturing outdoors.

In the program it has been possible to ask a question, and depending upon the answer, select an alternative statement for the computer to execute. The fragment of flowchart shown in Figure 6.1 illustrates a single branch that corresponds to this question.

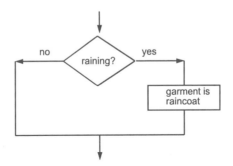

Figure 6.1 A one-way selection

C Syntax:

if ..

The syntax of the **if** statement is:

if (expression) statement

where the expression equates to either zero or nonzero. For example:

```
if (reply == yes) strcpy(garment, "raincoat");
```

Caution:

do not confuse the use of = with ==

The expression `reply == yes` is a conditional expression, where the symbol **==** represents the relational operator *equal to*. In the conditional expression `reply == yes`, pay particular attention to the data types being used. The data type for reply is `char`, and the identifier `yes` is declared as a constant assigned the value `'Y'`. This technique has been used to improve the readability of the program. An alternative method of coding the conditional expression could be `reply == 'Y'`, which is not as clear.

The conditional expression will either equate to nonzero, when the reply is equal to yes, or zero, when the reply is not equal to yes and, therefore, by implication may be equal to no. Only when the expression equates to nonzero will the statement immediately after the conditional expression be executed. If the conditional expression equates to zero, the computer will ignore the statement after the conditional expression and branch to the next executable statement. The end of the `if` statement, as far as the computer is concerned, follows the ; (semicolon) after the statement `strcpy(garment, "raincoat")`.

Remember that other than in a string declaration, it is not possible to assign a string literal to a string variable. In Chapter 3 we stated that a string must be assigned to a variable using the function `strcpy` from the `<string.h>` header found in the standard library. In this example, the function `strcpy` has been used to assign the variable `garment` with the string literal `"overcoat"` or with the string literal `"raincoat"`.

127

Conditional expressions in many high-level languages equate to either false or true. However, in C false and true are not keywords and conditions equate to either zero, corresponding to false, or nonzero, corresponding to true.

The relational operator == is not the only operator that can be used in an if statement. Table 6.1 lists the six relational operators that can be used in an if statement.

Table 6.1 Relational operators

operator	meaning
>	greater than
<	less than
==	equal to
>=	greater than or equal to
<=	less than or equal to
!=	not equal to

6.2 If .. Else

The following syntax notation indicates that there is more to the if statement than the previous section indicated.

C Syntax:

if .. else ..

if (conditional expression)
    statement_1
else
    statement_2

For example,

```
if (reply == yes)
    strcpy(garment, "raincoat");
else
    strcpy(garment, "overcoat");
```

The fragment of flowchart illustrated in Figure 6.2 shows this form of two-way selection.

128

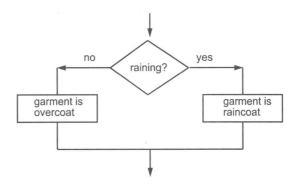

Figure 6.2 A two-way selection

In Program Example 6.2 the previous program has been modified to include the statement if .. else.

Program Example 6.2: If .. Else statement

The function of the program is exactly the same as before. If it was executed with the same data as the first program, then there would be no change in the output.

```
/*
chap_6\ex_2.c
program to demonstrate the if .. else statement
*/

#include <stdio.h>
#include <string.h>

void main(void)
{
        const   char    yes = 'Y';

        char    reply;
        char    garment[9];

        printf("is it raining outside? answer Y[es] or N[o] ");
        scanf("%c", &reply);

        if (reply == yes)
           strcpy(garment, "raincoat");
        else
           strcpy(garment, "overcoat");

        printf("before you go out today take your %s\n", garment);
}
```

There are, however, two differences in the construction of the program. The string variable `garment` has no initial assignment, and an if .. else statement has replaced the if .. statement in the previous program.

The action of the if .. else statement is very straightforward. If the result of the conditional expression `reply == yes` is nonzero (true), then the statement `strcpy( garment, "raincoat")` will be executed. However, if the result of the conditional expression is zero (false), then the statement `strcpy(garment, "overcoat");` will be executed. In both cases the computer branches to the `printf` statement after the if .. else statement has been executed.

Style Matters:

indentation

You should adopt the habit of indenting code within an if .. else statement. Indentation clarifies which statements are associated with the conditional expression being true and which statements are associated with it being false (after the else). Indentation of the statements after the else also indicates to the human reader where the if .. else statement finishes, since the next statement after the if .. else will be indented to the same distance from the margin as the *if* or the *else*.

In the previous example, only one statement was executed regardless of whether the conditional expression evaluated to zero or nonzero. What if more than one statement is to be executed? The answer is to treat the group of statements as a compound statement by introducing braces { }; for example,

```
if (alpha == beta)
{
   A = B;
   C = D;
}
else
{
   A = D;
   C = B;
}
```

Style Matters:

inclusion of braces

If only one statement is executed in a selection statement, the use of braces can improve the clarity of the code, even though the braces themselves are redundant. In Program Example 6.3, braces have been included in the selection statements purely to improve the readability of the code.

6.3 Nested If 's

The statement that follows the conditional expression in either if or if .. else statements can also be an *if* statement. This is also true of the statement that follows else, in an if .. else statement. In the previous examples if the weather had been warm then wearing either a raincoat or an overcoat could prove to be very uncomfortable. If a second item of data is included about the temperature then it is possible to more accurately specify what to wear whether it is raining or not. Let us therefore consider the following embellishments to the problem scenario.

Program Example 6.3: If .. Else ..

If it is raining and the temperature is less than 60 degrees Fahrenheit, then wear a raincoat; otherwise, if it is warmer, then take an umbrella. However, if it is not raining and the temperature is less than 60 degrees Fahrenheit, then wear an overcoat; otherwise, if it is warmer, then wear a jacket. The program has been reconstructed in Program Example 6.3 to take these new facts into account. The outer if .. else statement is used to determine which path to take depending upon whether it is raining. The inner if .. else statements are used to determine which path to take depending upon the temperature.

The flowchart in Figure 6.3 shows you the different paths that can be taken when the program runs.

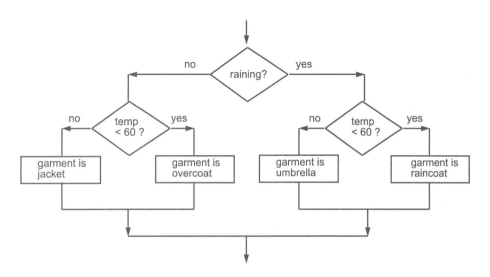

Figure 6.3 Flowchart showing nested if .. else ..

Notice also the use of the relational operator in the expression `temperature < 60`. The relational operator < means *less than*. Refer to Table 6.1 for the list of relational operators that can be used in conditional expressions.

```
/*
chap_6\ex_3.c
program to demonstrate nested if .. else statements
*/

#include <stdio.h>
#include <string.h>

void main(void)
{
        const   char    yes = 'Y';
```

```
char    reply;
char    garment[9];
int     temperature;

printf("what is the temperature outside today? ");
scanf("%d", &temperature);
getchar();

printf("is it raining outside? answer Y[es] or N[o] ");
scanf("%c", &reply);

if (reply == yes)
{
    if (temperature < 60)
        strcpy(garment, "raincoat");
    else
        strcpy(garment, "umbrella");
}
else
{
    if (temperature < 60)
        strcpy(garment, "overcoat");
    else
        strcpy(garment, "jacket");
}
printf("before you go out today take your %s\n", garment);
}
```

Results from the program being run four times

```
what is the temperature outside today? 50
is it raining outside? answer Y[es] or N[o] Y
before you go out today take your raincoat

what is the temperature outside today? 50
is it raining outside? answer Y[es] or N[o] N
before you go out today take your overcoat

what is the temperature outside today? 60
is it raining outside? answer Y[es] or N[o] Y
before you go out today take your umbrella

what is the temperature outside today? 60
is it raining outside? answer Y[es] or N[o] N
before you go out today take your jacket
```

In the program, after both the `temperature` and `reply` have been input, if the conditional expression `reply == yes` is true, then the statement after the conditional expression will be obeyed by another `if` statement! If the conditional expression `temperature < 60` is true, then the statement `strcpy( garment "raincoat")` will be executed; however, if the conditional expression `temperature < 60` is false, then the statement `strcpy(garment, "umbrella")` will be executed. In either case the computer will then branch to the next executable statement after the last statement in the outer `if .. else` statement.

If the conditional expression `reply == yes` is false, then the statement after `else` (in the outer `if .. else`) will be obeyed, and if the conditional expression `temperature < 60` is true, then the statement after the conditional expression `strcpy(garment, "overcoat")` will be executed; however, if the conditional expression `temperature < 60` is false, then the statement `strcpy( garment, "jacket")` will be executed.

If .. else statements can be nested to any depth; however, you should pay particular attention to the use of indentation and the grouping of else statements. In the following example, to which if statement does the single else statement belong?

```c
if (alpha == 3)
   if (beta == 4)
      printf("alpha 3 beta 4\n");
else
   printf("alpha beta not valid");
```

The indentation suggests that the `else` belongs to `if (alpha == 3)`, however, as you might expect this is wrong. The rule in C regarding which else belongs to which if is simple. An else clause belongs to the nearest if statement that has not already been paired with an else. This example can be rewritten taking into account the correct indentation.

```c
if (alpha == 3)
   if (beta == 4)
      printf("alpha 3 beta 4\n");
   else
      printf("alpha beta not valid");
```

If the `else` clause did belong to `if (alpha == 3)`, then braces would be introduced into the coding as follows:

```c
if (alpha == 3)
{
   if (beta == 4)
      printf("alpha 3 beta 4\n");
}
else
   printf("alpha beta not valid");
```

6.4 Enumerated Data Type

In order to clarify the coding in a computer program, it sometimes helps to replace integer values, such as 0 and 1, with meaningful names. An **enumeration** is a collection of integer values that have been given names by the programmer. All enumerated constants start with the integer value 0 unless otherwise specified by the programmer, and successive constants have successive integer values. The syntax of an enumeration is

C Syntax:

enumera-tion

enum { constant-1 , constant-2 , constant-3 ... }

For example, a condition in an `if` statement is regarded as false if it evaluates to zero and true if it evaluates to nonzero. By stating:

```
enum {false, true}
```

the names `false` and `true` become synonymous with the numbers 0 and 1 and can be used in place of 0 and 1. The enumeration can be regarded as a type having the values false and true.

In the C language, the **typedef** mechanism allows a programmer to explicitly associate a type with an identifier. The syntax of typedef is given as

C Syntax:

typedef

typedef type identifier

The Boolean data type is common in many high-level languages with the exception of C. In the following example, a data type `boolean` has been defined that contains the enumerated constants `false` and `true` where false = 0 and true = 1.

```
typedef enum {false, true} boolean;
```

A variable, in this example `error`, can be designated the data type `boolean` and initialized to the value `false`. For example,

```
boolean error = false;
```

By default, the value of the first enumeration constant is 0, the second is 1, and so on, with each constant being 1 greater than the previous constant. You can use an initializer to set an enumeration constant to a known value. For example, `enum {one=1, two, three}`; such that `one` is 1, `two` is 2 and `three` is 3. Notice that after initialization, the subsequent constants are greater than the initialization value.

In Program Example 6.3, how would the computer respond to data being input that did not match either yes or no in response to a reply? If the reply was neither `Y` or `N` then the conditional expression `reply==yes` would be false and the computer would assign `"overcoat"` to the variable `garment` if the temperature was less than sixty degrees, or would assign `"jacket"` to the variable `garment` if the temperature was warmer. This is clearly an undesirable feature of the program, and it is the responsibility of the programmer to trap any invalid data and report the exceptional circumstances to the user of the program.

The next program traps and reports on data being input that does not conform to the reply yes or no. The program introduces the explicitly defined type `boolean` whose values are `false` or `true`. A variable, `error`, has been declared as being `boolean`, which means that the values `false` or `true` can be assigned to it. In the program the variable `error` is initialized to `false` on the assumption that no invalid data will be input. However, as soon as invalid data is recognized, the value of `error` is changed to `true`.

Since `error` is of type `boolean` and only has the values `false` (zero) or `true` (nonzero) assigned to it, the variable may be used in place of a conditional expression. Notice in the last segment of the program code that if there has been an error, the message of what garment to take is suppressed and replaced by a data error message.

Program Example 6.4: Enumeration

```
/*
chap_6\ex_4.c
program to demonstrate the use of an enumeration type
*/

#include <stdio.h>
#include <string.h>

void main(void)
{
        typedef enum{false, true} boolean;

        const   char    yes = 'Y';
        const   char    no  = 'N';

        char    reply;
        char    garment[9];
        int     temperature;
        boolean error = false;

        printf("what is the temperature outside today? ");
        scanf("%d", &temperature);
        getchar();
        printf("is it raining outside? answer Y[es] or N[o] ");
        scanf("%c", &reply);
```

```
if (reply == yes)
{
    if (temperature < 60)
        strcpy(garment, "raincoat");
    else
        strcpy(garment, "umbrella");
}
else
{
    if (reply == no)
    {
        if (temperature < 60)
            strcpy(garment, "overcoat");
        else
            strcpy(garment, "jacket");
    }
    else
        error = true;
}

if (error)
    printf("DATA ERROR - reply not input as either Y or N\n");
else
    printf("before you go out today take your %s\n", garment);
}
```

Results from the program being run twice

```
what is the temperature outside today? 65
is it raining outside? answer Y[es] or N[o] Y
before you go out today take your umbrella

what is the temperature outside today? 65
is it raining outside? answer Y[es] or N[o] ?
DATA ERROR - reply not input as either Y or N
```

6.5 Conditional Expressions

From the discussion so far, it should be clear to you that conditional expressions can equate to one of two values, either zero (false) or nonzero (true). Examples of conditional expressions given so far are temperature < 60, reply == yes, reply == no and error.

Program Example 6.5: Multiple Conditional Expressions

Program Example 6.5 will input the name of a person and decide whether he or she is a suspect in a crime. We believe that the crime was committed by a person between 20 and 25 years of age, and between 66 and 70 inches tall. The program displays the name of the suspect if the person fits this description.

```
/*
chap_6\ex_5.c
program to display the name of a suspect to a crime who is aged between
20 and 25 years and between 66 inches and 70 inches tall
*/

#include <stdio.h>

void main(void)
{
    char    name[80];
    int     age;
    int     height;

    printf("input name of suspect ");
    gets(name);
    printf("age? ");
    scanf("%d", &age);
    printf("height? ");
    scanf("%d", &height);

    if (age >= 20 && age <= 25)
    {
      if (height >= 66 && height <= 70)
          printf("%s is a suspect and should be interrogated\n", name);
    }

}
```

Results

```
input name of suspect Artful Dodger
age? 23
height? 69
Artful Dodger is a suspect and should be interrogated
```

In Program Example 6.5, there is no output if a person is not a suspect.

The conditions used in this program are (age>=20), (age<=25), (height>=66), and (height<=70). It has been possible to combine these conditions into (age>=20 && age<=25) and (height>=66 && height<= 70) by using the logical operator AND (**&&**). A truth table for logical AND is given in Table 6.2. This table can be interpreted as follows.

If (age>=20) is condition X and (age<=25) is condition Y, then X && Y can only be true if both condition X is true and condition Y is true. In other words, both conditions (age>=20)   and (age<=25) must be true for the expression to be true. Therefore, if either condition X or condition Y or both happen to be false, the complete expression given by X && Y is false.

Similarly, both conditions in the Boolean expression (height>=66 && height<=70) must be true for the condition to be true. If either one condition or both conditions are false, then the conditional expression is false.

Table 6.2 Truth table for logical AND

condition X	condition Y	X && Y
FALSE	FALSE	FALSE
FALSE	TRUE	FALSE
TRUE	FALSE	FALSE
TRUE	TRUE	TRUE

If the age is between 20 and 25 years, then the computer executes the next if statement, and if the height is between 66 and 70 inches, then the name of the suspect is printed. This program can be reconstructed, by omitting the second if statement, and combining the conditions for age and height as follows:

```
if (age >= 20 && age  <= 25 && height >= 66 && height  <= 70)
    printf("%s is a suspect and should be interrogated\n", name);
```

The same program can be reconstructed yet again using different conditions and the logical operator OR (||). By considering the age and height to lie outside the ranges, it is possible to construct the following conditional expressions:

```
(age < 20 || age > 25)
(height < 66 || height > 70)
```

From the truth table for logical OR, given in Table 6.3, if (age<20) is condition X and (age>25) is condition Y, then X||Y is true if X is true or Y is true or both are true. Clearly both conditions cannot be true in this example.

Similarly, if (height<66) is condition X and (height>70) is condition Y, then X||Y is true if X is true or Y is true or both are true. Once again both conditions cannot be true in this example. The conditions for age and height can also be combined into

```
(age < 20 || age > 25 || height < 66 || height  > 70)
```

Thus if any one of the conditions is true, the entire conditional expression is true and the suspect is released. However, if all the conditions are false, then the entire conditional expression must be false, the suspect is between 20 and 25 years of age and between 66 and 70 inches tall, and is held for interrogation, as depicted in Program Example 6.6.

Table 6.3 Truth table for logical OR

condition X	condition Y	X || Y
FALSE	FALSE	FALSE
FALSE	TRUE	TRUE
TRUE	FALSE	TRUE
TRUE	TRUE	TRUE

Program Example 6.6: Logical OR

```
/*
chap_6\ex_6.c
program to display the name of a suspect to a crime who is aged between
20 and 25 years and between 66 inches and 70 inches tall
*/

#include <stdio.h>

void main(void)
{
        char    name[20];
        int     age;
        int     height;

        printf("input name of suspect ");
        gets(name);
        printf("age? ");
        scanf("%d", &age);
        printf("height? ");
        scanf("%d", &height);

        printf("%s", name);

        if (age < 20 || age > 25 || height < 66 || height > 70)
            printf(" is not a suspect and should be released\n");
        else
            printf(" is a suspect and should be interrogated\n");
}
```

Results from program being run twice

```
input name of suspect Bill Sykes
age? 44
height? 68
Bill Sykes is not a suspect and should be released

input name of suspect Artful Dodger
age? 23
height? 69
Artful Dodger is a suspect and should be interrogated
```

6.6 Else .. If

The complexity of nested if statements can be reduced by combining conditions using logical AND. For example, the following part of the nested selection in Program Example 6.4

```
if (reply == yes)
{
    if (temperature < 60)
        strcpy(garment, "raincoat");
    else
        strcpy(garment, "umbrella");
}
    .
    .
```

can be recoded as

```
if (reply == yes && temperature < 60)
    strcpy(garment, "raincoat");
else if (reply == yes && temperature >= 60)
    strcpy(garment, "umbrella");
    .
    .
```

An `else` clause followed by an `if` statement is very common in programming. In fact, in many high-level languages, except for C, there is an *else if* statement. In C we can write the `if` statement on the same line as the `else` clause as if it is one keyword, *elseif*. It is not, but indentation produces a very clear multibranch structure that is actually made of multiple two-branch `if else` statements.

In Program Example 6.4, if a user had typed either the values y or n, without depressing the shift key, in response to the question `is it raining outside? answer Y[es] or N[o]`, he or she would have been informed that the response was in error. Although the letter was correct, the user replied in lower-case, not upper-case as requested. Therefore, the program requires a means of converting the character to upper-case, if it is a lower-case letter of the alphabet. Look back at Table 2.1 ASCII codes for characters. What is the difference in the ASCII values between any lower-case letter and any upper-case letter? The answer is 32. For example, the letter *a* has code 97 and the letter *A* has code 65, difference 32; similarly the letter *b* has code 98 and the letter *B* has code 66, difference 32, etc.

A letter of the alphabet can be converted from lower case to upper case by using the following statement.

```
if ('a'<=reply && reply <='z') reply = reply - 32;
```

If the value of reply is input as a lower-case letter of the alphabet, then the condition is true and the value 32 is deducted from the ASCII code of the character. This action changes the ASCII code for the character to the ASCII code for the corresponding upper-case letter of the alphabet. If the condition is false, then the value of the reply remains unchanged.

Program Example 6.4 has been recoded to include the following features:

    ☐   A statement for the conversion of a lower-case character to an upper-case character.

    ☐   The use of the logical operator && to combine several conditions, reduce the complexity of the nested if statements and recode them as else if statements.

Program Example 6.7: The Else .. If Construct.

```
/*
chap_6\ex_7.c
program to demonstrate character conversion and the else .. if construct
*/

#include <stdio.h>
#include <string.h>

void main(void)
{
        typedef enum{false, true} boolean;

        const   char    yes = 'Y';
        const   char    no  = 'N';
        const   int     code_difference = 32;

        char    reply;
        char    garment[9];
        int     temperature;
        boolean error = false;

        printf("what is the temperature outside today? ");
        scanf("%d", &temperature);
        getchar();
        printf("is it raining outside? answer Y[es] or N[o] ");
        scanf("%c", &reply);
```

141

```
if ('a'<=reply && reply <='z') reply = reply - code_difference;

if (reply == yes && temperature < 60)
     strcpy(garment, "raincoat");
else if (reply == yes && temperature >= 60)
     strcpy(garment, "umbrella");
else if (reply == no && temperature < 60)
     strcpy(garment, "overcoat");
else if (reply == no && temperature >= 60)
     strcpy(garment, "jacket");
else
     error = true;

if (error)
     printf("DATA ERROR - reply not input as either Y or N\n");
else
     printf("before you go out today take your %s\n", garment);
}
```

The results from running this program are very similar to those shown earlier. The only exception is that a lower-case *y* or *n* can now be input in response to the question *is it raining outside? - answer Y[es] or N[o]* without resulting in an error.

6.7 Switch

An ordinal type has a value that belongs to an ordered set of items. For example, integers are ordinal types, since they belong to the set of values from -32768 to +32767. A character is an ordinal type, since it belongs to the ASCII character set of values from the *null* character (ASCII code 0) to the *del* character (ASCII code 127). Real numbers and strings are not ordinal types.

If selection is to be based upon an ordinal type then a switch statement can be used in preference to multiple if .. else statements.

The syntax of the **switch** statement is

C Syntax:

switch

switch (expression)
{
    case c1: statement(s)
    case c2: statement(s)

    .
    .

    default: statement(s)
}

The expression must evaluate to an ordinal value. Each possible ordinal value is represented as a case label, which indicates the statement to be executed corresponding to the value of the expression. Those values that are not represented by case labels will result in the statement after the optional default being executed.

For example,

```
scanf("%d", &number);
switch (number)
{
   case 1:   printf("one\n"); break;
   case 2:   printf("two\n"); break;
   case 3:   printf("three\n"); break;
   default:  printf("number not in range 1..3\n");
}
```

In the example a number is input from the keyboard. If this number is 1, then the string one will be output; if it is 2 then the string two will be output; if it is 3 then the string three will be output. If the number is not 1, 2, or 3, then the string number not in range 1..3 will be output.

It is necessary to include a method of exiting from the switch statement at the end of every case. Failure to exit from the switch will result in the execution of all the case statements following the chosen case. One method of exiting from a switch statement is through the use of a break statement at the end of every case list. The keyword **break** causes the switch to terminate, and execution resumes with the next statement (if any) following the switch statement. Other methods to exit from a switch statement are explained later in the book.

If the optional default statement was not present and the value of number had not been in the range 1 to 3 then the computer would branch to the end of the switch statement.

Program Example 6.8: Switch Statement

In Program Example 6.8, a user is invited to input a value for an exit on Highway 6 at Cape Cod. Depending upon the value of the exit from 1 to 12, the names, numbers, or both of the adjoining roads at that exit are displayed. If the value input is not in the range 1 to12, the statement after the default will warn the user of the data error.

The multiple selection in this problem can be highlighted by the use of the flowchart illustrated in Figure 6.4. The flowchart indicates the behavior of the switch statement.

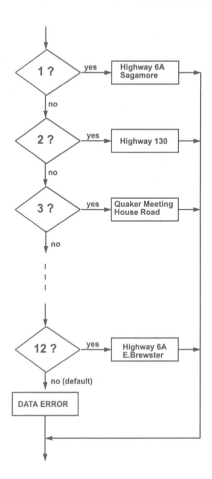

Figure 6.4 Multiple selection

```
/*
chap_6\ex_8.c
program to demonstrate the use of switch and break statements
*/

#include <stdio.h>

void main(void)
{
        int     exit_number;

        printf("input exit number on Highway 6 -> ");
        scanf("%d", &exit_number);
```

```
switch(exit_number)
{
    case 1:  printf("Highway 6A/ Sagamore Bridge\n"); break;
    case 2:  printf("Highway 130\n"); break;
    case 3:  printf("Quaker Meeting House Road\n"); break;
    case 4:  printf("Chase Road/ Scorten Road\n"); break;
    case 5:  printf("Highway 149/ Martons Mills\n"); break;
    case 6:  printf("Highway 132/ Hyannis\n"); break;
    case 7:  printf("Willow Street/ Higgins Crowell Road\n"); break;
    case 8:  printf("Union Street/ Station Avenue\n"); break;
    case 9:  printf("Highway 134/ S.Dennis\n"); break;
    case 10: printf("Highway 124/ Harwich Port\n"); break;
    case 11: printf("Highway 137/ S.Chatham\n"); break;
    case 12: printf("Highway 6A/ E.Brewster\n"); break;
    default: printf("DATA ERROR - incorrect exit number\n");
}
}
```

Results from the program being run three times

```
input exit number on Highway 6 -> 8
Union Street/ Station Avenue

input exit number on Highway 6 -> 2
Highway 130

input exit number on Highway 6 -> 13
DATA ERROR - incorrect exit number
```

By comparing the switch statement in the program with the syntax notation, the reader should note the following points.

An expression is any expression that will evaluate to an item of ordinal type. In this example the expression consists of a single variable exit_number of type integer, which is expected to evaluate to an integer in the range 1 .. 12.

A **case label** is any value that corresponds to the ordinal type in the expression. Case labels in this example represent the junction numbers 1, 2, 3, 4, 5, 6, 7, 8, 9, 10, 11, and 12. Case labels must be unique.

The optional default traps any values of the expression that are not represented as case labels. Without this option, no action would occur when a value was out of range.

In Program Example 6.8, only one case value was associated with a set of statements. What if more than one case value may be used for the same set of statements?

For example, if the requirement was to compute the number of days in a particular month in the year, a `switch` statement could be used. The variable `month` is an integer in the range 1 .. 12, indicating the months January .. December. Different case labels, separated by a colon, are used for each month of the year, for the months containing 31 days, 30 days and 28 days (assuming a non leap year).

```
switch(month)
{
    case 1: case 3: case 5: case 7: case 8: case 10: case 12:
                                    days_in_month = 31; break;
    case 4: case 6: case 9: case 11:
                                    days_in_month = 30; break;
    case 2:                         days_in_month = 28; break;
}
```

Case Study: Price of Food at Ben's Breakfast Bar

Write a program to find the price of food at Ben's Breakfast Bar (see Figure 2.3, in Chapter 2). You are required to display the items of food available, input the name of a single item of food and display the price of the food. In this solution you are expected to develop a function to return the price of the food.

Problem Analysis - The name of an item of food or drink from the menu is passed as an argument from the main function to the function price. This function returns a floating-point value that represents the price of the item of food or drink. For example, if the item of food was pancakes, then the function would return the value 4.00.

In this example, it is necessary to compare two strings for equality, for example, an item of food as a parameter with say, the string "pancakes". The function `strcmp` (string compare) from header file `<string.h>` (see Appendix A) will return zero if the two strings are identical. For example, `if (strcmp(item, "pancakes") == 0) return 4.00`.

Further work on the `strcmp` function will be covered in Chapter 7.

Algorithm for the Function main

1. display the menu of food and drink
2. input the name of an item of food or drink
3. call the function price and assign the value returned to the cost of the item
4. if the cost of the item is nonzero
5.   display the cost of the item
6. else
7.   display the food is not on the menu

Data Dictionary for the Function main - The argument to be passed to the function price is the name of the item of food or drink and is of type character string. The value returned by the function is the price of an item of food or drink and is assigned to a floating-point variable cost.

```
char    food[80];
float   cost;
```

Algorithm for the Function price

if   *item is eggs return 2.75*
else if   *item is pancakes return 4.00*
else if   *item is bagel return 1.50*
else if   *item is muffin or chocolate return 0.95*
else if   *item is yogurt or fries return 1.00*
else if   *item is hash return 1.75*
else if   *item toast or tea or coffee return 0.75*
else   *return 0.0*

Data Dictionary for the Function price - The formal parameter list for this function contains one item - the name of the item of food or drink - of data type character string. The function returns a floating-point value that represents the price of the item of food or drink. If the value returned is zero, this value implies that the item was not listed in the menu and its price could not be found. The function prototype is

```
float price(char item[]);
```

Test Data pancakes, eggs, chocolate, water

Desk Check of Function price Being Called Four Times

item	*price(item)*
pancakes	4.00
eggs	2.75
chocolate	0.95
water	0.00

```
+----------------------------------------------------------+
|                    Screen Layout                          |
+----------------------------------------------------------+
| 12345678901234567890123456789012345678901234567890        |
|                                                           |
| input an item of food from the following menu             |
|                                                           |
| eggs        pancakes bagel      muffin                    |
| yogurt      hash     toast      fries                     |
| tea         coffee   chocolate                            |
|                                                           |
| ? pancakes                                                |
| $4.00                                                     |
+----------------------------------------------------------+
```

147

```
/*
chap_6\ex_9.c
*/

#include <stdio.h>
#include <string.h>

float price(char item[])
/* function to return the price of an item of food at Ben's Breakfast Bar;
if an item cannot be matched the price is returned as zero */

{
    if      (strcmp(item, "eggs") == 0)
            return 2.75;
    else if (strcmp(item, "pancakes") == 0)
            return 4.00;
    else if (strcmp(item, "bagel") == 0)
            return 1.50;
    else if (strcmp(item, "muffin") == 0 || strcmp(item, "chocolate") == 0)
            return 0.95;
    else if (strcmp(item, "yogurt") == 0 || strcmp(item, "fries") == 0)
            return 1.00;
    else if (strcmp(item, "hash") == 0)
            return 1.75;
    else if (strcmp(item, "toast") == 0 || strcmp(item, "tea") == 0 ||
             strcmp(item, "coffee") == 0)
            return 0.75;
    else
            return 0.0;
}

void main(void)
{
    char    food[80];
    float   cost;

    printf("input an item of food from the following menu\n");
    printf("\neggs     pancakes    bagel    muffin");
    printf("\nyogurt   hash        toast    fries");
    printf("\ntea      coffee      chocolate\n\n");

    printf("? ");
    gets(food);
    cost = price(food);
    if (cost > 0.0)
       printf("$%-4.2f\n", cost);
    else
       printf("food not listed in menu\n");
}
```

Results

```
input an item of food from the following menu

eggs      pancakes   bagel      muffin
yogurt    hash       toast      fries
tea       coffee     chocolate

? pancakes
$4.00
```

Case Study: Validation of Dates Including Leap Years

The final program in this section validates a date. The format of the date is three integers representing month, day and year. The program checks that the number of months in a year should not exceed 12, and that the number of days in each month has not been exceeded. The program also reports on leap years.

Problem Analysis - The validation of the date has a three-part solution.

The first part is to validate a month as an integer in the range 1 to 12. If the month is treated as the ordinal value of a switch expression, with case labels occurring for each of the twelve months, then should a month not be in the range 1to12, the error can be trapped as the default.

The second part involves the calculation of a leap year, and clearly will only be considered if the month happens to be February. The calculation of a leap year uses the following rule:

> *if the year is evenly divisible by 4 and the year is not a century*
> *or the year is a century that is evenly divisible by 400*
> *then the year is a leap year*

This rule can be expressed as the following conditional expression:

```
if  (((year % 4 == 0) && (year % 100 != 0)) || (year % 400 == 0))
    printf("%d is a Leap Year\n", year);
```

The expression may be evaluated using the years 1992, 1993, 1900, and 2000 as test data.

$((1992 \% 4 == 0)$ && $(1992 \% 100 != 0)) || (1992 \% 400 == 0)$ is true

$((1993 \% 4 == 0)$ && $(1993 \% 100 != 0)) || (1993 \% 400 == 0)$ is false

$((1900 \% 4 == 0)$ && $(1900 \% 100 != 0)) || (1900 \% 400 == 0)$ is false

149

$((2000 \% 4 == 0) \&\& (2000 \% 100 != 0)) \,||\, (2000 \% 400 == 0)$ is true.

The third part of the solution involves the calculation of the number of days in a month. Since a switch statement is being used to select the appropriate month, the number of days in the month can be assigned according to the appropriate case label. For example, if the case label is either 1,3,5,7,8,10, or 12, then there are 31 days in the month; if the case label is 4, 6, 9, or 11, then there are 30 days in the month; however, if the case label is 2 and the year is a leap year then there are 29 days; otherwise, there are 28 days in the month.

Algorithm for the Function main

1. input date in format month, day, and year
2. validate the date
3. output the result

The validation of the date can be developed as a function.

After step 2, if there is an error in the date, then the error must be reported in step 3. Step 3 can be refined as follows:

3.1   if month is February and number of days = 29 then
3.2   report leap year
3.3   if day > number of days in month or error then
3.4   report error
3.5   else
3.6   report date is valid

Data Dictionary for the Function main - The numeric values for the month, day, year, and number of days in a month are represented as integers. A Boolean variable is declared to detect an error in the value for the month not being in the range 1 to 12.

```
int      month, day, year;
int      number_of_days;
boolean  error;
```

Algorithm for the Function days_in_month

The validation of both month and the number of days in a month, together with determining a leap year, can be incorporated into a switch statement. The syntax of the switch statement is not fully represented in the pseudocode; however, the functionality of the switch statement remains the same. Therefore, step 2 can be expanded into the following algorithm:

2.1	*switch month*		
2.2	*1,3,5,7,8,10,12*	:	*number of days in month is 31;*
2.3	*4,6,9,11*	:	*number of days in month is 30;*
2.4	*2*	:	*if leap year then*
2.5			*number of days in month is 29*
2.6			*else*
2.7			*number of days in month is 28*
2.9	*default*	:	*error in month number;*

Data Dictionary for the Function days_in_month - The formal-parameter list for this function contains two value parameters, month and year, of type integer and one reference parameter, error, of type Boolean. The function returns the number of days in a particular month. If the value for the month is illegal, then the parameter error is set at true. There are no local declarations. The function prototype is

```
int days_in_month(int month, int year, boolean *error);
```

Since the functions `days_in_month` and `main` both declare variables of type `boolean`, it will be necessary to declare the enumerated type at the beginning of the file and give it file scope so that it becomes visible to both functions.

Desk Check - Dates should be chosen that fully test the algorithm, for example, a valid date (3 18 1987), leap years (2 12 1992), (2 29 2000) and either a month or a day that is out of range (2 30 1987).

variable	*value(s)*			
month	3	2	2	2
day	18	12	29	30
year	1987	1992	2000	1987
number_of_days	31	29	29	28
error	false	false	false	true

If the names of the months are declared as the following enumerated constants:

enum {Jan=1, Feb=2, Mar=3, Apr=4, May=5, Jun=6, Jul=7, Aug=8, Sep=9, Oct=10, Nov=11, Dec=12}

the case labels 1 to 12 in the switch statement can be replaced by the names of the months so that the program becomes more readable.

```
                          Screen Layout
┌────────────────────────────────────────────────────────┐
│ 12345678901234567890123456789012345678901234567890      │
│                                                         │
│ input a date in the format MM DD YYYY                   │
│ 2 12 1992                                               │
│ 1992 is a Leap Year                                     │
│ date checked and is valid                               │
└────────────────────────────────────────────────────────┘
```

```c
/*
chap_6\ex_10.c
program to validate a date in the format MM DD YYYY
*/

#include <stdio.h>

typedef enum {false, true} boolean;

int days_in_month(int month, int year, boolean *error)
/* function to calculate and return the number of days in a month;
if the value for the month is illegal then set error to true  */
{
    enum   {Jan=1,Feb=2,Mar=3,Apr=4,May=5,Jun=6,
            Jul=7,Aug=8,Sep=9,Oct=10,Nov=11,Dec=12};

    switch (month)
    {
      case Jan: case Mar: case May: case Jul: case Aug: case Oct: case Dec:
                    return 31;
      case Apr: case Jun: case Sep: case Nov:
                    return 30;
      case Feb:{
                if (((year % 4 == 0) && (year % 100 != 0)) || (year % 400 == 0))
                    return 29;
                else
                    return 28;
               }
      default: *error = true;
    }
}

void main(void)
{
        int     month, day, year;
        int     number_of_days;
        boolean error = false;

        printf("input a date in the format MM DD YYYY\n");
        scanf("%d%d%d", &month, &day, &year);
        number_of_days = days_in_month(month, year, &error);

        if (month == 2 && number_of_days == 29)printf("%d is a Leap Year\n", year);

        if (day > number_of_days || error)
           printf("DATA ERROR - check day or month\n");
        else
           printf("date checked and is valid\n");
}
```

Results from the program being run four times

```
input a date in the format MM DD YYYY
3 18 1987
date checked and is valid

input a date in the format MM DD YYYY
2 12 1992
1992 is a Leap Year
date checked and is valid

input a date in the format MM DD YYYY
2 29 2000
2000 is a Leap Year
date checked and is valid

input a date in the format MM DD YYYY
2 30 1987
DATA ERROR - check day or month
```

Summary

☐ A conditional expression evaluates to either zero (false) or nonzero (true).

☐ Depending upon the result of the conditional expression, it is possible for the computer to select different statements in an if statement.

☐ The values false and true can be defined as enumerated constants that are equivalent to the values 0 and 1, respectively.

☐ By explicitly defining an enumerated type that contains the enumerated constants as false and true, it is possible to mimic the Boolean type found in other high-level languages.

☐ A programmer may change the default values of the enumerated constants by assigning new integer values at the time of the enumeration declaration.

☐ The programmer can use typedef to define an explicit data type.

☐ Conditional expressions can be combined into one expression by using the logical operators AND && and OR ||.

☐ If statements may be nested within each other.

☐ An else clause belongs to the nearest if statement that has not already been paired with an else.

☐ When selection is based upon an ordinal type, a switch statement may be used.

□ All `case` labels must be unique and of an ordinal type compatible with the selector type.

□ In this chapter eight new operators were introduced. The priority in which these operators are evaluated, compared with those introduced in Chapter 3, is illustrated in Table 6.4

Table 6.4 Priority of operators

priority level	type	operator	symbol	example

2	unary	negate
		plus
		size
			–
			+
			`sizeof`
				`-A`
				`+B`
				`sizeof(int)`

3	cast	a data type	`(type)`	`(float)`

4	multiplicative	multiply
		divide
		remainder
			*
			/
			%
				`A * B`
				`A / B`
				`A % B`

5	additive	add subtract	+ –	`A + B` `A - B`

7	relational	greater
		less
		greater or equal
		less or equal
			>
			<
			>=
			<=
				`A > B`
				`A < B`
				`A >= B`
				`A <= B`

8	equality	equal not equal	== !=	`A == B` `A != B`
12	logical	AND	`&&`	`(A<B) && (X>Y)`
13	logical	OR	`||`	`(A<B) || (X>Y)`
15	assignment	equals	=	`A = B`

Review Questions

1. What is the syntax of an `if` statement?

2. What value is associated with false in a conditional statement?

3. Distinguish between the operators = and ==.

4. What is the syntax of an `if..else` statement?

5. How many statements are allowed after the `if`?

6. How many statements are allowed after the `else`?

7. What is a conditional expression?

8. What symbols are used for the logical operators AND and OR?

9. What is the order of precedence, from highest to lowest, of the operators <, &&, =, ||, != and *?

10. Why do we indent statements in an `if..else` statement?

11. What are nested `if` statements?

12. What is an enumerated data type?

13. How can false and true be represented as constants in an enumerated type?

14. Explain the purpose of the `switch` statement.

15. Why should a `break` statement be used within a `switch` statement?

16. What are `case` labels?

17. When is the `default` label used in a `switch` statement?

18. If a statement corresponds to many `case` labels in a `switch` statement, how are the `case` labels organized?

Programming Exercises

19. If A=1, B=-2, C=3, D=4, E='S', and F='J', state whether the following conditions are true or false.

(a) A==B
(b) A>B
(c) (A<C && B<D)
(d) (A<C && B>D)
(e) (A>B || C<D)
(f) E>F
(g) ((A+C)>(B-D)) && ((B+C)<(D-A))

20. Code the following conditions in C.

(a) X is equal to Y
(b) X is not equal to Y
(c) A is less than or equal to B
(d) Q is not greater than T
(e) X is greater than or equal to Y
(f) X is less than or equal to Y and A is not equal to B
(g) A is greater than 18 and H is greater than 68 and W is greater than 75
(h) G is less than 100 and greater than 50
(i) H is less than 50 or greater than 100.

21. Trace through the following segment of code for each value of A,B, and C and state the output in each case.

(a) A=16, B=16, C=32
(b) A=16, B=-18, C=32
(c) A=-2, B=-4, C=16

```
if (A>0)
{
   if (B<0)
      printf("x");
   else
      if C>20
         printf("y");
}
else
   printf("z");
```

22. Trace through the following segment of code for each new value of the variable character and state the output.

(a) character = 'B';
(b) character = '4';
(c) character = 'a';

```
switch (character)
{
   case 'a': case 'b': case 'c' : printf("small letters\n"); break;
   case 'A': case 'B': case 'C' : printf("capital letters\n"); break;
   case '1': case '2': case '3' : printf("digits\n"); break;
   default                      : printf("error in data\n");
}
```

23. Correct the syntax errors in this program segment.

```
if y > 25
   x == 16;
   printf("x = %d\n", x);
else
   y = 20
```

Programming Problems

24. Modify Program Example 6.6 to cater for both sexes, and to eliminate all women from the list of suspects.

25. A worker is paid at the hourly rate of $8 per hour for the first 35 hours worked. Overtime is paid at 1.5 times the hourly rate for the next 25 hours worked and 2 times the hourly rate for additional hours worked. Write a program to input the number of hours worked per week and then calculate and output the overtime paid.

26. A student traveling to Florida for spring break will consider a particular airline if the round trip ticket costs less than $200 and has a layover of no longer than 4 hours; or if the ticket costs between $200 and $300 and has no layover. Write a program to input the name of an airline, cost of ticket, and layover time; output the name of the airline only if it meets the student's criteria.

27. A student choosing among payment plans for a college loan wants to keep the monthly payments to less than $200. If the initial amount of the loan is $5000 then write a program to calculate which plans are acceptable given different loan lengths and simple interest rates?

28. A researcher needs to screen individuals for certain characteristics before admitting them to a medical research study. The criteria for admittance are

gender: females only
age: 18 to 40 years
weight: no greater than 180 pounds
blood group: O only

Write a program to input the name of a person, together with his or her gender, age, weight, and blood group; display only the names of those individuals who meet the specified criteria.

29. A salesperson earns commission on the value of sales. Figure 6.5 shows the scale of the commission. Write a program to input a figure for the value of sales, and then calculate and output the commission.

value of sales	% commission
$1 - $999	1
$1000 - $9999	5
$10000 - $99999	10

Figure 6.5 Scale of commission

157

30. A barometer dial is calibrated into the following climatic conditions: STORM, RAIN, CHANGE, FAIR, and DRY. Write a program that will input one of these readings (abbreviated to the number assigned to the condition), and output clothing suggestions from the following rules:

1 STORM   wear overcoat and hat
2 RAIN   wear raincoat and take umbrella
3 CHANGE   behave as for FAIR if it rained yesterday and as for RAIN if it did not
4 FAIR   wear jacket and take umbrella
5 DRY   wear jacket

Hint: Create an enumeration `enum{STORM=1,RAIN,CHANGE,FAIR,DRY}` and use the numerical code as a selector in a switch statement with the corresponding enumerated constants as case labels in the same statement.

31. Write a program to mimic a calculator. Input two real numbers and state whether the numbers are to be added (+), subtracted (-), multiplied (*), or divided (/). Cater for the possibility of a denominator being zero in the division of two numbers.

32. A bicycle shop in Hyannis rents bicycles by the day at different rates throughout the year, according to the season (see Figure 6.6). The proprietor also gives a 25% discount if the rental period is greater than 7 days. Renters must also pay a $50 returnable deposit for each bicycle rented. Write a program to input the season and the number of days of rental and then calculate and display a total charge that includes the deposit.

Hint: Use a technique similar to that described in the previous question for the selection of the season.

season	charge
Spring	$5.00
Summer	$7.50
Autumn	$3.75
Winter	$2.50

Figure 6.6 Rental rates

Chapter 7
Repetition

In the previous chapter it was necessary to run some programs several times to demonstrate the effect that different items of input data would have on the results. At the time you might have thought that this approach was a little cumbersome. How much better it would be if we had a structure in the program that would allow statements to be repeated.

The purpose of this chapter is to introduce you to three methods for repeating statements that are based on the control structures known as while, do..while, and for. By the end of the chapter, you should have an understanding of the following topics.

☐   The concept of a loop.

☐   The syntax and appropriate use of *while*, *do..while*, and *for* loop statements.

☐   The use of postfix increment and decrement operators.

7.1 Loops

In writing computer programs it is often necessary to repeat part of a program a number of times. One way to achieve repetition is to write out that part of the program as many times as it is needed. This method is very impractical, since it produces a very lengthy computer program and the number of repetitions is not always known in advance.

A better way to repeat part of a program a number of times is to introduce a **loop** into the code. The flowchart segment in Figure 7.1 illustrates one mechanism for setting up a loop.

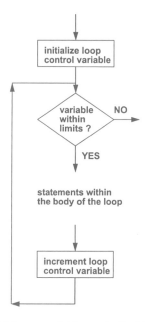

Figure 7.1 Loop variable controlled by counter

In this example a counter is used as a **loop control variable** to record the number of times part of the program is repeated. The following operations then take place on the loop control variable.

1. *The loop control variable must be initialized before the computer enters the loop.*
2. *The value of the loop control variable is tested to see whether it is within specified limits for looping to continue. If the loop variable is not within these limits, then the computer must exit from the loop.*
3. *The statements within the body of the loop are executed*
4. *The value of the loop control variable is incremented by one to indicate that the statements have been performed.*
5. *Go back to step 2, thereby completing the loop*

Notice from the flowchart that if the loop control variable is initialized to a value that is outside of the limits, then the loop will never be entered and the statements within the body of the loop will never be executed.

The loop control variable does not have to be assigned values from within the program. The initialization and incrementation of this variable can be replaced by reading data from an input device such as a keyboard. Figure 7.2 illustrates a flowchart for reading values of the loop control variable. Notice that a certain value will trigger the exit from the loop. This value is known as a **sentinel** value.

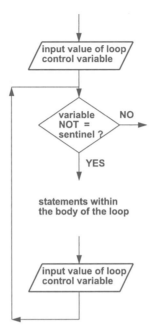

Figure 7.2 Loop variable controlled by data

7.2 While

A **while** loop will allow a statement to be repeated zero or more times and behaves in the same manner as depicted by the flowcharts in figures 7.1 and 7.2. The syntax of the while loop is

C Syntax:

while loop   *while (conditional expression) statement(s)*

Notice that many statements may follow the conditional expression. If more than one statement is to be repeated then it is necessary to enclose the statements within braces { } so the computer treats them as a compound statement. To conform with the syntax of the language a compound statement can be thought of as a single statement composed from many statements.

Loop Controlled by a Counter

The following segment of code uses a `while` loop and a loop variable controlled by a counter, as illustrated in Figure 7.1.

```
counter = 1;                  /* initialize loop control variable */
while (counter <= 5)          /* test if variable is within limits */
{
  printf("%d\t", counter);
  counter = counter + 1;      / * increment loop control variable */
}
```

The value of `counter` is initialized to 1; the condition (`counter <= 5`) is true; therefore, the value of the `counter` is output. The `counter` is incremented by 1 to the value 2; the condition (`counter <= 5`) is true, so the value of `counter` is output again. The process continues while the condition (`counter <= 5`) remains true. When `counter` is incremented to the value 6, the condition (`counter <= 5`) becomes false and the computer exits from the `while` loop.

Loop Controlled by Data

Consider the use of a `while` loop to display numbers on a screen while the numbers are not zero. The numbers are input from a keyboard, and the value 0 is the sentinel value. The following segment of code uses a `while` loop and a loop variable controlled by data, as illustrated in Figure 7.2.

```
scanf("%d", &number);        /* input value of loop control variable */
while (number != 0)          /* test if variable is sentinel value */
{
  printf("%3d",number);
  scanf("%d", &number);      /* input value of loop control variable */
}
```

If the first number to be read is zero, then the conditional expression `number != 0` will be false. The computer will not enter the loop but branch to the next executable statement after the end of the compound statement delimited by the braces { }. Since the loop was not entered, the loop is repeated zero times.

However, if the first number to be read was nonzero, the conditional expression would be true and the computer would execute the statements contained within the loop. To this end the number would be written on the screen, and the next number input at the keyboard. The computer then returns to the line containing the conditional expression, which is re-evaluated to test whether the new number is not zero. If the condition is true, the computer continues to execute the statements in the loop. If the condition is false, the computer will branch to the next executable statement after the end of the compound statement.

To restate the behavior of the while loop: if the first number read is zero, then the loop is not entered, and the statements within the loop have been repeated zero times. If the second number to be read is zero, the statements in the loop will have been repeated once. If the third number to be read is zero, the statements in the loop will have been repeated twice, etc. Therefore, if the hundredth number to be read is zero, the statements inside the loop will have been repeated ninety-nine times.

162

Note that for clarity, the body of the while loop is indented. As other kinds of loops are introduced in this chapter, we will follow the same pattern of indentation, since it makes for more readable programs. In addition, we will utilize indentation in writing the algorithms for such code. Getting into the habit of identifying the structure of a loop at the algorithm stage of program design will facilitate the eventual coding of the loop.

The outline program given in the second example has been developed into the following C program.

Program Example 7.1: While Loop with Numeric Sentinel

```
/*
chap_7\ex_1.c
program to demonstrate a while loop
*/

#include <stdio.h>

void main(void)
{
        int     number;

        printf("input an integer - terminate with 0 -> ");
        scanf("%d", &number);

        while (number != 0)
        {
                printf("%3d\n", number);
                printf("input an integer - terminate with 0 -> ");
                scanf("%d", &number);
        }
}
```

The specimen results from the program show (a) the statements within the loop being repeated twice and (b) the statements within the loop not being repeated at all.

(a) Results

```
input an integer - terminate with 0 -> 36
 36
input an integer - terminate with 0 -> 18
 18
input an integer - terminate with 0 -> 0
```

(b) Results

```
input an integer - terminate with 0 -> 0
```

Program Example 6.5 allowed us to input the age and height of an individual to determine whether he or she fits a certain criminal description. We will revise that program to include a while loop to allow the program to be repeated many times without rerunning the program.

Before the `while` loop is entered the user is requested to input the name of a suspect. If the word END is input, then this is the sentinel value to create an exit from the while loop. You might expect to construct the conditional expression `name != "END"` to control the `while` loop, for example, `while (name != "END")`. However, in C you cannot compare strings in this manner.

In Chapter 6 a brief mention was given about the function `strcmp`. You may recall that the header file `<string.h>` contains a function `strcmp` that allows two strings to be compared and returns the value zero if both strings are the same; otherwise it returns, a nonzero value. The format of this function is:

C Syntax: *strcmp(string_1, string_2)*

comparing strings   where *string_1* and *string_2* are string variables or constants. A specific example of the function is

```
strcmp(name, "END");
```

which compares the string variable `name` to the string literal `"END"`.

For our revised program example, the `strcmp` routine becomes part of a conditional expression `(strcmp(name, "END") == 0)`. If the contents of the string variable `name` is equal to the string `"END"`, then the result is true. If this expression is to be used in a `while` loop, it will be necessary to negate the condition, for example, `while (strcmp(name, "END") != 0)`. The `while` loop will then be exited only when the conditional expression `strcmp(name, "END")` is zero - in other words, when the string literal `"END"` has been input. As long as the string `"END"` is not input in response to the prompt to input the name of a suspect, the computer will continue to process the details of all suspects to the crime.

Program Example 7.2: While Loop with String Sentinel

```
/*
chap_7\ex_2.c
program to display the name of a suspect to a crime who is aged between
20 and 25 years and between 66 inches and 70 inches tall
*/

#include <stdio.h>
#include <string.h>
```

```
void main(void)
{
    char    name[20];
    int     age;
    int     height;

    printf("input name of suspect - terminate with END ");
    gets(name);

    while (strcmp(name, "END") != 0)
    {
        printf("age? ");
        scanf("%d", &age);
        printf("height? ");
        scanf("%d", &height);
        getchar();    /* flush input buffer */

        if (age >= 20 && age <= 25)

            if (height >= 66 && height <= 70)
                printf("%s is a suspect and should be interrogated\n", name);

        printf("input name of suspect - terminate with END ");
        gets(name);
    }
}
```

Results

```
input name of suspect - terminate with END Smith
age? 20
height? 68
Smith is a suspect and should be interrogated
input name of suspect - terminate with END Jones
age? 26
height? 68
input name of suspect - terminate with END Evans
age? 25
height? 69
Evans is a suspect and should be interrogated
input name of suspect - terminate with END END
```

7.3 Do .. while

The flowchart in Figure 7.3 illustrates another method for repeating statements within a program. Notice the absence of a decision diamond from the beginning of the loop, which implies that it is possible to execute the statements within the loop at least once. The decision diamond appears at the end of the loop. Thus the computer will exit from the loop only when the condition associated with this symbol is false.

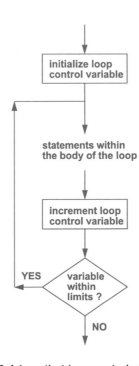

Figure 7.3 A loop that is executed at least once

Unlike a `while` loop a `do..while` loop always permits the statements within the loop to be executed at least once by the computer. The syntax of the `do..while` loop is:

C Syntax:

do .. while

do statement(s) while (conditional expression)

For example,

```
counter = 1;                  /* initialize loop control variable */
do
{
   printf("%d\t", counter);
   counter = counter + 1;     /* increment loop control variable */
} while (counter <= 5);       /* test if variable is within limits */
```

166

The value of counter is initialized to 1; the do .. while loop is entered and the value of counter is output. The counter is incremented by 1 to the value 2; the condition (counter<=5) is true, so the value of counter is output again. The process continues while the condition (counter <= 5) remains true. When the counter is incremented to the value 6, the condition (counter<=5) becomes false and the computer exits from the do .. while loop.

Notice that the computer enters the loop without any test for entry being made. Hence the contents of a do..while loop will always be executed at least once. There can be either a single statement or a compound statement between the reserved words do and while.

Like the while loop the do..while loop may also use a loop variable controlled by data as illustrated in Figure 7.4.

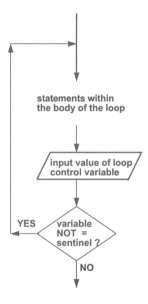

Figure 7.4 Loop controlled by data

Program Example 6.8 identified the road associated with each exit off a stretch of highway. We will revise that program to use a do .. while loop so that the program can be repeated many times without the need to rerun it. Program Example 7.3 uses data to control the loop as illustrated in Figure 7.4, by giving the user the option to continue executing the statements in the loop until the reply to the question is N (implying no). If the reply to continue is N then the conditional expression, reply == yes, will be false and the computer will branch to the next executable statement after the conditional expression. However, if the reply is Y (implying yes), then the conditional expression will be true and the computer will repeat all the statements within the loop.

In this example the conditional expression that controls the exit from the do..while loop compares the contents of a character variable with a character constant. The character constant yes had been declared as a constant in the program.

Recall that in Chapter 6 the following statement was used to convert a lower-case letter of the alphabet to an upper-case letter of the alphabet.

```
if ('a'<=reply && reply <='z') reply = reply - code_difference;
```

This statement can be replaced by the function `toupper` from the header file `<ctype.h>`. The prototype for this function is

```
int toupper(int character);
```

where the function returns the integer value of the ASCII code for the converted character. If the character is already an upper-case letter of the alphabet, then the function returns the ASCII code for that letter.

The `toupper` function is used in the following program as `reply = toupper(reply)`.

Program Example 7.3: Do .. While Loop

```
/*
chap_7\ex_3.c
program to demonstrate the use of the do..while statement
*/

#include <stdio.h>
#include <ctype.h>

void main(void)
{
    const char yes = 'Y';

    int     exit_number;
    char    reply;

    do
    {
        printf("input exit number on Highway 6 -> ");
        scanf("%d", &exit_number); getchar();

        switch(exit_number)
        {
            case 1:  printf("Highway 6A/ Sagamore Bridge\n"); break;
            case 2:  printf("Highway 130\n"); break;
            case 3:  printf("Quaker Meeting House Road\n"); break;
            case 4:  printf("Chase Road/ Scorten Road\n"); break;
            case 5:  printf("Highway 149/ Martons Mills\n"); break;
            case 6:  printf("Highway 132/ Hyannis\n"); break;
            case 7:  printf("Willow Street/ Higgins Crowell Road\n"); break;
            case 8:  printf("Union Street/ Station Avenue\n"); break;
            case 9:  printf("Highway 134/ S.Dennis\n"); break;
```

```
            case 10: printf("Highway 124/ Harwich Port\n"); break;
            case 11: printf("Highway 137/ S.Chatham\n"); break;
            case 12: printf("Highway 6A/ E.Brewster\n"); break;
            default: printf("DATA ERROR - incorrect exit number\n");
        }

        printf("continue? - answer Y[es] or N[o] ");
        scanf("%c", &reply);
        /* convert lower case to upper case */
        reply = toupper(reply);

    } while (reply == yes);
}
```

Results

```
input exit number on Highway 6 -> 8
Union Street/ Station Avenue
continue? - answer Y[es] or N[o] Y
input exit number on Highway 6 -> 2
Highway 130
continue? - answer Y[es] or N[o] y
input exit number on Highway 6 -> 13
DATA ERROR - incorrect exit number
continue? - answer Y[es] or N[o] y
input exit number on Highway 6 -> 12
Highway 6A/ E.Brewster
continue? - answer Y[es] or N[o] y
input exit number on Highway 6 -> 1
Highway 6A/ Sagamore Bridge
continue? - answer Y[es] or N[o] N
```

7.4 Increment/ Decrement Operators

At this point in the chapter it is worth digressing to the topic of incrementing and decrementing values, in particular in the context of control variables found in loops.

If you wanted to increase the value of an integer variable counter by one, then you would write

```
            counter = counter + 1
```

C Syntax:

The same result can be achieved by writing

postfix increment and decrement operators

```
            counter++
```

Similarly, if you wanted to decrease the value of counter by one, then you would write

```
            counter = counter - 1
```

The same result can be achieved by writing

    counter--

These new operators are known as **increment** and **decrement postfix** operators; they are written after the variable as ++ and -- respectively and can be used to increase or decrease a numeric variable by one.

The increment and decrement postfix operators are useful within loops as the next program illustrates.

The C language also has increment and decrement prefix operators, but they are not used in this book.

Program Example 7.4: Increment and Decrement Postfix Operators

```
/*
chap_7\ex_4.c
program to demonstrate the use of increment and decrement postfix operators
within while loops
*/

#include <stdio.h>

void main(void)
{
        const char ASCII_code_Z = 90;

        int counter = 10;
        int ASCII_code = 65;
                                        /* code to count down from 10 to 0 */
        printf("countdown ");
        while (counter >= 0)
        {
            printf("%2d", counter);
            counter--;                  /* same as counter = counter - 1 */
        }
        printf(" blast off!!\n\n");
                                        /* code to display the alphabet */
        printf("alphabet ");
        while (ASCII_code <= ASCII_code_Z)
        {
            printf("%c", ASCII_code);
            ASCII_code++;               /* same as ASCII_code = ASCII_code + 1 */
        }
        printf("\n");

}
```

```
    /* if expression_3 is omitted then the loop control variable
    must be incremented (or decremented) within the body of the loop
    */
    for (counter = 1; counter < 4;)
        printf("%2d", counter++);

}
```

Results

```
1 2 3
1 2 3
1 2 3
1 2 3
```

By omitting all three expressions in a `for` statement, it is possible to set up an **infinite** loop - one that repeats without ending! Unless you deliberately want your program to run forever, such programming practice should be avoided. For example, the following segment of code continues to print the message until the user interrupted the running of the program.

```
for ( ; ; )
    printf("forever and ever ... ");
```

Notice that even when the expressions are omitted in for loops, the semicolon separators must be present.

7.6 Which Loop?

You should by now understand the syntax and semantics of the three loop structures - while, do .. while, and for. However, knowing which loop to use in a program requires more explanation.

While

The first statement in a while loop contains a condition to exit from the loop. This condition guards entry into the loop. If the guarding condition is false, then entry into the loop will be denied. Whenever there is the possibility that you do not want the program to execute the statements within the loop, you should use a while loop.

In this example input data is used to control entry into the loop.

```
scanf("%d", &number);
while (number != sentinel)
{
    .
    .
    .
    scanf("%d", &number);
}
```

Notice that when data is used to control entry into a loop, it is necessary to read ahead for a datum in order to test the guarding conditional statement. It is also necessary to include a second read statement within the body of the loop to supply data for testing the conditional statement.

Do..While

The feature of this loop is that it is not guarded by any condition, and the computer will always execute the statements within the loop at least once. This feature can be useful when validating data. In the following example, the body of the loop will continue to be executed until a number is input that lies within the range 0 .. 100.

```
do
{
    printf("input number in the range 0 .. 100 ");
    scanf("%d", &number);
} while (number < 0 || number > 100);
```

For

A for loop is normally used for counting. However, since it behaves in a manner similar to the while loop, it can be used if the body of the loop needs to be guarded against initial entry. The following example illustrates the use of a for loop to control a counter to display the alphabet.

```
for (ASCII_code = 65; ASCII_code <= 90; ASCII_code++)
{
    printf("%c\t%d\t", ASCII_code, ASCII_code);
    if (ASCII_code % 2 == 0) printf("\n");
}
```

In this example the numeric variable ASCII_code acts as a counter from 65 .. 90. The control string in the printf statement contains %c to display the character with the ASCII code followed by %d to display the decimal value of the ASCII code. The if statement is used to generate a new line when two pairs of results have been output.

Case Study: Savings Account Interest

You open a savings account with a specified amount of money; the bank will pay 1.5% interest each quarter. You plan to make no deposits or withdrawals, but you want to see what each quarterly balance, including interest, will be over a period of time.

Problem Analysis - Calculating the interest for one quarter of a year is the product of the balance and the quarterly rate - *interest = balance * quarterly_rate*. Before you can calculate the interest for the next quarter, it is necessary to increase the balance by the interest for the first quarter - *balance = balance + interest*. This calculation of interest and balance continues for all the quarter years within the investment period.

Algorithm

1. input balance and term
2. output headings
3. calculate length of term in quarter years
4. for every quarter year in term
5.   calculate interest
6.   calculate balance
7.   output quarter year, interest, and balance

Data Dictionary - The quarterly rate can be declared in the program as a constant of value 0.015. The balance and interest are both quantities of money, and therefore, are declared as type float. The variable term, the length of the term in quarterly years, and the last quarter year are all declared as type integer.

```
const  float  quarterly_rate = 0.015;

float  balance;
float  interest;
int    term;
int    quarter_years;
int    last_quarter;
```

Desk Check - The initial balance is 2000 and the term 1 year.

balance	term	last_quarter	quarter_years	interest	(quarter_years <= last_quarter)
2000	1	4	1		
2030			2	30.00	true
2060.45			3	30.45	true
2091.36			4	30.91	true
2122.73			5	31.37	false

175

```
                        Screen Layout

12345678901234567890123456789012345678901234567890

input initial balance 2000
input length of investment in years 1
quarter    interest    balance

1          30.00       2030.00
2          30.45       2060.45
3          30.91       2091.36
4          31.37       2122.73
```

```c
/*
chap_7\ex_6.c
program to calculate accumulated interest payable on a savings account
*/

#include <stdio.h>

void main(void)
{
    const  float  quarterly_rate = 0.015;

    float  balance;
    float  interest;
    int    term;
    int    quarter_years;
    int    last_quarter;

    printf("input initial balance ");
    scanf("%f", &balance);
    printf("input length of investment in years ");
    scanf("%d", &term);

    /* output headings */
    printf("quarter\tinterest\tbalance\n\n");

    last_quarter = 4 * term;

    for (quarter_years = 1; quarter_years <= last_quarter; quarter_years++)
    {
        interest = balance * quarterly_rate;
        balance = balance + interest;
        printf("%-2d\t%-6.2f\t\t%-8.2f\n", quarter_years, interest, balance);
    }
}
```

Results

```
input initial balance 2000
input length of investment in years 1
quarter   interest balance

1           30.00    2030.00
2           30.45    2060.45
3           30.91    2091.36
4           31.37    2122.73
```

 **Case Study: Counting Words in a Sentence**

The following program counts the number of words in a sentence that is input at the keyboard.

Problem Analysis - We assume that only one space is used between words and the sentence is terminated by a period. The complete sentence is stored in the keyboard buffer. The following algorithm assumes that the input buffer is scanned one character at a time, analyzing the sentence before displaying the number of words.

Algorithm

1. initialize word count to zero (this may be performed in a declaration)
2. input character
3. while character not period
4.   if character is a space, increase word count by 1
5.   input character
6. increase word count by one (since end of sentence)
7. display word count

Data Dictionary - The word delimiters, a space and a period, can be represented as constants in the program. A single character is of type char, and the number of words in the sentence is of type integer and initialized to zero.

```
const   char    space = ' ';
const   char    period = '.';

char    character;
int     number_of_words = 0;
```

177

Desk Check - The sentence stored in the buffer as test data is *Have a nice day.*

character	number_of_words	period?	space?
H	0	false	false
a	0	false	false
v	0	false	false
e	0	false	false
<space>	1	false	true
a	1	false	false
<space>	2	false	true
n	2	false	false
i	2	false	false
c	2	false	false
e	2	false	false
<space>	3	false	true
d	3	false	false
a	3	false	false
y	3	false	false
. <period>	4	true	

Screen Layout

```
12345678901234567890123456789012345678901234567890123456789 0

input a sentence on one line - terminate with a period
Have a nice day.
number of words in sentence is     4
```

```c
/*
chap_7\ex_7.c
program to count the number of words in a sentence
*/

#include <stdio.h>

void main(void)
{
        const   char    space = ' ';
        const   char    period = '.';

        char    character;
        int     number_of_words = 0;
```

```
        printf("input a sentence on one line - terminate with a period\n");

        scanf("%c", &character);
        while (character != period)
        {
                if (character == space) number_of_words++;
                scanf("%c", &character);
        }

        number_of_words++;
        printf("number of words in sentence is %d", number_of_words);
}
```

Result from program being run twice

```
input a sentence on one line - terminate with a period
Have a nice day.
number of words in sentence is  4

input a sentence on one line - terminate with a period
To be or not to be that is the question.
number of words in sentence is  10
```

In this example the end of the sentence was detected by using the period as a sentinel. However, it is possible to detect the end of a line of data by testing for the end-of-line character. The end-of-line character is represented by ASCII code LF with a decimal code of 10.

Case Study: To Edit a Line of Text

The program in this example edits a single line of text. The input text includes an opening parenthesis, followed by some characters and a closing parenthesis. The text is to be output without the characters between and including the parentheses. You may assume that the opening parenthesis always appears before the closing parenthesis and that both characters will always be present.

Problem Analysis - Once again we assume that the keyboard buffer contains the line of text and that the algorithm is applied to each character, in succession, in the buffer. All the characters up to but not including the opening parenthesis are output; all those characters up to and including the closing parenthesis are flushed from the buffer; the remaining characters up to the end-of-line character are output.

179

Algorithm

1. input character
2. while character not opening parenthesis '('
3.   display character
4.   input character

5. while character not closing parenthesis ')'
6.   input character

7. input character in order to consume closing parenthesis
8. while character is not end of line
9.   display character
10.. input character

Data Dictionary - The end-of-line character can be stored as a character constant with value 10, and the character being examined from the input buffer as a variable of type char.

```
const   char     end_of_line = 10;
char    character;
```

Desk Check   - The line of text stored in the buffer is *printf("\n");*

character	(?)?	)?	end_of_line?	output
p	false			p
r	false			r
i	false			i
n	false			n
t	false			t
f	false			f
(	true			
"		false		
\		false		
n		false		
"		false		
)		true		
;			false	;
<return>			true	

Screen Layout
123456789012345678901234567890123456789012345678901234567890
input one line of text printf("\n"); printf;

180

```
/*
chap_7\ex_8.c
program to input a line of text, edit a portion of the text and
output the edited text
*/

#include <stdio.h>

void main(void)
{
        const   char    end_of_line = 10; /* ASCII code for LF */

        char    character;

        printf("input one line of text\n");

        /* read and write characters up to ( */
        scanf("%c", &character);
        while (character != '(')
        {
                printf("%c", character);
                scanf("%c", &character);
        }

        /* read characters up to ) */
        while (character != ')' )
        {
                scanf("%c", &character);
        }

        /* read and write characters as far as the end of the line */
        scanf("%c", &character);
        while (character != end_of_line)
        {
                printf("%c", character);
                scanf("%c", &character);
        }
}
```

Results

```
input one line of text
printf("\n");
printf;
```

Case Study: Count the Number of Words in a Sentence Spread over Many Lines

The program in this example allows a sentence to be input at the keyboard. The sentence may be written over several lines, be punctuated by commas, semicolons, colons, and spaces and be terminated by a question mark, exclamation mark, or period. However, it is assumed that a sentence will begin with a letter of the alphabet forming the first letter of a word. The purpose of the program is to count the number of words in the sentence and display this value. The user is given the opportunity to type more than one sentence.

Problem Analysis - Every time a character is input, it is checked for being either a terminator (question mark, exclamation mark, or period), or a word separator (comma, semicolon, colon, space, carriage return CR or line feed LF). In response to both types of word delimiters (terminator or separator), the word count must be increased by one. However, it is also necessary to detect the occurrence of multiple spaces or two separators together, in which case the word count must not be increased again.

Algorithm for Function main

1. do
2.   input and analyze sentence (this can be refined into a function called word_count)
3.   display word count
4.   ask user if there are more sentences
5. while more sentences to process

Data Dictionary for the Function main - The user reply about more sentences is a variable of type char. This value is compared with the character constant yes to determine whether to continue program execution.

```
const   char    yes = 'Y';

char     reply;
```

Algorithm for function word_count

2.1   initialize word count to zero (this may be performed in a declaration)
2.2   input character
2.3   while character not a sentence terminator
2.4   if character is a word separator
2.5   increase word count by 1
2.6   input character
2.7   while character is space, CR, or LF
2.8   input character
2.9   else
2.10   input character
2.11   increase word count by 1

Data Dictionary for the Function word_count - The sentence terminators ($'?'$, $'!'$, and $'.'$) and the word separators ($','$, $';'$, $':'$, $'\ '$, CR, and LF) are represented as character constants. The character being read from the input buffer and the number of words in a sentence are declared as character and integer variables, respectively. The number of words in the sentence can be initialized to zero in this declaration. Each time the function is called, the number of words will be reinitialized to zero. The function prototype is given as

```
int word_count(void);

const    char    question_mark = '?';
const    char    exclamation_mark = '!';
const    char    period = '.';
const    char    comma = ',';
const    char    semi_colon = ';';
const    char    colon = ':';
const    char    space = ' ';
const    char    LF = 10;
const    char    CR = 13;

char     character;
int      words = 0;
```

Desk Check - The following lines of text are stored one after another in the keyboard buffer.

To be
or not to be,
that is the question!

character	words	terminator?	separator?	space, CR, LF?
	0			
T	0	false	false	
o	0	false	false	
<space>	1	false	true	
b	1	false	false	false
e	1	false	false	
<CR>	2	false	true	
<LF>	2			true
o	2	false	false	false
r	2	false	false	
<space>	3	false	true	
n	3	false	false	false
o	3	false	false	
t	3	false	false	
<space>	4	false	true	
t	4	false	false	false
o	4	false	false	
<space>	5	false	true	

183

character	words	terminator?	separator?	space, CR, LF?
b	5	false	false	false
e	5	false	false	
,	6	false	true	
<CR>	6	false		true
<LF>	6	false		true
t	6	false	false	false
h	6	false	false	
a	6	false	false	
t	6	false	false	
<space>	7	false	true	
i	7	false	false	false
s	7	false	false	
<space>	8	false	true	
t	*8*	*false*	*false*	*false*
h	8	false	false	
e	8	false	false	
<space>	9	false	true	
q	9	false	false	false
u	9	false	false	
e	9	false	false	
s	9	false	false	
t	9	false	false	
i	9	false	false	
o	9	false	false	
n	9	false	false	
!	10	true		

The output from this desk check is the number of words in the sentence, which is 10.

Screen Layout

```
12345678901234567890123456789012345678901234567890
input a sentence, terminate with ? ! or .
To be
or not to be,
that is the question!

number of words in sentence 10

more sentences - answer Y[es] or N[o] N
```

```
/*
chap_7\ex_9.c
program to count the number of words in a sentence
*/

#include <stdio.h>
#include <ctype.h>

int word_count(void)
/* function to input a sentence and return the number of words */
{
    const   char    question_mark = '?';
    const   char    exclamation_mark = '!';
    const   char    period = '.';
    const   char    comma = ',';
    const   char    semi_colon = ';';
    const   char    colon = ':';
    const   char    space = ' ';
    const   char    LF = 10;
    const   char    CR = 13;

    char    character;
    int     words = 0;

    scanf("%c", &character);

    /* test for terminator */
    while (character != question_mark &&
           character != exclamation_mark &&
           character != period)
    {
        /* test for separator */
        if (character == comma ||
            character == semi_colon ||
            character == colon ||
            character == space ||
            character == LF)
        {
            words++;
            scanf("%c", &character);

            /* ignore further separators */
            while (character == space ||
                   character == CR ||
                   character == LF)
            {
                scanf("%c", &character);
            }
```

```
                }
                else
                    scanf("%c", &character);
        }
        words++;
        getchar(); /* flush input buffer */
        return words;
}

void main(void)
{
        const   char    yes = 'Y';

        char    reply;

        do
        {
            printf("input a sentence, terminate with ? ! or .\n");

            printf("\nnumber of words in sentence %d\n\n", word_count());

            printf("more sentences - answer Y[es] or N[o] ");
            scanf("%c",&reply);
            /* convert lower case to upper case */
            reply = toupper(reply);

            /* flush input buffer */
            getchar();
        } while (reply == yes);
}
```

Results

```
input a sentence, terminate with ? ! or .
To be
or not to be,
that is the question!

number of words in sentence 10

more sentences - answer Y[es] or N[o] Y
input a sentence, terminate with ? ! or .
This is a test of the program,
a full sentence can be input
over
as many lines as are required,
and, full account, will be taken of all
punctuation.
```

```
number of words in sentence 29

more sentences - answer Y[es] or N[o]  N
```

Summary

- ☐ The statements within a `while` loop can be executed zero or more times.

- ☐ The statements within a `do..while` loop are executed at least once.

- ☐ Both loops use conditional expressions to control the number of repetitions.

- ☐ All statements within a `while` loop and a `do..while` loop will be executed while the conditional expression is true.

- ☐ Counter variables may be increased or decreased by one by using postfix increment ++ and postfix decrement -- operators.

- ☐ A `for` loop is a generalized `while` loop and may contain up to three expressions.

- ☐ If the first expression in a `for` loop is omitted, then the initialization of the loop control variable can take place outside the loop.

- ☐ If the second expression in a `for` loop is omitted, then the loop does not terminate unless it contains a `break` statement.

- ☐ If the third expression in a `for` loop is omitted, then the loop control variable must be incremented or decremented within the body of the loop.

- ☐ By omitting all three expressions from within a `for` loop, it is possible to set up an infinite loop.

Review Questions

1. What is the purpose of a loop?

2. Is the conditional expression true or false upon exiting from the `while` loop?

3. What is the minimum number of times a `do..while` loop can be repeated?

4. How is a sentinel value used to control a `while` loop?

5. State the fundamental operations associated with using a `while` loop as a counter.

6. At what point in the loop does each expression in a `for` statement execute?

7. True or false - the statement `counter = counter - 1` is the same as the expression `counter--`.

187

8. What does the statement x++ do?

9. What is the purpose of the routine strcmp?

10. What is an infinite loop?

Programming Exercises

11. Desk check the following while loop. What is the output from the program segment?

```
counter = 1;
while (counter < 10)
{
   printf("%d\t", counter);
   counter = counter + 2;
}
```

12. Desk check the following do..while loop using the test data 10, -1 and 9. What is the purpose of the loop?

```
do
{
   scanf("%d", &digit);
} while (digit < 0 || digit > 9);
```

13. Desk check the following for loop. What is output?

```
for (counter = 65; counter <=90; counter++)
     printf("%c"; counter);
```

14. Discover the errors in the following segments of code.

(a)

```
i = 10;
while (i > 0);
{
   printf("T minus %d and counting\n", i);
   i--;
}
```

(b)

```
for (i=10; i>0; i--);
   printf("T minus %d and counting\n", i);
```

188

15. Use a `for` loop to rewrite the following segment of code.

```
x=30;
while (x >= 3)
{
    printf("%d\t", x);
    x--;
}
```

Programming Problems

16. Write a program that uses a loop to display the message *Hello World* ten times on the screen.

17. Write a program to input a message of your choice and the number of times you want to repeat it; then display the message repeatedly.

18. Write a program to output a table of conversion from miles to kilometres. The table should contain column headings for miles and kilometres. Miles should be output as integer values between 1 and 50, in steps of 1 mile. New headings should be printed at the beginning of the table and after 20 and 40 miles, respectively. Note: 1 mile = 1.609344 Km.

19. Write a program using `while` loops to output the following:

(a) The odd integers in the range 1 to 29.

(b) The squares of even integers in the range 2 to 20.

(c) The sum of the squares of the odd integers between 1 and 13.

(d) The alphabet in lower case.

20. Repeat question 19 using `for` loops.

21. Repeat question 19 using `do..while` loops.

22. Write a program to find and print the arithmetic mean of a list of nonzero numbers. The number of numbers is not known in advance. Terminate the sequence of numbers with zero.

23. Write a program to calculate and output the overtime pay for ten employees and the total overtime paid. Overtime is paid at $12.00 per hour for every hour worked over 40 hours per week. Assume that employees do not work for fractional parts of an hour.

24. Write a program to input a phrase and display the ASCII code for each character of the phrase.

25. Write a program to find and print the largest integer from ten integers input at the keyboard. Assume that numbers are input one per line.

26. Rewrite the program in Case Study: To Edit a Line of Text, so that it will output all the characters between the parentheses.

27. Write a program to input a phrase on one line and perform a classification of the vowels. Display the number of vowels in each category.

Before you answer the next two questions, return to your answers to questions 36 and 37 in Chapter 2 in which you drew flowcharts to convert between number systems.

28. Write a program to convert a decimal number to a hexadecimal number.

29. Write a program to convert an eight bit binary number to decimal. Treat each bit as a character.

30. The lengths of the four sides of a quadrilateral and one internal angle are input to a computer. Write a program to categorize the shape of the quadrilateral as a square, rhombus, rectangle, parallelogram, or irregular quadrilateral.

The rules for determining the shape of the quadrilateral are given in the following table:

name	all sides equal?	opposite sides equal?	right angle?
square	true	true	true
rectangle	false	true	true
rhombus	true	true	false
parallelogram	false	true	false

A suggested first-level design for this program is:

do

> *input angle and lengths of four sides*
> *analyze and display the name of the shape*

while more data

Use the following functions in your answer

```
void input_data(int *angle,
                float *side_1, float *side_2, float *side_3, float *side_4);
/* function to input one angle and the lengths of the four sides */

void analyse_shape(int angle,
                float side_1, float side_2, float side_3, float side_4,
                char name_of_quadrilateral[]);
/* function to return the name of the quadrilateral */

boolean more_data(void);
/* function to return true if more data is required otherwise re-
turn false */
```

Chapter 8
One-dimensional Arrays

Up to now all variables have been associated with discrete items of data, and little importance has been attached to the organization of data in the memory of a computer. This chapter introduces the array, which is the commonest of the data structures, is available in most high-level languages, and uses methods for accessing data that can lead to simple and more effective programming solutions. By the end of the chapter, you should have an understanding of the following topics:

- [ ] Concept of a one-dimensional array.
- [ ] The declaration of an array.
- [ ] Simple macros.
- [ ] Input and output of data stored in an array.
- [ ] Arrays of characters.
- [ ] String processing.

8.1 One-dimensional Array

Consider for a moment how you could store five integer values. The obvious answer is to create five variable names

```
int number_1, number_2, number_3, number_4, number_5;
```

and assign a value to each consecutive variable.

```
number_1 = 54;
number_2 = 26;
number_3 = 99;
number_4 = -25;
number_5 = 13;
```

If you adopted the same approach to storing fifty integer values, then the coding would become quite tedious. Clearly, we need a better method to store data of the same type, a method that reduces the amount of coding to a minimum.

Well, such a method is available and it is called an array. An **array** is a named collection of one or more items of data of the same type. Each individual element of data can be referenced by the name of the array and a numbered index indicating its position within the array. Arrays come in various dimensions, however, only one-dimensional arrays will be considered in this chapter.

Figure 8.1 A concept of a one-dimensional array

A one-dimensional array, containing five storage cells is illustrated in Figure 8.1. It is important to remember the following points:

- ☐ The contents of the array MUST be of the same data type. In other words, an array can contain all integers or all reals or all characters or all strings, but not a mixture of types.

- ☐ Each item in the array is stored in a separate cell. If an array contained five integers, then each integer would occupy a single cell.

- ☐ Each cell has a unique location value that shows the cell's position within the array. This location value is known as either a subscript or an index and starts at value 0.

- ☐ The array is given only ONE name, irrespective of the number of items it contains.

- ☐ Before an array can be used, it MUST be declared like any other variable.

- ☐ An item of data within a cell is accessed by using the name of the array followed by the position, subscript, or index number within square brackets.

The syntax for the declaration of a one-dimensional array is:

type-specifier array-name [constant expression]

For example, the array depicted in Figure 8.1 might be declared as `int numbers[5]`; this states that the name of the variable is `numbers`. It is an array containing five cells, having subscripts numbered 0 through to 4 respectively. The contents of the array is of type integer.

The following statement stores the number 54 at cell position 0 in the array.

```
numbers[0]=54;
```

To store number 26 at cell position 1 use

```
numbers[1]=26;
```

8.2 Simple Macros

A constant expression is used in the declaration of an array to specify the number of cells the array will contain, for example, `int numbers[5]`, where the constant expression 5 indicates that the array contains five cells.

A good programming practice is to replace the numeric literal that defines the number of cells in the array with a constant. Consequently, if the size of the array changes, the only statement in the program that needs to be modified is the declaration of the constant.

With this practice in mind, you might be tempted to write

```
const   int n=5;
        int numbers[n]; /* this statement is illegal */
```

However, such a declaration is illegal in ANSI C; therefore, we must look for an alternative method to implement the good programming practice. The use of a simple macro to define the size of an array will avoid this illegality.

A **simple macro** has the format:

#define identifier replacement-list

where the identifier represents the replacement-list, and wherever the identifier appears in the program the computer substitutes it for the replacement-list. The simple macro can appear anywhere in a program, however, it is normally given file scope so that replacement can be made to all identifiers that are visible in the source file. Notice that a semicolon is not required at the end of a simple macro. The declaration of the array depicted in Figure 8.1 can now be changed to:

```
#define size 5     /* simple macro defines the size of the array */

int numbers[size]; /* this statement is legal and
                       illustrates good practice */
```

193

8.3 Input and Output of Data

Figure 8.2 illustrates an array called `numbers` that contains five integers. These numbers can be stored in the array by either initialization at the time of declaring the array or by direct assignment.

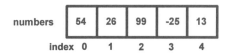

Figure 8.2 An array containing data

C Syntax: The syntax for array initialization is:

array initilization *type-specifier array-name [constant expression] = { data-list }*

For example the array illustrated in Figure 8.2 can be initialized with data by declaring

```
#define size 5
```

```
int numbers[size] = {54,26,99,-25,13};
```

If too few values are supplied to initialize an array, then the remaining cells are automatically set to zero.

The declaration of the maximum number of cells in the array can be omitted if initialization is present; therefore,

```
int numbers[] = {54,26,99,-25,13};
```

is also possible. However, the data-list must contain all the values to be stored in the array.

Alternatively the data may be directly assigned to each cell as follows:

```
numbers[0]=54;
numbers[1]=26;
numbers[2]=99;
numbers[3]=-25;
numbers[4]=13;
```

The contents of the array can be displayed on a screen by using `printf` statements. For example,

```
printf("%d\n", numbers[0]);
printf("%d\n", numbers[1]);
printf("%d\n", numbers[2]);
printf("%d\n", numbers[3]);
printf("%d\n", numbers[4]);
```

would display the contents of the array on five lines of a screen.

These statements have been incorporated into the following program so that the array `numbers` can be created and its contents displayed.

194

Program Example 8.1: Array Initialization

```
/*
chap_8\ex_1.c
program to assign numbers directly to the cells of an array
and display the contents of the cells
*/

#include <stdio.h>
#define size 5

void main(void)
{
        int numbers[size] = {54,26,99,-25,13};

        printf("contents of array\n\n");
        printf("cell 0 %d\n", numbers[0]);
        printf("cell 1 %d\n", numbers[1]);
        printf("cell 2 %d\n", numbers[2]);
        printf("cell 3 %d\n", numbers[3]);
        printf("cell 4 %d\n", numbers[4]);
}
```

Results

```
contents of array

cell 0   54
cell 1   26
cell 2   99
cell 3   -25
cell 4   13
```

The original idea of introducing an array to store the integers was to reduce the amount of coding required to assign the numbers to the store and output the numbers from the store. The previous example hardly inspires confidence that the original idea can be implemented! All it proves is that the same name, numbers, using different subscripts, 0 through 4, can be used in place of five different names. The program was introduced only to show you that it is possible to explicitly access any cell in the array.

To reduce the amount of coding, it is necessary to replace the explicit use of the subscript or index by a control variable identifier. Instead of explicitly coding numbers[0], numbers[1], numbers[2], numbers[3], and numbers[4], it is far easier to use numbers[index] and embed this statement in a for loop that changes the value of index from 0 to 4. For example, numbers can be input from a keyboard and stored in the array using

195

```
for (index=0; index < 5; index++)
   scanf("%d", &numbers[index]);
```

and the contents of each cell of the array can be displayed on a screen using

```
for (index=0; index < 5; index++)
   printf("%d", numbers[index]);
```

The next program demonstrates this idea of using a control variable identifier, in this case index, to control access to the contents of the array.

Program Example 8.2: Assigning Numbers to an Array During Program Execution

```
/*
chap_8\ex_2.c
program to input numbers into a one-dimensional array
and display the contents of the array
*/

#include <stdio.h>
#define size 5

void main(void)
{
        int numbers[size];
        int index;

        /* input numbers into the array */
        printf("input %d integers, one per line\n\n", size);
        for (index = 0; index < size; index++)
        {
            printf("cell %d ", index);
            scanf("%d", &numbers[index]);
        }
        printf("\n\n");

        /* output numbers from the array */
        printf("contents of array\n\n");
        for (index = 0; index < size; index++)
            printf("cell %d\t%d\n", index, numbers[index]);
}
```

Results

```
input 5 integers, one per line

cell 0 54
cell 1 26
cell 2 99
```

196

```
cell 3 -25
cell 4 13

contents of array

cell 0   54
cell 1   26
cell 2   99
cell 3   -25
cell 4   13
```

The use of a `for` statement to control the index to an array is not confined to input and output but can also be used to compare data between cells. In this next program five numbers are stored in an array, and the contents of the array are inspected to find the largest number.

The `for` loop controls the index so that it is possible to gain access to consecutive items of data and compare each item with the largest number found so far.

```
largest = numbers[0];
for (index = 1; index < size; index++)
    if (numbers[index] > largest) largest = numbers[index];
```

The variable `largest` is assigned the first value in the array. The control variable identifier is then set to access the remaining cells in the array. If a number in one of these cells is greater than the current value of the variable `largest`, then `largest` is assigned this value.

Program Example 8.3: Finding the Largest Number in an Array.

```
/*
chap_8\ex_3.c
program to input numbers into a one-dimensional array and find
and display the largest number in the array
*/

#include <stdio.h>
#define size 5

void main(void)
{
        int numbers[size];
        int largest;
        int index;

        /* input numbers into the array */
        printf("input %d integers, one per line\n\n", size);
```

```
    for (index = 0; index < size; index++)
    {
        printf("cell %d ", index);
        scanf("%d", &numbers[index]);
    }

    /* calculate and output the largest number in the array */
    largest = numbers[0];
    for (index = 1; index < size; index++)
        if (numbers[index] > largest) largest = numbers[index];

    printf("largest number in array is %d\n", largest);
}
```

Results

```
input 5 integers, one per line

cell 0 54
cell 1 26
cell 2 99
cell 3 -25
cell 4 13
largest number in array is 99
```

8.4 Array of Characters

A variable of string data type is represented as an array of characters where the lower bound for the array index starts at 0, and a null character automatically marks the end of a string. For this reason the declaration of the size of the array that holds a string must always be one cell larger than the number of characters in the string.

Figure 8.3 illustrates an array that contains ten characters. In the program that follows, despite the data being defined as a variable of type string, it is possible to access each cell of this array to display the contents of the array.

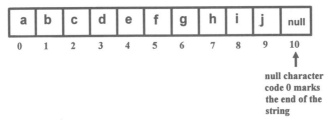

Figure 8.3 A string is an array of characters

198

Program Example 8.4: Array of characters.

```
/*
chap_8\ex_4.c
program to demonstrate that a string is an array of characters
*/

#include <stdio.h>
#define size 11

void main(void)
{
    char    characters[size];
    int     index;

    /* input a string */
    printf("input %d characters\n", size-1);
    gets(characters);

    /* output the contents of the string one character at a time */
    for (index = 0; index != size; index++)
        printf("%c",characters[index]);
}
```

Results

```
input 10 characters
abcdefghij
abcdefghij
```

Note: this program will fail if you input more than ten characters.

Program Example 8.5 finds the length of a string. The program assumes that a string is terminated by a null character. Therefore, starting at the beginning of the string (index = 0), the program examines each consecutive cell of the array until it discovers a null character. If the contents of a cell is not a null character, then the variable that keeps track of the length of the string is increased by 1.

Program Example 8.5: Finding the length of a string.

```
/*
chap_8\ex_5.c
program to find the length of a string
*/

#include <stdio.h>
#define max_size 255
```

```
void main(void)
{
     const  char null = 0; /* ASCII code for string terminator */

     char data[max_size];
     int  length = 0;

     printf("input a line of text\n"); gets(data);

     while (data[length] != null) length++;

     printf("length of text is %d characters\n", length);
}
```

Results

```
input a line of text
How many characters in this string?
length of text is 35 characters
```

Finding the length of a character string is a very common operation in programming. The C Standard library provides a function **strlen** in header file `<string.h>` that returns the number of characters that precede the terminating null character. The function `strlen` prototype is given as:

C Syntax:

length of string function strlen

$$size\_t\ strlen(const\ char\ *s);$$

where `size_t` is the length of the string and the parameter is character string `s`. For example,

```
strlen("abracadabra")
```

returns the value 11. Notice that the value returned by `strlen` is also the index of the null terminator of the string.

In the next example, the program examines each character of the line of text that is input from a keyboard. If a lower-case character is found, it is converted into an upper-case character; otherwise the character remains unchanged. The contents of the line of text is then displayed on the screen.

Program Example 8.6: Capitalizing Characters in a String

```
/*
chap_8\ex_6.c
program to change every alphabetic character in a string to upper case
*/

#include <stdio.h>
#include <ctype.h>
#define max_size 255

void main(void)
{
        const char  null = 0;
        char    text[max_size];
        int     index;

        printf("input a line of text\n");
        gets(text);

        for (index = 0; text[index] != null; index++)
            text[index] = toupper(text[index]);

        printf("capitalized text\n%s", text);
}
```

Results

```
input a line of text
This is a test to CAPITALIZE text .. and it works!
capitalized text
THIS IS A TEST TO CAPITALIZE TEXT .. AND IT WORKS!
```

8.5 Arrays as Parameters

We have just seen that a character string is represented as an array of characters. In Chapter 5 we noted that when the argument in a function call is a character string, then a local copy of the string is not created and not stored in the data area of the function being called. Instead, the argument passes to the corresponding function parameter a memory address of where the argument is located. The memory address is a reference to the argument.

Since character-string array parameters are passed by reference and since both the parameter and the argument are represented by the same array, any change to the contents of the formal array parameter must result in a change to the contents of the actual array parameter.

201

Program Example 8.7 illustrates how to pass a character-string array as a reference parameter. Notice the string array `characters` has block scope within the function `main`. There is no local copy of this character-string array in the function `capitalize`. The formal array parameter `string` makes reference to the string array `characters`, and it is the contents of array `characters` that changes.

Program Example 8.7: Passing a Character String Argument by Reference.

```
/*
chap_8\ex_7.c
program to demonstrate passing a character string array as a
reference parameter
*/
#include <stdio.h>
#include <ctype.h>
#include <string.h>

void capitalize(char string[], int size)
/* function to change the contents of an alphabetic
string to upper case letters only
*/
{
   int index;

   for (index=0; index != size; index++)
     string[index] = toupper(string[index]);

}

void main(void)
{
   char characters[] = "this string will change case ";
   int  length = strlen(characters); /* use strlen to find length of string */

   printf("original string - %s\n", characters);
   capitalize(characters, length);
   printf("converted string - %s\n", characters);
}
```

Results

```
original string - this string will change case
converted string - THIS STRING WILL CHANGE CASE
```

A natural conclusion to reach from this example is that all arrays, and not just character strings, can be used as parameters in functions, with the corresponding array argument being passed to the formal parameter by reference.

Program Example 8.8 illustrates how a numeric array is passed as an argument to a function. Since arrays are passed by reference, the function changes the contents of the argument `array`. Notice that the array is initialized using the statement `int array[size]={0};`. If enough values are not supplied to initialize an array, as in this example, then the remaining cells are automatically set to zero.

Program Example 8.8: Passing a Numeric Array by Reference

```
/*
chap_8\ex_8.c
program to demonstrate passing a numeric array as a reference parameter
*/

#include <stdio.h>
#define size 5

void supply_data(int data[], const int array_size)
/* function to input numbers and store them in a one dimensional array */
{
  int index;

  printf("input %d integers ", array_size);

  for (index=0; index != array_size; index++)
    scanf("%d", &data[index]);
  printf("\n");
}

void main(void)
{
  int array[size] = {0};
  int index;

  printf("original contents of array\n\n");
  for (index=0; index != size; index++)
    printf("%5d", array[index]);
  printf("\n\n");

  supply_data(array, size);

  printf("modified contents of array\n\n");
  for (index=0; index != size; index++)
    printf("%5d", array[index]);
  printf("\n");
}
```

Results

```
original contents of array

     0     0     0     0     0

input five integers 1 2 3 4 5

modified contents of array

     1     2     3     4     5
```

If an array is an argument in a function call and you do not want the argument to be modified by the calling function, then insert the reserved word `const` before the formal parameter declaration. In the following program segment, a function `length` returns the length of a string; on this occasion the contents of the string should not be modified by the function. Any attempt within the function `length` to reassign characters to the array `string` will result in a compilation warning or error.

```c
int length(const char string[])
{
    .
    .
    .
}

void main(void)
{
    char alphabet[] = "ABCDEFGHIJKLMNOPQRSTUVWXYZ";

    printf("length of string = %d\n", length(alphabet));
}
```

Case Study: Simulation of Rolling a Die

In rolling a die, one of the six sides will appear uppermost. If the die is rolled many thousands of times, each of the six sides should have an equal probability of appearing uppermost, provided the die was not biased (loaded!). Write a program that counts the number of times each of the six sides appears uppermost when rolled many number of times. At the end of the trial, display the number of times each of the six sides of the die appeared uppermost.

Problem Analysis - The solution to this problem uses an array that contains the frequency of occurrences of the spots on the sides of the die. An array containing seven cells is declared with indexes 0 .. 6. Cells 1..6 are used to store the frequency of occurrence of each side of the die. This strategy makes programming the final solution considerably clearer to read and understand than using array indexes 0 .. 5 to represent each side of the die. The first cell (0) is not used. Figure 8.4 illustrates the contents of the cells after 6000 trials (rolling the die 6000 times).

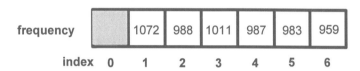

Figure 8.4 Representation of frequency of spots

How can we simulate rolling the die? What technique is available to produce the digits 1 .. 6 at random in the same way that the uppermost side of the die appears at random? The answer is to use a random number generator, which is a prewritten function **rand** from the header file `<stdlib.h>` that will return a random number each time it is called. The prototype for the function is :

C Syntax:

random
number
function
rand

int rand(void);

The function returns a pseudo-random number in the range 0 .. RAND_MAX. This value can then be converted into a random number in the range 1 .. 6 by using the expression (`rand() % 6 + 1`) and assigned to the number of spots that appears on any one side of the die. For example, the assignment `spots=6` implies that the side with six spots is uppermost.

If the value from this expression is used as a subscript to the array `frequency`, then the statement `frequency[spots]++` will increase the contents of the appropriate cell in the array by 1.

Algorithm for the function main

1. input the number of trials
2. while number of trials is positive do
3.   initialize the frequency of occurrences to zero
4.   roll the die for the number of trials (this can be represented by the function roll_die)
5.   display the frequency of occurrences of the spots
6.   input the number of trials

Data Dictionary for the Function main - The arguments to be passed to the function `roll_die` are the array `frequency` and the number of trials. The `main` function also contains a local variable used to count the number of spots. The integers used to represent the number of trials and the frequency of occurrence of each die face should be declared as long integers to allow a simulation of many millions of rolls.

```
      int   spots;
long  int   trials;
long  int   frequency[7];
```

Algorithm for the Function roll_die

4.1 for every trial
4.2   calculate a random number in the range 1 to 6 to represent the number of spots
4.3   increase the frequency by 1 for calculated number of spots

Data Dictionary for the Function roll_die - The formal parameter list for this function contains two items: the name of the array used to store the frequency of occurrences of the spots and the number of times the die is to be rolled (trials). The function does not return a value. The argument for the array parameter will change its values, since it is passed by reference. The function contains two local variables: one to count the number of trials and the second to represent the value of a spot.

```
void   roll_die(long int die[], long int trials);

long int  roll;
     int  spots;
```

Desk Check of Function roll_die - Test data 10 rolls.

spots	die[spots]	trials	roll	(roll<=trials)?
		10	1	true
3	1		2	true
5	1		3	true
2	1		4	true
3	2		5	true
1	1		6	true
3	3		7	true
4	1		8	true
2	2		9	true
6	1		10	true
3	4		11	false

```
                        Screen Layout
12345678901234567890123456789012345678901234567890
input number of trials (0 to exit) 6000
number of spots 1       2       3       4       5       6
frequency       1072    988     1011    987     983     959
```

```
/*
chap_8\ex_9.c
program to simulate throwing a die for different numbers of trials and
record the frequency that each side of the die (spots) appears in each
trial
*/

#include <stdio.h>
#include <stdlib.h>
#define sides 6

void roll_die(long int die[], long int trials)
/* function to update the frequency of occurrences of the spots 1..6
appearing on a die over a set number of trials */
{
     long int roll;
          int spots;

     for (roll=1; roll <= trials; roll++)
     {
         spots = rand() % sides + 1;
         die[spots]++;
     }
}

void main(void)
{
          int     spots;
     long int     trials;
     long int     frequency[sides + 1];

     printf("input number of trials (0 to exit) ");
     scanf("%ld", &trials);

     while (trials > 0)
     {

         /* initialize frequency of occurrences to zero */
```

207

```
        for (spots=1; spots<=sides; spots++)
            frequency[spots] = 0;

        /* simulate rolling the die for a given number of trials */
        roll_die(frequency, trials);

        printf("\nnumber of spots\t1      2      3      4      5      6\n");
        printf("frequency\t");
        for (spots=1; spots<=sides; spots++)
            printf("%-7ld", frequency[spots]);

        printf("\n\ninput number of trials (0 to exit) ");
        scanf("%ld", &trials);
    }
}
```

Results

```
input number of trials (0 to exit) 6000
number of spots    1        2        3        4        5        6
                   1072     988      1011     987      983      959
input number of trials (0 to exit) 0
```

emordnilap

?

Case Study: Is a Word a Palindrome?

Write a program to test for a word being a palindrome, that is a word spelled the same way backwards as forwards.

Problem Analysis - The method used to test the word is to inspect the characters at either end of the word. If these characters are the same, then the next two characters at either end of the word are compared. The comparisons continue until there is no match between the characters or there are no further comparisons possible. The movement of the indexes is shown in Figure 8.5.

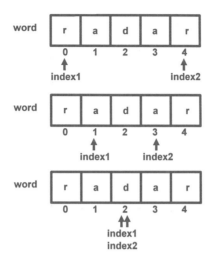

Figure 8.5 Comparison of characters in the array

Algorithm for the Function main

1. input a single word
2. if word is_palindrome (is_palindrome is a function that returns true or false)
3.   display word is a palindrome
4. else
5.   display the word is NOT a palindrome

Data Dictionary for the Function main - This contains just one variable, the declaration for the string being analyzed. The storage space allocated to this string is more than sufficient to accommodate the largest of words.

```
char word[80];
```

Algorithm for the Function is_palindrome

2.1 initialize the first index to point to the first letter in the word
2.2 initialize the second index to point to the last letter in the word
2.3 initialize a boolean flag to true, indicating that the letters being pointed at match (even if they don't)
2.4 while the first index is not larger than the second index and the letters pointed at match do
2.5   if the letters being pointed at are the same
2.6   increase the position of the first index by 1
2.7   decrease the position of the second index by 1
2.8   else
2.9   set the boolean flag to false to indicate that the letters being pointed at do not match

2.10 return the value of the boolean flag

In order to initialize the second index to point to the last letter in the word, we need to know the length of the word. This process uses the function `strlen` from header `<string.h>`.

Data Dictionary for the Function is_palindrome - The formal parameter list for this function is the array used to store the word to be analyzed. The function returns an enumerated `boolean` value `true` if the word is a palindrome; otherwise it returns the value `false`.

It is necessary to declare local integer variables for the two indexes, and the length of the word; and a Boolean flag to indicate whether the word is a palindrome or not.

```
boolean is_palindrome(const char word[]);

int       length;
int       index_1, index_2;
boolean   characters_match;
```

Desk Check of the function is_palindrome - Test data *radar*.

index_1	0	1	2	3
length	5			
index_2	4	3	2	1
characters_match	true			
(index_1 <= index_2 && characters_match)?	true	true	true	false
word[index_1]	r	a	d	
word[index_2]	r	a	d	
(word[index_1] == word[index_2])?	true	true	true	
is_palindrome(word)				true

Screen Layout

```
1234567890123456789012345678901234567890123456789012345678901234567890
input a single word radar
radar is a palindrome
input a single word mouse
mouse is NOT a palindrome
```

```
/*
chap_8\ex_10.c
program to input a word and test whether it is a palindrome
*/

#include <stdio.h>
#include <ctype.h>
#include <string.h>
#define size 80

typedef enum{false, true} boolean;

boolean is_palindrome(char word[])
/* function returns true if word is a palindrome otherwise returns false */
{

    int        length;
    int        index_1, index_2;
    boolean    characters_match;

    /* initialize indices and boolean flag */
    index_1 = 0;
    length = strlen(word);
    index_2 = length - 1;
    characters_match = true;

    /* compare characters in word */

    while (index_1 <= index_2 && characters_match)
        if (toupper(word[index_1]) == toupper(word[index_2]))
        {
            index_1++;
            index_2--;
        }
        else
            characters_match = false;

    return characters_match;
}

void main(void)
{
    char        word[size];

    printf("input a single word ");
    gets(word);
```

```
    if (is_palindrome(word))
        printf("%s is a palindrome\n", word);
    else
        printf("%s is NOT a palindrome\n", word);

}
```

Results from program being run twice

```
input a single word radar
radar is a palindrome
input a single word mouse
mouse is NOT a palindrome
```

Aa Ee Ii Oo Uu

vowels?

Case Study: Count the Number of Vowels in a Sentence.

Write a program to input a sentence and inspect each character. Keep a count of the numbers of different vowels that appear in the sentence and display these values when the end of the sentence is reached.

Problem Analysis - The solution to this problem is similar to that of the case study to simulate rolling a die. An array keeps a count of the frequency of occurrences of vowels in a sentence, rather than spots on a die. The array illustrated in Figure 8.6 indicates the frequency of occurrences of vowels in a sentence. Notice that it is more meaningful to use enumerated constants as subscripts rather than the integers 0..4 that they represent.

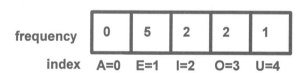

Figure 8.6 Frequency count of vowels

212

Algorithm for the Function main

This algorithm assumes that the sentence is stored in the input buffer. Each character from the buffer is then examined until the terminating period is located.

1. input character
2. while character is not a period do
3.   analyze character (this will refine into a function vowel_analysis)
4.   input next character
5. display the contents of the array for storing the vowel count

Data Dictionary for the Function main - The arguments to be passed to the function `vowel_analysis` are the integer array for keeping a count of the number of vowels and the current character to be analyzed. The contents of the array can be initialized to zero at its point of declaration. A local variable of type `vowel` is used as a subscript to the array, and a constant represents the terminating period at the end of a sentence.

```
const   char   period = '.';

int     frequency[5] = {0};
char    character;
vowel   letter;
```

Algorithm for the Function vowel_analysis

3.1 convert character to upper-case letter
3.2 switch letter
3.3   'A'   increase A-frequency by 1
3.4   'E'   increase E-frequency by 1
3.5   'I'   increase I-frequency by 1
3.6   'O'   increase O-frequency by 1
3.7   'U'   increase U-frequency by 1

Note: the letter cannot be used directly as a subscript to the array; therefore, a `switch` statement is used as a means of selecting the correct cell to increase in the array.

Data Dictionary for the Function vowel_analysis - The formal parameter list for this function contains two items; the integer array for counting the number of vowels in a sentence and a letter from the sentence to be analyzed.

```
void vowel_analysis(int vowel_count[], char letter);
```

Desk Check of Function vowel_analysis - Test data *Count the vowels in this sentence.*

letter	index	vowel_count[index]
C		
o	O	1
u	U	1
n		
t		
space		
t		
h		
e	E	1
space		
v		
o	O	2
w		
e	E	*2*
l		
space		
i	I	1
n		
space		
t		
h		
i	I	2
s		
space		
s		
e	E	3
n		
t		
e	E	4
n		
c		
e	E	5
.		

```
┌─────────────────────────────────────────────────────────────┐
│                      Screen Layout                          │
├─────────────────────────────────────────────────────────────┤
│12345678901234567890123456789012345678901234567890123456789 0│
│input a sentence - terminate with a period                   │
│Count the vowels in this sentence.                           │
│vowels   A  E  I  O  U                                       │
│         0  5  2  2  1                                        │
└─────────────────────────────────────────────────────────────┘
```

```c
/*
chap_8\ex_11.c program to count the number of vowels in a sentence
*/

#include <stdio.h>
#include <ctype.h>
#define size 5

typedef enum {A,E,I,O,U} vowel;

void vowel_analysis(int vowel_count[], char letter)
/* function to analyse a character and update the vowel frequency counter
*/
{
    letter = toupper(letter);

    switch(letter)
    {
    case 'A': vowel_count[A]++; break;
    case 'E': vowel_count[E]++; break;
    case 'I': vowel_count[I]++; break;
    case 'O': vowel_count[O]++; break;
    case 'U': vowel_count[U]++;
    }
}


void main(void)
{
    const  char   period = '.';
           int    frequency[size] = {0};
           char   character;
           vowel  letter;

    printf("input a sentence - terminate with a period\n");
    character = getchar();

    /* update vowel count */
    while (character != period)
    {
       vowel_analysis(frequency, character);
       character = getchar();
    }

    /* output contents of vowel count */
    printf("\n\nvowels\t\tA   E   I   O   U   \nfrequency\t");
    for (letter = A; letter <= U; letter++)
        printf("%-4d", frequency[letter]);
}
```

Results

```
input a sentence - terminate with a period
Count the vowels in this sentence.


vowels          A   E   I   O   U
                0   5   2   2   1
```

Summary

- ☐ A one-dimensional array is a data structure that can be used to store data of one type.

- ☐ An array is subdivided into cells. Each cell has a unique subscript or index value, and the first cell has an index of zero.

- ☐ The maximum number of cells that an array contains is declared in a program and remains constant. For this reason an array is known as a static data structure.

- ☐ It is good practice to declare the number of cells of an array as a constant using a simple macro.

- ☐ Simple macros are normally declared at the beginning of the source file to provide maximum file scope and hence visibility of the macro identifier.

- ☐ Access to any item of data in the array is through the name of the array, followed by the position of the data in the array, that is, the subscript or index value of the cell that contains the data.

- ☐ A loop control variable in a `for` statement is a useful way of representing the subscript or index of an array. By varying the value of the loop control variable, it is possible to access any cell within the array.

- ☐ An array of characters represents a variable of string data type. The initial subscript is zero, and a null character terminates the string.

- ☐ The contents of a variable of string data type can be accessed as individual characters stored from cell 0 in a one-dimensional array.

- ☐ Array parameters are passed by reference; therefore, any changes to the parameter will result in corresponding changes to the argument.

- ☐ Because array parameters are passed by reference, a local copy of the array is not made, and extra memory space, local to the function, is not required.

Review Questions

1. True or false - an array stores data of different types.

2. What is a subscript to an array?

3. Is the subscript of the first cell in an array always 0?

4. Declare an array named `real_numbers` to contain ten floating-point numbers.

5. Modify the declaration in question 4 to initialize the contents of every cell to zero.

6. What happens if we don't supply enough values to initialize the entire array?

7. Write a statement to show how you would you display a number in the third cell of the array declared in question 4.

8. How is a string of characters represented?

9. How does a function call pass array parameters?

10. Modify the array parameter in a formal parameter list so that the argument cannot be changed.

11. True or false - an array declaration may contain a constant expression defined by `const` to specify the number of cells in the array.

12. What is a simple macro?

13. True or false - a simple macro can be placed anywhere in a source program.

14. How may a simple macro be used in array declaration?

Programming Exercises

15. Desk check the following segment of code. What is the final value of the identifier `value` ?

```
int alpha[] = {-10, 16, 19, -15, 20};
int index;
int value = 0;

for (index=0; index != 5; index++)
   value = value + alpha[index];
```

16. What is the result of `alpha[3] - alpha[1]` in the array declared in question 15?

17. Given the declaration `char string[] = "abracadabra";` what is the value of `string[10]` and `string[11]`?

217

18. Desk check the following program and state the contents of the array when the program terminates.

```c
void function(char alpha[])
{
    alpha[1] = '*';
    alpha[3] = '!';
    alpha[5] = '?';
}

void main(void)
{
    char pasta[] = "spaghetti";

    function(pasta);
}
```

19. Desk check the following code and determine the final contents of the array.

```c
int  numbers[] = {5,2,8,7,0,3};
int  left=0;
int  right=5;

while (left <= right)
{
    numbers[right] = numbers[left];
    left++;
    right--;
}
```

20. Find the error in the following simple macro.

```c
#define size 255;
```

Programming Problems

21. Rewrite the following programs found in this chapter, so they contain the functions listed.

(a) Program Example 8.2   `void input_data(int array[], int N);`
`void display_data(int array[], int N);`

where the function `input_data` will allow keyboard input of N integers stored in the array and the function `display_data` will output to a screen the N integers stored in the array.

(b) Program Example 8.3   `int largest(int array[], int N);`

where the function `largest` will return the largest integer from the array containing N integers.

(c) Program Example 8.5   `int length(char array[]);`

where the function `length` will return the number of characters stored in the character string array. Do not use the terminating null character in the length of the string.

(d) Program Example 8.6   `void capitalize(char array[]);`

where the function `capitalize` will convert any lower-case letters in the array to upper-case letters.

22. Write a program to store the alphabet as characters in an array. The program should display:

(a) The entire alphabet.
(b) The first six characters of the alphabet.
(c) The last ten characters of the alphabet.
(d) The tenth character of the alphabet.

23. Write a program to input ten integers in numerical order into a one-dimensional array X; copy the numbers from array X to another one-dimensional array Y such that array Y contains the numbers in descending order. Output the contents of array Y.

24. The monthly sunshine record for a holiday resort follows.

month	JAN	FEB	MAR	APR	MAY	JUN	JUL	AUG	SEP	OCT	NOV	DEC
hours of sunshine	100	90	120	150	210	250	300	310	280	230	160	120

Write a program, structured into functions, to perform the following tasks:

(a) Store the hours of sunshine in a one-dimensional array and the names of the months in another one-dimensional array. The names of the months are themselves strings, which are represented by one-dimensional arrays. Therefore, the declaration becomes `char months[12][4]`.
(b) Calculate and display the average hours of sunshine over the year.
(c) Calculate and display the names of the months with the highest and lowest number of hours of sunshine.

Use the following functions, given by their respective prototypes, in your answer.

```
void sunshine_hours(int hours[]);
/* initialize array hours with hours of sunshine */
void names_of_months(char months[][4]);
/* initialize array names_of_months with abbreviated names of the months */
float average(int hours[]);
/* return the average hours of sunshine for a year */
```

```
void highest(int hours[], char months[][4], char highest[]);
/* find the month with the highest sunshine hours and return the name of
the month as a reference parameter */
void lowest(int hours[], char months[][4], char lowest[]);
/* find the month with the lowest sunshine hours and return the name of
the month as a reference parameter */
```

25. Code and test the following functions.

(a) **`void delete(char string[], int I, int N);`**
/* changes the value of the string by deleting N characters starting at the Ith character of the string.*/

(b) **`void insert(char string_1[], char string_2[], int I);`**
/* changes the value of string_2 by inserting string_1 at the Ith position of string_2 */

(c) **`void substring(char string[], int I, int N);`**
/* modifies the string by creating a substring, which is the N characters starting at the Ith position */

.

(d) **`void concat(char string_1[], char string_2[]);`**
/* modifies string_1 by the concatenation (joining together) of the string_1 and string_2 */

(e) **`int position(char string_1[], char string_2[]);`**
/* scans through the string_2 to find the first occurrence of the substring string_1 within string_2; the value returned is the index within string_2 of the first character of the matched substring */

Chapter 9
Pointers

Pointers are one of the most important features in C. We have already used pointers as part of the parameter passing mechanism in functions. You will learn from this chapter that they can also be used to declare and access elements in an array, to facilitate the creation of arrays at run time rather than at compile time, and to pass functions as parameters.

By the end of this chapter, you should have a knowledge of the following topics:

- ☐ The definition of a pointer.
- ☐ Pointer arithmetic.
- ☐ Accessing arrays through pointers.
- ☐ Strings.
- ☐ Dynamic arrays.
- ☐ Arrays of pointers.
- ☐ Using mathematical functions.
- ☐ Pointers to functions.

9.1 Pointers Revisited

Pointers were first introduced in Chapter 5 to explain a method in C for simulating the passing of reference parameters. You may recall that a **pointer** is an identifier that does not store data of type int, float, double, char, etc; but stores an address of where to find the data in memory. This address literally points to where the data is stored.

The syntax of a pointer declaration is:

> *type-specifier * identifier*

For example, the declaration int *IntPointer implies that the variable IntPointer is a pointer to an integer. The asterisk * in front of IntPointer instructs the compiler that IntPointer is a variable pointer and not a variable of type integer.

The statement IntPointer = &largest; assigns the address of largest to IntPointer, causing IntPointer to point at the variable largest, as depicted in Figure 9.1. Remember that **&** is an address operator and was described in Chapter 3.

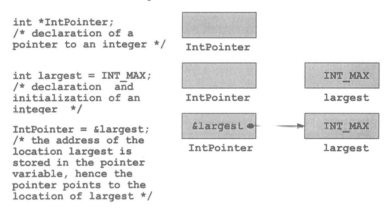

```
int *IntPointer;
/* declaration of a
pointer to an integer */

int largest = INT_MAX;
/* declaration   and
initialization of an
integer   */

IntPointer = &largest;
/* the address of the
location largest is
stored in the pointer
variable, hence the
pointer points to the
location of largest */
```

Figure 9.1 A pointer variable

The **indirection operator** * (asterisk) allows the programmer to identify the value of the datum that is being pointed at. The syntax of the indirection operator is

> *identifier

For example, in Figure 9.1, *IntPointer is the value INT_MAX. Do not confuse the use of the asterisk to declare a pointer as a variable, with the use of the asterisk to gain access to the value of what is being pointed at. The asterisk is used in two different contexts. The first is for declaration:

```
int *IntPointer;            /*declaration of a pointer to an integer */
```

and the second is for access to a datum:

```
printf("%d",*IntPointer); /* contents of the address being pointed at */
```

9.2 Pointer Arithmetic

In Chapter 8 subscripts or indexes were used to access elements in an array. However, it is also possible to use pointers to access the contents of an array. In the following code a pointer `ptr` has been declared and is made to point at the first cell of the array named `table`.

```
/* declaration and initialization of the array */
   int table[6] = {16,21,8,3,-7,9};
/* declaration of a pointer to an integer */
   int *ptr;

/* the pointer, which is an address, is assigned the address of the
   first cell in the array  */
   ptr = &table[0];
```

The result of this coding is illustrated in Figure 9.2.

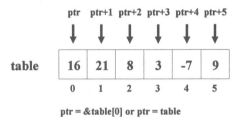

Figure 9.2 Pointer arithmetic

Note : when an array is declared, the name of the array is actually a pointer to the first element in the array. As a consequence array parameters are always passed to a function by reference.

Writing the array name `table` (a pointer) is the same as writing `&table[0]` (a pointer to the first element). The declaration of `int table[6];` implies that `*(table+0) = 16`. Similarly `*(table+1) = 21`, `*(table+2) = 8`, etc. But `table[0] = 16, table[1] = 21, table[2] = 8`, etc. Therefore, `*(table+i)` is the same as `table[i]`, where i = 0 to 5 in Figure 9.2.

It is possible to access the first cell through the pointer `ptr`. Thus `printf("%d", *ptr);` would display 16, the contents of cell 0. In order to allow the pointer `ptr` to traverse the addresses of the cells of the array, it is possible to perform arithmetic on a pointer. An integer can be added to a pointer to get it to point to another address; for example, `ptr = ptr + 1` (or `ptr++`) causes the pointer to point to the second cell in the array `table`.

The contents of the one-dimensional array `table` can be displayed using the following segment of code:

```
for (ptr=table; ptr <= table+6; ptr++)
  printf("%=4d", *ptr);
```

Two pointers can be subtracted as follows:

```
int  *ptr1, *ptr2;

ptr1=&table[5];
ptr2=&table[0];
```

Then `ptr1-ptr2` represents the difference in array elements of `&table[5]` and `&table[0]`, which is 5. However, if an integer is stored in two bytes, then by casting the pointer addresses to integer values `(int)ptr1-(int)ptr2`, the difference in memory locations is 10 bytes

Do not attempt to use pointer arithmetic to modify the name of an array. This value is a constant pointer and not a pointer variable.

The program that follows illustrates how the array can be accessed and its contents displayed.

Program Example 9.1: Access to an Array using Pointer Arithmetic

```
/*
chap_9\ex_1.c
program to demonstrate access to an array using pointers
*/

#include <stdio.h>

void main(void)
{
     int table[] = {16,21,8,3,-7,9};
     int *ptr, *ptr1, *ptr2;

     printf("contents of array is ");
     for (ptr = table; ptr < table+6; ptr++)
         printf("%-4d", *ptr);
     printf("\n\n");

     printf("number of array elements between &table[5] and &table[0] is ");
     ptr1 = &table[5];
     ptr2 = &table[0];
     printf("%d\n\n", ptr1 - ptr2); /* difference between array elements */

     printf("difference in bytes between these locations is %d\n",
            (int)ptr1 - (int)ptr2);
}
```

Notice that the difference in the pointers yields the same answer as the difference would be in the subscripts; however, it is necessary to use the difference in the integer values of `ptr1` and `ptr2` in order to calculate the difference in bytes between these two locations.

Results

```
contents of array 16   21   8    3    -7   9

number of array elements between &table[5] and &table[0] is 5

difference in bytes between these locations is 10
```

9.3 Strings

A string is stored as successive characters in the computer's memory with the last character of the string being the string terminator (a null character). The name of the string is a pointer to the first character of the string. For example,

```
char *magic = "abracadabra";
```

then magic is assigned as a pointer to the first character of "abracadabra", as depicted in Figure 9.3.

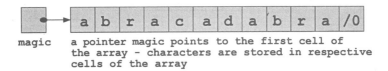

```
magic     a pointer magic points to the first cell of
          the array - characters are stored in respective
          cells of the array
```

Figure 9.3 A character string

The following program illustrates how to use pointer arithmetic to display a string array on the screen.

Program Example 9.2: Use of Pointers in a String

```
/*
chap_9\ex_2.c
program to demonstrate the use of a pointer to access a character string
*/

#include <stdio.h>

void main(void)
{
    const char null = 0;

    char *magic = "abracadabra";
    char *ptr;

    for (ptr = magic; *ptr != null; ptr++)
        printf("%c", *ptr);
}
```

225

Results

`abracadabra`

If the string is declared as a one-dimensional array and initialized as follows

`char magic[ ] = "abracadabra";`

then the same code can be used to display the contents of `magic` on the screen. Despite the same code being used to access the string, there are differences in the manner in which the string and the name of the string can be used. In the array declaration of the string, the contents of the string can be modified; however, in the pointer version, no attempt should be made to modify the string. In the array declaration, `magic` is the name of an array and it cannot point to a different array. By contrast, the pointer variable can be changed in the program so that it contains a different address and hence points to a different string!

9.4 Memory Allocation

When a pointer variable is declared, the declaration allocates storage space only for the pointer and does not allocate storage space for the information being pointed at by the pointer.

In Figure 9.4 P has been declared as a pointer to an address containing an integer by using the declaration `int *P`. Pointers are allocated memory from the system **heap** (a storage area for dynamically allocated variables) by the function **malloc** (memory allocation) and deallocated memory by the function **free**. The deallocated memory is returned to the system heap. The allocation, use, and deallocation of a pointer to memory is also illustrated in Figure 9.4.

C Syntax:

The prototype for the function `malloc` found in the header file `<stdlib.h>` is given as

memory
allocation
malloc

void *malloc(size_t size);

The function `malloc` allocates a block of bytes and returns a pointer to the block. The size of the bytes allocated depend on the data being pointed at. The `sizeof` operator returns the amount of storage space required for a value of the specified type. Hence the statement `P = malloc (sizeof(int))` will assign to P the address of the area of memory allocated from the heap to store an integer. The type `size_t` in ANSI C is an unsigned integral type.

If the heap is virtually empty and not enough memory can be allocated, then `malloc` returns a NULL pointer. **NULL** is an implementation-defined pointer constant defined in the header <stddef.h>. The header files <locale.h>, <stdio.h>, <stdlib.h>, <string.h>, and <time.h> all define NULL, so there is no need to include <stddef.h> if the program uses one of these.

`NULL` must not be confused with the null string terminator /0 - they have quite different meanings and are used in different contexts. `NULL` is a pointer, whereas null is an ASCII character used as a string terminator.

When you use `malloc` you should get into the habit of testing for the NULL pointer being returned; otherwise, you cannot be assured that enough memory has been allocated from the heap.

The function prototype for `malloc` contains the pointer `void *`. This is known as a **generic pointer** type and can be assigned a pointer value of any type.

Returning to Figure 9.4, the indirection operator * allows the programmer to identify the value of the integer that is being pointed at by P; therefore, the result of the assignment `*P = 10` is to store the value 10 at the area of memory pointed at by P.

The size of the heap is finite and clearly too many requests for storage space from the heap will exhaust the amount of memory available for allocation. For this reason, whenever allocated memory space is no longer required, it should be returned to the heap by using the function free.

C Syntax:

memory
re-alloca-
tion
free

The prototype for the function is given as:

> *void free(void *ptr);*

For example, `free(P)` returns the block of memory that P originally pointed at to the heap. Note: when a program terminates, all allocated memory will be returned to the heap regardless of whether or not free is used.

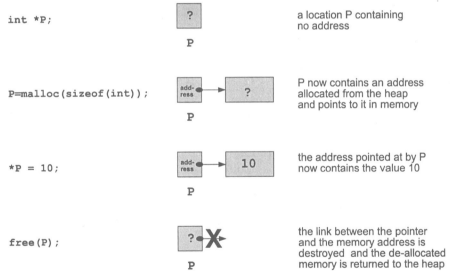

Figure 9.4 Allocation and deallocation of memory

Other pointers can be assigned to existing pointers as illustrated in Figure 9.5. Such assignment implies that both pointers point at the same address. For example, given the declaration of a pointer

```
int *Q;
```
and
```
P=malloc( sizeof (int));
```

227

then

```
Q =P;
```

implies that both P and Q point at the same address.

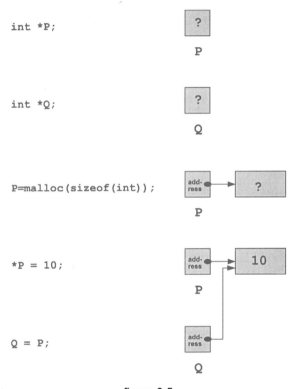

figure 9.5

C Syntax: The program that follows implements memory allocation and pointer assignment as illustrated in Figure 9.5. Note that in this program the function exit, defined in the header file <stdlib.h>, causes a program to terminate. The prototype of the function is given as:

termination of a program exit

void exit(int status);

For example, exit(errno), where errno is a variable defined in the header <errno.h>, can be set by library functions. The value of errno indicates the type of error that has occurred. A value of zero implies no error.

When using scanf to input a number or a character, the address of the variable is required. But variable P is a pointer and hence an address, so scanf("%d", &P) stores the input data at the address of P, which itself is another address. Therefore scanf("%d", P) is used correctly in the following program. Note also that *Q is the value of the integer that is being pointed at by Q.

Program Example 9.3: Creating Pointers to Integers.

```
/*
chap_9\ex_3.c
program to demonstrate the creation of a pointer to an integer,
and the re-assignment of another pointer to the same area of memory
*/

#include <stdio.h>
#include <stdlib.h>
#include <errno.h>

void main(void)
{

     int *P, *Q;  /* declare two pointers */

     P = malloc(sizeof(int));

     if (P == NULL)
     {
       printf("no memory allocated - program terminated\n");
       exit(errno);
     }

     printf("input a single integer ");
     scanf("%d",P);
     Q = P;
     printf("value of the integer being pointed at is %d\n", *Q);
     free(P);
}
```

Results

```
input a single integer 12345
value of integer being pointed at is 12345
```

9.5 Dynamic Arrays

In the previous chapter it was necessary to state the size of the array when a program was written. There was no opportunity to define the size of the array at run time. Hence the array was referred to as a static data structure. A **dynamic array** does not constrain you to specify its size at the time of writing the program. It allows you to define the size of the array when the program is running and hence tailor the storage requirements to the amount of data available.

When a pointer variable is declared, the declaration allocates storage space only for the pointer and does not allocate storage space for the information being pointed at by the pointer. For example, when a pointer variable to a string is declared as `char *string;` only the address of the pointer variable is allocated. Memory space needs to be allocated to store the characters in the string. The function `malloc` allocates memory. It requires one argument that represents the number of bytes requested and returns a pointer to the first byte. For example,

```
char    *string;
string = malloc(256);
```

allocates 256 bytes to the character array and the variable `string` points to the first character in this array.

The following program indicates how memory space is allocated to a character array being pointed at by `string`. A value for the string array is input using `gets(string)`. A further area of memory is allocated to a second array of characters pointed at by `copy`. The amount of memory allocated to the character array `copy` is determined by the length of string. The function `strlen` returns the length of a string. The string array is then copied into the `copy` array and the contents of this new array is output. The storage space allocated to `string` and `copy` is then returned to the heap using the function `free`. A separate function for memory allocation has been created to avoid a duplication of code.

Program Example 9.4: Creation of a Dynamic Array

```
/*
chap_9\ex_4.c
program to demonstrate the creation of a dynamic character array
*/

#include <stdio.h>
#include <stdlib.h>
#include <string.h>
#include <errno.h>

#define max_string 256

void *memory_allocation(size_t size)
/* function to return a pointer to a string */
{
   void *pointer;

   pointer = malloc(size);
   if (pointer == NULL)
   {
      printf("ERROR - no memory allocated\n");
      exit(errno);
   }
   return pointer;
}
```

```
void main(void)
{
    char *string, *copy;

    string = memory_allocation(max_string);
    printf("input string ");
    gets(string);

    copy = memory_allocation(strlen(string) + 1);
    strcpy(copy, string);
    printf("string input was %s\n", copy);

    free(copy);
    free(string);
}
```

Results

```
input string Peace on Earth? Maybe one day!
string input was Peace on Earth? Maybe one day!
```

C Syntax:

**memory
allocation
calloc**

Space allocation for arrays is also possible through the function **calloc** (contiguous allocation), also found in header <stdlib.h>. The prototype for calloc is:

void *calloc(size_t nmemb, size_t size);

This function requires two parameters: the first nmemb (number of members) represents the size of the array, and the second (size) represents the size of the data held in each cell of the array. If a one-dimensional array pointed at by table is to store integers, it could be declared as

```
int *table;
```

However, if the number of integers that table will hold is not known in advance, memory allocation for the array can be postponed until the size of the array is known. If the size of the array is found to be n during program execution, then memory can be allocated by using

```
table = calloc( n, sizeof(int));
```

Alternatively, memory allocation is still possible using malloc, and `table` could have been allocated memory by using the following statement:

```
table = malloc(n * sizeof(int));
```

Unlike `calloc`, the function `malloc` does not initialize the space in memory that it makes available. If there is no reason to initialize an array to zero, then use either `calloc` or `malloc`. The program that follows allows the user to create a dynamic array of integers at run time.

Program Example 9.5: Creation of a Dynamic Array of Integers

```
/*
chap_9\ex_5.c
program to dynamically declare the size of an integer array
*/

#include <stdio.h>
#include <stdlib.h>
#include <errno.h>

void *memory_allocation(int blocks, size_t size)
/* function to return a pointer to a block of memory */
{
   void *pointer;

   pointer = calloc(blocks, size);
   if (pointer == NULL)
   {
     printf("ERROR - no memory allocated\n");
     exit(errno);
   }

   return pointer;
}

void main(void)
{
    int *table; /* pointer to the array name table */
    int *ptr;   /* pointer used in place of subscript */
    int size;   /* size of the table declared at run-time */

    printf("input the number of cells in the table ");
    scanf("%d", &size);

    table = memory_allocation(size, sizeof(int)); /* allocate memory space */

    /* input numbers into table */
    printf("input numbers into array\n");
    for (ptr=table; ptr<table+size; ptr++)
        scanf("%d", ptr);

    /* display the contents of the table */
    printf("\ncontents of table\n");
    for (ptr=table; ptr<table+size; ptr++)
        printf("%-3d", *ptr);

    free(table);
}
```

Results

```
input the number of cells in the table 6
input numbers into array
21 13 -7 0 18 101

contents of table
21 13 -7 0   18 101
```

9.6 Arrays of Pointers

It is quite feasible to have a dynamic array in which each cell contains a pointer to another dynamic array. Figure 9.6 illustrates such a technique.

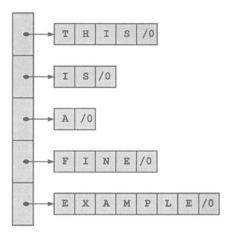

**An array of pointers to arrays
of character strings**

Figure 9.6 An array of pointers to strings

In the following program a dynamic array of pointers to dynamic arrays of characters is declared as

```
char* *array;
```

where `char*` declares the type as a pointer to char (hence pointer to an array of characters) and `*array` declares a pointer `array` (pointer to the first cell of the array of pointers). Hence `char * *array` is a pointer to an array containing data of type pointer to `char`.

The size of this array will be input during program execution, and enough memory space will be allocated to this array through the user-defined function `memory_allocation`.

The user will then be invited to enter a number of strings at the keyboard . Each string is temporarily stored in a single fixed-sized array known as a `string_buffer`. When the size of the input string is known, memory will be allocated to store the specific string in its own dynamic array. Notice from Figure 9.6 that the size of these arrays are customized to the size of the strings. The contents of the `string_buffer` are then copied into the customized character array.

When all the strings have been input, the program traverses the array of pointers, and displays the contents of each string.

Program Example 9.6: An Array of Pointers to Character Strings

```
/*
chap_9\ex_6.c
program to build an array of pointers to strings
then traverse the array and display the strings
*/

#include <stdio.h>
#include <stdlib.h>
#include <string.h>
#include <errno.h>

#define string_size 80

void *memory_allocation(size_t size)
/* function to allocate memory */
{
   void *pointer;

   pointer = malloc(size);
   if (pointer == NULL)
   {
     printf("no memory allocated - program terminated\n");
     exit(errno);
   }

   return pointer;
}


void main(void)
{
    char * *array;                 /* a pointer to an array of pointers to char */
    char    string_buffer[string_size];
    int     index;                 /* index to array of pointers */
    int     number_of_strings;
```

```
    printf("How many strings do you want to input? ");
    scanf("%d", &number_of_strings);
    getchar();

    array = memory_allocation(number_of_strings * sizeof(char *));

    for (index=0; index != number_of_strings; index++)
    {
        printf("string? ");
        gets(string_buffer);
        array[index] = memory_allocation(strlen(string_buffer) + 1);
        strcpy(array[index], string_buffer);
    }

    /* display the contents of the array */

    printf("\ncontents of dynamic arrays\n\n");

    for (index=0; index != number_of_strings; index++)
        printf("%s\n", array[index]);

}
```

Results

```
How many strings do you want to input? 5
string? ***** NEWS HEADLINES *****
string? BATMAN BEATS THE PENGUIN - SO WHAT'S NEW?
string? FLINTSTONES REVIVAL - DINOSAURS ARE A GO GO!!
string? DONALD DUCK GOES QUACKERS.
string? STOP PRESS - THE PENGUIN MAKES A COME BACK - ZAP, BIFF, POW!!!

contents of dynamic arrays

***** NEWS HEADLINES *****
BATMAN BEATS THE PENGUIN - SO WHAT'S NEW?
FLINTSTONES REVIVAL - DINOSAURS ARE A GO GO!!
DONALD DUCK GOES QUACKERS.
STOP PRESS - THE PENGUIN MAKES A COME BACK - ZAP, BIFF, POW!!!
```

In C, functions cannot be treated as data. It has not been possible to store a function in a variable, write a function that takes another function as a parameter, or write a function that returns a function - until now!

We can accomplish all of these goals by using pointers to functions, since pointers can be stored as variables, used as parameters, and returned by functions.

The quickest way to understand this topic is by example, and we will do so within the context of an integration problem, specifically, Simpson's rule.

The following example uses Simpson's rule, which provides a method of finding the area between a plotted function y=f(x), the x-axis, and the limits x=a, and x=b. An approximation to the area becomes $^1/_3 h(Y_0 + 4Y_1 + Y_2)$.

If the area under the plotted function is divided into strips, illustrated in Figure 9.7 and Simpson's rule is applied to each strip between the limits x=a and x=b, then clearly the more strips there are, the more accurate the estimation of the area will be. Also, the more strips there are, the smaller h will become. In Figure 9.7, h is the thickness of a strip, and is referred to as increment in Program Example 9.7.

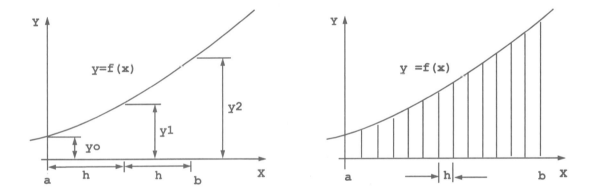

Figure 9.7 Area under a curve using Simpson's rule

In C it is possible to pass a pointer to a function as an argument in an actual parameter list. For example, if the function Simpson uses Simpson's rule to calculate the area under a curve between the limits x=a and x=b for any curve passed to the function, the prototype for the function would be defined as:

```
float Simpson(float a, float b, double (*f)(double));
```

where a and b are the upper and lower limits of integration and (*f) indicates that f is a pointer to a function that requires an argument of type double and returns a value that is of type double. The notation can be simplified, by replacing (*f)(double) with f(double).

The function Simpson can be called using a variety of mathematical functions. Up to now no mention has been made of mathematical functions in C. However, the language contains a repertoire of mathematical functions that can be found under the header file <math.h>. A description of the mathematical functions is given in Appendix A.

Program Example 9.7 uses Simpson's rule to perform the integrations defined in this section. Three standard mathematical functions sin, exp, and sqrt are passed as arguments to the function Simpson. For example,

```
Simpson(0, pi/2, sin);
Simpson(0,1, exp);
Simpson(0,9,sqrt);
```

where the functions sin, exp and sqrt are all described by the following prototypes:

```
double sin(double x);   /* returns the sine of angle x (radians) */
double exp(double x);   /* returns the exponential result of x */
double sqrt(double x);  /* returns the square root of x */
```

Program Example 9.7: Simpson's Rule

```
/*
chap_9\ex_7.c
program to illustrate the use of a pointer to a function
*/

#include <stdio.h>
#include <stdlib.h>
#include <math.h>

float Simpson(float a, float b, double f(double))
{
   const float increment = 0.001;

   float Y0, Y1, Y2;
   float area = 0.0;

   do
   {
      Y0 = f(a);
      Y1 = f(a+increment);
      Y2 = f(a+2*increment);
      area = area + (increment / 3) * (Y0+4*Y1+Y2);
      a = a + 2*increment;
   } while (a < b);
   return area;
}
```

```
void main(void)
{
    const float pi = 3.14159;

    printf("integral of sin(x) 0<=x<=pi/2 %f\n", Simpson(0,pi/2,sin));
    printf("integral of exp(x) 0<=x<=1 %f\n", Simpson(0,1,exp));
    printf("integral of sqrt(x) 0<=x<=9 %f\n", Simpson(0,9,sqrt));
}
```

Results

```
integral of sin(x) 0<=x<=pi/2 1.001187
integral of exp(x) 0<=x<=1 1.723699
integral of sqrt(x) 0<=x<=9 18.004187
```

Summary

☐ A pointer is an identifier that stores the address of an item of data.

☐ The declaration of a pointer variable allocates storage space only for the pointer and does not allocate storage space for the information being pointed at by the pointer.

☐ Storage allocation is through the functions malloc and calloc found in <stdlib.h>.

☐ The function calloc initializes the allocated memory to zero.

☐ Storage allocation is taken from the system heap. Storage space is reallocated back to the heap upon execution of the function free also found in <stdlib.h>.

☐ The indirection operator * is used to specify the contents of the memory being pointed at by the pointer variable.

☐ The address operator & is used to specify the memory address of a variable.

☐ The name of an array is a pointer to the first cell of the array. As a consequence, array parameters are always passed by reference.

☐ A pointer may be initialized to the address of the first cell of an array. The pointer may have arithmetic performed upon it to enable access to be gained to other cells within the array.

☐ The name of a string is a pointer to the first cell of the array that contains the string of characters.

☐ The header file <math.h> contains a repertoire of mathematical functions.

☐ A pointer to a function may be passed as an argument.

Review Questions

1. Explain the declaration `float *pointer`.

2. Given the declaration `float g = 32.0;` what is the meaning of `pointer = &g` where pointer was declared in question 1?

3. What is `*pointer` in relation to the assignment in question 2?

4. Distinguish between an address operator and an indirection operator.

5. Simplify the statement `j=*&i`.

6. True or false - the name of an array is a pointer to the first element in the array.

7. Given the declaration `int a[10]` how do you interpret the statement `*a=0`?

8. From the declaration in question 7, what is the meaning of `*(a+1)=1`?

9. True or false - given the declaration in question 7, the statement `a++` is legal.

10. If `ptr1=&a[10]` and `ptr2=&a[0]`, where ptr1 and ptr2 are both declared as `long int *ptr1, *ptr2`, what is the value of `ptr1 - ptr2`?

11. In the context of question 10, what is the value of `(long int)ptr1 - (long int)ptr2`, assuming a long integer uses four bytes of memory?

12. When an array is passed as an argument to a function, why is it treated as a reference parameter?

13. What is the heap?

14. True or false - the function `malloc` returns an amount of memory to store data.

15. True or false - the functions `malloc` and `calloc` are interchangeable as memory allocation functions.

16. True or false - `calloc` initializes all allocated memory to zero.

17. What is a `NULL` pointer?

18. What is a generic pointer?

19. True or false - one pointer may be assigned the value of another pointer.

20. True or false - the function `free` must be used when either the functions `malloc` or `calloc` appear in a program.

21. What is a dynamic array?

22. True or false - it is legal to declare a dynamic array as a pointer to the first cell of the array and then when the size of the array is known, it is legal to allocate memory from the heap to store the data in the array.

23. True or false - a function may be passed as an argument in a function call.

24. What type of argument is passed to the trigonometric functions defined in the header <math.h>? Inspect the contents of the header <math.h> before attempting to answer this question. This information is given in Appendix A.

25. What function would you use to find a natural logarithm? See <math.h> in Appendix A.

Programming Exercises

26. What is the effect of the following code?

```
int a[2];
int *p;

p=a;
*p=0;
p++;
*p=1;
```

27. Desk check the following code and determine the final value of sum.

```
#define N 5

int a[N] = {3,-2,9,1,-4};
int *p;
int sum - 0;

for (p=&a[0]; p < &a[N]; p++)
{
   sum = sum +(*p);
   p++;
}
```

28. The following function prototypes appear in the header <string.h>.

int strcmp(const char *S1, const char *S2);

char *strcpy(char *dest, const char *source);

size_t strlen(const char *S);

You have already seen these functions being used in earlier examples. Explain the meaning of the parameters and the value that is returned by each function.

29. Comment upon the errors in the following segment of code when it is called using `string = memory_allocation(sizeof(char))` where string is declared as `char *string`.

```c
char *memory_allocation(int size);
{
    char *pointer;

    pointer = calloc(size);
    if (pointer == null)
    {
        printf("no memory allocated - program terminated\n");
        exit();
    }

    return pointer;
}
```

30. Comment on the errors in the following program.

```c
#include <stdio.h>

float function(float f(float))
{
    return f(float);
}

void main(void)
{
    printf("%8.2f", function(sqrt(144.0)));
}
```

Programming Problems

31. Declare three pointers to the types `int`, `float` and `char`. Allocate memory from the heap to store values that are input of type `int`, `float` and `char` respectively. Display the contents of the addresses being pointed at by the three pointers. Deallocate memory back to the heap.

32. Create and test a function with the following prototype:

```c
char *to_upper(const char *array);
```

where the function `to_upper` converts any lower-case letters found in the array and returns a pointer to a string that contains upper-case characters. The advantage of this function is that the contents of the original array need not be changed.

33. This question should remind you how to use pointers to simulate reference parameters in a function call.

A carpenter has a supply of various lengths of wood. The carpenter wants to cut from them as many 5 foot lengths as possible, and where a 5 foot length cannot be cut, the carpenter will cut 2 foot lengths.

Write a program to input a length of wood and calculate and output the number of 5 foot, and 2 foot lengths and the amount of wasted wood. Repeat the program for different lengths of wood being input and keep a running total of the number of 5 foot and 2 foot pieces and the cumulative length of wasted wood. At the end of the data, output the total number of 5 foot and 2 foot pieces and the cumulative length of wasted wood.

A suitable function to calculate the number of pieces of wood that can be cut to a set size from a length of wood might have the following prototype:

```
void calculate(float *length, float size, int *pieces);
```

where the parameter `length` is reduced according to the number of `pieces` cut to `size`. The prototype implies that the reference value of length, after the function call, will give the length of wasted wood.

34. The letters of the alphabet A through Z can be represented in Morse code. Each letter is represented by a combination of up to four dots (.) and/or dashes (-) as illustrated in the Table 9.1

Table 9.1 Morse code

```
A .-        H ....      O ---       V ...-
B -...      I ..        P .--.      W .--
C -.-.      J .---      Q --.-      X -..-
D -..       K -.-       R .-.       Y -.--
E .         L .-..      S ...       Z --..
F ..-.      M --        T -
G --.       N -.        U ..-
```

The codes for the letters A through Z can be represented as the following character string. In these groups of characters spaces have been deliberately introduced to fill the code up to the maximum of four characters. However, the space does not represent part of the code.

```
char *MorseData = ".-  -...-.-.-.. .    ..-.--. ......  .----.- .-..--  "
                  "-.  --- .--.--.-.-. ... -    ..- ...-.-- -..--.----..";
```

Write a program to input a variable length message string and use the character string `MorseData` to convert the message into Morse code and display the result.

35. Figure 9.8 illustrates a data structure comprising a dynamic array for storing the names of children in a school class and a second dynamic array for storing pointers to strings. The strings are addresses to where the children live and are also to be treated as dynamic arrays.

The subscripts in the array of names corresponds with the subscripts to the array of pointers. Therefore the child `Lisa` corresponds with the pointer at subscript 0, which points to the address of where Lisa lives `125 River View`.

You will notice from Figure 9.8 that `Lisa` has a brother `Eric` who lives at the same address. Similarly the brothers `Frederick`, `Albert`, and `Jake` all live at `1076 Jefferson Ave`, whereas `Carol` has no brothers or sisters in the same class and lives at `76 Edmonton Walk`.

Write a program that will allow a user to input the size of the class and pairs of strings containing the name of a child and the address of that child. All the names of the children will be stored in the child array. An address that is input will be compared with the address strings that are already stored. If the address already exists in the structure, then the corresponding pointer for the child must be adjusted to point to the existing address; otherwise, the new address string is stored in the structure.

When the structure has been completed for all the children, display lists of brothers and/or sisters from the same class.

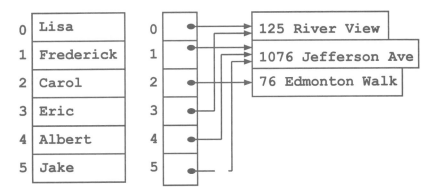

Figure 9.8 A dynamic data structure

36. Create a function that will display a tabular output for x and $f(x)$, where the range of values of x and the name of the function $f(x)$ are formal parameters.

Test your function with the following values:

function f(x)	*range of values of x*
tangent(x)	$0° <= x < 90°$ in steps of $5°$
cosine(x)	$-90° <= x <= +90°$ in steps of $10°$
logarithm$_{10}$(x)	$0 < x <= 10$ in steps of 0.5

Chapter 10
Text Files

In the previous chapters input was confined to entering data through a keyboard and output to displaying information on a screen. When there is a requirement to permanently store data, there is a need to create files. Data can be written to or read from files held on magnetic and optical media. Common media that you are likely to use for storing your files will be floppy disks that you can carry around or hard disks that are part of the computer.

You are already familiar with text files. All the source program files created using an editor have been text files. The text files used in this chapter have been created using either an editor or a specific program to produce a file in the format required.

This chapter covers the use of text files and the methods of accessing the information held on the files. By the end of the chapter, you should have an understanding of the following topics:

☐   Redirection of input and output from keyboard and screen to files held on a storage medium.

☐   Data streams.

☐   Library functions that permit file processing.

☐   Programs to read and create text files.

10.1 Redirection

Up to now when running a computer program, all data has been input at a keyboard and program results have been displayed on a screen. This technique can become impractical when you work with large amounts of data and results or you need to print a hard copy of your results.

Redirection can modify the use of a keyboard for input and a screen for output. Both MSDOS and UNIX permit redirection of keyboard input and screen output to other devices, such as magnetic file units. For example, data can be input to and output from a floppy disk unit.

A **text file** is a collection of ASCII characters, written in lines, with specific end-of-line markers, and an end-of-file marker inserted automatically by the operating system.

For example, the following text file can be input using an editor in the same way as you would input a computer program. The contents of the file are:

```
8
4
2
9
2
0
```

The file can be given the name numbers.txt and stored in a directory chap_10. If the disk is mounted on drive A, then the full pathname of the file becomes A:\chap_10\numbers.txt.

Program Example 10.1 reads numbers input at the keyboard, displays on the screen a running total for the numbers, and calculates and displays the average of the numbers.

The command to redirect input from the keyboard to the file numbers.txt and display the output on the screen is

```
A:\chap_10> ex_1 <numbers.txt
```

where A:\chap_10> is a screen prompt and ex_1 is an executable program file stored in the directory chap_10 on disk drive A. Redirection of the standard input, normally from a keyboard, can be altered using the redirection operator <, where input is taken from a named file.

MSDOS and UNIX Syntax:

redirection operators
< - input
> - output

If the output is to be written to a file called a:\chap_10\results.txt, then redirection is possible by modifying the command line statement used for running the program. The command line becomes

```
A:\chap_10> ex_1 <numbers.txt >results.txt
```

Redirection of the standard output, normally to a screen, can be altered using the redirection operator > so that the output overwrites or destroys the original contents, if any, of the data file results.txt.

Program Example 10.1: Redirection of Input and Output

```
/*
chap_10\ex_1.c
program to demonstrate redirection for input and output
*/

#include   <stdio.h>

void main(void)
{
     int    integer;
     int    sum = 0;
     int    counter = 0;
     float mean;

     scanf("%d", &integer);
     while (integer != 0)
     {
        sum = sum + integer;
        printf("sum of integers so far .. %d\n", sum);
        counter++;
        scanf("%d", &integer);
     }
     mean = (float) sum / counter;
     printf("mean value of integers is %6.1f\n", mean);
}
```

After the program has been executed, the contents of the text file `results.txt`, stored on disk drive
A in directory `chap_10` was:

```
sum of integers so far .. 8
sum of integers so far .. 12
sum of integers so far .. 14
sum of integers so far .. 23
sum of integers so far .. 25
mean value of integers is    5.0
```

This output was not visible on the screen because it had been redirected to the file. However, the output
can be viewed in several ways.

1. When working in MSDOS, use the command **type** to display the contents of a disk file on a screen.
For example, `type a:\chap_10\results.txt`.

2. When working in UNIX use the commands **cat** or **more** to display the contents of a disk file on a screen.
For example, `cat a:/chap_10/results.txt` or `more a:/chap_10/results.txt`.

3. When using an editor, open the file and view its contents on a screen.

4. When working in MSDOS, use the command **print** to output a file to a printer.
For example, `print a:\chap_10\results.txt`.

5. When working in UNIX, use the command **lpr** to output a file to a printer.
For example, `lpr a:/chap_10/results.txt`.

10.2 Streams

The term **stream** refers to any input source or output destination for data. The only streams that were used in the previous chapters were from keyboard input and screen output, but streams can use other devices, such as printers or disk drives.

A stream is represented by a file pointer, which is a value of type `FILE *`, and ANSI C has three standard streams whose file pointers have the following names:

`stdin`	standard input from a keyboard
`stdout`	standard output to a screen
`stderr`	standard output of error messages to a screen

The functions `scanf` and `printf` that relate to keyboard input and screen output have equivalent functions **fscanf** and **fprintf** for input and output from files held on other devices. Although the generic syntax of these functions is given here, they will be described in more detail later in the chapter.

*fscanf(FILE *stream, "control string", arg1, arg2, ... argn)*
*fprintf(FILE *stream, "control string", arg1, arg2, ... argn)*

Since `stdin` and `stdout` are file pointers, it is possible to use these streams with `fscanf` and `fprintf`, respectively, and retain input from the keyboard and output to the screen as if `scanf` and `printf` were being used. For example,

```
fscanf(stdin, "%d", &integer);
fprintf(stdout, "sum of integers so far .. %d\n", sum);
```

where `stdin` and `stdout` are streams for keyboard input and screen output.

Program Example 10.2 is similar to the previous example, but `fscanf` and `fprintf` replace the functions `scanf` and `printf`. This program demonstrates how input from the keyboard and output to a screen can be treated as input and output using standard streams. We do not use this method for keyboard input and screen output in future programs since both `scanf` and `printf` assume the default streams `stdin` and `stdout` respectively. The program is run without using redirection, so that input is taken from the keyboard and the output is directed to the screen.

Program Example 10.2: The Functions fscanf and fprintf to Read and Write using Standard Streams

```
/*
chap_10\ex_2.c
program to demonstrate input and output from the standard streams
stdin and stdout
*/

#include <stdio.h>

void main(void)
{
    int    integer;
    int    sum = 0;
    int    counter = 0;
    float mean;

    fscanf(stdin, "%d", &integer);
    while (integer != 0)
    {
        sum = sum + integer;
        fprintf(stdout, "sum of integers so far .. %d\n", sum);
        counter++;
        fscanf(stdin, "%d", &integer);
    }
    mean = (float) sum / counter;
    fprintf(stdout, "mean value of integers is %6.1f\n", mean);
}
```

Results

```
8
sum of integers so far .. 8
4
sum of integers so far .. 12
2
sum of integers so far .. 14
9
sum of integers so far .. 23
2
sum of integers so far .. 25
0
mean value of integers is    5.0
```

10.3 Opening and Closing Files

In using standard input and output streams as files, it was not necessary to open or close the streams, since this is performed automatically. However, when the programmer defines a new stream, a file must be opened before it can be used. Similarly, when a file is no longer required, or the mode of access changes from say, reading to writing, then the file should be closed.

A file can be opened using the function **fopen**, whose prototype declaration in the <stdio.h> library is

FILE *fopen(const char *path, const char *type);

where the function opens the file specified by path, and associates a stream with that file. The character string type specifies the access mode for the file. The function fopen returns a pointer to the open stream. If the stream could not be successfully opened a NULL pointer is returned. For example,

```
/* declaration of stream named text *
FILE *text;

/* open the file a:\numbers.txt in access mode read and associate it with
the stream text */
text = fopen("a:\numbers.txt", "r");
```

Two commonly used access modes to a file are string type specifiers "r" and "w".

1. String type specifier "r" - read only. The file must have already have been created using an editor or the output from a specific program. If the file has not been created, then a NULL pointer is returned by fopen.

2. String type specifier "w" - write only. If the file exists, it will be overwritten with new data causing the original data to be destroyed. However, if the file does not exist, then a new file will be created in order to write the new data.

A simple macro may be used to specify whether a file has been opened for reading or writing. This improves the readability of the program. For example,

```
#define read "r"
        .

        .
text = fopen("a:\numbers.txt", read);
        .
```

The name of a file can be input into a program in three ways.

1. The name can be implicitly contained in the fopen statement, for example:

```
FILE *text;
text = fopen("a:\text.txt", read);
```

where `a:\text.txt` implies that a file with the name `text.txt` may exist in the directory of the disk held on drive a.

2. The name of the file can be input at run time, prior to the file being opened, for example,

```
FILE *text;
char *filename;
{
   filename = malloc(30);
   printf("input the path and name of the file ");
   gets(filename);
   text = fopen(filename, read);
   .
```

3. The names of files can be passed as arguments in a command line when giving the command to run a program. For example, if an executable program file called `prog` had been created that required the names of the data files `file1.txt`, `file2.txt`, and `file3.txt` to be passed to the `main` function as parameters, the command line would be input as:

```
    prog    file1.txt    file2.txt    file3.txt
```

To accommodate these parameters the syntax of the function `main` must be modified to

C Syntax:

main (int argc, char *argv[])

passing arguments to the main function

where `argc` is the number of command line parameters including the name of the program, in this example argv is 4; `argv[]` is an array of pointers to the command line parameters, in this example `argv[0]` points to `prog`, `argv[1]` points to `file1.txt`, `argv[2]` points to `file2.txt`, `argv[3]` points to `file3.txt`, and `argv[4]` is a NULL pointer.

During run time, if a program attempted to open a file that did not exist, the program would be terminated automatically by the operating system. To overcome this problem, it is possible to check whether the number of command line arguments is correct and whether the files exist if they are to be read.

The following segment of code will check whether the correct number of parameters in the command line

```
    prog    file1.txt    file2.txt    file3.txt
```

are present.

```
void main (int argc, char *argv[])
{
   FILE *filename1, *filename2, *filename3;
   if (argc != 4)
   {
      fprintf(stderr, "ERROR - command line arguments\n");
      exit(errno);
   }
   .
```

The next segment of code can be used to check whether a file can be opened for reading.

```
   filename1 = fopen(argv[1], read);
   if (filename1 == NULL)
   {
      fprintf(stderr, "ERROR - file %s cannot be opened\n", argv[1]);
      exit(errno);
   }
   .
```

Caution:

Possible
Program-
ming
Error

When defining a path for a particular file, use the backslash with care. The compiler will treat \ in a string literal as the beginning of an escape character. For example, in the statement fopen("a:\new_file\text.txt, "w"); the compiler would treat \n and \t as escape characters and return a null pointer. When a backslash is required use \\; hence the statement is changed to fopen("a:\\new_file\\text.txt, "w").

Syntax:

Closing a
file
close

A file is closed by using the **fclose** function found in the header file <stdio.h>. The syntax of the prototype is defined as

int fclose(FILE *stream);

for example,

```
   fclose(filename1);
```

where the function dissociates a stream from a file and returns zero if the stream was closed successfully or EOF if any errors were detected. Note: EOF is defined in <stdio.h> and is a negative integral constant expression that is returned by several functions to indicate there is no more input from a stream.

The function `fclose` causes the stream pointed to by `stream` to be flushed. Any unwritten data for the stream are delivered to the host environment to be written to the file; any unread buffered data are discarded.

10.4 Reading and Writing

The following function prototypes, found in the header file <stdio.h>, are used to read from text files. They correspond to the functions `getchar`, `gets`, and `scanf` that you are already familiar with.

C Syntax:

*int fgetc(FILE *stream) ;*

reading characters, strings and formatted input from files using fgetc, fgets and fscanf respectively

`fgetc` reads a character from `stream`; if the end of the input file is reached or an error occurs, `fgetc` returns a negative integer constant EOF, otherwise `fgetc` returns the ASCII code for the character that was read. For example, `character = fgetc(text)` will get a single character from the stream `text` and assign it to the integer variable `character`.

*char *fgets(char *s, int n, FILE *stream) ;*

`fgets` reads from `stream` into the array that `s` points to, stopping at the first new-line character or when n-1 characters have been read. The new-line character, if read, is stored in the array. If the end of the input file is reached or an error occurs, the function returns a NULL pointer; otherwise the function returns a pointer to the string read. For example, `fgets(buffer, 80, text)` will read up to 79 characters into the character array `buffer`.

*int fscanf(FILE *stream, const char *format, ...) ;*

`fscanf` reads any number of data items from `stream`, using format to indicate the layout of input. If the end of the file is reached or an error occurs, the function returns a negative integer constant EOF. Otherwise, the function returns the number of items of data read. For example, `fscanf(text, "%f", &price)` will read the value of `price` as a floating-point number from the stream `text`.

A text file can be created from within a program by writing information to a file that has been opened in the appropriate mode.

The prototype of the function `fprintf` follows. It is found in the header file <stdio.h>, is similar to `printf`, and is used to create formatted output to a text file.

C Syntax:

*int fprintf(FILE *stream, const char *format, ...) ;*

writing formatted output to files using fprintf

`fprintf` writes a variable number of data items to an output `stream`, using a format string to control the appearance of the output. If an error occurs, `fprintf` returns a negative value; otherwise, it returns the number of characters that were written. For example, `fprintf(text, "%7.2f\n", price)` will write the value of `price` using the control string `"%7.2f\n"` to the stream `text`.

10.5 Detection of Events

The following function prototypes, found in the header file <stdio.h>, are used to detect events such as errors or the end of a file when processing files.

int ferror(FILE *stream);

ferror tests a stream's error flag. The function returns a nonzero value for an error; otherwise, it returns zero; for example, if (ferror(text)) printf("stream error").

int feof(FILE *stream);

feof returns a nonzero value if the end of stream has been reached.

To illustrate how the function feof can be used, it is necessary to introduce the logical operator ! which represents logical negation or logical NOT.

For example, the condition ! feof(text) implies NOT end of file, and when used in the statement

```
while (! feof(text))
{
   fgets(buffer, 80, text);
      .
      .
}
```

allows processing within the while loop to continue as long as the end of file is not reached.

Figure 10.1 illustrates what happens when a text file is opened with the name data and the file is read line by line. In opening the file for reading, a file position indicator points to the first line of the file to be read. At this stage the function feof(data) returns a value of zero, since the end of the file has not been encountered. The price and name of the appliance are read using the functions fscanf(data, "%f",&price) and fgets(appliance, string_length, data), respectively. The file position indicator moves to the next line and provided the end of the data file has not been encountered, the line can be read. The process of reading from the file continues while the end of the data file is not encountered.

text file - data	feof(data)?	fscanf(data,"%f",&price); fgets(appliance, string_length, data);
file position ⟶ 395.95 television 550.00 music center 149.95 freezer	0 (false)	price = 395.95 appliance = television
395.95 television file position ⟶ 550.00 music center 149.95 freezer	0 (false)	price = 550.00 appliance = music center
395.95 television 550.00 music center file position ⟶ 149.95 freezer	0 (false)	price = 149.95 appliance = freezer
395.95 television 550.00 music center 149.95 freezer file position ⟶	not 0(true)	

Figure 10.1 Reading lines from a text file

Program Example 10.3: Reading and Displaying the Contents of a Text File

The following information is used in Program Example 10.3. A text file contains data that relate to the insured values of several domestic appliances. For example, a television is insured for $395.95, a music center is insured for $550.00, a desk-top computer is insured for $995.95, and so on.

Note: this file has been created and stored on disk using an editor, in the same way as you would create and store a program source file. There is no new-line character after the last line in the file.

    395.95 television
    550.00 music center
    995.95 desk-top computer
    199.95 microwave oven
    299.99 washing machine
    149.95 freezer

The program demonstrates how to open the file and read and display the contents line by line. If the file cannot be opened, this fact is reported and the program is abandoned.

255

```
/*
chap_10\ex_3.c
program to read a file and display the contents on a screen
*/

#include <stdio.h>
#include <stdlib.h>
#include <errno.h>

#define filename "a:\\chap_10\\data.txt"
#define read "r"
#define string_length 20

void main(void)
{
    FILE *data;
    float price;
    char  appliance[string_length];

    /* attempt to open file */
    data = fopen(filename, read);
    if (data == NULL)
    {
        printf("%s cannot be opened - program terminated\n", filename);
        exit(errno);
    }

    /* read and display every line in the file */
    while (! feof(data))
    {
        fscanf(data, "%f", &price);
        fgets(appliance, string_length, data);
        printf("%6.2f\t%s", price, appliance);
    }

    /* close data file */
    fclose(data);
}
```

Results

```
395.95 television
550.00 music center
995.95 desk-top computer
199.95 microwave oven
299.99 washing machine
149.95 freezer
```

Program Example 10.4: Reading Data from a File, Updating the Data, and Writing it to a New File

When using files, output does not necessarily need to be directed to a screen. Output can also be directed to another text file. Program Example 10.4 modifies the contents of the file used in the previous program so that the price of each appliance is increased by the rate of inflation; the new price and the name of the appliance are written to a text file.

```
/*
chap_10\ex_4.c
program to read a file and update its contents and write
the new values to another file
*/

#include <stdio.h>
#include <stdlib.h>
#include <errno.h>

#define input_file  "a:\\chap_10\\data.txt"
#define output_file "a:\\chap_10\\new_data.txt"
#define read "r"
#define write "w"
#define string_length 20

void main(void)
{
    float inflation = 0.025; /* rate of inflation at 2.5% */

    FILE   *data;
    FILE   *new_data;
    float price;
    char   appliance[string_length];

    /* attempt to open files */
    data = fopen(input_file, read);
    new_data = fopen(output_file, write);

    if (data == NULL || new_data == NULL)
    {
       printf("file cannot be opened - program terminated\n");
       exit(errno);
    }

    /* read and update every line in the file
       and write the new values to another file */

    while (! feof(data))
    {
       fscanf(data, "%f", &price);
       fgets(appliance, string_length, data);
```

257

```
        price = price + (price * inflation);
        fprintf(new_data, "%7.2f\t%s", price, appliance);
    }

    /* close data files */
    fclose(data);
    fclose(new_data);
}
```

Results - contents of file new_data.txt

```
 405.85 television
 563.75 music center
1020.85 desk-top computer
 204.95 microwave oven
 307.49 washing machine
 153.70 freezer
```

Case Study: Stock Control of Books

The text file illustrated in Figure 10.2 has been created using an editor and stored under the name `books.txt`. Each line in the file contains the quantity in stock, the price of the book, and the title of a book. For example there is one copy of *Art in Athens* priced at *$8.95*. Note: there is no new-line character after the last line in the file. Write a program to read each line of the file and print a report similar to that illustrated in Figure 10.3.

```
1 8.95 Art in Athens
2 3.75 Birds of Prey
1 7.50 Eagles in the USA
3 5.20 Gone with the Wind
2 3.75 Hate, Lust and Love
3 5.95 Maths for Adults
3 3.75 Modern Farming
3 5.20 Raiders of Planet X
1 8.95 Splitting the Atom
1 3.75 The Invisible Man
2 3.75 The Otter
4 5.95 The Tempest
2 5.95 The Trojan Wars
2 3.75 Under the Seas
2 7.50 Vampire Bats
```

Figure 10.2 Contents of the file books.txt

```
                        Report Layout

12345678901234567890123456789012345678901234567890
              STOCK REPORT ON BOOKS

quantity    price              title

       1     8.95 *REORDER* Art in Athens
       2     3.75            Birds of Prey



number of books in stock 3
value of books in stock $ 16.45
```

Figure 10.3 The layout of the report on the books

Notice from the design of the document that when the stock level falls to one item, the report indicates that the stock should be replenished. Notice also that totals are calculated for the number of books and for the value of all the books in stock and printed at the end of the report.

Problem Analysis - The solution to the problem has two parts. The first part requires reading the text file and writing the same information to the report file. When the stock level falls to one book per title, the message to reorder that book title should be output to the file.

The second part calculates the cumulative totals for the number of books in stock and the total value of the books every time a new line from the file is read. When the end of the data file is detected, the information on cumulative totals should be written to the report. Note: the value of books of a specific title is the product of the quantity and the price.

Algorithm for the Function main

1. open input file for reading (refine into function open_file)
2. open output file for writing (refine into function open_file)
3. process files (refine into function process_files)
4. close input file
5. close output file

Data Dictionary for the Function main - This will consist of file pointers to the streams books, and report.

```
FILE *books;
FILE *report;
```

Algorithm for the Function open_file - This function can be used in steps 1 and 2 of the main program.

1.1   open file
1.2   if file cannot be opened
1.3   print warning message
1.4   terminate program
1.5   return pointer to stream

Data Dictionary for the Function open_file - This function contains one local variable to act as a file pointer when opening a file. The parameters are the file string containing the path-name, the name of the file, and the mode of access to the file. The function returns a pointer to the stream that has been opened. The function prototype is given as

```
FILE *open_file(const char filename[], const char mode[]);
FILE *file;
```

Algorithm for the Function process_files

3.1   write headings to the output file

3.2   while not end of input file
3.3   read quantity and price of book from input file
3.4   read title of book from input file
3.5   write quantity and price of book to output file

3.6   if quantity < reorder level then
3.7   write "REORDER" to output file
3.8   else
3.9   write blank spaces to output file

3.10   write title of book to output file
3.11   increase total quantity of books by quantity
3.12   increase total price of books by price

3.13   write total quantity of books to output file
3.14   write total price of books to output file

Data Dictionary for the Function process_files - This function will declare three local variables to represent the data to be found in each line of the file of books - `quantity`, `price`, and `title`. Since the function calculates the cumulative totals for `quantity` and `price`, it will be necessary to declare two local variables for `total_quantity` and `total_price`. Both these variables can be initialized at their point of declaration. Books will be reordered if they have reached the minimum value of 1 book; therefore, a reorder level can be declared as a local constant. The parameters to this function are both file pointers representing a stream for the book file and a stream for the report. The prototype for the function is

```
void process_files(FILE *books, FILE *report);

const int re_order_level = 1;

int     quantity;
float   price;
char    title[string_length];
int     total_quantity = 0;
float   total_price = 0.0;
```

Desk Check of Function process_files - Test data is the first three records in the books.txt file

```
1 8.95 Art in Athens
2 3.75 Birds of Prey
1 7.50 Eagles in the USA
```

! feof(books)?	true		true	true	false
quantity	1		2	1	
price	8.95		3.75	7.50	
title	Art in Athens		Birds of Prey	Eagles in the USA	
(quantity <= re_order_level)?	true		false	true	
total_quantity	0	1	3	4	
total_price	0.0	8.95	16.45	23.95	

Figure 10.4 illustrates a structure chart showing the three functions and the data that is passed between each function.

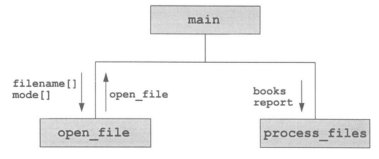

Figure 10.4 Structure chart showing functions

```
/*
chap_10\ex_5.c
program to read a file containing a stock list of books and write the
contents of the file, showing which books to reorder, and the total number
of books together with the total value of the stock, to another file
*/

#include <stdio.h>
#include <stdlib.h>
#include <errno.h>

#define input_file  "a:\\chap_10\\books.txt"
#define output_file "a:\\chap_10\\report.txt"
#define read "r"
#define write "w"
#define string_length 25

FILE *open_file(const char filename[], const char mode[])
/* function to open a file in a specific mode and return the name of the
stream if it can be opened, otherwise return a NULL pointer */
{
   FILE *file;

   file = fopen(filename, mode);
   if (file == NULL)
   {
     printf("%s cannot be opened - program terminated\n", filename);
     exit(errno);
   }

   return file;
}


void process_files(FILE *books, FILE *report)
/* function to read the books file and produce a stock report */
{
    const int re_order_level = 1;

    int quantity;
    float price;
    char   title[string_length];
    int total_quantity = 0;
    float  total_price = 0.0;
```

```
        /* write headings */

        fprintf(report, "              STOCK REPORT ON BOOKS\n\n");
        fprintf(report, "quantity price              title\n\n");

        /* process each line of the books text file */

        while (! feof(books))
        {
            fscanf(books, "%d%f", &quantity, &price);
            fgets(title, string_length, books);

            fprintf(report, "%8d%6.2f", quantity, price);

            if (quantity <= re_order_level)
                fprintf(report, " *REORDER* ");
            else
                fprintf(report, "            ");

            fprintf(report, "%s", title);

            total_quantity = total_quantity + quantity;
            total_price = total_price + (price * quantity);
        }

        /* write cumulative totals */

        fprintf(report, "\n\nnumber of books in stock %3d\n", total_quantity);
        fprintf(report, "value of books in stock $%7.2f\n", total_price);
}

void main(void)
{
        FILE    *books;
        FILE    *report;

        /* attempt to open files */
        books  = open_file(input_file, read);
        report = open_file(output_file, write);

        /* process files */
        process_files(books, report);

        /* close data files */
        fclose(books);
        fclose(report);
}
```

263

Results written to the file report.txt

```
              STOCK REPORT ON BOOKS

quantity price            title

        1   8.95 *REORDER*  Art in Athens
        2   3.75           Birds of Prey
        1   7.50 *REORDER*  Eagles in the USA
        3   5.20           Gone with the Wind
        2   3.75           Hate, Lust and Love
        3   5.95           Maths for Adults
        3   3.75           Modern Farming
        3   5.20           Raiders of Planet X
        1   8.95 *REORDER*  Splitting the Atom
        1   3.75 *REORDER*  The Invisible Man
        2   3.75           The Otter
        4   5.95           The Tempest
        2   5.95           The Trojan Wars
        2   3.75           Under the Seas
        2   7.50           Vampire Bats

number of books in stock  32
value of books in stock $ 170.15
```

10.6 Reading Ahead

It was stipulated that all the text files used in the previous examples had no new-line character at the end of the last line in the file. What if they had a new-line character? What difference would it make to processing the file?

When creating a text file it is important to know whether the last line in the file is terminated with a new-line character. If a new-line exists, then the last line containing text will be processed twice unless the technique of reading ahead is adopted. **Reading ahead** involves reading a line and then testing for the end of the file. Program Example 10.3 could be modified as follows to use the reading ahead technique if a new-line had been present after the last line in the file.

```
    fscanf(data,"%f",&price);                /* READ   */
    fgets(appliance,string_length,data);     /* AHEAD  */
    while (! feof(data))                      /* TEST FOR END OF FILE */
    {
        printf("%6.2f\t%s",price, appliance);
        fscanf(data,"%f",&price);             /* READ   */
        fgets(appliance,string_length,data);  /* AHEAD  */
    }
```

Notice with the reading-ahead technique that it is necessary to duplicate the code for reading the file. The first read is made outside of the while loop prior to the test for the end of the file. The second read is made inside and at the end of the while loop but prior to the test for the end of the file.

Case Study: Word-length Frequency Analysis

In the final example in this chapter, the poem *I Watched a Blackbird* by *Thomas Hardy 1840-1928* has been created using an editor and stored on disk under the filename Hardy.txt. A listing of the poem is given here, and it is assumed that a new-line character is present at the end of the last line.

Thomas Hardy 1840-1928

> *I watched a blackbird on a budding sycamore*
> *One Easter Day, when sap was stirring twigs to the core;*
> *I saw his tongue, and crocus-coloured bill*
> *Parting and closing as he turned his trill;*
> *Then he flew down, seized on a stem of hay,*
> *And upped to where his building scheme was under way,*
> *As if so sure a nest were never shaped on spray.*

Write a program to read the text file and process each line according to the following specifications.

1. Analyze the number of letters in each word, and record a frequency count for word size. For example, if an array frequency was used to store the number of word lengths, then frequency[1] is the number of one-letter words, frequency[2] is the number of two-letter words, frequency[3] is the number of three-letter words, and so on.

2. Write each line of text to a second file. Write the frequency of word lengths in the line on the next line of the file as depicted in Figure 10.5. For example, the first line of the poem contains 3 one-letter words, 1 two-letter word, 2 seven-letter words, 1 eight-letter word, and 1 nine-letter word.

Problem Analysis - The solution to this problem requires reading a line of the poem from the file and recording the frequency of the word lengths, then writing this information to a second file. The process continues until the end-of-the-poem file is encountered. Since there is a new-line character present at the end of the last line, you must use the reading-ahead technique before testing for the end of the file.

Before each line can be processed, it is important to initialize a one-dimensional array that is used to store the frequencies of the word lengths. The contents of this array will be updated during the processing of a single line.

```
┌─────────────────────────────────────────────────────────────────────────┐
│                              Report Layout                                │
├─────────────────────────────────────────────────────────────────────────┤
│123456789012345678901234567890123456789012345678901234567890123456789     │
│                                                                           │
│I watched a blackbird on a budding sycamore                                │
│                                                                           │
│letters in word   1  2  3  4  5  6  7  8  9  10  11  12  13  14  15         │
│word frequency    3  1  0  0  0  0  2  1  1  0   0   0   0   0   0          │
│                                                                           │
│One easter day, when sap was stirring twigs to the core;                   │
│                                                                           │
│letters in word   1  2  3  4  5  6  7  8  9  10  11  12  13  14  15         │
│word frequency    0  1  5  2  1  1  0  1  0  0   0   0   0   0   0          │
│                                                                           │
│I saw his tongue, and crocus-coloured bill                                 │
│                                                                           │
│letters in word   1  2  3  4  5  6  7  8  9  10  11  12  13  14  15         │
│word frequency    1  0  3  1  0  2  0  1  0  0   0   0   0   0   0          │
└─────────────────────────────────────────────────────────────────────────┘
```

Figure 10.5 Report layout for word-length analysis

To process a single line, it is necessary to analyze individual characters in the line by testing for the end of each word and counting the number of characters in a word. Use the number of characters in the word to update the `frequency` word-length array.

When a complete line has been processed, write it to a separate file, followed by the contents of the frequency word-lengths array that is also being written to the same file.

Algorithm for the Function main

1   open input file for reading (refined into function open_file)
2   open output file for writing
3   process line of text (refined into function process_line)
4   while not end of input file
5   write information to output file (refined into function write_info)
6   process line of text
7   close input file
8   close output file

Testing for the end of the file appears in the main function. Reading ahead requires processing a line of text prior to testing for the end of the file. The function to process a line of text will contain code to read a line from the file.

Data Dictionary for the Function main - All the declarations are local to the function `main`. This function assigns streams to text files and requires an input stream `text` for reading lines of the poem and an output stream `output` for writing lines of the poem and frequencies of word lengths.

A line of a poem is stored in a one-dimensional array `line` of size `max_length` (80 characters). The frequencies of the word lengths are stored in a one-dimensional array `frequency` of size `max_char`

(15 characters) + 1. The first cell (subscript 0) of this array is not used. The frequency of words with a length of one character are stored in cell 1, of two characters are stored in cell 2, and so on.

```
FILE    *text, *output;
int     frequency[max_char+1];
char    line[max_length];
```

Algorithm for the Function process_line

3   process line of text
3.1   initialize frequency count of words (refined into the function initialize)
3.2   read line from input file
3.3   analyze words in line (refined into the function analysis)

Data Dictionary for the Function process_line - This function contains no local declarations. The function prototype is

```
process_line(FILE *filename, char line[], int frequency[]);
```

Algorithm for the Function initialize

3.1   initialize frequency count of words
3.1.1 for number of letters in word from 1 to 15
3.1.2   set frequency of words to zero

Data Dictionary for the Function initialize - The function contains one local variable, a counter used as a subscript when initializing each cell of the array `frequency` to zero. The function prototype is

```
void initialize(int frequency[]);
int  counter;
```

Algorithm for the Function analysis

3.3   analyze words in line
3.3.1 obtain first character in line
3.3.2 while not end of line and not end of string
3.3.3   if character not a word delimiter then
3.3.4   increase letter counter by 1
3.3.5   else
3.3.6   increase frequency of counter-lettered word by 1
3.3.7   initialize letter counter to zero
3.3.8   obtain next character in line

Data Dictionary for the Function analysis - In analyzing a line of text, it is necessary to check for word delimiters. Local constants are declared for the following delimiters: space, hyphen, comma, period, colon, semicolon, carriage return CR, and line feed LF.

To inspect individual characters in a line of text stored in the one-dimensional array `line`, it is necessary to declare a subscript `index` to access each cell within the array. This `index` is advanced until either its value exceeds the maximum length of the line or a null character string terminator is found.

Local declarations are also necessary for a `counter` to record the length of a word and the `character` under investigation.

The function prototype is

```
void analysis(char line[], int frequency[]);

const int null = 0;
const int CR   = 13;
const int LF   = 10;

const char space     = ' ';
const char hyphen    = '-';
const char comma     = ',';
const char period    = '.';
const char colon     = ':';
const char semi_colon = ';';

int   index   = 0;
int   counter = 0;
char  character;
```

Desk check of the function analysis - Test data are the three words "I watched a " from the first line of the poem.

index	counter	character	frequency[counter]	index<=max_length && character != null ?	character != terminator?
0	0	I		true	true
1	1	space	1	true	false
2	0	w		true	true
3	1	a		true	true
4	2	t		true	true
5	3	c		true	true
6	4	h		true	true
7	5	e		true	true
8	6	d		true	true
9	7	space	1	true	false
10	0	a		true	true
11	1	space	2	true	false

At the end of this desk check, three words have been processed and the contents of `frequency` are:

`frequency[1]` = 2 illustrating there were two words of length one character;
`frequency[2]` to `frequency[6]` remained at zero indicating there were no words having lengths of 2 characters to 6 characters;
`frequency[7]` = 1 illustrating there was one word of length seven characters.

Algorithm for the Function write_info

5   write information to output file
5.1   write line of poem to output file
5.2   write "letters in word" to output file
5.3   for number of letters in word from 1 to 15
5.4   write number of letters in word to output file
5.5   write "word frequency" to output file
5.6   for number of letters in word from 1 to 15
5.7   write word frequency to output file
5.8   write blank lines to output file

Data Dictionary for the Function write_info - This function contains one local variable used as a subscript `counter` in a `for` loop. The function prototype is

```
void write_info(FILE *filename, const char line[], const int frequency[]);
int counter;
```

Algorithm for the Function open_file - This function is identical to `open_file` found in the previous case study; therefore, will not be listed here.

Data Dictionary for the Function open_file - This is identical to the previous case study.

Figure 10.6 illustrates a structure chart that shows the hierarchy of the functions. Notice that the function `main` calls the functions `open_file`, `write_info`, and `process_line`. The function `process_line` calls the functions `initialize` and `analysis`.

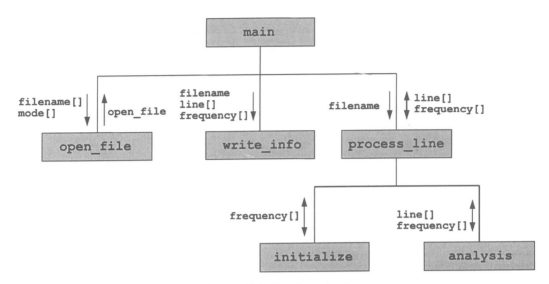

Figure 10.6 Structure chart

```
/*
chap_10\ex_6.c
program to analyze the size of words in a passage of text
*/

#include <stdio.h>
#include <stdlib.h>
#include <errno.h>

#define max_length 80
#define max_char 15
#define read "r"
#define write "w"
#define input_file "a:\\chap_10\\Hardy.txt"
#define output_file "a:\\chap_10\\results.txt"

void initialize(int frequency[])
/* function to initialize the frequency count of each word to zero */

{
    int counter;

    for (counter=1; counter <= max_char; counter++)
        frequency[counter] = 0;
}
```

```
FILE *open_file(const char filename[], const char mode[])
/* function to open a file in a specific mode and return the name of the
file if it can be opened, otherwise return NULL */
{
    FILE *file;

    file = fopen(filename, mode);
    if (file == NULL)
    {
        printf("%s cannot be opened - program terminated\n", filename);
        exit(errno);
    }
    return file;
}


void analysis(const char line[], int frequency[])
/* function to calclate the size of each word in one line of text;
the frequencies of word length are stored in an array called frequency */
{
    const int null         = 0;
    const int CR           = 13;
    const int LF           = 10;
    const char space       = ' ';
    const char hyphen      = '-';
    const char comma       = ',';
    const char period      = '.';
    const char colon       = ':';
    const char semi_colon  = ';';
    int  index   = 0;
    int  counter = 0;
    char character;

    character = line[index];
    while (index <= max_length && character != null)
    {
        if (character != space && character != hyphen &&
            character != comma && character != period &&
            character != colon && character != semi_colon &&
            character != CR && character != LF)
            counter++;
        else
        {
                frequency[counter]++;
                counter = 0;
        }
        index++;
        character = line[index];
    }
}
```

```
void write_info(FILE *filename, const char line[], const int frequency[])
/* function to copy a line to the output file (filename),
and write the frequency of word sizes on the next lines of
the output file
*/

{
    int counter;

    fprintf(filename, "%s", line);
    fprintf(filename, "\nletters in word ");

    for (counter=1; counter <= max_char; counter++)
        fprintf(filename, "%3d", counter);

    fprintf(filename, "\nword frequency  ");

    for (counter=1; counter <= max_char; counter++)
        fprintf(filename, "%3d", frequency[counter]);

    fprintf(filename, "\n\n");
}

void process_line(FILE *file, char line[], int frequency[])
/* function to read a line from the input file and return the line
as a string of characters
*/

{
    initialize(frequency);
    fgets(line, max_length, file);
    analysis(line, frequency);
}

void main(void)
{
    FILE *text, *output;
    int  frequency[max_char+1];
    char line[max_length];

    text   = open_file(input_file, read);
    output = open_file(output_file, write);

    process_line(text, line, frequency);
    while (! feof(text))
    {
        write_info(output, line, frequency);
        process_line(text, line, frequency);
    }
```

```
    fclose(text);
    fclose(output);
}
```

Results are stored on the file results.txt

I watched a blackbird on a budding sycamore

letters in word	1	2	3	4	5	6	7	8	9	10	11	12	13	14	15
word frequency	3	1	0	0	0	0	2	1	1	0	0	0	0	0	0

One easter day, when sap was stirring twigs to the core;

letters in word	1	2	3	4	5	6	7	8	9	10	11	12	13	14	15
word frequency	0	1	5	2	1	1	0	1	0	0	0	0	0	0	0

I saw his tongue, and crocus-coloured bill

letters in word	1	2	3	4	5	6	7	8	9	10	11	12	13	14	15
word frequency	1	0	3	1	0	2	0	1	0	0	0	0	0	0	0

parting and closing as he turned his trill;

letters in word	1	2	3	4	5	6	7	8	9	10	11	12	13	14	15
word frequency	0	2	2	0	1	1	2	0	0	0	0	0	0	0	0

Then he flew down, seized on a stem of hay,

letters in word	1	2	3	4	5	6	7	8	9	10	11	12	13	14	15
word frequency	1	3	1	4	0	1	0	0	0	0	0	0	0	0	0

And upped to where his building scheme was under way,

letters in word	1	2	3	4	5	6	7	8	9	10	11	12	13	14	15
word frequency	0	1	4	0	3	1	0	1	0	0	0	0	0	0	0

As if so sure a nest were never shaped on spray.

letters in word	1	2	3	4	5	6	7	8	9	10	11	12	13	14	15
word frequency	1	4	0	3	2	1	0	0	0	0	0	0	0	0	0

Summary

□ A text file is a collection of ASCII characters written in lines with a specific end-of-line marker and an end-of-file marker. A text file can be created using either an editor or a program.

□ Input and output can be redirected to files using command line parameters.

□ All input and output in C is from streams. A stream is associated with a file; however, it is not confined to disk or tape files but extends to other devices, such as keyboard, screen, and printer.

□ Files are opened and closed using the functions `fopen` and `fclose` respectively.

□ A file can be opened for reading as long as it exists. However, a file opened for writing need not already exist. If it does the original file will be overwritten. Access modes to files are `"r"` for reading and `"w"` for writing.

□ The name of a file can be input into a program in three ways:

   Implicitly at the time of writing the program.
   As a text string at run time.
   As a parameter in a command line at run time.

□ The <stdio.h> header file lists the following functions for processing text files:

   for output - `fprintf`;
   for input - `fgetc`, `fgets` and `fscanf`;
   for detecting the end of the file - `feof`;
   for detecting an error - `ferror`.

□ When creating a text file, it is important to know whether the last line in the file is terminated with a new-line character. If a new-line exists, then the last line containing text will be processed twice unless the technique of reading ahead is adopted. This technique involves reading a line and then testing for the end of the file.

Review Questions

1. What is the purpose of redirection?

2. Interpret the command line `run <a:\numbers.txt >a:\results.txt` where `run` is an executable program file.

3. If output is redirected to a file, how can you inspect the contents of the file?

4. What is a stream?

5. Name two standard streams.

6. Interpret the statement `fscanf(stdin, "%d", &integer)`.

7. How would you declare `text` in the statement `text = fopen("a:\numbers.txt", "r")`?

8. In question 7 `"r"` specifies the access mode to a file. What are the implications of using `"r"`?

9. Describe two methods to input the name of a file into a program at run time.

10. What does the function `fclose` do besides dissociating a stream from a file?

11. Describe a text file.

12. True or false - `fprintf` is used to write formatted information to a text file.

13. True or false - `fgets` is used to read a string from a text file.

14. What does the function `fgets` return?

15. True or false - the function `feof` returns zero at the end of a stream.

Programming Exercises

16. Desk check the following program segment and determine the output. The file `states.txt` contains the following lines of text:

    Arkansas
    Colorado
    Florida
    Georgia
    Illinois
    Massachusetts

```
        .
        .
        .
#define string_length 20

void main(void)
{
    FILE *text;
    char state_name[string_length];

    text = fopen("states.txt", "r");

    while (! feof(text))
    {
        fgets(state_name, string_length, text);
        printf("%s\n", state_name);
    }
        .
        .
        .
```

17. Find the errors in the following segment of code that opens a file.

```
        .
        .
        .
    FILE file;

    file = fopen(filename, "read");

    if (filename != NULL)
    {
      printf("file cannot be opened");
      exit;
    }
        .
        .
        .
```

18. If the command line to execute a program is given as run data.txt results.txt where the parameters in the main function are represented as main(int argc, char *argv[]), draw a diagram of the array argv and show its contents.

19. Desk check the following program segment. Assume the file numbers.txt contains the following data: 26 27 79 84 16.

```
    .
    .
    .
#define size 5

void main(void)
{
    FILE *text;
    int  array[size];
    int  index = 0;

    text = fopen("numbers.txt", "r");

    while (! feof(text))
    {
        fscanf(text, "%d", &array[index]);
        index++;
    }
    .
    .
    .
```

20. Desk check the following program segment and specify what will be written to the text file data.txt.

```
    .
    .
    .
    FILE *new_file;
    char letter;

    new_file = fopen("data.txt", "w");

    fprintf(new_file, "char\tcode\n\n");
    for (letter='A'; letter <= 'Z'; letter++)
      fprintf(new_file, "%c\t\t%d\n", letter, letter);
    .
    .
    .
```

Programming Problems

21. Use an editor to create a text file phrase.txt that contains the input data required for Case Study: Count the Number of Vowels in a Sentence in Chapter 8. Rerun this program using redirection, so that data is read from the text file that you have created and the output remains directed to the screen.

22. Using an editor create a text file words.txt containing a mixture of words, some of which are palindromes. The file layout should cater for one word per line. Modify Case Study: Is a Word a Palindrome? in Chapter 8 to cater for the input of words from a text file.

23. Use an editor to create a file `booze.txt` that contains the details of items of stock in a bar. Each line in the file contains the data: stock quantity, unit price, and description; for example, a line of text might contain: `3 30.00 Brandy`, which represents 3 bottles of Brandy at $30.00 per bottle.

Write a program to read each line from the text file `booze.txt` and create a report `stock.txt` similar to that illustrated in Figure 10.7, where the value of the stock is the product of the respective quantity and price.

```
                        Report Layout

12345678901234567890123456789012345678901234567890
              BAR STOCK REPORT

QUANTITY PRICE    VALUE DESCRIPTION

3         30.00   90.00 Brandy
5         18.50   92.50 Gin
5         17.00   85.00 Rum
10        15.50  155.00 Vodka
8         25.00  200.00 Whiskey

TOTAL         $   622.50
```

Figure 10.7 Report on bar stock

24. A text file `viewers.txt` contains the following three fields per line:

category code of program
estimated size of viewing audience (millions)
name of a television program

The category of program is coded using a single character as follows:

D - drama
L - light entertainment
M - music
S - science fiction

A typical record from the file might contain the following data:

`D 5.25 NYPD Blue`

The data indicate that 5.25 million viewers watched the television program NYPD Blue, and that the show is a drama.

Use an editor to create the text file with programs of your own choice so that the contents of your file are ordered on the category code as the key. Group all the drama programs together, all the light-entertainment programs together, and so on.

Write a computer program to input a category code and generate a report on the screen similar to that shown in Figure 10.8. This report lists the names of all the programs in the chosen category, the audience viewing figures, and the total number of viewers who watched programs in that category.

```
                        Report Layout

12345678901234567890123456789012345678901234567890123456789 0

 CATEGORY - DRAMA

audience          programme
millions

 5.25             NYPD Blue
 7.45             Murder She Wrote
 7.50             L.A.Law

20.20   total audience
```

Figure 10.8 Report on audience viewing figures

25. A multiple-choice questionnaire allows participants one of four possible answers per question. For example,

Question: *How many times a day do you brush your teeth?*

Answer: *a. never*
              b. once
              c. twice
              d. more than twice

In a survey it is possible to record a participant's answers as a string of letters, for example, the string

baaabdcbbbbbbdddddddaaaaacccdccccccccbbbb

may represent answers to forty questions from a questionnaire.

The string of data can at present be stored in forty bytes of storage (+ one byte for the terminating null character). If such information is to be stored for many hundreds of thousands of participants, then storage capacity of the order of Megabytes will be required.

If such strings are to be stored, then to save on storage space the strings can be compressed. For example, there is much repetition in this string

```
aaa
bbbbb
dddddd
.
.
```

If a character is repeated more than three times, then it may be encoded using a special symbol that indicates repetition @, followed by the number of characters being repeated, followed by the character being repeated.

aaa could be represented by @3a but this string does nothing to improve storage space;
bbbbb could be represented by @5b giving a saving of two bytes;
dddddd could be represented by @6d giving a saving of three bytes.

With this technique, the example string can be compressed into

<code>baaabdc@5b@6d@5acccd@9c@4b</code>

saving a total of fourteen bytes.

Create a text file `data.txt` containing lines of strings similar to the one shown in the example. The maximum string length should be restricted to 80 characters.

Write a program to read each line in the text file, encode each line using the technique described, and write the new encoded strings to both the screen and another text file `new_data.txt`. This program should maintain totals for the number of characters processed in `data.txt` and the number of characters written to the file `new_data.txt`. Use these figures to compute and display the percentage compression gained.

Extend the program to read each line in the file `new_data.txt`, decode the information, and display it on the screen.

Chapter 11

Structures and Arrays

This chapter introduces a method of representing data of different types as a single entity known as a structure.

Recall that in Chapter 8 one-dimensional arrays were introduced for the storage of data of one type only. This chapter shows how a mixture of data types may be stored in an array using structures.

We also cover the use of two-dimensional and three-dimensional arrays.

By the end of the chapter, you should have an understanding of the following topics:

- [ ] The format and organization of structures.
- [ ] Input and output of data stored as a structure.
- [ ] Structures as parameters and return values in functions.
- [ ] The union of different structures represented as a single data type.
- [ ] An array of structures.
- [ ] Searching structures in an array.
- [ ] Two-dimensional and three-dimensional arrays.

11.1 Structures

In order to treat a collection of different data types as a single entity, we need to introduce the concept of a structure. A **structure** is a collection of one or more members, which may be of different types, grouped together under a single name. In other high-level languages, a structure would be known as a record, and the collection of members would be known as fields.

Let us begin with an explanation of defining and initializing structures.

C Syntax: The generic syntax of a structure is

structure definition

```
struct tag {
        variable declarations
    };
```

where `struct` is a keyword that declares a structure designation; tag is the name of the structure, and variable declarations are the type definitions of member data items within the structure.

Figure 11.1 illustrates how a date can be divided into the members month, day, and year, where each member is of type integer.

```
  10        11        1953
 month      day       year
```

Figure 11.1 A date of birth as data in a structure

The structure illustrated in Figure 11.1 can be defined as:

```
struct date_of_birth {
                int month ;
                int day;
                int year;
            };
```

Defining a structure, as we have just done, is not the same as declaring it. Thus, we must next declare a variable of the type `struct date_of_birth`. The variable can be declared immediately with the structure definition, or separately. For example, continuing with Figure 11.1:

C Syntax:

structure declaration

```
struct date_of_birth {
                int month ;
                int day;
                int year;
            } birthday;
```

where `birthday` is the name of the variable whose type is `struct date_of_birth`. Alternatively, the variable may be declared on a separate line after the definition of the structure:

```
struct date_of_birth birthday;
```

C Syntax:

member operator (.)

Individual members of this structure are accessed by the variable name `birthday`, the **member operator** a dot (.), and the required member

```
birthday.month   birthday.day   birthday.year
```

The purpose of the member operator is to tie a specific member name to a specific structure variable, since we may have many different variable names of the same structure type.

Finally, the variable `birthday` may be initialized at the point of declaration using braces in a similar manner to initializing an array:

C Syntax:

structure initialization

```
struct date_of_birth {
                    int month ;
                    int day;
                    int year;
          } birthday = {10, 11, 1953};
```

or by assignment:

```
birthday.month = 10; birthday.day = 11; birthday.year = 1953
```

If two variables have the same structure then it is possible to assign the contents of one variable to another. For example, if two variables are defined as:

```
struct date_of_birth Fred = {3, 18, 1948};
struct date_of_birth Sue;
```

then the assignment `Sue = Fred` is legal and implies that Sue's age is the same as Fred's age.

An alternative means of dealing with structures is to define the structure as a type. The `typedef` mechanism was first introduced in Chapter 6 as a means of explicitly associating a type with an identifier. Typedef may be used in defining a structure to give a type name, not a tag, to a structure. For example,

```
typedef struct   {
                int   month;
                int   day;
                int   year;
          } date_of_birth;
```

Thus a variable `birthday`, of type `date_of_birth`, may then be declared as

```
date_of_birth birthday;
```

The author prefers this method of declaring structured types, since it more closely resembles other high-level languages.

Program Example 11.1 illustrates how a structure type `date_of_birth` is declared and used to store the members `month`, `day`, and `year` of a birthday. The contents of this structure are then displayed on a screen.

Program Example 11.1: Creation and Initialization of a Structure

```
/*
chap_11\ex_1.c
program to create a structure and display the contents
*/

#include <stdio.h>

void main(void)
{
      typedef struct {
                    int month;
                    int day;
                    int year;
                  } date_of_birth;

      date_of_birth birthday;

      printf("input a date of birth as MM DD YYYY ");
      scanf("%d%d%d", &birthday.month, &birthday.day, &birthday.year);

      printf("month %d\n", birthday.month);
      printf("day %d\n",   birthday.day);
      printf("year %d\n",  birthday.year);
}
```

Results

```
input a date of birth as MM DD YYYY 10 11 1953
month 10
day 11
year 1953
```

Note: alternative coding for the definition of the structure could have been

```
struct date_of_birth {
                    int month;
                    int day;
                    int year;
                  };
```

with the variable `birthday` being declared as

```
struct date_of_birth birthday;
```

The remainder of the program is the same.

11.2 Structures and Functions

In the previous example a structure was defined as a particular type `date_of_birth`. If data of this type is to be returned from a function, then it is acceptable to use the type in exactly the same manner as you would use any other type.

The second example is only a modification to the first example. A separate function `get_date` is used to input the date at the keyboard and return this value from the function. Notice that the function has been declared as returning the type `date_of_birth`. The declaration of this type has file scope so that it can be used in both functions without having to be declared separately in each function.

Program example 11.2: Returning the Contents of a Structure from a Function.

```
/*
chap_11\ex_2.c
program to return the contents of a structure from a function
*/

#include <stdio.h>

typedef struct {
                int month;
                int day;
                int year;
              } date_of_birth;

date_of_birth get_date(void)
{
   date_of_birth birthday;

   printf("input a date of birth as MM DD YYYY ");
   scanf("%d%d%d", &birthday.month, &birthday.day, &birthday.year);

   return birthday;
}


void main(void)
{

    date_of_birth birthday;

    birthday = get_date();

    printf("month %d\n", birthday.month);
    printf("day %d\n",   birthday.day);
    printf("year %d\n",  birthday.year);
}
```

285

Since structure types can used in the same manner as other data types, how then should we use a structure type as a parameter to a function? Once again, the first example in this chapter has been reprogrammed to include a function that returns a value for the birthday through a reference parameter and not, as in the previous example, as a value returned directly from the function.

Program Example 11.3: Returning the Contents of a Structure through a Parameter.

```
/*
chap_11\ex_3.c
program to return a structure as a parameter from a function
*/

#include <stdio.h>

typedef struct {
                int month;
                int day;
                int year;
              } date_of_birth;


void get_date(date_of_birth *birthday)
{
   printf("input a date of birth as MM DD YYYY ");
   scanf("%d%d%d", &birthday->month, &birthday->day, &birthday->year);
}

void main(void)
{
     date_of_birth birthday;

     get_date(&birthday);

     printf("month %d\n", birthday.month);
     printf("day %d\n",   birthday.day);
     printf("year %d\n",  birthday.year);
}
```

Notice from this example that the address of birthday, not the variable birthday, is passed as an argument. The corresponding formal parameter in the function get_date has been declared as a pointer to data of type date_of_birth. This technique of simulating reference parameters in C was explained fully in Chapter 5.

To store data in the appropriate fields month, day, and year of the structure requires using the contents of the item being pointed at - (*birthday).month, (*birthday).day and (*birthday).year. The parentheses are important because the member operator (.) has precedence over the

C Syntax:

structure
member
access
operator ->

indirection operator (`*`), and we want `birthday` to be evaluated as a pointer first and then directed to the `month`, `day`, and `year` members. This operation is common, but the notation is somewhat clumsy; therefore, C allows the notation `birthday->month` in place of `(*birthday).month`.

The operator `->` (a minus followed by a greater than) is known as a **structure member access operator** and is used to access the members of a structure via a pointer.

Because the members `month`, `day`, and `year` are not pointers, we must retain the address operator (`&`) in the `scanf` statement.

11.3 Unions - Variant Records

When information can be represented in more than one format, it is possible to define the different formats in a **union**. Although the compiler allocates sufficient storage to accommodate the largest member of the union, a union can hold only one of its components at a time. In principle you are using different identifiers to access the data in one set of memory locations. The declaration of a union looks exactly the same as the declaration of a structure; however, the keyword `union` replaces the keyword `struct`.

We again turn to an example that involves the representation of a date. Dates as you know can be written in different formats, for example, 6 / 6 /1944 and June 6 1944. The first date is composed of integers separated by slashes, and the second is a string of characters.

The structure of the date in the numeric format can be defined as:

```
typedef struct  {
               int month;
               int day;
               int year;
          } numeric_date;
```

The date in the string format can be defined as

```
char date_string[20];
```

If either format for the date is to be used in a program, then it is possible to represent both dates as one type using a union.

C Syntax:

union

```
typedef union {
               numeric_date   N_date;
               char           date_string[20];
          } dates;
```

It is then possible to declare a date as

```
dates D_Day;
```

and use either representation of the date, as the following example illustrates.

287

Program Example 11.4: Demonstration of a Union to Represent Dates in Various Formats

```c
/*
chap_11\ex_4.c
program to demonstrate a union of structures
*/

#include <stdio.h>
#include <stdlib.h>
#include <errno.h>
#include <ctype.h>

char menu(void)
{
   char reply;

   printf("do you want to input a date as\n");
   printf("N[umber]\n");
   printf("S[tring]\n\n");
   printf("input N or S ");

   reply = getchar();
   getchar();
   reply = toupper(reply);

   return reply;
}


void main(void)
{

   typedef struct {
                   int month;
                   int day;
                   int year;
                  } numeric_date;


   typedef union  {
                   numeric_date  N_date;
                   char          string_date[20];
                  } dates;

   dates D_Day;
   char  reply;
```

```
reply = menu();

  switch (reply)
{
    case 'N': printf("input date in format MM DD YYYY: ");
              scanf("%d%d%d", &D_Day.N_date.month,
                              &D_Day.N_date.day,
                              &D_Day.N_date.year);
            break;
    case 'S': printf("input date as one string: ");
              gets(D_Day.string_date);
              break;
    default : printf("wrong code - program terminated\n");
              exit(errno);
}


  printf("date input was ");
  if (reply == 'N')
      printf("%d/%d/%d\n", D_Day.N_date.month,
                           D_Day.N_date.day,
                           D_Day.N_date.year);
  else
      printf("%s", D_Day.string_date);

}
```

Results from program being run twice

```
do you want to input a date as
N[umber]
S[tring]

input N or S N

input date in format MM DD YYYY: 6 6 1944
date input was 6/6/1944

do you want to input a date as
N[umber]
S[tring]

input N or S S

input date as one string: June 6 1944
date input was June 6 1944
```

11.4 Structures and One-dimensional Arrays

In Chapter 8 we noted that the contents of all the cells in a one-dimensional array must be of the same data type. In other words, an array can contain all integers, all reals, or all characters, but not a mixture of each type. This statement is perfectly true; however, it does not preclude a mixture of data types being stored in each cell of an array provided the types come under the umbrella of a structure.

Program Example 11.1 can be extended to store more than one structure. The variable name `birth-day` needs to be redefined as an array that will store records of type `date_of_birth`:

```
date_of_birth  birthdays[5];
```

Each record that is input at the keyboard can then be stored into consecutive locations of this five-cell array, as depicted in Figure 11.2. When all five records have been stored, the contents of the array is displayed on a screen.

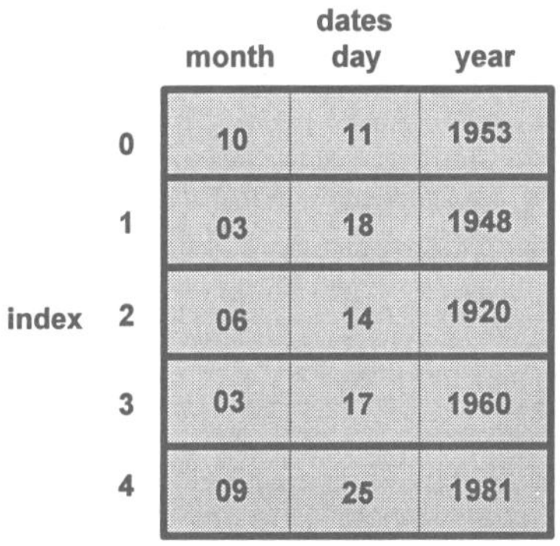

Figure 11.2 An array of records

Program Example 11.5: A One-dimensional Array of Records

```
/*
chap_11\ex_5.c
program to create an array of records and display the contents
*/

#include <stdio.h>

void main(void)
{
        typedef struct {
                        int month;
                        int day;
                        int year;
                    } date_of_birth;
```

```
date_of_birth birthdays[5] = {{10,11,1953},
                              { 3,18,1948},
                              { 6,14,1920},
                              { 3,17,1960},
                              { 9,25,1981}};
int index;

for (index=0; index < 5; index++)
     printf("%-3d%-3d%4d\n", birthdays[index].month,
                             birthdays[index].day,
                             birthdays[index].year);

}
```

Results

```
10 11 1953
3  18 1948
6  14 1920
3  17 1960
9  25 1981
```

Notice the use of braces when initializing the members of a structure, each data record must be contained within braces, and the initialization of the array is contained within outer braces. If not enough values are used to assign all the members of a structure, the remaining members are assigned the value zero by default.

It is possible for a member of a structure to also be another structure. For instance, in Figure 11.3 the structure has two fields: name and DOB. However, DOB has a data type date_of_birth, where date_of_birth had previously been defined as a structure type. As Figure 11.3 illustrates, a single member DOB of a structure can itself be a structure containing the fields month, day, and year.

Figure 11.3 A structure within a structure

The next program is merely an extension of the previous program. Instead of storing records containing dates of birth in an array, it stores the names of people and their corresponding dates of birth in an array. Figure 11.4 illustrates the storage of the new records in the array.

291

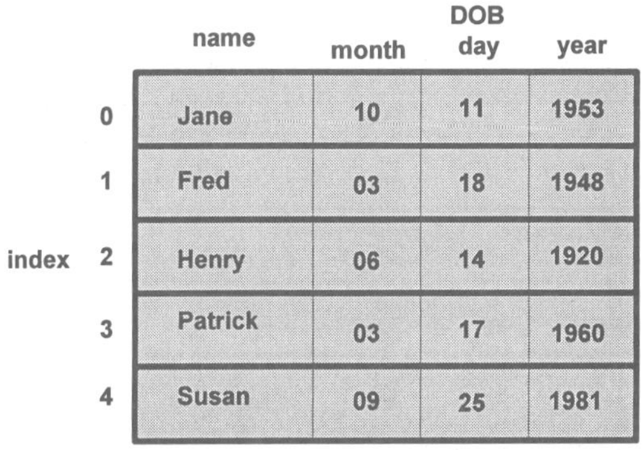

Figure 11.4 An array of records

The program illustrates that a structure must be defined before it can be used to define the data type of members in another structure.

Program Example 11.6: Defining a Structure that Lies Within Another Structure

```c
/*
chap_11\ex_6.c
program to create an array of records and display the contents
*/

#include <stdio.h>

void main(void)
{
    typedef struct {
                int    month;
                int    day;
                int    year;
            } date_of_birth;

    typedef struct {
                char            name[80];
                date_of_birth   birth_date;
            } names_dates;

    names_dates birthdays[5] =  {{"Jane",    10,11,1953},
                                {"Fred",     3, 18,1948},
                                {"Henry",    6, 14,1920},
                                {"Patrick",3, 17,1960},
                                {"Susan",    9, 25,1981}};
    int index;
```

292

```
    for (index=0; index < 5; index++)
        printf("%s\t%-3d%-3d%4d\n", birthdays[index].name,
                                    birthdays[index].birth_date.month,
                                    birthdays[index].birth_date.day,
                                    birthdays[index].birth_date.year);
}
```

Results

```
Jane       10 11 1953
Fred        3 18 1948
Henry       6 14 1920
Patrick     3 17 1960
Susan       9 25 1981
```

Program Example 11.7: A Serial Search of an Array

The final program in this section is an extension of the program to create an array of names and dates of birth. Having initialized the data in an array, the user is invited to type the name of a person, the array is searched for that name, and if a match is found, the date of birth for that person is displayed.

The method of searching the array is straightforward. Start at the first cell in the array and compare the name in the cell with the name input. If a match exits, return the subscript of cell. If there is no match, move to the next cell in the array and test again for a match. This process continues until either a match is found or there is no more data to inspect in the array. If no match is possible then the size of the array is returned to indicate that the array was searched until there was no more data to compare.

```
/*
chap_11\ex_7.c
program to create an array of records and given the name
of a person search the array for their date of birth
*/

#include <stdio.h>
#include <string.h>

#define max_char 80
#define array_size 5

typedef struct {
                int   month;
                int   day;
                int   year;
            } date_of_birth;
```

293

```
typedef struct {
                char            name[max_char];
                date_of_birth   birth_date;
            } names_dates;

int search(const char whose_birthday[], const names_dates birthdays[])
/* function to search the array and return the value of the index
when a match for the name is found, otherwise it returns the size
of the array */
{
    int index = 0;

    while (index != array_size)
    {
        if (strcmp(whose_birthday, birthdays[index].name) != 0)
            index++;
        else
            return index;
    }
    return index;
}

void main(void)
{
    names_dates birthdays[array_size] = {{"Jane",    10,11,1953},
                                        {"Fred",    3, 18,1948},
                                        {"Henry",   6, 14,1920},
                                        {"Patrick",3, 17,1960},
                                        {"Susan",   9, 25,1981}};

    char        whose_birthday[max_char];
    int         index;

    do
    {
      printf("name? ");
      gets(whose_birthday);

      index = search(whose_birthday, birthdays);

      if (index == array_size)
        printf("name not found\n");
      else
        printf("birthday %-3d%-3d%4d\n", birthdays[index].birth_date.month,
                                        birthdays[index].birth_date.day,
                                        birthdays[index].birth_date.year);
    } while (index != array_size);

}
```

Results

```
name? Henry
birthday  6  14 1920
name? Patrick
birthday  3  17 1960
name? Jane
birthday 10 11 1953
name? George
name not found
```

11.5 Two-dimensional Arrays

An array is not confined to one dimension (one subscript or index). In fact, an array can be extended to two dimensions and beyond in order to provide a flexible data structure for the solution to a problem. A two-dimensional array is a repetition of a one-dimensional array. The structure can be thought of as a matrix or grid. In Figure 11.5 the two-dimensional array named matrix is composed from three one-dimensional arrays.

Figure 11.5 A two-dimensional array

C Syntax: The declaration of the two-dimensional array in Figure 11.5 is given as

declaration of a two-dimensional array

```
int matrix[3][6];
```

Access to any element in the two-dimensional array is through a row subscript followed by a column subscript, for example, matrix[0][5] = 9; matrix[2][0] = 13; matrix[1][2] = 0.

The method to initialize the contents of the two-dimensional array is similar to the method used in one-dimensional arrays:

```
int matrix[3][6] = {{16,21,8,3,-7,9},
                    {-3,11,0,5,9,7},
                    {13,7,-64,19,14,2}};
```

The first row of initialization corresponds to the first row of the array, the second row of initialization corresponds to the second row of the array, and so on. If a row of initialization values does not contain enough values, then the remaining elements are set to zero. If there are not enough rows of initialization values, then the remaining rows are set to zero.

295

The contents of a two-dimensional array can be accessed and displayed using a double loop, as follows:

```
for (row=0; row < 3; row++)
{
   for (column=0; column < 6; column++)
     printf("%d\t", matrix[row][column]);

   printf("\n");
}
```

A desk check of the preceding code indicates how the `row` and `column` loop control variables are used to gain access to the cells of the two-dimensional array.

row	column	(row<3)?	(column<6)?	matrix[row][column]
0	0	true	true	16
0	1	true	true	21
0	2	true	true	8
0	3	true	true	3
0	4	true	true	-7
0	5	true	true	9
0	6	true	false	
1	0	true	true	-3
1	1	true	true	11
1	2	true	true	0
1	3	true	true	5
1	4	true	true	9
1	5	true	true	7
1	6	true	false	
2	0	true	true	13
2	1	true	true	7
2	2	true	true	-64
2	3	true	true	19
2	4	true	true	14
2	5	true	true	2
2	6	true	false	
3		false		

The following program stores the numbers found in the array depicted in Figure 11.5 and sums and displays the numbers in each column and the numbers in each row.

Program Example 11.8: Initializing and Processing a Two-dimensional Array

```
/*
chap_11\ex_8.c
program to store numbers in a two-dimensional array, display the contents
of the array and calculate and display the sum of each row and the sum of
each column
*/
```

```c
#include <stdio.h>

#define num_rows 3
#define num_cols 6

void display(const int matrix[][num_cols])
/* function to display the matrix */
{
    int row, column;

    for (row=0; row != num_rows; row++)
    {
        for (column=0; column != num_cols; column++)
            printf("%6d", matrix[row][column]);
        printf("\n");
    }
    printf("\n");
}

void sum_row(const int matrix[][num_cols])
/* function to sum and display numbers in each row */
{
    int row, column, row_sum;

    for (row=0; row != num_rows; row++)
    {
        row_sum = 0;
        for (column=0; column != num_cols; column++)
            row_sum = row_sum + matrix[row][column];
        printf("sum of row %d is %d\n", row, row_sum);
    }
    printf("\n");
}


void sum_column(const int matrix[][num_cols])
/* function to sum and display numbers in each column */
{
    int row, column, column_sum;

    for (column=0; column != num_cols; column++)
    {
        column_sum = 0;
        for (row=0; row != num_rows; row++)
            column_sum = column_sum + matrix[row][column];
        printf("sum of column %d is %d\n", column, column_sum);
    }
    printf("\n");
}
```

```
void main(void)
{
        int matrix[num_rows][num_cols] = {{16,21,8,3,-7,9},
                                          {-3,11,0,5,9,7},
                                          {13,7,-64,19,14,2}};

        /* display the contents of the array */
        display(matrix);

        /* display sum of each row */
        sum_row(matrix);

        /* display sum of each column */
        sum_column(matrix);
}
```

C Syntax:

two-dimensional array parameters

Notice that in passing a two-dimensional array as an argument, it is necessary to state at least the number of columns in the respective formal-parameter array. However, it is acceptable to declare both the number of rows and columns in the formal-parameter array.

The formal parameters have been declared as constant, since the functions do not change the contents of the array.

Results

```
   16    21    8    3   -7    9
   -3    11    0    5    9    7
   13     7  -64   19   14    2

sum of row 0 is 50
sum of row 1 is 29
sum of row 2 is -9

sum of column 0 is 26
sum of column 1 is 39
sum of column 2 is -56
sum of column 3 is 27
sum of column 4 is 16
sum of column 5 is 18
```

11.6 Three-dimensional Arrays

It is possible to create an array with more than two dimensions. A three-dimensional array is a repetition of two-dimensional arrays, a four-dimensional array is a repetition of three-dimensional arrays , and so on.

Figure 11.6 illustrates a three-dimensional array that consists of 4 two-dimensional arrays; each two-dimensional array consists of 2 one-dimensional arrays; each one-dimensional array contains 4 cells. Hence, the dimensions of the three-dimensional array are described as `[4][2][4]`, and since these arrays contain integers, a declaration for the complete structure might be `int array [4][2][4]`.

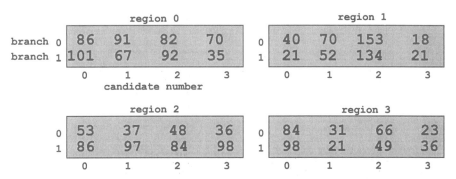

Figure 11.6 A three-dimensional array

The array is used to store the votes cast for the election of a union representative.

There are four regions in a city where voting takes place; these are designated regions 0, 1, 2, and 3 corresponding to the 4 two-dimensional arrays.

There are two union branches in every region; these are designated branches 0 and 1 corresponding to the 2 one-dimensional arrays in each region.

Finally, there are four candidates in the election; these are designated candidate numbers 0, 1, 2, and 3 corresponding to the 4 cells in each one-dimensional array.

In the program that follows, the three-dimensional array illustrated in Figure 11.6 has been initialized at the point of declaration. Pay particular attention to the grouping and the use of braces in the initialization of the array. This grouping corresponds with the data illustrated in Figure 11.6. Notice that each line in this initialization corresponds to the initialization of a two-dimensional array.

The program contains two functions in addition to the `main` function. Function `total_votes` returns the total number of votes cast for all the candidates. This calculation is performed by summing for each region and for each branch the votes cast for the four candidates.

The second function `candidate_votes` returns the number of votes cast for a particular candidate in all regions and all branches.

The purpose of the program is to display the percentage vote cast for each candidate. This figure is calculated for each candidate by dividing the number of votes cast for a particular candidate by the total number of votes and converting the fractional result into a percentage.

As a means of becoming familiar with the use of loop control variables to access the cells of a three-dimensional array, you are advised to desk check the code for the functions `total_votes` and `candidate_votes` before progressing with the remainder of the chapter.

Program Example 11.9: Initialization and Processing of a Three-dimensional Array

```c
/*
chap_11\ex_9.c
program to demonstrate a three-dimensional array
*/

#include <stdio.h>

#define regions 4
#define branches 2
#define candidates 4

int total_votes(const int three_D_array[][branches][candidates])
/* function to return the total number of votes cast for all candidates */
{
    int region, branch, candidate;
    int sum = 0;

    for (region=0; region != regions; region++)
    {
        for (branch=0; branch != branches; branch++)
        {
            for (candidate=0; candidate != candidates; candidate++)
            {
                sum = sum + three_D_array[region][branch][candidate];
            }
        }
    }

    return sum;
}


int candidate_votes(const int three_D_array[][branches][candidates], int candidate)
/* function to return the total number of votes cast for a specific candidate */
{
    int region, branch;
    int sum = 0;

    for (region=0; region != regions; region++)
    {
        for (branch=0; branch !=branches; branch++)
            sum = sum + three_D_array[region][branch][candidate];
    }
    return sum;
}
```

```
void main(void)
{
   int array[regions][branches][candidates] = {{{86,91,82, 70},{101,67,92, 35}},
                                                {{40,70,153,18},{21, 52,134,21}},
                                                {{53,37,48, 36},{86, 97,84, 98}},
                                                {{84,31,66, 23},{98, 21,49, 36}}};

   int   candidate;
   int   total;                /* total votes cast for all candidates */
   float percentage_vote;        /* percentage votes cast for any one candidate */

   total = total_votes(array);

   printf("candidate    percentage\n");
   printf("number       total vote\n\n");

   for (candidate=0; candidate != candidates; candidate++)
   {
      percentage_vote = 100.0 * ((float)candidate_votes(array,candidate)/(float)total)
      printf("%d            %4.1f\n", candidate, percentage_vote);
   }
}
```

Results

```
candidate    percentage
number       total vote

0            27.4
1            22.4
2            34.0
3            16.2
```

C Syntax:

three-dimensional array parameters

Notice that in passing a three-dimensional array as an argument, it is necessary to state at least the number of rows and columns in the respective formal-parameter array. However, it is acceptable to declare all three subscripts in the formal-parameter array.

The formal parameters have been declared as constant, since the functions do not change the contents of the array.

Case Study: Calculate Rainfall Over an Island

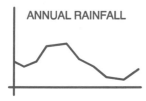

ANNUAL RAINFALL

The annual rainfall is recorded on a monthly basis over four regions of an island: North, South, East and West. Design and write a program to read rainfall data from a text file and store the data in a two-dimensional array. Calculate the average rainfall for each region over the year and the driest month taking the average rainfall for the four regions. The following table is an indication of the data.

Regions \ *Months*	Jan	Feb	Mar	Apr	May	Jun	Jul	Aug	Sep	Oct	Nov	Dec
North	14	13	11	9	5	3	1	1	4	8	9	12
South	17	18	15	13	11	9	7	8	9	10	13	15
East	9	8	6	4	2	1	0	1	3	7	9	10
West	12	11	9	6	4	2	1	3	5	8	10	13

The screen layout for the output from the program follows.

```
                        Screen Layout

12345678901234567890123456789012345678901234567890123456789012345678901234567890

                    rainfall
region      total       average
North       90          7
South       145         12
East        60          5
West        84          7

Jan Feb Mar Apr May Jun Jul Aug Sep Oct Nov Dec
13  12  10  8   5   3   2   3   5   8   10  12

dryest month is Jul
```

Problem Analysis - It is evident from the screen layout that the names of the four regions and the names of the months need to be displayed. These can be displayed as string literals or as the respective contents of 2 two-dimensional arrays. The latter approach will lead to succinct programming.

The first two-dimensional array to store the names of the months has twelve rows and four columns. If a three-character abbreviation is used for each month, then four columns will be needed for the three letters plus the null terminator. The second two-dimensional array to store the names of the regions has four rows and six columns. The longest string has five characters plus the null terminator. Both arrays are shown in Figure 11.7

```
   row     column          row     column
           0123                    012345

    0       Jan            0       North
    1       Feb            1       South
    2       Mar            2       East
    3       Apr            3       West
    4       May
    5       Jun          char regions[4][6]
    6       Jul
    7       Aug
    8       Sep
    9       Oct
   10       Nov
   11       Dec
```

char months[12][4]

Figure 11.7 Arrays to store the months and regions

To display the contents of either array, you do not need to use a column subscript. For example to display the abbreviation for the month of March printf("%s", months[2]) is all that is required. Similarly to display the region South printf("%s", regions[1]) is sufficient.

The solution to the problem divides into three areas:

1. Initialize the three two-dimensional arrays with the rainfall data, months, and regions, respectively. Read the rainfall data into the array from a text file. Initialize the arrays containing months and regions at declaration.

2. Calculate and display the average rainfall for each region.

3. Calculate and display by month the average rainfall in all regions and conclude which month is the driest.

Algorithm for the Function main

1. initialize the two-dimensional array with annual rainfall for regions
2. calculate and display the total and average rainfall for the regions
3. calculate and display the average rainfall for the regions and the driest month

Data dictionary for the Function main - This will contain declarations and initializations for the array to hold the names of the months and for the array to hold the names of the regions. The two-dimensional array used to store the monthly rainfall over the four regions is also declared.

```
char months[][4] = {"Jan","Feb","Mar","Apr","May","Jun",
                    "Jul","Aug","Sep","Oct","Nov","Dec"};
char regions[][6] = {"North","South","East","West"};
int rainfall[4][12];
```

Algorithm for the Function initialize

A text file will contain the following lines; each line represents a region's monthly rainfall.

14	13	11	9	5	3	1	1	4	8	9	12
17	18	15	13	11	9	7	8	9	10	13	15
9	8	6	4	2	1	0	1	3	7	9	10
2	11	9	6	4	2	1	3	5	8	10	13

1. initialize the two-dimensional array with annual rainfall for regions

1.1   open file to be read
1.2   if file cannot be opened, abandon program
1.3   set region subscript to zero
1.4   while not end of file
1.5   for every month
1.6   read file and store datum in rainfall array at the cell given by region and month
1.7   increase region subscript by 1
1.8   close file

Data Dictionary for the Function initialize - The formal-parameter list contains one entry - the two-dimensional array used to store the rainfall. There are three local variables: a file pointer to a stream that is associated with a physical file and two subscripts used to index the two-dimensional array. The prototype for the function is

```
void initialize(int rainfall[][max_months]);

FILE *filename;
int  region, month;
```

Algorithm for the Function average_rainfall

2. calculate and display the total and average rainfall for the regions

2.1   display the headings for total and average rainfall table

2.2   for each region
2.3   display the name of region
2.4   initialize total rainfall to zero

2.5   for each month
2.6   increase total rainfall by the rainfall for the month

2.7   calculate and display average annual rainfall for the region

Data Dictionary for the Function average_rainfall - The formal-parameter list for this function contains the array used to store the rainfall and the array used to store the names of the regions. Since the contents of both these arrays will not be changed by the function, they are both declared as being constants. The function does not return a value. There is a requirement to declare local variables to control the `for` loops for the regions and the months and local variables to store the total rainfall and the average rainfall over the twelve months. The function prototype is

```
void average_rainfall(const int  rainfall[][max_months],
                      const char regions[][6]);
int  region, month;
int  total_by_region, average_by_region;
```

Desk Check - For the test data, refer to data on rainfall per region per month. This data will be stored in a two-dimensional array with rows representing regions and columns representing months.

Desk check of the function average_rainfall (excludes screen output)

region	0	0	0	0	0	0	0	0	0	0	0	0
month	0	1	2	3	4	5	6	7	8	9	10	11
rainfall[region][month]	14	13	11	9	5	3	1	1	4	8	9	12
total_by_region	14	27	38	47	52	55	56	57	61	69	78	90
average_by_region												7

region	1	1	1	1	1	1	1	1	1	1	1	1
month	0	1	2	3	4	5	6	7	8	9	10	11
rainfall[region][month]	17	18	15	13	11	9	7	8	9	10	13	15
total_rainfall	17	35	50	63	74	83	90	98	107	117	130	145
average_rainfall												12

region	2	2	2	2	2	2	2	2	2	2	2	2
month	0	1	2	3	4	5	6	7	8	9	10	11
rainfall[region][month]	9	8	6	4	2	1	0	1	3	7	9	10
total_rainfall	9	17	23	27	29	30	30	31	34	41	50	60
average_rainfall												5

region	3	3	3	3	3	3	3	3	3	3	3	3
month	0	1	2	3	4	5	6	7	8	9	10	11
rainfall[region][month]	12	11	9	6	4	2	1	3	5	8	10	13
total_rainfall	12	23	32	38	42	44	45	48	53	61	71	84
average_rainfall												7

Algorithm for the Function monthly_rainfall

3. calculate and display the average rainfall for the regions and the driest month

3.1   for each month
3.2   display the name of the month

3.3   initialize amount of rain to a large value
3.4   for each month
3.5   initialize total rainfall to zero
3.6   for each region
3.7   increase total rainfall by rainfall for region for that month
3.8   calculate average rainfall over the four regions for that month

3.9   display average rainfall

3.10   if average rainfall < amount of rain
3.11   set amount of rain to average rainfall
3.12   set driest month to month

3.13   display driest month

Data Dictionary for the Function monthly_rainfall - The formal parameter list for this function contains the array used to store the rainfall and the array used to store the names of the months. Since the function does not change the contents of these arrays, they are described as constants. The function does not return a value. There is a requirement to declare local integer variables for the indexes region, month, and the driest month; totals for the amount of rain and the total rainfall; and the average rainfall over all the regions per month. The prototype of the function is

```
void monthly_rainfall(const int rainfall[][max_months],
                      const char months[][4]);

int region, month;
int driest_month;
int amount_of_rain, total_rainfall;
int average_by_month;
```

Desk Check - For the test data, refer to data on rainfall per region per month. This data will be stored in a two-dimensional array with rows representing regions and columns representing months.

Desk check of the function monthly_rainfall (excludes screen output and gives a sample for January, July, and December only).

average_rainfall	32767				13
month	0				
region	0	1	2	3	
rainfall[region][month]	14	17	9	12	
total_rainfall	14	31	40	52	
average				13	
(average < average_rainfall)?				true	
driest_month					0

.

average_rainfall	3				2
month	6				
region	0	1	2	3	
rainfall[region][month]	1	7	0	1	
total_rainfall	1	8	8	9	
average				2	
(average < average_rainfall)?				true	
driest_month					6

.

average_rainfall	10				12
month	11				
region	0	1	2	3	
rainfall[region][month]	12	15	10	13	
total_rainfall	12	27	37	50	
average				12	
(average < average_rainfall)?				false	
driest_month					6

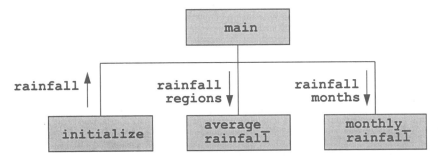

Figure 11.8 Structure chart of the program

```c
/*
chap_11\ex_10.c
program to store in a two-dimensional array the rainfall in each of four
regions per month, taken over the period of a year; calculate the
average rainfall for each region over the year and the driest month
taking the total rainfall for the four regions
*/

#include <stdio.h>
#include <stdlib.h>
#include <errno.h>
#include <limits.h>

#define data_file "a:\\chap_11\\rain.txt"
#define read "r"

#define max_regions 4
#define max_months 12

void initialize(int rainfall[][max_months])
/* function to read rainfall from file */
{
   FILE *filename;
   int region, month;

   filename = fopen(data_file, read);
   if (filename == NULL)
   {
     printf("file cannot be opened - program terminated\n");
     exit(errno);
   }

   region = 0;
   while (! feof(filename))
   {
      for (month=0; month != max_months; month++)
      {
         fscanf(filename, "%d", &rainfall[region][month]);
      }

      region++;
   }

   fclose(filename);

}
```

```
void average_rainfall(const int rainfall[][max_months], const char regions[][6])
/* function to calculate and display the total and average
annual rainfall over four regions */
{
        int region, month;
        int total_by_region, average_by_region;

        /* print heading */
        printf("        \t\t         rainfall\n");
        printf("region\t\tttotal\t\taverage\n");

        /* calculate the average rainfall for each region */
        for (region=0; region != max_regions; region++)
        {
                printf("%s\t\t", regions[region]);
                total_by_region = 0;

                for (month=0; month != max_months; month++)
                    total_by_region = total_by_region + rainfall[region][month];

                average_by_region = total_by_region / max_months;
                printf("%d\t\t%d\n", total_by_region, average_by_region);
        }
}

void monthly_rainfall(const int rainfall[][max_months], const char months[][4])
/* function to calculate and display the average rainfall per month
for all of the regions and the driest month on the island */
{
        int region, month;
        int driest_month;
        int amount_of_rain, total_rainfall;
        int average_by_month;

        printf("\n\n");

        /* display the names of the months */
        for (month=0; month < max_months; month++)
            printf("%s ", months[month]);
        printf("\n");

        /* calculate the driest month taking the total rainfall in all regions */
        amount_of_rain = INT_MAX;
        for (month=0; month < max_months; month++)
        {
                total_rainfall = 0;
                for (region=0; region < max_regions; region++)
                    total_rainfall = total_rainfall + rainfall[region][month];
                average_by_month = total_rainfall / max_regions;
```

```
            printf("%-4d", average_by_month);

            if (average_by_month < amount_of_rain)
            {
                amount_of_rain = average_by_month;
                driest_month = month;
            }
        }

        printf("\n\ndriest month is %s\n", months[driest_month]);
}

void main(void)
{

    char months[][4]  = {"Jan","Feb","Mar","Apr","May","Jun",
                         "Jul","Aug","Sep","Oct","Nov","Dec"};

    char regions[][6] = {"North","South","East","West"};

    int rainfall[max_regions][max_months];

    initialize(rainfall);
    average_rainfall(rainfall, regions);
    monthly_rainfall(rainfall, months);
}
```

Results

```
                    rainfall
region          total           average
North           90              7
South           145             12
East            60              5
West            84              7

Jan Feb Mar Apr May Jun Jul Aug Sep Oct Nov Dec
13  12  10  8   5   3   2   3   5   8   10  12

driest month is Jul
```

Case Study: Student Examination Results

The results of students taking four examinations are stored as records containing the following fields:

☐ A unique student number in the range 100 to 999.

☐ The name of the student (that may have duplicates in other records).

☐ The percentage marks in the four examinations.

Design and write a program that reads the student data from a text file and stores the records in an array; the contents of the array may be searched on student number or name. If a match is found for either the number or the name, then display the contents of the appropriate record together with the average mark attained over the four examinations.

Since the student number is unique, only one record may exist for a given number. However, this is not the case for a student name. Several students may have the same name; therefore, if a match for the name is found, the search must continue for further possible matches and display the required information after each match.

Problem Analysis - The structure of a record can be defined as

```
typedef struct    {
                  int   number;
                  char name[80];
                  int   marks[4];
              } record;
```

with the array containing the records being declared as

```
record students[number_of_students];
```

The arrays that are used in the solution to this problem are illustrated in Figure 11.9. Notice in this illustration that the array students contains ten records. The name of the student is a character string that must be represented as a separate array of characters. The four marks are stored in a separate array of integers.

311

```
100 Rankin,W    45 55 65 75
150 Jones,D     60 80 90 75
250 Smith,P     90 80 45 60
300 Davies,J    70 65 55 40
400 Smith,P     40 50 60 55
450 Adams,C     25 40 35 40
455 Collins,Z 55 87 43 20
501 Evans,M     65 75 70 95
525 Jones,D     45 80 75 55
550 Owens,H     45 55 65 70
```

`record students[number_of_students]`

`char name[80]`

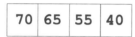

`int marks[4]`

Figure 11.9 Arrays used in the solution

The screen layout indicates the functionality of the program. From the menu the user can choose (1) to search on the student number, (2) to search on the student name, or (3) to finish using the program.

If the request is (1), the user is asked for the student number. If a match is found between the number and a record stored in the array, then the matched record is displayed and the average for the examination marks calculated and displayed. If the student number does not exist, the system prompts the user to choose from the menu again.

If the request is (2), the user is asked for the name of the student. If the name is repeated in the array of records, a record is displayed for each occurrence of the name and the average is calculated and displayed as before. If the name does not exist, the system prompts the user to make another choice.

```
┌─────────────────────────────────────────────────────────────┐
│                      Screen Layout                          │
│─────────────────────────────────────────────────────────────│
│ 12345678901234567890123456789012345678901234567890123456789 0│
│                                                             │
│ 1 - search on number                                        │
│ 2 - search on name                                          │
│ 3 - finish                                                  │
│                                                             │
│ ? 1                                                         │
│ input student number 300                                    │
│                                                             │
│ 300 Davies,J    70  65  55  40   average 57                 │
│                                                             │
│ 1 - search on number                                        │
│ 2 - search on name                                          │
│ 3 - finish                                                  │
│                                                             │
│ ? 2                                                         │
│ input student name Jones,D                                  │
│                                                             │
│ 150 Jones,D     60  80  90  75   average 76                 │
│ 525 Jones,D     45  80  75  55   average 63                 │
│                                                             │
│ 1 - search on number                                        │
│ 2 - search on name                                          │
│ 3 - finish                                                  │
│                                                             │
│ ? 3                                                         │
│                                                             │
└─────────────────────────────────────────────────────────────┘
```

In the development of this program it will be necessary to design and code functions to do the following.

A function `initialize` reads a text file containing data for each student and stores this information in the `students` array.

A function `search_number` searches the `students` array for the student number. If the number is found, the function returns the value of the index; else it returns the size of the array. Since the subscripting of an array starts at zero, the last entry in the array will appear at the subscript given by the number of records stored minus 1; therefore, returning the size of the array will indicate that the student number cannot be found.

A function `search_name` searches the `students` array for a student name. If the name is found, the function returns the value of the index; else it returns the size of the array. This function would work well if there were no duplicate names in the array. As it is currently described, it will always return the index of the first occurrence of a name and not the successive indexes. One solution is to introduce a second formal-parameter that marks the position in the array at which searching must take place. By changing the value of this parameter, it will be possible to step through the array every time a match is found.

A function `display_record` displays the contents of a record and requires a parameter that indicates the position of the record in the `students` array.

313

A function `average_mark` calculates and returns the average mark for a student and requires a parameter that indicates the position of the record in the `students` array.

Algorithm for the Function main

1. initialize the one-dimensional array with records for students
2. do
3.   display menu
4.   input menu code

5.   switch menu code
6.   '1':   input student number
7.   set index to value returned by function search_number
8.   if index not equal to the number of students
9.   call function to display_record
10.   display value returned by function average_mark
11.   '2':   input student name
12.   initialize start_at index to zero
13.   while start_at index less than number of students do
14.   set index to the value returned by the function search_name
15.   if index not equal to the number of students
16.   call function to display_record
17.   display value returned by function average_mark
18.   set start_at to value of index plus one
19.   '3':   set boolean flag for more to false
20.   default: display error message

21. while more data

Data Dictionary for the Function main - The array used to store student records must be declared. The function contains local variables to represent a student number, a student name, a menu code, and two integer indexes to gain access to the array.

```
record  students[number_of_students];
char    menu_code;
int     student_number;
char    student_name;
int     index;
int     start_at;
```

Algorithm for the function initialize

1. initialize the one-dimensional array with records for students

1.1	*open file to be read*
1.2	*if file cannot be opened abandon program*
1.3	*while not end of file*
1.4	*read datum and student number and store in array*
1.5	*read name of student and store in array*
1.6	*for every examination mark*
1.7	*read datum and store in array of marks*
1.8	*increase record index by 1*

Note: A student number and a student name appear on one line of the text file, and the student's four examination marks appear on the next line of the file. The format of these pairs of lines are repeated for each student held on the file. For example,

```
100Rankin,W
45 55 65 75
150Jones,D
60 80 90 75
      .
      .
```

When reading a student name from the file using the function `fgets`, the new-line character that appears after each name in the file is stored in the character string array used to store the name. No null character has been appended to the name. For this reason it is necessary to replace the stored new-line character with a null character in order to terminate the string correctly.

Data Dictionary for the Function initialize - This function contains one formal parameter: the array used to contain the records of the students. The information read from the file is stored in this one dimensional array. There are four local parameters: a file pointer to a stream that is associated with a physical file; a subscript, initialized to zero, to the records held in a one-dimensional array; a subscript to the four examination marks that are held in a different one-dimensional array; and a character string array used to store the name of the student temporarily. The prototype for this function is

```
void initialize(record students[]);

FILE *filename;
int  rec_index = 0;
int  mark_index;
char name_string[max_char];
```

315

Algorithm for the Function search_number - Figure 11.9 shows that the records have been entered into the array in student-number sequence. If a student number is less than the number it is being compared with, then it cannot exist in the array. If the student number is greater than the number it is being compared with, then the record may exist later in the array. If the student number is equal to the number it is being compared, then a match exists.

initialize array index to zero (subscript of the first cell)
initialize a boolean flag found to false

while array index is less than the number of students and the number is not found do
    if student number is equal to the number in the record in the array
        set boolean flag found to true
    else if student number is less than the number in the record in the array
        set array index to the number of students
    else
        increase the array index by 1 to point at the next record in the array

return the value of the array index

Data Dictionary for Function search_number - The function contains two formal parameters: the students record `array` and the integer `student_number`. The function returns the integer value of an index. There are also two local variables: an integer `index` used as a subscript to the array and a Boolean variable denoting whether a number has been found. The function prototype is

```
int        search_number(record array[], int student_number);

int        index = 0;
boolean    found = false;
```

Desk Check - The following desk checks assume that simple macros have been defined for `number_of_students` and `number_of_marks` that represent the ten records and four marks. The test data is student_number 400.

Desk check for function search_number using the data listed in Figure 11.9.

number_of_students	10					
student_number	400					
index	0	1	2	3	4	
found	false					true
(index < number_of_students && !found)?	true	true	true	true	true	false
array[index].number	100	150	250	300	400	
(student_number == array[index].number)?	false	false	false	false	true	
(student_number < array[index].number}?	false	false	false	false		

316

Algorithm for the Function search_name

initialize a boolean flag found to false
initialize array index to start at position

while array index is less than the number of students and the number is not found do
    if student name is equal to the name in the record in the array
        set boolean flag found to true
    else
        increase array index by 1 to point at the next record in the array

return the value of array index

Data Dictionary for the Function search_name - The function contains three formal parameters: the students record `array`, the `student_name` character string, and the value of the index `start_at`, for starting the search. The function returns the integer value of an index. There are also two local variables: an integer `index` used as a subscript to the array and a Boolean variable denoting whether a number has been found. The function prototype is

```
int       search_name(record array[], char student_name[], int start_at);

int       index;
boolean   found;
```

Desk Check - Use the data listed in Figure 11.9 and check twice with start_at 0 and 3. The test data is `student_name` Smith,P and `start_at` 0 and 3.

number_of_students	10			
student_name	Smith,P			
index	0	1	2	
found	false			true
(index < number_of_students && !found)?	true	true	true	false
array[index].name	Rankin,W	Jones,D	Smith,P	
(student_name equals array[index].name)?	false	false	true	
number_of_students	10			
student_name	Smith,P			
index	3	4		
found	false		true	
(index < number_of_students && !found)?	true	true	false	
array[index].name	Davies,J	Smith,P		
(student_name equals array[index].name)?	false	true		

317

Algorithm for the Function display_record

display the student number
display the student name
for each mark
    display mark

Data Dictionary for the Function display_record - The function contains two formal parameters: the student record `array` and the array index `at_index` of the record to be displayed. The function does not return a value. The function contains one local variable: an integer `index` used as a subscript to the array of marks. The function prototype is

```
void display_record(record array[], int at_index);

int   index;
```

Desk Check - Use the data listed in Figure 11.9 and the test datum 3 for `at_index`.

at_index	3					
number_of_marks	4					
array[at_index].number	300					
array[at_index].name	Davies,J					
index		0	1	2	3	4
(index < number_of_marks)?		true	true	true	true	false
array[at_index].marks[index]		70	65	55	40	

Algorithm for the Function average_mark

initialize total of marks to zero
for every mark
    increase total of marks by corresponding mark in array of marks for corresponding record

return the average of the total of marks

Data Dictionary for the Function average_mark - The function contains two formal parameters: the student record array and the array index `at_index` of the student record whose marks are to be averaged. The function returns the average of the marks for the selected record. The function contains two local variables: one keeps a running total of the marks, and the other is an integer index used as a subscript to the array of marks. The function prototype is

```
int average_mark(record array[], int at_index);

int total;
int index;
```

Desk Check - Use the data listed in Figure 11.9 and test datum 1 for `at_index`.

318

number_of_marks	4				
at_index	1				
index	0	1	2	3	4
(index < number_of_marks)?	true	true	true	true	false
array[at_index].marks[index]	60	80	90	75	
total	60	140	230	305	
total / number_of_marks					76

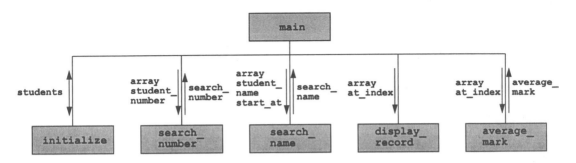

Figure 11.10 Structure chart of the program

```
/*
chap_11\ex_11.c

program to create an array of records that contains the following data

- student number (unique 3 digit number)
- student name (may contain duplicates)
- percentage marks in four final examinations

from the program it is possible to perform the following

- search the array on student number
- search the array on student name

and if the record is found then

- display the contents of a chosen record
- calculate and display the average mark for any student

*/
```

319

```c
#include <stdio.h>
#include <stdlib.h>
#include <errno.h>
#include <string.h>
#define data_file "a:\\chap_11\\marks.txt"
#define read "r"
#define number_of_students 10
#define number_of_marks 4
#define max_char 80
#define null 0

typedef struct {
                int   number;
                char  name[max_char];
                int   marks[number_of_marks];
          } record;

typedef enum{false, true} boolean;

void initialize(record students[])
/* function to read lines of a text file and store
them as records in an array */
{
   FILE *filename;
   int  rec_index = 0;
   int  mark_index;
   char name_string[max_char];

   filename = fopen(data_file, read);
   if (filename == NULL)
   {
     printf("file cannot be opened - program terminated\n");
     exit(errno);
   }

   while (! feof(filename))
   {
     fscanf(filename, "%d", &students[rec_index].number);

     fgets(name_string, max_char, filename);
     name_string[strlen(name_string) - 1] = null; /* replace new line with null */
     strcpy(students[rec_index].name, name_string);

     for (mark_index=0; mark_index != number_of_marks; mark_index++)
         fscanf(filename, "%d", &students[rec_index].marks[mark_index]);
     fgetc(filename); /* flush unwanted CR */
     rec_index++;
   }
}
```

```
int search_number(const record array[], int student_number)
/* function to search the array for the student_number,
if found return the value of the index, else return the
size of the array */
{
     int      index = 0;
     boolean found = false;

     while (index < number_of_students && !found)
         if      (student_number == array[index].number)
                 found = true;
         else if (student_number < array[index].number)
                 index = number_of_students;
         else
                 index++;

     return index;
}

int search_name(const record array[], const char student_name[], int start_at)
/* function to search the array for the student_name from the index
value start_at in the array, if found return the value of the index,
else return the size of the array */
{
     int      index;
     boolean found = false;

     index = start_at;
     while (index < number_of_students && !found)
        if (strcmp(student_name, array[index].name) == 0)
           found = true;
        else
           index++;

     return index;
}

void display_record(const record array[], int at_index)
/* function to display the contents of a record in the array
at_index position */

{
     int index;

     printf("\n%-4d%s\t", array[at_index].number, array[at_index].name);
     for (index=0; index < number_of_marks; index++)
        printf("%-4d", array[at_index].marks[index]);
}
```

```c
int average_mark(const record array[], int at_index)
/* function to calculate and return the average mark for a
student whose record is located at_index in the array */

{
    int total = 0;
    int index;

    for (index=0; index < number_of_marks; index++)
        total = total + array[at_index].marks[index];

    return total / number_of_marks;
}

void main(void)
{
    record students[number_of_students];

    char    menu_code;
    int     student_number;
    char    student_name[80];
    int     index;
    int     start_at;
    boolean more = true;

    initialize(students);

    do
    {
        printf("\n\n");
        printf("1 - search on number\n");
        printf("2 - search on name\n");
        printf("3 - finish\n\n");
        printf("? ");
        menu_code = getchar();
        getchar();

        switch (menu_code)
        {
        case '1' : printf("input student number ");
                   scanf("%d", &student_number); getchar();
                   index = search_number(students, student_number);
                   if (index != number_of_students)
                   {
                       display_record(students, index);
                       printf("average %d\n", average_mark(students, index));
                   }
                   break;
```

```
        case '2' : printf("input student name ");
                   gets(student_name);
                   start_at = 0;
                   while (start_at < number_of_students)
                   {
                     index = search_name(students, student_name, start_at);
                     if (index != number_of_students)
                     {
                        display_record(students, index);
                        printf("\taverage %d\n", average_mark(students, index));
                     }
                     start_at = index+1;
                   }
                   break;

        case '3' : more = false;
                   break;

        default  : printf("error in menu code try again\b\n");
      }
   }
   while (more);

}
```

Results

```
1 - search on numbers
2 - search on name
3 - finish

? 1
input student number 300

300 Davies,J  70  65  55  40    average 57


1 - search on numbers
2 - search on name
3 - finish

? 2
input student name Jones,D

150 Jones,D   60  80  90  75    average 76

525 Jones,D   45  80  75  55    average 63
```

323

```
1 - search on numbers
2 - search on name
3 - finish

? 3
```

Summary

☐ A structure is defined as a collection of one or more members, which may be of different types, grouped together under a single tag or name.

☐ A variable may be declared as a structure type.

☐ Structure variables may be initialized at the point of declaration.

☐ Individual members of a structure can be accessed by qualifying the corresponding structure variable with each member using the member operator.

☐ If two variables have the same structure, it is possible to assign the contents of one variable to another.

☐ A structure may be passed as a parameter in a function or returned as a value from a function.

☐ A union allows its members to be referred to as one type.

☐ An array may contain mixed data types within the umbrella of a structure.

☐ An array can have more than one dimension.

☐ An N-dimensional array can be thought of as a repetition of $(N-1)$-dimensional arrays.

☐ Arrays of any dimension may be initialized at the point of declaration.

Review Questions

1. True or false - a structure must have a tag.

2. What is the purpose of a tag?

3. True or false - a structure can be initialized at its point of declaration.

4. True or false - the declaration `struct date today;` is legal provided the structure `date` has been defined.

5. True or false - a member operator is used to access the members of a structure.

6. True or false - if two variables have the same structure the contents of one variable can be assigned to the second variable.

7. If a structure is defined as a type, is there a need to supply a tag?

8. If the return type of a function is a structure with the tag `alpha`, how would you express the prototype of the parameterless function `beta`?

9. If a reference parameter is a structure with a tag `gamma`, how would you express the prototype of the single parameter function `epsilon` that does not return a value?

10. What is the purpose of a union?

11. True or false - a variable whose type is defined by a union can store all the members of the union at one time.

12. True or false - an array of records is the same as a two-dimensional array.

13. When is it permissible to define a structure that contains another structure?

14. What is the order, in terms of rows and columns, when subscripting a two-dimensional array?

15. Describe the contents of the array declared as `int alpha[3][4] = {0};`

16. Define a two-dimensional array.

17. How does a three-dimensional array differ from a two-dimensional array?

18. Illustrate how you might visualize an array declared as `char string[3][2][10];`

Programming Exercises

19. Comment on the errors in the following structure:

```
time {
      int HH
      int MM
   } time_of_day
```

325

20. Detect the errors in the following declaration:

```
struct details {
                char name[];
                int  age;
        } {"Joey", 21};
```

21. Use tagged structures to rewrite the following segments of code.

```
typedef struct {
                int HH;
                int MM;
        } time;


time get_time(void);


void change_time(time *new_time);
```

22. What are the values of `time_of_day.HH` and `time_of_day.MM`, from the following declaration

```
typedef struct {
                int HH;
                int MM;
        } time;


time time_of_day = {12,49};
```

23. Use the declarations given in question 22 to interpret the meaning of

`time *wand, (*wand).HH and wand -> MM.`

24. How many bytes of storage are used to represent data in the following union?

```
typedef union {
                int date;
                char date_string[8];
        } dates;
```

25. Use the data from Figure 11.2 to determine the values of the following expressions:

```
birthdays[3].month;
birthdays[0].year;
birthdays[1].day;
```

26. Use the data from Figure 11.4 to determine the values of the following expressions:

```
birthdays[3].name;
birthdays[1].birth_date.month;
birthdays[0].birth_date.day?
```

27. Use the data from Figure 11.5 to determine the values of the following expressions:

```
matrix[2][4];
matrix[0][2];
matrix[3][1];
```

28. Use Figure 11.5 to determine what values are printed with the following code:

```
for (column=0; column != 6; column++)
{
    sum = 0;
    for (row = 0; row != 3; row++)
        sum = sum + matrix[row][column];

    printf("%d\n", sum);
}
```

29. Use Figure 11.6 to determine the values of the following expressions:

```
array[3][1][3];
array[0][0][0];
array[1][0][2];
```

30. Use Figure 11.6 to determine the values printed with the following code:

```
for (branch=0; branch != 2; branch++)
{
    for (region=0; region != 4; region++)
        printf("%d", array[region][branch][3]);
}
```

Programming Problems

31. Write a program to store the names of foods and their prices, as displayed at Ben's Breakfast Bar (section 2.1), as records in an array. Extend the program to

(a) Input the name of an item of food and display the price.
(b) Input an amount of money and display all the individual items of food that cost the same or less than the amount of money.

32. Define three structures of types `triangle`, `circle`, and `ellipse` with members to represent the area and length of three sides of a triangle, the area and radius of a circle, and the area and lengths of the two half axes of an ellipse.

Declare a union of the three structures as a type `shapes`.

Define a further structure of type `figures` with a member to represent a single code for a shape (T-triangle, C-circle, and E-ellipse) and a member containing the data for the corresponding shape.

Create the following functions defined by their prototypes.

```
char menu(void);
/* function to display a menu of the shape T, C or E and return a
valid menu code */
figures get_data(void);
/* function to input and return the data for a shape */
figures calculate_area(figures data);
/* function to calculate and return the area of a figure */
void display_area(figures data);
/* function to display the area of the figure */
```

Write a program to repeatedly input data for a particular shape and display the area of the shape.

Note: since shapes is declared as a union, it is possible to process the appropriate shape without the need for separate functions for each shape.

33. Write a program to input and store in an array the ten records illustrated in Figure 11.11. The records contain the names of towns and their corresponding telephone area codes for Scotland. Include a procedure to search for the name of the town when given the area code. Display the result of the search.

```
Aberdeen        01224
Ayr             01292
Dundee          01382
Edinburgh       0131
Falkirk         01324
Fort William    01397
Glasgow         0141
Inverness       01463
Perth           01738
Stirling        01786
```

Figure 11.11 Telephone area dialling codes

328

34. Write a program to store two 20-digit integers as characters of a string and perform the operations of addition and subtraction on the two integers. Output the answer as a string of digits.

35. Towns in three states have populations as shown in Figure 11.12.

state	town/ city	population
Massachusetts	Boston	574,283
	Worcester	169,759
	Marlborough	31,813
North Carolina	Raleigh	207,951
	Winston-Salem	143,485
	Gastonia	54,732
Texas	Austin	465,622
	Abilene	106,654
	Houston	1,630,553

Figure 11.12 Populations of towns

Initialize the following arrays:

(a) A two-dimensional array containing the names of the states.
(b) A two-dimensional array containing records of the names of the towns and their respective populations, where each row represents a different state, in the order given in the first array.

Use the arrays from (a) and (b) to write procedures to input the name of a state and the name of a town, perform a serial search on the first two-dimensional array to match the state and obtain a row subscript, and perform a serial search on the corresponding row of the second two-dimensional array to match the town and obtain a column subscript. Use the row and column subscripts to access the second two-dimensional array and display the value for the population of the chosen town.

Write procedures to input the name of a state and output the total population for the towns listed in the state. Also express this figure as a percentage of the population of all the towns defined in the array.

Note: the population figures are for 1990 and were taken from the *Microsoft Encarta Multimedia Encyclopaedia (1994)*.

36. From the saying "Thirty days hath September, April, June and November, and all the rest have thirty-one, except for February that has twenty-eight days clear and twenty-nine in a leap year", write a program to perform the following functions:

(a) Store the names and number of days in each month as records in an array.
(b) Display a calendar for any year between 1997 and 2099, and print the year and the names of the months. Print the value for the date under the name of the day.

37. Design and write a program to enable the user to construct a crossword similar to that illustrated in Figure 11.13. The user will be required to input the starting and finishing coordinates of a word and the word string. The computer will store the letters of the word either across or down the 15x15 array, depending upon the values of the coordinates. Display the contents of the array after each word has been stored.

columns

	1	2	3	4	5	6	7	8	9	10	11	12	13	14	15
1	J	U	I	C	E										
2	A				L	A	U	N	C	H					
3	M	O	D	E	M			A							
4								U							
5								G							
6								H							
7								T							
8								Y							
9															
10															
11															
12															
13															
14															
15															

rows

Figure 11.13 Layout of the crossword

38. Rewrite Program Example 11.9: Initialization and Processing of a Three-dimensional Array, to cater for the following changes:

(a) Create a text file containing the votes for the candidates. Initialize the three-dimensional array by reading the data from this file.

(b) The names of the union representatives are Adams, Davies, Jones and Smith. A two-dimensional array is initialized at declaration with these names.

(c) The names of the four regions are Bay View, Metropolis, Parkside, and Suburbia. A two-dimensional array is initialized at declaration with these names.

(d) Calculate and display in a table the total vote in each named region for each of the four named candidates.

(e) Display the name of the winner of the election with the total number of votes cast.

39. A computerized minefield is divided into a 10x10 matrix as illustrated in Figure 11.14. Write a game program to generate the random position of the mines in the field. The number of mines is also a random number in the range 1 to 10. Invite a player to input pairs of coordinates of a path through the minefield. The computer generates the starting position at any column in row 9 of the matrix, and the only legal move a player can make is to any adjacent position in the matrix. The object of the game is to trace a path through the field without stepping on a mine and to finish at the northern perimeter of the matrix. Only at the end of the game should the computer reveal the positions of the mines.

In order to generate a different number of mines and a different starting position each time the game is played you need to generate a new seed value for the random number generator. If a value for elapsed time is used as the seed in the function srand, then a new starting point will be possible in the random number generator. From the header file <time.h> it is possible to obtain elapsed time in seconds by using the function time(&tt), where tt is of type time_t.

A call to srand((unsigned)tt) will cause a new starting position to be chosen when using the random number generator rand().

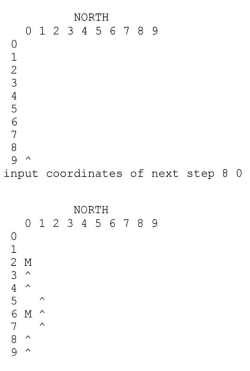

Figure 11.14 Matrix of minefield

The first level of design of this program might be as follows.

initialize the matrix by generating a number of mines, their positions and the starting position
display the matrix without showing the positions of the mines
do
> *do*
>> *input coordinates of next adjacent step*
> *while illegal move*

> *search for mine in current position and plot current position*

> *if area mined*
>> *display the matrix with the positions of the mines*
> *else*
>> *display the matrix showing the route taken so far*

while no mine found or not reached the northern perimeter
if no mine found display the matrix showing the safe route

Implement a program that contains the following function prototypes:

```
void initialize(int *last_row, int *last_column);
/* function to plant the mines in the minefield */
boolean mine(int row, int column);
/* return true if a mine is found at the coordinates [row,column]*/
void display(boolean reveal);
/* function to display the path taken across the minefield and the
positions of the mines if reveal is true */
```

40. Write a program to play tic-tac-toe against the computer. Use a two-dimensional array to store the noughts (O's) and crosses (X's). Let the computer be the cross and use a random number generator to create the position of play by the computer. Display the board and the final result of the game, on the screen as illustrated in figure 11.15.

For the reader who has not played tic-tac-toe before, the rules are as follows:

Each player places either a cross "X" or a nought "O" in a square on the board. The object of the game is to prevent your opponent from completing any horizontal, vertical, or diagonal line of crosses or noughts which will result in a winning line. If after several moves either competitor cannot make a winning line, then a stale-mate results.

However in this simulation, the computer will not deliberately attempt to block the opponent's line of noughts. The computer is to be programmed to place a cross in any randomly generated free space. Use the method of generating random numbers suggested in the previous question.

In this simulation, the game results in a stale-mate only when every square on the board has been filled without a successful line of noughts or crosses.

```
X|   |
---------
  |   |
---------
  |   |

input position of play 2 2

X|   |
---------
  | O |
---------
  |   |

X|   |
---------
  | O |
---------
  |   |X

input position of play 1 2

X| O |
---------
  | O |
---------
  |   |X

X| O |
---------
  | O |X
---------
  |   |X

input position of play 3 2

X| O |
---------
  | O |X
---------
  | O |X

you win - smarty pants!!
```

Figure 11.15 A game of tic-tac-toe

Use the following functions, described by their prototypes, in your program

void display(void);
/* display the contents of the board on a screen */
void initialize(void);
/* fill the noughts and crosses board with spaces and generate a
new seed for the random number generator */
void play(player who);
/* function to allow a player to make a particular move, where
player is an enumerated type containing the constants computer and
you, respectively */
boolean check_position(int row, int column);
/* check to see if the position given by the coordinates
[row,column] on the board is free */

```
boolean check_winner(player who);
/* check to see if the current player wins */
```

The first level of design of this program might be as follows:

do
    initialize the board
    set number of moves to zero
    do
        set computer to current player
        play the move
        display the move
        increase the number of moves by 1
        check for winner
            if computer wins display message that computer has won
            if no winner and the number of moves is less than 9
                set person (computer user) to current player
                play the move
                display the move
                increase the number of moves by 1
                check for winner
                if person wins display message that user has won
    while no winner and number of moves is less than 9

    if no winner and number of moves is equal to 9 display stale-mate
    request for another game
while another game requested

Chapter 12
Recursion, Sorting, and Searching

This chapter is divided into three topics with the first topic - recursion - finding its way into the second and third topics - sorting and searching.

You are already familiar with the process of calling one function from within another function. For example from within the function `main` other functions can be called. The calling of one function from within another function is quite acceptable. But what if the function being called from within a function is the same function? When the function is in effect calling itself, the technique is known as recursion.

Methods used to organize information must provide a means of sorting information using a defined key or keys and a means of searching through the information efficiently using a particular key. This chapter considers both nonrecursive and recursive methods for sorting and searching. By the end of the chapter, you should have an understanding of the following topics:

    ☐   A definition of recursion.

    ☐   The use of recursive functions.

    ☐   The development of a nonrecursive sorting algorithm.

    ☐   The recursive Quicksort algorithm.

    ☐   The development of a nonrecursive searching algorithm that relies upon the data being sorted.

    ☐   The recursive binary search algorithm.

    ☐   The efficiency of various sorting and searching algorithms.

    ☐   The Quicksort and binary search algorithms as standard C functions.

12.1 Recursion

Program Example 12.1 introduces the subject of recursion with a function to output the value of the variable level, in the range from 1 to 5. Rather than constructing a loop, the value of level is updated and output in the function, and the function is then called recursively to repeat updating level and to output the value of level. The function is called recursively until level becomes equal to 5.

Program Example 12.1: Recursive Calls to a Function

```
/*
chap_12\ex_1.c
program to demonstrate recursive calls and returns
*/

#include <stdio.h>

void output(int level)
{
    level++;
    printf("recursive call to level %d\n", level);

    if (level < 5)
        output(level); /* recursive call made here */
    else
        return;

    printf("returning through level %d\n", level);
}

void main(void)
{
    output(0);
}
```

Results

```
recursive call to level 1
recursive call to level 2
recursive call to level 3
recursive call to level 4
recursive call to level 5
returning through level 4
returning through level 3
returning through level 2
returning through level 1
```

Figure 12.1 illustrates that a recursive call to a function produces another instance or **level** of the function, depicted by the code being superimposed upon the calling code.

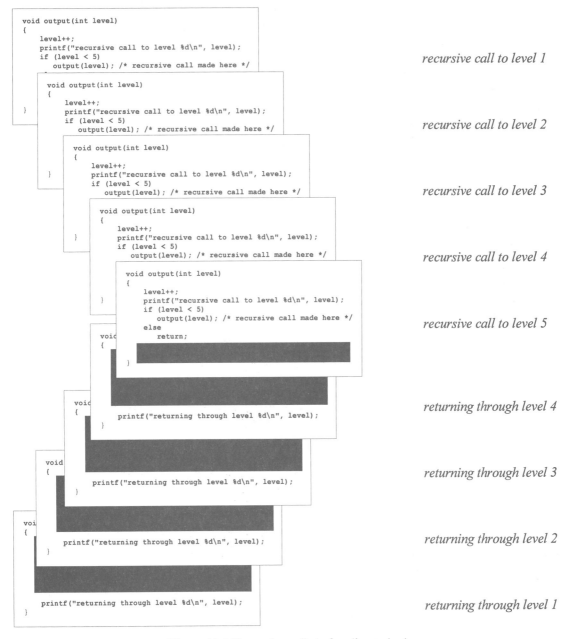

Figure 12.1 Recursive calls to function output

The remaining code after `output(level)` is not shown in the recursive calls to levels 1, 2, 3, and 4, since this is not yet executed. Level 5 serves as the terminating case in which the parameter `level` is equal to 5. No further recursion is possible and the code

```
if (level < 5)
    output(level); /* recursive call made here */
else
    return;
```

will cause `return` to be executed. The computer must return through each level or instance of the code before the program can finish. Since the computer is returning to the function that invoked the call, the next statement after the call, `output(level)`, will be executed. However, `output(level)` was in one branch of a selection; therefore, the next statement to be executed `printf("returning through level %d\n", level);` will be after the selection statement. Consequently, all the code that had been executed is now blacked-out because it will not be used as the computer returns through the levels, or instances, of the function. Notice also, that within each level the value of `level` remains what it was when the `level` was originally invoked. Hence, in returning through the levels, the parameter `level` is output as 4, 3, 2, and 1 respectively.

You may wonder how the computer remembers the values of the parameters at each level of recursion and where to return to from a level of recursion?

The computer stores information in a data structure known as a **stack**. Stacks will be explained fully in Chapter 14, but for now you may think of a stack as being analogous to a pile of trays in a self-service restaurant. You place a tray on the top of the pile, and you remove a tray from the top of the pile. Thus access to the pile of trays is based on a last-in-first-out (LIFO) principle in which access to a tray is from one end only, in this case the top of the pile of trays.

A stack operates on a LIFO principle in which the computer stores and removes information from one end of the stack only. The computer associates a stack frame with each level of recursion. A **stack frame** contains the values of the parameters and local variables for any one level of recursion and the memory address of where the computer should return to after the level of recursion is complete. Figure 12.2 illustrates a single stack frame for Program Example 12.1. This stack frame contains a value for the `level` parameter and the next statement after the function call. In this example it is not practical to include the memory address of the statement.

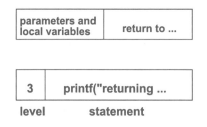

Figure 12.2 An example of a stack frame

Figure 12.3 illustrates how each frame is stored at the top of a stack for every recursive call to the function `output` and how each frame is removed from the stack as the computer returns through the levels of recursion. The figure should be read first from top left to bottom left, which represents how frames are stored on the stack at each recursive call. After the terminating case `level = 5` has been reached, the figure should be read from bottom right to top right where the computer removes each frame from the top of the stack. The removed frame contains the level number of the value of the parameter for that particular instance of recursion and the statement of where to return to after that instance of recursion is complete.

The computer continues to remove frames from the stack as it returns through each level of recursion until the stack is empty and the computer has returned to the end of the main function.

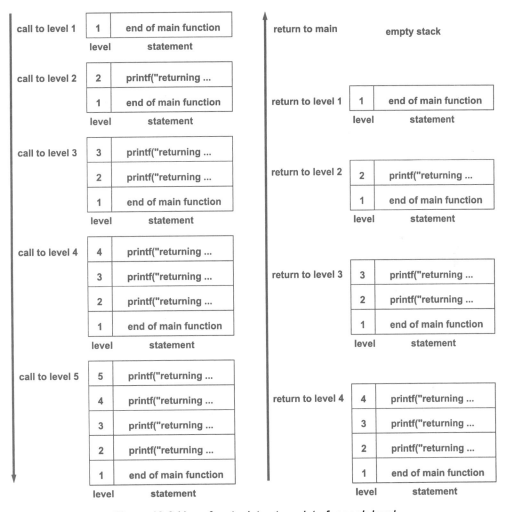

Figure 12.3 Use of a stack to store data for each level

It is tempting to offer a simple definition of recursion as a function that calls itself. However, this definition is incomplete, since there is no mention of how the called function gets closer to the solution or how to stop the function repeatedly calling itself.

Recursion can be regarded as a technique for performing function R, by performing a similar function R_i. The function R_i is exactly the same in nature as the original function R, however, it represents a solution to a smaller problem than R.

Thus function R recursively calls function R_1; function R_1 recursively calls function R_2; function R_{n-1} recursively calls function R_n. In this scenario, R_n is a solution to a smaller problem than R_{n-1}; R_2 is a solution to a smaller problem than R_1; R_1 is a solution to a smaller problem than R. Eventually the recursive calls must lead to a solution R_n, which cannot allow for further recursive calls, because a terminating criterion has been reached.

With these facts in mind, you should always address the following three questions before constructing a recursive solution.

- How can you define the solution in terms of a smaller solution of the same type?

- In what manner is the size of the solution diminished at each recursive call?

- What instance or level of the solution can serve as the terminating case, and does the manner in which the solution size is diminished ensure that this terminating case will always be reached?

In the context of Program Example 12.1, consider the three questions about constructing a recursive algorithm.

A smaller solution has been defined, since only one value of `level`, not all five values, is output by the function.

Since `level` is being increased by 1 after each recursive call, `level` will eventually become equal to 5. The size of the solution is being diminished as the value of level approaches 5.

The terminating case is when `level` is equal to 5. No further recursion is possible, and all values in the range 1 to 5 have been output.

12.2 Examples of Recursion

The two programming examples In this section will be fully explained with the aid of diagrams. You should work as carefully and slowly through this section as you need to in order to understand the technique of recursion.

The first program illustrates how a function can be called recursively to output the contents of a string backwards.

Program Example 12.2: Recursively Writing a String Backwards

```
/*
chap_12\ex_2.c
program to print a string backwards
*/

#include <stdio.h>

char alphabet[]="abcdefghijklmnopqrstuvwxyz";

void write_backwards(const char alpha_string[], int index)
{
        if (index >= 0)
        {
            printf("%c", alpha_string[index]);
            write_backwards(alpha_string, index-1);
        }
}

void main(void)
{
        write_backwards(alphabet, 25);
}
```

Results

```
zyxwvutsrqponmlkjihgfedcba
```

We can make two observations from the preceding program and Figure 12.4.

The identifier index is set at the last cell of the array and the contents, z, output. The index is then reduced by 1 and a recursive call to write_backwards outputs y; index is then reduced by 1 and write_backwards is recursively called again. The output of characters continues until the index is less than zero. The condition to terminate recursion is index >= 0 becoming false.

The recursive call write_backwards(alpha, index-1) is the last executable statement of the function write_backwards, and although the computer must return through each level of function write_backwards, no further output is possible.

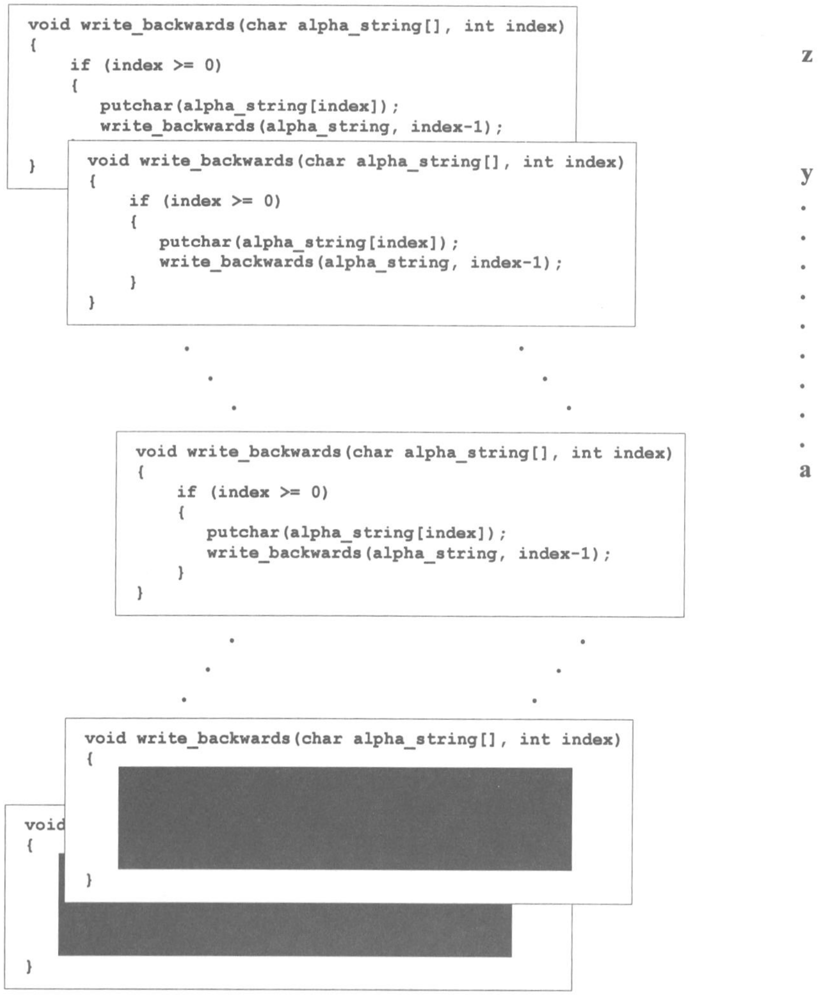

Figure 12.4 Recursive calls to function write_backwards

The second program in this section illustrates how a function can be called recursively to calculate the factorial value of a number.

Factorial *n*, written as *n!*, is defined as: *n*(n-1)*(n-2) .. 3*2*1*. Hence 5! = 5*4*3*2*1 = 120.

Program Example 12.3: Calculating the Factorial Value of a Number.

```
/*
chap_12\ex_3.c
program to calculate the factorial of a number
*/

#include <stdio.h>

long int factorial(int n)
{
        if (n==0)
            return 1;
        else
            return n * factorial(n-1);
}

void main(void)
{
        int number;

        printf("input a number in the range 1..12 ");
        scanf("%d", &number);

        while (number >= 1 && number <= 12)
        {
            printf("%d!\t%ld\n", number, factorial(number));
            printf("input a number in the range 1..12 ");
            scanf("%d", &number);
        }
}
```

Results

```
input a number in the range 1..12
3!      6
input a number in the range 1..12
4!      24
input a number in the range 1..12
5!      120
input a number in the range 1..12
6!      720
input a number in the range 1..12
```

In this example the value of the factorial of a number cannot be calculated until the function has recursively reached factorial(0). Upon returning to the lower level of factorial(1), the value 1*factorial(0) can then

343

be calculated. Returning to the lower level of factorial(2), the value 2*factorial(1) can then be calculated. Finally, returning to the lower level of factorial(3), the value 3*factorial(2) can be calculated. This information is illustrated in Figure 12.5.

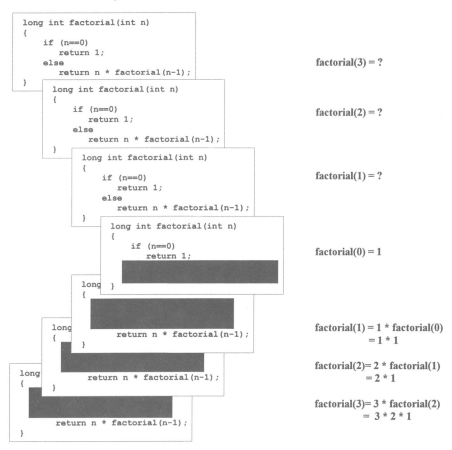

Figure 12.5 Recursive call to the function factorial

12.3 Recursion Versus Iteration

Style Matters:

Recursion or Iteration?

Recursion can be used as an alternative to iteration; however, recursion is not a wise choice if it merely replaces a straightforward iteration. The true value of recursion is its use in solving problems for which there is no simple nonrecursive solution.

Recursion is a powerful problem-solving tool that, compared with iteration, can lead to succinct solutions to the most complex problems. Recursion's strength will be demonstrated later in this chapter with searching and sorting algorithms and also in Chapter 14 in the context of dynamic data structures that lend themselves to iterative techniques.

There are, however, drawbacks related to efficiency when recursion is compared with iteration. These drawbacks may be summarized as follows.

- ☐ There is the overhead of the extra memory space associated with a call to a function. Memory space must be set aside for storing parameters, local variables, and the return address of the next statement to be executed in the calling function. Recall for a moment the use of the stack frame for storing this information. Every time a recursive call is made the computer must allocate memory space to store the information. This overhead is magnified by a recursive function, since a single initial call to the function can generate a large number of recursive calls. For example the function `factorial(n)` generates n recursive calls.

- ☐ There is the overhead of the computer time it takes to make recursive function calls. Although fast computers make this overhead negligible.

- ☐ Finally, some recursive algorithms can be inherently inefficient in the way they process data. This inefficiency has nothing to do with how recursion is implemented on a computer, but is tied to the method of solution in the algorithm.

12.4 Sorting

We now turn our attention to methods for sorting data. In this section one nonrecursive method and one recursive method for sorting numbers held in an array will be explained. Both methods will be compared in terms of their efficiency to sort differing amounts of data.

Sorting methods used in computing can be classified as internal sorting or external sorting. Internal sorting involves the storage in main memory of all the data to be sorted. However, when the amount of data is too large to be stored and sorted in the main memory, the data is stored on an external secondary storage medium, such as tape or disk, and successive parts of the data are sorted in the main memory. Such a technique is known as external sorting. The type of sorting method for a specific task depends on at least one of the following factors:

- ☐ The amount of information to be sorted. Clearly, it would be very time consuming to use a relatively inefficient sorting method on a large quantity of data.

- ☐ The computer configuration being used - the size of the main memory and the number of tape or disk units.

- ☐ The nature of the application and the urgency of the results.

Only internal sorting methods will be considered in this text.

Selection Sort

The first internal nonrecursive sorting algorithm we will consider is known as the selection sort. Figure 12.6 illustrates the movement of integers in a one-dimensional array when a selection sort is used to place the integers into ascending order (lowest value to highest value).

The contents of the cells from 0 to 4 are inspected for the largest number (18), which is swapped with the number in cell 4. The contents of the cells from 0 to 3 are inspected for the largest number (15), which is swapped with the number in cell 3. The contents of the cells from 0 to 2 are inspected for the largest number (13), which is swapped with the number in cell 2. The contents of the cells from 0 to 1 are inspected for the largest number (8), which is swapped with the number in cell 1. When only the contents of cell 0 remains to be inspected the numbers are assumed to have been sorted into ascending order.

To generalize, if N represents the number of integers to be sorted, in the cells of an array from 0 to N-1, the largest number in 0 to N-1 cells is found and swapped with the number in cell N-1. The process is repeated, with N being decreased by 1 each time, until N = 0.

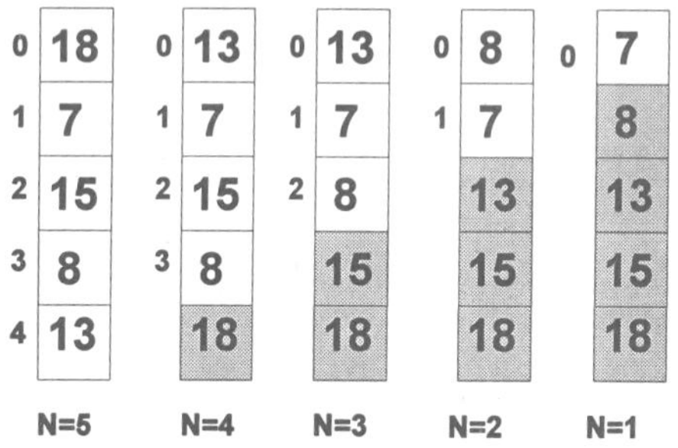

Figure 12.6 A selection sort

Although the selection sort can be implemented as a single function, it is clearer if the implementation is based upon two functions. The first function `position_of_largest` will return the subscript of the largest element in an array `numbers` of size `limit`.

```
int position_of_largest(int numbers[], int limit)
/* function to return the position of the largest number in the array
numbers with bounds 0..limit */
{
        int largest = numbers[0];
        int index;
        int index_of_largest = 0;

        for (index=1; index<=limit; index++)
            if (numbers[index] > largest)
            {
                largest = numbers[index];
                index_of_largest = index;
            }
```

```
        return index_of_largest;
}
```

The second function `selection_sort` calls the first function to find the largest number in the N-element array, where N is equal to size. This number is then swapped with the number at the end of the array. The process is repeated for N-1 elements, then N-2 elements, and so on, until N is reduced to zero.

```
void selection_sort(int numbers[], int size)
/* function to sort an array of integers into ascending order */
{
        int index, position, temp_store;

        for (index=size-1; index > 0; index--)
        {
            /* find the position of the largest number in the
            array bounds 0 .. index */
            position = position_of_largest(numbers, index);

            /* if the numbers are not the same swap the numbers */
            if (index != position)
            {
                temp_store = numbers[index];
                numbers[index] = numbers[position];
                numbers[position] = temp_store;
            }
        }
}
```

Desk check of `selection_sort` function using test data from Figure 12.6

size	index	position	index != position?	temp_store	numbers[index]	numbers[position]
5	4	0	true	13	18	13
	3	2	true	8	15	8
	2	0	true	8	13	8
	1	0	true	7	8	7
	0					

Program Example 12.4 initializes an array with the numbers in Figure 12.6, sorts the numbers into ascending order in the array, and displays the contents of the sorted array.

Program Example 12.4: Sorting Numbers into Ascending Order Using the Selection Sort.

```c
/*
chap_12\ex_4.c program to demonstrate a selection sort
*/

#include <stdio.h>

int position_of_largest(int numbers[], int limit)
/* function to return the position of the largest number
in the array numbers with bounds 0..limit */
{
        int largest = numbers[0];
        int index;
        int index_of_largest = 0;

        for (index=1; index<=limit; index++)
            if (numbers[index] > largest)
            {
                largest = numbers[index];
                index_of_largest = index;
            }

        return index_of_largest;
}

void selection_sort(int numbers[], int size)
/* function to sort an array of integers into ascending order */
{
        int index, position, temp_store;

        for (index=size-1; index > 0; index--)
        {
            position = position_of_largest(numbers, index);

            if (index != position)
            {
                temp_store = numbers[index];
                numbers[index] = numbers[position];
                numbers[position] = temp_store;
            }
        }
}
```

```
void main(void)
{
        int numbers[5] = {18,7,15,8,13};
        int index;

        selection_sort(numbers, 5);

        for (index=0; index<5; index++)
            printf("%d\t", numbers[index]);
}
```

Results

7	8	13	15	18

In analyzing the efficiency of the selection sort it is important to look at the number of comparisons on the data being sorted. If there are N items of data, then

the number of comparisons on the first pass through the array is N-1;
the number of comparisons on the second pass through the array is N-2;
the number of comparisons on the third pass through the array is N-3;

.

.

the number of comparisons on the N-1th pass through the array is 1.

The selection sort algorithm is blind to the original order of the numbers. The number of comparisons, regardless of the order of the numbers, will be the sum of the sequence of numbers (N-1)+(N-2)+(N-3) + ... +1 which as the sum of a series is N(N-1)/2. Don't worry you are not expected to know the mathematics of summing a series! Expanding this expression, the number of comparisons is $N^2/2 - N/2$. If we omit the fractional part of this expression, we may conclude that the selection sort has an order of magnitude of N^2 comparisons and is referred to as a *quadratic* algorithm. The time it takes to sort an array will be proportional to the amount of work the computer must do to compare and swap data.

The algorithm is suitable for sorting only a small amount of data; otherwise, the time to complete the sorting algorithm, proportional to N^2, will become lengthy.

Quicksort

By way of a contrast to the selection sort, the next sorting algorithm is normally considerably quicker in sorting data stored in an array. The algorithm is recursive and is known as the Quicksort created by C.A.R.Hoare and described in his paper "Quicksort" (*Computer Journal*, Vol. 5, No. 1, 1962).

Figure 12.7 illustrates integers stored in a one-dimensional array with subscript bounds *first .. last*. Quicksort relies upon a routine to find a value, known as a **pivot**, in the array. When the pivot is placed in its correct position, all the numbers between the subscripts *first .. pivot_index-1* are less than or equal to its value and all the numbers between the subscripts *pivot_index+1 .. last* are greater than its value.

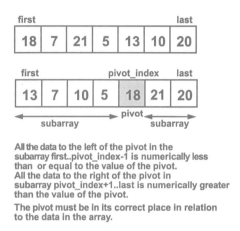

Figure 12.7 Properties of a pivot value

The array has been divided into two subarrays by the pivot value. Since the pivot is in its correct position regarding the remainder of the data, there is no need to include this value in any further data to be sorted. The problem has been reduced to sorting two subarrays as depicted in Figure 12.8.

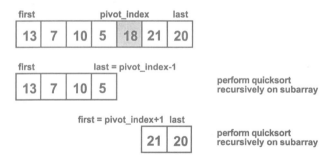

Figure 12.8 Quicksort performed on subarrays

Quicksort is then applied recursively to the left subarray contained between subscripts *first .. pivot_index-1* and then recursively to the right subarray contained between subscripts *pivot_index+1 .. last*. The algorithm can be expressed by the following function.

```
void quicksort(int array[], int first, int last)
{
    int pivot_index;

    if (first < last)
    {
        pivot_index = partition(array, first, last);

        quicksort(array, first, pivot_index - 1);
        quicksort(array, pivot_index+1, last);
    }
}
```

The recursive algorithm is applicable only when the first < last. If first = last, then there is only one element in the subarray and is therefore sorted. The case when first > last indicates that the array bounds do not classify a subarray.

Figure 12.9 illustrates the operations on the array that are necessary to move the pivot to its correct position in the array.

A value for the pivot is chosen from the array. When we are selecting the pivot, if the arrays are initially randomly ordered, then it really does not matter which element is used as the pivot value. In this example the pivot is chosen to be the first number in the array.

```
pivot = array[first];
```

In order to access the array from different ends, the subscripts lo and hi are used. In Figure 12.9 lo is initialized to first and will be incremented to move up the array (to the right); hi is initialized to last and will be decremented to move down the array (to the left).

```
lo = first;
hi = last;
```

The value contained in the array at lo is compared with the pivot. If this value is less than or equal to the pivot, the value of lo is increased by 1. The comparison continues while the value in the array at subscript lo is less than or equal to the pivot and the value of lo has not exceeded the subscript last.

```
while ((array[lo] <= pivot) && (lo <= last)) lo++;
```

When the comparisons stop because the value in the array at subscript lo is greater than the pivot or lo exceeds last, attention must switch to the data at subscript hi. The value contained in the array at hi is compared with the pivot. If this value is greater than the pivot, the value of hi is decreased by 1. The comparison continues while the value in the array at subscript hi is greater than the pivot.

```
while (array[hi] > pivot) hi--;
```

351

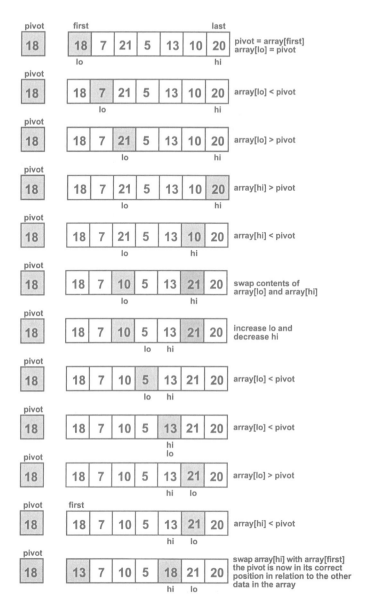

Figure 12.9 Moving a pivot to the correct position

When the comparisons stop because the value in the array at subscript hi is less than or equal to the pivot, the two values in the array at subscripts hi and lo are swapped as long as lo is less than hi. The subscripts lo and hi are then increased and decreased, respectively.

```
    if (lo < hi)
    {
        swap(&array[lo], &array[hi]);
        lo++;
        hi--;
    }
```

As long as the subscripts `lo` and `hi` do not cross over each other, the algorithm is repeated with `lo` moving up the array to the right and `hi` moving down the array to the left. When this condition becomes false, the iteration ceases and the `pivot` value is moved to its correct place in the array.

```
swap(&array[first], &array[hi]);
```

The following program demonstrates the Quicksort on an array of integers.

Program Example 12.5: Demonstration of the Quicksort.

```
/*
chap_12\ex_5.c
program to demonstrate the Quicksort
*/

#include <stdio.h>

#define size 7

void swap(int *X, int *Y)
/* function to swap (exchange) the values of *X and *Y */
{

    int temp;

    temp = *X;
    *X = *Y;
    *Y = temp;
}

int partition(int array[], int first, int last)
/* function to return the subscript of array, such that
all values less than or equal to array[subscript] are
stored in the range first..subscript-1 and all values
greater than array[subscript] are stored in the range
subscript+1..last */

{
    int pivot;
    int lo, hi;

    pivot = array[first];
```

```
   lo = first;
   hi = last;

   while (lo <= hi)
   {
      while ((array[lo] <= pivot) && (lo <= last)) lo++;

      while (array[hi] > pivot) hi--;

      if (lo < hi)
      {
         swap(&array[lo], &array[hi]);
         lo++;
         hi--;
      }
   }

   swap(&array[first], &array[hi]);
   return hi;
}


void quicksort(int array[], int first, int last)
/* function to sort an array with subscripts first..last, by
recursively sorting the smaller array first..pivot_index-1 followed by
recursively sorting the smaller array pivot_index+1..last */
{
    int pivot_index;

    if (first < last)
    {
       pivot_index = partition(array, first, last);

       quicksort(array, first, pivot_index - 1);
       quicksort(array, pivot_index+1, last);
    }
}

void display(int array[])
/* function to display the contents of the array */
{
   int index;

   for (index=0; index != size; index++)
     printf("%3d", array[index]);
   printf("\n");
}
```

```
void main(void)
{
   int array[] = {18,7,21,5,13,10,20};

   printf("unsorted array ");
   display(array);
   quicksort(array, 0, size-1);
   printf("sorted array    ");
   display(array);
}
```

Results

```
unsorted array   18   7 21   5 13 10 20
sorted array      5   7 10 13 18 20 21
```

The Quicksort algorithm works more efficiently for some arrays than it does for others. The best results are found when the partitioning process splits each subarray into two subarrays of approximately the same size. In such cases the time to perform a Quicksort is proportional to the order of N log₂N where N is the number of elements to be sorted. Hence Quicksort is known as a *logarithmic* algorithm. The worst results occur when the array is already sorted, the `pivot` remains in position `first`, and the remainder of the elements are in the subarray subscripted `2..last`. In such cases the time to perform the Quicksort is no faster than the time to perform a selection sort; the efficiency deteriorates to the order of N^2.

Figure 12.10 illustrates the comparative efficiency of the selection sort and the Quicksort for increasing values of N. Notice that the time to sort identical arrays is proportional to N^2 and Nlog₂N respectively, and increases dramatically for the selection sort as the number of elements (N) increases.

N	N^2 Selection sort	$Nlog_2 N$ Quicksort
32	1024	160
64	4096	384
128	16384	896
256	65536	2048
512	262144	4608

Figure 12.10 Efficiency of sorting algorithms

12.5 Function qsort

The ANSI C library contains a function associated with the header file <stdlib.h> for sorting an array of data using the Quicksort algorithm. The prototype for the function is:

```
void qsort(const void *base, size_t num, size_t width,
                int (*compare) (const void *e1, const void *e2));
```

where   *base*   is the array being sorted;
            num   is the number of elements in the array;
            width   represents the number of bytes required to store an element;
            compare   is a pointer to a user supplied function that compares array elements
                           (e.g. *e1 and *e2) and returns an integer value indicating their relationship:

$$\text{if } *e1 < *e2, \text{ return} < 0$$
$$\text{if } *e1 == *e2, \text{ return} = 0$$
$$\text{if } *e1 > *e2, \text{ return} > 0$$

The array is ordered by increasing value. Reversing the sense of less than and greater than in compare will cause the array to be ordered by decreasing value. The original array is overwritten with the sorted array. The following program illustrates how to use the library function qsort, and replaces the quicksort function developed in the previous example to sort the same array of integers.

Program Example 12.6: Demonstration of the Function qsort.

```
/*
chap_12\ex_6.c
program to demonstrate qsort from <stdlib.h>
*/

#include <stdio.h>
#include <stdlib.h>
#define size 7

int compare(const void *n1, const void *n2)
{
        return *((int *)n1) - *((int *)n2);
}

void main(void)
{
        int numbers[size] = {18,7,21,5,13,10,20};
        int index;
        qsort(numbers, size, sizeof(int), compare);

        for (index=0; index < size; index++)
            printf("%3d", numbers[index]);
}
```

If you examine the user defined function, the formal-parameter list contains two parameters that are `void` (generic) pointers . These pointers have been described as constant, since the values of the data they point to cannot be changed within this function.

In returning the difference between the values being pointed at, you might expect to write `*n1 - *n2`, however, because the parameters are declared as `void *` pointers, you will need to type cast them into a compatible type `(int *)`. Therefore, the value `*((int *)n1) - *((int *)n2)` is returned as an integer of value less than zero, zero or greater than zero depending upon the values of `*n1` and `*n2`.

12.6 Searching

The concept of searching was first introduced in Chapter 11. In this section, we will cover in detail two major methods, the sequential search and the binary search.

Sequential Search

In Chapter 11 a function was developed for searching for a student number `search_number`, knowing that the number in the array appeared in ascending sequence. This algorithm can be adapted to cater for searching for strings that are ordered in an array. When the information held in an array is sorted into search key order, it is not always necessary to search through an entire array before discovering that the information is not present. Consider for a moment the following information held in the array depicted in Figure 12.11. Alphabetically Adams is before Davies, Davies is before Evans, Evans is before Farthing, and so on.

0	Adams	18 Milestone Road
1	Davies	72 Sherwood Avenue
2	Evans	433 Lake Street
3	Farthing	10 Almond Avenue
4	Fielding	21 Turnpike Boulevard
5	Hewitt	30 Chester Street
6	Jones	336 Cornwallis Road
7	Mowbray	45 Brookside Avenue
8	Peters	113 Flemming Avenue
9	Quayle	212 Wiltshire Boulevard
10	Rankin	732 High Road

Figure 12.11 An array of records

If we search the contents of the array for the key Ellis, then we must perform the following comparisons, illustrated in Figure 12.12, before we discover that Ellis is not in the array. Ellis is alphabetically greater than both Adams and Davies, so may be found further on in the array. Ellis is alphabetically less than Evans; therefore, an entry for Ellis cannot exist in the array because the names are ordered into alphabetical sequence. By sorting the contents of the array into alphabetical order on the name of each person, only three key comparisons are necessary to discover that Ellis does not exist in the array. If the array is not sorted by name, then we have to compare every name in the array in order to discover that Ellis does not exist in the array.

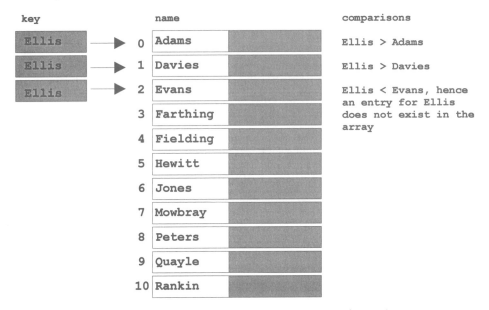

Figure 12.12 A sequential search on an array of records

Assuming that the records are stored into consecutive array locations from 0 to 10, the following algorithm is used in searching for a surname in the array.

```
boolean sequential_search(names_addresses table[],
                     int size, char key[], int *position)
/* function to search the records of an ordered array for a key */
{
    int      index=0;

    while (index < size)
    {
        if (strcmp(key, table[index].name) == 0)
        {
            *position = index;
            return true;
        }
    }
```

358

```
        else if (strcmp(key, table[index].name) < 0)
            return false;
        else
            index++;
    }
    return false;
}
```

The index used to access each cell of the array is initialized to 0, the first cell position of the array.

While the value of the index is within the limits of the array [0 .. 10], the search for the key continues. If the key is equal to the surname in the cell being examined, the information is found and the Boolean value true is returned. The position in the array of the located record, that is the value of the index, is assigned to the contents of what is being pointed at by the pointer variable position.

If the key is less than the name field in the cell being examined, then the surname cannot exist in the array and the search can stop. The value false is returned as long as it is understood that the value of the pointer to the variable position has not been determined and should not be used.

If the key is greater than the name field in the cell being examined, then the surname may exist further down the array and the value of the index is increased to examine the contents of the next cell.

This algorithm is implemented as the function sequential_search in the following program that stores eleven records containing surnames and addresses in a one-dimensional array in alphabetical order of surname. A user is invited to input a name, and the array is searched for a key match. If the key is found, the corresponding address is output.

Program Example 12.7: Sequential Search on an Array of Records

```
/*
chap_12\ex_7.c
program to create an array of records and given the name
of a person search the array for the corresponding address
*/

#include <stdio.h>
#include <string.h>

typedef enum {false, true} boolean;

typedef struct {
                char    name[20];
                char    address[40];
           }    names_addresses;
```

```
boolean sequential_search(names_addresses table[],
                          int size, char key[], int *position)
/* function to search the records of an ordered array for a key */
{
    int     index=0;

    while (index < size)
    {
        if (strcmp(key, table[index].name) == 0)
        {
            *position = index;
            return true;
        }
        else if (strcmp(key, table[index].name) < 0)
            return false;
        else
            index++;
    }
    return false;
}

void main(void)
{
    #define number_of_entries 11

    names_addresses table[number_of_entries] =
    {{"Adams",     "18 Milestone Road"},
     {"Davies",    "72 Sherwood Avenue"},
     {"Evans",     "433 Lake Street"},
     {"Farthing",  "10 Almond Avenue"},
     {"Fielding",  "21 Turnpike Boulevard"},
     {"Hewitt",    "30 Chester Street"},
     {"Jones",     "336 Corwallis Road"},
     {"Mowbray",   "45 Brookside Avenue"},
     {"Peters",    "113 Flemming Avenue"},
     {"Quayle",    "212 Wiltshire Boulevard"},
     {"Rankin",    "732 High Road"}};


    int     index;
    char    name_key[20];
    boolean found;

    do
    {
        printf("name? ");
        gets(name_key);
```

```
        found = sequential_search(table, number_of_entries, name_key, &index);

        if (found)
          printf("address %s\n", table[index].address);
        else
          printf("name not found\n");

      } while (found);
}
```

Results

```
name? Quayle
212 Wiltshire Boulevard
name? Fielding
21 Turnpike Boulevard
name? Ellis
name not found
```

Binary Search

This method requires that the keys are sorted prior to the search and that the information is stored in an array. From Figure 12.13 the array is divided into two parts by the midpoint. The midpoint is calculated as (first+last)/2, and in this example it is assigned to the variable location. The key *Quayle* is compared with the key at location. Since *Quayle > Hewitt*, *Quayle* may be found in the lower subarray within the bounds (location+1 .. last). The process is repeated with a new midpoint being calculated as (location+1+last)/2 and assigned to the variable location. The key *Quayle* is compared with the key at the location. Since *Quayle > Peters*, *Quayle* may be found in the lower subarray within the bounds (location+1 .. last). The process is repeated again with a new midpoint being calculated. Note when a sublist contains an even number of keys the midpoint may be taken to be the next lowest key from the center. A match for the key *Quayle* exists at location=9. If the value for first had exceeded the value for last, then no match can be found for the key. Notice that only three comparisons are necessary compared with ten comparisons if a serial or sequential search had been performed.

A binary search can be implemented succinctly using recursion. The search involves calculating a midpoint from the lowest and highest indexes of an array and, if the key is in the lower half of the subarray, repeating the process within the bounds (first .. location-1). However, if the key is in the upper half of the subarray, we repeat the process within the bounds (location+1 .. last). Recursion continues until the bounds of the subarray cross (first > last), or a match for the key is found.

Figure 12.13 A binary search for a surname in an array

The function `binary_search` has the following prototype:

```
boolean binary_search(names_addresses table[], char key[],
                      int first, int last, int *location);
```

where `table` is the array to be searched, `key` is a string to be matched with the keys in the array, `first`, `last`, and `location` are as described. The following program uses the binary search to locate the address of a person given the surname as key. The results are similar to those found in the previous section, but the method of searching for a key is different.

Program Example 12.8: Binary Search of an Array of Records

```c
/*
chap_12\ex_8.c
program to create an array of records and given the name
of a person binary search the array for the correct address
*/

#include <stdio.h>
#include <string.h>

typedef enum {false, true} boolean;
```

362

```
typedef struct {
                char    name[20];
                char    address[40];
        } names_addresses;


boolean binary_search(names_addresses table[], char key[],
                int first, int last, int *location)
/* function to binary search the records of an ordered array for a key */
{
    if (first > last)
       return false;
    else
    {
       *location = (first+last) / 2;
       if (strcmp(key, table[*location].name)==0)
          return true;
       else if (strcmp(key, table[*location].name) < 0)
          return binary_search(table, key, first, *location-1, location);
       else
          return binary_search(table, key, *location+1, last, location);
    }
}

void main(void)
{
    #define number_of_entries 11

    names_addresses table[number_of_entries] =
    {{"Adams",    "18 Milestone Road"},
     {"Davies",   "72 Sherwood Avenue"},
     {"Evans",    "433 Lake Street"},
     {"Farthing", "10 Almond Avenue"},
     {"Fielding", "21 Turnpike Boulevard"},
     {"Hewitt",   "30 Chester Street"},
     {"Jones",    "336 Corwallis Road"},
     {"Mowbray",  "45 Brookside Avenue"},
     {"Peters",   "113 Flemming Avenue"},
     {"Quayle",   "212 Wiltshire Boulevard"},
     {"Rankin",   "732 High Road"}};

    int   first = 0;
    int   last  = number_of_entries-1;
    int   location;
    char  name_key[20];
    boolean found;
```

```
do
{
  printf("name? ");
  gets(name_key);

  found = binary_search(table, name_key, first, last, &location);

  if (found)
    printf("address %s\n", table[location].address);
  else
    printf("name not found\n");

} while (found);
}
```

Figure 12.14 illustrates the performance of a sequential search and a binary search.

N sequential search	$\log_2 N$ binary search
32	5
64	6
128	7
256	8
512	9

Figure 12.14 Efficiency of searching algorithms

12.7 Function bsearch

C Syntax: The ANSI C library contains a function in the header file <stdlib.h> for searching an array of data using the binary search algorithm. The prototype for the function is

binary search function bsearch

```
void *bsearch(const void *key, const void *base, size_t num, size_t width,
              int (*compare) (const void *e1, const void *e2));
```

where   *key*   is a pointer to the element being sought;
             base   is a pointer to the base of the array to be searched;
             num   is the number of elements in the array;
             width   represents the number of bytes required to store an element;
             compare   is a pointer to a user supplied function that compares array elements
                      (e.g. *e1 and *e2) and returns an integer value indicating their relationship:

if *e1 < *e2, return < 0
if *e1== *e2, return = 0
if *e1 > *e2, return > 0

The function returns a pointer to the first matching element if found; otherwise the value NULL is returned.

Notice that the return type is a generic pointer `void *`, since we do not know from the prototype what the data type being pointed at will be.

The following program illustrates how to use the library function `bsearch`, and replaces the `binary_search` function developed in the previous example.

Note: in the function `compare` that the *indirection* operator (`*`) has been used to reference the structure to which `n1` and `n2` point. The *selection* operator (`.`) is then applied to select a member with this structure.

Similarly, the contents of the record being pointed at by `result` is given as `result->address`, which is the same as `(*result).address`.

Program Example 12.9: Demonstration of the Function bsearch

```
/*
chap_12\ex_9.c
program to demonstrate bsearch from <stdlib.h>
*/

#include <stdio.h>
#include <string.h>
#include <stdlib.h>

typedef struct {
                char    name[20];
                char    address[40];
        }   names_addresses;


int compare(const names_addresses *n1, const names_addresses *n2)
{
    return strcmp( (*(names_addresses *)n1).name, (*(names_addresses *)n2).name);
}
```

```
void main(void)
{
    #define number_of_entries 11

    names_addresses table[number_of_entries] =
    {{"Adams",    "18 Milestone Road"},
     {"Davies",   "72 Sherwood Avenue"},
     {"Evans",    "433 Lake Street"},
     {"Farthing", "10 Almond Avenue"},
     {"Fielding", "21 Turnpike Boulevard"},
     {"Hewitt",   "30 Chester Street"},
     {"Jones",    "336 Corwallis Road"},
     {"Mowbray",  "45 Brookside Avenue"},
     {"Peters",   "113 Flemming Avenue"},
     {"Quayle",   "212 Wiltshire Boulevard"},
     {"Rankin",   "732 High Road"}};


    names_addresses *result;
    char            name_key[20];

    do
    {
       printf("name? ");
       gets(name_key);
       result = bsearch(name_key, table, number_of_entries,
                        sizeof(names_addresses), compare);
       if (result)
         printf("address %s\n", result->address);
       else
         printf("name not found\n");

    } while (result != NULL);
}
```

Summary

☐ A recursive function will repeatedly call itself until a criterion for terminating is satisfied.

☐ The computer must return through each level of the recursive function that has been invoked.

☐ Each level of a recursive function represents a smaller solution to a problem; all the levels represent the complete solution to the problem.

☐ In the selection sort the largest item of data is located and transferred to the end of the structure holding the data. The area over which the structure is examined is reduced by one storage unit, and the largest item of data is located and transferred to the end of the structure. These operations continue until the size of the structure is reduced to one storage unit. The contents of the original structure have then been ordered.

☐ In the Quicksort algorithm an array is divided into two partitions by a pivot key. Keys in each partition are compared for an ordered sequence with the pivot key. When an ordered sequence in each partition is no longer possible, the offending keys are swapped. Further comparisons and swapping of keys continue until each key in each partition has been compared. All the keys in one partition will be less than or equal to the pivot key, and all the keys in the other partition will be greater than the pivot key. The partitions themselves are not yet ordered. The algorithm is then applied to each partition recursively until the subpartitions contain only one item of data.

☐ Searching for data held in an array is made more efficient when the data is ordered on key value. If the value of the key is greater than the item being inspected, then the key may be found further on in the array. However, if the value of the key is less than the item being inspected, then the key cannot exist in the array and the search must be abandoned.

☐ The binary search algorithm relies upon the fact that the contents of the array must be ordered. The technique repeatedly divides an array into smaller arrays that are likely to contain the key until either a key match is possible or the array cannot be subdivided further.

Review Questions

1. What is a recursive call to a function?

2. What is a level of recursion?

3. True or false - the computer must pass back through each level of recursion before returning to the initial function call.

4. True or false - a stack is a queue of items with access to the queue from both ends.

5. In recursion, what is normally contained in a stack frame?

6. How does the computer use stack frames when executing recursive calls to a function?

7. If function R calls function R_1 and function R_1 calls function R_2, where R, R_1, and R_2 are the same functions, at what level of function should a terminating case exist?

8. True or false - in question 7 R is a smaller solution than R_1, and R_1 is a smaller solution than R_2.

9. When would you use iteration in place of recursion?

10. Why is recursion considered to have drawbacks over iteration?

11. Distinguish between internal and external sorting.

12. If an array contained 32 integers, proportionally how long would it take to sort the numbers using a selection sort?

13. What changes should you make to the selection sort to reverse the order of the sorted numbers, that is highest to lowest?

14. When will it take as long to sort numbers using Quicksort as it does using the selection sort?

15. If an array contained 128 integers distributed at random, give an order of time that it would take to sort the integers using Quicksort. Compare this to sorting the array using the selection sort.

16. What is a sequential search?

17. What is the proportional saving in time when using a sequential search versus a binary search to search for an items that does exist?

18. In a sequential search, what is the consequence of knowing that the value of the search key is less than the item in the array that is being compared?

19. True or false - the contents of an array do not have to be ordered for a binary search.

20. How many key comparisons are necessary in a binary search when there are 32 items in an array and the key does exist in the array?

Programming Exercises

21. Desk check the following segment of code and comment upon your observations.

```c
void counter(int N)
{
   N++;
   printf("%d\n", N);
   counter(N);
}

void main(void)
{
   int N;

   counter(0);
}
```

22. To sort by name the data in Program Example 12.9 into descending alphabetical order using the `qsort` function, how would you change the `compare` function? Modify `compare` so that it does not allow for type casting but uses local variables.

23. Desk check the code for the function `quicksort` given in Program Example 12.5. Show how the contents of the stack change at each level of recursion.

368

24. When the data in an array is already sorted, Quicksort will return the slowest possible time being proportional to N^2 to sort the data . Derive this value based upon the pivot being the first element in the array.

25. Desk check the following code that searches an array of nonordered strings for a particular key entry. The number of entries in the array is defined as `size`. Comment upon the efficiency of the searching algorithm.

```
int linear_search(char array[][80], char key[])
{
    int index;

    for (index=0; index != size; index++)
    {
        if (strcmp(key, array[index])==0)
            return index;
    }

    return size;
}
```

Programming Problems

26. Write recursive functions to

(a) sum a one-dimensional array containing positive integers only;

(b) raise a number to a power, for example $X^n = X * X^{n-1}$ where $n > 0$;

(c) find the greatest common divisor of two positive integers;

(d) generate the first fifteen numbers in a Fibonacci series where the nth element is the sum of the (n-2) and (n-1) elements for $n > 2$, for example, 1 1 2 3 5 8 13 21 ...

Test each function by embedding it into a separate program.

27. The median of a set of numbers is the number that has the same number of values above and below it. For example, in the set [1,3,9,18,7,5,4], the median is 5 because three numbers [7,9,18] are larger and three numbers [1,3,4] are smaller than 5. Write a program to compute the median of a set of nonzero integers input to the computer in any order for

    (a) an odd number of values;
    (b) an even number of values.

Note: For an odd number of values, the median will be the central value of the ordered set of numbers. An even number of values will have two, not one, central values. The median is the average of the two central values.

28. Write a program to store positive integers in a one-dimensional array, so that the numbers are not in any predefined order. Compare adjacent numbers in the array and swap the numbers so that the first number of the pair is always smaller than the second number of the pair. Repeat the process for all the adjacent numbers in the array.

Repeat the process described in the previous paragraph until all the numbers are sorted into ascending order, that is, no swapping is necessary. This algorithm is known as a *bubble* sort.

Derive the order of magnitude of this sorting algorithm.

29. Implement the `selection_sort` as a recursive function and modify Program Example 12.4 to test your answer.

30. Use an editor to create a text file of up to 100 lines of text where each line contains a student number and a student name, for example, `100Adams, J`.

Write a program to read the text file and store each line as a record in a one-dimensional array. Each record has the following format:

```
typedef struct    {
                    int   number;
                    char name[20]
                } student_id;
```

where `number` is a unique student number that corresponds with the `name` of a student.

Sort the array on the key `number` using `qsort`.

Given a `number` search the array using `bsearch` for the name of the student and display this name if it is found.

Chapter 13
Binary Files

You are already familiar with the concepts involved when processing text files. Text files, however, do not always offer the best possible advantages for the storage and processing of data.

This chapter continues the theme of file processing by introducing you to a method for storing data in binary files using the internal binary format of data held in main memory.

The chapter incorporates many of the features of the C language already explained in the previous three chapters and demonstrates various techniques for processing multiple files.

By the end of the chapter, you should have an understanding of the following topics:

- The difference between text and binary files.
- The advantages and disadvantages of text and binary files.
- Reading and writing to binary files.
- Merging of data stored on two files.
- Updating a master file from a transaction file.
- Direct access to records held in a binary file.

13.1 Binary Versus Text Files

In chapter 10 you were introduced to text files that are composed from lines of characters. However, in creating these files it is necessary to represent all numbers in a character format. Therefore, it is necessary to convert the numbers from their internal form of representation to characters using the appropriate format string in an `fprintf` statement. Similarly, it is necessary to convert numbers stored as characters back into their correct internal representation by using the correct format string in an `fscanf` statement.

Text files attempt to match the internal storage of data to the typical formatting of text for the operating system being used. For example, in C a new-line character is represented as (\n), whereas under MSDOS a new-line is represented as a carriage return and a line feed - a two-character combination. Therefore, a single-character new-line in memory is translated into two characters when written to a file. Similarly, when the combination carriage return and line feed is read from a file, it is converted and stored as a single new-line character (\n) in the main memory.

A text stream does *not* guarantee a one-to-one mapping between what is written to a file and what is actually stored in the file, and vice versa.

Binary files assume nothing about the operating system and as such make no translations on the data. The contents of main memory will be written to the file using the internal binary representation of the data and vice versa. A binary stream *does* guarantee a one-to-one mapping between the internal representation of the data and what appears on the file.

Binary files have the following advantages over text files.

- [ ] There is no need to worry whether a binary file is terminated with a new line in order to process the file using the read-ahead technique. All binary files will be processed in this manner.

- [ ] Data are often grouped together in structures and as such can be written to a file as a series of records.

- [ ] There is some saving in file space, since the internal representation of the data is stored.

- [ ] There is some saving in processing time, since there is no need to translate numbers into characters and vice versa.

The use of binary files causes the following inconveniences rather than disadvantages.

- [ ] A binary file consists of a sequence of arbitrary bytes that is not in a human-readable form, since the contents of the bytes are stored as the internal representation of the data.

- [ ] Such files can be created only by a specific program; unlike text files, binary files cannot be created using an editor.

C Syntax:

binary file mode

Whether a stream is text or binary depends upon the mode in which it is opened. The mode for text files was described in Chapter 10 as `r` or `w` for read and write, respectively. A file opened in a binary mode is qualified with the letter `b`, for example, `rb` is a binary file opened for reading and `wb` is a binary file opened for writing.

13.2 Reading and Writing

There are two functions **fread** and **fwrite** associated with the reading and writing of binary files. These functions allow us to copy information to and from main memory, without any translation process taking place, using a binary file. The prototype of `fread` is

$$size\_t\ fread(void\ *ptr,\ size\_t\ size,\ size\_t\ nmemb,\ FILE\ *stream);$$

The function reads into the array pointed to by `ptr` up to `nmemb` elements whose size is specified by `size` from the stream pointed to by `stream`.

For example, if a structure is declared as being of the type `team_record`

```
typedef struct   {
                    char    name[20];
                    int     points;
                 } team_record;
```

an array is declared as:

```
team_record buffer[1];
```

and a data stream as:

```
FILE *data_file;
```

then the statement used to read a record from the `data_file` and store it in the array `buffer` is

```
fread(buffer, sizeof(team_record), 1, data_file);
```

The function `fread` returns the number of complete items read. If this value is less than `nmemb`, we use `feof` or `ferror` to determine whether the end of file was reached or whether another error occurred.

The `fwrite` function has a format similar to `fread`, and its prototype is given as

$$size\_t\ fwrite(const\ void\ *ptr,\ size\_t\ size,\ size\_t\ nmemb,\ FILE\ *stream);$$

The function writes from the array pointed to by `ptr` up to `nmemb` elements whose size is specified by `size` to the stream pointed to by `stream`.

For example, if the requirement is to write just one record from the array `buffer` to the stream `data_file`, assuming that it was opened in the appropriate mode, then the following statement is used.

```
fwrite(buffer, sizeof(team_record), 1, data_file);
```

The function returns the number of complete items actually written. If an error or end-of-file condition occurs, this number will be less than `nmemb`. Again the functions `ferror` or `feof` should be used to determine which condition caused `fwrite` to terminate. If either `nmemb` or `size` is zero, the return value will be zero and no bytes are written.

C will keep track of the byte position of the next item to access in a file by using a **file position indicator**. When a file is opened in either the reading or writing mode, the file position indicator is positioned at the start of the file (byte position zero or character number zero). The system maintains the file position indicator after every read or write to the file so that an orderly progression through the file can be made.

For both the fread and fwrite functions, the file position indicator for a particular stream is advanced by the number of characters successfully read or written, respectively. If an error occurs, the resulting value of the file position indicator for the stream is indeterminate.

Case Study: Creation of a Binary File

Create a binary file to contain information about members of a swimming club. Each record of the file contains information on the name, sex, age, and competition results for each member and can be represented by the following structure:

```
typedef struct   {
                     char name[20];
                     char sex;
                     int  age;
                     int  results[3];
                 } record;
```

Typical records in the file named members.bin might contain the following data:

```
    Jones      M 17 1 2 3
    Evans      F 15 1 0 1
```

The entry for competition results shows the placing (1) first, (2) second, (3) third, and (0) not placed or absent from the competition for a member over the previous three swimming competitions.

Problem Analysis - The solution to this problem involves inputting the data via a keyboard for each swimmer and storing it in a one-dimensional array. Once the array contains all the records for the swimmers, it is simply copied to the binary file.

Algorithm for the Function main

1. *open members file for writing*
2. *fill an output buffer (array) with records*
3. *write the contents of the buffer (array) to the members file*
4. *display the contents of the buffer (array)*
5. *close members file*

Data Dictionary for the Function main - This function will contain three local variables. The first is a file pointer to the stream, the second is the array used to store the records of the swimmers, and the third is the number of records stored in the array.

```
FILE    *members;
record buffer[buffer_size];
int     size;
```

Note the `buffer_size` is defined as a simple macro specifying a theoretical maximum number of records that can be accommodated. The variable `size` refers to the actual number of records stored.

Algorithm for the Function open_file

1 open members file for writing
1.1   open file
1.2   if file cannot be opened
1.3   print warning message
1.4   terminate program
1.5   return pointer to stream

Data dictionary for the Function open_file - This function contains one local variable to act as a file pointer when opening a file. The parameters are the file string containing the path name, the name of the file, and the mode of access to the file. The function returns a pointer to the stream that has been opened. The function prototype is given as

```
FILE *open_file(const char filename[], const char mode[]);
FILE *file;
```

Algorithm for the Function fill_buffer

2   fill an output buffer (array) with records
2.1   do
2.2   create a record and store in the next consecutive location of the buffer (array)
2.3   while more records to create
2.4   return the size of the buffer (array)

Data Dictionary for the Function fill_buffer - The function has two reference formal-parameters: the array `buffer` containing the records input at the keyboard and the number of records `size` in the array. There are two local variables, an index used to subscript the array buffer and a character to represent the users' reply for whether they want more data. The function prototype is given as

```
void fill_buffer(record buffer[], int *size);

int  index = 0;
char more_data;
```

Algorithm for the Function create_record - This function returns a complete record for a swimmer. The record is then stored in the array `buffer` declared in the function `fill_buffer`.

2.2   create a record and store in the next consecutive location of the buffer (array)
2.2.1   input name, sex and age of swimmer
2.2.2   input the last three competition results for the swimmer
2.2.3   return the record for the swimmer

Data Dictionary for the Function create_record - This function has no formal parameters and returns a record for a swimmer. The function has one local variable a record for a swimmer. The function prototype is given as

```
record create_record(void);
record swimmer;
```

Algorithm for the Function display_buffer

4   display contents of buffer (array)
4.1   for every entry in the buffer (array)
4.2   display name, sex and age of swimmer
4.3   display the last three results of the swimmer

Data Dictionary for the Function display_buffer - This function contains two formal parameters: the array `buffer` whose contents are to be displayed and the number of records `size` in the array. There is one local variable `index` used as a subscript to the array. The function prototype is given as

```
void display_buffer(const record buffer[], int size);
int index;
```

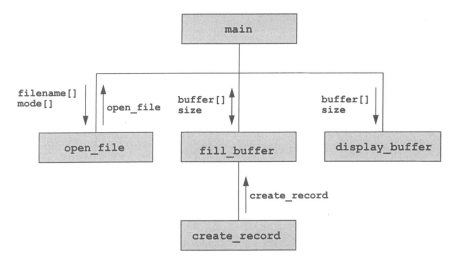

Figure 13.1 Structure chart for creating a binary file

376

```
/*
chap_13\ex_1.c
program to produce a binary file
*/

#include <stdio.h>
#include <stdlib.h>
#include <errno.h>
#define members_file "a:\\chap_13\\members.bin"
#define buffer_size 100
#define write_bin "wb"

typedef struct {
                char name[20];
                char sex;
                int  age;
                int  results[3];
            } record;

FILE *open_file(const char filename[], const char mode[])
/* function to open a file in a specific mode and return
the name of the file if it can be opened, otherwise
return NULL
*/
{
    FILE *file;

    file = fopen(filename, mode);
    if (file == NULL)
    {
       printf("%s cannot be opened\n", filename);
       exit(errno);
    }
    else
       return file;
}

record create_record(void)
/* function to supply the data fields of a single record */
{
        record swimmer;

        printf("name? ");
        gets(swimmer.name);
        printf("sex? ");
        swimmer.sex = getchar();
        printf("age? ");
        scanf("%d", &swimmer.age);
        printf("results? ");
```

377

```
            scanf("%d%d%d", &swimmer.results[0],
                            &swimmer.results[1],
                            &swimmer.results[2]);
            getchar();
            return swimmer;
}

void fill_buffer(record buffer[], int *size)
/* function to fill the output buffer with records */
{
        int  index = 0;
        char more_data;

        do
        {
           buffer[index] = create_record();
           index++;
           printf("more data Y[es] or N[o]? ");
           more_data=toupper(getchar()); getchar();
        }
        while (more_data == 'Y');
        *size = index;
}


void display_buffer(const record buffer[], int size)
/* function to display the contents of a file buffer */
{
        int index;
        for (index=0; index < size; index++)
           printf("%s\t%c %3d %2d%2d%2d\n",
                   buffer[index].name, buffer[index].sex, buffer[index].age,
                   buffer[index].results[0],
                   buffer[index].results[1],
                   buffer[index].results[2]);
}

void main(void)
{
        FILE   *members;
        record buffer[buffer_size];
        int    size;

        members = open_file(members_file, write_bin);
        fill_buffer(buffer, &size);
        fwrite(buffer, sizeof(record), size, members);
        display_buffer(buffer, size);
        fclose(members);
}
```

Partial results, including screen listing of contents of the binary file

```
name? Jones
sex? M
age? 17
results? 1 2 3
more data Y[es] or N[o]? Y
  .
  .
  .
```

```
Jones     M 17 1 2 3
Holmes    M 18 1 1 1
Evans     F 15 1 0 1
Peters    F 14 1 1 0
Nichols   M 18 1 2 2
Adams     F 15 1 1 2
Betts     M 17 3 1 1
Jenkins   M 16 1 0 1
Patel     F 15 2 0 1
Morgan    F 15 1 0 3
Phelps    M 17 1 2 1
Smith     F 16 1 1 3
```

Case Study: Splitting a Binary File into Two New Files

 The binary file of members that has been created can be used to create two new files of swimmers: a file of male swimmers in the age range (16 < age <= 18) and a file of female swimmers in the age range (14 < age <= 16). The files will contain the names of the eligible members and the total number of points scored by each member over the previous three competitions. The structure of a record in the file is defined as

```
typedef struct   {
                char  name[20];
                int   points;
         } team_record;
```

A points system is used to signify how well a swimmer did in the last three competitions. Three points are awarded for first place, two points for second place, and one point for third place. No points are awarded for not being placed or being absent from a competition. For example, a member with two first places and one second place is awarded eight points.

Problem Analysis - The contents of the members file is read into an array. Each record in the array is then processed to calculate the total number of points for a swimmer. If the swimmer is male and within the age limits, his name and points are written to the file of male swimmers; however, if the swimmer is female and within the age limits, her name and points are written to the file of female swimmers.

The number of points can be calculated by inspecting the array `results` which contains the results from the last three competitions. For nonzero values, calculate the points as *(4 - place in competition)*. For example, if a swimmer had the results from the last three competitions as 1   1   2, the calculation for the total is (4-1) +(4-1) +(4-2) = 8 points.

Apart from using separate functions to open a file and display the contents of a file, all the processing can be confined to the main function.

Algorithm for the Function main

1. open members file for reading
2. open males and females files for writing
3. split members file into males and females files (refined into the function split_file)
4. close members, males, and females files

5. open males and females files for reading
6. display contents of males file
7. display contents of females file
8. close males and females files

Data Dictionary for the Function main - The function contains local variables that represent pointers to the three data streams.

```
FILE *members, *males, *females;
```

Algorithm for the Function open_file - This algorithm has already been given in the preceding case study.

Algorithm for the Function split_file

3. split members file into males and females files (refined into the function split_file)

3.1   read entire contents of members file into a buffer (array)
3.2   for each record in the buffer (array)
3.3   initialize the points to zero
3.4   calculate the points based on the competition results
3.5   if swimmer is male and aged between 16 and 18 then
3.6   copy name and points to male record buffer
3.7   write contents of male record buffer to male file
3.8   else if swimmer is female and aged between 14 and 16 then
3.9   copy name and points to female record buffer
3.10   write contents of female record buffer to female file

Data Dictionary for the Function split_files - The function contains three formal parameters that are pointers to the data streams `members`, `males`, and `females`. There are local variables for the array containing all the swimmers records and arrays containing a single record for the male and female swimmers, subscripts to allow access to arrays, and a variable to represent the number of points scored by each swimmer. The function prototype is given as

```
void split_files(FILE *members, FILE *males, FILE *females);
```

```
record buffer[buffer_size];        /* array containing records of swimmers */
team_record male_buffer[1];        /* array with record of male swimmer */
team_record female_buffer[1];      /* array with record of female swimmer */
int size;                          /* number of records for all swimmers */
int index, competition;            /* subscripts to buffer and results */
int points;                        /* total number of points per swimmer */
```

Algorithm for the Function display_file - can be used in algorithmic steps 6 and 7 in the main function to display the contents of the males and females files.

read one record from the file
while not end of file
    display the number of points and the name of the swimmer
    read one record from the file
display new line

Data Dictionary for the Function display_file - The function contains one formal parameter, which is a pointer to a data stream for the file to be displayed. There is one local variable: an array for storing one record at a time from the file. The function prototype is given as

```
void display_file(FILE *name);
```

```
team_record buffer[1];
```

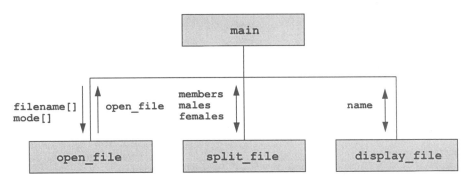

Figure 13.2 Structure chart for splitting the file

```
/*
chap_13\ex_2.c
program to read a binary file and create two new binary files
*/

#include <stdio.h>
#include <stdlib.h>
#include <string.h>
#include <errno.h>

#define members_file "a:\\chap_13\\members.bin"
#define male_file    "a:\\chap_13\\males.bin"
#define female_file  "a:\\chap_13\\females.bin"
#define buffer_size 100
#define write_bin "wb"
#define read_bin "rb"

typedef struct {
                char name[20];
                char sex;
                int  age;
                int  results[3];
            } record;

typedef struct {
                char name[20];
                int  points;
            } team_record;

FILE *open_file(const char filename[], const char mode[])
/* function to open a file in a specific mode and return
the name of the file if it can be opened, otherwise
return NULL
*/
{
    FILE *file;

    file = fopen(filename, mode);
    if (file == NULL)
    {
       printf("%s cannot be opened\n", filename);
       exit(errno);
    }
    else
       return file;
}
```

```
void split_file(FILE *members, FILE *males, FILE *females)
/* function to take the members file and split it into two files
based upon age and sex criteria */
{
    record       buffer[buffer_size];
    team_record  male_buffer[1], female_buffer[1];
    int          size;
    int          index, competition;
    int          points;

    size = fread(buffer, sizeof(record), buffer_size, members);

    for (index=0; index < size; index++)
    {
       points=0;
       for (competition=0; competition < 3; competition++)
           if (buffer[index].results[competition] > 0)
               points = points + 4 - buffer[index].results[competition];

       if (buffer[index].sex == 'M' &&
           buffer[index].age > 16 && buffer[index].age <=18)
       {
           strcpy(male_buffer[0].name, buffer[index].name);
           male_buffer[0].points = points;
           fwrite(male_buffer, sizeof(team_record), 1, males);
       }
       else if (buffer[index].sex == 'F' &&
               buffer[index].age > 14 && buffer[index].age <= 16)
       {
           strcpy(female_buffer[0].name, buffer[index].name);
           female_buffer[0].points = points;
           fwrite(female_buffer, sizeof(team_record), 1, females);
       }
    }
}

void display_file(FILE *name)
/* function to display the contents of a binary file */
{
    team_record buffer[1];

    fread(buffer, sizeof(team_record), 1, name);
    while (! feof(name))
    {
       printf("%3d %s\n", buffer[0].points, buffer[0].name);
       fread(buffer, sizeof(team_record), 1, name);
    }
    printf("\n");
}
```

```
void main(void)
{
     FILE          *members, *males, *females;

     members = open_file(members_file, read_bin);
     males   = open_file(male_file, write_bin);
     females = open_file(female_file, write_bin);

     split_file(members, males, females);

     fclose(members);
     fclose(males);
     fclose(females);

     males = open_file(male_file, read_bin);
     females = open_file(female_file, read_bin);

     display_file(males);
     display_file(females);

     fclose(males);
     fclose(females);
}
```

Results indicating the contents of the males and females files

```
6 Jones
9 Holmes
7 Nichols
7 Betts
8 Phelps

6 Evans
8 Adams
5 Patel
4 Morgan
7 Smith
```

Case Study: Processing a Binary File

After splitting the members file into two separate files, the next requirement is to read each file and produce a list of the three best male swimmers and the three best female swimmers based upon the highest number of points scored over the previous three competitions.

Problem Analysis - The simplest way to solve this problem is to treat it as two separate problems by processing the males and females files separately. A file is read and its contents stored in an array. The array is then sorted using the function qsort into descending order on points as the key. Provided there are at least three records in the array, then the first three records are displayed, thus giving the top three swimmers for that file. Remember the function qsort will require a separate function compare to allow data in the array to be compared.

Algorithm for the Function main

1. open males file for reading
2. read the entire contents of the males file into a buffer
3. sort the contents of the buffer into descending order on points scored
4. if size of buffer >= 3 then
5.   display top three swimmers from the buffer (refined into function top_three)
6. close males file

This algorithm is repeated again in the main function for the females file.

Data Dictionary for the Function main - The function contains local variables that declare pointers to the streams for the males and females files, an array to store the contents of either file, and a variable that represents the number of records in each file.

```
FILE          *males, *females;
team_record   buffer[buffer_size];
int           size;
```

Algorithm for the Function open_file - already described in Case Study: Creation of a Binary File.

Algorithm for the Function top_three

5. display top three swimmers from the buffer

5.1   for the first three records in the array
5.2   display the points scored and the name of the swimmer
5.3   display new lines

Data Dictionary for the Function top_three - The function has one formal parameter which is the array containing the records from a particular file. The one local variable is used as a subscript to access records from the array. The prototype for the function is given as

```
void top_three(const team_record buffer[]);
```

```
int index; /* subscript to the array */
```

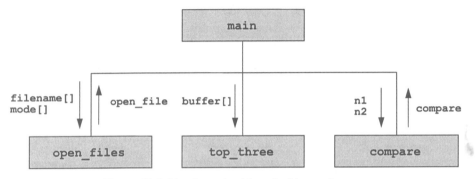

Figure 13.3 Structure chart to select top swimmers

```
/*
chap_13\ex_3.c
program to read a binary files sort them on points scored and
display the first three records in each file
*/

#include <stdio.h>
#include <stdlib.h>
#include <errno.h>

#define male_file    "a:\\chap_13\\males.bin"
#define female_file  "a:\\chap_13\\females.bin"
#define buffer_size 100
#define read_bin "rb"

typedef struct {
                char name[20];
                int  points;
            } team_record;

FILE *open_file(const char filename[], const char mode[])
/* function to open a file in a specific mode and return
the name of the file if it can be opened, otherwise
return NULL
*/
```

```
{
    FILE *file;

    file = fopen(filename, mode);
    if (file == NULL)
    {
        printf("%s cannot be opened\n", filename);
        exit(errno);
    }
    else
        return file;
}

void top_three(const team_record buffer[])
/* function to display the first three records from an array */
{
    int index;

    for (index=0; index < 3; index++)
        printf("%2d %s\n", buffer[index].points, buffer[index].name);

    printf("\n\n");
}

int compare(const void *n1, const void *n2)
{
    return (*(team_record *)n2).points - (*(team_record *)n1).points;
}


void main(void)
{
    FILE        *males, *females;
    team_record buffer[buffer_size];
    int         size;

    males   = open_file(male_file, read_bin);
    females = open_file(female_file, read_bin);

    size = fread(buffer, sizeof(team_record), buffer_size, males);
    qsort(buffer, size, sizeof(team_record), compare);
    if (size >= 3)
    {
        printf("male swimming team\n");
        top_three(buffer);
    }

    size = fread(buffer, sizeof(team_record), buffer_size, females);
    qsort(buffer, size, sizeof(team_record), compare);
```

```
    if (size >= 3)
    {
        printf("female swimming team\n");
        top_three(buffer);
    }

    fclose(males);
    fclose(females);
}
```

Results

```
male swimming team
  9 Holmes
  8 Phelps
  7 Nichols

female swimming team
  8 Adams
  7 Smith
  6 Evans
```

13.3 Merging Files

If two binary files contain records that are already sorted on a key, then it is possible to create a third file using the contents of the original two files. The information held on the third file is also sorted on the same key.

The technique of merging two binary files involves the interleaving of the records to form a new binary file. The algorithm for merging the two files relies upon the fact that both files are already sorted on a key.

First the keys of the two files to be merged are compared. If the keys are in ascending order, the record with the lower key value is written to the new file. The file that supplied the record is then read again and processing continues until the end of both files is encountered.

In the following algorithm to merge two files, it is necessary to compare the key of *file_a* with the key of *file_b*. However, when the end of either file is reached, it is necessary to set the key field of the file that has ended to a higher value than all the other keys in the two files. The purpose of this practice is to force the remaining records in the remaining file to be copied to *file_c*. A ~ (ASCII code 126), replaces the first character in the key field, thus setting the key to *high_key*.

The action of reading a record must be followed by testing for the end of the file, and if this condition is true, then setting the key field to a *high_key*.

open file_a and file_b for reading (the two files to be merged)
open file_c for writing (the file that eventually contains the records from file_a and file_b)
read file_a, at end of file set key of file_a to high_key
read file_b, at end of file set key of file_b to high_key
while not end of both files
   if key file_a < key file_b
      write file_a record to file_c
      read file_a, at end of file set key of file_a to high_key
   else
      write file_b record to file_c
      read file_b, at end of file set key of file_b to high_key
close all files

Desk check the preceding algorithm with the data displayed after the program in Case Study: Splitting a Binary File into Two New Files is run, but first manually sort the data for each file on the key surname.

Consider how you would modify the algorithm to merge two files that had been sorted on a key into descending order.

In Program Example 13.1 the binary data files `males.bin` and `females.bin` are both sorted using the surname as the key. The files are then merged using the two-way merging algorithm, and the contents of the new file containing the merged data are then displayed on the screen.

Program Example 13.1: Merging Two Sorted Files.

```
/*
chap_13\ex_4.c
program to sort two binary files into alphabetical sequence
merge the files into one and display the contents of the new file
*/

#include <stdio.h>
#include <stdlib.h>
#include <string.h>
#include <errno.h>

#define male_file      "a:\\chap_13\\males.bin"
#define female_file    "a:\\chap_13\\females.bin"
#define merged_file    "a:\\chap_13\\merged.bin"
#define buffer_size 100
#define read_bin "rb"
#define write_bin "wb"
#define tilde "~"  /* high value */
```

```
typedef struct {
                    char name[20];
                    int  points;
             } team_record;

FILE *open_file(const char filename[], const char mode[])
/* function to open a file in a specific mode and return
the name of the file if it can be opened, otherwise
return NULL
*/
{
    FILE *file;

    file = fopen(filename, mode);
    if (file == NULL)
    {
        printf("%s cannot be opened\n", filename);
        exit(errno);
    }
    else
        return file;
}

void write_records(const team_record buffer[], int size, FILE *name)
/* function to copy the contents of the buffer to a binary file */
{
    fwrite(buffer, sizeof(team_record), size, name);
}

void merge_files(FILE *file_1, FILE *file_2, FILE *file_3)
/* function to perform a two-way merge to produce a third file */
{
    const char  high_value[2] = tilde;
    team_record buffer_1[1], buffer_2[1];

    fread(buffer_1, sizeof(team_record), 1, file_1);
    if (feof(file_1)) strcpy(buffer_1[0].name, high_value);
    fread(buffer_2, sizeof(team_record), 1, file_2);
    if (feof(file_2)) strcpy(buffer_2[0].name, high_value);

    while (! feof(file_1) || ! feof(file_2))
    {
        if (strcmp(buffer_1[0].name, buffer_2[0].name) < 0)
        {
            fwrite(buffer_1, sizeof(team_record), 1, file_3);
            fread(buffer_1, sizeof(team_record), 1, file_1);
            if (feof(file_1)) strcpy(buffer_1[0].name, high_value);
        }
        else
```

```
        {
            fwrite(buffer_2, sizeof(team_record), 1, file_3);
            fread(buffer_2, sizeof(team_record), 1, file_2);
            if (feof(file_2)) strcpy(buffer_2[0].name, high_value);
        }
    }
}

void display_file(FILE *name)
/* function to display the contents of a binary file */
{
    team_record buffer[1];

    fread(buffer, sizeof(team_record), 1, name);
    while (! feof(name))
    {
        printf("%3d %s\n", buffer[0].points, buffer[0].name);
        fread(buffer, sizeof(team_record), 1, name);
    }
    printf("\n");
}

int compare(const void *n1, const void *n2)
{
    return strcmp((*(team_record *)n1).name, (*(team_record *)n2).name);
}


void main(void)
{
    FILE        *males, *females, *merged;
    team_record buffer[buffer_size];
    int         size;

    males   = open_file(male_file, read_bin);
    females = open_file(female_file, read_bin);

    /* read files independently into buffer, sort records and write
       records back to files */

    size = fread(buffer, sizeof(team_record), buffer_size, males);
    qsort(buffer, size, sizeof(team_record), compare);
    fclose(males);
    males = open_file(male_file, write_bin);
    write_records(buffer, size, males);
    fclose(males);

    size = fread(buffer, sizeof(team_record), buffer_size, females);
    qsort(buffer, size, sizeof(team_record), compare);
```

```
    fclose(females);
    females = open_file(female_file, write_bin);
    write_records(buffer, size, females);
    fclose(females);

    /* open files male and female files for reading and merged
       file for writing */

    males   = open_file(male_file, read_bin);
    females = open_file(female_file, read_bin);
    merged  = open_file(merged_file, write_bin);

    /* perform a two-way merge on the male and female files
       writing the result to the merged file */

    merge_files(males, females, merged);

    fclose(males);
    fclose(females);
    fclose(merged);

    /* open merged file for reading so that its contents
       can be displayed */

    merged = open_file(merged_file, read_bin);

    display_file(merged);

    fclose(merged);
}
```

Results

```
8 Adams
7 Betts
6 Evans
9 Holmes
6 Jones
4 Morgan
7 Nichols
5 Patel
8 Phelps
7 Smith
```

13.4 File Maintenance

Information that is contained in data files is not always static; it can change. Such changes to the information will come about through the insertion, amendment, and deletion of records. The process of changing information held on data files is known as updating.

The most common types of files used in an updating situation are the **master** file and the **transaction** file.

Master files are files of a permanent nature, for example, a stock file, a personnel file, a customer file. A feature to note is that master files undergo regular updating to show a current position. For example, when orders are processed, the amount of stock in the stock file should be decreased. It is seen, therefore, that master records contain data of a static nature, for example, a stock number, description of stock, and a minimum reorder level, as well as data that changes each time a transaction occurs, for example, the depletion of a stock level.

A transaction file is made up from the various transactions created from source documents, for example, sales invoices. In a stock control application, the file will contain a list of stock items that have been sold. The transaction file will be used to update the master file. As soon as it serves this purpose, the transaction file is no longer required. It will, therefore, have a very short life because it will be replaced by another transaction file containing the next list of stock items that have been sold.

In the following example, a master file contains the names and addresses of friends in a particular city.

The format of a record is defined as

```
typedef struct   {
                char name[20];
                char address[40];
            } record;
```

and an example of the master file is

Adams	18 Milestone Road
Davies	72 Sherwood Avenue
Evans	433 Lake Street
Farthing	10 Almond Avenue
Fielding	21 Turnpike Boulevard
Hewitt	30 Chester Street
Jones	336 Cornwallis Road
Mowbray	45 Brookside Avenue
Peters	113 Flemming Avenue
Quayle	212 Wiltshire Boulevard
Rankin	732 High Road

This file is to be updated. Friends have moved away from the city and are to be deleted from the file. New friends have been made in the city; therefore, new records are to be inserted into the file. Finally, some existing friends have changed their addresses in the city; therefore, these records must be amended.

The transaction file that contains the data to be updated follows.

Adams	
Barrington	22 Lake Court
Collins	432 Parkside
Farthing	298 Sycamore Drive
Hewitt	
Patel	1016 Long Drive
Ramirez	57 Presidents Court
Rankin	35 Station Road
Tomlinson	794 High Road

If only the name is present in the record, then the friend has moved from the city and is to be deleted from the master file. By comparing transaction file records with master file records, it should be evident that names appearing in the transaction file only (with the address field present) are names of new friends and are to be inserted into the master file. When the same names appear in both files and the records have the address field present but with different addresses, then the record in the master file is to be amended.

The following algorithm can be used to update the master file from the transaction file. The algorithm requires presorting both files into ascending order on the name of the friend. The master file is not overwritten, but instead a new master file is created using a selection of records from both the transaction and master files.

open transaction file and master file for reading
open new master file for writing
read transaction file, at end of file set transaction key to a high value
read master file, at end of file set master key to a high value

while not end of both the transaction and master files
  if transaction key < master key
    write transaction record to new master file
    read transaction file, at end of file set transaction key to a high value
  else if transaction key = master key
    if address field of transaction file is empty
      read transaction file, at end of file set transaction key to a high value
      read master file, at end of file set master key to a high value
    else
      write transaction record to new master file
      read transaction file, at end of file set transaction key to a high value
      read master file, at end of file set master key to a high value
  else
    write master record to new master file
    read master file, at end of file set master key to a high value

close all files

Desk check the preceding algorithm using the data from the transaction and master files.

Program Example 13.2: Updating a Master File from a Transaction File.

```
/*
chap_13\ex_5.c
program to maintain a master file from a transaction file
*/

#include <stdio.h>
#include <stdlib.h>
#include <string.h>

#define trans_file "a:\\chap_13\\trans.bin"
#define master_file "a:\\chap_13\\master.bin"
#define new_master_file "a:\\chap_13\\new_mast.bin"

#define buffer_size 100
#define read_bin "rb"
#define write_bin "wb"
#define tilde "~" /* high value */

typedef struct {
            char name[20];
            char address[40];
        } record;


FILE *open_file(const char filename[], const char mode[])
/* function to open a file in a specific mode and return
the name of the file if it can be opened, otherwise
return NULL
*/
{
    FILE *file;

    file = fopen(filename, mode);
    if (file == NULL)
    {
        printf("%s cannot be opened\n", filename);
        exit(errno);
    }
    else
        return file;
}
```

```
void read_file(FILE *stream, record buffer[])
/* function to read a record in the file */
{
   const char high_value[2]=tilde;

   fread(buffer, sizeof(record), 1, stream);
   if (feof(stream)) strcpy(buffer[0].name, high_value);
}

void update_file(FILE *trans, FILE *master, FILE *new_master)
{
     const char null[2]="";

     record buffer_1[1], buffer_2[1];

     /* read ahead transaction and master files */
     read_file(trans, buffer_1);
     read_file(master, buffer_2);

     /* process files while not end of both files */
     while (! feof(trans) || ! feof(master))
     {
       if (strcmp(buffer_1[0].name, buffer_2[0].name) < 0)
       {
         fwrite(buffer_1, sizeof(record), 1, new_master);
         read_file(trans, buffer_1);
       }
       else if (strcmp(buffer_1[0].name, buffer_2[0].name) == 0)
       {
         if (strcmp(buffer_1[0].address,null)==0)
         {
           read_file(trans, buffer_1);
           read_file(master, buffer_2);
         }
         else
         {
           fwrite(buffer_1, sizeof(record), 1, new_master);
           read_file(trans, buffer_1);
           read_file(master, buffer_2);
         }
       }
       else
       {
         fwrite(buffer_2, sizeof(record), 1, new_master);
         read_file(master, buffer_2);
       }
     }
}
```

```
void main(void)
{
    FILE    *trans, *master, *new_master;
    record buffer_1[1];

    /* open files */
    trans = open_file(trans_file, read_bin);
    master = open_file(master_file, read_bin);
    new_master = open_file(new_master_file, write_bin);

    /* update master file from transaction file and write the result
       to the new master file */
    update_file(trans, master, new_master);

    /* close files */
    fclose(trans);
    fclose(master);
    fclose(new_master);

    /* display the contents of the new master file */
    new_master = open_file(new_master_file, read_bin);

    read_file(new_master, buffer_1);
    while (! feof(new_master))
    {
      printf("\t\t\t%s\r%s\n",buffer_1[0].address, buffer_1[0].name);
      read_file(new_master, buffer_1);
    }

    fclose(new_master);
}
```

Results showing the contents of the new master file

Barrington	22 Lake Court
Collins	432 Parkside
Davies	72 Sherwood Avenue
Evans	433 Lake Street
Farthing	298 Sycamore Drive
Fielding	21 Turnpike Boulevard
Jones	336 Cornwallis Road
Mowbray	45 Brookside Avenue
Patel	1016 Long Drive
Peters	113 Flemming Avenue
Quayle	212 Wiltshire Boulevard
Ramirez	57 Presidents Court
Rankin	35 Station Road
Tomlinson	794 High Road

Before leaving this program, it is worth commenting on how the contents of the new master file were displayed on the screen using

```
printf("\t\t\t%s\r%s\n",buffer_1[0].address, buffer_1[0].name);
```

Notice that a new escape character has been introduced into the control string **\r** that represents a carriage return; in other words, it returns the cursor to the beginning of the line without generating a new line. The control string is processed as follows. Three tabulations are made across the screen followed by an address being displayed; the cursor is then returned to the beginning of the same line, and the name is displayed followed by a new line. Since both the name and address strings are of variable length, this method ensures that both the name and address are printed in two columns. Without this technique the output of the address would appear ragged across the screen.

13.5 Direct Access

The organization of text and binary files means that it is necessary to read each record in a file until the required record is located. If file is not sorted on a particular key, it may be necessary to compare the key of every record in the file before discovering that the record is not present. However, if a file is sorted, then key comparisons are necessary only until the record is found or until it becomes evident from key values that the record cannot exist in the file.

With **direct access** it is possible to go directly to the record that is required without having to search through the records in the file.

The function **fseek** found in the header `<stdio.h>` moves the file position indicator (**fpi**) associated with the specified stream. The file position indicator is moved to a location that is offset bytes from the specified origin. The next operation on the stream will take place at the new location.

C Syntax: The prototype of `fseek` is

fseek

int fseek(FILE *stream, long offset, int origin);

where `stream` specifies the file name, `offset` the number of bytes to move from the origin, and `origin` specifies the reference location for the move; `origin` must be one of the following values:

SEEK_SET	beginning of the file;
SEEK_CUR	current file position;
SEEK_END	end of file.

For example,

```
fseek(filename, 0L, SEEK_SET);   /* fpi moved to start of file */
fseek(filename, 0L, SEEK_END);   /* fpi moved to the end of the file */
fseek(filename, N, SEEK_SET);    /* fpi moved to the Nth byte of the file */
fseek(filename, N, SEEK_CUR);    /* fpi moved ahead by N bytes */
```

398

Case Study: Direct Access to Records in a Binary File

A compact disk player enables the user to select the tracks on a compact disk in random order. This idea can be incorporated into a program to demonstrate the use of direct access to a file by allowing a user to select a track at random and then displaying the artist's name, title of the song/ tune, and the length of playing time on a screen.

Problem Analysis - Rather than having to enter the data for each song/tune on the compact disk at the keyboard, the information on the duration of a track, the name of the artist, and the title of the song/tune is initially stored in a text file.

The contents of the text file taken from the album *Soulemotion* from *Polygram Record Operations Ltd*, follows. Each line in the text file is ordered by track number, starting at track 1 and followed by track 2, and so on, which implies that *Simply Red* is at track 1, *Robert Palmer* at track 2, and so on.

3.23 Simply Red	If you don't know me by now
4.48 Robert Palmer	Mercy mercy me I want you
4.09 Paul Young	Wherever I leave my hat
3.35 Tina Turner	Let's stay together
4.14 Lisa Stansfield	Change
4.43 Whitney Houston	One moment in time
2.46 Dionne Warwick	Walk on by
3.22 Stephanie Mills	Never knew love like this before
3.57 Omar	There's nothing like this
4.51 Kenny Thomas	Thinking about your love
4.22 Cathy Dennis	Too many walls
4.00 Quartz	It's too late
4.13 Phyllis Nelson	Move closer
2.46 James Brown	It's a man's man's man's world
2.26 Wilson Pickett	In the midnight hour
4.01 Barry White	Can't get enough of your love
4.33 Earth Wind and Fire	After the love has gone
3.23 Ashford and Simpson	Solid

Each line in the text file is transferred to the binary file as a structure defined as

```
typedef struct    {
                float   duration;
                char    artist_title[60];
            } information;
```

The size of each record is determined by the operator sizeof(information); therefore, it is possible to change the position of the file position indicator by using the following fseek function:

```
fseek(filename, (long int) (track-1) * sizeof(information), SEEK_SET);
```

If a track is input as 1, the file position indicator will be moved to the start of the file; if a track is input as 2, the file position indicator will be moved through `sizeof(information)` bytes to the next record. A track value of 10 will move the file position indicator through `9*sizeof(information)` bytes to the starting position of the tenth record.

Algorithm for the Function main

1. open music text file for reading
2. open CD binary file for writing
3. transfer data from the music text file to the CD binary file (refined into the function transfer)
4. close music text file
5 . close CD binary file
6. open CD binary file for reading
7. read CD binary file by direct access and display information (refined into function track_selector)
8. close CD binary file

Data Dictionary for the Function main - There are three local variables: two file pointers for the data streams data and compact_disk and one integer variable that represents the number of tracks on a disk.

```
FILE *data;          /* text file */
FILE *compact_disk;  /* random access binary file */
int  tracks;         /* number of tracks on the disk */
```

Algorithm for the Function open_file - already described earlier in the chapter in the case Study: Creation of a Binary File.

Algorithm for the Function transfer

3   transfer data from music text file to the CD binary file

3.1   while not end of music text file
3.2   read line of music text file into buffer
3.3   copy contents of buffer to CD binary file
3.4   increase line count by 1
3.5   return number of lines read from music text file

Data Dictionary for the Function transfer - This function has two formal parameters that are pointers to the data streams for the text file and binary file. The function returns the number of records transferred to the binary file. The function has two local variables: a single-element array used to store a record and a counter to return the number of records written to the binary file. The prototype for this function is given as

```
int transfer(FILE *file_1, FILE *file_2);

information buffer[1];
int         lines= 0;
```

400

Algorithm for the Function track_selector

7   read CD binary file by direct access and display information

7.1   input track required
7.2   while track number in range of CD file
7.3   seek track on CD file
7.4   read record into buffer
7.5   display information from track
7.6   input track required

Data Dictionary for the Function track_selector - The function has two formal parameters. The first is a pointer to the data stream for the binary file, and the second is the total number of tracks on the disk. There are also two local variables: one stores the track request and the other is an array that stores a record from the binary file. The prototype for the function is

```
void track_selector(FILE *name, long int max_track);

int track;
information buffer[1];
```

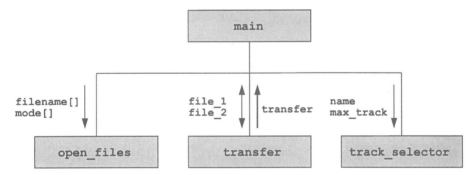

Figure 13.4 Structure chart

```
/*
chap_13\ex_6.c
program to demonstrate random access to a binary file
*/

#include <stdio.h>
#include <stdlib.h>
#include <errno.h>

#define music_file "a:\\chap_13\\music.txt"
#define cd_file    "a:\\chap_13\\cd.bin"

#define read "r"
#define read_bin "rb"
#define write_bin "wb"

typedef struct {
                float duration;
                char  artist_title[60];
            } information;

FILE *open_file(const char filename[], const char mode[])
/* function to open file in a specific mode and return
the name of the file if it can be opened otherwise return NULL
*/
{
    FILE *file;

    file = fopen(filename, mode);
    if (file == NULL)
    {
        printf("%s cannot be opened\n", filename);
        exit(errno);
    }
    else
        return file;
}


int transfer(FILE *file_1, FILE *file_2)
/* function to read a text file, transfer the information to a
   binary file and return the number of lines read */
{
    information buffer[1];
    int         lines = 0;

    while (! feof(file_1))
    {
        /* read a single line from the text file */
```

```
            fscanf(file_1, "%f", &buffer[0].duration);
            fgets(buffer[0].artist_title, 60, file_1);

            /* transfer this line to the binary file */
            fwrite(buffer, sizeof(information), 1, file_2);
            lines++;
        }
        return lines;
}

void track_selector(FILE *name, long int max_track)
/* function to select the information stored on a particular track */
{
        int          track;
        information buffer[1];

        printf("track? "); scanf("%d", &track);
        while (track > 0 && track <= max_track)
        {
            fseek(name, (long int) (track-1) * sizeof(information), SEEK_SET);
            fread(buffer, sizeof(information), 1, name);
            printf("duration:      %5.2f minutes\n", buffer[0].duration);
            printf("artist/title: %s\n", buffer[0].artist_title);
            printf("track? "); scanf("%d", &track);
        }
}

void main(void)
{

        FILE *data;          /* text file */
        FILE *compact_disk;  /* random access file */
        int tracks;

        data         = open_file(music_file, read);
        compact_disk = open_file(cd_file, write_bin);

        tracks = transfer(data, compact_disk);
        fclose(compact_disk);

        compact_disk = open_file(cd_file, read_bin);
        track_selector(compact_disk, tracks);

        fclose(data);
        fclose(compact_disk);
}
```

403

Results

```
track? 10
duration:      4.51 minutes
artist/title: Kenny Thomas      Thinking about your love

track? 5
duration:      4.14 minutes
artist/title: Lisa Stansfield   Change

track? 3
duration:      4.09 minutes
artist/title: Paul Young        Wherever I lay my hat

track? 0
```

Summary

- ☐ A binary file contains data in the same format as it is stored in the main memory, that is to say, in an internal binary format.

- ☐ Text files, however, store data as a series of characters. There is not always a one-to-one correspondence between the data stored in the memory and the data stored in a text file.

- ☐ Binary files use less storage space than text files.

- ☐ Since there is no character conversion between main memory and a binary file and vice versa, file processing should be faster with a binary file than it is with a text file.

- ☐ Binary files cannot be created using an editor; they are a product of a specific program. Information is read or written to binary files in blocks of data using the functions `fread` and `fwrite`, respectively.

- ☐ Direct access files are normally binary files. The position of any record in the file can be specified relative to either the beginning of the file (SEEK_SET), current file position (SEEK_CUR), or end of file (SEEK_END). The file position is then located using the function `fseek`.

Review Questions

1. What is the difference in the way a text file and a binary file store data?

2. How many bytes are required to store the integer 32767 in a text file and in a binary file?

3. True or false - a binary file will guarantee a one-to-one mapping between what is written to the file and what is actually stored in the file.

4. True or false - a binary file can be created using an editor.

5. True or false - the function `fwrite` writes the binary representation of data held in main memory to a binary file.

6. What does the function `fread` return?

7. What is a file position indicator?

8. What is the difference between a master file and a transaction file?

9. Explain the term direct access.

10. What is the purpose of the function `fseek`?

11. What is the position of the file position indicator after the statement fseek(filename, N, SEEK_CUR) is executed?

12. If N is negative in question 11, deduce the position of the file position indicator?

Programming Exercises

13. Given the following declarations:

```
#define number_of_items 10;

typedef struct   {
                    int     stock_id;
                    int     quantity;
                    float   cost;
                  } stock_record;

stock_record *item;
FILE         *stream;
```

what is wrong with the following statement?

```
fread(item, sizeof(stock_record), number_of_items, stream);
```

14. Using the declarations from question 13, discuss the errors in the following statement:

```
fwrite(item, sizeof(item), 1, stream);
```

15. In section 13.3 you were asked to consider how you would modify the algorithm to merge two files that had been sorted on a key into descending order. Describe the algorithm.

16. If a transaction file contained only records with unique keys for amending existing records in a master file, describe an algorithm to update the master file. You may assume that both files are sorted into ascending key order.

Programming Problems

17(a). Write a program to create a binary file *account.bin* that contains records about a person's transactions for a credit card account. A format for a record is given as:

date of transaction - format MM/DD/YY
amount of transaction - maximum value 9999.99
credit or debit C or D
description of the transaction - maximum 80 characters

A typical transaction record might contain the following information:

```
12/18/94 75.50 D Good Food Restaurant
```

The file should, at the time of creation, be ordered on the date of the transaction.

(b). Write a second program to read the file *account.bin* and create a text file *statement.txt* containing a monthly credit card statement similar to the one shown in Figure 13.5. Assume for the purpose of this exercise that the name and address of the account, account number, and date of issue are literals coded in the program rather than variables.

```
                            Report Layout

12345678901234567890123456789012345678901234567890123456789012345678901234567890
                  CREDIT CARD ACCOUNT

Mr.Henry J.Smithers                5115 0042 2345 6000
Boulevard Walk
Boston                             12/31/94


12/01/94   550.00      balance outstanding
12/10/94   250.00      XYZ Supermarket
12/13/94   150.00      Toy Fair
12/18/94    75.50      Good Food Restaurant
12/21/94   250.00CR    payment received - thank you
12/24/94   350.00      Speedy Travel Co

           $1125.50    new balance
```

Figure 13.5 Monthly credit card statement

18(a). A distributor for a chain of music shops receives compact disks from the manufacturer and distributes the disks to individual music shops. Each distribution of a batch of compact disks is entered as a record in a binary file. The format for each record on the file is:

name of music shop - maximum of twenty characters
title and artist on compact disk - maximum of forty characters
quantity distributed - integer
retail price per disk - float

At the end of each month the records in the file are sorted on the name of the music shop into ascending sequence.

Write a program to create the file and sort the data as described.

(b). Read the file created in 18(a) and produce a report similar to that illustrated in Figure 13.6 that shows for each music shop a listing of the title, artist, quantity, and price for each of the compact disks distributed as well as the total value of all the disks.

```
ABC Music

5   Salute to Disney - Arthur Fiedler @ $15.50
10  The Best Country Album @ $11.75
3   Compact Jazz @ $7.50


Total $217.50

Dial-a-Disk

4   Festival of Carols @ %5.50
15  Moods @ $9.35
20  Soulemotion @ 11.75
1   Crocodile Shoes/ Jimmy Nail $12.99


Total $410.24


Fab Four-Hundred Club

    .
    .
    .
```

Figure 13.6 An example of the stock report

19. Three binary files contain lists of words as keys in alphabetical sequence and their meanings. Each word and meaning occupies one record. Write a program that can be reused to create the three different files. Write a second program that will merge the three files to produce a fourth file containing an alphabetical listing of the words and their meanings. Display the contents of this file.

20(a). In a simplified weekly wages system, factory employees are allocated one record per employee on a wages master file. The format of a record on this file follows.

Employee number - integer
Employee name - maximum of 20 characters
Hourly rate of pay - float
Total gross income to date -float
Total FIT to date - float
Total FICA to date - float
Total savings plan to date - float
Total retirement to date - float
Total health insurance to date - float

For every employee the deductions are as follows:

FIT rate - 19% of gross pay
FICA rate - 6.2% of gross pay
Savings plan - 3% of gross pay
Retirement - 8.5% of gross pay
Health insurance $3.75 per employee

A transaction file contains records with the following information:

Employee number - integer
Hours worked in week (including overtime if any) - float

Write a program to produce binary files for the master file and transaction file. Sort the records in each file into ascending order on employee number as key. The number of employees on the transaction file is less than those on the master file and only amendments to the master file are required (no deletions or insertions).

(b). Write a program to process the transaction file against the master file and produce an updated master file and pay-slips similar to those illustrated in Figure 13.7 for each employee on the transaction file.

Check that the values in the master file have been correctly updated after program execution is complete.

```
          ACME DELTA COMPANY - PaySlip

     Employee # 1234   Name: Smith, Arthur

     Rate: $15.75/hr     Hours: 35.75

     Gross pay before deductions: $563.06
     Deductions
     FIT                           106.98
     FICA                           34.91
     Savings Plan                   16.89
     Retirement Plan                47.86
     Health Insurance                3.75
     Total                         210.39

     Pay after deductions:         352.67
```

Figure 13.7 An example of a payslip

21. An alphabetic key is used to access a record position in a direct access file. The size of the file is limited to just twenty records. The alphabetic key must first be transformed into a number in the range 0..19, using a hashing algorithm, before access to the file is possible.

For example, the name George can be transformed into a number by summing the corresponding ASCII code for each letter and finding the remainder after dividing the sum by 20 (the maximum number of records in the file).

G = 71; **e** = 101; **o** = 111; **r** = 114; **g** = 103; **e** = 101

The alphabetic key George is transformed into the numeric key:

$(71+101+111+114+103+101)$ modulus 20
$= 601$ modulus 20
$= 1$

The name George has generated a record position 1; therefore, information relating to the key George may be stored at this record position in a direct access file. However, using the same hashing algorithm, there may be other names that also generate the same record position as George. This is known as a collision.

(a). Write a program to input and store ten names together with the annual birth date for the corresponding person in a direct access file. Generate the record positions using the hashing algorithm described. If a name causes a collision, then use different names until the collision is avoided. When ten names and birth dates have been stored, display the positions and contents of these records. For example, part of this listing might contain the following information:

```
record      person      birthdate
position

0           Hazel       September 23
1           George      February 18
2           Jane        October 11
3
.
.
```

(b). Either adapt part (a) or write a second program to input a name, and convert the name into a record position using the same hashing algorithm. Access a record in the direct access file using the record position generated, compare the name key with the name stored in the record, and if this is the same, then display the birth date of the person.

22(a). A binary file is used to store the details of aircraft departures from an airport in the U.S.A. The format of a record on the file follows.

Departure time (24-hour clock) - long integer
Flight number - maximum of six characters
Destination - maximum of thirty characters

The records are organized into departure-time order.

Write a program to create this aircraft departures file from data held in a text file.

(b). Write a program to read the aircraft departures file created in 22(a) and output a real-time display of the next ten flights that are scheduled to depart from the airport. Figure 13.8 illustrates a typical departure board for this problem. Update the departures board every minute from the information in the binary file. Display the contents of the departure board once every minute.

The following functions found in the Standard Library header <time.h> should be used to solve this problem.

time(&time_now); will give you the time in seconds,

asctime(localtime(&time_now)); will give you the date and time as a string of characters where time_now is of type time_t.

When you refresh the departure board, you may want to clear the screen prior to displaying the board. The control character required to clear a screen depends upon the type of monitor being used and is therefore system dependent. You are advised to consult the reference manual for the version of C you are using in order to find out how to clear the screen.

```
          D E P A R T U R E S

Fri Feb 10 18:59:32 1995

TIME     FLIGHT       DESTINATION
1900     BA147        LONDON HEATHROW
1910     AA202        BOSTON
1925     AA204        BOSTON
1930     LU110        MUNICH
1945     LU120        FRANKFURT
2000     BA654        LONDON GATWICK
2015     BA655        IRELAND SHANNON
2020     AA200        SAN FRANCISCO
2025     SA156        SINGAPORE
2035     SA276        HONG KONG
```

Figure 13.8 An example of a departure board

Chapter 14

Dynamic Data Structures

In Chapter 9 you were introduced to the concept of a pointer and the creation of dynamic arrays. Within this chapter the subject of dynamic data structures is taken further through the discussion of linked lists, queues, stacks, and binary search trees. The purpose of this chapter is to introduce you to these topics so that you may pursue them in greater depth on a later course. By the end of the chapter, you should have an understanding of the following topics:

☐   Creating a linked list.

☐   Traversing and displaying a linked list.

☐   Searching a linked list and inserting and deleting nodes.

☐   Using first-in-first-out (FIFO) queues.

☐   Using last-in-first-out (LIFO) stacks.

☐   Creating a binary search tree.

☐   Traversing a binary tree.

☐   Searching a binary tree and deleting nodes.

14.1 Linked List

Figure 14.1 illustrates a structure containing two members; the first `word` will store a string of characters, and the second `link` is a pointer to data of type `struct record`. The structure is of type `struct record`; therefore, `link` is in effect pointing at data of the same type as the structure and for this reason is known as a **self-referential structure**. The structure has been defined as a type `node`, which may be visualized as a record containing the fields `word` and `link`. The pointer `link` points at data of the same type as `node`, in other words, to another record of the same type.

```
struct record {
                char word[80];
                struct record *link;
              };
typedef struct record node;
```

Figure 14.1 Data type node

A **linked list** is a sequence of nodes in which each node is linked or connected to the node following it as illustrated in Figure 14.2. This list has a pointer `head` pointing at the first node in the list. The first member of this node contains the word `apple`, and the second member of the node is a pointer to the next node. The second node contains the word `banana`, and a pointer to the third node. The third node contains the word `date`. Since this is the last node in the list, `link` cannot point to another node and is therefore given a `NULL` value signified by a *slash* in the figure. To summarize, the linked list illustrated has the following constructional features:

☐   A named pointer variable `head` that points to the first node in the linked list.

☐   A list in which the order of the nodes is determined by an explicit pointer member of each node, rather than by the physical order of the components in memory (as is the case with an array).

☐   A `NULL` pointer indicating the end of the linked list.

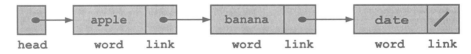

Figure 14.2 An example of a linked list

A linked list may be used in preference to an array for storing data in the main memory when the following circumstances apply.

- ☐ The number of data records to be stored is not known in advance of the program being executed. The linked list is truly a dynamic data structure, since main memory is allocated for storing the records at runtime without having to specify the number of nodes in the list. Although it was stated in Chapter 9 that an array could be dynamic, it was still necessary to specify at runtime the maximum number of elements the array would hold.

- ☐ Nodes need to be inserted into a list or deleted from a list. During the insertion or deletion of nodes in a linked list, there is no movement of the data records in memory, only changes in pointer values. By contrast, the insertion or deletion of records in an array would involve the movement of the records in main memory.

14.2 Creating a Linked List

The linked list illustrated in Figure 14.2 may be created using two functions. The first function create_node allocates space for a new node and stores a word together with a NULL pointer in the node, and the second function create_list allows the user to input words into the list and manipulates the pointer to the next node.

```
node *create_node(node *next, char text[])
/* function to create a node and return a pointer to it */
{
        next=malloc(sizeof(node));

        if (next == NULL)
        {
          printf("no memory allocated - program terminated\n");
          exit(errno);
        }

        strcpy(next->word, text);
        next->link = NULL;
        return next;
}
```

The structure member access operator -> was described in Chapter 11 and is used to access the members of a structure via a pointer; for example, next->word is the same as (*next).word.

An illustration of how function create_node builds a node is given in Figure 14.3.

function create_node - creates a single node
containing data and returns a pointer to this item

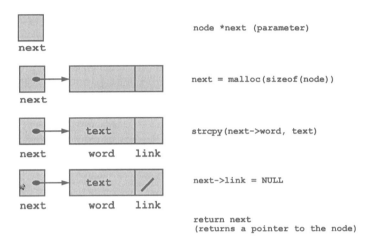

Figure 14.3 Creation of a node using create_node

```
node *create_list(node *head)
/* function to create a linked list and return a pointer
to the head of the linked list */
{
      node *last;
      char word[80];

      printf("input word - enter ! to exit ");
      gets(word);

      while (strcmp(word, "!") != 0)
      {
          if (head == NULL)              /* list empty */
          {
             head = create_node(head, word);
             last = head;
          }
          else                          /* list not empty */
          {
             last->link = create_node(last->link, word);
             last = last->link;
          }
          printf("input word - enter ! to exit ");
          gets(word);
      }
      return head;
}
```

function create_list - successively calls create_node supplying data for each new node

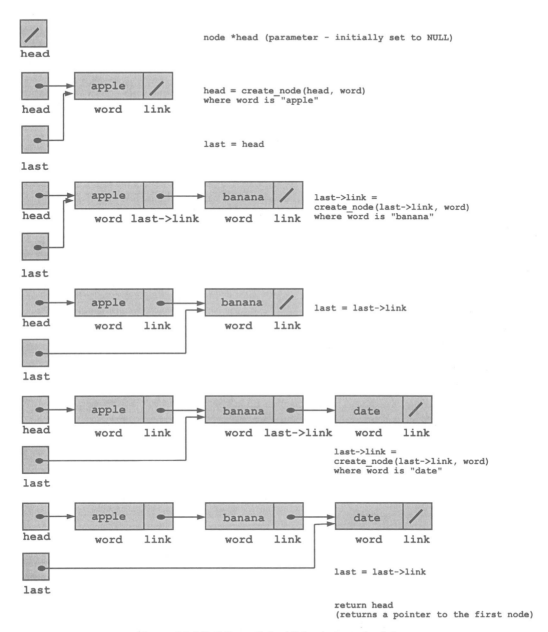

Figure 14.4 Building a linked list using create_list

417

The process of building a linked list is illustrated in Figure 14.4 and should be studied in conjunction with the code in functions create_list and create_node. Initially the pointer head is assigned the value NULL and passed as a parameter to the function create_list. Upon entering create_list, the user is invited to type a word at the keyboard, and provided it is not the terminating character, both the head of the list and the word are passed as parameters to the function create_node. The function create_node stores the word in a node, assigns the link as NULL, and returns a pointer to the newly created node. Upon returning to create_list, the pointer head is assigned the value returned by create_node, resulting in the head pointing to the first node in the linked list. Another pointer last is also assigned to point to the first node in the list.

The user inputs a second word, and provided it is not the terminating symbol, the function create_node is called again, this time passing a pointer last_link to the next node to be created and the word to be inserted into the new node. Upon returning from create_node, last->link is updated to point at the second node and last is then assigned to point at the second node. The process continues until the user inputs the terminating symbol.

Desk check the functions create_list and create_node so that you understand fully how these functions are used to create a linked list.

14.3 Displaying a Linked List

The following function list_out and Figure 14.5 illustrate how to traverse a linked list in order to display its contents on a screen. The technique requires writing the contents of current->word, and then replacing the value of the pointer current by current->link, which is a pointer to the next node in the list. When the value of current is NULL, the end of the list will have been reached.

```
void list_out(node *head)
/* function to display the contents of a linked list */
{
        node *current;

        current = head;
        printf("\n\n");

        if (current == NULL)
           printf("list empty\n");
        else
        {
           while (current != NULL)
           {
                printf("%s\n", current->word);
                current = current->link;
           }
        }
}
```

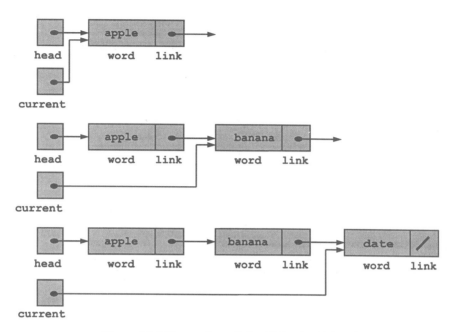

Figure 14.5 Traversing a linked list using list_out

14.4 Destroying a Linked List

Finally when the linked list is no longer required, the storage allocated to the linked list should be returned to the heap. This process is performed in the function `clean_up`, which should be studied in conjunction with Figure 14.6. The method of traversing the linked list is similar to that to output the contents of the list. Starting at the head of the list, two pointers are introduced: `current` points at the first node and `temporary` points at the second node. Deallocating the storage space for the node being pointed at by `current` leaves both `head` and `current` with nothing to point at, as a consequence, they are known as **dangling pointers**. Dangling pointers can lead to some error-prone situations, so care must be maintained to avoid them!

Caution:

possible programming error

The pointer `current` is assigned the value of the pointer `temporary`, and later in the algorithm, the pointer `head` is assigned a `NULL` value.

The pointer `current` is in effect pointing at the first node in the list, and the pointer `temporary` must be arranged to point at the second node in the list. The node being pointed at by `current` is deallocated, and the algorithm continues as before. Eventually `temporary` will be assigned the value `NULL` when there is only one node remaining in the linked list. After this node has been deallocated, `current` is assigned to `temporary`, and therefore, `current` is set to `NULL`.

Since there is no more deallocation of storage to perform on the linked list and the linked list is in effect empty, `head` is set at the value `NULL`.

Note: dynamic structures are allocated memory from the heap only during the running of a program. The function clean_up is not strictly necessary, since after the program terminates, the memory allocated to the data structure is automatically restored to the heap.

```
node *clean_up(node *head)
/* function to deallocate storage space for nodes and
return memory back to the heap */
{
        node *current, *temporary;

        current = head;
        while (current != NULL)
        {
                temporary = current->link;
                free(current);
                current = temporary;
        }
        head = NULL;
        return head;
}
```

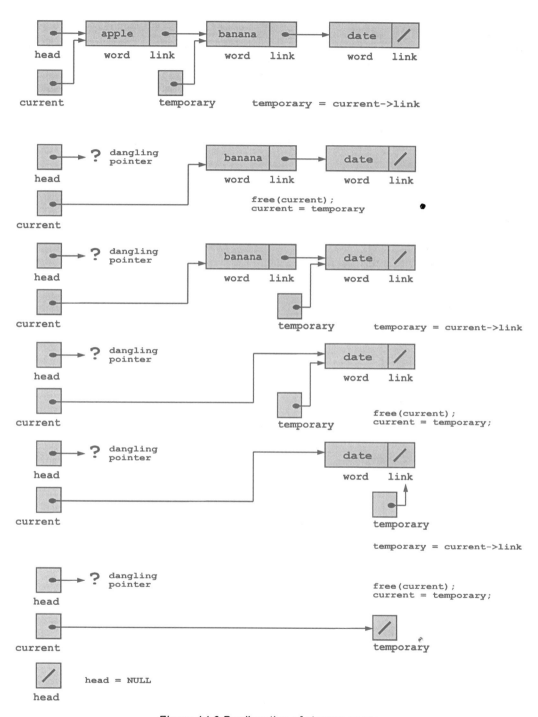

Figure 14.6 Deallocation of storage space

14.5 Searching a Linked List

The method of searching a linked list will depend upon how the data is arranged in the list. If the data has not been input in any specific order, then it will be necessary to compare each item in the list before a key can be located. It may even be necessary to search the entire contents of the list before discovering that there is no entry for the required data.

If the data is ordered, then as long as the key value is greater than the key being compared in the list, the item that is required may be found later in the list. If, however, the key value is less than the key being compared in the list, then the item required cannot exist in the list.

These facts are not new to you; they were explained in Chapter 12 in the context of searching an array of records.

In order to maintain a linked list, it will be necessary to insert new nodes into the list and delete redundant nodes from the list. The method of insertion and deletion of nodes is straightforward but relies on the list having first been searched for the position in which to insert a new node or the position from which to remove an existing node. The prototype for the function `search` is given as

```
node *search(node *head, char key[], boolean *found);
```

The function `search` relies upon the fact that the contents of the list must be ordered on a particular key, and it is the responsibility of the data entry person to ensure that the data has been input in alphabetical sequence. When searching for a node that already exists in order to delete it, if the node is found, the function returns a pointer to the previous node unless the node is at the head of the list, in which case the function returns a `NULL` value.

When searching for the position to insert a new node, the `search` function will return a pointer to the position where the node should be inserted.

Figure 14.7 illustrates how the `search` function works. These illustrations should be viewed in conjunction with the following code:

```
node *search(node *head, char key[], boolean *found)
{
     node *previous, *current;

     *found = false;
     current = head;
     previous = current;

     while (current != NULL)
     {
        if (strcmp(key, current->word) == 0)
        {
           *found = true;
           break;
        }
        else if (strcmp(key, current->word) < 0)
           break;
        else
        {
           previous = current;
           current = current->link;
        }
     }
     if (current == head)
        return NULL;
     else
        return previous;
}
```

1. The key is located as the first node in the ordered list

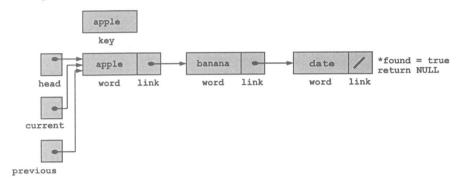

2. The key is located in any position after the first node in the ordered list

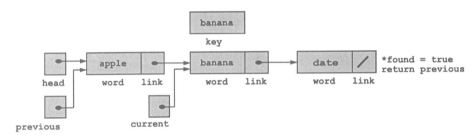

3. The key does not lie within the range of values

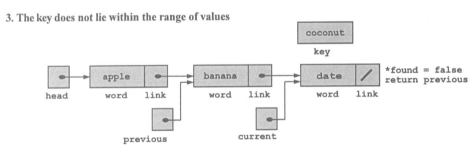

4. The search for the key has reached the end of the list without success

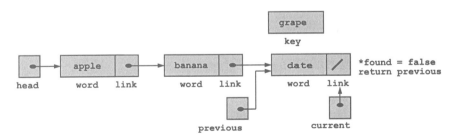

Figure 14.7 Search function mechanism

14.6 Insertion and Deletion of Nodes

The prototype for the function `insert_node` is

```
node *insert_node(node *head, node *previous, char key[]);
```

where `head` is a pointer to the head of the linked list, `previous` is the value returned by the `search` function indicating where the new node is to be inserted, and `key` is the value to be inserted. Figure 14.8 illustrates how the node containing the word `almond` and the node containing the word `artichoke` are inserted into a linked list. These illustrations should be viewed in conjunction with the following `insert_node` function:

```c
node *insert_node(node *head, node *previous, char key[])
/* function to insert a node into a linked list and return
the head of the linked list*/
{
    node *new_node, *temp;

    new_node = malloc(sizeof(node));
    if (new_node == NULL)
    {
        printf("no memory allocated - program terminated\n");
        exit(errno);
    }
    strcpy(new_node->word, key);
    if (previous == NULL) /* insert node into head of list */
    {
        temp = head;
        head = new_node;
        new_node->link = temp;
    }
    else
    {
        temp = previous->link;
        previous->link = new_node;
        new_node->link = temp;
    }
    return head;
}
```

1. Insertion of a new node at the head of the list having first searched for the key and returned null

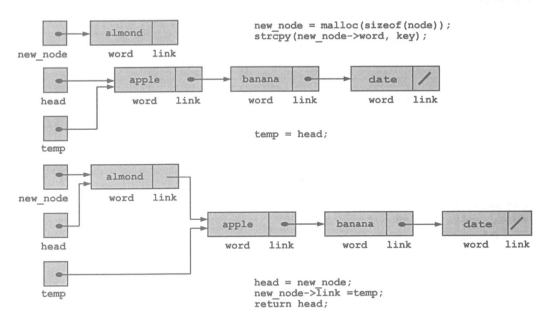

2. Insertion of a new node into a list other than at the head having first searched for the key and returned previous

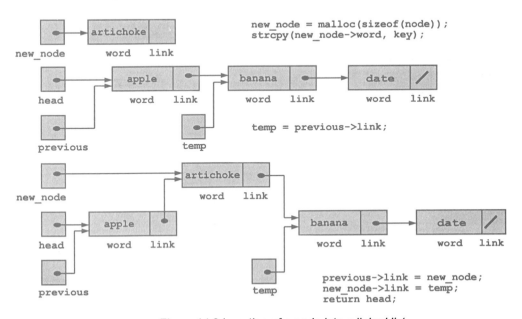

Figure 14.8 Insertion of a node into a linked list

The prototype for the function `delete_node` is

```
node *delete_node(node *head, node *previous);
```

where `head` is a pointer to the head of the linked list and `previous` is the value returned by the `search` function indicating where the new node is to be deleted. Figure 14.9 illustrates how to delete a node from the head of a linked list and how to delete a node from the remainder of the linked list. These illustrations should be viewed in conjunction with the following `delete_node` function:

```
node *delete_node(node *head, node *previous)
/* function to delete a node from the linked list */
{
    node *temp;

    if (previous == NULL) /* delete node at head of list */
    {
        temp = head;
        head = head->link;
    }
    else
    {
        temp = previous->link;
        previous->link = temp->link;
    }
    free(temp);
    return head;
}
```

1. Deletion of a node at the head of the list having first searched for the key

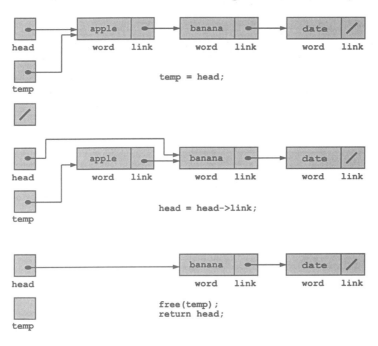

2. Deletion of a node other than at the head of the list having first searched for the key

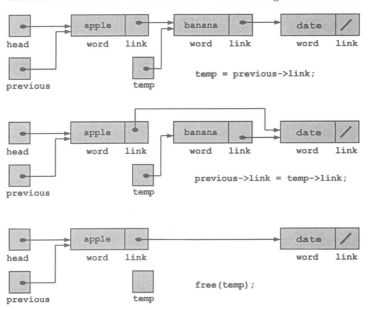

Figure 14.9 The deletion of a node from a linked list

Program Example 14.1: Linked List Maintenance

Program Example 14.1 is devised to maintain a linked list containing words. The words to be stored in the linked list are initially held in a text file in alphabetical sequence. The function create_list used in an earlier section has been modified so that words are read from the text file and not the keyboard. Once the linked list has been created, the user is given the opportunity to insert new words, delete existing words, examine the contents of the linked list, or quit from the program. Prior to exiting from the program, the contents of the linked list are written back to the original text file and the memory space used to build the list is deallocated back to the system heap.

```
/*
chap_14\ex_1.c
program to maintain a linked list
*/

#include <stdio.h>
#include <stdlib.h>
#include <string.h>
#include <ctype.h>
#include <errno.h>

#define insert  'I'
#define delete  'D'
#define examine 'E'
#define quit    'Q'
#define read  "r"
#define write "w"
#define word_length 80
#define string_terminator 0
#define data_file "a:\\chap_14\\data.txt"

struct record {
                char        word[80];
                struct record *link;
            };

typedef struct record node;
typedef enum {false, true} boolean;

node *create_node(node *next, char text[])
/* function to create a node and return a pointer to it */
{
        next=malloc(sizeof(node));
        if (next == NULL)
        {
          printf("no memory allocated - program terminated\n");
          exit(errno);
        }
```

```
            strcpy(next->word, text);
            next->link = NULL;
            return next;
}

node *create_list(node *head, char filename[])
/* function to create a linked list from the contents of
a text file and return a pointer to the head of the linked list */
{
        node *last;
        char word[word_length];
        FILE *file;

        file = fopen(filename, read);
        if (file == NULL)
        {
            printf("%s cannot be opened\n", filename);
            exit(errno);
        }
        fgets(word, word_length, file);
        while (! feof(file))
        {
            word[strlen(word)-1]=string_terminator; /* eliminate newline */
            if (head == NULL)
            {
                head = create_node(head, word);
                last = head;
            }
            else
            {
                last->link = create_node(last->link, word);
                last = last->link;
            }
            fgets(word, word_length, file);
        }
        fclose(file);
        return head;
}

node *search(node *head, char key[], boolean *found)
/* function to search an ordered linked list for a word,
   if found return the pointer to the previous node unless
   the node is at the head of the list in which case return NULL
   else return the pointer to the position where the node
   should be inserted */
{
        node *previous, *current;
        *found = false;
        current = head;
```

```
       previous = current;
       while (current != NULL)
       {
           if (strcmp(key, current->word) == 0)
           {
               *found = true;
               break;
           }
           else if (strcmp(key, current->word) < 0)
               break;
           else
           {
               previous = current;
               current = current->link;
           }
       }
       if (current == head)
           return NULL;
       else
           return previous;
}

node *insert_node(node *head, node *previous, char key[])
/* function to insert a node into a linked list and return
the head of the linked list*/
{
    node *new_node, *temp;

    new_node = malloc(sizeof(node));
    if (new_node == NULL)
    {
        printf("no memory allocated - program terminated\n");
        exit(errno);
    }
    strcpy(new_node->word, key);
    if (previous == NULL) /* insert node into head of list */
    {
        temp = head;
        head = new_node;
        new_node->link = temp;
    }
    else
    {
        temp = previous->link;
        previous->link = new_node;
        new_node->link = temp;
    }
    return head;
}
```

```
node *delete_node(node *head, node *previous)
/* function to delete a node from the linked list */
{
    node *temp;

    if (previous == NULL) /* delete node at head of list */
    {
        temp = head;
        head = head->link;
    }
    else
    {
        temp = previous->link;
        previous->link = temp->link;
    }

    free(temp);
    return head;
}

void list_out(node *head)
/* function to display the contents of a linked list */
{
        node *current;

        current = head;
        printf("\n\n");
        if (current == NULL)
           printf("list empty\n");
        else
        {
           while (current != NULL)
           {
                printf("%s\n", current->word);
                current = current->link;
           }
        }
}

void save_list(node *head, char filename[])
/* function to transfer the contents of the linked list
to a text file */
{
        FILE *file;
        node *current;

        file = fopen(filename, write);
        if (file == NULL)
        {
```

```c
            printf("%s cannot be opened\n", filename);
            exit(errno);
        }

     current = head;
     while (current != NULL)
     {
          fprintf(file, "%s\n", current->word);
          current = current->link;
     }

     fclose(file);
}

node *clean_up(node *head)
/* function to deallocate storage space for nodes and
return memory back to the heap */
{
     node *current, *temporary;

     current = head;
     while (current != NULL)
     {
          temporary = current->link;
          free(current);
          current = temporary;
     }
     head = NULL;
     return head;
}

char menu(void)
/* function to return an appropriate menu code
from a given selection */
{
    char reply;

    printf("\ndo you want to: \n");
    printf("I[nsert] a new entry \n");
    printf("D[elete] an existing entry \n");
    printf("E[xamine] the list \n");
    printf("Q[uit] \n");
    printf("input I, D, E or Q ");
    reply = getchar(); getchar();
    reply = toupper(reply);
    return reply;
}
```

```c
void main(void)
{
        node    *head = NULL;
        node    *previous;
        char    key[word_length];
        boolean found;

        head = create_list(head, data_file);

        for (;;)
        {
            switch (menu())
            {
                case insert:printf("input word ");
                            gets(key);
                            previous = search(head, key, &found);
                            if (! found)
                                head = insert_node(head, previous, key);
                            else
                                printf("\n\nERROR WORD EXISTS\n\n");
                            break;
                case delete:printf("input word ");
                            gets(key);
                            previous = search(head, key, &found);
                            if (found)
                                head = delete_node(head, previous);
                            else
                                printf("\n\nERROR WORD NOT FOUND\n\n");
                            break;
                case examine: list_out(head);
                            break;
                case quit:  save_list(head, data_file);
                            clean_up(head);
                            exit(errno);
                default:    printf("\n\nERROR - MENU CODE\n\n");
            }
        }
}
```

Results

```
do you want to:
I[nsert] a new entry
D[elete] an existing entry
E[xamine] the list
Q[uit]
input I, D, E or Q E
```

```
apple
banana
date

do you want to:
I[nsert] a new entry
D[elete] an existing entry
E[xamine] the list
Q[uit]
input I, D, E or Q I
input word almond

do you want to:
I[nsert] a new entry
D[elete] an existing entry
E[xamine] the list
Q[uit]
input I, D, E or Q E

almond
apple
banana
date

do you want to:
I[nsert] a new entry
D[elete] an existing entry
E[xamine] the list
Q[uit]
input I, D, E or Q D
input word date

do you want to:
I[nsert] a new entry
D[elete] an existing entry
E[xamine] the list
Q[uit]
input I, D, E or Q E

almond
apple
banana

do you want to:
I[nsert] a new entry
D[elete] an existing entry
E[xamine] the list
Q[uit]
input I, D, E or Q D
```

435

```
input word date

ERROR WORD NOT FOUND

do you want to:
I[nsert] a new entry
D[elete] an existing entry
E[xamine] the list
Q[uit]
input I, D, E or Q I
input word apple

ERROR WORD EXISTS

do you want to:
I[nsert] a new entry
D[elete] an existing entry
E[xamine] the list
Q[uit]
input I, D, E or Q Q
```

14.7 Queues

Queues are a familiar aspect of everyday life. People often queue in orderly lines to wait for buses or to wait to be served in a bank. There are many examples in computing of the use of queues. In a real-time system, queues of processes wait to use a processor or queues of jobs wait to use a resource such as a printer. The general concept of a queue is a line of objects that has a front and a rear. The first object in the queue is said to be at the front of the queue, whereas the last object in the queue is said to be at the rear of the queue. In a first-in-first-out (FIFO) queue, an object can join the queue only at the rear and leave only at the front.

Queues can be built out of linked lists. To allow a node to join a FIFO queue requires a new node temporary. This node will contain the details of the last member to join the queue. The function insert_node to insert a new node into the rear of a FIFO queue relies upon the existence of two further functions: queue_empty will return a Boolean value indicating whether the queue is empty or not, and find_rear will return a pointer to the last node in the FIFO queue. Both of these functions are listed in Program Example 14.2. The code required to insert a new node at the rear of the queue follows and should be read in conjunction with Figure 14.10.

In this example the contents of the FIFO queue are not ordered.

```
node *insert_node(node *front, char text[])
/* function to insert a node into the rear of the queue
and return a pointer to the front node */
{
    node *rear, *temporary;

    temporary = malloc(sizeof(node));
    if (temporary == NULL)
    {
        printf("no memory allocated - program terminated\n");
        exit(errno);
    }
    strcpy(temporary->word, text);
    temporary->link = NULL;

    if (! queue_empty(front))
    {
        rear = find_rear(front);
        rear->link = temporary;
        return front;
    }
    else
        return temporary;
}
```

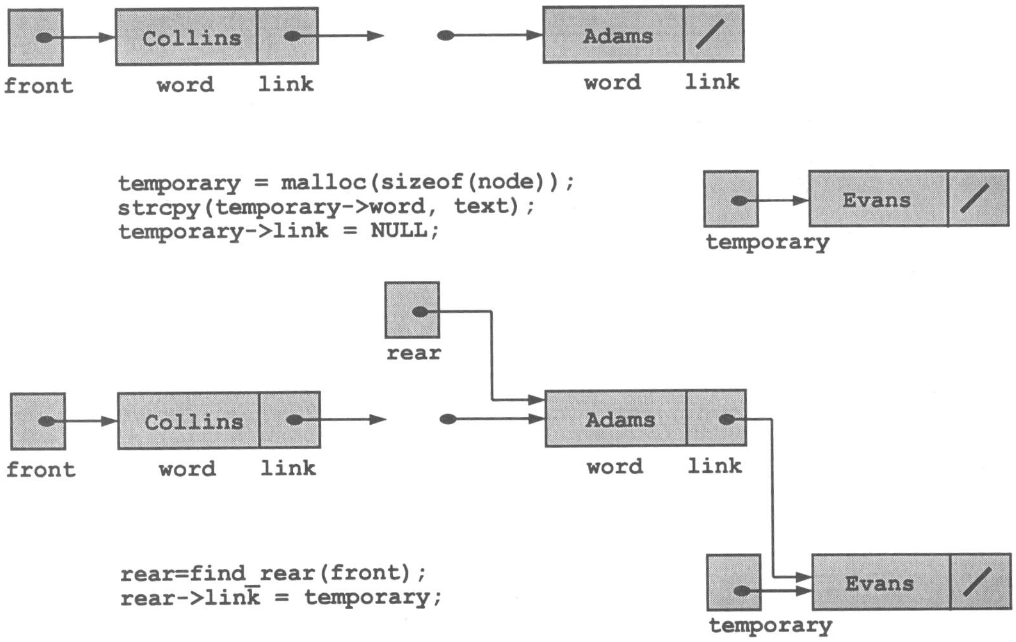

Figure 14.10 Insert into the rear of a FIFO queue

437

Members of a FIFO queue can leave only from the front. Figure 14.11 illustrates how a node can be removed from the front of a queue. This figure should be viewed in conjunction with the function `remove_node`. The function `remove_node` also relies upon the existence of the function `queue_empty`. If the queue is empty, then `remove_node` will return a NULL value.

```
node *remove_node(node *front)
/* function to remove a node from the front of the queue
and return a pointer for the new front */
{
    node *temporary;

    if (! queue_empty(front))
    {
        temporary = front->link;
        free(front);
        return temporary;
    }
    else
        return NULL;
}
```

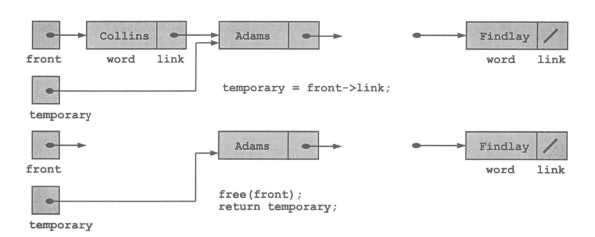

Figure 14.11 Removal from the front of a FIFO queue

Program Example 14.2: Inserting and Removing Nodes from a FIFO Queue

```
/*
chap_14\ex_2.c
program to insert and remove nodes from a FIFO queue
*/

#include <stdio.h>
#include <stdlib.h>
#include <string.h>
#include <errno.h>

struct record {
                char            word[80];
                struct record *link;
            };

typedef struct record node;
typedef enum {false, true} boolean;

boolean queue_empty(node *front)
/* function to test and return whether a queue is empty */
{
     if (front != NULL)
        return false;
     else
        return true;
}

node *find_rear(node *front)
/* function to find and return the position of the rear of the queue */
{
    node *rear = NULL;

    while (front != NULL)
    {
       rear  = front;
       front = front->link;
    }
    return rear;
}

node *remove_node(node *front)
/* function to remove a node from the front of the queue
and return a pointer for the new front */
{
    node *temporary;
```

```
    if (! queue_empty(front))
    {
        temporary = front->link;
        free(front);
        return temporary;
    }
    else
        return NULL;
}

node *insert_node(node *front, char text[])
/* function to insert a node into the rear of the queue
and return a pointer to the front node */
{
    node *rear, *temporary;

    temporary = malloc(sizeof(node));
    if (temporary == NULL)
    {
     printf("no memory allocated - program terminated\n");
     exit(errno);
    }

    strcpy(temporary->word, text);
    temporary->link = NULL;

    if (! queue_empty(front))
    {
        rear = find_rear(front);
        rear->link = temporary;
        return front;
    }
    else
        return temporary;
}

void list_out(node *front)
/* function to display the contents of a FIFO queue */
{
        node *current;

        current = front;
        printf("\n\n");
        if (current == NULL)
            printf("queue empty\n");
        else
        {
            while (current != NULL)
            {
```

```
                printf("%s\n", current->word);
                current = current->link;
            }
        }
}

void main(void)
{
        node *queue = NULL;


        queue = insert_node(queue, "Collins");
        list_out(queue);
        queue = insert_node(queue, "Adams");
        list_out(queue);
        queue = insert_node(queue, "Evans");
        list_out(queue);
        queue = remove_node(queue);
        list_out(queue);
        queue = remove_node(queue);
        queue = remove_node(queue);
        list_out(queue);

}
```

Results

```
Collins

Collins
Adams

Collins
Adams
Evans

Adams
Evans

queue empty
```

14.8 Stacks

You first met the term **stack** in Chapter 12 where it was introduced to describe how the computer stores information to allow recursive calls to functions. A stack is a data structure in which members can join and leave at one end only. The stack operates on a last-ln-first-out (LIFO) principle. The entry/ exit point of the stack is known as the **stack top**, and a stack pointer controls the position of this stack top. An item that joins the stack is said to be **pushed** on to the stack. An item that leaves the stack is said to be **popped** from the stack. The methods used for pushing and popping items from a stack are given in the functions push and pop, respectively, and should be read in conjunction with Figures 14.12 and 14.13. Stacks like queues can be implemented as linked lists. The function push inserts a node at the front of a linked list and returns a pointer to the new stack top.

```
node *push(node *stack_top, char text[])
/* function to insert a node into the top of the stack
and return a pointer to the new stack top */
{
    node *temporary;

    temporary = malloc(sizeof(node));
    if (temporary == NULL)
    {
        printf("no memory allocated - program terminated\n");
        exit(errno);
    }
    strcpy(temporary->word, text);
    temporary->link = stack_top;
    return temporary;
}
```

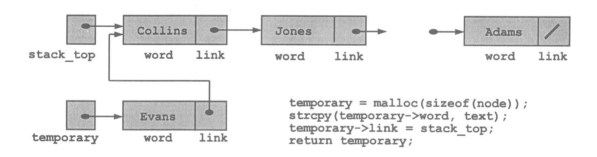

Figure 14.12 Pushing an item on a stack

The function pop removes a node from the stack top and returns a pointer to the new stack top. The function pop relies upon another function stack_empty that returns a Boolean value of true if there are no nodes in the stack. The function stack_empty is listed in Program Example 14.3.

```
node *pop(node *stack_top, char text[])
/* function to remove a node from the top of a stack
and return a pointer for the new stack top; text contains
the contents of the top of the stack prior to removal */
{
    node *temporary;

    if (! stack_empty(stack_top))
    {
        strcpy(text, stack_top->word);
        temporary = stack_top->link;
        free(stack_top);
        return temporary;
    }
    else
        return NULL;
}
```

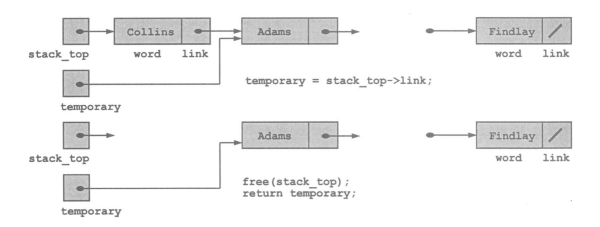

Figure 14.13 Popping an item from a stack

443

Program Example 14.3: Inserting and Removing Words from a Stack

```c
/*
chap_14\ex_3.c
program to push and pop items on a stack
*/

#include <stdio.h>
#include <stdlib.h>
#include <string.h>
#include <errno.h>

struct record {
                char        word[80];
                struct record *link;
            };

typedef struct record node;
typedef enum {false, true} boolean;

boolean stack_empty(node *stack_top)
/* function to test and return whether a stack is empty */
{
    if (stack_top != NULL)
       return false;
    else
       return true;
}


node *pop(node *stack_top, char text[])
/* function to remove a node from the top of a stack
and return a pointer for the new stack top; text contains
the contents of the top of the stack prior to removal */
{
    node *temporary;

    if (! stack_empty(stack_top))
    {
       strcpy(text, stack_top->word);
       temporary = stack_top->link;
       free(stack_top);
       return temporary;
    }
    else
       return NULL;
}
```

```c
node *push(node *stack_top, char text[])
/* function to insert a node into the top of the stack
and return a pointer to the new stack top */
{
    node *temporary;

    temporary = malloc(sizeof(node));
    if (temporary == NULL)
    {
    printf("no memory allocated - program terminated\n");
    exit(errno);
    }

    strcpy(temporary->word, text);
    temporary->link = stack_top;
    return temporary;
}

void list_out(node *stack_top)
/* function to display the contents of a linked list */
{
        node *current;

        current = stack_top;
        printf("\n\n");
        if (current == NULL)
           printf("stack empty\n");
        else
        {
           while (current != NULL)
           {
               printf("%s\n", current->word);
               current = current->link;
           }
        }
}

void main(void)
{
        node *stack = NULL;
        char word[80];

        stack = push(stack, "Jones");
        stack = push(stack, "Collins");
        stack = push(stack, "Evans");
        list_out(stack);
        stack = pop(stack, word);
        list_out(stack);
        stack = pop(stack, word);
```

445

```
        stack = pop(stack, word);
        list_out(stack);
}
```

Results

```
Evans
Collins
Jones

Collins
Jones

stack empty
```

14.9 Binary Tree

The dynamic data structures described so far had nodes that contained only one pointer to point to the next node in a linked list, queue, or stack. However, it is possible for a node to contain more than one pointer. Figure 14.14 illustrates a **binary tree**. The **root pointer** points at the first node or **root node** of the binary tree and is used to reference the tree structure in the same way as the head of a linked list was used to reference a linked list structure. Notice that each node contains two pointers: a left pointer and a right pointer. Each pointer points to a node at a lower level in the tree if one exists; otherwise, the pointer is set at NULL.

A parent-child relationship exists between the nodes of a binary tree. The root node (A) is a parent node that points to two child nodes (B) and (E). In turn node (B) is a parent node that points two child nodes (C) and (D). For any node in a tree, the left pointer of the node is the root pointer of the left subtree of the

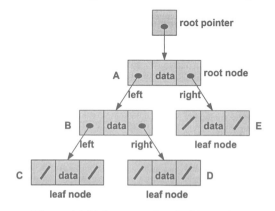

Figure 14.14 An example of a binary tree

node. For example, the left pointer of node A is the root pointer to the subtree containing nodes B, C, and D. Similarly, the right pointer is the root pointer of the right subtree of the node. In this example the right pointer of node A is a root pointer to the subtree containing node E. Nodes such as C,D, and E, whose left and right pointers are both NULL, are called **leaf nodes**.

Despite Figure 14.14 showing only five nodes in the tree, the only limit imposed upon the size of a tree is the amount of main memory available from the heap used to store the nodes of the tree.

Notice that no reference has been made to the data stored in the tree. The data forms part of the members of a node and is therefore unique to different applications. For example, you may want to store numbers, names, addresses, or exam marks at each node in the tree depending upon the nature of the program.

If a linked list offers the following advantages:

☐ A data structure that can be built though dynamic memory allocation in which the size of the structure need not be known at run-time.

☐ The insertion and deletion of nodes can be accomplished through pointer changes and not the shifting of data in memory.

What advantages can be gained by using a binary tree to store data in the main memory?

A binary tree has all the advantages of a linked list. However, if the binary tree is arranged such that the key in any node is greater than all the keys in the left subtree and less than all the keys in the right subtree, then the tree is known as a **binary search tree** and it offers the following advantages over a linked list. This definition of a binary search tree precludes duplicate entries in the tree.

☐ Regardless of the order in which the data is inserted into a binary search tree, it can be retrieved in an ordered format.

☐ An efficient searching algorithm can be used to search for components in a binary search tree.

14.10 Binary Search Tree

In this section you will be shown how to create a binary search tree for storing numbers. The structure of a node in this tree is illustrated in Figure 14.15.

```
struct record {
                struct record *left;
                int            number;
                struct record *right;
             };
typedef struct record tree;
```

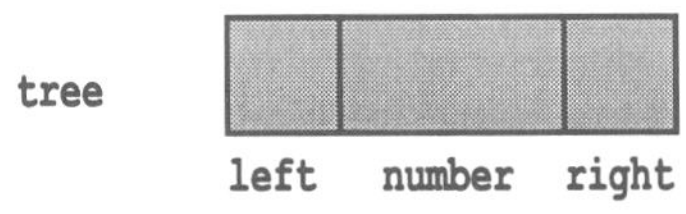

Figure 14.15 The structure of a binary tree node

Initially in building a binary search tree, if the root of the tree (parent) is `NULL`, then the tree is said to be empty. The algorithm used to insert a node into the tree can be coded as

```
parent = malloc(sizeof(tree));
parent->left = NULL;
parent->number = number;
parent->right = NULL;
```

In this example `number` is the value of a random number 56 to be inserted into the tree. This information is represented in Figure 14.16.

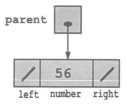

Figure 14.16 Inserting a node into a binary tree

To insert a second node containing the random number 78 into the tree such that the property of the binary search tree is preserved, the reasoning is

*if number to be inserted is **less than** number in parent node then*
  branch left
else
  branch right

Therefore, if the next random number to be inserted into the binary tree is 78, a node must be attached to the right of the parent node because 78 is greater than 56. This situation is illustrated in Figure 14.17. Note the new parent to the new node becomes `parent->right`.

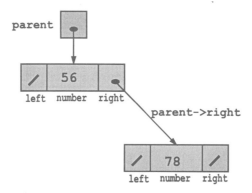

Figure 14.17 Inserting another node into the binary tree

448

If the random numbers 31, 3, 17, 67, and 99 are also to be inserted into this binary tree, the tree will grow as depicted in the set of Figures 14.18 to 14.22.

The number 31 is compared with `parent->number` (56). Since 31 < 56 and `parent->left` is NULL, the new node is built to the left of the parent node. Notice that the parent pointer to this new node is `parent->left`.

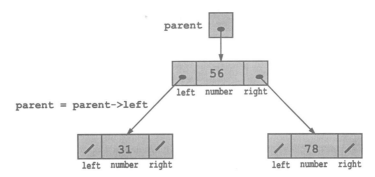

Figure 14.18 Since 31 < 56 it forms a left node

The number 3 is compared with `parent->number` (56). Since 3 < 56, branch left to make the new value of the parent equal to `parent->left` and to make a further comparison with `parent->number` (31). Since 3 < 31 and `parent->left` is NULL, the new node is built to the left of the parent node. Notice that the parent pointer to this new node is `parent->left`.

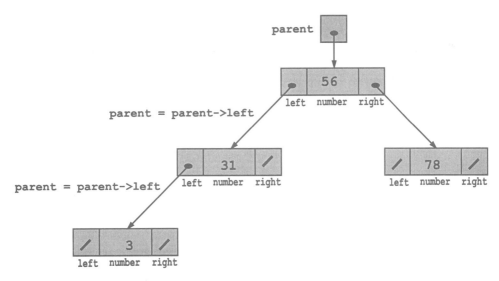

Figure 14.19 Since 3 < 31 it also forms a left node

The number 17 is compared with `parent->number` (56). Since 17 < 56, branch left to make the new value of the parent equal to `parent->left` and to make a further comparison with `parent->number` (31). Since 17 < 31, branch left to make the new value of parent equal to `parent->left` and to make a further comparison with `parent->number` (3). Since 17 > 3 and `parent->right` is NULL, the new node is built to the right of the parent node. Notice that the parent pointer to this new node is `parent->right`.

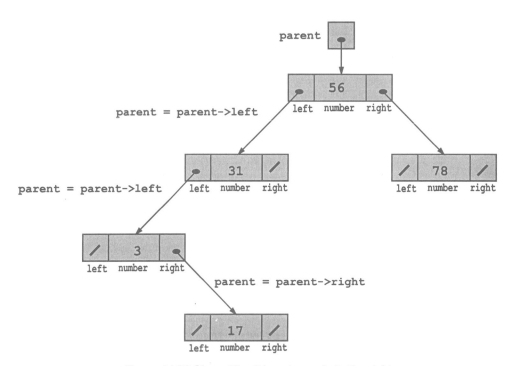

Figure 14.20 Since 17 > 3 insert a node to the right

The number 67 is compared with `parent->number` (56). Since 67 > 56, branch right to make the new value of the parent equal to `parent->right` and to make a further comparison with `parent->num-ber` (78). Since 67 < 78 and `parent->left` is NULL, the new node is built to the left of the parent node. Notice that the parent pointer to this new node is `parent->left`.

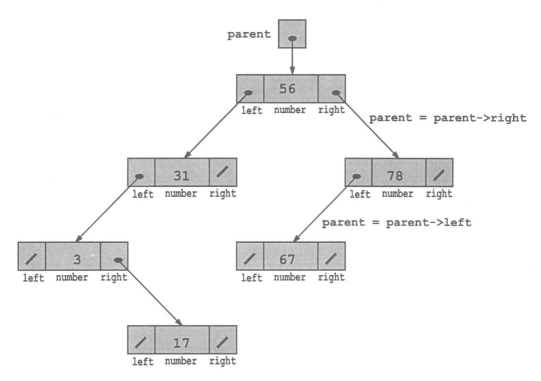

Figure 14.21 Since 67 < 78 insert node to the left

The number 99 is compared with `parent->number` (56). Since 99 > 56, branch right to make the new value of the parent equal to `parent->right` and to make a further comparison with `parent->num-ber` (78). Since 99 > 78 and `parent->right` is NULL, the new node is built to the right of the parent node. Notice that the parent pointer to this new node is `parent->right`.

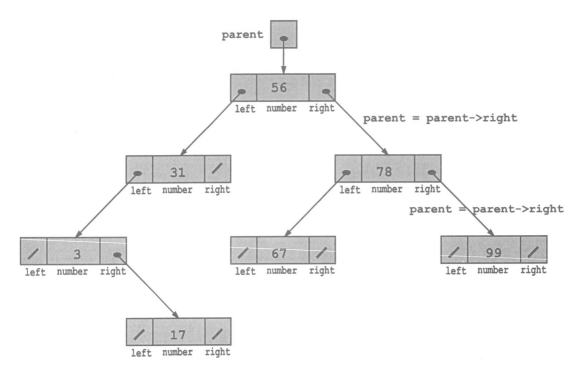

Figure 14.22 Since 99 > 78 insert node to right

The function used to attach a node to a tree has the following prototype:

```
tree *attach_node(tree *parent, int number, boolean *success);
```

where the root pointer (parent) is passed as a parameter, together with the number to be input into the tree. The parameter `success` is a reference parameter and is assigned the boolean value `true` if the number is attached to the tree; otherwise, it is assigned the Boolean value `false` if the number already exists in the tree. This algorithm, therefore, does not cater for duplicate entries in the same tree.

If the pointer parent (initially the root of the tree) is `NULL`, then space for the root node is allocated from the heap and the value for the number inserted into the node. The left and right pointers are also set at `NULL`.

If the random number is less than the number found in the root node, then the function is recursively called again, but this time the parent is the value of `parent->left`. Similarly, if the random number is greater than that found in the root node, then the function is recursively called again, but this time the parent is the value `parent->right`.

Upon returning from each recursive call, the value of the parent pointer for the node of the subtree is returned by the function.

The code for the function `attach_node` follows and should be read in conjunction with Figure 14.23.

```c
tree *attach_node(tree *parent, int number, boolean *success)
/* function to attach a node to a binary tree */
{
    if (parent == NULL)
    {
        parent = malloc(sizeof(tree));
        if (parent == NULL)
        {
            printf("no memory allocated - program terminated\n");
            exit(errno);
        }
        parent->left = NULL;
        parent->number = number;
        parent->right = NULL;
        *success = true;
    }
    else if (number < parent->number)
        parent->left = attach_node(parent->left, number, success);
    else if (number > parent->number)
        parent->right = attach_node(parent->right, number, success);
    else
        *success = false;

    return parent;
}
```

Having built the binary tree, the method of displaying the contents of the tree in sequential order uses an **in-order** tree traversal. During an in-order traversal, the contents of each node are displayed after all the nodes in its left subtree have been visited and before any node in its right subtree is visited. The following function `display_tree` is used to display the contents of a binary tree. The reader is advised to desk check this recursive algorithm using the tree depicted in Figure 14.22 to gain an understanding of why the algorithm should display the numbers in sequential order.

```c
void display_tree(tree *parent)
/* function to output the contents of the tree in order */
{
    if (parent != NULL)
    {
        display_tree(parent->left);
        printf("%3d", parent->number);
        display_tree(parent->right);
    }
}
```

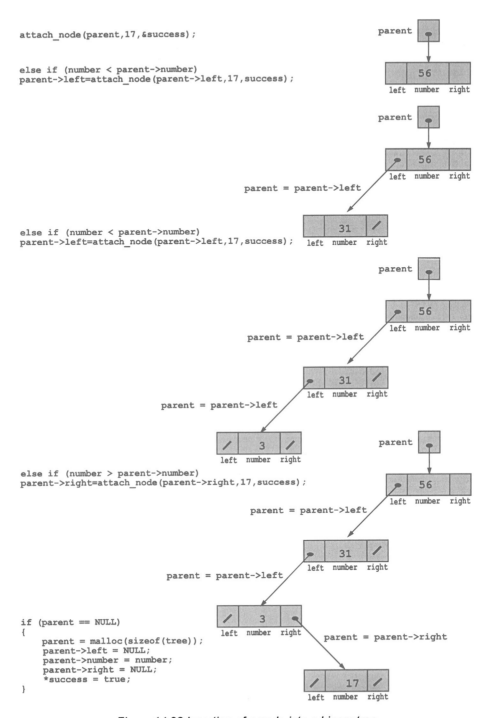

```
attach_node(parent,17,&success);

else if (number < parent->number)
parent->left=attach_node(parent->left,17,success);
```

```
else if (number < parent->number)
parent->left=attach_node(parent->left,17,success);
```

```
else if (number > parent->number)
parent->right=attach_node(parent->right,17,success);
```

```
if (parent == NULL)
{
    parent = malloc(sizeof(tree));
    parent->left = NULL;
    parent->number = number;
    parent->right = NULL;
    *success = true;
}
```

Figure 14.23 Insertion of a node into a binary tree

454

To digress for a moment, there are two other algorithms for traversing a binary tree - **preorder** and **postorder** traversals. In a preorder traversal, a node is processed before the computer traverses either of the node's subtrees. However, with postorder traversal, both the subtrees of a node are traversed before processing the node.

The preorder algorithm is coded as

```
void display_tree_pre_order(tree *parent)
/* function to output the contents of the tree in preorder */
{
    if (parent != NULL)
    {
        printf("%3d", parent->number);
        display_tree_pre_order(parent->left);
        display_tree_pre_order(parent->right);
    }
}
```

and displays the numbers 56, 31, 3, 17, 78, 67, 99 from Figure 14.22.

The postorder algorithm is coded as

```
void display_tree_post_order(tree *parent)
/* function to output the contents of the tree in postorder */
{
    if (parent != NULL)
    {
        display_tree_post_order(parent->left);
        display_tree_post_order(parent->right);
        printf("%3d", parent->number);
    }
}
```

and displays the numbers 17, 3, 31, 67, 99, 78, 56 from Figure 14.22.

Program Example 14.4 Creating a Binary Tree of Random Numbers.

Program Example 14.4 consolidates the work of this section by enabling a user to build a binary tree that contains fifteen random numbers and to display the contents of the tree.

```
/*
chap_14\ex_4.c
program to build a binary tree of random numbers
and display the contents of the binary tree
*/

#include <stdio.h>
#include <stdlib.h>
#include <errno.h>

#define number_of_nodes 15

struct record {
                struct record *left;
                int            number;
                struct record *right;
            };

typedef struct record tree;
typedef enum {false, true} boolean;

tree *initialize_tree(void)
/* initialize the root of the tree to NULL */
{
    return NULL;
}

tree *attach_node(tree *parent, int number, boolean *success)
/* function to attach a node to a binary tree */
{
    if (parent == NULL)
    {
        parent = malloc(sizeof(tree));
        if (parent == NULL)
        {
          printf("no memory allocated - program terminated\n");
          exit(errno);
        }
        parent->left = NULL;
        parent->number = number;
        parent->right = NULL;
        *success = true;
    }
```

```
    else if (number < parent->number)
        parent->left = attach_node(parent->left, number, success);
    else if (number > parent->number)
        parent->right = attach_node(parent->right, number, success);
    else
        *success = false;

    return parent;
}

void display_tree(tree *parent)
/* function to output the contents of the tree in order */
{
    if (parent != NULL)
    {
        display_tree(parent->left);
        printf("%3d", parent->number);
        display_tree(parent->right);
    }
}

void main(void)
{
    tree    *parent;
    int     count;
    boolean success;
    int     number;

    parent = initialize_tree();
    for (count=1; count <= number_of_nodes; count++)
    {
      do
      {
        number = rand() % 100;
        parent = attach_node(parent, number, &success);
        if (success) printf("%3d", number);
      }
      while (! success);
    }
    printf("\n\n");
    display_tree(parent);
}
```

Results

```
23 89 43  2 17 99 56 66 34 19 73 59 81 91 13

 2 13 17 19 23 34 43 56 59 66 73 81 89 91 99
```

457

14.11 Removing Nodes

When a node is to be removed from a tree, it is necessary to search the tree for that node. Figure 14.24 illustrates how the number 17 is found prior to removing the node. The method of searching through the tree is similar to that depicted in Figure 14.23 when it was necessary to search for the correct place to insert the new node.

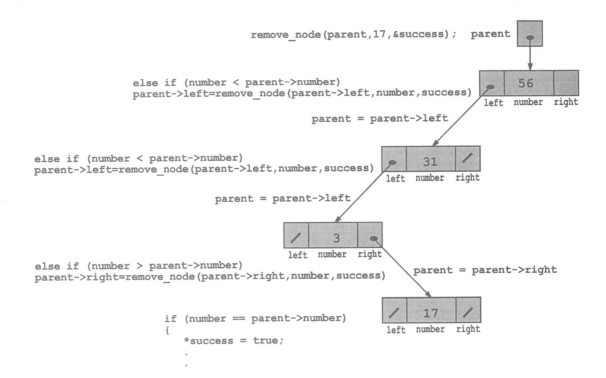

Figure 14.24 A recursive search for a node

Removing a node from a tree is not as simple a matter as attaching a new node to the tree. When the node to be removed has been located, it might be a leaf node (no children), a node with either the left or right pointers NULL (one child), or a node with both left and right pointers pointing at two respective subtrees (two children). Figures 14.25 to 14.27 illustrate how to delete the node in each of the three cases. These figures should be studied in conjunction with the following code:

```
tree *remove_node(tree *parent, int number, boolean *success)
/* function to remove a node from a tree */
{
    tree *temp;
    int  new_number;

    if (parent != NULL)
    {
        if (number == parent->number)
        {
            *success = true;
            if (parent->left == NULL && parent->right == NULL)
            {
                temp = parent;
                free(temp);
                parent = NULL;
            }
            else if (parent->left == NULL)
            {
                temp = parent;
                parent = parent->right;
                free(temp);
            }
            else if (parent->right == NULL)
            {
                temp = parent;
                parent = parent->left;
                free(temp);
            }
            else
            {
                parent->right = successor(parent->right, &new_number);
                parent->number = new_number;
            }
        }
        else if (number < parent->number)
            parent->left = remove_node(parent->left, number, success);
        else
            parent->right = remove_node(parent->right, number, success);
    }
    else
        *success = false;
    return parent;
}
```

When a node that has pointers to two children is to be removed, it is necessary to search the right subtree of this node for the left-most entry. It is this node that will replace the node to be deleted. The function successor is necessary in finding the contents of a node that is the next in sequence to the node to be removed.

```
tree *successor(tree *parent, int *number)
/* function to locate the left-most word in a subtree */
{
    tree *temp;

    if (parent != NULL)
    {
        if (parent->left == NULL)
        {
            *number = parent->number;
            temp = parent;
            parent = parent->right;
            free(temp);
        }
        else
            parent->left = successor(parent->left, number);
    }
    return parent;
}
```

When the left-most node is found (`parent->left == NULL`), the reference parameter `number` is assigned the random number stored at this node. A temporary pointer is assigned to point at this node in readiness for its removal. The value of the parent pointer is then reassigned so that it points to whatever the pointer in the right node is pointing to. This pointer may point to another subtree, or it may be `NULL`. The storage space associated with the temporary pointer is then deallocated, which removes the node from the tree.

The reference parameter number found in the formal-parameter list of `successor` contains the number required to replace the number in the node to be deleted. Note: the contents of this node are only replaced; the node is not physically deleted from the tree.

1. removal of the leaf node containing the number 17

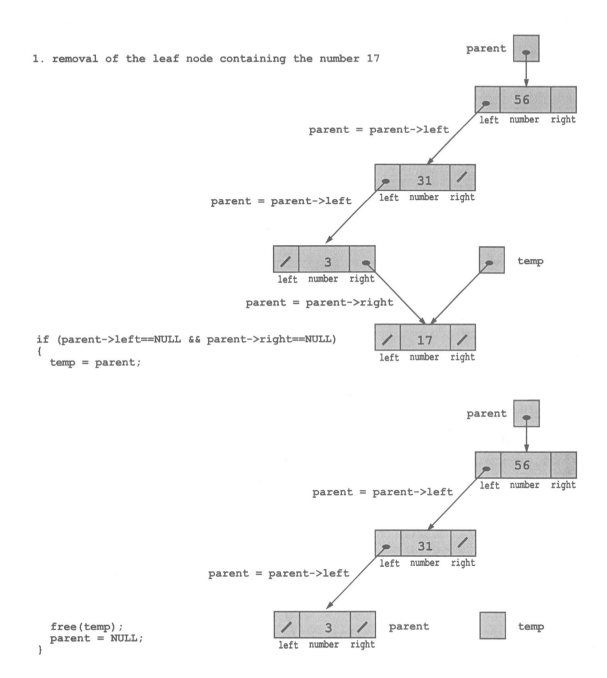

```
if (parent->left==NULL && parent->right==NULL)
{
  temp = parent;
```

```
  free(temp);
  parent = NULL;
}
```

Figure 14.25 Removal of a leaf node (no children)

461

Removal of a node with only one child and containing
the number 31

```
if (number == parent->number)
{
.
.
    else if (parent->right == NULL)
    {
        temp = parent;
```

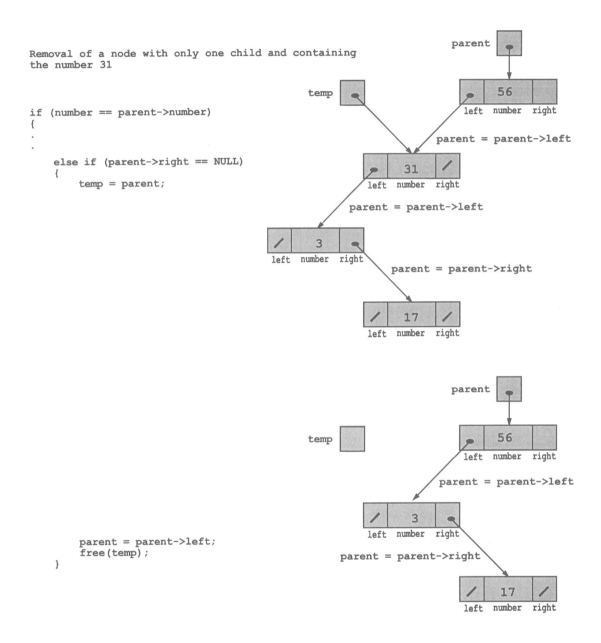

```
        parent = parent->left;
        free(temp);
    }
```

Figure 14.26 Removal of a node with one child

Removal of a node containing two
children and containing the
number 56

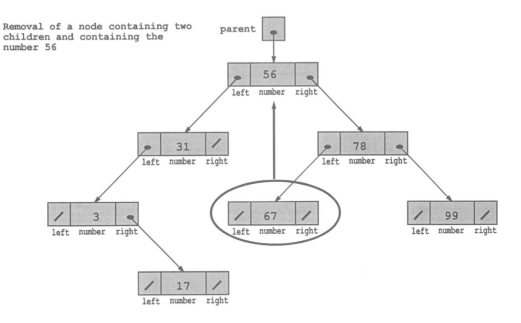

The node to be deleted must be replaced with a number that is larger than all the
numbers in the left sub-tree. This element is the left-most element (67) in the
right sub-tree and can be found using the function successor.

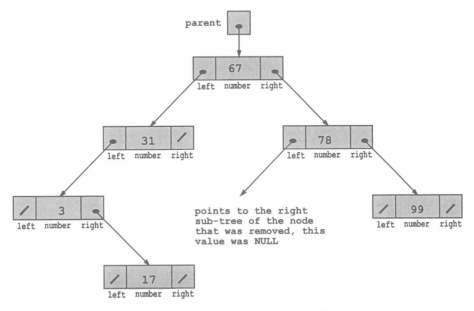

Figure 14.27 Removal of a node with two children

Summary

☐ A node is a self-referential structure, since it contains a member with a pointer to the same structure.

☐ A linked list is a sequence of nodes in which each node is linked or connected to the node following it. A named pointer variable points to the first node in the linked list. A NULL pointer is used to indicate the end of the linked list.

☐ A linked list offers the following advantages over an array:

(a) A list is created at run time through dynamic memory allocation.

(b) The insertion and deletion of nodes in a list requires changing pointers only and not moving data about main memory.

☐ If the keys representing data in a linked list are ordered, then the insertion and deletion of nodes in the list are made easier by virtue of a search function. If the keys are not ordered, then it will still be necessary to search the list prior to insertion or deletion; however, the searching algorithm used cannot be as efficient as if the list had been ordered.

☐ A linked list can be used to represent queues and stacks.

☐ A FIFO queue will have records inserted into the end of a linked list and records deleted from the head of a linked list.

☐ A LIFO stack will have records inserted (pushed) into the head of the linked list and records deleted (popped) also from the head of the linked list. The head of a LIFO stack is known as the stack top.

☐ A named pointer variable, the root pointer, points at the root node in a binary tree. Every node in the tree contains left and right pointers that are the root pointers to left and right subtrees, respectively. If the left and right pointers in a node are both NULL, then the node is known as a leaf node.

☐ In a binary search tree, if the data to be stored in the tree is less than the contents of the current node, the data is stored in the subtree indicated by the left-hand pointer; otherwise, the data is stored in the subtree indicated by the right-hand pointer.

☐ Owing to the manner in which data can be stored in a binary search tree, an inorder tree traversal will result in the contents of each node being accessed in sequence; therefore, the data can be accessed as if it was sorted.

☐ Data in a binary search tree can be accessed efficiently by using the property of the storage of data in the tree.

Review Questions

1. Explain the term self-referential structure.

2. How do you make reference to a linked list?

3. How does the use of the main memory differ for the storage of cells in an array and, for nodes in a linked list?

4. Why is it easier to insert or delete nodes into a linked list rather than to insert or delete records into an array?

5. What is a dangling pointer?

6. True or false - if the contents of a linked list are not ordered, it makes no difference where a new node is inserted into the list. Assume the list may contain nodes storing identical data.

7. True or false - members of a FIFO queue join and leave the queue at one end only.

8. True or false - a LIFO structure is known as a stack.

9. How do you make reference to a binary tree?

10. What is a subtree?

11. What is a leaf node?

12. Describe a property of a binary search tree.

13. What benefits does a binary search tree have over a linked list for storing data?

14. Describe an inorder traversal of a binary tree.

15. As a method of deleting a parent node that points to two child nodes, what node would you use to replace the parent node that points to two child nodes?

Programming Exercises

16. Draw diagrams to show how the following algorithm will build a linked list.

```
void create_list(node *head)
{
   node *temp;
   head = NULL;
   do
   {
     temp = head;
     head = malloc(sizeof(node));
     head->number = rand() % 100;
     head->link =temp;
   } while (head->number != 0);
}
```

17. Write a function to return the number of nodes in the linked list that was created in question 16.

18. Write a recursive function to display the contents of the linked list that was created in question 16.

19. Write a recursive function to search for a specific number in the binary search tree described in Program Example 14.4.

20. Use the binary tree created in Figure 14.22 to desk check the function `remove_node` (see section 14.11) to delete the root node containing the number 56.

Programming Problems

21. Write a program to create a linked list of nonzero integer random numbers stored in key disorder. Build a second linked list that contains the integers from the first linked list sorted into key order. Find the largest number in the first linked list and copy this to the second linked list. As each integer is used from the first linked list, delete it from the first linked list. Repeat the process until the first linked list is empty. Display the contents of the second linked list.

22. Figure 14.28 illustrates a circular linked list containing integers. Notice that the pointer at the end of the list points to the head of the list, thus allowing the traversal of the list to take a continuous or circular path. Write a program to store 10 random numbers in the range 0 to 99 in respective nodes of a linked list. In this question the numbers are not ordered in the list. Traverse the list and display the numbers stored at the nodes. Stop traversal when the first number is displayed for the second time.

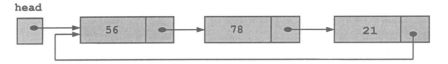

Figure 14.28 A circular linked list

23. Figure 14.29 illustrates a circular, double-linked list structure containing a dummy node at the head of the list.

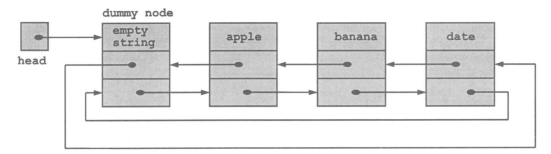

Figure 14.29 A circular double linked list

Note that the dummy node contains a null or empty string; therefore, all nodes to be inserted into the structure must have words alphabetically greater than the dummy node. By using the dummy node, there is no special case to consider for the insertion or deletion at the head of the linked list. The dummy node is always present and should not be removed. The backward pointer in each node greatly facilitates the search function, since there is no need to maintain a separate pointer that always points to the previous node.

Rewrite Program Example 14.1 to maintain a circular, double-linked list. The structure of a record in this type of list may be declared as:

```
struct record {
            char word[80];
            struct record *link_backward;
            struct record *link;
        };
```

Examine the contents of the list both in forward and backward order.

24. The following strings are examples of infix and postfix expressions.

infix	postfix
a*b+c	ab*c+
a*(b+c/d)	abcd/+*
a*b+c/d	ab*cd/+
u+f*t	uft*+

The values of operands from these expressions are stored in a linked list similar to that illustrated in Figure 14.30. The following algorithm evaluates a postfix expression. Traverse the expression from left to right and continue to push operands on a stack until an operator is encountered. For a binary operator, pop two operands from the stack, evaluate the result, and push the answer back on the stack. Continue traversing the postfix expression until the end of the string; then pop the contents of the stack and display this value.

head

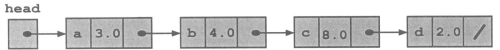

Figure 14.30 A linked list for storing operands

Write a program to input a postfix expression together with values for the operands of the expression and store the operands together with their respective values in a linked list. Modify the functions push and pop given in Program Example 14.3 to store and retrieve floating-point numbers and incorporate these functions into the program to evaluate the postfix expression.

Using the postfix expressions given in this question, check each answer by evaluating, by hand, the equivalent infix expression using the same operands.

25. In addition to the left and right pointers, a node of a binary tree may contain the following information about a student's course results.

```
typedef struct {
                char id[10];        /* unique student id number */
                char name[40];      /* student name */
                char course[40];    /* the name of study course */
                int  average;       /* average % mark to date */
        } student;
```

(a) Write a program to create a binary file of records with this format.

(b) Write a second program that will read the contents of the binary file built from running the program in (a) and store the records as nodes in a binary tree. Allow a user to

(i)   insert a new student record into the tree;
(ii)   delete an existing student record from the tree;
(iii)   examine the contents of the tree;
(iv)   display the records of all those students on a particular course, and the mean mark of the averages for those students on the course;
(v)   search the tree on name only and display the records of all those students with the same name;
(vi)   search the tree on student_id and display the record of the corresponding student;
(vii)   quit the program, but before exiting copy the contents of the tree back to the same binary file.

Note: when a tree is written to a file, it is wise to use a *preorder* traversal of the tree so that the root node is written first. An *inorder* traversal would result in the contents of the tree being stored as an ordered sequence. Unfortunately, this sequence would cause the tree to be built as a linked list the next time the file is read.

Chapter 15
Further Topics

Although the major topics of the C language have already been covered, we must still deal with several more topics to give you the complete picture of the C language. These topics are presented as an assortment of subjects, which in themselves would not warrant a separate chapter for each topic. This chapter covers the following material:

- ☐ Modes of storage for variables and functions.

- ☐ Program implementation using more than one source file.

- ☐ Macros - simple, parameterized, and predefined.

- ☐ Preprocessor directives for conditional compilation.

- ☐ Grouping of operators in compound assignments.

- ☐ Manipulation and use of bits.

- ☐ Functions containing a variable number of arguments.

- ☐ Statements that permit conditional and unconditional branching.

15.1 Storage Classes

C Syntax:

storage
classes

Four storage classes can be assigned to variables - static, auto, register, and extern. The syntax of the declaration is

storage-class type identifier

For example,

```
static int character;
```

Static variables are allocated storage for the life of the program and not just the life of a function. In the following example the variable character has been described as being static. Although this value is initialized to 65 (the ASCII code for the character 'A') in the function another_one, repetitive calls to the function use the updated value of character character++ and not the original value initialized to 65.

Program Example 15.1: Static Storage of Variables

```
/*
chap_15\ex_1.c
program to demonstrate the use of static storage
*/

#include <stdio.h>

void another_one(void)
{
    static int character = 65;

    printf("%c", character);
    character++;
}

void main(void)
{
    another_one();
    another_one();
    another_one();
}
```

Result

ABC

Global variables, variables with file scope, are also static by default, since their values are preserved for the life of a program, and not just the life of the functions.

All the variables used in the functions in the programs prior to this chapter were, by default, **auto** variables and have the same meaning as *local* variables in other languages. Since these are the default variables, there is no need to precede the type with the storage class auto. When an auto variable is allocated storage space, it contains garbage unless specifically initialized. An auto variable has a meaningful value only for the life of a function. The next time a function is called, the values of the auto variables cannot be determined unless they are reinitialized.

In Program Example 15.1, if the variable character was not declared as being static, then by default it would be an auto variable, and upon every call to the function another_one, the value of character would be reinitialized to 65 and the output from the program would be AAA.

When the same variables are frequently used, execution speed might improve if the variables are stored in the central processing unit registers by declaring them as **register** storage class. A variable declared as register storage class has the same properties as auto storage class.

A variable can also be accessed from another source file by declaring the variable as **extern**. This implies that the variable has already been allocated storage in another source file and is not allocated any additional storage. In Program Example 15.2, two source files first.c and second.c contain function main and function change_char, respectively. A variable character is declared and initialized in the file first.c, and the character is declared as being extern in the file second.c. Both files are separately compiled and then linked together to form one executable program.

Program Example 15.2: The Use of the extern Storage Class.

```
/*
chap_15\first.c
*/

#include <stdio.h>

extern void change_char(void);

int character = 65; /* global variable */

void main(void)
{
   printf("%c", character);
   change_char();
   printf("%c", character);
}
```

471

```
/*
chap_15\second.c
*/

extern int character;

void change_char(void)
{
   character++;
}
```

Results

AB

declaration
of the same
variables
in files

When declarations of the same variable appear in different files, the compiler cannot check that the declarations are consistent. It is not usually advisable to make variables global in this way.

Function declarations, like variable declarations, may include a storage class. The only options available are extern and static. The extern storage class indicates that a function may be called from other files. In Program Example 15.2 a prototype for the function change_char was declared as being extern in the file first.c. The static storage class indicates that a function may be called only within the file in which it is defined. If no class is specified, then the function is assumed to be extern.

15.2 Make

Style
Matters:

a program
may consist
of several
files

Program Example 15.2 introduced a new concept in the way in which programs may be constructed. Throughout the book we have stored every program in one source file as a matter of convenience. However, there is no requirement that all the functions and declarations should be present in the same source file. Each function or group of functions can be stored in separate source files, and all included headers from the Standard Library, constants, types, structures, external declarations, prototypes, and macros that are required by the functions can be stored in a separate header file.

For example, Program Example 14.4 could have been constructed using three separate files: the first file as a header file; the second file to store the functions initialize_tree, attach_node, and display_tree; and the third file to store the function main.

A full listing of the header file follows.

```
/* chap_15\header.h */

/* Standard C Library header files */
#include <stdio.h>
#include <stdlib.h>
#include <errno.h>

/* constants, structures and types */
#define number_of_nodes 15

struct record {
                struct record *left;
                int           number;
                struct record *right;
            };

typedef struct record tree;
typedef enum {false, true} boolean;

/* function prototypes */
extern tree *initialize_tree(void);
extern *attach_node(tree *parent, int number, boolean *success);
extern void display_tree(tree *parent);

/* end of file header.h */
```

The header file is included in the remaining two source files. To avoid repeating the entire code from Program Example 14.4, the following files illustrate an abbreviation of the code required for each function. Notice that user-defined header files are not included between < > as with Standard C Library headers, but instead written as a string delimited by quotation marks.

```
/* chap_15\treefile.c */

#include "a:\chap_15\header.h"

tree *initialize_tree(void)
/* initialize the root of the tree to NULL */
{
      .
      .
}

tree *attach_node(tree *parent, int number, boolean *success)
/* function to attach a node to a binary tree */
{
      .
      .
}
```

```
void display_tree(tree *parent)
/* function to output the contents of the tree in order */
{
        .
        .
}

/* end of file treefile.c */

/* chap_15\mainfile.c */

#include "a:\chap_15\header.h"

void main(void)
{
    .
    .
}

/* end of file mainfile.c */
```

The obvious disadvantage of this approach is seen when changes are made to either the header file or function files. All the files dependent upon the changes will need to be recompiled! But not to worry; help is at hand in the form of the **make** facility.

Make is a UNIX tool that is now widely available for MSDOS and is included with most C compilers. The make facility requires a **makefile**, which contains commands to show what files are to be compiled and linked. For example, a UNIX makefile contains the following lines to create an executable program named run by compiling and linking treefile.c and mainfile.c where both files are dependent upon header.h.

```
run: treefile.o mainfile.o
  cc treefile.o mainfile.o -o run
treefile.o mainfile.o:header.h
```

The creation of makefiles for different systems is beyond the scope of this book. You are therefore advised to consult your C programming manual for details of building a makefile for your particular operating system and C compiler.

When the make command is invoked, every function file listed in the makefile is compiled automatically. If compilation is successful, the files are linked to form an executable run-time file. However, if changes are made to any of the function files or the header file, then when the make facility is invoked for a second time, only those files that depend on the changes are recompiled automatically.

15.3 Macros

An unusual feature of C is the preprocessing phase that precedes the actual compilation of a program. Prior to the compilation of a C program, a **preprocessor** is automatically invoked by the system to preprocess every source file before compilation takes place.

During preprocessing the C program source text is modified according to the preprocessing directives that are embedded in the program. Examples of directives already encountered are #include and #define.

□   Directives always begin with a # symbol.

□   Directives always end at the first new-line character unless explicitly continued. To continue a directive to the next line we must precede the new-line character by a \ symbol.

□   Directives can appear anywhere in a program although it is customary to put preprocessing directives at the beginning of a file.

□   Comments may appear on the same line as a directive.

The #define directive instructs the preprocessor to replace one set of characters with another. We refer to this replacement as a **macro**.

Simple Macros

C Syntax:

macro definition

You may recall that the syntax of a simple macro is:

#define identifier replacement-list

for example,

```
#define FALSE 0
```

where any occurrence of FALSE in a program would be replaced by the preprocessor with the numeric literal 0.

C Syntax:

macro undefined

The scope of a macro normally covers the entire source file from the definition of the macro to the end of the source file. A macro can be undefined as a method of limiting its scope. The syntax is

#undef identifier

for example,

```
#undef FALSE
```

Although #define can also be used to specify constants in a program, this approach is quite different from using const to specify constants.

□   #define is not subject to the same scope rules as variables; its scope is from its point of declaration to either the end of the source file or the statement #undef identifier. By contrast the scope of a global constant is from its point of declaration to the end of the source file, or if it is a local declaration, from its point of declaration to the end of the function.

- ☐ #define allows constants to be used in any constant expression, for example, in the declaration of the size of an array.

- ☐ #define allows the definition of a macro that represents only a numerical value, character, pointer, or string constant; however, const can be used to create read-only items of any type.

Parameterized Macros

An alternative syntax for a macro will allow parameters to be included in the identifier

C Syntax:

> *#define identifier(p1, p2 ... pn)   replacement-list*

parameter-zed macros

where p1, p2 .. pn are the macro's formal parameters. For example, in the <stdio.h> header file, the identifier putchar, which will output a single character to the standard output stream, is described as a macro - not as a function - by the definition

```
#define putchar(c) fputc((c), stdout)
```

where the function fputc writes a single character c to the standard output stream stdout.

C Syntax:

To digress for a moment, C contains a conditional operator ?: (the symbols ? and : are considered to be a single operator), which requires three operands whose syntax is

conditional operator

> *expression_1 ? expression_2 : expression_3*

The expression is evaluated as follows: expression_1 is evaluated to either zero (false) or nonzero (true). If the value of expression_1 is nonzero (true), then the entire expression takes on the value of expression_2. However, if the value of expression_1 is zero (false), then the entire expression takes the value of expression_3.

The parameterized macro expression

```
#define smallest(X,Y) ((X)<(Y) ? (X):(Y))
```

implies that if X<Y is true, the value of X is returned; otherwise, if X<Y is false, the value of Y is returned.

Further examples of parameterized macros are

```
#define to_upper(c) ('a'<= (c) && (c) <='z' ? (c) - 32 : (c))
```

In this macro expression if the parameter (c) is a lower-case letter, then the expression (c)−32 will be evaluated, giving the upper-case equivalent of the letter. If the letter is already in upper case then it remains as (c).

```
#define digit(x) ('0'<=(x) && (x)<='9' ? TRUE : FALSE)
```

can be used to validate a character being a decimal digit.

```
#define letter(L) ('A'<=to_upper(L) && to_upper(L) <= 'Z' ? TRUE : FALSE)
```

can validate a character as being either in the range A to Z or a to z. Notice that it is permissible to include in a macro previously defined macros, such as TRUE, FALSE, and to_upper(L).

Using a parameterized macro instead of a function call has the following advantages:

- ☐ The program code may run slightly faster, since a function call often requires information to be saved to effect the function call, return, and copy parameters. A macro invocation requires no such run-time overhead.

- ☐ A macro can be used with parameters of any type, since the formal parameters of a macro, unlike the formal parameters of a function, have no particular type. For example, the previously defined macro smallest can be used to find the smallest of two values of types int, long int, float, double, and so on.

The disadvantages of using a macro instead of a function are as follows:

- ☐ Because the replacement list is inserted in-line with the program code, the compiled code will often be larger.

- ☐ Macros cannot be passed as parameters in a function call. Remember, C has the concept of a pointer to a function to allow functions to be passed as parameters. However, macros are removed during preprocessing, so there is no possibility of having a pointer to a macro.

- ☐ A macro may evaluate its parameters more than once, whereas a function evaluates its parameters only once. Consider the following expression:

  ```
  min=smallest(X,smallest(Y,Z));
  ```

  This expression would be preprocessed as

  ```
  min = ((X)<smallest(Y,Z))?(X):(smallest(Y,Z))
  min = ((X)<(((Y)<(Z)?(Y):(Z)))?(X):(((Y)<(Z)?(Y):(Z))))
  ```

  Here smallest has evaluated its first parameter X once and the second parameter smallest(Y,Z) twice.

Program Example 15.3: Use of Parameterized Macros.

```
/*
chap_15\ex_3.c
program to demonstrate the use of macros
*/

#include <stdio.h>
#define TRUE   1
#define FALSE  0
#define smallest(X,Y) ((X)<(Y) ? (X):(Y))
#define to_upper(c) ('a'<=(c) && (c)<='z' ? (c)-32:(c))
#define digit(x) ('0'<=(x) && (x)<='9' ? TRUE:FALSE)
#define letter(L) ('A'<=to_upper(L) && to_upper(L)<='Z' ? TRUE:FALSE)

void main(void)
{
        int     first, second;
        char    letter;
        int     character;

        printf("input a pair of integers ");
        scanf("%d%d", &first,&second);
        getchar();
        printf("smallest number is %d\n", smallest(first, second));

        printf("input a single alphabetic character ");
        scanf("%c", &letter);
        getchar();
        printf("upper case letter is %c\n", to_upper(letter));

        printf("input a single character ");
        scanf("%c", &character);
        if digit(character)
           printf("digit\n");
        else if letter(character)
           printf("letter\n");
        else
           printf("cannot classify\n");

}
```

Results

```
input a pair of integers 25 3
smallest number is 3
input a single alphabetic character q
upper case letter is Q
input a single character %
cannot classify
```

Predefined Macros

A number of predefined macros may be used, but these macros must not be undefined or redefined. The names of the macros are as follows:

__FILE__	supplies the current source file name as a string literal;
__LINE__	supplies the current source code file line number as a decimal integer;
__DATE__	supplies the compilation date in the form of a string literal having the format Mmm dd yyyy;
__TIME__	supplies the compilation time in the form of a string literal having the format hh:mm:ss;
__STDC__	supplies the integer constant 1 if the compiler conforms to the ANSI standard.

Note: predefined macros use a double underscore __ before and after each identifier as part of the identifier. Program Example 15.4 uses several predefined macros.

Program Example 15.4: Predefined Macros.

```
/*
chap_15\ex_4.c
program to demonstrate the use of predefined macros
*/

#include <stdio.h>

void main(void)
{
        printf("%s\n", __FILE__);
        printf("%d\n", __LINE__);
        printf("%s\n", __DATE__);
        printf("%s\n", __TIME__);
}
```

Results

```
ex_4.c
11
Jan  6 1996
16:27:56
```

Operators # and

Program Example 15.5 introduces the **#** operator, and illustrates how a parameterized macro can be used as a template for code that is used many times in a program. The # operator converts a macro parameter into a string literal; for example, in the definition

```
#define   printer(x)  printf(#x "=%d\n", x)
```

479

#x will be replaced by the string literal for x. The statement `printer(A)` would display A = 3 if the value of A is 3. Notice in the following macro definition, that it is possible to include more than one statement in a replacement list provided the statements are separated by commas.

```
#define   input(y)  (printf("input " #y " "), scanf("%d",&y))
```

The **##** operator is used to *paste* symbols together. For example,

```
#define   var(i)  Y##i
```

when used in the declaration **float var(0), var(1), var(2)**, would produce

```
float Y0, Y1, Y2
```

Program Example 15.5: Demonstration of the # Operator

```
/*
chap_15\ex_5.c
program to demonstrate the use of the # operator
*/

#include <stdio.h>

#define printer(x) printf(#x "=%d\n", x)
#define input(y) (printf("input a value for " #y " "), scanf("%d",&y))

void main(void)
{
    int a,b;

    input(a);
    input(b);
    printer(a+b);
    printer(a-b);
    printer(a*b);
    if (a != 0) printer(b/a);
}
```

Results

```
input a value for a 15
input a value for b 24
a+b=39
a-b=-9
a*b=360
b/a=1
```

15.4 Conditional Compilation

There is a group of preprocessor directives that can be used to stipulate which segments of code are to be compiled. The directives use a version of the `if` and `else` statements that you are already familiar with. The syntax of the six directives and a brief explanation of their respective meanings follow.

C Syntax:	*#if identifier*	- <u>if</u> condition true
preproces-	*#ifdef identifier*	- <u>if</u> macro <u>defined</u>
sor	*#ifndef identifier*	- <u>if</u> macro <u>not</u> <u>defined</u>
conditional	*#elif identifier*	- <u>else</u> <u>if</u> condition true
compilation	*#else*	- <u>else</u> condition false
directives	*#endif*	- <u>end</u> <u>if</u> statement

Commenting-out Code

When testing a program, it is common practice to disable parts of the program code by converting the code to comments. This process is known as **commenting-out** the source code and can be achieved by placing / * at the beginning and * / at the end of the code you don't want to compile. This practice cannot be achieved in C if the code already contains comments. However, by using the preprocessor directives `#if..#endif`, it is possible to delimit a segment of program that should not be compiled.

```
#define FALSE 0
#if FALSE
   .
   .
   .
#endif
```

Since the expression after `#if` is (0), the compiler will ignore all the statements up to `#endif`. If the macro definition was rewritten as `#define FALSE 1,` then the expression after `#if` would be true and the statements after the expression would be compiled.

Debugging Code

Conditional compilation is a useful way of including debugging statements in a program. For example, by including the code:

```
#ifdef DEBUG_PROGRAM
   printf("X=%d\tY=%d\n",X,Y);
#endif
```

The compiled program will display the values of X and Y if the macro is defined by the statement **#define DEBUG_PROGRAM** earlier in the program. On the other hand, if the macro is not defined, the `printf` statement will be ignored. Notice from the simple macro `#define DEBUG_PROGRAM` that it is legal for the replacement list to be empty.

Default Definition of a Macro

When a program includes header files, it may not be clear whether a particular macro has been defined in one of the files. Conditional compilation allows us to provide a definition for a macro if one did not exist. In the following example if the SIZE_OF_ARRAY was not defined, then it is now defined to be 1000

```
#ifndef SIZE_OF_ARRAY
#define SIZE_OF_ARRAY 1000
#endif
```

Declaration of External Variables

External variables are declared outside the body of a function and can be shared by several functions in different files.

If the function main(void), stored in file main.c, contained the code

```
#define MAIN
#include <definition.h>
int flag; /* global variable */
```

then the declaration of the integer variable flag would not need to be declared as an external variable in this function. This fact would be ensured if the header file definition.h contained the statement:

```
#ifndef MAIN
   extern int flag;
#endif
```

In the file main.c, MAIN has been defined, therefore, the declaration of flag as an external integer is not required. However, in other files that include the header file <definition.h>, the identifier flag will be declared as an external integer variable.

15.5 Compound Assignment

C Syntax:

compound assignment arithmetic operators

A **compound assignment** is a shorthand notation that can be used in an assignment statement. For example, count=count+10 can be written as count+=10. The advantage of such an operator is that count is evaluated only once in count+=10 compared with twice in count=count+10. Similar compound assignment statements can be constructed for the other binary additive and multiplicative operators -=, *=, /=, and %=. For example,

alpha=alpha-5 is equivalent to alpha-=5;
beta=beta*15 is equivalent to beta*=15;
gamma=gamma/20 is equivalent to gamma/=20, and
epsilon=epsilon % 11 is equivalent to epsilon%=11.

15.6 Bit Manipulation

One advantage of C over many other languages is its ability to access the computer memory at bit level. One reason for working at this level is to write software that will execute rapidly, for example, graphics programs and game simulations.

Since you were introduced to number bases and number conversion in Chapter 2, you should be conversant with binary and hexadecimal numbers and know how to convert between them. If your knowledge of these topics is a bit rusty, then please reread sections 2.7 and 2.8.

Six operators operate on integer and character operands at the bit level.

The first two are shift operators.

C Syntax:

left shift

<< left shift is an operator to shift bits to the left; the value of a << b is the result when a is shifted left b positions. Zero bits are added at the right end to replace the bits that are shifted out.

For example, if a = 0xFABA (hexadecimal), a = 1111101010111010 (binary); then a << 5 gives a result 0101011101000000.

C Syntax:

right shift

>> right shift is an operator to shift bits to the right; the value of a >> b is the result when a is shifted right b positions. If a is unsigned or nonnegative, then zero bits are added to the left of the number. If the number is negative the result is implementation dependent.

For example, if a = 0111101010111010 then a >> 4 gives the result 0000011110101011.

In addition to the shift operators, there are bit operators that have the following meanings:

C Syntax:

bitwise
NOT

Bitwise complement ~ is a unary operator that is also known as a one's complement or bitwise NOT. The operator examines each bit position in turn and changes 1 for 0 and 0 for 1, as illustrated in the truth table in Figure 15.1.

C	01101110
~C	10010001

Figure 15.1 Bitwise complement ~

C Syntax:

bitwise
AND

Bitwise AND & is a binary operator that examines each bit position of both values in turn. The result is a bit value of 1 if both bit values are 1; otherwise, the result is a bit value of 0, as illustrated in the truth table in Figure 15.2.

C	00001011
D	11111000
C&D	00001000

Figure 15.2 Bitwise AND &

C Syntax: bitwise inclusive OR

Bitwise inclusive OR | is a binary operator that examines each bit position of both values in turn. The result is a bit value of 1 if either or both values are 1; otherwise, if both bit values are 0 the result is 0, as illustrated in the truth table in figure 15.3.

C	00001001
D	11111100
C|D	11111101

Figure 15.3 Bitwise inclusive OR |

C Syntax: bitwise exclusive OR

Bitwise exclusive OR ^ is a binary operator that examines each bit position of both values in turn. The result is a bit value of 1 if either, but not both, values are 1; otherwise, the result is a bit value 0 as illustrated in Figure 15.4.

C	00001001
D	11111100
C^D	11110101

Figure 15.4 Bitwise exclusive OR ^

Caution! bitwise operators and logical operators

The bit operators & and | are not equivalent to the logical operators && and ||.

Program Example 15.6: Bit Manipulation.

```
/*
chap_15\ex_6.c
program to illustrate bit manipulation
*/

#include <stdio.h>
#define print(x) printf(#x "= %d\n", x);

void main(void)
{
        int i=0x00FF; /* i=0000000011111111 */
        int j=0x000F; /* j=0000000000001111 */

        print(i);
        print(j);
        print(i << 8);      /* shift left by 8 bits */
        print(j >> 2);      /* shift right by 2 bits */
```

```
    print(~j);              /* take one's complement of j */
    print(i & j);           /* bitwise i AND j */
    print(i | j);           /* bitwise i inclusive OR j */
    print(i ^ j);           /* bitwise i exclusive OR j */
}
```

Results

```
i= 255
j= 15
i << 8= -256
j >> 2= 3
~j= -16
i & j= 15
i | j= 255
i ^ j= 240
```

C Syntax:

shift and bitwise compound assignment operators

The shift operators **<<** and **>>**, and the bit operators **&**, **^**, and **|** can be combined with **=** to provide compound assignment operators **<<=**, **>>=**, **&=**, **^=**, and **|=**, respectively, where the result is always stored in the first of the binary operands.

A **bit mask** is a group of bits that acts as a filter by allowing only certain bits through when operated upon another group of bits. For example, the bit mask `0x8000` (hexadecimal), `1000000000000000` (binary), will set the sign bit (most significant bit or left-most bit) of a 16-bit number (`i`) when used with bitwise inclusive OR (`i |= 0x8000`), as illustrated in the truth table in Figure 15.5.

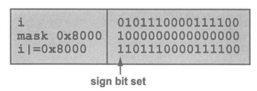

sign bit set

Figure 15.5 Use of a bit mask to set a sign bit

The bit mask `0x7FFF` (hexadecimal), `0111111111111111` (binary), will clear the sign bit of a 16-bit number when used with bitwise AND (`j &= 0x7FFF`), as illustrated in the truth table in Figure 15.6.

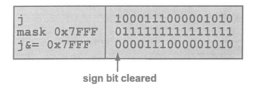

sign bit cleared

Figure 15.6 Use of a bit mask to clear a sign bit

A group of consecutive bits can be cleared by using a bit mask in which each bit to be cleared is set to zero. For example, the bit mask 0xFFC7 (hexadecimal), 1111111111000111 (binary), is used in conjunction with bitwise AND to clear bits 5, 4, and 3, as illustrated in the truth table in Figure 15.7. Note - the right-most or least-significant bit is bit 0.

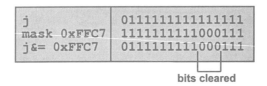

bits cleared

Figure 15.7 Use of a bit mask to clear a group of bits

Individual bits can then be set by the use of a bit mask. The truth table in Figure 15.8 illustrates that bit 4 can be set by using the bit mask 0x0010 (hexadecimal), 0000000000010000 (binary), in conjunction with bitwise inclusive OR.

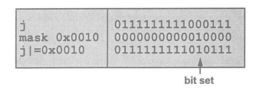

bit set

Figure 15.8 Use of a bit mask to set individual bits

Finally a group of bits can be retrieved by masking out unwanted bits and shifting the result. For example, in Figure 15.9 if bits 12, 13, and 14 are required (bit 15 is the sign bit), the bit mask 0x7000 (hexadecimal), 0111000000000000 (binary), would be used in conjunction with bitwise AND on the number. The result would then be shifted twelve places to the right in order to obtain the value of the group of bits.

486

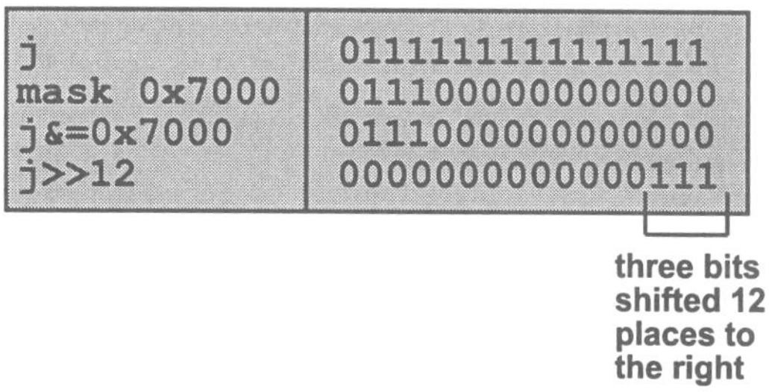

three bits
shifted 12
places to
the right

Figure 15.9 Use of a bit mask and shift to extract bits

Individual bits can be extracted using bit masks and tested in an if statement where (0) is false and (1) is true. Program example 15.7 illustrates the use of bit masks.

Program Example 15.7: Use of Bit Masks.

```c
/*
chap_15\ex_7.c
program to illustrate access to bits
*/

#include <stdio.h>
#define print(x) printf(#x "=%d\n", x)

void main(void)
{
        int i=0x0000, j=0xFFFF;

        print(i);
        print(j);

        print(i |= 0x8000);     /* set the sign bit */
        print(j &= 0x7FFF);     /* clear the sign bit */

        if (i & 0x8000)
        {
           printf("sign bit set ");
           print(i);
        }

        if (~j & 0x8000)
        {
           printf("sign bit is cleared ");
           print(j);
        }

        print(j & 0xFFC7 | 0x0010); /* modifying a bit field */
        print((j & 0x7000) >> 12);  /* retrieving a bit field */
}
```

Results

```
i=0
j=-1
i  |=0x8000=-32768
j  &=0x7FFF=32767
sign bit set i=-32768
sign bit cleared j=32767
j & 0xFFC7 | 0x0010=32727
(j & 0x7000) >> 12=7
```

We have just seen that bitwise operators can be used with masks to access groups or individual bits. However, by using a structure, it is possible to name bits or groups of bits as structure members. These members are known as **bit fields**. The syntax of a structure member expressed as a bit field is

C Syntax:

bit fields within a structure

> *type identifier : number-of-bits*

In Program Example 15.8, a six-digit date is represented by a structure containing bit fields for month, day, and year. It is possible to define the number of bits in each field. In this example four bits giving a range of 0 to15 represent the month; five bits giving a range of 0 to 31 represent the day; and seven bits giving a range of 0 to 127 represent the year. Within these ranges the month values 1 to 12, day values 1 to 31, and year values 0 to 99 can be accommodated. The total number of bits to represent a date is sixteen, or two bytes. If the fields month, day and year had each been coded as `short int`, the number of bytes required to store a date would have been three. Therefore, defining the number of bits in a field is a useful way in which to compress information.

```
typedef struct{
                unsigned int month : 4;
                unsigned int day   : 5;
                unsigned int year  : 7;
            } date;
```

A field may not overlap an integer boundary. If the bit-field width would cause this to happen, the field is aligned at the next integer boundary.

Bit fields must be considered as machine dependent. ANSI C permits an implementation to choose to use `long` instead of `int` when a bit field is defined with more bits than a single precision `int`.

Field members are restricted to type `int`. Arrays of fields are not allowed. Fields cannot be addressed directly by pointers, and the address operator cannot be applied to a bit-field member.

Program Example 15.8 illustrates the use of bit fields. Both a date of birth and the current date are stored in a compressed format using the bit fields described above. From this information the age of a person is calculated and displayed.

Program Example 15.8: Use of Bit Fields

```
/*
chap_15\ex_8.c
program to demonstrate the use of bit fields;

the program calculates the age of a person given their
date of birth and the current date;
the program is written for the twentieth century only
*/

#include <stdio.h>

typedef struct {
            unsigned int month :4; /* least significant bits */
            unsigned int day   :5;
            unsigned int year  :7; /* most significant bits */
        } date;

void main(void)
{
    date date_of_birth, today;
    int  mm, dd, yy;
    int  age;

    printf("input all dates in the format mm dd yy\n\n");
    printf("date of birth? ");
    scanf("%d%d%d", &mm, &dd, &yy);

    date_of_birth.month = mm;
    date_of_birth.day   = dd;
    date_of_birth.year  = yy;

    printf("today's date? ");
    scanf("%d%d%d", &mm, &dd, &yy);

    today.month = mm;
    today.day   = dd;
    today.year  = yy;

    /* calculate age */
    if ((today.month > date_of_birth.month) ||
        (today.month == date_of_birth.month &&
         today.day > date_of_birth.day))
```

```
        age = today.year - date_of_birth.year;
    else
        age = today.year - date_of_birth.year - 1;

    printf("current age is %d years\n ", age);
}
```

Results

```
input all dates in the format mm dd yy

date of birth? 3 18 48
today's date? 1 6 96
current age is 47 years
```

15.7 Variadic Functions

Variadic functions are functions that can take a variable number of arguments. Such functions are not entirely unfamiliar to you, since both `scanf` and `printf` cater for different numbers of arguments. However, the functions created by the programmer have, up to now, had only a fixed number of arguments.

In Program Example 15.9, a function is defined to calculate the arithmetic mean of a set of numbers. A prototype for this function may be declared as

`float mean(int number, ...);`

The ellipsis . . . appearing at the end of the argument list indicates that the function can take a variable number of arguments.

The header file `<stdarg.h>` provides a new type called `va_list` and three macros that operate on items of this type called `va_start`, `va_arg`, and `va_end`.

A variable `args` needs to be declared of type `va_list`.

`va_list args;`

Before the variable argument list can be accessed, the macro `va_start` must be called.

`va_start(args, number);`

where `number` is the number of arguments to follow in the actual-parameter list of the function call.

The actual arguments can be accessed sequentially by the macro `va_arg`; for example,

`arg = va_arg(args, int);`

where `arg` is the value of an actual parameter and `int` represents the data type of the parameter.

Finally when all the arguments have been processed, the macro va_end should be called. For example,

```
va_end(args);
```

Program Example 15.9: Variadic Functions to Calculate the Mean of a Series of Numbers.

```
/*
chap_15\ex_9.c
demonstration of a function with a variable number of arguments
*/

#include <stdio.h>
#include <stdarg.h>

float mean(int number, ...)
/* function to return the mean for any number of parameters */
{
    va_list     args;
    int         arg;
    int         count, total = 0;

    va_start(args, number);
    for (count=0; count < number; count++)
    {
        arg = va_arg(args, int);
        total += arg;
    }
    va_end(args);
    return (float) total/number;
}

void main(void)
{
    printf("average %4.1f\n", mean(2,10,20));
    printf("average %4.1f\n", mean(4,10,20,30,40));
    printf("average %4.1f\n", mean(10,1,2,3,4,5,6,7,8,9,10));
}
```

Results

```
average 15.0
average 25.0
average  5.5
```

15.8 Branching

Branching implies changing the order in which the computer executes statements. Throughout the book, branching has been achieved using function calls, `return`, `if`, `switch`, `break`, and `exit` statements. All the forms of branching have led to well-structured programs and have not resulted in haphazard changes to the order in which statements are executed.

Further statements that permit a controlled form of branching follow.

Break Statement

C Syntax:

break

A `break` statement, first discussed in Chapter 6, can be used in conjunction with an `if` statement anywhere in a loop to terminate the loop. For example,

```
for (;;)
{
    .
    .
    if (exit_condition) break;
    .
    .
}
```

Continue Statement

C Syntax:

continue

A `continue` statement causes the computer to branch to the end of the last statement in a loop, but not outside the loop. If used in conjunction with an `if` statement, statements inside the loop can be by-passed if a particular condition happens to be true. Note: `continue` is different from `break` in so much as the computer remains in the loop; with `break` the computer was taken outside the loop or selection statement. For example,

```
for (;;)
{
    .
    .
    if (by_pass-condition) continue;
    .
    .
}
```

Unconditional branching, however, should be avoided where possible, since it may lead to programs that violate the normal use of sequence, selection, repetition, and function calls. Tracing through a program that contains excessive unconditional branching is like trying to find the ends of lengths of string that have become tangled together. Unconditional branching is possible with the following statement.

492

Goto Statement

C Syntax:

goto

A `goto` statement permits unconditional branching and should be avoided whenever possible. The `break` and `continue` statements all permit a restricted form of unconditional branching and it should not usually be necessary to use `goto`. However, the statement is part of the language and a brief mention is all it will receive. The format of a `goto` statement is: `goto label;` where the `label` is an identifier.

A label must be followed by a statement and any statement can have more than one label. In the example that follows, the label is `end` and it is followed by the statement `printf("unconditional branch");`

```
        {
                .
  ┌──────── goto end;
  │             .
  └────────▶ end: printf("unconditional branch");
                .
        }
```

C Syntax:

null statement

If the label in the last example had been at the end of the compound statement, it would still need to be followed by a statement. The **null** statement is represented by a semicolon (`;`) and is used whenever a statement is required to complete the syntax, as in `end : ;`

A null statement can be used in the body of a loop if the body must be kept empty, for example,

```
while ((character = getchar()) == space)
; /* this is the body of the loop and contains a null statement */
```

Caution!

This loop will keep receiving input from a keyboard as long as the character is a space, or in other words, it will ignore all space characters.

use of null statements

Be very careful where you place null statements in relationship to if, while, and for statements, since accidentally putting a semicolon after the parenthesis in these statements ends the statement prematurely and the computer cannot detect this as an error.

Summary

☐ The storage classes `auto`, `static`, `register`, and `extern` can be assigned to variables.

☐ Functions may be `extern` or `static`.

☐ A program may be either stored in a single file or built from individual files and header files.

☐ Use a header file to encompass all the included headers from the Standard Library, constants, types, structures, external declarations, prototypes, and macros that are required by the functions in a program.

☐ The `make` facility requires a makefile (or equivalent in non-UNIX systems) that contains commands to show what files are to be compiled and linked.

☐ The `make` command enables all function files within the makefile to be compiled and linked. Changes to individual function files will result in only those files being recompiled. The `make` facility examines all function and header files for all dependencies.

☐ Simple macros may be introduced into a program as an alternative to constants.

☐ Parameterized macros can be used in place of explicitly coded functions.

☐ A set of five macros are predefined and must not be redefined or undefined. They are

    `__FILE__ , __LINE__ , __DATE__ , __TIME__` and `__STDC__`

☐ The scope of a macro covers its point of declaration (`#define`) through to either the end of the file or the declaration of the end of the macro (`#undef`).

☐ It is possible to replace a preprocessing token parameter with a string literal token by using the operator #.

☐ If, in the replacement list, a parameter is immediately preceded or followed by the ## processing token, the parameter is replaced by the corresponding argument's preprocessing token sequence.

☐ The preprocessor can be used to selectively include/ exclude lines of source code from further processing by the compiler, by using `#if`, `#ifdef`, and `#ifndef` directives.

☐ Using the operators ~, <<, and >>, it is possible to one's complement, left shift, or right shift, respectively, a group of bits.

☐ Groups of bits may have the operations of bitwise AND &, inclusive OR |, and exclusive OR ^ applied to respective bits in the corresponding bit strings.

☐ Compound operators +=, -=, *=, /=, %=, <<=, >>=, &=, ^=, and |= store the result in the first operand of the binary operators.

☐ Bit masks may be used to modify the contents of bit strings.

☐ Members of a structure can be composed from a set number of bits and are known as bit fields.

☐ A function may be allowed to take on a variable number of arguments. In such cases, a number of macros from the library `<stdarg.h>` must be used when processing the arguments.

☐ A `break` statement used in conjunction with an `if` statement can terminate a loop.

☐ A `continue` statement used in conjunction with an `if` statement can branch to the end of a loop.

☐ A `goto` statement permits unconditional branching, and its use should be avoided if possible.

Review Questions

1. Distinguish between a `static` variable and an `auto` variable in terms of the life of a program and the life of a function.

2. True or false - a variable declared as being `extern` has been allocated storage space in another file.

3. What is the purpose of declaring a function as being `extern`?

4. True or false - a program may be constructed by storing individual functions in separate files.

5. True or false - a programmer-defined header file may contain all the constants, types, structures, external declarations, prototypes and macros that are required in a program.

6. What is a makefile and how is it associated with a `make` command?

7. What are the advantages of using a simple macro rather than a constant?

8. What are the advantages of using a parameterized macro in place of a function?

9. True or false - a predefined macro may be redefined.

10. True or false - comments may be nested in the C language.

11. Describe three uses for conditional compilation.

12. True or false - the variable in a compound assignment statement is evaluated only once.

13. True or false - the bitwise operators & and | are equivalent to the logical operators && and ||.

14. What is a bit mask and how is it used?

15. What bit mask and bitwise operator would you use to clear (set to zero) bits 12,11,10, 1, and 0 in a group of 16 bits? Give your answer in both binary and hexadecimal.

16. What is a bit field?

17. True or false - a function may have a variable number of arguments.

18. What is the difference between a `break` and a `continue` statement?

19. What is the purpose of a `goto` statement?

20. What is a null statement, and why should it be used with care in `if`, `while`, and `for` statements?

Programming Exercises

21. What are the values of the x variables, and what is displayed when the following program is executed? Note: function `printf` returns the number of characters output.

```c
#include <stdio.h>
int x=68;

void display(void)
{
   static int character = 100;
   int x;

   x = printf("%c", character);
   character +=10;
}

void main(void)
{
   display();
   display();
   display();
}
```

Write parameterized macros as answers to questions 22 to 24.

22. Test characters for being hexadecimal.

23. Test whether the second number in a set of three numbers represents a maximum value.

24. Calculate and display the area of a triangle given the lengths of two sides a and b and the included angle C. The formula for the area of a triangle is 1/2*a*b*sin(C).

25. Evaluate the following:

(a) 0xABCD << 7

(b) 0x1FBB ^ 0x0CDE

(c) 0xABCD & 0xFF00

(d) (0x7AAA | 0x1FFF) >> 10

Programming Problems

26. Return to Chapter 11 and rewrite the program given in Case Study: Student Examination Results. You should create your own header file that contains directives to include all the necessary header files from the Standard Library, constant definitions, type declarations, and function prototypes. Modify each function to include your new header file and store each function in a separate file.

Create a makefile for your specific system.

Invoke the `make` command to compile and link the files specified in the makefile.

Run the program.

27. Write parameterized macros for the following:

(a) to swap two items;

(b) to order two items into ascending order.

Using these macros write a program to sort data held in an array into ascending sequence. The choice of data is left to you.

28. Rewrite Program Example 15.9 to contain a function to return both the maximum and minimum values from a set of integers. Hint: return these values as two fields of a structure.

29. A nonstandard library function `biosequip` reports on the hardware configuration of an IBM PC or compatible microcomputer. The prototype of this function is given as

```
int biosequip(void);
```

and it returns an unsigned 16-bit integer where the following bits represent information about the equipment of the computer.

Bit(s)	Meaning
0	set to 1 if the system boots from disk
1	set to 1 if a coprocessor is installed
2-3	indicates motherboard RAM size:
	00 16K
	01 32K
	10 48K
	11 64K
4-5	initial video mode
	00 unused
	01 color card 40x25 BW mode
	10 color card 80x25 BW mode
	11 monochrome card 80x25 BW mode

497

6-7	number of disk drives
	00 1 drive
	01 2 drives
	10 3 drives
	11 4 drives, but only if bit 0 is 1
8	set to 0 if machine does not have DMA; set to 1 otherwise
9-11	number of serial ports
12	set to 1 if a game port is attached
13	set to 1 if a serial printer is attached
14-15	number of parallel printers installed

(a) Using bit masks and shifts, write a program to report on the hardware configuration of your PC.

(b) Rewrite your answer to part (a) using bit fields and unions.

Note: if you do not have access to the library function `biosequip`, then you will not be able to run your answer to this question on your computer.

30. Using bit manipulation, devise functions to

(a) rotate either counter-clockwise or clockwise a specified number of bits of a 16-bit word;

(b) multiply two 8-bit binary integers that can be either positive or negative.

Incorporate these functions into suitable test programs and run the programs.

Chapter 16

An Introduction to C++

In 1980 Bjarne Stroustrup of AT&T Bell Laboratories Computing Research Centre began work on extending the C language with the intention of using it for simulation applications. By 1983 the extended language was renamed as C++; the ++ indicating the incremental increase of C.

C++ is essentially a superset of ANSI C, meaning that everything that is available in C is also available in C++. Work on the ANSI standardization of C++ began in 1990 and at the time of this publication has not yet been completed.

Using your knowledge from learning and understanding C, this chapter focuses your attention upon many of the differences between C and C++ as a procedural language. As the title suggests, the material covered in this chapter is only an introduction to C++. C++ is also the topic of the final two chapters of the book. By the end of this chapter, you should have an understanding of the following topics:

☐   Input and output in C++.

☐   C++ enhancements to C.

☐   Functions in C++.

☐   Overloading functions.

☐   Incompatibilities between C and C++.

16.1 Stream Output

The term *stream* was first introduced in Chapter 10, and you may recall that it was used to define any input source or output destination for data. The standard streams that you are already familiar with are stdin, stdout, and stderr from the library <stdio.h>. The stream stdin was associated with data from a keyboard, and both stdout and stderr were associated with output being directed to the screen of a terminal.

The C++ header file associated with output is <iostream.h>. In the <iostream.h> library, the standard output stream is named **cout** and the error stream is named **cerr**; the streams correspond to the stdout and stderr streams found in C.

Two programs follow. The first is written in C++, and the second program listed along side the first is written in C. If both programs produce identical results, what do you think the output from the C++ program will be?

```
/* C++ program */              /* C program */
#include <iostream.h>          #include <stdio.h>
void main(void)                void main(void)
{                              {
   cout << "Hello World\n";       printf("Hello World\n");
}                              }
```

If you deduced that the string Hello World followed by a new-line character is output to a screen, then you are correct.

C++ feature In the preceding C++ program, the operator **<<** implies output or an **insertion** into the standard output stream cout. You may remember that the **<<** operator has been used before to represent a bitwise left **operator** shift. The use of the same operator, but in a different context, is known as **operator overloading** and is **overloading** common practice in C++. The compiler resolves the intended use for the symbol by examining the context in which the symbol is being used. But more of this later!

Notice from the C++ program that it is permissible to include escape characters in a string, and their meaning will be interpreted the same as for C. Hence the \n at the end of the string will generate a new line after the string.

The following segment of code illustrates how the values for different types of numeric variables may be output. You may assume that the values of the variables integer, real, and large_real have been initialized to 127, 378.29 and 9.87654321E+30, respectively.

As before, the equivalent C code has been listed to the right of the C++ code to enable you to compare how output statements differ between C++ and C.

```
/* C++ program */               /* C program */
#include <iostream.h>           #include <stdio.h>

void main(void)                 void main(void)
{                               {
   int    integer;                 int    integer;
   float  real;                     float  real;
   double large_real;              double large_real;

   .                               .
   cout << integer << "\n";        printf("%d\n",integer);
   cout << real << "\n";           printf("%f\n",real);
   cout << large_real;             printf("%e", large_real);

   .                               .
```

The output from the segments of code are

```
127                             127
378.29                          378.290009
9.87654e+30                     9.876543e+30
```

Several observations should be made about the output of numbers in the C++ segment.

First, it is not necessary to introduce a control string, as with `printf`, to indicate the type of number to be displayed. Notice that the C++ program does not use a control string to distinguish between integer, real, and double-precision numbers.

Second, additional output can be introduced into the output stream by using additional insertion operators; therefore, it is possible to terminate each number with a new-line character by including `<<"\n"`.

When using the insertion operator, the field width is automatically adjusted to fit the number being output and real numbers are output to a fixed number of decimal places. Notice the minor variations in the output of the numbers between the C++ and C segments. This variation is caused by the different defaults in the printing routines in C++ and C.

C++ feature C++ uses the following manipulators, found in the library header file `<iomanip.h>`, to format output.

format manipulators
```
setw(n)
```

sets the field width to n unless the number of digits in a number is larger than n, in which case the instruction is ignored.

```
setprecision(n)
```

sets the floating-point precision to n digits unless the number of digits after the decimal point is less than n, in which case the statement is irrelevant.

```
endl
```

inserts a new-line and can be used in place of `"\n"`.

501

The previous segment of C++ code has been modified to include manipulators.

```
#include <iostream.h>
#include <iomanip.h>

void main(void)
{
   int    integer;
   float  real;
   double large_real;
    .
   cout << setw(5) << integer;
   cout << setw(10) << real << endl;
   cout << setw(15) << setprecision(4) << large_real;
    .
```

The output from this segment of code is

```
^^127^^^^378.29
^^^^^9.8765e+30
```

where the symbol ^ indicates the position of a space.

C++ feature

number conversion manipulators

Three manipulators permit integer number conversion.

```
dec
```

converts an integer to base 10 (decimal), this is the default.

```
oct
```

converts an integer to base 8 (octal).

```
hex
```

converts an integer to base 16 (hexadecimal).

The following segment of code uses the manipulators oct and hex to convert a decimal integer, assumed to have the value 127, to octal and hexadecimal values, respectively.

```
#include <iostream.h>
#include <iomanip.h>

void main(void)
{
   int integer = 127;

   cout << integer << endl;          /* displays a decimal integer */
   cout << oct << integer << endl;   /* displays an octal integer */
   cout << hex << integer;           /* displays a hexadecimal integer */
    .
```

The output from this segment of code is

```
127
177
7F
```

16.2 Stream Input

The header file associated with input is also `<iostream.h>`. In the `<iostream.h>` library, the standard input stream is named **cin** and corresponds to the `stdin` stream found in the library `<stdio.h>`.

The input of data is from the standard input stream **cin**. Input is accomplished by using the **extraction** operator **>>**. The following segments of code show how data is input in C++ and C.

```
/* C++ code */                /* C code */

void main(void)              void main(void)
{
   int    integer;              int    integer;
   float  real;                 float  real;
   double large_real;           double large_real;

   cin >> integer;              scanf("%d", &integer);
   cin >> real;                 scanf("%f", &real);
   cin >> large_real;           scanf("%le",&large_real);
   .                            .
```

Both segments of code will allow values for `integer`, `real`, and `large_real` numbers to be input via the keyboard. There is no need to specify the type for the data being input in C++ as is the case when using the function `scanf` in C.

Characters and strings can also be input and output to streams in C++. The following segment of code is used to input a single character and output its value.

```
#include <iostream.h>

void main(void)
{
   char character;

   cout << "input a single character ";
   cin >> character;
   cout << "character input was " << character;
   .
```

A string can be input and output in a similar manner. The previous segment of code has been modified to input and output a single string of up to eighty characters in length.

503

```
#include <iostream.h>

void main(void)
{
    char string[80];

    cout << "input a string of characters ";
    cin >> string;
    cout << "character string input was " << string;
    .
```

Note: white-space characters in the input string are regarded as string delimiters.

Finally, all the input and output functions that are applicable to C can also be used in C++. However, input and output in C++ is safer than in C, for the following reasons:

- ☐ There are no conversion specifications or format strings to get wrong as in `printf` and `scanf`.

- ☐ There is no address operator to forget to include as in `scanf`.

16.3 C++ Enhancements to C

In this section, we will briefly consider some of the fundamental differences between C and C++. This coverage is not meant to be exhaustive, but rather introductory in nature. In many cases, the C++ statements represent improvements over the equivalent C statements, and whenever reasonable, we will consider specifically how C++ is better or more functional than C.

Single-line Comments

C++ allows single-line comments, which begin with // and terminate at the end of the line. Single-line comments are regarded as being safer than the old-style comments, since they cannot accidentally be left not terminated. For example,

C++ feature

single line comments

```
// program to create an array of integers; calculate the sum and
// arithmetic mean of the numbers, and display this information
```

However, old-style comments can still be used, and either style comment delimiter can be commented out using the other. For example,

```
/*
    // these comments
    // are commented out
*/


// /*
    // these comments
    // are commented in
// */
```

Filenames of Source Files

C++ feature

filename
extension

Programs written in C++ are stored as text files, normally with **.cpp** as an extension to the filename.

```
// chap_16\ex_1.cpp
```

Reference Parameters

The difference between reference and value parameters was first discussed in Chapter 5. In C, parameters, except for arrays and pointers, are passed by value. Therefore, changing the value of a parameter affects only the function's local copy. For a C function to modify an actual parameter, the function must be passed an address of the actual parameter. You may remember that the technique of passing an address of the actual parameter and using the indirection operator upon the parameter was the method of simulating a reference parameter in C. However, C++ provides an alternative way to modify an actual parameter using the symbol **&** to declare the formal parameter a reference parameter, as illustrated in the following prototype of the function mean.

C++ feature

reference
parameters

```
float mean(int size, int *table, int &sum);
```

The parameter size is a value parameter; *table is a pointer to the first cell of an array, and sum is a reference parameter. The actual parameter total, corresponding to sum in the function call, is not preceded by the & operator but simply treated as a variable, as illustrated by the following statement:

```
average = mean(length, array, total);
```

The compiler arranges for the address of total to be passed to the function mean. Whenever sum is used inside the function, for example, sum = sum + table[index], the indirection operator is automatically applied to this address. The effect is that sum behaves as though it were equivalent to total. We say that sum is an **alias** for total.

The relationships between the arguments in the function call to mean found in the main function and the formal parameters in the function mean are illustrated in Figure 16.1.

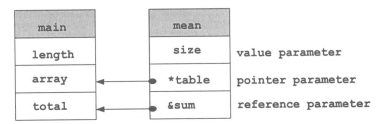

Figure 16.1 Arguments in main and parameters in mean

Dynamic Storage Allocation and Deallocation

C++ feature

dynamic
memory
allocation

In C dynamic storage allocation is made by using the functions `calloc` or `malloc`. C++ provides an alternative to these functions through the operator **new**. The operator `new` can be used to dynamically allocate memory for a single item or an array of items and returns a `NULL` pointer if there is no memory to allocate.

An example of an allocation for a single item follows.

```
int *int_pointer;        // declaration of a pointer to an integer

int_pointer = new int;  // allocation of memory for an integer
```

An example of an allocation for an array follows. Notice that the size of the array `length` is enclosed between square brackets `[]` after the data type.

```
int *array;              // declaration of a pointer to an array

array = new int[length];  // allocation of memory for an array
```

will allocate enough memory to create the variable `array`, subscripted in the range `0 .. length-1`.

Recall for a moment how you would allocate memory using `calloc`.

```
array = calloc(length, sizeof(int));
```

The disadvantage of this approach stems from the programmer's ability to correctly name the data type for which storage space is required - in this example `int`. If a mistake is made in the type, the compiler will not generate an error, yet the wrong amount of space may have been requested from the heap. Clearly the use of `new` is a safer alternative!

The deallocation of memory is possible by using the C++ operator **delete** in place of the C function `free`.

C++ feature

dynamic
memory
deallocation

The operator has two formats, depending upon whether the pointer variable points at a single item or an array.

For a single item the statement

```
delete int_pointer;
```

and for an array

```
delete [ ] array;
```

In this latter case the empty square brackets `[]` must be included to signify that the memory space for an array is being deallocated. Applying `delete` to a pointer that has not been returned by `new` is illegal, and applying `delete []` to a nonarray or `delete` without `[]` to an array will give unpredictable results.

For Loop

C++ feature

declaration of for loop control variable

In C++ the first expression in the `for` statement, for initializing the loop variable, may contain a type declaration for the loop variable. In this example the type declaration `int` has been declared with the initialization of the variable `index`. This feature allows the `for` statement to declare its own loop control variable without the declaration being made outside the loop.

```
for (int index=0; index!=size; index++)
    table[index]=(rand()%25)+1;
```

The scope of the declared loop variable extends to the end of the enclosing block. In this example, the block is the one in which the `for` statement appears. If a `for` statement is declared in one branch of an `if` statement, the scope of the loop control variable is confined to the `if` statement and does not exist outside this statement.

Explicit Type Conversion

C++ feature

type conversion

In C, explicit type conversions are performed using *cast* expressions. C++ allows an alternative notation in which the type name is used as though it were a function. In this example both `float(sum)` and `float(size)` temporarily convert the type of the variables `sum` and `size` to floating-point.

```
return float(sum) / float(size);
```

Mixing Data Declarations and Statements

C++ feature

declarations

In a C++ function, declarations can be mixed with statements. For example, the declaration of the variable `average` as `float` appears in the same statement as the assignment. The scope of such a variable extends from its declaration to the end of the enclosing block.

```
float average = mean(size);
```

The following case study consolidates the features that have been explained in the first three sections of this chapter.

Case Study: Sum and Arithmetic Mean of Numbers

integers
sums
averages

The first case study in this section generates an array of variable size in the range 1 to 10 and stores random integers in the range 1 to 25 in the array. The program then calculates the sum and arithmetic mean of the numbers in the array and displays the number of cells in the array, the numbers that are stored in the array, and the sum and mean of the numbers.

Problem Analysis - If this program is to produce various size arrays containing different numbers every time the program is executed, then a new set of random numbers must be generated each time the program is run. This process is made possible by the function **srand**, which is found in the header file `<stdlib.h>` and sets the starting point for the pseudo random number generator. The prototype for `srand` is

```
void srand(unsigned seed);
```

The value of the `seed` must be different each time the function is executed in order to generate a different set of random numbers. A value for the `seed` that changes can be a number dependent upon time. The function **time**, found in the header `<time.h>`, will return the number of seconds elapsed since midnight, January 1, 1970. The prototype for time is

```
time_t time(time_t *elapsed_time);
```

where type **time_t** is defined in the header file `<time.h>`.

The following expression can be used to select a new set of random numbers every time the program is run.

```
srand(unsigned (time(&elapsed_time)%INT_MAX));
```

where `elapsed_time` is declared of type `time_t`.

The function **rand** found in header `<stdlib.h>` returns a pseudo random number in the range `0..RAND_MAX`.

The size of the table in the range 1..10 is generated using the expression

```
(rand()%10)+1;
```

and a single random number in the range 1..25 is generated using the expression

```
(rand()%25)+1;
```

The program has been divided into four functions including the `main` control function as depicted in the structure chart in Figure 16.2. The function `GetData` fills the array with random numbers in the range 1..25. The function `mean` calculates the arithmetic mean of the numbers stored in the array. The function `display` prints the size of the array and the contents of the array on the screen. Finally, the function `main` generates the size of the array and dynamically allocates enough memory to store the array. The function `main` calls `GetData` and then calls the function `display` to display the size of the array and the contents of the array. The function `main` then calls `mean` to calculate the arithmetic mean of the numbers and displays this value. Finally `main` deallocates the memory used for the array.

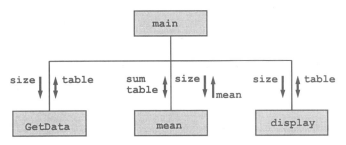

Figure 16.2 Structure chart

Algorithm for the Function main

1. set starting point for pseudo random number generator
2. generate the size of the array
3. dynamically allocate space for storing the array
4. generate data at random and store in the array
5. display the size and contents of the array
6. calculate the sum and arithmetic mean of the numbers in the array
7. display the sum and arithmetic mean
8. deallocate the storage space for the array

Data Dictionary for the Function main - The array variable `array` is declared as a pointer to an integer. The size of the array - `length`, and the sum of the numbers in the array - `total` are both declared as integers. The arithmetic mean `average` is declared as `float`, and the time variable as `elapsed_time` having type `time_t`.

```
int     *array;
int     length;
int     total;
float   average;
time_t elapsed_time;
```

Algorithm for the Function GetData

4.1   for every cell in the array
4.2   generate and store in the array a random number in the range 1 to 25

Data Dictionary for the Function GetData - The function contains two formal parameters: the size of the array and a pointer to the array. There is one local variable `index` that is used to declare the loop control variable to gain access to the table; however, this variable can be declared as part of the `for` statement.

```
void GetData(int size, int *table);
int  index;
```

509

Desk Check of the Function GetData - Assume that the size of the array is 8 and that the numbers are generated at random in the range 1 to 25.

variable	value(s)							
size	8							
index	0	1	2	3	4	5	6	7
table[index]	22	14	11	20	7	2	12	4

Algorithm for the Function display

5.1 display the size of the array
5.2 for every cell in the array
5.3 display the number stored in the cell
5.4 display a new-line

Data Dictionary for the Function display - The function contains two formal parameters: the size of the array and a pointer to the array. Once again the loop control variable can be declared within the `for` loop.

```
void display(int size, int *table);
int  index;
```

Algorithm for the Function mean

6.1 initialize sum to zero
6.2 for every cell in the array
6.3 increase the value of sum by the number stored in the cell
6.4 calculate and return the arithmetic mean

Data Dictionary for the Function mean - The function contains three formal parameters: the size of the array, a pointer to the array, and a reference parameter for the sum of the numbers stored in the array. The function returns a value for the arithmetic mean. The loop control variable `index` can be defined within the `for` loop.

```
float   mean(int size, int *table, int &sum);
int     index;
```

Desk Check of the Function mean - The data is the same as that defined in the desk check for the function GetData.

variable	value(s)							
size	8							
table[index]		22	14	11	20	7	2	12	4
sum	0	22	36	47	67	74	76	88	92
index		0	1	2	3	4	5	6	7
returned value	11.50							

```
                        Screen Layout
 12345678901234567890123456789012345678901234567890

 size of table 8
    22   14   11   20    7    2   12    4
 sum of numbers 92
 average of contents 11.5
```

All the new features in C++ that have been previously described appear in second color in the following program.

```cpp
// chap_16\ex_1.cpp
// program to create an array of integers; calculate the sum and
// arithmetic mean of the numbers, and display this information

#include <iostream.h>
#include <iomanip.h>
#include <time.h>
#include <stdlib.h>
#include <limits.h>

void GetData(int size, int *table)
// function to fill the array with integers in the range 1 to 25

{
        for (int index=0; index!=size; index++)
            table[index] = (rand()%25)+1;
}
```

could generate same no ?

```cpp
float mean(int size, int *table, int &sum)
// function to calculate the arithmetic mean of the numbers in the array
{
        sum=0;

        for (int index=0; index!=size; index++)
                sum=sum+table[index];

        return float(sum) / float(size);
}
```

```
void display(int size, int *table)
{
        cout << "size of table " << size << endl;
        for (int index=0; index!=size; index++)
        {
                cout << table[index] << "\t";
        }
        cout << endl;
}


void main(void)
{
        int     total;
        time_t  elapsed_time;

        // set starting point for pseudo random number generator
        srand(unsigned(time(&elapsed_time)%INT_MAX));

        // generate size of table
        int length=(rand()%10)+1;

        // allocate space for storing table
        int *array = new int[length];

        GetData(length, array);
        display(length, array);

        float average = mean(length, array, total);

        cout << "sum of numbers " << total << endl;
        cout << "average of contents " << average << endl;
        // de-allocate memory for array
        delete [] array;
}
```

Results

```
size of table 8
   22   14   11   20    7    2   12    4
sum of numbers 92
average of contents 11.5000
```

We continue to look at C++ enhancements to C by considering further improvements in the use of tags in enumerations; structures, and unions; array initialization; and in-line functions.

Tags

In C++, unlike C, tags are automatically visible as type names. Therefore, with the following enumerated type

```
enum answer {no, yes};
```

the tag `answer` can be used to declare a variable or function of type `answer`; for example,

```
answer MoreData(void)
```

Similarly, a structure such as

```
struct PayDetails   {
                      float taxable_income;
                      float pension;
                      float tax;
                      float salary;
                   };
```

could be used to define a variable of type `PayDetails`; for example,

```
void calculations(income person, PayDetails &wages)
```

Unions

In C, a union variable or union member must always have a name. By contrast, in C++ this restriction is lifted, provided there is no ambiguity. A union with no name is known as an **anonymous union**.

```
struct income {
                float   AnnualSalary;
                char    status;
                union   {
                          int single;
                          int married;
                        };
              };
```

The members of the union are directly accessible as illustrated by the following code:

```
if (person.status == 'M' || person.status == 'm')
{
  person.married = MarriedAllowance;
  return MarriedAllowance;
}
else
{
  person.single = SingleAllowance;
  return SingleAllowance;
}
```

Initialization of Arrays

C++ feature

array
initializa-
tion

Recall that in C we used a simple macro to define the number of elements in an array, since it was not possible to use a constant. This restriction is lifted in C++, so a constant may appear in a constant expression. For example, the constant `tax_bands` is used to declare the size of the array `tax_rate`.

In C++, all initializers may contain references to previously declared variables and functions. In the following example, `tax_bands` and `basic_rate` are declared as constants.

```
const int   tax_bands  = 5;
const float basic_rate = 0.20;

float tax_rate[tax_bands] = {0,
                            basic_rate,
                            1.5*basic_rate,
                            2.0*basic_rate,
                            2.5*basic_rate};
```

Inline Functions

C++ feature

in line
functions

In C, it is common practice to write small functions as macros, either with or without parameters. In C++ the preferred method is to define an **inline** function. A function declared as being `inline` causes a copy of the function code to be placed in the program at the point where the function is called, without the overhead of a function call. The compiler is not obliged to honor the request, especially if the `inline` function contains loops or selections. A general rule is to restrict an inline function to no more than two or three statements. For example,

```
inline void format(void)
// function to set the format for printing numbers
{
   cout << setprecision(5);
   cout << setw(12);
}
```

The following case study is used to put these new enhancements into context.

Case Study: Tax Affairs

TAXMAN!

In this second example a C++ program has been written to calculate income tax, in an unspecified country, according to the following rules:

A tax allowance is given according to marital status: a single person is allowed $3000; a married person $5000, which is allowed only against one salary if both partners are working.

The pension contribution is 6% of the gross annual salary. Taxable income is the sum of the single/ married allowance and the pension contribution, subtracted from the gross annual salary

Income tax is based upon taxable income and is levied at the following rates:

Tax Band 0	*The first $5000 of taxable income attracts tax at 0%.*
Tax Band 1	*A taxable income of up to $20,000 attracts tax at the rate of 20% for any amount over $5000.*
Tax band 2	*A taxable income of up to $30,000 attracts tax at the rate of 30% for any amount over $20,000.*
Tax Band 3	*A taxable income of up to $40,000 attracts tax at the rate of 40% for any amount over $30,000.*
Tax Band 4	*A taxable income in excess of $40,000 attracts tax at the rate of 50%.*

Problem Analysis - The data to be input is the gross annual salary and the marital status of [m]arried or [s]ingle. The information supplied by the program is the allowance for a married or single person, the annual pension contribution, the annual taxable income, the annual income tax, and the net annual salary. Some of this information can be represented by the following structures:

```
struct income {
            float   AnnualSalary;
            char    status;
            union {
                    int single;
                    int married;
                };
        };
```

where `single` or `married` will be used to represent the appropriate personal allowance.

```
struct PayDetails   {
                float taxable_income;
                float pension;
                float tax;
                float salary;
            };
```

The rates of income tax can be stored in a one-dimensional array as illustrated in Figure 16.3, where the subscripts 0 to 4 represent the five tax bands. At band 0 (subscript 0) the rate of tax is 0%; at band 1 (subscript 1) the rate of tax is 20%, and so on.

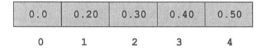

Figure 16.3 Rates of tax over five bands

This array might be declared and initialized as follows:

515

```
float tax_rate[tax_bands] = {0,
                             basic_rate,
                             1.5*basic_rate,
                             2.0*basic_rate,
                             2.5*basic_rate};
```

where the `tax_bands = 5` and the `basic_rate = 0.20` are both declared as constants.

The values for the tax thresholds can also be stored in a one-dimensional array as depicted in Figure 16.4. Cells 0 and 5 contain the lowest and highest taxable incomes respectively. Cells 1 to 4 contain the tax thresholds at which different rates of tax will apply.

0	5000	20000	30000	40000	LONG_MAX
0	1	2	3	4	5

Figure 16.4 Tax thresholds

This array is declared and initialized as follows:

```
long int tax_threshold[tax_bands + 1] = {0,
                             basic_threshold,
                             4*basic_threshold,
                             6*basic_threshold,
                             8*basic_threshold,
                             LONG_MAX};
```

where `basic_threshold = 5000` and is declared as a constant. The constant LONG_MAX from the header `<limits.h>` is used for the maximum upper limit of income, which will be far in excess of the largest income.

If the following constant and variables are declared

```
const float    superannuation = 0.06;
income         person;
PayDetails     wages;
```

then the pension is calculated as

```
wages.pension = superannuation * person.AnnualSalary
```

The taxable income is calculated as

```
wages.taxable_income =
person.AnnualSalary - allowance(person) - wages.pension;

if (wages.taxable_income < 0) wages.taxable_income = 0;
```

where the function `allowance` returns the personal allowance of a `person`.

Two expressions are used for calculating the income tax.

For each tax band, if the taxable income is greater than the next tax band, then apply the expression

```
wages.tax =
wages.tax +
(tax_threshold[band+1] - tax_threshold[band]) * tax_rate[band];
```

However, if the taxable income is not greater than the next tax band, then apply the expression

```
wages.tax =
wages.tax +
(wages.taxable_income - tax_threshold[band]) * tax_rate[band];
```

where the value of band represents the current tax band.

The program is divided into seven functions including the main function as illustrated in Figure 16.5.

The function DataIn allows a person to input the gross annual salary and the marital status. Function allowance returns a value for the allowance based upon the marital status. The function calculations calculates the pension, taxable income, income tax, and net salary. The function InfoOut displays the allowance, pension, taxable income, income tax, and salary after deductions. The function format is used to format numbers being output. The function MoreData simply asks whether the user has more data. Finally, the main function allows the user to input data through DataIn, calls for calculations to be made on this data, displays the results through InfoOut, and asks for more data.

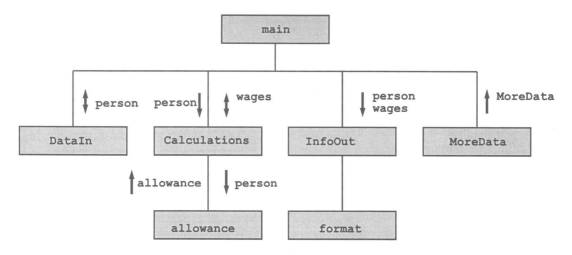

Figure 16.5 Structure chart

Algorithm for the Function main

1. do
2.   input data for a person
3.   calculate tax information
4.   output tax information
5. while more data

Data Dictionary for the Function main - The data input and output is stored in the fields of the structures discussed earlier; therefore, the only data is of type income and PayDetails.

```
income      person;
PayDetails  wages;
```

The statement *while more data* will use the function MoreData to capture a user's request to continue processing. The algorithm for MoreData is given later in the development of the program.

Algorithm for the Function DataIn

2.1   input annual salary
2.2   input marital status

Data Dictionary for the Function DataIn - The function contains just one formal parameter of type income. The function does not return a value, since the parameter is declared as a reference parameter and not as a value parameter.

```
void DataIn(income &person);
```

Algorithm for the Function calculations

3.1   calculate pension
3.2   calculate taxable income
3.3   set income tax to zero
3.4   if taxable income > zero
3.5   for every tax band
3.6   if taxable income > next tax band
3.7   increase income tax by tax rate over the entire current tax band
3.8   else
3.9   increase income tax by tax rate over residue of tax band
3.10   exit for loop
3.11   calculate net salary

Data Dictionary for the Function calculations - The formal parameter list for this function needs to contain information for both the input data and calculated results. There are two formal parameters; one of type income and the other of type PayDetails. Constants are declared for the number of tax bands, basic rate of income tax, the basic threshold from which tax is calculated, and the rate of superannuation. Local variables are declared for the arrays tax_rate and tax_threshold. A local variable needs to be declared to represent a tax band. This variable will be used as a loop control variable and can be declared in the for loop.

```
void calculations(income person, PayDetails &wages);

const int    tax_bands       = 5;
const float  basic_rate      = 0.20;
long  int    basic_threshold = 5000;
const float  superannuation  = 0.06;

float tax_rate[tax_bands] = {0,
                             basic_rate,
                             1.5*basic_rate,
                             2.0*basic_rate,
                             2.5*basic_rate};

long int tax_threshold[tax_bands+1] = {0,
                                       basic_threshold,
                                       4*basic_threshold,
                                       6*basic_threshold,
                                       8*basic_threshold,
                                       LONG_MAX};


int band; // loop control variable
```

Desk Check of the Function calculations - The basic rate of tax is assumed to be 20%, the lowest threshold $5000, and the superannuation is 6%. If the annual salary is $15000 and the person is married, then the algorithm should produce the following results:

variables	value(s)		
AnnualSalary	15000		
status	m		
allowance	5000		
taxable_income	9100		
pension	900		
tax	0	0	820
taxable income > 0?	yes		
band	0	1	
taxable income > next threshold?	yes	no	
salary	13280		

The problem analysis stated that a function was introduced to calculate a person's allowance. This function is called when calculating a person's taxable income.

Algorithm for the Function allowance

if personal status is married
  set allowance to married allowance
  return married allowance
else
  set allowance to single allowance
  return single allowance

519

Data Dictionary for the Function allowance - The formal parameter list for this function contains information for the input data to ascertain whether a person is married. The function returns the value of the personal allowance. The prototype for this function is given as

```
int allowance(income person);
```

Algorithm for the Function InfoOut

4.1 display personal allowance
4.2 display pension contribution
4.3 display taxable income
4.4 display income tax
4.5 display net salary

Data Dictionary for the Function InfoOut - The formal parameter list for this function needs to contain information for both the input data and the calculated results. There are two formal parameters: one of type `income` and the other of type `PayDetails`.

```
void InfoOut(income person, PayDetails wages);
```

Prior to displaying numerical information the function `InfoOut` calls a function `format` that sets the precision and the field width of the number to be displayed.

Algorithm for the Function MoreData

do
    display prompt for more data
    input reply
    convert reply to upper case
while reply not in correct format
display new line
return reply

Data Dictionary for the Function MoreData - There is no formal parameter for this function. However, the function does return an enumerated constant `yes` or `no` of type `answer`. The function contains one local variable to represent the user's reply.

```
answer MoreData(void);
char reply;
```

```
                            Screen Layout
-------------------------------------------------------------------------
12345678901234567890123456789012345678901234567890123456789012345678901234567890

input annual salary 15000
married or single? m
allowance                        5000
pension contribution              900
taxable income                   9100
income tax                        820
net salary                      13280

MORE DATA? [Y]es [N]o y

input annual salary 10000
married or single? m
allowance                        3000
pension contribution              600
taxable income                   6400
income tax                        280
net salary                       9120

MORE DATA? [Y]es [N]o n
```

All the new features of C++ described for this case study are printed in second color in the following program.

```cpp
// chap_16\ex_2.cpp
// program to demonstrate the use of tags, anonymous unions,
// initializers, constants and inline functions in C++
// the program computes the personal allowance,
// income tax and pension contributions on a person's annual salary

#include <iostream.h>
#include <iomanip.h>
#include <limits.h>
#include <ctype.h>

enum answer {no, yes};

struct income {
            float  AnnualSalary;
            char   status;
            union {
                  int single;
                  int married;
                };
        };
```

```
struct PayDetails {
                  float    taxable_income;
                  float    pension;
                  float    tax;
                  float    salary;
            };


int allowance(income person)
// function that receives status of a person and returns the allowance
{
        const int  MarriedAllowance = 5000;
        const int  SingleAllowance = 3000;

        if (person.status ==  'M' || person.status == 'm')
        {
           person.married = MarriedAllowance;
           return MarriedAllowance;
        }
        else
        {
           person.single = SingleAllowance;
           return SingleAllowance;
        }
}




void DataIn(income &person)
// function to input the annual salary and marital status
{
        cout << "input annual salary ";
        cin >> person.AnnualSalary;
        cout << "married or single? ";
        cin >> person.status;
}


void calculations(income person, PayDetails &wages)
// function to calculate the taxable income, pension, income tax and net salary
{
        const int    tax_bands       = 5;
        const float  basic_rate      = 0.20;
        long  int    basic_threshold = 5000;
        const float  superannuation  = 0.06;
```

```
        float tax_rate[tax_bands] = {0,
                                     basic_rate,
                                     1.5*basic_rate,
                                     2.0*basic_rate,
                                     2.5*basic_rate};

        long int tax_threshold[tax_bands+1] = {0,
                                               basic_threshold,
                                               4*basic_threshold,
                                               6*basic_threshold,
                                               8*basic_threshold,
                                               LONG_MAX};

        // calculate pension
        wages.pension = superannuation * person.AnnualSalary;

        // calculate taxable income
        wages.taxable_income =
        person.AnnualSalary - allowance(person) - wages.pension;
        if (wages.taxable_income < 0) wages.taxable_income = 0;

        // calculate income tax
        wages.tax = 0;

        if (wages.taxable_income > tax_threshold[0])
        {
           for (int band=0; band <= tax_bands; band++)
              if (wages.taxable_income > tax_threshold[band+1])
                 wages.tax =
                 wages.tax +
                 (tax_threshold[band+1] - tax_threshold[band])
                  * tax_rate[band];
              else
              {
                 wages.tax =
                 wages.tax +
                 (wages.taxable_income - tax_threshold[band])
                 * tax_rate[band];
                 break;
              }
        }


        // calculate net salary
        wages.salary = person.AnnualSalary - wages.tax - wages.pension;
}
```

```
inline void format(void)
// function to set the format for printing numbers
{
        cout << setprecision(5);
        cout << setw(12);
}


void InfoOut(income person, PayDetails wages)
// function to display details of allowance, deductions and wage
{
        cout << "allowance\t\t";
        format();
        cout << allowance(person) << endl;
        cout << "pension contribution\t";
        format();
        cout <<  wages.pension << endl;
        cout << "taxable income\t\t";
        format();
        cout << wages.taxable_income << endl;
        cout <<  "income tax\t\t";
        format();
        cout << wages.tax << endl;
        cout << "net salary\t\t";
        format();
        cout << wages.salary << endl;
}


answer MoreData(void)
// function to capture a yes/no reply
{
        char reply;

        do
        {
            cout << "\n\nMORE DATA? [Y]es  [N]o ";
            cin >> reply;
            reply = toupper(reply);
        } while (reply != 'Y' && reply != 'N');

        cout << endl;
        return (reply=='Y') ? yes : no;
}
```

524

```
void main(void)
{
        income      person;
        PayDetails   wages;

        do
        {
                DataIn(person);
                calculations(person, wages);
                InfoOut(person, wages);
        }
        while (MoreData());
}
```

Results

```
input annual salary 15000
married or single? m
allowance               5000
pension contribution     900
taxable income          9100
income tax               820
net salary             13280

MORE DATA? [Y]es [N]o Y

input annual salary 10000
married or single? s
allowance               3000
pension contribution     600
taxable income          6400
income tax               280
net salary              9120

MORE DATA? [Y]es [N]o N
```

16.4 Functions Revisited

C++ feature

formal parameters with default values

In C++, the formal parameters of a function can be initialized. For example, the following function prototype has the three default values `operation = '+'`, `a=10`, and `b=5`. Although these values are constants, the default arguments can be expressions; they do not have to be a constant value.

```
int calculator(char operation = '+', int a=10, int b=5);
```

In this example all three arguments have default values. However, if some arguments do not have default values, then arguments without default values must appear in the formal-parameter list before the arguments that have default values. For example,

```
int calculator(char operation, int a=10, int b=5);
```

Function calls may omit parameters with default values, starting from the right-hand end of the formal-parameter list. For example, using the function

```
int calculator(char operation = '+', int a=10, int b=5);
```

it is legal to call `calculator` with the following actual-parameter lists:

```
calculator();              // all three defaults assumed
calculator('*');           // operation='*', a and b use defaults
calculator('/', 30);       // operation='/', a=30, b uses default
calculator('*', 30, 40);   // operation='*', a=30 and b=40
```

Program Example 16.1 illustrates some of the function calls that are possible using default arguments.

Program Example 16.1: Default Arguments in Function Calls in C++

```cpp
// chap_16\ex_3.cpp
// program to demonstrate the use of default arguments

#include <iostream.h>

int calculator(char operation = '+', int a=10, int b=5)
// function to return the result of the calculation (a operation b)
{
        switch (operation)
        {
                case '+': return a+b;
                case '-': return a-b;
                case '*': return a*b;
                case '/': if (b==0) return 0;
                          else return a/b;
                default : cout << "ILLEGAL OPERATOR"; return 0;
        }
}
```

```
void main(void)
{
        cout << calculator() << endl;
        cout << calculator('-') << endl;
        cout << calculator('*', 20) << endl;
        cout << calculator('/', 32767, 128) << endl;
}
```

Results

```
15
5
100
255
```

Caution!

default values

Default values for the same parameter cannot appear more than once in the same file, even if the values of the parameters are the same.

However, multiple declarations of a function in the same file may supply additional default values. Therefore,

```
int calculator(char operation = '+', int a, int b);
int calculator(char operation, int a=10, int b);
int calculator(char operation = '+', int a, int b=5);
```

are the same as

```
int calculator(char operation = '+', int a=10, int b=5);
```

An alternative strategy for declaring default values is to put them in a header file. For example, if the contents of the header file "a:\chap_16\ex_3.h" is

```
int calculator(char operation = '/', int a=99, int b=11);
```

then the header may be included in a modified version of the previous program as follows. The inclusion of the header permits the prototype of the function with its defaults to be included at the beginning of the program file before the function is called.

```
// program to demonstrate the use of default arguments using a
// header file containing a declaration of the default values

#include <iostream.h>
#include "a:\chap_16\ex_3.h"

int calculator(char operation, int a, int b)
    .
```

527

Results from running modified Program Example 16.1

```
9
88
220
255
```

In a C program, functions within the same scope must be given unique names; however, this restriction is lifted in C++. When two or more functions within the same scope have the same name, the function name is said to be **overloaded**.

You may wonder how the compiler can resolve calls to an overloaded function? The answer is by examining the types in the formal-parameter list. For example, in the two prototypes for the function `calculator` that follow

```
long int calculator(char operation, long int a, long int b = 1);
long int calculator(char operation, char *stringA, char *stringB);
```

the types in the formal parameter lists are quite different. A call of `calculator('+', 47567, 69856)` would be to the first function, since the last two actual parameters are both long integers, whereas a call of `calculator('*', "32767", "128")` would be to the second function, since the last two actual parameters are both explicitly stated as strings.

If overloaded functions have a different number of formal parameters, then argument matching is straightforward and based upon a match with a function call containing the same number of arguments. However, when the number of parameters is the same, then the compiler attempts to find the best match for any one parameter by using the following rules in the order given.

(1.) Exact match. The compiler determines that the actual parameter is the same type as the formal parameter.

(2.) Match with promotions. The compiler attempts to convert the actual parameter by applying integral promotions: `float` to `double` to `long double` or `int` to `unsigned int` to `long int` to `unsigned long int`.

(3.) Match with standard conversions. The compiler attempts to convert the actual parameters to other numeric or character types, for example, `long` to `int` or `char*` to `void*`.

(4.) Match with ellipsis. The compiler matches the actual parameter with an ellipsis in the formal parameter list. Functions that take an unlimited number of parameters are declared with an ellipsis . . . This match is the worst case and will not be used if there is any other match. If two or more formal-parameter lists are equally as good, then the function call is illegal.

Argument matching may not always produce the expected result. For example, it is easy to forget that floating-point literals have type double instead of float.

528

In Program Example 16.2, the function `strtol` from the library `<stdlib.h>` has been used to convert a string to a long integer. The `strtol` function stops scanning the string at the first character that cannot be interpreted as part of a numerical value. This character may be the terminating null character.

The function returns a long integer value that corresponds with the digits in the string. If the value cannot be converted, then `endptr` is set to `string`. The prototype for the function is

```
long strtol(const char *string, char **endptr, int base);
```

where `string` points to the string to be converted,
`endptr` is set to point at the character that stopped the scan, and
`base` signifies the number base being used, which may be in the range 0 to 36.

Program Example 16.2: Overloaded Functions

```cpp
// chap_16\ex_4.cpp
// program to demonstrate the use of overloaded functions

#include <iostream.h>
#include <stdlib.h>

long int calculator(char operation, long int a, long int b = 1)
{
        switch (operation)
        {
                case '+' : return a+b;
                case '-' : return a-b;
                case '*' : return a*b;
                case '/' : return a/b;
                default : return 0;
        }
}

long int calculator(char operation, char *stringA, char *stringB)
{
        char *endchar;

        long int a=strtol(stringA, &endchar, 10);
        long int b=strtol(stringB, &endchar, 10);

        switch (operation)
        {
                case '+' : return a+b;
                case '-' : return a-b;
                case '*' : return a*b;
```

```
                case '/' : return a/b;
                default : return 0;
        }
}

void main(void)
{
        cout << calculator('+', 47567, 69856) << endl;
        cout << calculator('*', "32767", "128") << endl;
        cout << calculator('-', 32768) << endl;
}
```

Results

```
117423
4194176
32767
```

Case Study: Sorting Numbers and Strings

SORTING NUMBERS AND STRINGS The final case study in this section demonstrates the use of function overloading in using functions with the same names to sort an array of real numbers and to sort an array of strings. Both functions use the selection sort. The overloading of function names continues with two functions having the same names being used to display the contents of an array of real numbers and an array of strings.

Problem Analysis - Before you continue with reading through the solution to this problem, you would be well advised to look back at a full description of the selection sort in Chapter 12.

Algorithm for the Function main

1. display contents of numbers array
2. display contents of strings array
3. sort numbers array
4. sort strings array
5. display contents of numbers array
6. display contents of strings array

Data Dictionary for the Function main - The arrays used to store the real numbers and the strings are initialized within the `main` function, as illustrated here. The `main` function contains local variables to declare and initialize the `numbers` array and the `strings` array.

```
float numbers[] = {16.5, 31.75, -45.20, 121.1, -99.25};
char strings[][80] = {"Leon", "Adam", "Zak", "Beth", "Louise"};
```

Algorithm for the Function display

for each cell in the array
  display contents of cell

Data Dictionary for the Function display - The formal-parameter lists for the functions with the name `display` are sufficiently different for the compiler to distinguish the correct context. The function prototypes are

```
void display(float numbers[], int size);
void display(char strings[][80], int size);
```

Notice that both functions cater for arrays of different sizes.

The `for` loop control variable can be defined implicitly within the `for` loop.

Algorithm for the Function selection_sort

Refer to Chapter 12 for this algorithm.

Data Dictionary for the Function selection_sort - The formal-parameter lists for the functions with the name `selection_sort` are sufficiently different for the compiler to distinguish the correct context. The function prototypes are

```
void selection_sort(float numbers[], int size);
void selection_sort(char strings[][80], int size);
```

Both functions contain local variables to define the temporary store used in swapping the data and the value of the position of the largest item of data in the subarray.

```
int   position;
float temp_store;
```

and

```
int   position;
char  temp_store[80];
```

In both functions the `for` loop control variable `index` can be defined implicitly within the `for` loop.

The implementation of the selection sort used another function, `position_of_largest`, to return a subscript for the position of the largest item of data in the subarray being searched. The function prototypes for these functions are

```
int position_of_largest(float numbers[], int limit);
int position_of_largest(char strings[][80], int limit);
```

Both functions contain local variables to declare the largest item and the position of the largest item.

```
int largest = numbers[0];
int index_of_largest = 0;
```

and

531

```
        char largest[80];
        int  index_of_largest = 0;
```

In both functions the `for` loop control variable `index` can be defined implicitly within the `for` loop.

```
┌────────────────────────────────────────────────────────────┐
│                     Screen Layout                          │
├────────────────────────────────────────────────────────────┤
│12345678901234567890123456789012345678901234567890123456789 0│
│                                                            │
│UNSORTED                                                    │
│16.5    31.75   -45.2 121.1   -99.25                        │
│Leon    Adam    Zak   Beth    Louise                        │
│                                                            │
│SORTED                                                      │
│-99.25 -45.2  16.5   31.75   121.1                          │
│Adam    Beth   Leon   Louise Zak                            │
└────────────────────────────────────────────────────────────┘
```

```cpp
// chap_16\ex_5.cpp
// program to demonstrate the overloading of function names
// to sort and display arrays of either numbers or strings

#include <iostream.h>
#include <iomanip.h>
#include <string.h>

int position_of_largest(float numbers[], int limit)
{
        int largest = numbers[0];
        int index_of_largest = 0;

        for (int index=1; index <= limit; index++)
            if (numbers[index] > largest)
            {
                largest = numbers[index];
                index_of_largest = index;
            }

        return index_of_largest;
}
```

```
void selection_sort(float numbers[], int size)
{
        int   position;
        float temp_store;

        for (int index=size-1; index > 0; index--)
        {
                position = position_of_largest(numbers, index);

                if (index != position)
                {
                        temp_store = numbers[index];
                        numbers[index] = numbers[position];
                        numbers[position] = temp_store;
                }
        }
}

int position_of_largest(char strings[][80], int limit)
{
        char largest[80];
        int  index_of_largest = 0;

        strcpy(largest, strings[0]);
        for (int index=1; index <= limit; index++)
            if (strcmp(strings[index], largest) > 0)
            {
                    strcpy(largest, strings[index]);
                    index_of_largest = index;
            }

        return index_of_largest;
}

void selection_sort(char strings[][80], int size)
{
        int   position;
        char  temp_store[80];

        for (int index=size-1; index > 0; index--)
        {
                position = position_of_largest(strings, index);

                if (index != position)
                {
                        strcpy(temp_store, strings[index]);
                        strcpy(strings[index], strings[position]);
                        strcpy(strings[position], temp_store);
                }
```

```
          }
}

void display(float numbers[], int size)
// function to display numbers in an array
{
   for (int index=0; index < size; index++)
      cout << numbers[index] << "\t";
   cout << endl;
}

void display(char strings[][80], int size)
// function to display strings in an array
{
   for (int index=0; index < size; index++)
      cout << strings[index] << "\t";
   cout << endl;
}

void main(void)
{
   float numbers[]    = {16.5, 31.75, -45.20, 121.1, -99.25};
   char strings[][80] = {"Leon","Adam","Zak","Beth","Louise"};

   cout << "UNSORTED\n";
   display(numbers, 5);
   display(strings, 5);

   selection_sort(numbers,5);
   selection_sort(strings,5);

   cout << "\n\nSORTED\n";
   display(numbers, 5);
   display(strings, 5);
}
```

Results

```
UNSORTED
16.5    31.75   -45.2   121.1   -99.25
Leon    Adam    Zak     Beth    Louise

SORTED
-99.25  -45.2   16.5    31.75   121.1
Adam    Beth    Leon    Louise  Zak
```

16.5 Incompatibilities

If C++ can be regarded as a superset of ANSI C, then it must follow that a program written in C will compile using a C++ compiler. To a large extent this statement is true; however, some features in C will no longer operate correctly under C++. There are also cases where a C program can have a different meaning when compiled using a C++ compiler.

A list of the known incompatibilities between the two languages follows.

External Linkage

The linkage of a variable determines the extent to which it may be shared. A variable with external linkage may be shared by all files in a program. However, a variable with internal linkage is restricted to a single file.

In C, constants defined by `const` have external linkage by default. In C++, such constants have internal linkage by default. As a result, a C file that refers to a `const` in another file will not link using C++.

```
/* file_1.c */

const float pi = 3.14159;


/* file_2.c */

#include <stdio.h>
extern const float pi;

void main(void)
{
    printf("%f\n", pi);
}
```

Both files will compile using a C compiler and link giving a result of 3.14159. Both files will compile using a C++ compiler; however, a link error is reported as *pi is unresolved in file_2*.

Size of char and int

In C, character constants have type `int`; in C++, character constants have type `char`. Thus `sizeof('A')` in C is `sizeof(int)` and `sizeof('A')` in C++ is `sizeof(char)`. These changes will affect the meaning of a C program compiled in C++.

When the following program is compiled on a personal computer using a C compiler, the result 2   2 is displayed; however, when the same program is compiled using a C++ compiler, the result 2   1 is displayed.

```
#include <stdio.h>

void main(void)
{
    printf("%d\t", sizeof(int));
    printf("%d\n", sizeof('x'));
}
```

Multiple Definitions of the Same Variable

In C, a global variable can be defined more than once in a source file; in C++, a variable can be defined only once. In C these declarations are known as **tentative** definitions, and the compiler treats them as a single definition. When the following program is compiled in C++, the error message *number is already defined* is given.

```
int number;

void function(void)
{
    /* empty */
}

int number;

void main(void)
{
    function();
}
```

Character Array Initialization

In C, a character array can be initialized by a string of the same length; in C++, the array must be at least one character longer than the string to store the terminating null character.

When the following program is compiled using a C++ compiler, the error message *too many initializers* is given. However, if the same program is compiled using a C compiler, there are no errors, but a potential disastrous situation arises when attempting to output a string that has not been terminated by a null character.

```
#include <stdio.h>

void main(void)
{
    char name[6] = "Freddy";

    printf("%s",name);
}
```

Function Declaration

C allows a function to be called without a prior declaration or definition; C++ does not. A C program that has not included the header file `<stdio.h>`, yet uses the function `printf`, will compile in C but not in C++. Attempting to omit `<stdio.h>` in the previous example will cause the C++ compiler to generate the error message *undeclared identifier 'printf'*.

Visibility of Tags

In C, the words `struct`, `union`, and `enum` must precede structure, union, and enumeration tags, for the tags to become visible when declaring data to be of the said type. In C++, tags are visible without being preceded by `struct`, `union`, or `enum`. Both the structure and enumeration tags would be legal in C, but not in C++. This discrepancy can cause problems as the following code illustrates.

This program compiles and runs in C, and displays an answer of 2 2. However, in C++ compilation fails with the error message *redeclaration of identifier 'days'* being given.

```
#include <stdio.h>
typedef enum {Sun, Mon, Tue, Wed, Thu, Fri, Sat} days;
struct days {
               int number;
            };

days        WEEK;
struct days NUMBER;

void main(void)
{
    WEEK = Tue;

    NUMBER.number = 2;

    printf("%d\t", WEEK);
    printf("%d\n", NUMBER.number);
}
```

Scope of Global Variables and Tags

The following program compiles and runs without errors in both C and C++; however, in C the result is 2, and in C++ the result is 6. In C the global integer variable `alpha` is used in `function`, since the tag `alpha` is not visible; however, in C++ the tag `alpha` has become visible in `function` and temporarily hides the global declaration of the integer `alpha`. Hence the size of `alpha` is reported as 6 bytes, which is the size of the structure member.

537

```
#include <stdio.h>

int alpha;

void function(void)
{
    struct alpha {
                    char name[6];
                };

    int beta = sizeof(alpha);
    printf("%d\n", beta);
}

void main(void)
{
    function();
}
```

Enumeration

In C, values of an enumerated type are freely convertible to and from integers. In C++, values of an enumeration type are automatically converted to integers when necessary; however, integers are not automatically converted to enumeration values. The following program will compile and run in C and yield an answer of true. However, the program will not compile in C++ and displays the error message *return value is not compatible with return type*.

```
#include <stdio.h>

typedef enum {false, true} boolean;

boolean is_lower(char c)
{
    return 'a' <= c && c <= 'z';
}

void main(void)
{
    if (is_lower('a'))
        printf("true");
    else
        printf("false");
}
```

Generic Pointers

In C, a pointer of any type can be assigned to a variable of type `void*`, and `void*` pointers can be assigned to variables of other pointer types. In C++, any pointer can be assigned to a variable of type `void*` only.

Since `malloc` and `calloc` both return a generic pointer type `*void`,

```
int *integer_pointer;
integer_pointer = malloc(sizeof(int));
```

is legal in C, but not in C++; therefore, the returned value must be changed via a cast as a pointer to integer.

```
integer_pointer = (int *) malloc(sizeof(int));
```

Goto Statements

C allows a `goto` statement to jump over any declarations at the beginning of a block; in C++, a `goto` statement may not jump over a declaration that contains an initializer; however, it can bypass an entire block.

Keywords

Finally, the following C++ keywords are not part of C.

```
asm       friend    private    try
catch     inline    protected  this
class     new       public     throw
delete    operator  template   virtual
```

C programs that use any of these keywords as identifiers (variable names, constants, types, function names, etc) will not compile using a C++ compiler.

Summary

Compared with C, C++ offers the following enhancements at the procedural level of programming.

- ☐ An input/ output library `<iostream.h>`, using streams `cin, cout, cerr`.

- ☐ Data is extracted from an input stream and inserted into an output stream by the use of the operators >> and <<, respectively.

- ☐ Library `<iomanip.h>` contains a set of manipulators `setw, setprecision, oct, dec,` and `hex`. The first two manipulators are used to format numbers, and the remaining manipulators are used in number conversion to different bases.

- ☐ Single line comments using `//`.

- ☐ Source filenames are normally appended with .cpp.

- ☐ Formal parameters can be reference parameters.

- ☐ Memory allocation and deallocation from the heap with `new` and `delete`.

- ☐ Format of the `for` loop includes a declaration for the type of the loop control variable.

- ☐ Explicit type conversion by using the type in a manner similar to a function name.

- ☐ Declarations can occur anywhere in a block, provided there is no attempt to use the identifier before it is declared.

- ☐ Tags for structures, unions, and enumerations can be used to define types without the need to precede the tag with `struct`, `union`, or `enum`, respectively.

- ☐ Unions do not need to be tagged; they can be anonymous.

- ☐ Array sizes can be declared using a constant.

- ☐ Arrays can be initialized using previously declared constants, variables, and functions.

- ☐ Inline functions are preferred to macros.

- ☐ Formal parameters can be given default values. Defaults can be omitted from the actual-parameter list when the function is called.

- ☐ Default values can be changed by using different actual parameters in a function call or by using header files containing prototypes of the function with different default values.

- ☐ Functions can have the same names within the same scope. The names are overloaded, and the compiler uses a set of rules based on the formal and actual-parameters to resolve which function to use.

- ☐ C programs will compile using a C++ compiler; however, there are some features of C that will no longer operate under C++. In some instances C programs may take a different meaning when compiled as C++ programs. Incompatibilities are likely to take place in the following areas:

  External linkage
  Size of char and int
  Multiple definitions of the same variable
  Character array initialization
  Function declaration
  Visibility of tags
  Global variables and tags
  Enumeration
  Generic pointers
  Goto statements
  Keywords

Review Questions

1. What is the name of the header file associated with input and output in C++?

2. What do the streams `cin`, `cout`, and `cerr` correspond to in C?

3. What is operator overloading?

4. True or false - the extraction operator is denoted by $<<$.

5. What will the following statement output if $i = 5$?

```
cout << i << "\t" << i*i;
```

6. Give an example of an output manipulator.

7. What will the following statement output if $j = 137.89765$?

```
cout << setw(15) << setprecision(4) << j;
```

8. What is the output from the following statement?

```
cout << hex << 32767;
```

9. Comment on the behavior of the following line of code.

```
cin >> alpha;
```

10. How are comments written in C++ ?

11. What is a reference parameter, and when should it be used?

12. What is the purpose of the operators `new` and `delete`, and what do they replace in C?

13. Where are you allowed to declare variables in a C++ program that you cannot do in a C program?

14. What is the scope of a loop control variable when it is declared as part of the `for` loop?

15. What is the difference between the cast operation in C and explicit type conversion in C++?

16. How would you declare a data type in C++ for the date expressed as a structure containing the fields month, day, and year?

17. What is an anonymous union?

18. How has the initialization of `arrays` been extended in C++?

19. What is an `inline` function, and when should it be used?

20. Can the formal parameters of a function be initialized?

21. If the answer to question 20 is yes, then what restrictions are placed on the order of the formal parameters?

22. How can actual-parameter lists be used in conjunction with formal-parameter lists to initialize variables?

23. Can default values for the same parameter appear more than once in the same file?

24. Describe a strategy for declaring a set of alternative default values.

25. If overloaded functions have the same number of formal parameters, then how can the compiler resolve the correct function call?

26. True or false - the number of bytes allocated to an integer is the same as a character in C++.

27. True or false - the following declaration will cause an error in C++.

```
char name[7]="Freddy";
```

28. True or false - in C++ tags must be preceded with either `struct` or `enum` when declaring a type.

29. True or false - in C++ integers are automatically converted to enumeration constants.

30. Would the following program compile without errors in C++?

```
#include <stdio.h>
char operator;

void main(void)
{
   printf("%c", operator);
}
```

Programming Exercises

31. What are the errors in the following segments of C++ code?

(a)

```
float alpha(void)
{
   int a, b;
   c = a+b;
   return float(c);
}
```

(b)

```
int j, n=10;
if (n > 0)
   for (int i = 1; i != n; i++)
      cout << i;
else
   j=i;
```

(c)
```
void beta(int i = 0, float j);
```

(d)

```
void gamma(char a, int b =10, float c = 3.14);
```

   (i)   `gamma(,,);`
   (ii)   `gamma(*, , 3.14159);`
   (iii) `gamma(67);`

32. Comment on the legality of the following function calls in C++.

(a)

```
void alpha(int, char);
void alpha(float, int);
```

   (i)   `alpha(1, 2);`
   (ii)   `alpha(1.0, 2);`
   (iii) `alpha(1, 2.0);`
   (iv) `alpha(1.0, 2.0);`

(b)

```
void beta(const int *);
void beta(int *);
int *p;
const int *q;
```

   (i) `beta(p);`
   (ii)`beta(q);`

(c)

```
void gamma(int&);
void gamma(float);
int i;
double d;

   gamma(i);
   gamma(d);
```

(d)

```
void epsilon(signed char);
void epsilon(unsigned char);
char c;

   epsilon(c);
```

Programming Problems

33. Return to Chapter 11 and rewrite the program in Case Study: Student Examination Results using as many of the new features of C++ as applicable.

Modify three of the functions in this program, and consequently the `main` function, so they conform to the following prototypes:

```
void search_number(record array[], int student_number, int &index);

void search_name(record array[], char student_name[],
                 int start_at, int &index);

void average_mark(record array[], int at_index, int &mean);
```

34. Write a program in C++ to demonstrate overloading the function name *area* for the calculation of the area of a triangle, given

(a) the lengths of three sides (a, b, and c) and *area = sqrt(s*(s-a)*(s-b)*(s-c))* where s is the semiperimeter;

(b) base length (b) and perpendicular height (h) and *area = 0.5*b*h*;

(c) two sides (a and b) and an included angle C and *area = 0.5*a*b*sin C*.

Chapter 17
Data Abstraction

Abstraction is the process of ignoring details in order to concentrate on essential characteristics. The method of programming used up to now in the book has been procedural abstraction. We have divided a program into a set of functions and hidden the details of the solution within these functions. This method enabled you to construct a main function that was not cluttered with detail and was, therefore, easier to read and understand.

Although procedural abstraction is universally accepted as a valid method of programming, it has increased the cost of software production over the years. One way of containing this cost is to reuse software without extensive revision, retesting and revalidation of the code. A cornerstone in this approach is to write software that should be an entity in itself, defining its own data types and operations upon data of that type.

This chapter describes the programming method known as data abstraction and marks the point where we stop considering C++ enhancements to C and turn to the C++ language features that support data abstraction.

This chapter covers the following topics:

- □ Abstract data types.
- □ Classes.
- □ Member functions within classes.
- □ Creation of objects.
- □ Constructors and destructors.
- □ Objects as parameters and return values.
- □ Operator overloading.
- □ Friends of classes.

17.1 Abstract Data Type

Traditional procedural programming involves creating data types and writing functions to access and manipulate the data. This fact is illustrated in Figure 17.1, where functions are shown to operate upon data of a particular type.

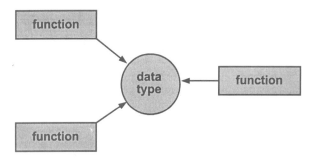

Figure 17.1 Functions operate upon data

The key behind creating an abstract data type is **encapsulation**. Encapsulation is the grouping together of a data type and a set of functions to perform actions on data of that type. Encapsulation is illustrated in Figure 17.2. Access to the data is allowed only via specific interface functions. The implementation of the data type, functions and interface functions are all hidden from the user. An encapsulated group such as this, consisting of a data type and its associated functions, is called an **abstract data type**.

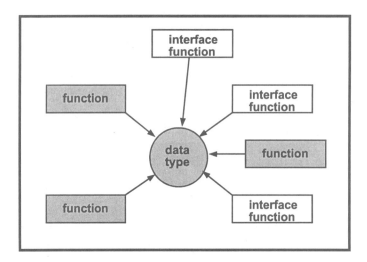

Figure 17.2 Encapsulation of data and functions

This concept of an abstract data type is not new. Consider for a moment the data type `int` (integer). Data of type integer can apply the operations of **+** (addition), **−** (subtraction), ***** (multiplication), **/** (division), and **%** (remainder) to the data.

The method of implementing the data type `int` is hidden from the user. Without consulting a technical manual for the internal representation of integers, there is no way of knowing the internal format of an integer.

Similarly the implementations of the operations **+**, **−**, *****, **/**, and **%** are hidden from the user. There is no direct way of inspecting how these operations are carried out.

A user may declare variables of type `int` and apply any of the set of operators to variables of this type.

The integer example demonstrates the following features that embody the requirements of the abstract data type.

- The abstraction has created a data type `int`.
- The declaration of variables of a specific type, for example, `int value;`
- The type contains a set of operators (**+,− ,*,/,** and **%**).
- The implementation of the type, behind the scenes, uses whatever data and functions are necessary.
- User access to the type is through a restricted interface with the implementation details being hidden from the user of the type.

Throughout the following sections, we shall see how C++ supports these requirements.

17.2 Classes

An abstract data type is a programmer-defined data type that can be manipulated in a manner similar to the system-defined data type for `int`, explained in section 17.1. C++ uses a **class** to implement an abstract data type. A class is similar to a structure in C but may contain functions as well. A class is a new data type with the following generic syntax:

C++ Syntax

class declaration

```
class identifier {
            private:
                declaration(s)
            public:
                declaration(s)
        };
```

For example, the abstract data type `string_1`, illustrated in Figure 17.3 can be represented by the following class definition:

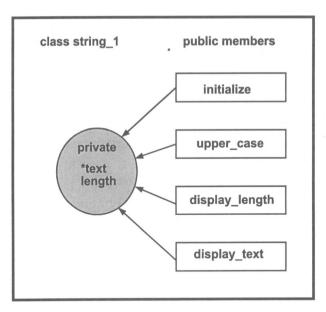

Figure 17.3 Abstract data type string_1

```
// chap_17\string_1.h

#ifndef CLASS_STRING_1
#define CLASS_STRING_1

class string_1
{
   private:
      char *text;    // pointer to the first character of a string
      int   length;  // length of the string

   public:
      void initialize(const char *value); // set text to a value
      void upper_case(void);               // convert text to upper case
      void display_length(void);           // display length of text
      void display_text(void);             // display the text
};

#endif //CLASS_STRING_1
```

The data declarations for the class `string_1` declare a pointer `*text` to the first character in a string, represented by an array of characters, and the `length` of the string. These declarations are **private**, implying the variables cannot be accessed from outside of the class.

The function prototype declarations are the only means of accessing and manipulating the private data variables. Since all declarations within a class are private by default, it is necessary to label the function prototypes as being **public**, implying they can be used outside of the class to access the data. The function prototypes are interface functions to the private data. The functions `initialize`, `upper_case`, `display_length`, and `display_text` are all capable of accessing the private data and are known as **member** functions of the class `string_1`.

You can use the private and public labels as often as you want in a class definition. However, many programmers group the private members together and the public members together. All class definitions begin with the `private` label as the default mode; however, explicitly labeling all sections improves readability.

To recapitulate, private data and functions are accessible only by other class member functions; public data and functions can be accessed by any part of a program, though it is not good practice to have public data.

In C++ it is common practice to place the class definitions in a header file. The class `string_1` has been stored in the header file `string_1.h`. Notice that the header file uses the `#ifndef` preprocessor directive, first defined in Chapter 15, to prevent multiple inclusions of the same header file in a multimodule program.

The implementations of the member functions declared in the class are stored in a separate source file. For example, the implementation of the member functions for the class `string_1` has been stored in the source file `string_1.cpp`. The implementation of the class should have restricted access and is of no consequence to the user.

Before describing the implementation of the member functions, it is necessary to digress for a moment to describe the **scope resolution operator**. In C a local variable takes precedence over a global variable with the same name. In the scope of the local variable, the global variable has in effect become invisible. In C++ you can instruct the compiler to use the global variable in the scope of the local variable by **C++ Syntax** prefixing the global variable with the scope resolution operator. The syntax is

scope resolution operator   *:: identifier*

For example, from the following program segment

```
int counter = 123; // global variable

void main(void)
{
    int counter = 456;          // local variable
    cout << ::counter << endl;  // display global variable
    cout << counter << endl;    // display local variable
```

the output would be

```
123
456
```

C++ Syntax

scope resolution operator used with methods in a class

The scope resolution operator is also used in the implementation of a function to show that the function belongs to a particular class. The syntax of the scope resolution operator is modified to

class_name :: function_name

For example, `void string_1 :: initialize(const char *value)`

This indicates that each function is a member of the class and that its name has class scope. Without this notation a C++ compiler would regard the function `initialize` as an ordinary function that did not belong to the class `string_1`. The implementation of the class methods for `string_1` follows.

```cpp
// chap_17\string_1.cpp

#include "a:\chap_17\string_1.h"
#include <ctype.h>
#include <string.h>
#include <iostream.h>
#include <iomanip.h>

void string_1::initialize(const char *value)
{
   length = strlen(value);
   text   = new char[length+1];
   strcpy(text, value);
}

void string_1::upper_case(void)
{
   for (int index=0; index != length; index++)
     text[index] = toupper(text[index]);
}

void string_1::display_length(void)
{
   cout << "length of string ";
   cout << length <<endl;
}

void string_1::display_text(void)
{
   cout << text << endl;
}
```

17.3 Object Declaration

A class does not declare any actual data. In the same way as we declare variables, for example, `int value;` we can create actual data of our abstract data type. Such data is known as an instance of the class and is called an **object**.

Like any other data declaration, the data to be declared is preceded by its type. For example,

C++ Syntax

```
string_1 name;
```

instantiating an object and invoking a method

creates an object `name` containing its own data items that can be manipulated using the class methods already described. To invoke a method on an object we use

object_name.method_name(arguments);

For example:

```
name.initialize("Freddy Fox");
name.display_length();
```

The object `name` has its private data initialized to `Freddy Fox`, the string pointed at by `*text` whose `length` is 10 characters.

Each instance of a class contains its own set of member variables, which are stored in separate data structures. Each object has its own clearly defined state as determined by the values stored in its member variables. The exception is when the mode of storage of a data member is declared as `static`, in which case only one copy of the data member is allocated, no matter how many instances of the class are declared. Figure 17.4 illustrates how the data is stored for the object `name` in a structure in memory. The address of the data structure is a special pointer called **this**, which is accessible to member functions. The `this` pointer points to the object for which the member function is called. Every time a member function accesses one of the class's data members, it is implicitly using the `this` pointer.

Within the implementation of the class `string_1`, it would be acceptable to access the private data through the `this` pointer. For example, `this->text` would gain access to the contents of the `text` variable, and `this->length` would gain access to the contents of the `length` variable. Similarly the expressions `(*this).text` and `(*this).length` could also be used to access the private data.

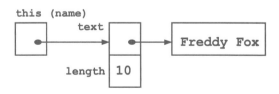

Figure 17.4 The this pointer

551

Program Example 17.1 includes the implementation of the class `string_1` in the program, instantiates an object `name`, and applies the class methods to the object.

Program Example 17.1: Invoking Class Methods

```
// chap_17\ex_1.cpp

#include "a:\chap_17\string_1.cpp"

void main(void)
{
   string_1 name; // instantiate an object

   name.initialize("Freddy Fox");
   name.display_text();
   name.upper_case();
   name.display_text();
   name.display_length();
}
```

Results

```
Freddy Fox
FREDDY FOX
length of string 10
```

Since C++ allows us to define our own abstract data types, it is reasonable to assume that these types should have the same capabilities as the built-in data types such as `int`. That is to say, abstract data types should support at least the following capabilities:

☐ Define one or more variables - `int value_1, value_2;`

☐ Initialize a variable at definition - `int value = 3;`

☐ Assign a value to a variable - `value = 20;`

☐ Assign one variable's value to another variable - `value_1 = value_2;`

☐ Perform mathematical operations - `value_1 * value_2;`

☐ Perform comparisons on data - `if (value_1 > value_2)`

We have already seen how to define a variable `string_1 name;` and this definition may be extended to more than one variable, for example, `string_1 name_1, name_2;`. The rest of the chapter considers the remainder of the capabilities listed.

17.4 Constructors and Destructors

When we declare our own data types, we may need a way to tell the compiler how to create, initialize, and destroy the data. We do so by using two special functions: **constructors** tell the compiler to create an instance of the class, and **destructors** tell the compiler to tidy up the data when it goes out of scope.

Up to now, the only method of initializing data of a class has been through the `initialize` member function. C++ offers an alternative technique that conforms to the syntax of the language. A **constructor** is used for class data initialization, it looks like a function, and it has the same name as the class. The syntax of a constructor is *class_name (optional parameters)*

C++ Syntax For example, `string_2(); string_2(const char *value);`

constructor The definition of the class `string_1` has been modified into class `string_2` to include two constructors as follows:

```
// chap_17\string_2.h

#ifndef CLASS_STRING_2
#define CLASS_STRING_2

class string_2
{
    private:
        char *text;   // pointer to the first character of a string
        int   length; // length of the string

    public:

        // constructors
        string_2();
        string_2(const char *value);

        // destructor
        ~string_2();

        // member functions
        void upper_case(void);            // convert text to upper case
        void display_length(void);        // display length of text
        void display_text(void);          // display the text
};

#endif //CLASS_STRING_2
```

The first constructor `string_2()` is the default constructor and is used to initialize objects to some default value. The second constructor `string_2(const char *value)` is used to initialize the object to a specified value through a member initialization list.

A constructor has a dual purpose: to declare an object and to initialize the data of the object. For example, the declaration `string_2 first_name, second_name("Freddy Fox");` uses the two constructors. Objects `first_name` and `second_name` are declared with initial values of NULL pointer, 0 and `Freddy Fox`, 10 for the contents and length of the strings, respectively. A study of the implementation of the constructors will reveal how this is possible.

```
string_2::string_2()
{
   text=NULL;
   length=0;
   cout << "default constructor called" << endl;
}
```

```
string_2::string_2(const char *value)
{
   length = strlen(value);
   text   = new char[length+1];
   strcpy(text, value);
   cout << "constructor called" << endl;
}
```

Observe that the function names of the constructors have been overloaded and the correct function is obtained through argument matching. It is also possible to use default arguments when invoking constructors, although not with this example.

Introducing constructors into class `string_2` eliminates the requirement for the member function `initialize`, and for this reason, it has been deleted.

If you do not include a constructor in your class definition, the compiler will supply a **null constructor** for you. However, such a constructor is not very useful, since it expects no arguments and has an empty body.

The second capability of an abstract data type is now realized, since it is possible to initialize a variable at definition.

C++ Syntax

destructor

A class is allowed only one **destructor**, which has no return type, and no formal parameters. The name of the destructor is the same name as the class with a preceding tilde ~ symbol. The name of the destructor can be thought of as the complement of the name of the constructor. The syntax of the destructor is: *~class_name()*, for example, `~string_2();`

The destructor is automatically called when an object ceases to exist. Note that a `static` object exists throughout the execution of a program, so its destructor will not be called until the program terminates. An object's storage mode is `auto` by default, and it ceases to exist when its enclosing block completes execution. A *dynamic* object ceases to exist when it is deallocated using *delete*.

The order of construction of the member instances is the order in which they are defined in the class. Destruction is in the reverse order.

A destructor for the class string may be implemented as

```
string_2::~string_2()
{
   delete [] text;
   cout << "destructor called" << endl;
}
```

Like constructors, a default do-nothing destructor is provided by the C++ compiler in the absence of an explicit destructor. Unlike constructors, however, there can be only one destructor function per class.

The memory the object occupies can be deallocated by using the destructor. For example, the statement

```
        second_name.~string_2();
```

is sufficient to deallocate the memory used to store the string and restore this memory back to the heap. Destructors usually do not have to be explicitly invoked from within an application program unless memory space is running short and it is necessary to return memory to the heap to allow the program to continue. Normally, destructors are invoked automatically before the program terminates and are called the same number of times as constructors were called.

The following implementation of class string_2 includes constructors and destructors.

```
// chap_17\\string_2.cpp

#include "a:\chap_17\string_2.h"
#include <ctype.h>
#include <string.h>
#include <iostream.h>
#include <iomanip.h>

string_2::string_2()
{
   text=NULL;
   length=0;
   cout << "default constructor called" << endl;
}

string_2::string_2(const char *value)
{
   length = strlen(value);
   text   = new char[length+1];
   strcpy(text, value);
   cout << "constructor called" << endl;
}
```

```
string_2::~string_2()
{
   delete [] text;
   cout << "destructor called" << endl;
}

void string_2::upper_case(void)
{
   for (int index=0; index != length; index++)
      text[index] = toupper(text[index]);
}

void string_2::display_length(void)
{
   cout << "length of string ";
   cout << length << endl;
}

void string_2::display_text(void)
{
   cout << text << endl;
}
```

Program Example 17.2 illustrates the use of constructors and destructors. Notice from the results that the default constructor is called for the declaration of first_name. This object is initialized to a NULL pointer and appears as a blank line in the output with a length of zero. The constructor is then called for the second_name, and the contents of the string and its length are displayed. Notice that although the destructor has not been explicitly called in the program, the results indicate that the destructor was automatically invoked twice for the destruction of each object when the program was executed.

Program Example 17.2: Use of Constructors and Destructors

```
// chap_17\ex_2.cpp

#include "a:\chap_17\string_2.cpp"

void main(void)
{
   string_2 first_name;

   first_name.display_text();
   first_name.display_length();

   string_2 second_name("Freddy Fox");

   second_name.display_text();
   second_name.display_length();
}
```

Results

```
default constructor called

length of string 0
constructor called
Freddy Fox
length of string 10
destructor called
destructor called
```

17.5 Copy Constructors

A class object that contains a pointer to dynamically allocated memory can be copied in two ways, as illustrated in Figure 17.5.

If an object W had been initialized to the string "data", then by **memberwise** initialization, a second object can also be initialized to this value. The statement

```
string_2 W("data"), X = W;
```

creates a second pointer to the string that W is pointing to. This is fine until the destructor for either X or W is invoked:

```
X.~string_2();
```

in which case the destructor destroys the string belonging to the other string_2 object as well. However, even if the destructor was not explicitly invoked, at the end of a program the destructor is automatically invoked and would attempt to release the same area of memory more than once! To overcome this problem, a **copy constructor** must initialize an object from another object of the same class. The class string_2 has been modified to include a prototype and implementation of the copy constructor. The class has been renamed as string_3 and contains the following insertions:

In file string_3.h the prototype

```
string_3(const string_3 &value);  // copy constructor
```

and in the implementation file string_3.cpp the copy constructor

```
string_3::string_3(const string_3 &value)
{
   length = strlen(value.text);
   text = new char[length+1];
   strcpy(text, value.text);
   cout << "copy constructor called" << endl;
}
```

The dot notation (.) may be used to access the private data of an object in an implementation of the class. For example, value.text is the character string of the object value. However, text refers to the character string for the new object that is being created by the constructor. Given the declaration

```
string_3 Y("data"), Z=Y;
```

value is the object Y; value.text is the string **data**; text is the data member for the object Z. This initialization creates a copy of the original data being pointed at by Y.

This type of constructor is automatically invoked when an object of class string_3 is initialized using another object of the same class.

In Figure 17.5 object Z points to a separate copy of the data used by object Y. In these circumstances if a destructor had been invoked for object Y, the memory storing the data for object Z would not be reallocated to the heap. Furthermore, at the end of a program the destructors would be invoked the same number of times as the constructors had been invoked, and there would be no attempt to release the same area of memory more than once.

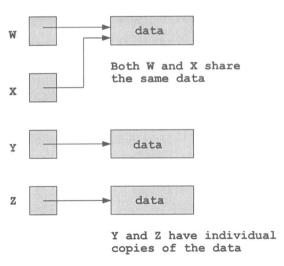

Figure 17.5 Two methods for copying data

Program Example 17.3 illustrates the use of a copy constructor. In the declaration and initialization of Y, a constructor string_3(const char *value); is called; however, in the declaration and initialization of Z=Y, the copy constructor string_3(const string_3 &value); is called. The values of Y and Z are then displayed. The destructor for object Z is called. The value of Y is then displayed, showing that a separate copy of the data has been made; otherwise, the link to the data would have been destroyed by the destructor. The destructor is then automatically called twice to complement the original creation of Y and Z.

558

Program Example 17.3: Use of a Copy Constructor

```
// chap_17\ex_3.cpp

#include "a:\chap_17\string_3.cpp"
#include <iostream.h>
#include <iomanip.h>

void main(void)
{
   string_3 Y("data"), Z=Y;

   cout << "values of Y and Z respectively" << endl;
   Y.display_text();
   Z.display_text();

   Z.~string_3();
   cout << "value of Y only after destructor used on Z" << endl;
   Y.display_text();
}
```

Results

```
constructor called
copy constructor called
values of Y and Z respectively
data
data
destructor called
value of Y only after destructor used on Z
data
destructor called
destructor called
```

17.6 Passing and Returning Objects

A copy constructor may be called when a function takes an object as a parameter or when a function returns an object.

In the following program segment, the function display_data is passed a string object by value. This means that the function gets its own local copy of the object. The compiler must implicitly call the copy constructor to create the local copy.

```
void display_data(string parameter)
{
   parameter.display_text();
}

void main(void)
{
   string data("Have a nice day!");
   display_data(data);
}
```

If you don't define a copy constructor to create a local copy of parameter in display_data, the parameter shares data defined in the main function. When the function display_data finishes executing, parameter goes out of scope and a destructor is called to destroy the object. The implication is that data will have a pointer to deleted memory, which makes it unsafe to use after the function has completed.

Clearly, an overhead is involved in calling a copy constructor every time an object is passed by value to a function. If you pass a reference to a constant object, then the effect is the same as passing a parameter by value, but without the copy constructor call, and hence no destructor call when parameter goes out of scope.

The function display_data can be modified as follows:

```
void display_data(const string &parameter)
{
   parameter.display_text();
}
```

A reference is initialized with the object being passed. The compiler performs the equivalent of the code const string &parameter = data; and as a result the function uses the same object as the caller. The const keyword is used so that the function display_data cannot modify the parameter.

A similar situation arises when a function returns an object.

```
string get_data()
{
   string value("Object-oriented programming");
   return value;
}

void main(void)
{
   string data;
   data = get_data();
   data.display_text();
}
```

The compiler calls the copy constructor to create a hidden temporary object in the caller's scope. This hidden temporary object is then used as the right-hand of the assignment statement. If the copy constructor is not available, the hidden temporary object shares the object `value`'s data. When the function `get_data` finishes executing, `value` goes out of scope and is destroyed. There is no guarantee that the assignment to `data` will work correctly!

Returning a reference to a function can also be more efficient than returning an object. However, you must use caution when returning a reference to objects or variables other than `*this`.

17.7 Operator Overloading

Operator overloading was first encountered in Chapter 16, where the left shift << and right shift >> operators had been overloaded to represent insertion and extraction from streams. Most C++ operators may be overloaded; however, the following restrictions on operator overloading exist.

- ☐ You cannot extend the language by inventing new operators.

- ☐ Overloaded operators retain their original number of operands as well as their original precedence and associativity (see Appendix B regarding associativity).

- ☐ You cannot change the way an operator works with built-in types.

- ☐ You cannot overload the following operators:

`::`	scope resolution operator
`.`	class member operator
`.*`	pointer-to-member operator
`?:`	conditional expression operator

You should overload operators only when the meaning is clear. For example, the arithmetic operators **+**, **−**, *****, and **/** are meaningful when applied to a numeric classes such as fractions and complex numbers.

Let us consider adding operators to the string classes already discussed. A new string class can be created called `string`. In addition to the constructors, destructors, and member functions, it will contain new member functions to assign strings, concatenate strings, and compare strings for being greater than, less than, and equal to using the overloaded operators **=**, **+**, **>**, **<**, and **==**, respectively.

Given a declaration of `string A("Hello "), B("World"), C;`

it is possible to write programs that contains statements such as

```
C = A;   C = A + B; if (B > A) ..; if (A < B) ..; if (A == B) ..;
```

to show how the operators **=**, **+**, **>**, **<**, and **==** have been overloaded.

We shall consider in detail one example of implementing an overloaded operator and use several overloaded operators in the next program.

A prototype for overloading the **+** operator to represent string concatenation is

```
const string& operator+(const string &s);
```

Figure 17.6 illustrates the meaning of each part of the first line of the method, followed by the implementation of the overloaded string concatenation operator.

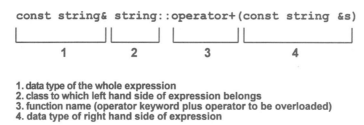

1. data type of the whole expression
2. class to which left hand side of expression belongs
3. function name (operator keyword plus operator to be overloaded)
4. data type of right hand side of expression

Figure 17.6 Interpretation of a method's first line

```
const string& string::operator+(const string &s)
{
    char *temp;                  // pointer to temporary string
    length = length+s.length;    // increase length of text by length of s
    temp = new char[length+1];   // allocate space to store concatenated string
    strcpy(temp, text);          // copy text to temporary string
    strcat(temp, s.text);        // concatenate temp and string s
    delete [] text;              // re-allocate old storage back to heap
    text = temp;                 // assign text to point at the new string
    return *this;                // return the result of concatenation
}
```

Given the declaration `string A("Hello "), B("World");` the method of evaluating the expression A+B is described as follows:

When the binary operator + is defined as a member function, the first operand is the object for which it is called and the second operand is the parameter.

For example, with the expression A+B, A is the object for which the operator is called, therefore, any implementation has immediate access to the private data `text` and `length` for object A. In this example, object B is the second operand and is passed as a parameter to s. Within the implementation, the private data for `text` and `length` of the second operand B is accessed through `s.text` and `s.length`, respectively.

The length of object A is increased by the length of s (`s.length`), ready to accommodate the concatenated string. Space is allocated to a temporary pointer `temp` for storing the concatenated string. The current text of A is copied to the temporary string. The text from B (`s.text`) is concatenated with the temporary string. The memory space for `text` is returned to the heap. The character string pointer `text` is then reassigned to point at the temporary string. The concatenation operator returns the new values of `text` and `length` to the object A. Figure 17.7 illustrates how the function works when the two objects are instantiated and concatenated using A+B.

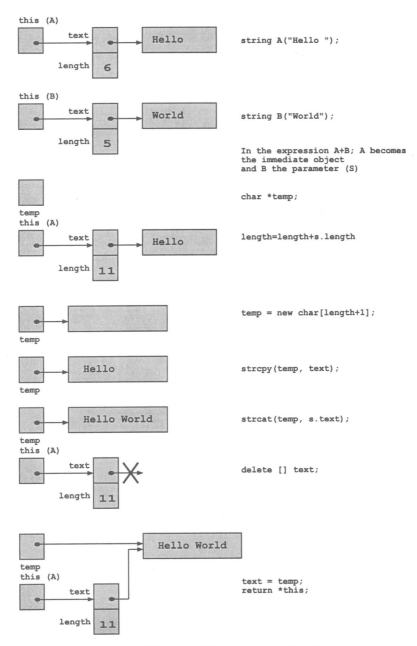

Figure 17.7 Instantiation and concatenation

Copies of the files `string.h` and `string.cpp` illustrate the definition and implementation of the class `string`. Program Example 17.4 tests the implementation of the overloaded operators.

```cpp
// chap_17\string.h

#ifndef CLASS_STRING
#define CLASS_STRING

class string
{

        private:
                char *text;
                int  length;

        public:
                // constructors
                string();
                string(const char *value);
                string(const string &value);   // copy constructor

                // destructor
                ~string();

                // overloaded operators
                // string assignment
                const string& operator=(const string &s);

                // string concatenation
                const string& operator+(const string &s);

                // string comparison > == <
                int operator>(const string &s);
                int operator<(const string &s);
                int operator==(const string &s);

                // methods
                // display string on screen
                void display_text(void);

};

#endif //CLASS_STRING
```

```
// chap_17\string.cpp

#include <iostream.h>
#include <iomanip.h>
#include <string.h>
#include "a:\chap_17\string.h"

string :: string()
{
        text = NULL;
        length = 0;
}

string :: string(const char *s)
{
        length = strlen(s);
        text = new char[length+1];
        strcpy(text, s);
}
string :: string(const string &s)
{
        length = strlen(s.text);
        text = new char[length+1];
        strcpy(text, s.text);
}

string :: ~string()
{
        delete [] text;
}

const string& string :: operator=(const string &s)
{
        delete [] text;
        length=s.length;
        text=new char[length+1];
        strcpy(text, s.text);
        return *this;
}

const string& string :: operator+(const string &s)
{
        char *temp;

        length = length+ s.length;
        temp = new char[length+1];
        strcpy(temp, text);
        strcat(temp, s.text);
        delete [] text;
```

```
        text = temp;
        return *this;
}

int string::operator>(const string &s)
{

    if (strcmp(text, s.text) > 0)
       return (1);
    else
       return (0);
}

int string::operator<(const string &s)
{
    if (strcmp(text, s.text) < 0)
       return (1);
    else
       return (0);
}

int string::operator==(const string &s)
{
    if (strcmp(text, s.text) == 0)
       return (1);
    else
       return (0);
}

void string :: display_text(void)
{
        cout << text << endl;
}
```

Program example 17.4 Test of the Overloaded Operators from the Class string.

```
// chap_17\ex_4.cpp

#include "a:\chap_17\string.cpp"

void main(void)
{
   string A("Hello "), B("World"), C;

   // test assignment
   C=A;
   C.display_text();
```

```
// test concatenation
C=A+B;
C.display_text();

// test for string comparisons
if (B>A)
    cout << "greater than operator OK" << endl;

if (A<B)
    cout << "less than operator OK" << endl;

A=B;

if (A==B)
    cout << "equality operator OK" << endl;
}
```

Results

```
Hello
Hello World
greater than operator OK
less than operator OK
equality operator OK
```

17.8 Friends

In the spirit of data encapsulation, a class's data members should be kept private so that they are not accessible to functions outside of the class. The C++ **friend** mechanism allows the programmer to by-pass class access restrictions. Since this feature goes against the spirit of data encapsulation it should be used sparingly.

Friend Classes

You may find that one class needs to have access to another class's private data, yet it would be inefficient for the class to use its access functions.

Consider the following segments of code:

```
class A
{
    friend class B;
};

class B
{
    friend class C;
};
```

```
class C
{
   .
   .
   .
};
```

Class A declares that class B is a friend. This permits member functions of class B to directly read or modify the private data of class A. B is a friend of A, so B can access A's private data and methods. Friends have rights that others don't.

Class B declares that class C is a friend, which permits member functions of class C to directly read or modify the private data of class B. Class B cannot access the private data and methods of class C. Friendship can only be given; it cannot be taken.

Class C cannot access the private data and methods of class A. Friends of friends are not automatically friends of yours!

Friend Functions

A single function may be declared with the `friend` keyword, instead of an entire class. A friend is not a member function. However, a function that is defined as a `friend` has access to all members of the class, including private members, as though it were a member itself. A `friend` declaration can be placed into either the private or public section of a class.

In contrast to an operator being defined as a member function where the first operand is the object for which it is called and the second object is the parameter, when an operator is defined as a `friend`, both operands are parameters to the function.

You cannot define a friend and a member function that define the same operator. For example, if a `friend` function was defined for string concatenation, in place of the member function, it would be written as follows:

```
friend string operator+(const string &s1, const string &s2);
```

and may appear in either the private or public sections of the class definition. The implementation of the `friend` function would appear in the equivalent `.cpp` file, in this case `stack.cpp` as follows:

```
string operator+(const string &s1, const string &s2)
{
   string s;

   s.length = s1.length + s2.length;
   s.text = new char[s.length+1];
   strcpy(s.text, s1.text);
   strcat(s.text, s2.text);
   return s;
}
```

The `<iostream.h>` header file contains classes for input and output streams **istream** and **ostream**, respectively, where the standard stream `cin` belongs to the `istream` class and the standard stream `cout` belongs to the `ostream` class. C++ output/input uses overloaded versions of the left and right shift operators << and >>, respectively, for stream insertion (output) and stream extraction (input). Furthermore, these operators are overloaded many times to provide for the input and output of all the standard built-in data types such as `char`, `char *`, `int`, `float`, `double`, etc.

We can define additional overloaded versions of >> and << in order to read and write objects of a user-defined class.

To overload the << operator so that it will insert an object of class X, include the following operator function in the definition of class X.

```
friend ostream& operator<<(ostream &output, const X &object);
```

The implementation of this in class `string` would be as follows:

```
friend ostream& operator<<(ostream &output, const string &s)
{
    return output << s.text;
}
```

To overload the >> operator so that it will extract an object of class X, include the following operator function in the definition of class X.

```
friend istream& operator>>(istream &input, X &object);
```

The implementation of this in class `string` would be as follows:

```
friend istream& operator<<(istream &input, const string &s)
{
    return input >> s.text;
}
```

17.9 Inline functions

Up to now the header file for the class definition has included only the prototypes of the constructors, destructors, and methods used to access the private data. When the implementation of either the constructors, destructors, or methods is reasonably short you may code these directly into the header file.

For example, in the implementation of the `string` class a constructor might have been coded as follows:

```
#ifndef CLASS_STRING
#define CLASS_STRING

class string
{
    .
    public:
```

```
        // constructor
        string();
        .
};

inline string::string()
{
    text = NULL;
    length = 0;
}


    .


#endif // CLASS_STRING
```

Alternatively, you may dispense with the separate inline entry and write the code directly after the function name in the header file. Do not insert a semicolon after the function name.

```
class string
{
    .
  public:
        // constructor
        string()
        {
          text = NULL;
          length = 0;
        }
          .
};
```

Let us consider a programming problem that utilizes friend functions and inline functions.

Suppose we want to devise a class for the addition, subtraction, multiplication, and division of rational numbers (fractions). The class should also contain a function to display a rational number. Operator overloading will be used for the operators **+**, **−**, *****, and **/**, and **<<** to output to the `ostream`.

In performing arithmetic on fractions, it is necessary to find the greatest common divisor (gcd) between two integers m and n. This is achieved by using Euclid's algorithm as follows:

divide m by n and find the remainder
while remainder is not zero
*   assign n to m*
*   assign remainder to n*
*   divide m by n and find remainder*
assign n to gcd

Euclid's algorithm is used in a private function that converts a numerator and denominator into a rational number by dividing by the greatest common denominator and adjusting the sign of the fraction according to the signs of the numerator and denominator. Program Example 17.5 illustrates the desired coding.

Program Example 17.5: Arithmetic of Fractions

```cpp
// chap_17\rational.h

#ifndef CLASS_RATIONAL
#define CLASS_RATIONAL
#include <iostream.h>

class rational
{
        private:
                int numerator;
                int denominator;
                void MakeRational(void);
        public:
                // in-line constructors
                rational()
                {
                        numerator = 0;
                        denominator = 1;
                }
                rational(int num, int denom = 1)
                {
                        numerator=num;
                        denominator = denom;
                        MakeRational();
                }
                ~rational(){};  // destructor

                rational rational::operator+(const rational&);
                rational rational::operator-(const rational&);
                rational rational::operator*(const rational&);
                rational rational::operator/(const rational&);

                // friend function
                friend ostream& operator<<(ostream&, const rational&);
};

#endif // CLASS_RATIONAL
```

```
// chap_17\rational.cpp

#include <stdlib.h>
#include "a:\chap_17\rational.h"

// Euclid's algorithm for evaluating the greatest common divisor
// between two positive integers m and n
int Euclid(int m, int n)
{
        int remainder=m % n;

        while (remainder!=0)
        {
                m=n;
                n=remainder;
                remainder=m % n;
        }
        return n;
}

void rational :: MakeRational(void)
{
        int gcd; // greatest common divisor
        int divisor;

        gcd = Euclid(numerator, denominator);
        numerator = numerator/gcd;
        denominator = denominator/gcd;

        if (numerator == 0 || denominator == 0)
            denominator = abs(denominator);
        else
        {
            divisor = Euclid(abs(numerator), abs(denominator));
            if (denominator > 0)
            {
                numerator /= divisor;
                denominator /= divisor;
            }
            else
            {
                numerator /= (-divisor);
                denominator /= (-divisor);
            }
        }
}
```

```
rational rational::operator+(const rational &A)
{
        int n = A.numerator * denominator + numerator * A.denominator;
        int d = A.denominator * denominator;
        return rational(n,d);
}

rational rational::operator-(const rational &A)
{
        int n = numerator * A.denominator - A.numerator * denominator;
        int d = A.denominator * denominator;
        return rational(n,d);
}

rational rational::operator*(const rational &A)
{
        int n = A.numerator * numerator;
        int d = A.denominator * denominator;
        return rational(n,d);
}

rational rational::operator/(const rational &A)
{
        int n = numerator * A.denominator;
        int d = denominator * A.numerator;
        return rational(n,d);
}

ostream& operator<<(ostream& output, const rational& A)
{
        if (A.denominator == 1)
           return output << A.numerator;
        else
           return output << A.numerator << "/" << A.denominator;
}
```

```
// chap_17\ex_5.cpp

#include "a:\chap_17\rational.cpp"

// program to test the data abstraction for rational numbers

void main(void)
{
        rational a(8,3), b(9,4);

        cout << a << endl;
        cout << b << endl;
        cout << a+b << endl;
        cout << a-b << endl;
        cout << a*b << endl;
        cout << a/b << endl;
}
```

Results

```
8/3
9/4
59/12
5/12
6
32/27
```

RAILWAY SHUNTING YARD ALGORITHM

Case Study: Converting Infix Notation to Reverse Polish Notation

Normal algebraic notation is often termed infix notation, since the binary arithmetic operator appears between the two operands to which it is being applied. Infix notation may require parenthesis to specify the desired order of operations. For example, in the expression a/b+c, the division will occur first followed by the addition. If we want the addition to occur first, we must parenthesize the expression as a/(b+c).

Using postfix notation (also called reverse Polish notation after the nationality of its originator Jan Lukasiewicz), the need for parenthesis is eliminated because the operator is placed directly after the two operands to which it applies.

The infix expression a/b+c would be written as the postfix expression ab/c+, which is interpreted as divide a by b and add c to the result.

574

The infix expression a/(b+c) would be written as abc+/ in postfix notation, which is interpreted as add b to c then divide that result into a.

In compiler writing it is more convenient to evaluate arithmetic expressions written in reverse Polish notation than it is to evaluate arithmetic expressions written in infix notation. The following algorithm, known as the Railway Shunting Yard algorithm, since data are shunted to and from a stack, can be used to convert infix notations to reverse Polish notations.

The operators [and] are used to delimit the infix expression. For example, the expression a*(b+c/d) will be coded as [a*(b+c/d)].

The algorithm uses operator priorities as defined in Figure 17.8.

operator	priority
[	0
(	1
–	2
+	2
/	3
*	3
^	4

Figure 17.8 Operator priorities

Use Figure 17.9 to trace the following explanation of the algorithm.

diagram (i) If brackets [or (are encountered, each is pushed on to the stack.

diagram (ii) All operands that are encountered, for example a, b, and c, are displayed on the screen.

diagrams (iii), (iv), & (v) When an operator is encountered, its priority is compared with that of the operator's priority at the top of the stack.

diagram (vi) If when comparing priorities the operator encountered is not greater than the operator on the stack, the stack operator is popped and displayed. This process is repeated until the encountered operator has a higher priority than the stack top operator. The encountered operator is then pushed on to the stack.

diagrams (v) & (vi) When a) is encountered, all the operators up to, but not including (, are popped from the stack one at a time and displayed. The operator (is then deleted from the stack.

diagram (vi)& (vii) When the operator] is encountered, all the remaining operators, up to but not including [, are popped from the stack one at a time and displayed. The string of characters that is displayed will be the reverse Polish string.

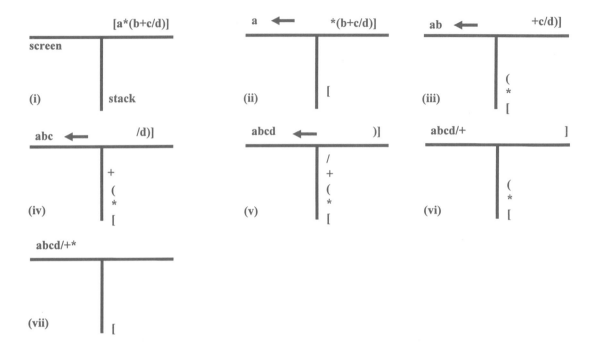

Figure 17.9 The use of a stack in the algorithm

Using the techniques of data abstraction, write a header file stack.h that defines a stack for storing single characters and an implementation of this file stack.cpp containing functions to manipulate data on the stack.

Write a program that includes the stack.cpp file and will enable strings of expressions written in infix notation to be converted to reverse Polish notation.

Problem Analysis - A full description of a stack was given in Chapter 14. The functions described in the header file stack.h must cater for a constructor to initialize the stack, together with functions to test for an empty stack and to push and pop characters to and from the stack.

```
// chap_17\stack.h

#ifndef CLASS_STACK
#define CLASS_STACK

class node
{
        friend class stack;

        private:
                char    datum;
                node*   link;
};

class stack
{
        private:
                node*   stacktop;

        public:
                        stack();        // constructor
                        ~stack(){};     // destructor
                int     empty(void);
                void    push(char value);
                char    pop(void);
};

#endif // CLASS_STACK
```

The implementation of the constructor and functions is given in the following file stack.cpp.

```
// chap_17\stack.cpp

#include <stdlib.h>
#include "a:\chap_17\stack.h"

stack :: stack()
{
        stacktop=NULL;
}

int stack :: empty(void)
{
    return (stacktop==NULL);
}
```

```
void stack :: push(char value)
{
        node* temp;

        temp=new node;
        temp->datum = value;
        temp->link = stacktop;
        stacktop = temp;
}

char stack :: pop(void)
{
        node* temp;
        char   value=stacktop->datum;

        if (! empty())
        {
                temp=stacktop;
                stacktop=stacktop->link;
                delete temp;
                return value;
        }
        else
          return 0;
}
```

The operators depicted in Figure 17.8 are stored as structures in a one-dimensional array as illustrated in Figure 17.10. One member of the structure represents the operator, and the second member, the priority.

Figure 17.10 Storage of operators and their priorities

This array is declared as

```
operator_priorities operators[MaxOperators] = {{'[',0},
                                                {'(',1},
                                                {'-',2},
                                                {'+',2},
                                                {'/',3},
                                                {'*',3},
                                                {'^',4}};
```

578

For convenience in this example, the infix expressions to be converted to reverse Polish notation are stored in a two-dimensional array as illustrated in Figure 17.11.

```
0   [a*b+c]
1   [a*(b+c/d)]
2   [a*b+c/d)]
3   [u+f*t]
4   [b^2-4*a*c]
5   [h*(a+4*b+c)/3]
6   [w*1-1/(w*c)]
```

Figure 17.11 Storage of data used in the problem

The contents of this array can be declared as

```
const char* InfixData[MaxData] = {  "[a*b+c]",
                                    "[a*(b+c/d)]",
                                    "[a*b+c/d]",
                                    "[u+f*t]",
                                    "[b^2-4*a*c]",
                                    "[h*(a+4*b+c)/3]"
                                    "[w*1-1/(w*c)]"};
```

The program has been divided into four functions including the `main` control function, as depicted in the structure chart illustrated in Figure 17.12 The function `priority` returns a value for the hierarchical priority of a symbol. The function `priority_stacktop` returns the priority of the character that is currently at the top of the stack. The function `analysis` implements the Railway Shunting Yard algorithm by determining whether a character should be placed on the stack, pushed from the stack, or displayed on the screen.

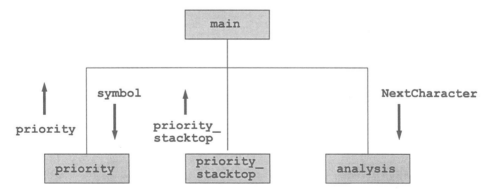

Figure 17.12 Structure chart

Algorithm for the Function main

1. for each infix expression stored in the two-dimensional array
2.   copy the expression into a temporary array
3.   for every character in the infix expression
4.   isolate the character from the expression
5.   analyze the character in relation to the stack
6.   display a new line

Data Dictionary for the Function main - The `main` function has four local variable declarations: an array of characters for temporarily storing an infix expression; the next character in the string; and two indexes, `index` and `position` for processing the two-dimensional array of infix expressions and the characters of a single infix expression, respectively. Since the indexes are both used in a for loop, they need not be declared outside the scope of these loops.

```
char    temp[MaxString+1];
char    NextCharacter;
int     index;
int     position;
```

Algorithm for the Function priority

for every cell in the one-dimensional array containing the operators and priorities
*   if symbol is equal to the operator found in the cell*
*   return the corresponding priority*
*   exit from the function*
*   else*
*   return error value (-1)*

Data Dictionary for the Function priority - The function contains one formal parameter, the symbol whose priority is to be found, and if found, returns the priority value. There is one index, and it can be declared within the for loop.

```
int    priority(char symbol);
int    index;
```

Desk Check of the Function priority - The input parameter can be assumed to be the symbol +.

variable	value(s)
symbol	+
index	0 1 2 3
operators[index].operator_	[(- +
symbol==operators[index].operator_?	no no no yes
return operators[index].priority_	3

580

Algorithm for the Function priority_stack

pop the contents of the stack and assign this value to a local variable symbol
push symbol back to the stack to restore the status quo
return the value of the priority of symbol

Data Dictionary for the Function priority_stack - The function returns an integer value representing the priority of the stack top. One local character variable for the symbol is popped from the stack.

```
int priority_stacktop(void);
char symbol;
```

Algorithm for the Function analysis

if next character is closing parenthesis ')'
  pop character from stack
  while character not opening parenthesis '('
    display character
    pop character from stack

else if next character is closing bracket ']'
  pop character from stack
  while character not opening bracket '['
    display character
    pop character from stack

else if next character is opening parenthesis '(' or opening bracket '['
  push next character onto stack

else if next character arithmetic symbol
  while priority of next character is less than or equal to priority of stack top character
    pop character from stack
    display character
  push next character onto stack

else
  display next character

Data Dictionary for the Function analysis The function has just one formal parameter and one local declaration for the character being popped from the stack.

```
void analysis(char& NextCharacter);
char character;
```

581

Desk Check of the Function analysis - The test data is assumed to be [a*(b+c/d)]

diagram (figure 17.9)	(i)	(ii)			(iii)	(iv)		(v)			(vi)
NextCharacter	[	a	*	(	b	+	c	/	d	)		
NextCharacter ==')'?	no	no	no	no	no	no	no	no	no	yes		
NextCharacter == ']'?	no	no	no	no	no	no	no	no	no			
NextCharacter =='(' || '['?	yes	no	no	yes	no	no	no	no	no			
arithmetic operator?		no	yes		no	yes	no	yes	no			
character											/	+
character not '('											no	no
character not '['												
priority <= priority stack top			no			no		no				
stack	[		*	(		+		/				
character displayed		a			b		c		d		/	+

diagram (figure 17.9)	(vii)		
NextCharacter	]		
NextCharacter ==')'?	no		
NextCharacter == ']'?	yes		
NextCharacter =='(' || '['?			
arithmetic operator?			
character	(	*	[
character not '('	no	yes	
character not '['			no
priority <= priority stack top			
stack			
character displayed		*	

```cpp
// chap_17\ex_6.cpp

// program to convert an infix expression to a reverse polish expression

#include <iostream.h>
#include <string.h>
#include "a:\chap_17\stack.cpp"

const int MaxOperators=7;
const int MaxData=7;
const int MaxString=15;

struct operator_priorities  {
                              char operator_;
                              int  priority_;
                            };
```

```
operator_priorities operators[MaxOperators] = {{'[',0},
                                                {'(',1},
                                                {'-',2},
                                                {'+',2},
                                                {'/',3},
                                                {'*',3},
                                                {'^',4}};

const char* InfixData[MaxData] = {"[a*b+c]",
                                  "[a*(b+c/d)]",
                                  "[a*b+c/d]",
                                  "[u+f*t]",
                                  "[b^2-4*a*c]",
                                  "[h*(a+4*b+c)/3]",
                                  "[w*1-1/(w*c)]"};

stack OperatorStack; // declare object of type stack


// function to find the priority of a symbol
int priority(char symbol)
{
        for (int index=0; index!=MaxOperators; index++)
            if (symbol==operators[index].operator_)
            {
                return operators[index].priority_;
                break;
            }

        return -1;

}


// function to find the priority of the symbol at stacktop
int priority_stacktop(void)
{
        char symbol;

        // obtain and replace the symbol at stacktop
        symbol=OperatorStack.pop();
        OperatorStack.push(symbol);

        return priority(symbol);
}
```

```
void analysis(char& NextCharacter)
{
        char character;

        if (NextCharacter == ')')
        {
                character=OperatorStack.pop();
                while (character != '(')
                {
                        cout << character;
                        character=OperatorStack.pop();
                }
        }
        else if (NextCharacter == ']')
        {
                character=OperatorStack.pop();
                while (character != '[')
                {
                        cout << character;
                        character=OperatorStack.pop();
                }
        }
        else if (NextCharacter == '(' || NextCharacter == '[')
                OperatorStack.push(NextCharacter);
        else if (NextCharacter == '^' || NextCharacter == '*' ||
            NextCharacter == '/' || NextCharacter == '+' ||
            NextCharacter == '-')
             {
                        while (priority(NextCharacter) <= priority_stacktop())
                        {
                                character=OperatorStack.pop();
                                cout << character;
                        }
                        OperatorStack.push(NextCharacter);
             }
        else
           cout << NextCharacter;
}
```

```
void main(void)
{
        char   temp[MaxString+1];
        char   NextCharacter;

        for (int index=0; index!=MaxData; index++)
        {
            strcpy(temp, InfixData[index]);
            for (int position=0; position!=int(strlen(temp)); position++)
            {
                NextCharacter=temp[position];
                analysis(NextCharacter);
            }
            cout << endl;
        }
}
```

Results

```
ab*c+
abcd/+*
ab*cd/+
uft*+
b2^4a*c*-
ha4b*+c+*3/
w1*1wc*/-
```

Summary

☐   Data abstraction is the technique of combining a data type with a set of operations on data of the same type.

☐   A `class` is a data type that contains both data members and function members. Access to the private data members is through the function members.

☐   A class can contain at least two sections, `private` and `public`. Outside the class, access to the private members is prohibited and access to public members only is permissible.

☐   The definition of an abstract data type is normally organized into two header files. The first header, appended with the abbreviation .h, should be made accessible to the user of the class. This file contains the definition of the members of the class. The second file, appended with the abbreviation .cpp, should be given restricted access. This file contains the implementation of the members of the class and is not intended to be made visible to the user of the class.

☐ The implementation of class member functions can be made in the definition file for the class, in which case the functions are treated as inline. This technique is advisable only for short functions. A preferred method is to implement the member functions in a separate .cpp file. Each function in this file needs to be qualified with a scope resolution operator; otherwise, the C++ compiler will not associate the function as a class member.

☐ Identifiers that would normally be hidden can be made visible using the scope resolution operator.

☐ All instances of a class are known as objects of the class. Objects can be thought of as self-contained units that comprise both data and the instructions that operate on the data.

☐ The `this` pointer points to the object for which the member function is called.

☐ Objects can be copied and used for initialization, passed as parameters, or returned by functions. In the latter case it is advisable to declare the formal parameter or function return type as a reference to avoid the overhead of copying the object.

☐ Constructors are used to create an instance of a class. An object is normally initialized through a constructor. When an object goes out of scope, a destructor is used to destroy the data structure associated with the object.

☐ Constructors, as functions, can be overloaded.

☐ Copy constructors are used to provide a copy of the data structure associated with an object. Without a copy constructor, only memberwise initialization is possible, and a separate copy of the object is not made.

☐ Operators as well as functions can be overloaded. However, there is a restricted set of operators that may be overloaded.

☐ A friend is not a class member function but a means of by-passing the class access restrictions to access all the members of a class.

Review Questions

1. What is an abstract data type?

2. True or false - data abstraction permits users to access data using their own functions.

3. What is a class?

4. True or false - items of data defined by a class can be accessed using dot (.) notation.

5. Why can class data be defined as private?

6. What is the purpose of the reserved word public?

7. What is the instance of a class?

8. What is an object?

9. What is the purpose of the reserved word `this`?

10. How can you resolve a name conflict between a class function and a global function?

11. What is a constructor?

12. How many constructors may be defined in a class?

13. Can C++ automatically define its own constructor for a class if one is not present?

14. What is the purpose of a destructor?

15. How many destructors is a class allowed?

16. What is memberwise initialization of an object?

17. What is the purpose of a copy constructor?

18. How is an object passed by value to a function?

19. Why is it better to pass a reference to a constant object when passing a parameter to a function?

20. What is operator overloading?

21. True or false - all operators in C++ may be overloaded.

22. What is the purpose of the reserved word `friend`?

23. True or false - friendship can only be given; it cannot be taken.

24. True or false - a friend declaration must appear in the public section of a class.

Programming Exercises

25. Rewrite the overloaded operator = function found in `string.h` so that the function checks to see that it is not assigning the same object.

26. Implement as overloaded operators **+=**, **-=**, ***=**, and **/=** for the class `rational` described in section 17.9

Programming Problems

27. Using the `string` class, create an array of objects for the names of people and a separate array of objects for the addresses of these people. Concatenate the contents of both arrays into a third array containing the names and addresses of people.

Use the selection sort, and hence overloaded operators for comparison and assignment, to sort the contents of this third array into ascending order on the name of a person as the key. Display the contents of the array before and after the sort.

28. Devise a class for the addition, subtraction, multiplication, and division of complex numbers. The class should also contain a function to display complex numbers. As with the previous question, overload the operators +, -, *, /, and <<.

A complex number has two parts (A, iB) where A is the real part, B is the imaginary part, and i=sqrt(-1). The following expressions show how arithmetic can be performed on two complex numbers, so that a real part (R) and an imaginary part (I) are evaluated.

addition   R = A.real + B.real
            I = A.imaginary + B.imaginary

subtraction   R = A.real - B.real
               I = A.imaginary - B.imaginary

multiplication   R = (A.real * B.real) - (A.imaginary * B.imaginary)
                  I = (A.real * B.imaginary) + (A.imaginary * B.real)

division   T = A *(B.real - B.imaginary)
            N = B.real * B.real - B.imaginary * B.imaginary
            R = T.real / N
            I = T.imaginary / N

29. If floating-point computations are performed on amounts of money, inaccuracies can occur in the results. Devise a class money that will cater for arithmetic using the overloaded operators +, -, *, /, and % (remainder); comparisons using the overloaded operators ==, !=, >, <, >=, and <=; and the overloaded operator << on ostream for displaying an amount of money.

30. Return to Chapter 14 and refresh your knowledge of binary search trees. Create a class `tree` that is implemented as a binary search tree. You will need methods to test for a tree being empty, attach nodes, remove nodes and display the contents of the tree. Write a program to instantiate an object of type `tree` and maintain the data contained in this object.

Chapter 18

Object-oriented Programming

In the previous chapter the technique of data abstraction was introduced as the cornerstone of better programmer productivity. Although the goal of saving software development and production costs through the use of data abstraction was mentioned, there was no indication of how this goal could be achieved.

This final chapter extends your knowledge of data abstraction by introducing you to object-oriented programming and explains how software can be reused without extensive revision, retesting and revalidation of code. This chapter covers the following topics:

- ☐ The advantages of object-oriented programming.

- ☐ Classes receiving the characteristics of other classes through inheritance.

- ☐ The use of a class method throughout a range of classes through polymorphism.

- ☐ Implementation of polymorphism through virtual methods.

- ☐ Object-oriented design and programming.

18.1 Introduction

The increasing popularity of object-oriented programming, OOP for short, owes its success to many factors.

Back in the 1940s when computers were developed, the applications tended to be mathematical. Therefore, it should come as no surprise that by 1957 the first commercially available high-level language was FORTRAN, used for mathematical applications. The seeds of procedural programming had been sown, and for years languages followed the procedural method.

Software costs are related directly to human productivity and contribute substantially toward the cost of project development. Over the last decade the cost of hardware has decreased rapidly, yet the cost of writing software has remained reasonably constant.

One way to increase programmer productivity is to create code that can be reused without extensive revision, testing, and revalidation. The techniques of reuse are not particularly appropriate to procedural languages; hence the need to search for other approaches to software development.

With the emergence of graphical user interfaces (GUIs) such as windows-based environments, the use of procedural languages became impractical and an object-oriented approach to programming became essential.

Object-oriented programming uses the technique of data abstraction developed in the previous chapter. The concept of defining class types and functions that allow you to access the data associated with such types is fundamental to OOP.

Object-oriented programming has the following advantages over traditional procedural programming.

- ☐ **Improved data typing**. In object-oriented code, data types are used that relate to the problem to be solved. Such types have meaningful names and behavior.

- ☐ **Reusability**. Once an abstract data type has been created it can be reused in other applications. OOP positively encourages the use of libraries of objects. Software can not only be reused but also extended, which in turn should help to reduce development costs.

- ☐ **Maintainability**. Object-oriented code is easier to maintain and modify, since you simply add or modify public methods.

- ☐ **Fewer errors**. Owing to the encapsulation of types and methods, errors can be localized and thus become easier to locate and to fix. Hence the reliability of the software is improved.

- ☐ **Lower costs**. Software development time is shorter and development costs are lower.

A disadvantage of the technique is the time it takes most programmers to learn how to use it well.

18.2 Inheritance

Figure 18.1 illustrates how different car models are derived from a fundamental concept of a vehicle. The concept of the vehicle is a blueprint of the generic car and specifies such features as four wheels, an engine, a transmission unit, and a saloon body shell. Different models of motor car can be derived from this concept of a vehicle, and each derivation incorporates a plan for a specific car such as a VW Beetle, Jaguar, or Rolls-Royce. All three vehicles have inherited the characteristics of the generic car; that is to say, they all have four wheels, they all contain engines and transmission units, and they are all built with a saloon body shell. However, each particular model has a different set of four wheels, a different engine and transmission unit, and a different shape of body shell.

The concept or blueprint of the vehicle is the base class. The VW Beetle, Jaguar, and Rolls Royce all inherit characteristics from the base class and represent derived classes.

The cars themselves are the objects, since they are instances, created in the factory, of a particular model or class of car.

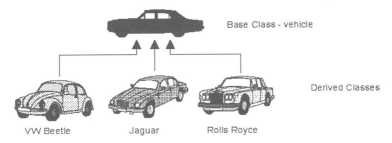

Figure 18.1 Base and derived classes

Figure 18.1 illustrates the class hierarchy between the base class vehicle and the derived classes VW Beetle, Jaguar, and Rolls Royce. By convention, the arrows always point from the derived class to the base class.

This example illustrates some of the fundamental features of inheritance.

Inheritance is the process by which one class receives the characteristics of another class.

The initial class is called the **base** or parent class. The receiving class is called the **derived** or child class. Instead of having to define the derived class fully, it is necessary to define only how it differs from the base class. Inheritance is usually used where similar types of classes are required.

Turning our attention to a computing example, the base class of the C++ input/ output classes is the class `ios`. This class provides operations, data, and values common to input and output. The `ios` class defines a number of useful methods, such as

```
int ios::eof(void);      // returns true if end of file
int ios::fail(void);     // returns true if operation failed
```

Figure 18.2 illustrates that the classes `istream` and `ostream` are derived from the `ios` class.

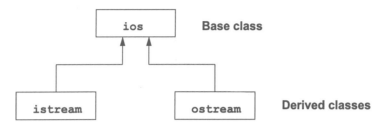

fig 18.2 Derived classes from the ios base class

The classes `istream` and `ostream` provide facilities for providing specific types of input/ output. They use the methods and values provided by `ios` and also define new methods. These new methods can be different for each class. For example,

```
// input of binary data
istream& istream::read(char *buffer, int buffer_size);
// output data in binary format
ostream& ostream::write(char *buffer, int buffer_size);
```

The following program segment illustrates how the inherited characteristics from the `ios` class may be used in both the `istream` and `ostream` classes. Notice that two lines of code have deliberately been incorrectly written to focus your attention on the use of methods within appropriate classes.

```
const int buffer_size 255;
istream input_stream;
ostream output_stream;
char buffer[buffer_size];

if (!input_stream.eof())
    input_stream.read(buffer, buffer_size);
else
    output_stream.read(buffer, buffer_size);   // THIS LINE IS WRONG

output_stream.write(buffer, buffer_size);

if (output_stream.fail())
  input_stream.write(buffer, buffer_size);     // THIS LINE IS WRONG
```

Notice that the methods `eof` and `fail` defined in the `ios` class have been inherited by the `istream` and `ostream` classes. For this reason both methods may be legitimately used by objects from both classes. Since `read` is a method within the class `istream` and `write` is a method within the class `ostream`, you cannot read from the object `output_stream` or write to the object `input_stream`.

Inheritance is often more complex than a single class being derived from another. Figure 18.3 illustrates that the class `iostream` is derived from `ostream` and `istream`. The class `iostream` inherits properties from both parents and can be used for input and output from a terminal. A further class derived from `ios` is `fstreambase`, which provides the basic facilities for accessing files. The class `ofstream` is derived from both `ostream` and `fstreambase` and provides facilities for output to files.

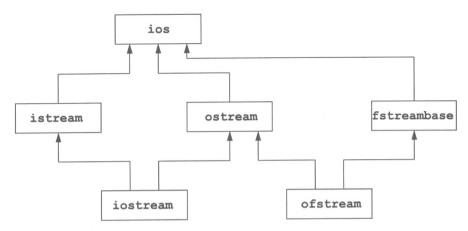

Figure 18.3 Further inheritance

Figure 18.4 illustrates that the class `ifstream` is derived from both `istream` and `fstreambase` and provides facilities for input from files.

The class `fstream` is derived from `iostream` and `fstreambase` and provides facilities for input from and output to files.

The classes `ios`, `iostream`, and `fstreambase` (all shaded in Figure 18.4) are **abstract** classes. The compiler will allow other classes to be derived from abstract classes but will not allow actual instances of the classes to be created.

For example, the `fstreambase` class is useful as a parent for the file access classes `fstream`, `ifstream`, and `ofstream`. However, it would be no use to create an `fstreambase` object, since the class does not have any input/ output methods - they must be inherited from `ostream` or `istream`.

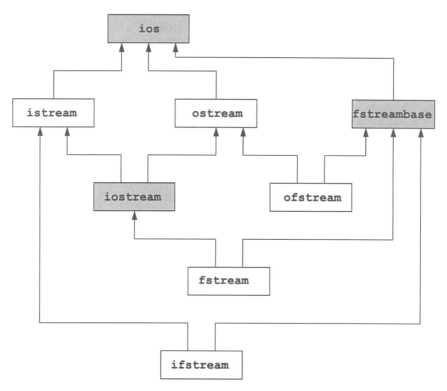

Figure 18.4 An example of abstract classes

The generic syntax of a derived class from a single class is

C++ Syntax

single inheritance

class derived-class : mode-of-inheritance base-class
{
    .
    .
    .
};

where the mode of inheritance is one of the keywords **public** or **private**.

As we have seen from the `ios` class it is possible for a derived class to inherit from many classes, in which case the syntax is modified to

C++ Syntax

multiple inheritance

class derived-class : mode-of-inheritance base-class-1, mode-of-inheritance base-class-2, ...
{
    .
    .
    .
};

Public Inheritance - In public inheritance, the derived class will look exactly like the base class. All private and public members of the base class will become private and public members of the derived class. A derived class can modify the existing functionality by redefining base-class methods. In other words, everything is inherited unless overridden by the derived class. As well as inheriting functionality from the base class, a derived class can add its own functionality. For example,

```
class base_class
{
  private:
    int value;
  public:
    void function_1(void);
};

class derived_class : public base_class
{
  public:
    void function_2(void);
};
```

The derived class may be viewed as containing the following data and methods:

```
class derived_class : public base_class
{
  private:
    int value;
  public:
    void function_1(void);
    void function_2(void);
};
```

Had function_2 in the derived class been replaced by a new function_1, then function_1 in the derived class would override the inherited function_1 from the base class.

The derived class cannot access the private areas of the base class; therefore, the only access to the private data value is through function_1. To overcome this restriction, it is necessary to declare the private members of the base class as being **protected**. Derived classes which inherit protected members are allowed direct access to them. However, as far as other classes and nonmember functions are concerned, protected members are like private members and cannot be accessed.

Private Inheritance - With private inheritance everything is hidden unless otherwise specified in the derived class. Here we have specified private inheritance for the derived class.

```
class base_class
{
  public:
    int value;
  public:
    void function_1(void);
    void function_2(void);
};

class derived_class : private base_class
{
  // no methods specified
};
```

If a call is made to a method of the derived class, the corresponding base-class method will be invoked.

For example,

```
base_class.function_1();
derived_class.function_1();
```

are effectively two identical calls.

Methods of the derived class can still access the public and protected methods of the base class. However, these methods are not visible by default as methods of the derived class. All the methods inherited from the base class are hidden due to private inheritance.

We can selectively export those attributes of the base class that we require.

```
class derived_class : private base_class
{
  protected:
    base_class::function_1;
  public:
    base_class::function_2;
};
```

Often when a derived class method is redefined, a call to the original base-class version of the method is required. This association can be done by using the scope resolution operator : : for example,

```
base_class::function_1;
```

To export an attribute we must specify the base-class and the method name. You can export only attributes that have the same or reduced privacy. Therefore, public attributes can be exported as public or protected attributes, however, protected attributes can be exported only as protected.

The following example illustrates how the derived class cross inherits from the base class point. Both classes have constructors and destructors and methods to plot and erase the corresponding shape (point or cross). The base class methods get_x and get_y return the coordinates of the point; however, these are inherited by the class cross and can be used to return the coordinates of the center of the cross.

```
// chap_18\shapes_1.h

class point
{
        protected:
                short int x,y;

        public:
                // constructors
                point() {x=0; y=0;}
                point(const short int &X, const short int &Y) {x=X; y=Y;}

                // destructor
                ~point(){};

                // methods
                void plot(void);
                void erase(void);
                short int get_x(void);
                short int get_y(void);
};


class cross: public point
{
        public:
                // constructors
                cross() {x=0; y=0;}
                cross(const short int &X, const short int &Y) {x=X; y=Y;}

                // destructor
                ~cross(){};

                // overridden methods
                void plot(void);
                void erase(void);
};
```

The implementation of these classes assumes an IBM-compatible PC environment. The functions to draw the shapes are taken from the nonstandard header file <graph.h> used in the Microsoft implementations of C and C++.

The functions used in the implementation of the classes point and cross are described briefly.

short far _getcolor(void) returns the current color used by functions that write to the graphics screen.

long far _getbkcolor(void) function returns the current background color.

short far _setcolor(short col) sets the current color to the value specified in col.

short far _setpixel(short x, short y) sets the pixel at the logical point whose horizontal and vertical coordinates correspond to the arguments x and y, respectively.

struct xycoord far _moveto(short x, short y) moves the current graphics output position to the logical point specified by the parameters.

short far _lineto(short x, short y) draws a line from the current graphics position to the logical point specified by the arguments.

short far _setvideomode(short mode) selects a screen mode suitable for a particular configuration; the mode parameter will take on the following values:

_VRES16COLOR 640x480 pixel color graphics mode with 16 colors used for a VGA adapter.
_DEFAULTMODE specifies the default video mode for the given hardware configuration.

A **pixel** is the smallest element of a visual display. A pixel may have one or more attributes of color, brightness, and flashing.

The axes on the graphics screen have their origin in the top left corner of the screen. In this application the maximum value along the x-axis is 640 pixels, and the maximum value down the y-axis is 480 pixels. The application assumes the display to have a VGA adapter displaying 16 colors in a grid of 640x480 pixels.

```
// chap_18\shapes_1.cpp

#include <graph.h>
#include "a:\chap_18\shapes_1.h"

void point :: plot(void)
{       _setcolor(_getcolor());
        _setpixel(x,y);
}
```

```
void point :: erase(void)
{
        short int color;

        color=_getcolor();
        _setcolor(_getbkcolor());
        _setpixel(x,y);
        _setcolor(color);
}

short int point :: get_x(void)
{
        return x;
}

short int point :: get_y(void)
{
        return y;
}

void cross :: plot(void)
{
        _setcolor(_getcolor());
        _moveto(x-2,y);
        _lineto(x+2,y);
        _moveto(x,y-2);
        _lineto(x,y+2);
}

void cross :: erase(void)
{
        short int color;

        color=_getcolor();
        _setcolor(_getbkcolor());
        _moveto(x-2,y);
        _lineto(x+2,y);
        _moveto(x,y-2);
        _lineto(x,y+2);
        _setcolor(color);
}
```

Program Example 18.1 illustrates how two objects, a point and a cross, are created and plotted on the screen. The inherited methods to return the coordinates of the cross are used to create a new cross relative to the position of the first cross. The new cross is then plotted.

The program also contains a function to delay the appearance of the graphics on the screen.

This nonstandard function is stored in the separate header file `chap_18\delay.cpp` as follows (for more information on the header file `<time.h>`, see Appendix A):

```cpp
#include <time.h>

void delay(int seconds)
{
        time_t initial_time, time_now;

        time(&initial_time);
        time(&time_now);
        while (time_now - initial_time < seconds)
                time(&time_now);
}
```

Program Example 18.1: The Creation of Objects and Use of Inheritance

```cpp
// chap_18\ex_1.cpp

#include "a:\chap_18\shapes_1.cpp"
#include "a:\chap_18\delay.cpp"

void main(void)
{
        short int X, Y;   // coordinates

        // instantiate class point to create object POINT
        point POINT(200,150);
        // instantiate class cross to create object CROSS
        cross CROSS(300,150);

        _setvideomode(_VRES16COLOR);

        // plot point and cross on screen
        POINT.plot();
        CROSS.plot();

        delay(5);

        // get coordinates of cross
        X = CROSS.get_x();
        Y = CROSS.get_y();

        // instantiate class cross to create object NEW_CROSS
        cross NEW_CROSS(X+100, Y);
```

```
    // plot cross on screen
    NEW_CROSS.plot();

    delay(5);

    _setvideomode(_DEFAULTMODE);
}
```

The output from this program displays a point . (illuminated pixel) at the coordinates 200,150 and a small cross **+** at coordinates 300,150. After a timed delay of 5 seconds, a new cross is displayed on the screen at the coordinates 400, 150.

18.3 Polymorphism

Polymorphism, Greek for "many shapes", allows you to use an object of a child class as though it were an object of the parent class.

Polymorphism is a way of giving an action one name that is shared up and down an object hierarchy, with each object in the hierarchy implementing the action in a way appropriate to itself. Polymorphism applies only for a specific set of actions. To write polymorphic classes we require two things.

☐ The classes must be part of the same inheritance hierarchy.

☐ The classes must support the same set of required methods.

For example, we have already seen that we can define << operator that will output objects to ostream.

```
ostream& operator<<(ostream &output, const string &str)
{
    output << str.text();
    return(output);
}
```

From Figure 18.4 notice that the classes fstream and ofstream both inherit from ostream. Note fstream is not an immediate child of ostream but inherits from iostream, which itself inherits from ostream. Both fstream and ofstream support an operator << to output a character pointer data type. The net effect is that the << operator we have defined can be used with an ofstream or fstream object without further declaration. For example a line can be written to the stream output.

```
string str="a line in the file\n";
ofstream output("a:\filename.txt");
output << str;
```

The operator << is polymorphic, since it can be used up and down the object hierarchy without having to be redefined.

Consider the following segment of code.

```
class base_class
{
  private:
    .
  public:
    void function_1(void);   void _base_class_function_1(void);        F100:0100
};

class derived_class : public base_class
{
  public:
    void function_1(void);   void _derived_class_function_1(void);     F100:0200
    .
};

base_class      base_variable;
derived_class   derived_variable;

base_variable.function_1();      _base_class_function_1();        jsr F100:0100
derived_variable.function_1();   _derived_class_function_1();     jsr F100:0200
```

The compiler will assign a unique name to every function that is declared; for example, void **_base_class_function_1 (void)** is assigned to method function_1 in the base_class. When a call is made to a method, the compiler looks at the type of the object variable to decide which function is to be called.

The linker will assign a memory location to each function and ensure that the correct function is called; for example, **F100:0100** to function_1 in the base_class is called using **jsr F100:0100**.

This is known as **compile-time binding**, as the jump from the function call to the appropriate function code is bound during the compilation process.

Compile-time binding works fine when manipulating objects directly but may fall down when indirect manipulation is used.

Often we will wish to manipulate an object of a derived type using a base class pointer as the following code illustrates.

```
class base-class
{
      .
  void function_1(void);
};

class derived_class : public base_class
{
      .
  void function_1(void);
};

base_class      base_variable;
derived_class   derived_variable;

base_class      *base_ptr;
```

`base_ptr = &base_variable;`	we can set a pointer to point tothe variable base_variable and use this to invoke function_1(); when the compiler processes the call it will decide which function to call by the type base_ptr
`base_ptr = &derived_variable;` `base_ptr-> function_1();`	unfortunately when the compiler tries to process the second invocation it assumes that anything the pointer points to is the base_object - so the program invokes the base class function as a derived class object

There are many times when the compiler will not know at compile time what objects are being processed. This is especially true when functions are concerned. Consider the following code:

```
void function(base_class *base_ptr)
{
  base_ptr -> function_2();
}
```

`function(&base_variable);` `function(&derived_variable);`	this function does not know what type of object it will be dealing with until the call to the function is made

The same situation applies when references are used instead of pointers.

```
void function(base_class &base_ref)

{
  base_ref. function_2();
}

function(base_variable);
function(derived_variable);
```

Since we cannot be sure what type of object we are going to receive until we actually run the program, we want to put off the decision about what function to call until this time. This technique is known as **run-time binding**.

18.4 Virtual Methods

The **virtual** keyword tells the compiler to use run-time binding for the specified method. Once declared as virtual in the base class, a method is automatically virtual in all derived classes.

When a virtual function is invoked indirectly, the compiler will set up code that inspects the type of object being used and invokes the appropriate function for that type of object.

When writing a base class, it is a good idea to follow these rules.

☐ Never declare constructors as virtual because you must know what type of object you want in order to create it.

☐ Always declare the destructor as virtual.

☐ Declare all other methods as virtual unless you explicitly want the base class method always to be invoked.

☐ If a base class method is not virtual, do not redefine this method in any derived class.

The following listing shows how methods in the class definitions for point and cross have been qualified by the reserved word virtual. Notice that once a parent method is tagged as virtual, all the descendant types that implement a method of the same name must tag that method as virtual.

```
// chap_18\shapes_2.h

class point
{
        protected:
                short int x,y;

        public:
                // constructors
```

604

```
                        point() {x=0; y=0;}
                        point(const short int &X, const short int &Y) {x=X; y=Y;}

                        // destructor
                        virtual ~point(){};

                        // methods
                        virtual void plot(void);
                        virtual void erase(void);
                        short int get_x(void);
                        short int get_y(void);
                        void move(const short int &toX, const short int &toY);
};


class cross: public point
{
        public:
                        // constructors
                        cross() {x=0; y=0;}
                        cross(const short int &X, const short int &Y) {x=X; y=Y;}

                        // destructor
                        virtual ~cross(){};

                        // overridden methods virtual by implication
                        void plot(void);
                        void erase(void);
};
```

The method move is inherited by the class cross from the class point. Both plot and erase have been described as being virtual; therefore, when move is used on a cross, the correct implementation of plot and erase will be used and not the implementation for a point.

Dynamic binding is implemented in C++ through the use of a **virtual method table** or VMT. This is an array of method pointers that the compiler constructs for every class that uses a virtual function. The VMT contains one method pointer for each virtual function in the class. Each pointer points to the version of the method that is appropriate to that class. The VMT for a point has pointers to point::plot and point::erase, while the VMT for a cross has pointers to cross::plot and cross::erase. This fact is illustrated in Figure 18.5.

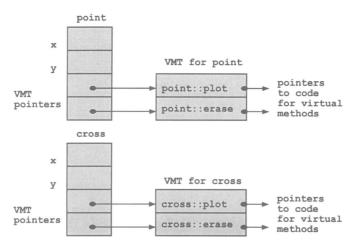

Figure 18.5 VMT's for point and cross

When multiple instantiations are made on a single class, there is only one VMT for the class, as illustrated in Figure 18.6.

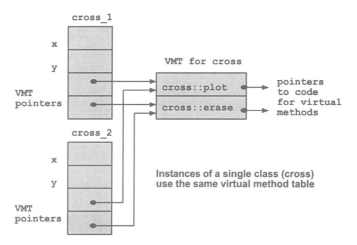

Figure 18.6 VMT for multiple instances of a class

The new implementation of the modified class for `point` follows. This implementation is very similar to the original implementation, and for this reason only the additions to the file are shown.

```
// chap_18\shapes_2.cpp

#include <graph.h>
#include "a:\chap_18\shapes_2.h"


          .


void point :: move(const short int &toX, const short int &toY)
{
        erase();
        x=toX;
        y=toY;
        plot();
}


          .
```

Program Example 18.2 illustrates how the function move can be used to move either a point or a cross. The method move is truly polymorphic, since it can be used up and down the hierarchy with the correct implementations for plot and erase being used regardless of whether a point or a cross is being moved.

Program Example 18.2: Demonstration of a Polymorphic Method


```
// chap_18\ex_2.cpp

#include "a:\chap_18\shapes_2.cpp"
#include "a:\chap_18\delay.cpp"

void main(void)
{
        short int X,Y; // coordinates

        // define positions of shapes
        point      POINT(150,50);
        cross      CROSS(200,50);

        _setvideomode(_VRES16COLOR);

        // plot shapes
        POINT.plot();
        CROSS.plot();

        delay(5);
```

```
            // move point
            POINT.move(100,100);

            delay(5);

            // get position of cross
            X=CROSS.get_x();
            Y=CROSS.get_y();

            // move cross relative to original position
            CROSS.move(X+100,Y+50);

            delay(5);

            _setvideomode(_DEFAULTMODE);
}
```

The results from running the program are that a point is plotted at coordinates (150,50) followed by a cross plotted at coordinates (200,50). After a 5-second delay, the point is moved to coordinates (100,100), and after another 5-second delay, the cross is moved to coordinates (300, 100).

Dynamic binding makes it possible for you to provide a library of classes that other programmers can extend, even if they don't have your source code. All you need to distribute are the header files and the compiled object code files for the hierarchy of classes you have written and for the methods that use those classes. Other programmers can derive new classes from yours and redefine the virtual functions that you declared. Then the functions that use your classes can handle the classes they have defined.

In section 18.2 we stated that an abstract class is one from which the compiler will allow other classes to be derived, but it will not allow actual instances of the classes to be created, since the class does not support any suitable methods. A class that defines **pure virtual functions** is known as an abstract class, because you cannot declare any instances of it. For example,

```
class base_class
{
  public:
    virtual void function_1() const = 0;  // pure virtual
};
```

A pure virtual function requires no definition; you don't have to write the body of base_class ::function_1, since it is intended to be redefined in all derived classes. In the base_class the function serves no purpose except to provide a polymorphic interface for the derived classes.

If a derived class does not provide a definition for a pure virtual function, the function is inherited as pure virtual and the derived class becomes an abstract class as well.

When an object of a derived class goes out of scope, the destructor for the derived class is called and then the destructor for the base class is called. When destroying dynamically created objects with the `delete` operator, if `delete` is applied to a base class pointer, the compiler calls the base class destructor, even if the pointer points to an instance of a derived class. The solution is to declare the base class's destructor as virtual, which causes the destructors of all derived classes to be virtual. If `delete` is applied to a base class pointer, the appropriate destructor is called no matter what type of object the pointer is pointing to.

18.5 Object-oriented Design

Program design has featured prominently throughout this book. The method normally used pseudocode to described the major steps that the program must perform. Each step was then refined into smaller steps until each step could be translated into statements in C or C++.

Object-oriented design differs dramatically from this technique in that you don't analyze a problem in terms of top-down decomposition starting with an abstract view of the program and ending with a detailed view. Object-oriented design requires you to do the following:

☐ Identify the classes

☐ Assign attributes and behavior

☐ Find relationships between the classes

☐ Arrange the classes in hierarchies

These stages are not mutually exclusive, each step in the process may alter the assumptions you made in the previous step, requiring you to go back and repeat that step with new information. Object-oriented design is a repetitive process in so much as you successively refine you class descriptions throughout the design process.

Identifying Classes

One technique for identifying classes is to write a description of the program's purpose, list all the nouns that appear in the description , and then choose your classes from that list. For example, a rectangle class and an ellipse class are obvious candidates for a graphic drawing program.

Attributes and Behavior

Once you have identified a class, the next step is to determine what responsibilities it has. Responsibilities fall into two categories.

☐ The information that an object of a class must maintain

☐ The operations that an object can perform or that can be performed on it

Every class has attributes, which are the properties or characteristics that describe it. Every instance of a class has a state that it must remember. An object's state consists of the current values of all its attributes. An attribute's value can be stored as data, or it can be computed each time it is needed. For example, a cross has an attribute of its position on the screen, and this value is stored as data x and y. Once you have identified the attributes and behavior of a class, you have some candidate member functions for the class's interface. The behavior you have identified usually implies member functions. Some attributes require members functions to query or set their state.

Relationships Between Classes

Classes can build upon and cooperate with other classes. Often one class depends upon another class because it cannot be used unless the other class exists.

Another way in which one class can depend on another is when the other class is embedded within it, that is it contains objects of the other class as members. For example, a circle object might have a point object representing its center, as well as an integer representing its radius.

Most relationships between classes arise because one class's interface depends on another.

Arranging the Classes into Hierarchies

Creating class hierarchies is an extension of the first step, identifying classes, but it requires information gained during the second and third steps. By assigning attributes and behavior to classes, you have a clearer idea of their similarities and differences; by identifying the relationships between classes, you see which classes need to incorporate the functionality of others.

Case Study: Drawing and Animation.

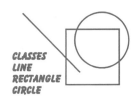

CLASSES
LINE
RECTANGLE
CIRCLE

As an extension of the point and cross classes discussed so far, this case study introduces classes for a straight line, rectangle, and circle. Objects can then be instantiated from these classes to build the shape of a motor vehicle. Once the vehicle is drawn on the screen, it will be programmed to move across the screen from right to left.

Problem Analysis - In the solution to this problem, it is assumed that you have access to the Microsoft library header <graph.h> or equivalent library. In addition to the functions described earlier from this header, two more functions will be used in the example.

short far _rectangle(short fill, short x1, short y1, short x2, short y2) draws a rectangle bounded by the specified upper-left (x1,y1) and lower-right (x2,y2) points; fill is a constant where _GBORDER implies draw only an outline of the figure.

short far _ellipse(short fill, short x1, short y1, shortx2, short y2) draws an ellipse within a rectangle whose boundaries are specified as (x1,y1) coordinates of upper-left corner and (x2,y2) coordinates of lower-right corner. If the coordinates represent the boundaries of a square, then a circle will be drawn; fill is a constant _GBORDER.

Figure 18.7 illustrates the figure to be displayed on the screen. The numbers represent values on the X and Y axis. Notice that the Y values increase as you move down the screen.

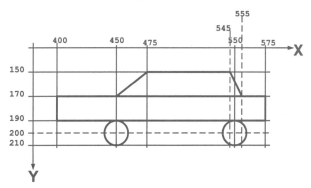

Figure 18.7 An illustration of the figure to be drawn

As you can see from the drawing, the wheels are made by two circles, the body of the car by a rectangle, and the front and rear screens and the roof of the car by three straight lines.

Identification of Classes - The classes have already been identified as `line`, `rectangle`, and `circle`; in addition to the original classes of `point` and `cross`.

Assign Attributes and Behavior - Drawing a straight line, rectangle, and circle will require different sets of coordinates.

A straight line requires coordinates (X1, Y1) representing the left-most end of the line and (X2, Y2) representing the right-most end of the line.

A rectangle will also require coordinates (X1, Y1) representing the upper-left corner and (X2, Y2) representing the lower-right corner.

A circle requires the coordinates of the center (x, y) and the radius R. From these values the coordinates (X1, Y1) and (X2, Y2) that represent the upper-left and lower-right corners of the square that surrounds the circle can be calculated.

The midpoint of each shape (x, y) must also be computed, since it will be used to move a shape to a new position on the screen.

Since the straight line, rectangle, and circle will need to be reconstructed with respect to the midpoint after being moved, it will be necessary to store the distance of (X1, Y1) or (X2, Y2) from the midpoint as values Xinc and Yinc respectively.

All three shapes will need to be plotted on the screen at the coordinates stated and then erased from the screen; therefore methods to `plot` and `erase` each shape will need to be present.

611

Relationships Between Classes - The method `move` can be inherited by all derived classes from the class `point`. This method was listed earlier and uses the methods `erase` and `plot` to move a shape from one position to another. If the methods `erase` and `plot` are to be used correctly throughout the hierarchy, it will be necessary to declare them as `virtual` functions. This declaration will ensure that `move` can be used in a polymorphic manner throughout the classes.

Class Hierarchy - Figure 18.8 illustrates the hierarchy between the classes. The class `line` has inherited from `point` so that it may include the protected data for the midpoint (`x`, `y`). Classes `rectangle` and `circle` inherit from `line` so they may include the pairs of coordinates that represent the upper-left and lower-corners of the rectangle and square, respectively. In addition these classes will also inherit the midpoint (`x`, `y`) and the distances `Xinc` and `Yinc` between the midpoint and either set of coordinates of the rectangle or square. All derived classes inherit the methods `move`, `get_x` and `get_y`; however, all three methods use the midpoint (`x`, `y`) of every shape.

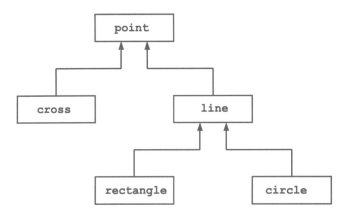

Figure 18.8 Class hierarchy

```
// chap_18\shapes_3.h

class point
{
        protected:
                short int x,y;

        public:
                // constructors
                point() {x=0; y=0;}
                point(const short int &X, const short int &Y) {x=X; y=Y;}

                // destructor
                virtual ~point(){};

                // methods
                virtual void plot(void);
                virtual void erase(void);
                short int get_x(void);
                short int get_y(void);
                void move(const short int &toX, const short int &toY);
};


class cross: public point
{
        public:
                // constructors
                cross() {x=0; y=0;}
                cross(const short int &X, const short int &Y) {x=X; y=Y;}

                // destructor
                virtual ~cross(){};

                // methods
                void plot(void);
                void erase(void);
};

class line: public point
{
        protected:
                short int X1,Y1,X2,Y2;
                short int Xinc, Yinc;
        public:
                // constructors
                line() {x=0; y=0; X1=0; Y1=0; X2=0; Y2=0; Xinc=0; Yinc=0;}
                line(const short int & _X1, const short int & _Y1,
                    const short int & _X2, const short int & _Y2);
```

```
                // destructor
                virtual ~line(){};

                // methods
                void plot(void);
                void erase(void);
};

class rectangle: public line
{
        public:
                // constructors
                rectangle() {x=0;y=0;X1=0;Y1=0;X2=0;Y2=0;}
                rectangle(const short int & X1, const short int & Y1,
                        const short int & X2, const short int & Y2);

                // destructor
                virtual ~rectangle(){};

                // methods
                void plot(void);
                void erase(void);
};

class circle: public line
{
        protected:
                 short int R;
        public:
                // constructors
                circle() {x=0; y=0; R=0;}
                circle(const short int & X, const short int & Y,
                        const short int & R);

                // destructor
                virtual ~circle(){};

                // methods
                void plot(void);
                void erase(void);
};
```

```
// chap_18\shapes_3.cpp

#include <graph.h>
#include <math.h>
#include "a:\chap_18\shapes_3.h"

const float pi = 3.14159;

void point :: plot(void)
{       _setcolor(_getcolor());
        _setpixel(x,y);
}

void point :: erase(void)
{
        short int color;

        color=_getcolor();
        _setcolor(_getbkcolor());
        _setpixel(x,y);
        _setcolor(color);
}

short int point :: get_x(void)
{
        return x;
}

short int point :: get_y(void)
{
        return y;
}

void point :: move(const short int &toX, const short int &toY)
{
        erase();
        x=toX;
        y=toY;
        plot();
}

void cross :: plot(void)
{
        _setcolor(_getcolor());
        _moveto(x-2,y);
        _lineto(x+2,y);
        _moveto(x,y-2);
        _lineto(x,y+2);
}
```

```
void cross :: erase(void)
{
        short int color;

        color=_getcolor();
        _setcolor(_getbkcolor());
        _moveto(x-2,y);
        _lineto(x+2,y);
        _moveto(x,y-2);
        _lineto(x,y+2);
        _setcolor(color);
}

line :: line(const short int & X1, const short int & Y1,
            const short int & X2, const short int & Y2)
{
        X1=_X1; Y1=_Y1; X2=_X2; Y2=_Y2;
        x=(X1+X2)/2; y=(Y1+Y2)/2;
        Xinc=(short int)fabs((double)(x-X1));
        Yinc=(short int)fabs((double)(y-Y1));
}


void line :: plot(void)
{
        // obtain the correct orientation of the line

        if (X1<X2 && Y1<Y2)
        {
                X1=x-Xinc; Y1=y-Yinc;
                X2=x+Xinc; Y2=y+Yinc;
        }
        else if (X1<X2 && Y1>Y2)
        {
                X1=x-Xinc; Y1=y+Yinc;
                X2=x+Xinc; Y2=y-Yinc;
        }
        else if (X1>X2 && Y1<Y2)
        {
                X1=x+Xinc; Y1=y-Yinc;
                X2=x-Xinc; Y2=y+Yinc;
        }
        else
        {
                X1=x+Xinc; Y1=y+Yinc;
                X2=x-Xinc; Y2=y-Yinc;
        }
```

```
        _setcolor(_getcolor());
        _moveto(X1,Y1);
        _lineto(X2,Y2);
}

void line :: erase(void)
{
        short int color;

        color=_getcolor();
        _setcolor(_getbkcolor());
        _moveto(X1,Y1);
        _lineto(X2,Y2);
        _setcolor(color);
}

rectangle :: rectangle(const short int &_X1, const short int &_Y1,
                       const short int &_X2, const short int &_Y2)
{
        X1=_X1;Y1=_Y1;X2=_X2;Y2=_Y2;
        x=(X1+X2)/2; y=(Y1+Y2)/2;
        Xinc=(short int)fabs((double)(x-X1));
        Yinc=(short int)fabs((double)(y-Y1));
}


void rectangle :: plot(void)
{
        X1=x-Xinc; Y1=y-Yinc;
        X2=x+Xinc; Y2=y+Yinc;

        _setcolor(_getcolor());
        _rectangle(_GBORDER,X1,Y1,X2,Y2);
}

void rectangle :: erase(void)
{
        short int color;

        color=_getcolor();
        _setcolor(_getbkcolor());
        _rectangle(_GBORDER,X1,Y1,X2,Y2);
        _setcolor(color);
}

circle :: circle(const short int &_X, const short int &_Y,
                 const short int &_R)
{
        x=_X; y=_Y; R=_R;
```

617

```
          X1=x-(R*cos(pi/4));
          Y1=y-(R*sin(pi/4));
          X2=x+(R*cos(pi/4));
          Y2=y+(R*sin(pi/4));
          Xinc=(short int)fabs((double)(x-X1));
          Yinc=(short int)fabs((double)(y-Y1));
}


void circle :: plot(void)
{
          X1=x-Xinc; Y1=y-Yinc;
          X2=x+Xinc; Y2=y+Yinc;

          _setcolor(_getcolor());
          _ellipse(_GBORDER, X1,Y1,X2,Y2);
}

void circle :: erase(void)
{
          short int color;

          color=_getcolor();
          _setcolor(_getbkcolor());
          _ellipse(_GBORDER, X1,Y1,X2,Y2);
          _setcolor(color);
}
```

Algorithm for the Function main

1. initialize shapes to draw vehicle
2. set video mode to suitable graphics mode
3. plot shape of vehicle at initial position on screen
4. delay
5. for every value of a counter in the range 0..limit
6.   get coordinates of each part of the vehicle
7.   move each part of the vehicle
8 delay
9. restore video mode to default settings

Data Dictionary for the Function main - The shapes that are used to represent the parts of the vehicle are circles for the wheels, a rectangle for the body and straight lines for the front and rear screens and the roof. Objects front_wheel, rear_wheel, body, front_screen, roof, and rear_screen must be instantiated from the appropriate classes and initialized to the coordinates inferred from Figure 18.7.

In addition the function requires constants that specify by how far the vehicle is to be moved before it is redrawn and the number of times the vehicle is to be redrawn.

```
const short int Xinc = 2;
const short int counting_limit = 200;

circle front_wheel(450,200,10);
circle rear_wheel(550,200,10);
rectangle body(400,170,575,190);
line screen(450,170,475,150);
line roof(475,150,545,150);
line rear_screen(545,150,555,170);
```

Test Data - The data chosen has been taken from Figure 18.7. The coordinates inferred from this figure assume that the vehicle is starting on the right-hand side of the screen with the front of the vehicle at position x=400. If the vehicle is to move from right to left across the screen, then a distance of two pixels is deducted from the abscissa of the midpoint value of each of the vehicle's graphic components prior to the vehicle being moved. This calculation is repeated two hundred times to allow the front of the vehicle to reach the left-hand edge of the screen.

```
// chap_18\ex_3.cpp

// program to display the shape of a vehicle
// and move the vehicle across the screen

#include "a:\chap_18\shapes_3.cpp"
#include "a:\chap_18\delay.cpp"

void main(void)
{
        const short int Xinc = 2; // incremental distance to move vehicle
        const short int counting_limit = 200;

        // initialization of shapes to draw vehicle

        circle front_wheel(450,200,10);
        circle rear_wheel(550,200,10);
        rectangle body(400,170,575,190);
        line screen(450,170,475,150);
        line roof(475,150,545,150);
        line rear_screen(545,150,555,170);

        _setvideomode(_VRES16COLOR);
```

```
// plot shape of vehicle

front_wheel.plot();
rear_wheel.plot();
body.plot();
screen.plot();
roof.plot();
rear_screen.plot();

delay(1);

for (int counter=0; counter!=counting_limit; counter++)
{
        // get coordinates of each vehicle part
        // and move that part

        short int X,Y; // coordinates

        X=front_wheel.get_x();
        Y=front_wheel.get_y();
        front_wheel.move(X-Xinc,Y);

        X=rear_wheel.get_x();
        Y=rear_wheel.get_y();
        rear_wheel.move(X-Xinc,Y);

        X=body.get_x();
        Y=body.get_y();
        body.move(X-Xinc,Y);

        X=screen.get_x();
        Y=screen.get_y();
        screen.move(X-Xinc,Y);

        X=roof.get_x();
        Y=roof.get_y();
        roof.move(X-Xinc,Y);

        X=rear_screen.get_x();
        Y=rear_screen.get_y();
        rear_screen.move(X-Xinc,Y);
}

delay(1);

_setvideomode(_DEFAULTMODE);

}
```

Summary

□ In C++ objects are implemented as instances of classes.

□ A subclass (child) may be derived from a base class (parent), allowing all the protected and public members of the base class to be inherited by the derived class.

□ A derived class may inherit from more than one base class.

□ Inherited methods can be overloaded in the derived class.

□ Polymorphism is a way of giving an action one name that is shared up and down an object hierarchy, with each object in the hierarchy implementing the action in a way appropriate to itself.

□ Virtual methods allow methods declared in a base class to be implemented differently in derived classes.

□ Virtual functions support polymorphism in C++.

Object-oriented programming techniques have the following benefits:

□ OOP encourages the use of libraries of objects. Software can be reused and can also be extended, which in turn should help to reduce development costs.

□ The maintainability of software is improved in terms of better standards of documentation, and changes to software can take place at a local level.

□ Software development time is shorter and development costs are lower.

□ Reliability of software is improved.

Review Questions

1. Name a factor that led to the necessity for object-oriented programming.

2. State three advantages of object-oriented programming over conventional procedural programming.

3. Distinguish between the terms parent class and child class.

4. Define the term inheritance.

5. True or false - a class may inherit from more than one parent class.

6. What is an abstract class?

7. True or false - with public inheritance everything is inherited unless overrriden by a derived class.

8. True or false - a derived class can access the private areas of a base class.

9. True or false - with private inheritance everything is hidden unless otherwise specified in the derived class.

10. Define the term polymorphism.

11. True or false - for methods to be polymorphic, they must be part of the same inheritance hierarchy.

12. What is compile-time binding?

13. What is run-time binding?

14. True or false - run-time binding requires certain methods to be described as being virtual.

15. What is a virtual method table?

16. True or false - constructors cannot be virtual.

17. Why and when should destructors be declared as being virtual?

18. True or false - it is necessary to declare only the base class methods as being virtual.

19. What is a pure virtual function?

20. Describe the four stages that should be followed in object-oriented design.

Programming Exercises

21. Study the following segment of code.

(a) Is the definition of `function_2` valid?

(b) If a *global* function called `function_2` does not belong to any class, how could this function be invoked from within a method of `derived_class`?

```
class base_class
{
  private:
    int value;
  public:
    void function_1(void);
};

class derived_class : public base-class
{
  public:
    void function_2(void){ function_1(); value = 10;}
};
```

22. Study the following segment of code.

```
class base_class
{
  private:
    int value;
  protected:
    void initialize_value(int val){value=val};
  public:
    void function_1(void);
    void function_1(int value);
    void function_2(void);
};

class derived_class : public base-class
{
  public:
    void function_3(void);
    void function_1(void);
};


base_class object_1;
derived_class object_2;
```

Which of the following lines of code are not valid?

```
(a)    object_1.function_1();
(b)    object_1.function_1(20);
(c)    object_1.function_2();
(d)    object_1.function_2(30);
(e)    object_1.function_3();
(f)    object_2.function_1();
(g)    object_2.function_1(20);
(h)    object_2.function_2();
(i)    object_2.function_2(30);
(j)    object_2.function_3();
```

23. Discover the errors in the following segment of code.

```
class shapes
{
  public:
    void draw_at(int X, int Y) =0;
    void move_to(int X, int Y);
};

class circle  public shapes
{
  private:
    int radius;
  public:
    virtual circle(int rad):radius(rad){};
    void draw_at(int X, int Y);
};

void main(void)
{
  shapes S;
  circle C(a);
  shapes *shape_ptr = &C;

  shape_ptr -> draw_at(110,115);
  C.move_to(200,200);
}
```

Programming Problems

24. (a) Extend the definition and implementation of the classes found in the files shapes_3.h and shapes_3.cpp, respectively, to include the class of a triangle in any orientation. The coordinates of the vertexes are (X1,Y1), (X2,Y2) and (X3,Y3).

(b) Write a program to test the constructors and methods of the triangle class created in part (a).

25.(a) Employees in a company are divided into the classes of *employee, hourly_paid, sales_commissioned,* and *executive* for the purpose of calculating their weekly wages or monthly salaries.

The data to be maintained for each class may be summarized as follows:

employee class	name of employee
hourly_paid class	rate of pay
	total weekly hours worked
sales_commissioned class	percentage commission on total sales
	total sales for month
executive class	incremental point on annual salary scale

The methods used in each class may be summarized as follows:

employee class	get_name
	compute_pay- as a pure virtual function
hourly_paid class	get_rate
	get_hours
	compute_pay
sales_commissioned class	get_percentage
	get_sales
	compute_pay
executive class	get_increment
	compute pay

Note: to compute the monthly gross wage of an executive, it will be necessary to construct a one-dimensional array containing an increasing annual salary scale. Each subscript to the array equates to an incremental point on the salary scale.

Draw a hierarchy diagram for the classes and create files that define and implement the classes.

(b) Write a program to test the constructors and methods of the classes created in part (a).

Appendix A - Summary of ANSI C Standard Library Functions

The ANSI C library is divided into fifteen sections, with each section being described by one of the following header files.

```
<assert.h>    <ctype.h>     <errno.h>     <float.h>     <limits.h>
<locale.h>    <math.h>      <setjmp.h>    <signal.h>    <stdarg.h>
<stddef.h>    <stdio.h>     <stdlib.h>    <string.h>    <time.h>
```

Many of the header files contain function declarations, type definitions, constant definitions and/or macro definitions. If a source file contains a reference to any of these items then the appropriate header file should be included using **#include** at the beginning of the source file.

Within this appendix the contents of all the header files has been summarised.

A.1 <assert.h> Diagnostics

void assert(expression);

This header contains only the assert macro which enables a program to perform self-checks. If *expression* is zero (false), assert prints a message to stdout and calls abort. The message has the format:

```
Assertion failed: expression, file filename, line linenumber
```

Note - If #define NDEBUG 1 occurs prior to #include <assert.h> the call to assert is ignored.

```
/*
app_A\p1.c program to demonstrate the assert function
*/

#include <stdio.h>
#include <assert.h>

void test(char character)
{

    /* assertion character is lower case letter or digit */
    assert(islower(character) || isdigit(character));
    printf("character %c lower case or digit\n", character);
}

void main(void)
{
    test('3');
    test('a');
    test('!');
}
```

Results

```
character 3 lower case or digit
character a lower case or digit
Assertion failed: islower(character)||isdigit(character),file p1.c,line 12
Abnormal Program Termination
```

A.2 `<ctype.h>` Character Handling

The header contains functions for testing and converting characters. In the following list, the declaration of each function is followed by a description of the value returned by each function. Note - a return value of `!=0` (non-zero) implies *true* when used in a conditional statement.

`int isalnum(int c);`	!=0 if c is an alphanumeric character in range 'A'-'Z', 'a'-'z', or '0'-'9'
`int isalpha(int c);`	!=0 if c is an alphabetic character in range 'A'-'Z' or 'a'-'z'
`int iscntrl(int c);`	!=0 if c is a control character in range 0x0 - 0x1F or 0x7F
`int isdigit(int c);`	!=0 if c is a digit in range '0'-'9'
`int isgraph(int c);`	!=0 if c is a printable character (excluding space) in range 0x21 - 0x7E
`int islower(int c);`	!=0 if c is lower case letter in range 'a'-'z'
`int isprint(int c);`	!=0 if c is a printable character in range 0x20 - 0x7E
`int ispunct(int c);`	!=0 if c is a punctuation character in range 0x21 - 0x2F, 0x3A - 0x40, 0x5B - 0x60, 0x7B - 0x7E
`int isspace(int c);`	!=0 if c is a white space character in range 0x9 - 0xD or 0x20
`int isupper(int c);`	!=0 if c is upper case letter in range 'A'-'Z'
`int isxdigit(int c);`	!=0 if c is a hexadecimal digit in range '0'-'9', 'A'-'F' or 'a'-'f'
`int tolower(int c);`	return lower case value of character c in range 'a'-'z'
`int toupper(int c);`	return upper case value of character c in range 'A'-'Z'

A.3 `<errno.h>` Errors

If this header is included in a program, then it is possible to detect whether an error has occurred during calls to certain library functions. After an error occurs the system variable `errno` will contain information about the error. The following symbolic constants are defined in the header file `<errno.h>` in response to either the DOS or UNIX error codes.

/* Dos Error Codes */

EZERO	0	/* No Error	*/
EINVFN	1	/* Invalid function code	*/
ENOENT	2	/* File not found	*/
ENOPATH	3	/* Path not found	*/
EMFILE	4	/* Too many open files	*/
EACCES	5	/* Access denied	*/
EBADF	6	/* Invalid handle	*/
E2BIG	7	/* Memory blocks destroyed	*/
ENOMEM	8	/* Insufficient Memory	*/
EINVMEM	9	/* Invalid memory block address	*/
EINVENV	10	/* Invalid environment	*/
EINVFMT	11	/* Invalid format	*/
EINVACC	12	/* Invalid access code	*/
EINVDAT	13	/* Invalid data	*/

```
ENODEV    15        /* Invalid drive                      */
ECURDIR   16        /* Attempt to remove CurDir           */
ENOTSAM   17        /* Not same device                    */
ENMFILE   18        /* No more files                      */
```

/* RTL error codes */

```
EINVAL      19      /* Invalid argument                   */
ENOTDIR     20      /* Not directory                      */
EISDIR      21      /* Is directory                       */
ENOEXEC     22      /* Corrupted exec file                */
EMLINK      32      /* Cross-device link                  */
EDOM        33      /* Math argument                      */
ERANGE      34      /* Result too large                   */
EDEADLOCK   36      /* file locking deadlock              */
EEXIST      80      /* File exists MSDOS 3.0 +            */
EFAULT      -1      /* Unknown error                      */
EPERM       -1      /* UNIX - not in  MSDOS               */
ESRCH       -1      /* UNIX - not in  MSDOS               */
EINTR       -1      /* UNIX - not in  MSDOS               */
EIO         -1      /* UNIX - not in  MSDOS               */
ENXIO       -1      /* UNIX - not in  MSDOS               */
ECHILD      -1      /* UNIX - not in  MSDOS               */
EAGAIN      -1      /* UNIX - not in  MSDOS               */
ENOTBLK     -1      /* UNIX - not in  MSDOS               */
EBUSY       -1      /* UNIX - not in  MSDOS               */
ENFILE      -1      /* UNIX - not in  MSDOS               */
ENOTTY      -1      /* UNIX - not in  MSDOS               */
ETXTBSY     -1      /* UNIX - not in  MSDOS               */
EFBIG       -1      /* UNIX - not in  MSDOS               */
ENOSPC      -1      /* UNIX - not in  MSDOS               */
ESPIPE      -1      /* UNIX - not in  MSDOS               */
EROFS       -1      /* UNIX - not in  MSDOS               */
EPIPE       -1      /* UNIX - not in  MSDOS               */
EUCLEAN     -1      /* UNIX - not in  MSDOS               */
```

```
/*
app_A\p2.c program to demonstrate header <errno.h>
*/

#include <stdio.h>
#include <errno.h>
#include <math.h>
#include <limits.h>

void main(void)
{
    printf("%10.2G\n", sqrt(-1.0));
    printf("%d\n", errno);
    printf("%10.2G\n", exp(INT_MAX));
    printf("%d\n", errno);
}
```

Results

```
       0
33
  1.8E+308
34
```

Notice from the output that errno 33 (EDOM) indicates an error with the maths argument in sqrt(-1.0) and errno 34 (ERANGE) indicates that the result exp(INT_MAX) is too large.

A.4 <float.h> Characteristics of Floating Types

Supplies macros that define the range and accuracy of floating-point types.

```
DBL_DIG          15                        /* decimal digits of precision  */
DBL_MANT_DIG     53                        /* bits in mantissa             */
DBL_MAX_10_EXP   308                       /* maximum decimal exponent     */
DBL_MAX_EXP      1024                      /* maximum binary exponent      */
DBL_MIN_10_EXP   -307                      /* minimum decimal exponent     */
DBL_MIN_EXP      -1021                     /* minimum binary exponent      */
DBL_RADIX        2                         /* exponent radix               */
DBL_ROUNDS       1                         /* addition rounding            */
DBL_EPSILON      2.2204460492503131e-016   /* 1.0+DBL_EPSILON != 1.0       */
DBL_MAX          1.7976931348623151e+308   /* maximum value                */
DBL_MIN          2.2250738585072014e-308   /* minimum positive value       */
```

631

```
FLT_DIG            6                          /* decimal digits of precision      */
FLT_GUARD          0
FLT_MANT_DIG       24                         /* bits in mantissa                 */
FLT_MAX_10_EXP     38                         /* maximum decimal exponent         */
FLT_MAX_EXP        128                        /* maximum binary exponent          */
FLT_MIN_10_EXP     -37                        /* minimum decimal exponent         */
FLT_MIN_EXP        -125                       /* minimum binary exponent          */
FLT_NORMALIZE      0
FLT_RADIX          2                          /* exponent radix                   */
FLT_ROUNDS         1                          /* addition rounding chops          */
FLT_EPSILON        1.192092896e-07            /* smallest such that 1.0+FLT_EPSILON != 1.0 */
FLT_MAX            3.402823466e+38            /* maximum value                    */
FLT_MIN            1.175494351e-38            /* minimum positive value           */

LDBL_DIG           19                         /* decimal digits of precision      */
LDBL_EPSILON       5.42101086242752217 06e-20
                                              /* smallest such that 1.0+LDBL_EPSILON != 1.0 */
LDBL_MANT_DIG      64                         /* bits in mantissa                 */
LDBL_MAX           1.189731495357231765e+4932L  /* maximum value                 */
LDBL_MAX_10_EXP    4932                       /* maximum decimal exponent         */
LDBL_MAX_EXP       16384                      /* maximum binary exponent          */
LDBL_MIN           3.3621031431120935063e-4932L /* minimum positive value */
LDBL_MIN_10_EXP    (-4931)                    /* minimum decimal exponent         */
LDBL_MIN_EXP       (-16381)                   /* minimum binary exponent          */
LDBL_RADIX         2                          /* exponent radix                   */
LDBL_ROUNDS        DBL_ROUNDS                 /* addition rounding                */
```

A.5 `<limits.h>` Sizes of Integral Types

Supplies macros that define the range of integer and character types.

```
CHAR_BIT           8                 /* number of bits in a char                */
CHAR_MIN           (-128)            /* minimum if signed char, otherwise (0)   */
CHAR_MAX           127               /* maximum if signed char, otherwise (255) */
MB_LEN_MAX         1                 /* multiple byte length - maximum 1 byte   */
SCHAR_MAX          127               /* maximum signed char                     */
SCHAR_MIN          (-128)            /* minimum signed char                     */
UCHAR_MAX          255               /* maximum unsigned char                   */
```

```
SHRT_MAX      32767              /* maximum short integer           */
SHRT_MIN      (-32767-1)         /* minimum  short integer          */
USHRT_MAX     65535U             /* maximum unsigned short integer  */
INT_MAX       32767              /* maximum integer                 */
INT_MIN       (-32767-1)         /* minimum integer                 */
UINT_MAX      0xFFFFU            /* maximum unsigned integer        */
LONG_MAX      2147483647L        /* maximum long integer            */
LONG_MIN      (-2147483647L-1)   /* minimum long integer            */
ULONG_MAX     4294967295UL       /* maximum unsigned long integer   */
```

A.6 <locale.h> Localization

The header provides functions to control aspects of the library that depend upon the country or other geographical location. These include the character used as the decimal point, the currency symbol and the appearance of the date and the time.

struct lconv *localeconv(void);

The function localeconv returns a pointer to the structure specifying the current locale and is specified as follows in the header file <locale.h>

```
struct lconv    {
                char *decimal_point;
                char *thousands_sep;
                char *grouping;
                char *int_curr_symbol;
                char *currency_symbol;
                char *mon_decimal_point;
                char *mon_thousands_sep;
                char *mon_grouping;
                char *positive_sign;
                char *negative_sign;
                char int_frac_digits;
                char frac_digits;
                char p_cs_precedes;
                char p_sep_by_space;
                char n_cs_precedes;
                char n_sep_by_space;
                char p_sign_posn;
                char n_sign_posn;
                };
```

char *setlocale(int category, const char *locale);

The function `setlocale` may be used to set or query the program's current locale, where category specifies the action requested and can take one of the following values.

LC_ALL	specifies the entire locale
LC_COLLATE	specifies the behaviour of functions `strcoll` and `strxfrm`
LC_CTYPE	specifies the behaviour of the character and multi-byte functions
LC_MONETARY	specifies the formatting information returned by `localeconv`
LC_NUMERIC	specifies the decimal point character for the formatted I/O functions and string conversion functions
LC_TIME	specifies the behaviour of the `strftime` function

`locale` points to a specification for the locale. A value of "C" for `locale` specifies the minimal C environment; a value of "" specifies the native environment.

If a valid string is given for the `locale` argument, the area of the locale specified by `category` is changed to that value. If an error occurs a `NULL` value is returned. If the value of `locale` is "", the current setting for that portion of the locale is returned and the locale remains unchanged.

```c
/*
app_A\p3.c program to demonstrate <locale.h>
*/

#include <stdio.h>
#include <locale.h>
#include <limits.h>

void main(void)
{
    struct lconv *current_locale;

    current_locale = localeconv();

    printf("%s\n", current_locale->decimal_point);
    printf("%s\n", current_locale->currency_symbol);
    printf("%d\n", current_locale->frac_digits);

    setlocale(LC_MONETARY, "");

    current_locale = localeconv();
    printf("%s\n", current_locale->currency_symbol);
}
```

Results

```
  .
  $
127
  £
```

634

A.7 <math.h> Mathematics

The header provides trigonometric, hyperbolic, exponential, logarithmic and several miscellaneous mathematical functions. These functions normally expect parameters of type `double` and return values of type `double`.

`double acos(double x);`	returns the arc cosine of x
`double asin(double x);`	returns the arc sine of x
`double atan(double x);`	returns the arc tangent of x
`double atan2(double x, double y);`	returns the arc tangent of y/x
`double ceil(double x);`	returns the result of rounding x towards infinity to the nearest integer
`double cos(double x);`	returns the cosine of x
`double cosh(double x);`	returns the hyperbolic cosine of x
`double exp(double x);`	returns the exponential result of x
`double fabs(double x);`	returns the absolute value of x
`double floor(double x);`	returns the result of rounding x towards zero to the nearest integer
`double fmod(double x, double y);`	returns the remainder after the division x/y
`double frexp(double val, int *exptr);`	function returns the mantissa and stores the exponent in the location pointed at by exptr
`double ldexp(double x, int exp);`	returns $x*2^{exp}$
`double log(double x);`	returns the natural logarithm of x
`double log10(double x);`	returns the base 10 logarithm of x
`double modf(double x, double *intptr);`	returns the signed fractional part of x and stores the integer part at the location pointed at by intptr
`double pow(double x, double y);`	returns x raised to the power of y
`double sin(double x);`	returns the sine of x
`double sinh(double x);`	returns the hyperbolic sine of x
`double sqrt(double x);`	returns the square root of x
`double tan(double x);`	returns the tangent of x
`double tanh(double x);`	returns the hyperbolic tangent of x

A.8 `<setjmp.h>` Non-local Jumps

If function `main` calls function `A`, and in turn function `A` calls function `B`, then control normally passes back to `A` upon exiting from `B`, and then to `main` upon exiting from `A`. However, it is possible to return from function `B` directly to `main` without returning via function `A`. Such a change in behaviour is possible by using the following functions.

```
void longjmp(jmp_buf env, int retval);
int setjmp(jmp_buf env);
```

The `longjmp` function restores the processor environment previously saved in `env` by `setjmp`. These functions provide a mechanism for executing inter-function gotos, and are usually used to pass control to error recovery code.

A call to `setjmp` causes the current processor environment to be saved in `env`. A following call to `longjmp` restores the saved environment and causes execution to resume at a point immediately after the corresponding `setjmp` call. Execution continues with `retval` as the return value from `setjmp`.

As long as `longjmp` is called before the function calling `setjmp` returns, all variables local to the routine will have the same value as when `setjmp` was called. However, register variables may not be restored. Use the `volatile` keyword to ensure that local variables are properly restored.

Essentially `setjmp` marks a place in a function so that `longjmp` can be used to return to that place later.

The function `setjmp` returns 0 after saving the processor environment. If `setjmp` returns after a call to `longjmp`, it returns the value argument of `longjmp`, which is guaranteed to be non-zero.

```
/*
app_A\p4.c program to demonstrate the use of non-local jumps
*/

#include <stdio.h>
#include <setjmp.h>

typedef enum {false, true} boolean;
jmp_buf mark;

void B(void);

void A(void)
{
    printf("function A\n");
    B();
    printf("returned to function A\n");
}
```

```
void B(void)
{
    static boolean jump = false;

    if (jump)
        longjmp(mark, 1);
    else
        printf("function B\n");

    jump = true;
}

void main(void)
{
    int counter = 0;

    for (; counter <= 1; counter++)
    {
        printf("function main\n");
        if (setjmp(mark))
            printf("jumped back to main from B\n");
        else
            A();
    }
}
```

Results

```
function main
function A
function B
returned to function A
function main
function A
jumped back to main from B
```

A.9 <signal.h> Signal Handling

The header provides facilities for handling exceptional conditions including interrupts and run-time errors.

`int raise(int sig);`

The function `raise` sends a signal, `sig` to the current process. The default action for that signal will be taken unless a new action was defined previously by a call to signal. The return value is 0 if this call is successful and non-zero otherwise.

```
void (* signal(int sig, void(*func)(int))) (int) ;
```

The function `signal` sets the signal handler for signal `sig` to the value `func`. The function returns the previous value of the signal handler. If an error occurred, a value of `SIG_ERR` is returned and `errno` is set to `EINVAL`, indicating an invalid value for `sig`.

The argument `sig` can take any one of the following values defined in `<signal.h>`

```
SIGINT          /* interrupt - corresponds to DOS 3.x int 23H     */
SIGILL          /* illegal op code                                */
SIGFPE          /* floating point error                           */
SIGSEGV         /* segment violation                              */
SIGTERM         /* Software termination signal from kill          */
SIGABRT         /* abnormal termination triggered by abort call   */
```

The argument `func` must be one of the following constants or the function address of a user defined signal handler.

```
SIG_DFL         /* default signal action    */
SIG_IGN         /* ignore                   */
```

```c
/*
app_A\p5.c program to demonstrate the functions raise and signal
*/

#include <stdio.h>
#include <signal.h>

void warning(void)
{
    printf("interrupt - Ctrl C pressed\n");
}

void abort_program(void)
{
    printf("program termination - raised SIGABRT\n");
    exit(errno);
}

void main(void)
{
    signal(SIGINT, warning);
    getchar();
    signal(SIGABRT, abort_program);
    raise(SIGABRT);
}
```

Results

```
^C
interrupt - Ctrl C pressed

program termination - raised SIGABRT
```

A.10 <stdarg.h> Variable arguments

The header provides functions that allow the programmer to write functions containing variable-length parameter lists. The variable argument list macros provide a portable method of accessing arguments to a function taking a variable number of arguments.

```
type va_arg(va_list argptr, type);   returns the current and succeeding arguments
void va_end(va_list argptr);          sets the argument pointer to NULL
void va_start(va_list argptr);        sets the argument pointer (argptr), declared as
                                      type va_list, to the first argument in the list passed
                                      to the function
```

A.11 <stddef.h> Common Definitions

The header provides definitions of frequently used types and macros. A partial listing of the header illustrates definitions for the types ptrdiff_t, size_t, wchar_t and macros offset and NULL.

```
typedef int ptrdiff_t;

typedef unsigned size_t;

typedef unsigned char wchar_t;

#define offsetof(st, member) (size_t)(&((st*)0)->member)

#define NULL    0
```

A.12 `<stdio.h>` Input/ Output

The header provides functions for text and binary I/O and file operations.

`void clearerr(FILE *st);` clears the `error` and EOF flags on stream `st`.

`int fclose(FILE *st);` closes the stream `st`, flushing any buffer associated with the stream; returns 0 if `st` was successfully closed, otherwise returns EOF.

`int feof(FILE *st);` determines whether the stream `st` has reached the end of the file; returns non-zero for end of file, otherwise returns 0.

`int ferror(FILE *st);` tests stream `st`'s error flag; returns non-zero if an error has occurred, otherwise returns 0.

`int fflush(FILE *st);` flushes the stream `st`; if the last operation involving the stream was output, the contents of the buffer are written to the associated file; if the stream's last operation was input, the state of the stream remains unaltered; returns 0 if successful, otherwise returns EOF.

`int fgetc(FILE *st);` reads an unsigned character (converted to an `int`) from the current position of stream `st`, and increments the stream pointer, if any; returns the character read from stream `st` as an integer value; otherwise returns EOF.

`int fgetpos(FILE *st, fpos_t *fp);` gets the current value of the stream's file position indicator and store this value in the object to which `fp` points; if successful returns 0, otherwise returns non-zero.

`char *fgets(char *string, int num, FILE *st);` reads a string from the stream `st` and stores it at `string`; num specifies the maximum length for `string`; returns the string read from the stream `st`; if error occurs returns NULL.

`int flushall(void);` flushes all open streams; if the last operation involving the stream was output, the contents of the buffer are written to the associated file; if the stream's last operation was input, the state of the stream remains unaltered; returns the number of open streams.

`FILE *fopen(const char *path, const char *type);` opens the file specified by `path` and associates a stream with that file; the character string `type` specifies the access mode for the file, and can be any of the following:

`"r"`   read only - file must exist
`"w"`   write only - if the file exists its contents will be overwritten, otherwise it is created
`"a"`   append - write only from the end of the file
`"r+"`   read and write - file must exist
`"w+"`   read and write
`"a+"`   read and append - if the file does not exist it is created

In addition to these values , the characters t or b may be included after the first character of type to specify text or binary translation modes.

If successful the function returns a pointer to the open stream, otherwise returns a NULL pointer.

int fprintf(FILE *st, const char *format, ...); provides formatted output to the stream st; returns the number of characters printed.

int fputc(int c, FILE *st); writes a character c (converted to an unsigned char) to the current position of stream st, and increments the stream pointer; if successful returns the character written as an integer value, otherwise returns -1 indicating an error or end of file condition.

int fputs(const char *string, FILE *stream); writes string to the specified stream at the current position in the stream; the null terminator is not copied; if successful the function returns the last character written, otherwise the function returns EOF.

size_t fread(void *buffer, size_t size, size_t nritems, FILE *stream); reads into array buffer, up to nritems, each of specified size from the stream; returns the number of complete items read.

void free(void *buffer); de-allocates a block of memory previously allocated with malloc, calloc or realloc.

FILE *freopen(const char *path, const char *type, FILE *stream); closes the file specified by stream and then reassigns the stream to the file specified by path; the character string type specifies the access mode for the file (see function fopen); returns a pointer to the open stream, otherwise returns a NULL pointer.

int fscanf(FILE *stream, const char *format, [arguments] ...); reads data from the current position in the specified stream; the data are read into locations specified by arguments, each of which must be a pointer to an appropriate type; the types are determined by the contents of the format string. The function returns the number of fields successfully converted and assigned, otherwise returns 0 indicating that no fields were assigned or returns EOF indicating an attempt to read past the end of file.

int fseek(FILE *stream, long offset, int origin); moves the file pointer associated with the specified stream to a location that is offset bytes from the specified origin - the next operation on the stream will take place at the new location; if successful returns 0, otherwise returns non-zero.

int fsetpos(FILE *st, const fpos_t *fp); sets the current value of the stream st's file position indicator to the value pointed to by fp; if successful returns 0, otherwise non-zero.

long ftell(FILE *st); returns the current position of the file pointer relative to the beginning of the file associated with stream st, otherwise returns -1L for an error.

int fwrite(const void *buffer, size_t size, size_t num, FILE *st); writes up to num blocks, each of size bytes, from buffer to stream st; the stream pointer is incremented by the number of bytes written; returns the number of complete items actually written; if an error occurs the returned value will be less than num.

int getc(FILE *st); reads a character from the current position of stream st and increments the stream pointer; returns the character read as an integer value, otherwise returns EOF.

int getchar(void); reads a character from stdin; returns the character read as an integer, otherwise returns EOF.

char *gets(char *buf); reads a string from the stream stdin and stores it at buf; returns buf if successful, otherwise returns NULL.

void perror(const char *message); prints an error message to stderr; the argument message is printed first, followed by the system defined error message for the last error that occurred.

int printf(const char *format[, argument] ...); formats and prints a series of arguments to stdout; format is a string consisting or ordinary characters, escape sequences and format specifications corresponding to the list of arguments passed to printf after format. The function returns the number of characters printed.

int putc(int ch, FILE *st); writes a character ch on to the stream st at the current position and increments the stream pointer; returns the character written as an integer, otherwise returns EOF.

int putchar(int ch); writes a character ch on the steam stdout; returns the character written as an integer, otherwise returns EOF.

int puts(const char *s); copies the string s to stdout, replacing the string's terminating null character with a new line character (\n); returns 0 if successful, otherwise returns EOF.

int remove(const char *path); deletes the file specified by path; returns 0 if the file was successfully deleted, otherwise returns -1.

int rename(const char *oldname, const char *newname); changes the name of the file or directory specified by oldname to newname - oldname must exist; returns 0 if the file was successfully renamed, otherwise returns -1.

void rewind(FILE *st); sets the file pointer associated with st to the beginning of the file and clears the error and end of file indicators

int scanf(const char *format, [arguments] ...); reads characters from stdin and stores the converted data in the locations given by arguments; format is a string consisting or ordinary characters, escape sequences and format specifications corresponding to the list of arguments passed to scanf after the format argument. The function returns the number of fields converted and assigned; return value 0 indicates that no fields were assigned; return value -1 indicates an attempt was made to read past the end of file.

void setbuf(FILE *st, char *buffer); allows the user to control buffering for stream st - st refers to an open stream before it has been read or written; if buffer is not NULL it must point to a character array of at least BUFSIZ defined in <stdio.h>. If the argument buffer is NULL the stream will be unbuffered.

int setvbuf(FILE *st, char *buffer, int type, size_t size); allows the user to control buffering for stream st; the arguments st and buffer are the same as for setbuf; type specifies the buffering mode:

_IOFBF   full buffering
_IOLBF   line buffering - buffer flushed whenever a line-feed character is output
_IONBF   no buffer used

The argument `size` specifies the size of the buffer to be used. The function returns 0 if successful, otherwise returns non-zero.

`int sprintf(char *s,const char *format, ...);` provides formatted output to a character string.

`int sscanf(const char *s, const char *format, ...);` provides formatted input, taking its input from a character string.

`FILE *tmpfile(void);` creates a temporary file, opening it for updating in a binary mode; the file is automatically deleted when it is closed or when the current process terminates; returns a pointer to the temporary file's stream; if the file cannot be created the value `NULL` is returned.

`char *tmpnam(char *sptr);` creates a unique file name which can be used as a temporary file; `sptr` is a pointer to an array of characters; returns a pointer to the newly created filename, otherwise returns a `NULL` pointer.

`int ungetc(int c, FILE *st);` puts the character `c`, converted to an unsigned integer `char`, back on to stream `st`; returns the character put back, otherwise returns `EOF`.

A.13 `<stdlib.h>` General Utilities

The header provides functions for converting numbers to strings and strings to numbers, random number generation, memory management, searching, sorting, operations upon multi-byte characters and strings, and miscellaneous functions.

`void abort(void)`; writes the message `Abnormal Program Termination` to `stderr` and calls `raise(SIGABRT)`

`int abs(int num)`; returns the absolute value of `num`

`int atexit(void (*func)(void))`; places the function pointer `func` onto a stack to be called from the function `exit` when the process terminates; functions are called on a LIFO basis and cannot take parameters or return any value. The function returns 0 if a function was successfully placed on the stack, otherwise returns a non-zero value if the stack was full.

`double atof(const char *s)`; converts the string argument `s` to double precision; returns the result of the conversion, otherwise returns 0 if the input string cannot be interpreted as a number.

`int atoi(const char *s)`; converts the string argument `s` to an integer value; returns the result of the conversion, otherwise returns 0 if the input string cannot be interpreted as a number.

`long atol(const char *s)`; converts the string argument `s` to a long integer value; returns the result of the conversion, otherwise returns 0 if the input string cannot be interpreted as a number.

```
void *bsearch( const void *key,
               const void *base,
               size_t num,
               size_t width,
               int (*compare)(const void *e1, const void *e2));
```

performs a binary search on a sorted array; returns a pointer to the first matching element if found, otherwise the value `NULL` is returned.

`void *calloc(size_t number, size_t size)`; allocates a specified `number` of elements, each of `size` bytes, from the heap; returns a pointer to the allocated storage, otherwise returns `NULL` to indicate insufficient storage

`div_t div(int num, int den)`; divides `num` by `den`, returning the quotient in the `div_t` structure member `quot` and the remainder in the structure member `rem`.

`void exit(int status)`; terminates the calling process.

`char *getenv(const char *name)`; searches the environment variables for an entry corresponding to `name`; returns a pointer to the environment variable containing the string value of `name`; if the variable is not defined the return value will be `NULL`.

`long labs(long num)`; returns the absolute value of its long integer argument `num`.

struct ldiv_t ldiv(long num, long den); divides num by den, storing the quotient in the structure member quot and the remainder in the structure member rem; returns a structure of type ldiv_t which contains members for quotient and remainder. Note ldiv_t is defined in stdlib.h as:

```
typedef struct {
             long quot;
             long rem;
        } ldiv_t;
```

void *malloc(size_t size); allocates a block of at least size bytes from the heap; returns a void pointer to the allocated space, otherwise returns NULL.

int mblen(const char *s, size_t n); determines the number of bytes comprising the multi-byte character to which s points where n specifies the maximum number of bytes in a multi-byte character. If s points to a null character returns 0, otherwise returns 1. (Note implementation dependent).

size_t mbstowcs(wchar_t *pwcs, const char *s, size_t n); converts a sequence of multi-byte characters pointed to by s and stores them as codes at the addresses to which pwcs points; returns the number of characters copied.

int mbtowc(wchar_t *pwc, const char *s, size_t n); converts up to n bytes comprising the multi-byte character pointed to by s to a code representing that character and stores this code at pwc, provided that pwc is not NULL. If s points to the null character returns 0, otherwise returns 1. (Note implementation dependent).

void qsort(const void *base,
**   size_t num,**
**   size_t width,**
**   int(*compare)(const void *e1, const void *e2));**

qsort is an implementation of the Quicksort algorithm for sorting an array.

int rand(void); returns a pseudo-random number in the range 0 - RAND_MAX. A preceding call to srand can be used to set the random starting point.

void *realloc(void *buffer, size_t size); changes the size of a memory block (buffer) previously allocated from the heap by a call to calloc, malloc or realloc; size is the new number of bytes requested; returns a void pointer to the allocated space; if no space is available returns a NULL pointer.

void srand(unsigned seed); sets the starting point for the pseudo random number generator.

double strtod(const char *s, char **endptr); converts a string s to a double precision floating-point value; returns the double precision floating-point value. Note endptr is set to point at the character that stopped the scan. If the value could not be converted or if endptr is not NULL, endptr is set to s.

long strtol(const char *s, char **endptr, int base); converts a string s to a long integer value; returns the long integer value. Note endptr is set to point at the character that stopped the scan. If the value could not be converted or if endptr is not NULL, endptr is set to s.

unsigned long strtoul(const char *s, char **endptr, int base); converts a string s to an unsigned long integer value; returns the unsigned long integer value. Note endptr is set to point at the character that stopped the scan. If the value could not be converted or if endptr is not NULL, endptr is set to s.

size_t wcstombs(char *s, const wchar_t *pwcs, size_t n); converts the codes stored at the location to which pwcs points; these codes are converted to multi-byte characters and stored at the location to which s points; n is the maximum number of bytes to convert; returns the number of characters created.

int wctomb(const char *s, wchar_t wchar); returns the number of bytes needed to represent the code wchar as a multi-byte character and stores the multi-byte character at s. If s points to the null character returns 0, otherwise wctomb returns 1. (Note implementation dependent).

A.14 <string.h> String Handling

The header provides functions that perform string operations.

void *memchr(const void *buf, int c, size_t num); searches for character c in the first num bytes of buf; if c found returns a pointer to the first occurrence, otherwise returns NULL.

int memcmp(const void *s1, const void *s2, size_t num); compares the first num bytes of s1 and s2; returns an integer indicating the relationship of s1 and s2; if s1 is greater than, equal to or less than s2, return greater than zero, zero and less than zero respectively.

void *memcpy(void *dest, const void *source, size_t num); copies num bytes from source to dest; does not ensure that overlapping regions of memory are correctly copied; returns a pointer to dest.

void *memmove(void *dest, const void *source, size_t num); copies num bytes from source to dest; if regions of memory overlap, these regions are copied before being overwritten; returns a pointer to dest.

void *memset(void *s, int c, size_t num); sets the first num bytes of s to a specified character c; returns a pointer to s.

char *strcat(char *dest, const char *source); appends source to dest, terminating the new string with a null character; returns a pointer to the new string.

char *strchr(const char *s, int c); returns a pointer to the first occurrence of character c in string s; if character not found a NULL pointer is returned.

int strcmp(const char *s1, const char *s2); compares strings s1 and s2 and returns a value representing their relationship; if s1 is greater than, equal to or less than s2, return greater than zero, zero and less than zero respectively.

int strcoll(const char *s1, const char *s2); compares strings s1 and s2, both interpreted as appropriate to the LC_COLLATE category of the current locale, otherwise similar to strcmp.

char *strcpy(char *dest, const char *source); copies string source to dest and returns a pointer to dest.

size_t strcspn(const char *s1, const char *s2); returns the index of the first character in s1 that belongs to the set of characters in s2. Returns the length of the substring of s1 that contains no characters from s2. If the first character in s1 is contained in s2, the function will return 0.

char *strdup(const char *s); allocates storage space for a copy of string s and copies string s to this new location; returns a pointer to the new copy of s, otherwise returns NULL if storage could not be allocated.

char *strerror(int errnum); maps errnum to an error message, returning a pointer to the error message string.

size_t strlen(const char *s); returns the length of string s excluding the terminating null character.

char *strncat(char *dest, const char *source, size_t num); appends up to num characters from string source to string dest, terminating the new string with a null character; returns a pointer to the new string.

int strncmp(const char *s1, const char *s2, size_t num); compares up to num characters from strings s1 and s2 and returns a value representing their relationship; if s1 is greater than, equal to or less than s2, return greater than zero, zero and less than zero respectively.

char *strncpy(char *dest, const char *source, size_t num); copies up to num bytes from string source to string dest; returns a pointer to dest.

char *strnset(char *s, int ch, size_t num); sets up to num bytes of string s to character ch; returns a pointer to string s.

char *strrchr(const char *s, int c); returns a pointer to the last occurrence of character c in string s, otherwise returns a NULL pointer if c is not found in s.

char *strrev(char *s); reverses the order of the characters in string s (except for the terminating null character); returns a pointer to string s.

char *strset(char *s, int ch); sets the bytes of string s to character ch; returns a pointer to string s.

size_t strspn(const char *s1, const char *s2); returns the index of the first character in s1 that does not belong to the set of characters in s2. The function returns the length of the substring of s1 that contains characters from s2. If the first character in s1 is not contained in s2, the function will return 0.

char *strstr(const char *s1, const char *s2); returns the address of the first occurrence of string s2 in s1. If the target st ing is not found, a NULL pointer is returned.

char *strtok(char *s1, const char *s2); separates string s1 into a series of tokens, with string s2 as the set of delimiters for the tokens; returns a pointer to a token.

size_t strxfrm(char *s1, const char *s2, size_t n); copies up to n bytes from string s2 to string s1; returns a pointer to s1.

A.15 <time.h> Date and Time

The header provides functions for manipulating the date and time.

char *asctime(const struct tm *time); converts time as a structure to a formatted character string containing exactly 26 characters; returns a pointer to the character string result.

time_t clock(void); returns a number that gives the number of seconds elapsed since the start of the current process if divided by the macro CLOCKS_PER_SECOND.

char *ctime(const time_t *tt); converts time tt seconds, stored as a time_t to a formatted character string; returns a pointer to a formatted character string.

double difftime(time_t t1, time_t t2); calculates the difference between two times t1 and t2; returns the elapsed time in seconds t1-t2.

struct tm *gmtime(const time_t *tt); converts the time value stored at tt to a structure tm; returns a pointer to the structure result.

struct tm *localtime(const time_t *tt); converts time stored at tt to a structure; the function uses global variables timezone and daylight to calculate local time; returns a pointer to the structure result.

time_t mktime(struct tm *timeptr); converts the local time, stored in the structure timeptr, into the format that would have been returned by a direct call to the function time; returns the encoded time.

```
size_t strftime( char *s,
                 size_t maxsize,
                 const char *format,
                 const struct tm *timeptr);
```

places characters into the array pointed to by s according to the format string format. No more than maxsize characters are output. Where s - specifies the location into which characters are to be placed; maxsize - specifies the maximum number of characters to place into the s array; format - specifies the format for the output and timeptr is a pointer to the structure containing the time. The format string consists of zero or more conversion specifiers and ordinary characters. Each conversion specifier is replaced by characters as specified in the following list. Other characters are output directly.

char	meaning
%a	abbreviated weekday name
%A	full weekday name
%b	abbreviated month name
%B	full month name
%c	date and time representation
%d	day of month as a decimal number 00 - 31
%H	hour as a decimal number 00 - 23
%I	month as a decimal number 01 - 12
%j	day of the year as a decimal number 001 - 366
%m	month as a decimal number 01 - 12
%M	minute as a decimal number 00-59
%p	AM or PM
%S	second as a decimal number
%U	week number of the year, with Sunday as day 1 - 00 - 53
%w	week day as a decimal number, with Sunday = 0 - 0 - 6
%W	week number of the year, with Monday as day 1 - 00 - 53
%x	date representation
%X	time representation
%y	year without century 00 - 99
%Y	year with century
%%	is replaced by %

time_t time(time_t *tt); returns the number of seconds elapsed since 00:00:00 Greenwich Mean Time, January 1st 1970

In a listing of the <time.h> file the following definitions are available

```
typedef long   time_t;
typedef long   clock_t;
#define CLOCKS_PER_SEC 100

struct tm {
          int   tm_sec;
          int   tm_min;
          int   tm_hour;
          int   tm_mday;
          int   tm_mon;
          int   tm_year;
          int   tm_wday;
          int   tm_yday;
          int   tm_isdst;
     };
```

```
/*
app_A\p6.c program to demonstrate the functions asctime,
clock, gmtime, localtime, strftime and time
*/

#include <stdio.h>
#include <time.h>

#define max_size 64

void main(void)
{
    time_t    time_now;
    struct tm *time_ptr;
    char      string[max_size];

    time(&time_now); /* get time in seconds */

    /* display local time */
    printf("%s\n\n", asctime(localtime(&time_now)));

    /* custom build the format of the date/ time */
    time_ptr = gmtime(&time_now);
    strftime(string, max_size, "%H:%M %p", time_ptr);

    /* display new format string */
    printf("%s\n\n", string);

    getchar(); /* introduce a delay */

    /* display elapsed time in seconds since start of program */
    printf("%d\n\n", (int) clock() / CLOCKS_PER_SEC);
}
```

Results

```
Fri Feb 10 18:59:32 1995

18.59 PM

10
```

Appendix B
Miscellany

☐ Various C operators have been introduced throughout the book with the culmination in the later chapters of the use of overloading operators. This appendix provides you with a summary of all the operators used in C together with their precedence and associativity.

☐ Only a small selection of escape sequence characters appear in the text. This appendix provides you with a complete list of all the escape sequence characters.

Symbol(s)	Name	Precedence	Associativity
[]	array subscripting	1	left
()	function call	1	left
.	structure and union member	1	left
->		1	left
++	increment (postfix)	1	left
--	decrement (postfix)	1	left
++	increment (prefix)	1	right
--	decrement (prefix)	1	right
&	address of	2	right
*	indirection	2	right
+	unary plus	2	right
-	unary minus	2	right
~	bitwise complement	2	right
!	logical negation	2	right
sizeof	size	2	right
()	cast	3	right
*	multiplicative	4	left
/		4	left
%		4	left
+	additive	5	left
-		5	left
<<	bitwise shift	6	left
>>		6	left
<	relational	7	left
>		7	left
<=		7	left
>=		7	left
==	equality	8	left
!=		8	left
&	bitwise and	9	left
^	bitwise exclusive or	10	left
|	bitwise inclusive or	11	left
&&	logical and	12	left
||	logical or	13	left
?:	conditional	14	right
=	assignment	15	right
*=		15	right
/=		15	right
%=		15	right
+=		15	right
-=		15	right
<<=		15	right
>>=		15	right
&=		15	right
^=		15	right
|=		15	right
,	comma	16	left

Table B.1 C Operators, their precedence and associativity

Table B.1 contains a complete table of C operators, showing the precedence and associativity of each operator.

The highest precedence is 1 and the lowest is 15. Operators of precedence 1 are postfix operators. Operators of precedence 2 (unary operators) are prefix operators, as is the `cast` operator of precedence 3. All the remaining operators, with the exception of the conditional operator, are binary operators.

The expression `- a * b - c` is equivalent to `((- a) * b) - c`, since unary minus has a precedence of 2, multiplication has a precedence of 4 and subtraction a precedence of 5.

When an expression contains two or more operators with the same precedence, associativity must be taken into consideration before the expression can be evaluated. When an operand is between two operators that have the same precedence, the operand is grouped with one or other of the operators depending on its associativity. For example, the addition and subtraction operators are both left-associative, so the following expression is evaluated from left to right.

`a = b + c - d;` is evaluated as `a = (b + c) - d;`

The indirection operator `*` is right associative with a precedence of 2 and the structure and union member `.` is left associative with a precedence of 1. The expression:

`*this.data` must be written as `(*this).data` otherwise the order of evaluation is incorrect.

Escape sequence characters, from the following set, can be represented in a control string.

\a	alert (bell)
\b	backspace
\f	form feed
\n	new-line
\r	carriage return
\t	horizontal tabulation
\v	vertical tabulation
\\	backslash
\?	question mark
\'	single quote
\"	double quote
\ddd	where ddd is an octal number in the range 0 to 377 and represents the ASCII code for the character
\xdd	where dd is a hexadecimal number in the range 0 to FF and represents the ASCII code for the character

Appendix C
Selected Answers

This appendix contains answers to selected questions taken from the Programming Exercises and Programming Problems sections from each chapter.

Chapter 1 - Programming Environment

28.

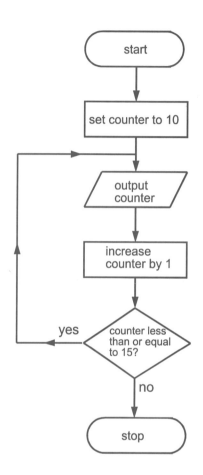

Desk Check

counter	counter <= 15?
10	
11	yes
12	yes
13	yes
14	yes
15	yes
16	no

30.

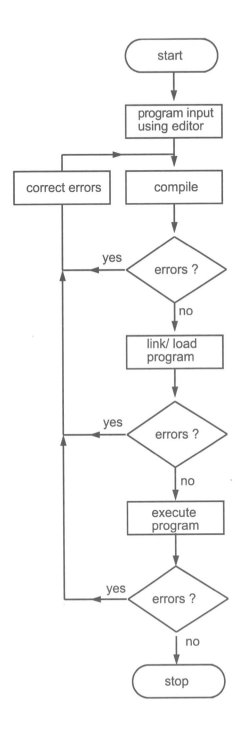

31.

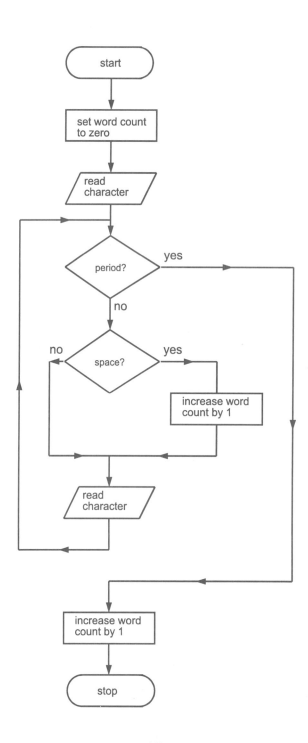

34(b).

The following listing shows the error message from the compiler. There is no semi-colon at the end of the line `printf("Computing can be fun ")`

```
#include <stdio.h>
void main(void)
{
   printf("Computing can be fun ")
   print("provided you get it right!");
}

Compiling...
c:\c1_34a.c
c:\c1_34a.c(5) : error C2146: syntax error : missing ';' before identifier
'print'
 CL returned error code 2.
C1_34A.EXE - 1 error(s), 0 warning(s)
```

(d).

The following listing shows the error message from the linker. In Standard C there is no statement to `print`; the statement must be changed to `printf`, similar to the line above it.

```
#include <stdio.h>
void main(void)
{
   printf("Computing can be fun ");
   print("provided you get it right!");
}

Compiling...
c:\c1_34c.c
Linking...

C1_34C.OBJ(c:\c1_34c.c) : error L2029: '_print' : unresolved external
```

(f).

The following listing shows the corrected program, with no compilation or linking errors. The text beneath the `0 error(s), 0 warning(s)` illustrates the output from the program to the screen.

```
#include <stdio.h>
void main(void)
{
  printf("Computing can be fun ");
  printf("provided you get it right!");
}
```

```
Compiling...
c:\c1_34e.c
Linking...
Binding resources...
Creating browser database...
C1_34E.EXE - 0 error(s), 0 warning(s)
```

```
Computing can be fun provided you get it right!
```

Chapter 2 - Data

27.

(b) `net-pay` embedded hyphen is illegal

(d) `cost of paper` embedded spaces are illegal

(f) `?X?Y` characters other than alphabetic, numeric digits or underscore are illegal

(g) `1856AD` identifier must begin with an alphabetic character or an underscore

(h) `float` is a keyword so illegal variable name

30.

(a) -8.74458E+02

(b) +1.23456E-03

(c) 1.234567890E+08

31.

(a) 0.3016E+40 overflow if stored as `float`, change to `double`.

(b) 1.23456E+09 accuracy of number cannot be maintained, change to `long double` to improve accuracy.

(c) -0.456E-42 underflow if stored as `float`, change to `double`.

32.

(a) 0.37948E+17 mantissa and exponent are correctly represented

(b) -0.263948E+01 loss of digits in the mantissa

(c) 0.739462E+03 loss of digits in the mantissa

(d) -0.176943E+40 exponent greater than 38 hence number too large to store - overflow

(e) 0.471E-40 exponent less than -38 hence number too small to store - underflow

33.

```
(a) const unsigned int octal_number = 0213;
(b) const int decimal_number = 45678;
(c) const unsigned long int hex_number = 0xFABC46;
(d) const char New_York[15] = "The Big Apple!";
```

34.

(a) $0234 = 2 \times 8^2 + 3 \times 8^1 + 4 \times 8^0 = 156$

(b) $0x56ABC = 5 \times 16^4 + 6 \times 16^3 + 10 \times 16^2 + 11 \times 16^1 + 12 \times 16^0 = 355004$

(c) $01011011 = 2^6 + 2^4 + 2^3 + 2^1 + 2^0 = 91$

38.

The variable declaration is `char single_character;`

A possible output from the program follows.

```
input a single character A
65
```

The significance of the number 65 is that it is the ASCII code for the letter A.

39.

The program containing the edits should appear as follows.

```
#include <stdio.h>
void main(void)
{
    char single_character;
```

```
    printf("input a single character ");
    scanf("%c",&single_character);
    printf("%d\n", single_character);
    printf("%o\n", single_character);
    printf("%X\n", single_character);
}
```

Possible results from running this program are given below.

```
input a single character A
65
101
41
```

The significance of the three numbers are that 101 and 41 are the octal and hexadecimal representations respectively of the decimal number 65.

Chapter 3 - Arithmetic, Input and Output

21.

(a)

A	B	C	D
36	36	36	36

(b)

A	B	C	D
10	14	29	89

(c)

A	B
48	50

(d)

X	Y
19	-13

(e)

X	Y	Z
18	3	54

(f)

A	B
12.5	2.0

(g)

A	B	X - assuming A, B and X are integers
16	3	5

(h) C   D   Y
     19   5   4

(i) D
     35

22.

(a) `(A+B)/C`
(b) `(W-X)/(Y+Z)`
(c) `(D-B)/(2*A)`
(d) `(A*A + B*B)/2`
(e) `(A-B)*(C-D)`
(f) `B*B-(4*A*C)`
(g) `(A*X*X)+(B*X)+C`

23.

(a) `AxB`
       ^ illegal operator
(b) `X*-Y`
       ^ combined operators do not produce an error, however clearer to write `X*(-Y)`
(c) `(64+B)/-6`
              ^ combined operators do not produce an error, however,
                clearer to write `(64+B)/(-6)`
(d) `(A-B)(A+B)`
            ^ no operator between parenthesis
(e) `-2/A+-6`
       ^ combined operators do not produce an error, however clearer to write `-2/A+(-6)`
(f) `1*(X-Y)`
     `2`
     ^ illegal division operator

26.

(a) control string should be `"%f"` and statement should be terminated with semi-colon

(b) no address operator, should be `&beta`, also statement should be terminated with semi-colon

(c) control string does not contain enough type declarations, should be `"%2d%2d%2d";` also a space appears before `day` and it should be `&day`

(d) control string specifies the type for a signed integer - don't worry at this stage about the type for an unsigned integer since you will rarely use it in this book - however, it happens to be u; also the address operator is missing.

31.

```
#include <stdio.h>

void main(void)
{
    const int secs_in_hour   = 3600;
    const int secs_in_minute = 60;

    long int elapsed_time;
         int hours, minutes, seconds;

    printf("input the elapsed time in seconds since Midnight ");
    scanf("%ld",&elapsed_time);

    hours = elapsed_time / secs_in_hour;
    elapsed_time = elapsed_time % secs_in_hour;

    minutes = elapsed_time / secs_in_minute;
    seconds = elapsed_time % secs_in_minute;

    printf("%d:%d:%d\n",hours, minutes, seconds);
}
```

Chapter 4 - Program Design

11.

(i) Structure Chart

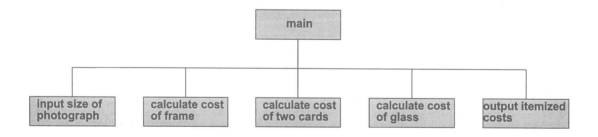

(ii) Algorithm

first level

1. input size of photograph
2. calculate costs
3. output itemized quotation

second level

1.1 input length of photograph
1.2 input width of photograph

2.1 calculate cost of frame
2.2 calculate cost of cards
2.3 calculate cost of glass
2.4 calculate total cost

3.1 display heading
3.2 display cost of frame
3.3 display cost of cards
3.4 display cost of glass
3.5 display total cost

(iii) Desk Check

size of photograph 12 inches x 8 inches
size of frame 18 inches x 14 inches
length of wood 64 inches
cost of wood 5 foot 4 inches @ $2.50 per foot = $13.33

size of card 17.5 inches x 13.5 inches
area of two cards 3.28 square feet [note 144 square inches in a square foot]
cost of cards 3.28 square feet @ $1.50 per square foot = $4.92

area of glass 1.64 square feet
cost of glass 1.64 square feet @ $5.50 per square foot = $9.02

Total cost of materials = $27.27

(iv) Data Dictionary

The constants can be categorized into two groups. The constants and conversion factors used to calculate the sizes of the materials and the costs of the wood for the frame, backing cards and glass. The variables are the length and width of the photograph; length of wood, area of backing card and area of glass; the cost of the wooden frame, backing cards, glass and total cost of all the materials.

```
/* constants */

const int    frame_excess = 6;
const float card_excess = 5.5;
const int    inches_per_foot = 12;
const int    sq_inches_per_sq_foot = 144;

const float wood = 2.50;  /* $2.50 per foot */
const float card = 1.50;  /* $1.50 per square foot */
const float glass = 5.50; /* $5.50 per square foot */

/* variables */

float length, width;
float length_wood, area_card, area_glass;
float cost_wood, cost_card, cost_glass;
float total;
```

(v) Screen layout

```
                          Screen Layout

12345678901234567890123456789012345678901234567890123456789012345678901234567890

input length of photograph (inches) 12.0
input width of photograph (inches) 8.0

QUOTATION FOR FRAMING PHOTOGRAPH

length of wood 5.33 feet @ $2.50 per foot                    $13.33
area of two cards 3.28 square feet @ $1.50 per square foot   $ 4.92
area of glass 1.64 square feet @ $5.50 per square foot       $ 9.02

Total cost of materials                                      $27.27
```

13.

```
#include <stdio.h>

void main(void)
{
   const int    frame_excess = 6;  /* frame 6 inches longer and wider than photo */
   const float card_excess = 5.5; /* card 5.5 inches longer and wider than photo */
```

666

```
const int    inches_per_foot = 12;
const int    sq_inches_per_sq_foot = 144;

const float wood = 2.50;  /* $2.50 per foot */
const float card = 1.50;  /* $1.50 per square foot */
const float glass = 5.50; /* $5.50 per square foot */

float length, width;
float length_wood, area_card, area_glass;
float cost_wood, cost_card, cost_glass;
float total;

/* input size of photograph */

printf("input length of photograph (inches) ");
scanf("%f", &length);
printf("input width of photograph (inches) ");
scanf("%f", &width);

/* calculate costs */

length_wood = (2*(length+frame_excess+width+frame_excess))/inches_per_foot;
cost_wood = wood * length_wood;

area_card = 2*(length+card_excess)*(width+card_excess)/sq_inches_per_sq_foot;
cost_card = card * area_card;

area_glass = area_card / 2.0;
cost_glass = glass * area_glass;

/* adjust total for any rounding errors */
total = (float)((int)(100 *(cost_wood+cost_card+cost_glass)))/100;

/* output itemized quotation */

printf("\nQUOTATION FOR FRAMING PHOTOGRAPH\n\n");
printf("length of wood %5.2f feet @ $%4.2f per foot
       $%5.2f\n", length_wood, wood, cost_wood);
printf("area of two cards %4.2f square feet @ %4.2f per square foot
       $%5.2f\n", area_card, card, cost_card);
printf("area of glass %4.2f square feet @ $%4.2f per square foot
       $%5.2f\n\n", area_glass, glass, cost_glass);

printf("Total cost of materials
       $%5.2f\n",total);
}
```

Chapter 5 - Functions

23.

sum 25 [note - the function returns the sum of A and B]

25.

sum 38 [note - A and B are passed the values 25 and 13 respectively]

27.

X=40 Y=30 [note - X and Y are passed by reference, therefore, any changes to A and B result in changes to X and Y]

29.

The function does not return a value (void), therefore, return 2*number cannot be possible. The function prototype should be changed to:

int alpha(int number);

33.

```
#include <stdio.h>

/* global declarations */

const float wood  = 2.50;  /* $2.50 per foot */
const float card  = 1.50;  /* $1.50 per square foot */
const float glass = 5.50;  /* $5.50 per square foot */

float cost_of_frame(float length, float width, float *length_wood)
{
   const int frame_excess    = 6;
   const int inches_per_foot = 12;

   *length_wood = 2*(length+frame_excess+width+frame_excess)/inches_per_foot;
   return wood * (*length_wood);
}

float cost_of_card(float length, float width, float *area_card)
{
   const float card_excess          = 5.5;
   const int   sq_inches_per_sq_foot = 144;

   *area_card = 2*(length+card_excess)*(width+card_excess)/sq_inches_per_sq_foot;
```

```
   return card * (*area_card);
}

float cost_of_glass(float length, float width, float *area_glass)
{
   const float glass_excess           = 5.5;
   const int   sq_inches_per_sq_foot = 144;

   *area_glass = (length+glass_excess)*(width+glass_excess)/sq_inches_per_sq_foot;
   return glass * (*area_glass);
}

void main(void)
{

   float length, width;
   float length_wood, area_card, area_glass;
   float cost_wood, cost_card, cost_glass;
   float total;

   /* input size of photograph */

   printf("input length of photograph (inches) ");
   scanf("%f", &length);
   printf("input width of photograph (inches) ");
   scanf("%f", &width);

   /* calculate costs */

   cost_wood = cost_of_frame(length, width, &length_wood);
   cost_card = cost_of_card(length, width, &area_card);
   cost_glass = cost_of_glass(length, width, &area_glass);

   /* adjust total for any rounding errors */
   total = (float)((int)(100 *(cost_wood+cost_card+cost_glass)))/100;

   /* output itemized quotation */

   printf("\nQUOTATION FOR FRAMING PHOTOGRAPH\n\n");
   printf("length of wood %5.2f feet @ $%4.2f per foot
           $%5.2f\n", length_wood, wood, cost_wood);
   printf("area of two cards %4.2f square feet @ %4.2f per square foot
           $%5.2f\n", area_card, card, cost_card);
   printf("area of glass %4.2f square feet @ $%4.2f per square foot
           $%5.2f\n\n", area_glass, glass, cost_glass);

      printf("Total cost of materials
              $%5.2f\n",total);
}
```

669

Chapter 6 - Selection

19.

(a) false
(b) true
(c) true
(d) false
(e) true
(f) true
(g) true

21.

	A	B	C	output
(a)	16	16	32	y
(b)	16	-18	32	x
(c)	-2	-4	16	z

23.

```
if (y>25)
{
   x=16;
   printf("x = %d\n", x);
}
else
   y = 20;
```

25.

```
#include <stdio.h>

void main(void)
{
        const   float   normal_hours = 35.0;
        const   float   threshold = 60;
        const   float   rate_1 = 12.00;
        const   float   rate_2 = 16.00;

                float   hours_worked;
                float   overtime_pay;
```

```
        printf("input number of hours worked ");
        scanf("%f", &hours_worked);
        if (hours_worked > threshold)
        {
            overtime_pay = (threshold - normal_hours) * rate_1
                        + (hours_worked - threshold) * rate_2;
        }
        else
        {
            if (hours_worked > normal_hours)
                overtime_pay = (hours_worked - normal_hours) * rate_1;
            else
                overtime_pay = 0.0;
        }

        printf("overtime pay is $%-7.2f\n", overtime_pay);
}
```

Chapter 7 - Repetition

11.

output from while loop

```
1 3 5 7 9
```

13.

output from for loop - [note characters are output and not numbers since the control string is "%c"]

```
ABCDEFGHIJKLMNOPQRSTUVWXYZ
```

15.

```
for (x=30; x>=3; x--)
  printf("%d\t", x);
```

18.

```c
#include <stdio.h>

void main(void)
{
        const    float   conv_factor = 1.609344;

        unsigned int    miles = 1;
                float    kilometres;

        printf("MILES\t\tKILOMETRES\n\n");
        for (; miles <= 50; miles++)
        {
                if (miles % 20 ==0)
                    printf("\nMILES\t\tKILOMETRES\n\n");

                kilometres = miles * conv_factor;
                printf("%d\t\t%-12.2f\n", miles, kilometres);
        }
}
```

19.

```c
#include <stdio.h>

void main(void)
{
        int    counter = 1;
        int    sum;
        char   letter;

        while (counter <= 29)
        {
                printf("%3d", counter);
                counter = counter + 2;
        }

        printf("\n");
        counter = 2;
        while (counter <= 20)
        {
                printf("%5d", counter*counter);
                counter = counter + 2;
        }
        printf("\n");
        counter = 1;
```

```
        sum = 0;
        while (counter <= 13)
        {
                sum = sum + counter * counter;
                counter = counter + 2;
        }
        printf("sum of squares of odd integers from 1..13 %d\n", sum);

        letter = 'a';
        while (letter <= 'z')
        {
                printf("%c", letter);
                letter++;
        }

}
```

22.

```
#include <stdio.h>

void main(void)
{
        int     sum = 0;
        int     counter = 0;
        int     number;
        float   mean;

        printf("number? - terminate with zero ");
        scanf("%d", &number);
        while (number != 0)
        {
                sum = sum + number;
                counter++;
                printf("number? - terminate with zero ");
                scanf("%d", &number);
        }

        if (counter != 0)
        {
                mean = (float) sum / counter;
                printf("mean of %d numbers is %-10.2f\n", counter, mean);
        }
}
```

Chapter 8 - One-dimensional Arrays

15.

alpha[0]	-10						
alpha[1]	16						
alpha[2]	19						
alpha[3]	-15						
alpha[4]	20						
index		0	1	2	3	4	5
value	0	-10	6	25	10	30	

Final value of the dentifier `value` is 30.

17.

string[10] is the letter 'a' and string[11] contains the string terminator `null` character.

19.

numbers[0]	5				
numbers[1]	2				
numbers[2]	8				
numbers[3]	7			8	
numbers[4]	0		2		
numbers[5]	3	5			
left		0	1	2	3
right		5	4	3	2
left <= right?		true	true	true	false

22.

```
#include <stdio.h>

void main(void)
{
        int index;
    const char alphabet[] = "abcdefghijklmnopqrstuvwxyz";

    printf("%s\n\n", alphabet);

    for (index=0; index < 6; index++)
        printf("%c", alphabet[index]);
    printf("\n\n");
```

```
    for (index=16; index < 26; index++)
        printf("%c", alphabet[index]);
    printf("\n\n");

    printf("%c", alphabet[9]);
}
```

Chapter 9 - Pointers

26.

An array a is declared as having two cells. The pointer p is set to point at the first cell. The contents of what p is pointing at a[0] is set to 0. The pointer p is advanced to the next cell a[1]. The contents of what p is pointing at a[1] is set to 1.

28.

```
int strcmp(const char *S1, const char *S2);
```

The parameters are pointers S1, S2 to character strings; the const implies the parameters will not be changed. The function returns an integer value.

```
char *strcpy(char *dest, const char *source);
```

The parameters are pointers dest and source to character strings; the const implies that only the source character string will not change its value. The function returns a pointer to the dest.

```
size_t strlen(const char *s);
```

The parameter is a pointer s to a character string. The function returns a value of type size_t that happens to be the length of the string being pointed at by s.

30.

No inclusion of <math.h> for the function sqrt.

Function sqrt takes a parameter of type double and returns a value of type double and not float as stated in the question.

The correct code is written as:

```
#include <math.h>
#include <stdio.h>

double function(double f(double))
```

```
{
  return f(double);
}

void main(void)
{
  printf("%15.2e", function(sqrt(144.0)));
}
```

31.

```
#include <stdio.h>
#include <stdlib.h>

void main(void)
{
    int   *P;
    float *Q;
    char  *R;

    P=malloc(sizeof(int));
    Q=malloc(sizeof(float));
    R=malloc(sizeof(char));

    printf("input data of the types int, float and char respectively\n");
    scanf("%d",P);
    scanf("%f",Q);
    getchar();
    scanf("%c",R);
    printf("values input are \n%d\n%f\n%c\n",*P,*Q,*R);

    free(P);
    free(Q);
    free(R);
}
```

Chapter 10 - Text Files

17.

The stream `file` has not been declared as a pointer of type `FILE`. A file opened for reading is `"r"` and not "read". The logical name of the file must be used and not the name found in the directory. The keyword `exit` should be given the argument `errno`.

The correct syntax is:

.
```
FILE *file;

file = fopen(filename, "r");
if (file != NULL)
{
  printf("file cannot be opened");
  exit(errno);
}
```
.

19.

array[0]	26	26	26	26	26	
array[1]		27	27	27	27	
array[2]			79	79	79	
array[3]				84	84	
array[4]					16	
index	0	1	2	3	4	5

When the end of the file numbers.txt is encountered the values held in the file will have been copied to consecutive locations in the array.

23.

```
#include <stdlib.h>
#include <stdio.h>
#include <errno.h>

#define input_file  "c:\\booze.txt"
#define output_file "c:\\stock.txt"
#define read "r"
#define write "w"
#define string_length 20

void main(void)
{
    FILE  *booze;
    FILE  *stock;
    int   quantity;
    float price;
    char  description[string_length];
```

```
   float value;
   float total = 0;

   /* attempt to open files */
   booze = fopen(input_file, read);
   stock = fopen(output_file, write);

   if (booze == NULL)
   {
      printf("file cannot be opened\n");
      exit(errno);
   }

   /* print headings */
   fprintf(stock, "          BAR STOCK REPORT\n\n");
   fprintf(stock, "QUANTITY PRICE   VALUE DESCRIPTION\n\n");

   /* read every line in the file and write the report */

   while (! feof(booze))
   {
      fscanf(booze, "%d%f", &quantity, &price);
      fgets(description, string_length, booze);
      value = price * quantity;
      total = total + value;

      fprintf(stock, "%-9d%5.2f%8.2f%s",
                   quantity, price, value, description);
   }

   fprintf(stock, "\n\nTOTAL          $%8.2f", total);

   /* close data files */
   fclose(booze);
   fclose(stock);
}
```

Chapter 11 - Structures and Arrays

19.

The structure is missing the keyword `struct`. There are no semicolons after every variable name. The correct format is:

```
struct time  {
              int HH;
              int MM;
          } time_of_day;
```

21.

```
struct time_tag  {
                  int HH;
                  int MM;
              };

struct time_tag get_time(void);

void change_time(struct time_tag *new_time);
```

23.

`time *wand` declares a pointer `wand` to a structure of type `time`;

`(*wand).HH` specifies the contents of the member `HH` of the structure being pointed at by `wand`;

`wand->MM` specifies the contents of the member `MM` of the structure being pointed at by `wand`.

26.

Patrick
3
11

27.

14
8
A deliberate error since there is no fourth row corresponding to `matrix[3][1]`

28.

26
39
-56
27
16
18

31.

```c
#include <stdio.h>
#include <string.h>

typedef struct {
                char   name[26];
                float price;
          } food;

float cost(char item[], food prices[])
/* function to search array for the price of an item of food,
if the item cannot be found returns the value zero */
{
     int index;

     for (index=0; index < 11; index++)
         if (strcmp(item, prices[index].name)==0)
             return prices[index].price;

     return 0.0;
}

void search(float amount, food prices[])
/* function to serach array and display the items of food and prices
that are equal to or below an amount of money */
{
     int index;

     for (index=0; index < 11; index++)
         if (amount >= prices[index].price)
             printf("%s %4.2f\n", prices[index].name, prices[index].price);
}
```

```
void main(void)
{
        food prices[11] = {{"Eggs - scrambled or fried",2.75},
                            {"Blueberry Pancakes",4.00},
                            {"Bagel with cream cheese",1.50},
                            {"English Muffin",0.95},
                            {"Yogurt",1.00},
                            {"Corned Beef Hash",1.75},
                            {"Toast",0.75},
                            {"Home Fries",1.00},
                            {"Tea",0.75},
                            {"Coffee",0.75},
                            {"Hot Chocolate",0.95}};

        char  menu_item[26];
        float charge, amount;

        do
        {
           printf("input name of food ");
           gets(menu_item);
           charge = cost(menu_item, prices);
           printf("price of food $%4.2f\n", charge);
        }
        while (charge != 0.0);

        printf("input an amount of money "); scanf("%f",&amount);
        search(amount, prices);
}
```

Chapter 12 - Recursion, Sorting and Searching

22.

To sort the data into descending alphabetical sequence reverse the order of n1 and n2 in the `return` statement.

```
int compare(const names_addresses *n1, const names_addresses *n2)
{
return strcmp((*(names_addresses *)n2).name, (*(names_addresses *)n1).name);
}
```

The modification of function compare using local variables and no type casting follows.

```
int compare(const void *X, const void *Y)
{
   const names_addresses *n1 = X;
   const names_addresses *n2 = Y;
   int   difference;

   difference = strcmp(n1,n2);

   if (difference >=0)
     return -1;
   if (difference == 0)
     return 0;
   return 1;
}
```

24.

With the pivot value at one end of the array the number of comparisons will be N-1.
In the first level of recusion the number of comparisons will be N-2.
In the second level of recursion the number of comparisons will be N-3

.

.

In the N-1 th level of recursion the number ofcomparisons will be 1.

Hence the number of comparisons will be the sum of these values giving an order of magnitude of N^2 comparisons similar to that of the Selection Sort.

26 (a).

```
#include <stdio.h>
#define max_array 100

int input_data(int array[])
/* function to input numbers into the array
and return the size of the array */
{
    int index = 0;
    int datum;

    printf("input positive integers - terminate with negative value\n");
    scanf("%d", &datum);
    while (datum > 0)
    {
        array[index] = datum;
```

```
        index++;
        scanf("%d", &datum);
    }
    return index;
}

int sum(int array[], int max_index)
/* recursive function to sum the contents of the array of integers */
{
    if (max_index < 0)
        return 0;
    else
        return array[max_index]+sum(array, max_index-1);
}

void main(void)
{
    int array[max_array];
    int size;

    size = input_data(array);
    printf("sum of integers in array is %d\n", sum(array, size-1));
}
```

(b).

```
#include <stdio.h>

long int power(int X, int n)
/* function to raise X to the power of n and return the result */
{
    if (n==0)
        return 1;
    else
        return X * power(X,n-1);
}

void main(void)
{
    int X, n;

    printf("input a value for X ");
    scanf("%d", &X);
    printf("input a value for n ");
    scanf("%d", &n);
    printf("X raised to the power of n is %ld", power(X,n));
}
```

(c).

```c
#include <stdio.h>

int greatest_common_divisor(int first, int second)
{
   int remainder;

   remainder = first % second;
   if (remainder == 0)
     return second;
   else
     return greatest_common_divisor(second, remainder);
}

void main(void)
{
   int first, second;

   printf("input two integers ");
   scanf("%d%d",&first, &second);

   printf("greatest common divisor is %d\n",
          greatest_common_divisor(first, second));
}
```

(d).

```c
#include <stdio.h>

int Fibonacci(int n)
/* recursive function to generate n terms in a Fibonacci sequence */
{
     if (n==1 || n==2)
        return 1;
     else
        return Fibonacci(n-2)+Fibonacci(n-1);
}

void main(void)
{
     int n;

     for (n=1; n<=15; n++)
         printf("%4d", Fibonacci(n));
}
```

Chapter 13 - Binary Files

13.

There is a syntax error in the definition of `number_of_items`; the line should not be terminated with a semi-colon. Hence `number_of_items` is not recognised in the `fread` statement.

Without the `number_of_items` error the `fread` statement is still incorrect. Although `item` is a pointer to data of type `stock_record` there has been no allocation of memory space from the heap to store data being read from the `stream`. The variable `item` should have been defined as a one-dimensional array containing data of type `stock_record`.

```
stock_record item[number_of_items];
```

15.

The keys of the two files to be merged are compared. If the keys are in descending order, the record with the **higher** key value is written to the new file. The file that supplied the record is then read again and processing continues until the end of both files is encountered.

However, when the end of either file is reached it is necessary to set the key field of the file that has ended to a **lower** value than all the other keys in the two files. The purpose of this practice is to force the remainder of the records in the reamining file to be written to the merged file. A suitable low value might be the **null** character.

The algorithm is described as follows.

open file_a and file_b for reading
open file_c for writing
read file_a, at end of file set key of file_a to low_value
read file_b, at end of file set key of file_b to low_value
while not end of both files
    if key file_a > key file_b
        write file_a record to file_c
        read file_a, at end of file set key of file_a to low_value
    else
        write file_b record to file_c
        read file_b, at end of file set key of file_b to low_value
close all files

17 (a).

```
/*
program to produce a binary file
*/

#include <stdlib.h>
#include <stdio.h>
#include <errno.h>

#define account_file "c:\\account.bin"
#define buffer_size 10
#define write_bin "wb"

typedef struct {
                char    date[9];
                float   amount;
                char    cr_db;
                char    description[80];
        } record;

FILE *open_file(char filename[], char mode[])
/* function to open a file in a specific mode and return
the name of the file if it can be opened, otherwise
return NULL
*/
{
    FILE *file;

    file = fopen(filename, mode);
    if (file == NULL)
    {
        printf("%s cannot be opened\n", filename);
        exit(errno);
    }
    else
        return file;
}

record create_record(void)
/* function to supply the data fields of a single record */
{
        record transaction;

        printf("date? MM/DD/YY ");
        gets(transaction.date);
        printf("amount? ");
        scanf("%f", &transaction.amount);
        getchar();
```

```
            printf("credit/debit? ");
            transaction.cr_db = getchar();
            getchar();
            printf("description? ");
            gets(transaction.description);

            return transaction;
}

void fill_buffer(record buffer[], int *size)
/* function to fill the output buffer with records */
{
        int  index = 0;
        char more_data;

        do
        {
            buffer[index] = create_record();
            index++;
            printf("more data Y[es] or N[o]? ");
            more_data=toupper(getchar());
            getchar();
        }
        while (more_data == 'Y');
        *size = index;
}


void display_buffer(record buffer[], int size)
/* function to display the contents of a file buffer */
{
        int index;

        for (index=0; index < size; index++)
            printf("%s\t%6.2f%c\t%s\n",
                    buffer[index].date,
                    buffer[index].amount,
                    buffer[index].cr_db,
                    buffer[index].description);
}

void main(void)
{
        FILE    *account;
        record buffer[buffer_size];
        int     size;
```

```
        account = open_file(account_file, write_bin);
        fill_buffer(buffer, &size);
        fwrite(buffer, sizeof(record), size, account);
        display_buffer(buffer, size);
        fclose(account);
}
```

(b).

```
/*
program to produce a report from a binary file
*/

#include <stdlib.h>
#include <stdio.h>
#include <errno.h>
#include <math.h>

#define account_file    "c:\\account.bin"
#define statement_file "c:\\statemnt.txt"
#define buffer_size 10
#define read_bin "rb"
#define write      "w"

typedef struct {
                    char   date[9];
                    float  amount;
                    char   cr_db;
                    char   description[80];
                } record;

FILE *open_file(char filename[], char mode[])
/* function to open a file in a specific mode and return
the name of the file if it can be opened, otherwise
return NULL
*/
{
    FILE *file;

    file = fopen(filename, mode);
    if (file == NULL)
    {
        printf("%s cannot be opened\n", filename);
        exit(errno);
    }
    else
        return file;
}
```

```
void main(void)
{
    FILE    *account;
    FILE    *statement;
    record buffer[buffer_size];
    int     size;
    int     index;
    float   balance = 0.0;

    account   = open_file(account_file, read_bin);
    statement = open_file(statement_file, write);

    size = fread(buffer, sizeof(record), buffer_size, account);

    fprintf(statement, "                  CREDIT CARD ACCOUNT\n\n");
    fprintf(statement, "Mr.Henry J.Smithers            5115 0042 2345 6000\n");
    fprintf(statement, "Boulevard Walk\n");
    fprintf(statement, "Boston                             12/31/94\n\n");
    fprintf(statement, "_____\n\n");


    for (index=0; index < size; index++)
    {
        fprintf(statement, "%s  ", buffer[index].date);
        fprintf(statement, "%6.2f", buffer[index].amount);

        if (buffer[index].cr_db == 'c')
        {
            fprintf(statement, "CR  ");
            balance = balance + buffer[index].amount;
        }
        else
        {
            fprintf(statement, "    ");
            balance = balance - buffer[index].amount;
        }

        fprintf(statement, "%s\n", buffer[index].description);
    }

    if (balance < 0)
        fprintf(statement, "\n          $%7.2f  ", fabs((double)balance));
    else
        fprintf(statement, "\n          $%7.2fCR", balance);
    fprintf(statement, "  new balance\n");

    fclose(account);
    fclose(statement);
}
```

Chapter 14 - Dynamic Data Structures

17.

```
int counter(node *head)
{
   node *temp;
   int number_of_nodes = 0;

   temp = head;
   while (temp != NULL)
   {
      number_of_nodes++;
      temp = temp->link;
   }
   return number_of_nodes;
}
```

19.

If we assume the declaration of:

```
typedef enum (false, true) boolean;
```

the function to find a number in a binary tree follows. The function will return a pointer to the node containing the number.

```
tree find_number(tree *parent, int number, boolean *success)
/* function to find a number in a binary search tree */
{
   if (parent == NULL)
   {
      *success = false;
      return NULL;
   }
   else if (number < parent->number)
      parent->left = find_number(parent->left, number, success);
   else if (number > parent->number)
      parent->right = find_number(parent->right, number, success);
   else
   {
      *success = true;
      return parent;
   }
}
```

21.

```c
#include <stdio.h>
#include <stdlib.h>

#define max_numbers 10

struct record {
                int             number;
                struct record *link;
            };

typedef struct record node;


node *create_node(node *next)
/* function to create a node and return a pointer to it */
{
        next=malloc(sizeof(node));
        next->number = (rand()%100) + 1;
        next->link = NULL;
        return next;
}

node *create_list(node *head)
/* function to create a linked list of max_number random numbers
and return a pointer to the head of the linked list */
{
        node *last;
        int  counter;

        for (counter=1; counter <= max_numbers; counter++)
        {
            if (head == NULL)
            {
                head = create_node(head);
                last = head;
            }
            else
            {
                last->link = create_node(last->link);
                last = last->link;
            }
        }
        return head;
}
```

```
int largest(node *head)
/* function to return the largest integer in a linked list */
{
        node *current;
        int  maximum;

        maximum = head->number;
        current = head->link;
        while (current != NULL)
        {
            if (current->number > maximum)
                maximum = current->number;

            current = current->link;
        }
        return maximum;
}


node *build(node *head, int maximum)
/* function to build a new linked list inserting new nodes at
the head of the list, thereby creating a list of numbers sorted
into ascending order */
{
    node *temp;

    if (head == NULL)
    {
        head = malloc(sizeof(node));
        head->number = maximum;
        head->link   = NULL;
    }
    else
    {
        temp = head;
        head = malloc(sizeof(node));
        head->number = maximum;
        head->link   = temp;
    }
    return head;
}


node *delete_node(node *head, int maximum)
/* function to delete the node containing the number maximum */
{
    node *current, *last;

    current = head;
    last    = head;
```

```
   while (current->number != maximum)
   {
      last = current;
      current = current->link;
   }

   if (head == current)
      head = head->link;
   else
      last->link = current->link;

   free(current);
   return head;
}

void list_out(node *head)
/* function to display the contents of a linked list */
{
      node *current;

      current = head;
      if (current == NULL)
         printf("list empty\n");
      else
      {
         while (current != NULL)
         {
            printf("%d\n", current->number);
            current = current->link;
         }
      }
      printf("\n");
}

void main(void)
{
      node    *head     = NULL;
      node    *new_head = NULL;
      int     number;

      head = create_list(head);
      printf("list of random numbers\n");
      list_out(head);

      while (head != NULL)
      {
            number = largest(head);
            new_head = build(new_head, number);
            head = delete_node(head, number);
```

```
    }

    printf("sorted list of random numbers\n");
    list_out(new_head);
}
```

Chapter 15 - Further Topics

21.

The value of the variable x with file scope (global variable) remains at 68.

The value of the auto variable x in the function `display` has a value of 1 every time the function is called.

When the program is executed the function `display` is called three times, and the values of the static variable `character` are 100, 110 and 120 at each repective function call. The values output from this function will be the corresponding ASCII chararacters `dnx`.

23.
```
#define TRUE 1
#define FALSE 0
#define maximum(i,j,k) ((j>i && j>k) ? TRUE : FALSE)
```

25.

(a)   0xE680
(b)   0x1365
(c)   0xAB00
(d)   0x001F

27.

```
#include <stdio.h>

#define swap(X,Y) {int temp; temp=X; X=Y; Y=temp;}
#define order(X,Y) if (X>Y) swap(X,Y)

void main(void)
{
   int array[10] = {45,16,67,29,33,4,8,-12,13,9};
   int index, passes, size = 10;
```

```
`for (passes=0; passes != size; passes++)
 {
     for (index=0; index != size-1; index++)
        order(array[index],array[index+1]);
 }

 for (index=0; index != size; index++)
     printf("%d\n", array[index]);
}
```

Chapter 16 - An Introduction to C++

31.

(a) The data type for variable c has not been declared. The type conversion of `float(c)` after the statement c=a+b does not compensate for the missing type for c. The function can be corrected by writing `int c=a+b;`

(b) When a `for` statement declares a variable in one branch of an `if` statement the variable does not exist outside the `if` statement, or in the other branch of the `if` statement. The statement `j=i;` is illegal since i is outside the scope of the declaration of i in the `for` statement.

(c) When only some of a function's parameters have default values, these parameters must come last in the parameter list.

(d)
    (i) commas illegal; parenthesis should be empty `gamma()`.
    (ii) parameters cannot be omitted from the middle of a parameter list, only from the right of the list; the commas are also illegal.
    (iii) The parameter lists do not match, (67) is not a character.

34.

```
#include <math.h>
#include <iostream.h>

// program to demonstrate overloading of a function name

// parameters - lengths of three sides
double area(double a, double b, double c)
{
        double s=(a+b+c)/2; //semi-perimeter

        return sqrt(s * (s-a) * (s-b) * (s-c));
}
```

```
// parameters - lengths of two sides and an included angle
double area(double a, double b, int C)
{
        const pi=3.14159;

        return 0.5 * a * b * sin(double(C*pi/180.0));
}


// parameters - length of base and perpendicular height
double area(double b, double h)
{
        return 0.5 * b * h;
}

void main(void)
{
        double a=3.0, b=4.0, c=5.0;
        int    angleC=90;

        cout << area(a,b,c) << endl;
        cout << area(a,b,angleC) << endl;
        cout << area(a,b) << endl;
}
```

Chapter 17 - Data Abstraction

25.

```
const string& string :: operator=(const string &s)
{
   if (this != s.this)
   {
     delete [] text;
     length=s.length;
     text=new char[length+1];
     strcpy(text, s.text);
   }
   return *this;
}
```

27.

```cpp
#include <iostream.h>
#include <iomanip.h>
#include "a:\chap_17\string.cpp"

void store_data(string array[], const int size)
{

   // creation of arrays of objects

   string names[5] = {string("Hewitt "),
                      string("Quayle "),
                      string("Evans "),
                      string("Adams "),
                      string("Farthing ")};

   string addresses[5] = { string("30 Chester Street"),
                           string("212 Wiltshire Boulevard"),
                           string("433 Lake Street"),
                           string("18 Milestone Road"),
                           string("21 Turnpike Boulevard")};

    // concatenate arrays

    for (int index=0; index!=size; index++)
     array[index]=names[index]+addresses[index];
}

int position_of_largest(string array[], int limit)
{
     string largest = array[0];
     int    index_of_largest = 0;

     for (int index=1; index <= limit; index++)
       if (array[index] > largest)
       {
         largest = array[index];
         index_of_largest = index;
       }

     return index_of_largest;
}


void selection_sort(string array[], const int size)
{
        int    position;
        string temp_store;
```

```
            for (int index=size-1; index > 0; index--)
            {
                position = position_of_largest(array, index);

                if (index != position)
                {
                    temp_store = array[index];
                    array[index] = array[position];
                    array[position] = temp_store;
                }
            }
}

void output_data(string array[], const int size)
{
            for (int index=0; index!=size; index++)
                array[index].display_text();
            cout << endl << endl;
}

void main(void)
{
            const int  size=5;
            string   array[size];

            store_data(array, size);
            output_data(array, size);
            selection_sort(array, size);
            output_data(array, size);
}
```

Chapter 18 - Object-oriented Programming

22.

The following statements are not valid.

(d) `function_2` does not take a parameter

(e) `function_3` does not belong to the base class

(g) `function_1` has been overridden in the derived class and does not take a parameter

(i) the inherited `function_2` does not take a parameter

24(a).

```
// shapes_3.h

class triangle: public line
{
        protected:

        short int X3,Y3;
        short int x1,y1,x2,y2,x3,y3;
        short int X1inc, Y1inc, X2inc, Y2inc, X3inc, Y3inc;

        public:
                // constructors
        triangle() {X1=0; Y1=0; X2=0; Y2=0; X3=0; Y3=0;
                x1=0;y1=0;x2=0;y2=0;x3=0;y3=0;
                X1inc=0;Y1inc=0;X2inc=0;Y2inc=0;X3inc=0;Y3inc=0;}

        triangle(const short int & X1,  const short int & Y1,
                const short int & X2, const short int & Y2,
                const short int & X3, const short int & Y3);

        // destructor
        virtual ~triangle(){};
        // methods
        void plot(void);
        void erase(void);
        void move(const short int &toX, const short int &toY);
};




// shapes_3.cpp

triangle :: triangle(const short int & X1, const short int & Y1,
                const short int & X2, const short int & Y2,
                const short int & X3, const short int & Y3)
{
        X1=_X1; Y1=_Y1; X2=_X2; Y2=_Y2; X3=_X3; Y3=_Y3;

        x1=(X1+X2)/2; y1=(Y1+Y2)/2;
        x2=(X2+X3)/2; y2=(Y2+Y3)/2;
        x3=(X3+X1)/2; y3=(Y3+Y1)/2;

        X1inc=(short int)fabs((double)(x1-X1));
        Y1inc=(short int)fabs((double)(y1-Y1));
```

```
        X2inc=(short int)fabs((double)(x2-X2));
        Y2inc=(short int)fabs((double)(y2-Y2));

        X3inc=(short int)fabs((double)(x3-X3));
        Y3inc=(short int)fabs((double)(y3-Y3));

}

void draw_line(short int X1, short int Y1,
        short int X2, short int Y2,
        short int x,  short int y,
        short int Xinc, short int Yinc)
{
        if (X1<X2 && Y1<Y2)
        {
                X1=x-Xinc; Y1=y-Yinc;
                X2=x+Xinc; Y2=y+Yinc;
        }
        else if (X1<X2 && Y1>Y2)
        {
                X1=x-Xinc; Y1=y+Yinc;
                X2=x+Xinc; Y2=y-Yinc;
        }
        else if (X1>X2 && Y1<Y2)
        {
                X1=x+Xinc; Y1=y-Yinc;
                X2=x-Xinc; Y2=y+Yinc;
        }
        else
        {
                X1=x+Xinc; Y1=y+Yinc;
                X2=x-Xinc; Y2=y-Yinc;
        }

        _setcolor(_getcolor());
        _moveto(X1,Y1);
        _lineto(X2,Y2);
}

void triangle :: plot(void)
{

        draw_line(X1,Y1,X2,Y2,x1,y1,X1inc,Y1inc);
        draw_line(X2,Y2,X3,Y3,x2,y2,X2inc,Y2inc);
        draw_line(X3,Y3,X1,Y1,x3,y3,X3inc,Y3inc);
}
```

```
void triangle :: erase(void)
{
        short int color;

        color=_getcolor();
        _setcolor(_getbkcolor());
        _moveto(X1,Y1);
        _lineto(X2,Y2);
        _lineto(X3,Y3);
        _lineto(X1,Y1);
        _setcolor(color);
}

void triangle :: move(const short int &toX, const short int &toY)
{

        erase();
        Xinc = toX - X1;
        Yinc = toY - Y1;
        X1=toX;
        Y1=toY;
        X2 = X2+Xinc;
        Y2 = Y2+Yinc;
        X3 = X3+Xinc;
        Y3 = Y3+Yinc;

        x1=(X1+X2)/2; y1=(Y1+Y2)/2;
        x2=(X2+X3)/2; y2=(Y2+Y3)/2;
        x3=(X3+X1)/2; y3=(Y3+Y1)/2;

        X1inc=(short int)fabs((double)(x1-X1));
        Y1inc=(short int)fabs((double)(y1-Y1));

        X2inc=(short int)fabs((double)(x2-X2));
        Y2inc=(short int)fabs((double)(y2-Y2));

        X3inc=(short int)fabs((double)(x3-X3));
        Y3inc=(short int)fabs((double)(y3-Y3));
        plot();
}
```

(b).

```cpp
#include "c:\shapes_3.cpp"
#include "c:\delay.cpp"

void main(void)
{

    triangle X(0,200,200,200,200,100);

    _setvideomode(_VRES16COLOR);
    X.plot();
    delay(5);
    X.move(300,100);
    delay(5);
    X.erase();
    delay(5);
    _setvideomode(_DEFAULTMODE);
}
```

Index